DECISION SUPPORT AND DATA WAREHOUSE SYSTEMS

DECISION SUPPORT AND DATA WAREHOUSE SYSTEMS

Efrem G. Mallach

University of Massachusetts at Lowell

Irwin
McGraw-Hill

Boston   Burr Ridge, IL   Dubuque, IA   Madison, WI   New York   San Francisco   St. Louis
Bangkok   Bogotá   Caracas   Lisbon   London   Madrid
Mexico City   Milan   New Delhi   Seoul   Singapore   Sydney   Taipei   Toronto

McGraw-Hill Higher Education

A Division of The **McGraw-Hill** *Companies*

DECISION SUPPORT AND DATA WAREHOUSE SYSTEMS

 This book is printed on acid-free paper.

1 2 3 4 5 6 7 8 9 0 DOC/DOC 0 9 8 7 6 5 4 3 2 1 0

ISBN 0–07–289981–6

Vice president/Editor-in-chief: *Michael W. Junior*
Publisher: *David Kendric Brake*
Senior sponsoring editor: *Rick Williamson*
Project manager: *Karen J. Nelson*
Production supervisor: *Kari Geltemeyer*
Freelance design coordinator: *Pam Verros*
Cover illustration: *© Photodisc*
Supplement coordinator: *Craig S. Leonard*
Compositor: *Shepherd Incorporated*
Typeface: *10.5/12 Times Roman*
Printer: *R. R. Donnelley & Sons Company*

Library of Congress Cataloging-in-Publication Data

Mallach, Efrem G.
  Decision support and data warehouse systems / Efrem G. Mallach.
    p. cm.
  ISBN 0–07–289981–6 (alk. paper)
  1. Decision support systems. 2. Data warehousing. I. Title.

  T58.62 M25 2000
  658.4'03—dc21   99-054014

http://www.mhhe.com

To my students, who have taught me more than I have taught them

PREFACE

WHY THIS BOOK?

Decision Support and Data Warehouse Systems is intended as a textbook for a one-semester course in decision support systems (DSS), with data warehousing playing the same starring role in the course as it does in today's decision support picture. With the addition of enrichment material in data warehousing, much of which can be found on the Web, it also fits a quarter system: the DSS portion of the book fits one quarter, and the data warehousing portion can easily be expanded to fill another. The book suits these environments:

- Management (business administration) programs, at the advanced undergraduate or master's level.
- Programs in computers and information systems (CIS) or in application-oriented computer science programs, typically at the advanced undergraduate level. (My own DSS courses, while offered in our College of Management, attract computer science majors as well.)
- Workshops for practicing professionals who need a grasp of this important area of technology.

I wrote this book for the same reason that most authors write textbooks: I had taught the subject for several semesters and was not satisfied with any of the available texts. It is meant to offer several advantages over its alternatives.

- It has a realistic objective: to help the student understand decision support systems, not to create an experienced professional.
- It was written as a unified whole in which each chapter relates its content to what went before and is, in turn, related to what will follow.

- As a result, topics are reinforced by continued use rather than being touched upon and subsequently forgotten.
- It gets away from the conventional wisdom, often repeated in textbook after textbook, long after actual practice has left it in the dust, to reflect how the real world works.
- It focuses throughout, not just on how things are, but on *why* they are that way. It does not present facts or research results without explanation and context.
- Along the same lines, it does not attempt to provide exhaustive coverage of every fact or research result that exists. It focuses on what is (in the author's opinion) important.
- It makes realistic assumptions about what students have already studied. It neither presumes they remember every nuance of their introductory IS course nor insults them by assuming they never saw the subject.
- It offers many accessible, often nontechnical (even homey) examples of difficult concepts.
- It includes a running case that enables the students to apply the concepts in the chapters to a familiar situation.

A learning tool for the twenty-first century must be more than well planned, though. It must be current. No technology is changing the world as quickly as information technology. The decision support field is no exception to this general truth. A book that is not up-to-date, a book that merely gives the content of the 1980s a new look, will not serve its students well. The content of this book is as current as possible.

- The technology is up-to-date throughout. This is most evident in Chapter 5, where hardware issues are covered, but shows up in most other areas as well.
- The Web pervades this book as much as it pervades our world. It is discussed explicitly as a DSS platform. In the data warehousing arena, WOLAP is covered with examples.
- The last third of the book is devoted totally to the new and vital area of data warehousing. Nobody can claim to understand DSS today without having studied this key topic in depth. This section covers the approaches in use today, arranging them so the student can understand how they relate to each other and enabling the reader to sort through competing vendor claims.
- Material on expert systems, long a staple of DSS texts, has been cut back to one chapter.

HOW THIS BOOK IS ORGANIZED

Decision Support and Data Warehouse Systems is divided into three major parts. They are described further in Section 1.6, "The Plan of This Book." Each major part opens with a brief introduction to the entire part.

Part I, Chapters 1 to 4, provides an overview of decision support system fundamentals: how people make decisions, how systems work, where models fit into the DSS picture, what the benefits of DSS are, and several ways to classify them. The purpose of this classification is this: if we know something about the types of decisions and the types of DSS, and we know what DSS have been useful with certain decisions in the past, we have a head start in developing a DSS for a similar decision today.

Part II, Chapters 5 to 11, covers technical and nontechnical DSS development issues. Chapters 5 and 6 cover the hardware and software technologies that go into DSS. The nontechnical side, including implementation and some ethical issues, is in Chapter 7. The intent throughout is to enable the student to apply the best method to a new situation. Chapters 8 through 11 then go into particular types of DSS and important aspects of many DSS in more detail. These chapters cover, respectively, the major kinds of models that are useful for decision support, optimization, group decision support systems, and expert systems.

Part III, Chapters 12 to 15, covers data warehousing. It opens with an introduction to this area and continues through their database, analyzing their contents, and implementation.

Finally, Chapter 16 summarizes the book. It is followed by an Appendix with nine real-world cases that bridge chapter boundaries to reinforce the material.

Each chapter includes:

- A chapter outline.
- A set of learning objectives for the chapter.
- An introduction, which explains why the subject of the chapter is worth taking time to study.
- A summary, which recaps the major points made in the chapter.
- A list of key terms introduced in the chapter.
- A set of simple review questions to check the reader's understanding. These require only reference to the appropriate paragraph(s) of the chapter.
- A set of more involved discussion questions to apply the material. These require additional thought. Some also require, or can benefit from, the use of a computer.
- References, covering both citations in the chapter and sources of further depth in the chapter topics.
- A case, about the fictional Fort Lowell Trading Company department store chain,[1] to show how the concepts and principles of that chapter work out in practice. FLTC is introduced at the end of Chapter 1. Each episode of this running case includes discussion questions.

SUPPLEMENTS

Adopters of this book can obtain the following items, in addition to the book itself:[2]

- An instructor's manual with suggestions for presenting the material, for class projects, and other information that will help make a DSS course successful.

---

[1]The overlap between this name and that of the university where I teach is a coincidence. As explained in Chapter 1, the store was named for the first Anglo settlement newr what is now Tucson, Arizona.
[2]These items may accompany *Decision Support and Data Warehousing Systems*. Please consult your McGraw-Hill representative for policies, prices, and availability, as some restrictions may apply.

- A test bank, which instructors can use to develop exams.
- A set of PowerPoint presentations for every chapter.[3]

ACKNOWLEDGMENTS

No person can sit down unaided at a word processor and hope to arise some time later with a finished manuscript. I am indebted to many people for much that is in these pages. In particular, I wish to thank:

- The more than 100 DSS students at the University of Massachusetts, Lowell, who suffered through several versions of this book in manuscript form and whose comments improved it substantially.
- The thousands of DSS students and teachers who used *Understanding Decision Support Systems and Expert Systems* (Irwin, 1994) and whose feedback led to many of the improvements in the present book.
- The reviewers, both the anonymous ones and the ones whose names I know, who pointed out many errors and opportunities for improvement in earlier drafts. Since I ignored their advice in a few places, I retain the blame for any remaining problems.
- The editors and production staff at Irwin/McGraw-Hill, who kept after me to ensure that the book was as good as I was capable of making it.
- The many educators and MIS professionals who have worked in DSS and related fields over the past several decades and who have taken the time to record what they have learned. I hope I have added some useful insight here and there but, as with any textbook, I can claim originality for only a small part of its content.
- The software vendors who have provided examples of how decision support software works, often with screen photographs to enhance the book.
- The administration of the University of Massachusetts, Lowell, which granted me sabbatical leave to develop the manuscript for this book.
- My family, who understood the needs of someone trying to do creative work. They gave me the schedule flexibility to write it and supported my sometimes-unusual needs during the process.

If *Decision Support and Data Warehouse Systems* helps students develop into practicing professionals who understand what DSS are about and how to construct systems that meet decision makers' support needs, it will have achieved its most important objective.

Efrem G. Mallach

---

[3]Requires Microsoft PowerPoint 97 (Windows) or 98 (Macintosh), or compatible software.

BRIEF CONTENTS

PART IV

Summary

CONTENTS

PART II

Building and Implementing Decision Support Systems

PART III

Data Warehousing

INTRODUCTION TO DECISION SUPPORT SYSTEMS

CHAPTER 1

Introduction to Decision Support Systems

CHAPTER OUTLINE

Introduction

This chapter will introduce you to decision support systems, the subject of this book. In a nutshell, decision support systems are information systems that help people make decisions. In this chapter you'll get an idea of what decision support systems are, how they were originally used, how they are used today, what benefits they provide to organizations, and why it makes sense for you to study them over the next few months.

CHAPTER OBJECTIVES

After you have read and studied this chapter, you will be able to:

1. Define decision support systems.
2. Describe how decision support systems evolved.
3. Discuss where decision support systems fit into the information systems picture.

4. Identify how all types of information systems can also be used for decision support.
5. Outline the benefits of decision support systems.
6. Understand why it is important to study decision support systems.

1.1 HOW DECISION SUPPORT SYSTEMS EVOLVED

As you learned in your introductory MIS course, early computers were used to automate repetitive calculations. The first ones processed numerical data, as in solving equations. Many advances in computing were made under the pressure of World War II needs. During that conflict, computers calculated the effective range of depth charges and optimal trajectories for artillery shells. Computing power in that era was typically measured by the roomfuls of mathematicians that an "electronic brain" could replace, a popular comparison that ignored the difference between a clerk with a desk calculator and a true mathematician.

Electronic computers found commercial uses in the 1950s. The first large-scale system to process businesslike data was a Univac I at the U.S. Census Bureau in 1951. It has been stated that, without computers, data for the 1950 census could not have been tabulated before the next census began a decade later.

By the mid-1950s, large corporations had adopted computers for their own repetitive calculations, such as processing the corporate payroll. This activity was known as **automatic data processing**—a term that previously referred to electro-mechanical punched card processing—or **electronic data processing (EDP).** These terms were shortened to **data processing (DP)** as computers came into wide use and manual data processing became a historical relic. Later, when the term *data processing* came to encompass all the computer applications of an organization, the term **transaction processing** was coined to describe the repetitive processing of common business events and the recording of their associated data.

Managers were quick to realize that suitably summarized transaction data had potential decision-making value. They asked their organizations' data processing staffs for information that could be obtained from data that was already stored in their computers. At the time, direct-access storage devices and on-line terminals, to say nothing of integrated databases with query software, were not in general use. There was, therefore, no easy way to obtain a single data element upon request. The only way to satisfy such a request was to produce a voluminous report containing every data element which could possibly be relevant. **Information reporting systems (IRS)** thereby arose. Managers found thick reports, typically on 17-inch-wide paper with green and white horizontal bars across the page, on their desks every Monday morning. Some of these reports got lots of use; others were discarded unread when the next Monday's report arrived.

Outmoded as paper-based IRS might seem at the dawn of a new century, the reports did demonstrate that computers contained a great deal of useful management data. As technology evolved to permit instant access to this data, the concept of a **management information system (MIS)** evolved with it. The idea behind MIS was to store all of a firm's data: customers, orders, inventory, production schedules, suppliers, employees, payroll, and so forth, for access and correlation on

DSS at Omni Healthcare (from [OMNI97])

"We needed a tool that would allow our managers to independently seek answers to their questions and facilitate their decision making processes," said John Volkober, Chief Financial Officer of this Northern California health maintenance organization. The answer: a decision support system. More than 50 people now use it to make better decisions. The types of people who use Omni's DSS include:

- Actuaries—to review costs of supplies and services, enabling the organization to negotiate the best possible contracts.
- Marketing—to analyze membership demographics, pinpoint successful marketing tactics and reach new markets.
- Membership Accounting—to track premium payments and conduct audits.
- Provider Group, which is responsible for signing up new providers (such as physicians and other health professionals who provide services to Omni members). They use it to decide where more providers are needed and to analyze costs in contract negotiations.
- Medical Management—to analyze Omni's competitive standing in its industry, enabling them to make strategic and policy decisions that will improve that standing.

This system enabled Omni to turn data it already had into a competitive weapon.

California Daylighting (from [MILL98])

In 1992 the California State Automobile Association trashed the plans for their next office building and went for a more energy-efficient design. With the help of Pacific Gas and Electric Company, they cut energy use (heating, cooling, lighting and ventilation) by three-quarters and saved money in the process.

Hundreds of design decisions affect a building's energy usage. For instance, every wooden stud in an exterior wall creates "thermal bridging"—letting outside heat or cold penetrate the building no matter how much insulation is placed between them. So, spacing studs 24 inches apart instead of the standard 16 inches can save energy. In that case, though, 2×6 studs must be used rather than the usual 2×4s, increasing costs. The thicker wall can, however, accommodate more insulation . . . there are layers within layers, wheels within wheels.

The building designers turned to computers to analyze over 300 possible energy efficiency measures. A computer model predicted energy consumption for each possible combination. As one example, they found that reorienting the axis of the building from northwest/southeast to north/south allowed for improved use of natural light, while changing the design from two-story to one-story allowed them to use skylights instead of electrical lighting during daylight hours. Many of these decisions would not have been obvious, even to a trained and environmentally aware architect, and would have been impossible to optimize by hand.

The net effect was a reduction in energy costs from an estimated $23,500 per year, for a standard design, to $5,000 per year for the CSAA building as constructed. The savings of $18,500 per year were achieved for an additional construction cost of $115,000, yielding an annual return of over 16% on the initial investment. In addition, dollars not spent on energy are expended elsewhere in the state economy, creating more jobs than if they were spent on conventional energy sources. The new building also reduces yearly emissions by 106,900 lb (48,640 kg) of carbon dioxide (CO_2), 42 lb (19 kg) of sulfur dioxide (SO_2), and 387 lb (176 kg) of nitrogen oxides (NO_x).

FIGURE 1–1   Knowledge Worker Looking at Report

demand by nontechnical managers. This dream did not come true in that form at that time, in part because all the necessary enabling technologies such as distributed databases were not yet available and the systems of that era were not user-friendly. A product of those early efforts is the current use of the term *MIS* to refer to commercially oriented information systems overall. There is an excellent chance that your introductory information systems course, its textbook, or both, went by that name.

Despite their lack of general success, efforts to produce a corporate MIS showed that decision-making data did not have to come from thick reports. This lack of success may have been a benefit in disguise: Managers saw that they didn't need a total MIS in order to obtain useful information. As a result, more modest systems to help make specific types of decisions came to the fore in the 1970s. These were, and are, called **decision support systems (DSS).**[1] Decision support systems evolved further during the 1980s to provide easier end-user access to the data they contain. In the 1990s, data for decision making evolved into the **data warehouse,** which is a close approximation of the early MIS concept. Figure 1–2 depicts the place of a typical DSS in a corporate structure. This book is about such systems: what they do, how they do it, how they are built, and how they are used.

---

[1]We'll use the abbreviation DSS to stand for both decision support system in the singular and decision support systems in the plural. You can determine which form is intended from the context.

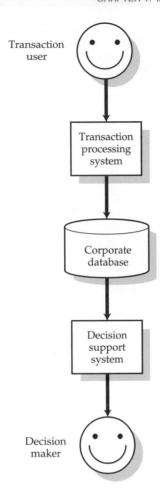

FIGURE 1–2 Flow Diagram of Transaction Data Feeding DSS

Figure 1–3 compares some characteristics of three types of information systems you just read about. You may also encounter these types of information systems:

- **Office information systems (OIS),** also called *Office automation systems (OAS),* improve the efficiency and effectiveness of handling information (words, images, schedules, and other items) in an office.
- **Executive information systems (EIS)** enable top managers of an organization to obtain information to guide their decisions. This makes EIS a type of DSS. We'll discuss EIS in Chapter 12 of this book.
- **Personal information systems** are developed and used by one individual (in a process often known as **end-user computing**) to improve his or her personal productivity and effectiveness. That effectiveness can involve decision making. A personal information system used for this purpose is a DSS, too.

System Characteristic	Transaction Processing Systems	Information Reporting Systems	Decision Support Systems
User community	Clerical and supervisory	Supervisory and middle management	Individual knowledge workers, all management levels
Usage volume	High	Moderate	Moderate to low
Database usage	Some reading, heavy updating	Read-only	Primarily read-only
Typical software base	Third-generation languages	Third- and fourth-generation languages	Specialized languages, packages
Emphasis on ease of use	Low	Moderate	High
Emphasis on processing efficiency	High	Moderate	Low
Reason for development	Cost savings, customer service	Reporting requirements, basic information for decision making	Improved decision-making effectiveness

FIGURE 1–3   **Comparison of TPS/IRS/DSS Characteristics**

- **Workgroup information systems** are used to improve communication and co-ordination among members of a group who collaborate on a set of joint tasks. These systems can often support group decision making. For that reason, they're a big part of Chapter 10.
- **Expert systems** follow rules similar to those a person might use in order to reach a recommendation or conclusion from available data. If the rules are those a human might follow to reach a decision, an expert system can be a DSS also. You'll read about expert systems in Chapter 11.
- **Strategic information systems (SIS)** enable an organization to obtain a competitive advantage over its rivals or prevent its rivals from obtaining a competitive advantage over it.

These are not distinct categories. They overlap, interact, and supplement each other. Several types, as noted above, are closely related to DSS. Some, such as workgroup systems and expert systems, are technologies as much as they are types of information systems.

Take the first, and oldest, transaction processing systems. Although it is easy to put these down as "old hat," no modern organization could function for long without them. In addition, today's transaction processing systems often form the foundation for powerful strategic information systems. Examples include airline reservation systems and the Home Shopping Club's "Tootie" automated order entry system, which uses entry from the customer's Touch-Tone telephone to adjust prices on the air using up-to-the-second order rate data. The combination of transaction processing and an on-line link to the customer, on which both these applications are based, is a powerful one. In both of these cases, it is hard to define exactly where the TPS stops and where the SIS begins. Fortunately, we don't have to.

We could find similar examples for any of the other areas. Applying information technology intelligently can transform the way an organization works. It is no exaggeration to state that information systems can reshape the nature of competition in an industry.

Information Systems and Decision Support   Consider the types of information systems listed above. Each type can help people make decisions, such as the following:

- Transaction processing system: A telephone order entry operator sees that maroon bath towels are out of stock and asks the customer if another color would be acceptable. The customer must decide whether to wait two weeks for the requested maroon towels, select another color, or look for a store that has maroon towels in stock.
- Information reporting system: An accounting clerk looks at an aged accounts receivable report and decides which customer to call for payment.
- Executive information system: The vice president for strategic planning sees that the company's Model A-100 is gaining market share and decides to expand that market segment with a smaller Model A-80 and a larger Model A-150.
- Office information (automation) system: A marketing director, having been informed by an automated calendar and scheduling system that six product managers can't meet as a group for the next three weeks, decides to meet with four of them the day after tomorrow and talk to the other two individually later.
- Personal information system: A department manager tries out several different budget possibilities before deciding which one to submit upward.
- Workgroup information system: Regional sales managers must decide, as a group, which of three proposed national advertising campaigns they think would be most effective for their firm.
- Expert system: A family doctor decides how to treat a patient with a rare blood disease which that physician had never seen before.
- Strategic information system: Airline reservation systems and Tootie, both mentioned previously, support customer decisions. Airline passengers and their travel agents use information from on-line reservation systems to choose their flights. Home Shopping Club viewers make purchase decisions on the basis of the price offered at the moment: If it's too high, they won't buy; if it's too low, HSC loses potential revenue. These customer decisions tie directly to business decisions: To the airline, what flights should we schedule? To HSC, how should we adjust the price of the product now being sold on the air?

The point here is that *computer support of decision making is all-pervasive.* We can't put it in a slot called "DSS" with walls between that slot and adjacent slots. All types of information systems have some ability to help people make decisions. Decision support systems are at one end of a spectrum. We can visualize this spectrum as in Figure 1–4. Note that transaction processing systems are visibly above the zero point on the scale. Even they can provide useful decision-making information!

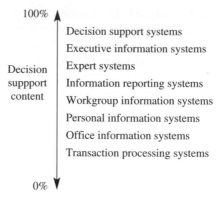

100%

Decision
suppport
content

Decision support systems
Executive information systems
Expert systems
Information reporting systems
Workgroup information systems
Personal information systems
Office information systems
Transaction processing systems

0%

FIGURE 1–4 **Approximate Decision Support Content of Different Types of Information Systems**

1.2 WHAT IS A DSS?

Now that you have a general idea of what DSS are, it's time to get more specific. This is not easy: as Davis points out in the preface to [DAVI88]: "Ask someone to explain the concept and application of DSS, and the answer given will most often depend on who you ask."

One way to try to understand the essence of decision support systems is to look at several definitions that have been put forth. A sampling follows, organized from the oldest to the most recent.[2] Some of these definitions were taken from popular introductory MIS textbooks, perhaps including the one you used. Others are from more specialized writings in the DSS field.

> Decision support implies the use of computers to (1) assist managers in their decision processes in semistructured tasks; (2) support, rather than replace, managerial judgment; (3) improve the effectiveness of decision making rather than its efficiency. [KEEN78]

> Information systems featuring an integrated system composed of decision models, database, and decision maker to support decision making. [SPRA79]

> A computer-based system that is used on an ongoing basis by managers themselves, or their immediate staffs, in direct support of managerial decision making. [KEEN79]

> A set of computer-based tools used by a manager in connection with his or her problem-solving and decision-making duties. [LEIG86]

> Decision support systems are used for less structured problems, where the art of management is blended with the science. [KANT92]

> . . . a computer-based information system that affects or is intended to affect how people make decisions. [SILV91]

> . . . a set of tools, data, models, and other resources that managers and analysts use to understand, evaluate and solve problems . . . [in] unstructured problem domains. [KROE92]

> An integrated set of computer tools that allow a decision maker to interact directly with computers to create information useful in making unanticipated semistructured and unstructured decisions. [HICKS93]

---

[2]Some were first put forth by their authors in earlier writings than those cited here.

Decision support systems are analytic models used to increase managerial or professional decision making by bringing important data to view. [FREN96]

. . . an organized collection of people, procedures, software, databases and devices used to support problem-specific decision making. [STAI97]

. . . computer-based information systems designed to help managers select one of many alternate solutions to a problem. [OZ98]

. . . computer-based information systems that provide interactive information support to managers during the decision-making process. [OBRI99]

Ralph Sprague, in his pioneering work on DSS [SPRA80], made a serious attempt to define DSS from a theoretical point of view and in terms of what it means in practice. His compromise, based on observing many DSS of that era, includes these four characteristics:

- They tend to be aimed at the less well-structured, underspecified problems that upper level managers typically face.
- They attempt to combine the use of models or analytic techniques with traditional data access and retrieval functions.
- They specifically focus on features which make them easy to use by noncomputer people in an interactive mode.
- They emphasize flexibility and adaptability to accommodate changes in the environment and the decision-making approach of the user.

We can derive several themes from these definitions:

1. *Decision support systems are information systems.* This might seem obvious, but this seemingly trivial statement has great significance. It means that everything you have studied and have learned about information systems applies to DSS as well.
2. *Decision support systems are used by managers.* Although this is part of many definitions of DSS, it's too restrictive. A manager is someone who achieves results through other people. DSS are used by the broad category of **knowledge workers.** Knowledge workers include nonmanagement staff such as stockbrokers, urban planners, production coordinators, travel agents, college admissions officers, and many more. Anyone who makes decisions, in business, in government, in the nonprofit sector, or even in many areas of personal living, is a potential DSS user.
3. *Decision support systems are used in making decisions.* Making decisions is the foundation of corporate success: What products should we manufacture? What services should we provide? How should we market and sell them? How should we raise capital? Who should be assigned to each task? Such decisions are fundamental to any organization. DSS can therefore have an enormous impact on an organization's "bottom line."[3]

---

[3]From time to time we'll use terms such as *corporate* and *bottom line* that imply a profit-making corporation. This is done for convenience. However, everything applies equally to nonprofit organizations such as museums or hospitals, to government agencies at all levels, and to any other organization that has objectives and must make decisions in order to reach them.

4. *Decision support systems are used to support, not to replace, people.* Decision support systems are not decision-making systems, though the dividing line can be fuzzy at times and borderline cases exist. If there isn't, at a minimum, some human review of the system's recommendation, it isn't a DSS.
5. *Decision support systems are used when the decision is "semistructured" or "unstructured."* We'll discuss the concept of decision "structure" more completely in Chapter 2. For now, lack of structure means essentially that we can't program a computer to make a decision to our total satisfaction in all cases. A decision that is not structured is a decision that requires some human judgment. This point goes along with the previous one: If we could program a computer to make the decision, we'd need a decision-making system, not a decision support system.
6. *Decision support systems incorporate a database*[4] *of some sort.* That is because all decisions are based on information. A database is where computers store information. (More precisely, it is where computers store data that we can process into, or interpret as, information.)
7. *Decision support systems incorporate models.* A **model** is a computer representation of a real-life system that lets us investigate the impact of a possible decision affecting that system.[5] This capability, to forecast the impact of a decision without actually putting it into effect, is of great value when corporate future hangs in the balance.

Two points are worth noting about these elements of DSS. These are:

• The very name DSS reflects points 1, 3, and 4. In contrast to many other MIS terms, this one actually makes sense.
• The first four points are true of all DSS, whereas the last three are typical of most DSS but may not apply to a particular one. Figure 1–5 illustrates the seven characteristics of DSS. DSS experts differ on their importance. When we encounter one of the last three points in a definition intended to characterize all DSS, as we did in a few of the definitions quoted previously, it tells us something about the author's perspective and the types of DSS on which we can expect that author to focus.

The definition of DSS that we'll use in this book is the following:

> A decision support system is a computer-based information system whose primary purpose is to provide knowledge workers with information on which to base informed decisions.

This definition incorporates the essential elements of the previously listed definitions without restricting us to a specific technology, approach, set of system elements, or mode of use (such as interactivity). The definition deliberately doesn't

---

[4]The term *database* is used in an informal sense here. We'll get more precise about database concepts in Chapter 6.
[5]This is not a general definition of a model but applies to most models used in DSS. We'll look at models in more detail in Chapters 3 and 9.

All DSS . . .

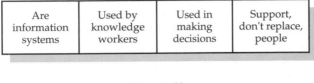

And some DSS . . .

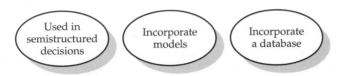

FIGURE 1–5   Seven Characteristics of DSS: Four Are Held in Common and Three Are Optional

indicate where the information that a DSS provides originates. The DSS might read it directly out of a database, for example, or it may result from long and complex computations. This is, in other words, a broad definition. We can't avoid this generality in a definition that must cover all the existing types of DSS. As we proceed further in our study of DSS, we will uncover many specific types of DSS with narrower definitions.

Note the words *primary purpose* in our definition. Many DSS provide, as a by-product, reports or other aspects of conventional data processing systems. These incidental features, which often cost little or nothing to add, do not make a system non-DSS-like as long as they are secondary to the main reason for developing it. Conversely, as you've seen, many other information systems provide, as by-products, information that can sometimes help someone decide something. If providing information for decision making was not a major purpose of developing the system, however, then it's not (for our purposes) a DSS. Yet because decision support is not the sole province of a particular category of system, what you learn about computer-based support for decision making in a pure DSS context will help you work with other types of systems as well.

1.3 WHY DECISION SUPPORT SYSTEMS MATTER

Ask most people what they think when they hear *computers,* and they will discuss desktop microcomputer operators running spreadsheets, preparing newsletters, and surfing the Web. Tell them that you mean corporate-level applications, and you'll hear about accounting, payroll, and tracking inventory—all applications designed to improve the **efficiency** of existing business processes.

Improving efficiency is a common use of computers, but improved efficiency can have only a limited impact on the corporate bottom line. We can look at the payroll process as an example to see why this is so. Let's go through an approximate calculation, step by step.

First, the maximum amount a firm can save by automating any task is the cost of doing it manually. Processing payroll manually means hiring payroll clerks. The most we can save by automating our payroll processing therefore is the salary and benefits of those clerks (assuming the costs of calculators, paper, pens, and other supplies are negligible by comparison).

To continue our cost estimate of manual payroll processing and of how much automation of the process could save, we must know how many employees each clerk can handle. Assuming employees are paid weekly, we must calculate how many paychecks a clerk can produce per week. The clerk has to look at the number of hours each person worked (on a time card), multiply that number by that employee's hourly wage (in a wage list), adjust for overtime and weekend or holiday work, calculate tax withholding and other deductions, figure the resulting net pay, and write it on a check and in the pay register. Suppose this takes 10 minutes. (It shouldn't take that long, but if our estimate is off, we would prefer it to be on the high side.)

There are 480 minutes in an eight-hour work day. To allow for breaks and simplify the numbers, let's assume each clerk works 400 minutes. At 10 minutes per check, that's 40 checks per day, 200 checks in a five-day week.

In other words, if we do the payroll process manually, we need one clerk per 200 employees to handle the paperwork. That's 1/200th, or one-half of 1 percent, of our staff. It would require less than one-half of 1 percent of our total personnel costs, however, because payroll clerks are among the lower-paid employees in most organizations. And, since a payroll clerk doesn't need raw materials, inventory, or expensive equipment, the position comprises an even smaller fraction of our total costs. So let's say that the cost of all the required payroll clerks represents one-quarter of 1 percent of our revenue (see Figure 1–6).

This being the case, *the most we can possibly save by automating payroll processing is 0.25 percent of our revenue.* And we will never save all of that because computers are not free; programs to calculate payroll are not free; and people who operate computers don't work for free—in fact, they probably earn more than payroll clerks. So our net saving from automating payroll processing will probably be about 0.1 percent (not 0.1, but 0.1 percent, or 1/1000th) of our revenue. If a firm's pretax profits are 10 percent of its revenue, payroll automation can increase them to 10.1 percent of revenue.

We shouldn't scorn these small savings or reject them out of hand. One-tenth of 1 percent of the annual revenue of General Motors, for example, is about $100 million. We should take savings wherever we can find them. No sensible person would suggest doing payroll by hand just because automating it will save only a small fraction of revenues. (Automating payroll also has other benefits, such as producing fewer errors and more legible checks and having the data readily available in computers for other purposes.) But, compared with the difference that other uses of information technology can make in corporate profits, saving 0.1 percent of revenue isn't the best place for top management to focus its attention.

We could do a similar calculation for other potential uses of automation to improve efficiency: accounts payable and receivable, customer billing, general

FIGURE 1–6 **Manual versus Computerized Payroll Processing**

ledger, and so forth. We would reach the same conclusion each time. The savings may justify the cost of automation but are too small to make a strategic impact on a firm. Automation can't help decide what kind of products to make, where to put the next store, or whether to raise funds by borrowing or issuing new stock. Those decisions have *high leverage;* in other words they make a big difference in organizational success. Most importantly, improvements in business efficiency don't help attract or retain customers. Did *you* ever choose a restaurant or a clothing store because it processed payroll efficiently or produced its general ledger a particular way?

For computers to make a real difference, we must look beyond improved efficiency, which is doing the same things as before, with the same results, but more quickly or less expensively. We must look instead at improved effectiveness: doing things better than they were done before. One place where every organization wants to do the best possible job is in making important decisions. This type of improved **effectiveness** is what decision support systems, and this book, are about.

Who Uses DSS?   The types of information systems we've been discussing span all levels of every organization. Yet each type is not necessarily used at every level. It is unlikely that the CEO of Galactic Industries, Inc., will personally update its accounts payable files. It is equally unlikely that an accounts payable clerk will make the final decision on the per-share price that Galactic offers for its chief rival, Universal Manufacturing, in a merger proposal. Each type of system has its main purpose, its primary user community, and its business impact.

The impact of pure transaction processing systems is usually in improving the efficiency of existing processes. TPS tend to be used primarily by employees at lower levels of the organization and tend to be used in high volume. Even though organizations have grown dependent on them and couldn't continue to function without them for long, the difference between one organization's TPS and another's generally has little bottom-line impact.

The benefits that come from providing managers with information to make better decisions are far greater. That's where DSS come in: in making the organization more effective and giving it a competitive advantage. DSS are typically used by fewer people than use TPS, though their usage is increasing as organizations empower more workers to make decisions independently. DSS users typically use DSS less frequently: Some decisions are made only at intervals, and in other cases some "think time" is needed between computer runs. For both these reasons, they usually consume only a small fraction of the firm's computer resources. Yet DSS make a bigger bottom-line difference than the transaction processing applications that eat up so many CPU cycles. This is analogous to the management hierarchy: People near the top are few in number compared to those further down, but they have a disproportionately large impact—for good or for bad—on the future of the organization.

Figure 1–7 shows the analogy graphically. It shows no dividing lines because the boundaries are, at best, fuzzy. It gives a general idea of the relationships. Don't let it force your thinking into narrow boxes where each type of system "should" fit.

Increased use of information for decision making, as opposed to control, is a clear trend. Management guru Peter Drucker has written extensively on his vision of the twenty-first century corporation [DRUC88]. He sees it as having fewer levels of management and far fewer managers than does today's typical corporation. These managers will be empowered to make decisions on their own, as the massive controlling structures of today will no longer exist. They will make these decisions on the basis of organized feedback from colleagues, customers, and corporate headquarters: in short, on information. This information-based, knowledge-based organization will depend heavily on computer-based DSS.

FIGURE 1–7 Twin Pyramids of Organizational Structure and Information System Usage

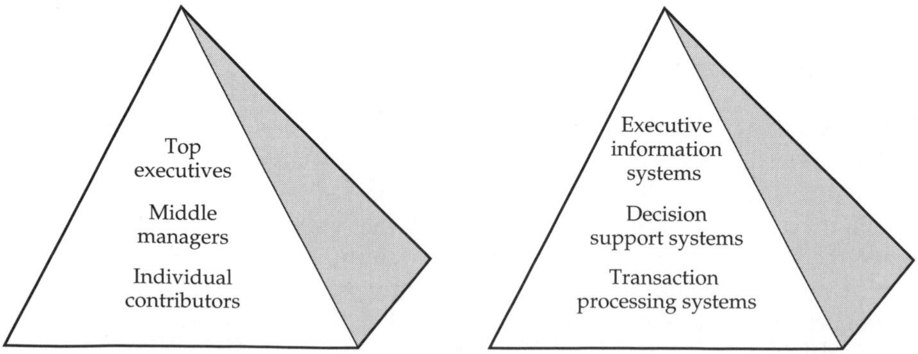

1.4 DSS BENEFITS

Consider the following decision problems.

1. We have budgeted $100,000 to advertise our new line of nongreasy green, pink, and yellow sunscreen lotion next summer. We know something about the types of people who buy sunscreen lotion. (We have decided to concentrate on converting existing sunscreen lotion users to our product, rather than persuading nonusers to start using sunscreen lotion. Computers might have helped us make that decision as well.) Demographic survey data tell us what types of people read various magazines and watch various TV shows. We can relate such demographic data to what we know about sunscreen buyers. Research studies have provided data about the impact of size and color usage in a print ad, and the impact of commercial duration for TV and radio, on brand awareness. We want to spend our $100,000 to give our ads the greatest brand awareness impact on our target market.

Decision impact: success or failure of a product line.

2. We have budgeted $100,000 to invest in common stocks. We have decided that we want to invest in firms with a good growth record from the past five years, which have had a recent drop in earnings so their stock price is down, and which pay a dividend of under 3 percent so they can reinvest their earnings in more growth.[6] Thousands of stocks on major stock exchanges might meet these criteria.

Decision impact: losing or multiplying the invested funds.

3. We have budgeted $100,000 for new equipment to improve the productivity of our factory. There are dozens of things we could do with the money: upgrade our milling machines, install conveyor belts, buy robotic assembly systems, install a computer to schedule jobs better, hire more workers, rearrange the existing equipment, give our current work force a raise, and so on.

Decision impact: the ability to price the factory's products competitively and still make money, or not to. (Question: What happens if we can't?)

People can make all these decisions, and many others like them, more effectively (not necessarily more efficiently, though this often happens, but more effectively) with computers. One possible way—not necessarily the best—in which a computer could help us make each decision might be the following:

1. *Advertising budget.* We enter a combination of print ads and commercials into a computer, which already has the cost of specific advertising vehicles in its database, so the computer can figure the cost of this combination. We repeat this process until we have a program that costs approximately $100,000. The computer then figures out its awareness impact on our target market by using

---

[6]This is not necessarily a good strategy. If you try it and lose money, don't blame this book.

impact formulas and readership demographic data, which are also in its database. We repeat this process several times until we are happy with the results or decide that we can't improve them much more. (You can read about an actual system of this type in [RATH92].)

2. *Investment decision.* We have a computer scan a database on the New York and American Stock Exchanges for stocks that meet these criteria. The third one, dividend rate, is easy to get from current price data. Several publicly available databases have five-year stock price records. We must define "recent earnings drop" more precisely if we want the computer to scan for that as well. Even without that, the computer can give us a short list of all the stocks that meet the other two criteria and print their earnings history for us to inspect.

3. *Factory upgrade.* We can develop a model of our production process: what steps each product goes through, how long each step takes, what equipment is required for it, what has to happen between each step and the next. We can calibrate our model by plugging in data for our present production process and verifying that the model predicts its present output with acceptable accuracy. We can then enter possible changes to the process, such as a milling machine that carries out step 6 in half the time or a conveyor belt that reduces the time between steps 8 and 9, and see the effect of each $100,000 mix of alternatives. To figure out the effect of giving our workers a raise, we would have to make assumptions about the impact of a raise on job performance, employee turnover (which affects performance), or other factors that affect factory output.

All three of these possible computer systems are decision support systems. If you take another look at the seven themes that we derived from the definitions of a DSS in Figure 1–5, you can see that all three of these example DSS meet the first five points. The first and third DSS presented here use models: Example 1 uses a model of responses to advertising; example 3 uses a model of factory production. The value of these DSS is largely in their ability to carry out many complex calculations quickly so we can use the results. The first and second DSS both use databases: an advertising medium demographics database in the first case, one or more corporate financial history and stock performance databases in the second. The second DSS doesn't do much computing. Its value to an investor lies primarily in its ability to scan these massive databases far more quickly than a person could.

Categorizing the Benefits of DSS

Organizations, and people within organizations, adopt decision support systems such as those already discussed in order to improve some aspect of their operation. We must make this vague desire more specific if we are to plan and develop effective DSS. DSS can help an organization in a number of specific ways. These benefits are not mutually exclusive. It is possible, indeed desirable, for one DSS to help an organization in more than one way. For example, a DSS that **facilitates communication** (see item 3 below) may also, if managers are part of the improved communication process, increase organizational control (see item 5 below).

These categories of DSS benefits were first described by Steven Alter in [ALTE80]. We've changed the titles a bit but kept his basic categories. Although

Alter's research is 20 years old, we'll cite it several times because people and their decision-making needs haven't changed much. Today's DSS technologies would impress an observer from the late 1970s, but the benefits of those technologies in supporting decisions—with a few noted exceptions to follow—are much the same.

1. Improving Personal Efficiency   Many DSS don't do anything a person couldn't do himself or herself. People prepared budgets for centuries before spreadsheet software came into use. DSS help them do it far faster and with less chance of error. Today, few spreadsheet users would willingly revert to manual techniques.

We mustn't confuse efficiency with effectiveness or productivity. Suppose a planner is considering different budgets for a department. A spreadsheet may allow the planner to assess the consequences of a set of choices in a few seconds. People in this situation often fall into the trap of repeating the process long after the incremental benefit has passed the point of diminishing returns. Without a spreadsheet program, our planner might have spent a day on the budget, tried five options, and stopped with a fully satisfactory result. With the program, the same person might try 200 options in two days with no measurable improvement in the outcome. Efficiency went up 20-fold, from five options evaluated per day to 100. Effectiveness, however, was exactly the same, since both final budgets were equally good. Productivity was cut in half, since the process took two days instead of one.

2. Improving Problem Solving   The previous category referred to efficiency in carrying out a specific calculation or data retrieval task. This category of DSS benefits refers to solving the overall problem of which that task is a part. A DSS can make it possible for a person or a group to solve a problem *faster* or *better* than they could without it. There is a relationship between the two, of course: Increased efficiency in a small task, if properly applied, hopefully contributes to solving the problem as a whole.

Solving a problem *faster* is self-explanatory. Some decisions must be made quickly, before the value of a correct decision erodes or more nimble competitors move in. In other cases, a job consists largely of making decisions, and productivity is a direct function of the time spent on each. If the planner of the previous section had the self-discipline to stop after five or ten trial budgets, his or her productivity could have increased enormously. A loan officer who can approve or turn down two applications per hour is twice as productive, all else being equal, as one who evaluates just one per hour. A bank that can double the productivity of its loan officers needs only half as many of them, saving the costs associated with the other half. If those savings exceed the cost of the system that makes the savings possible, the system is financially justified. (If such a system is introduced and half the loan officers are displaced, there are the social costs of job elimination and dislocation. These are separate issues, but managers must not ignore them as it is increasingly important, for both legal and social reasons, to consider these costs.)

Solving a problem *better* may reflect objectively improved decision quality. If a stockbroker without a DSS can pick stocks that perform 20 percent better than the market average, and an equally capable broker with a DSS can select stocks that outperform the market by 30 percent, the benefits of the DSS are clear. The benefit of improved problem solving—better performance of the selected portfolio—is distinct from the increased efficiency with which the DSS retrieves stock information or compares alternative investments. DSS that are used many times for similar decisions, and that replace manual systems which performed the same task in the past, allow us to quantify their benefits in this way.

Solving a problem better may also mean an increased *consistency* of decisions. Here we are not improving the quality of one individual decision, but are improving the effect of a set of related decisions by making them consistent with each other.

Judicial sentencing is an example of this. Intelligent and well-informed individuals have debated "correct" sentencing for millennia without agreement. Most people agree, however, that sentencing should be consistent. One motorist, for example, should not get 30 days in jail for passing a stopped school bus if one in the next courtroom—all other circumstances being similar—is fined $10 and sent home. A DSS can help ensure consistency in sentencing, as well as in other less emotion-laden decisions.

DSS can improve consistency by providing decision makers with information about similar decisions that have been made in the past, or information that constrains a set of similar decisions to be made in the future. Salary increases are an example of data about a group of future decisions. Many large firms give their managers salary increase guidelines but allow managers latitude in interpreting these guidelines. A persuasive low-level manager can obtain a larger-than-average slice of a higher-level manager's salary increase budget, or one manager can give widely varying increases that average out to the right figure while another keeps all raises within 1 percent of the prescribed average. Such inconsistencies are bad for morale. They can be reduced with a DSS.

DSS can also help ensure consistency by making sure that all decision makers use the same assumptions and formulas in reaching their decisions. If all budget analysts in a firm use the same set of economic assumptions (such as inflation) in their work, the overall corporate budget will be better than if they had used different ones.

The technology of expert systems can improve consistency by recommending, on a consistent and unemotional basis, decisions that make sense when given a particular set of facts. That's one of the many close connections between expert systems technology and decision support applications. We'll look at expert systems in detail in Chapter 11.

3. Facilitating Communication   Alter found that DSS facilitate interpersonal communication in several ways. In addition, technology developments that have occurred since his research have opened up new ways for DSS to provide this benefit. One way in which DSS facilitate communication is when used as a tool for persuasion. The system can indicate when a particular action should be taken in the future (**offensive use**) or when a particular action was justified in the past (**defensive use**).

- *Example of offensive use.*   A carefully constructed spreadsheet can persuade a manager to approve a subordinate's budget request. That subordinate may, as a result, obtain more resources than subordinates whose requests are not as well documented. (This is not necessarily unethical. A manager can hardly be expected to approve budget requests that are not well justified.)
- *Example of defensive use.*   A financial forecast can explain, after the fact, why a project that failed was still a good bet based on what was known when it was approved.

Both these examples involve decisions that initially appear to be individual decisions, but that turn out to be group decisions when viewed in a broader organizational context. The proliferation of graphic embellishment capabilities in modern spreadsheet packages is eloquent testimony to the importance of using spreadsheets for persuasion in the business world.

DSS also facilitate communication by providing a common basis for decision making, including standardization of concepts, mechanics, and vocabulary. These are important in group decisions. For example, two people may disagree over the implications of a decline in last year's sales, when the real disagreement is over just what last year's sales comprise. Does the term refer to sales in units, as production people normally measure them, or in dollars, as marketing people do? (If prices are dropping, a firm can have increasing unit sales and decreasing revenue.) Does it encompass the previous calendar year, or the most recent 12 months? Does it count what was booked, what was shipped, what was accepted by customers, what was installed, or what was paid for? Does it include returns made this year of goods sold last year? If the word *sales* is defined in terms of specific data elements to be retrieved from a database, this source of disagreement is eliminated.

A new form of DSS that is designed specifically to provide this type of benefit is called **groupware.** Groupware is decision support software designed to accommodate the way in which a group reaches decisions and to support its activities as a group. To deal effectively with group interactions during the decision-making process, groupware must fulfill an interpersonal communication function. We'll discuss groupware further in Chapter 10.

Some forms of groupware facilitate communication by providing more convenient communication vehicles than were formerly available. Electronic mail is an elementary example of this genre, as are computerized bulletin boards and various forms of electronic conferencing. Others provide clerical support to decision makers, such as by automatic scheduling of meetings for times when all participants are available. These capabilities are helpful—decision makers do send messages, and they do sometimes have to meet—but they are more properly classified as office automation tools or office information systems than as DSS. (This is another example of the point we made earlier: The boundaries between types of information systems are seldom clear-cut.)

True group DSS reflect the nature of the group decision-making process. This may appear in automatic routing of documents so that each participant in a group decision can contribute at the right time. Insurance claims can be routed to the right people in the right order, with each person having available what was done before and being able to add his or her contribution in the right place.

4. Promoting Learning or Training   Improved learning was seldom a goal of early DSS. However, it often occurred as a by-product of their use. Today it is often deliberately incorporated into DSS design. Learning via a DSS occurs when a DSS is used repeatedly: Its user gets to see the types of decisions it favors under different situations, and experience over time lets the user see the results of these decisions. The sort of DSS that facilitates learning, therefore, has to go beyond one that simply retrieves data from a database and presents the data to its user. There isn't much one can learn from a DSS that does that, though such a DSS can be valuable in other ways.

Improved learning is often associated with DSS that follow a humanlike process in reaching a decision, as opposed to DSS that simply provide information for humans to use. Expert systems, which we cover in Chapter 11, can be designed to provide this type of benefit. Most expert systems include an interface facility which allows users to ask why the system made a particular recommendation and receive an answer in nontechnical terms. After seeing many such explanations, their users begin to understand the reasoning of the experts who contributed to the system's development. They can then make better decisions on their own than they could have made previously; learning has thereby taken place.

Using a DSS can also help people learn more about using computers and about the software packages that are in the DSS. Although this is seldom a specific objective of developing the DSS, it can be a valuable by-product.

5. Increasing Organizational Control   This factor refers to using a DSS to constrain individual decisions to conform to organizational norms, guidelines, or requirements. By requiring managers to develop salary increase forecasts using a computerized system, a firm can ensure a level of consistency across organizational units. Another example of this type of consistency occurs in judicial sentencing. Both of these were also used as examples of improved problem solving; they are both. Managers believe that consistent decisions are better than inconsistent ones in these situations and wish to control the organization to ensure that consistency is achieved.

Some DSS can also report information about an individual's decisions to his or her manager. This information can then be used to assess the productivity of the individuals in question, in terms of how many decisions they make or how good their decisions turn out to be. Such capabilities, even if available in a system, should be used with caution. Their use may encourage people to make "safe" decisions, which may not be in the organization's best interests. They can also damage morale. If taken to an extreme, this use of DSS also raises legal and ethical privacy issues.

You can see that these categories overlap. Improving decision quality through increased consistency clearly involves some interpersonal communication. So does increasing organizational control. One value of these categories is that they help us think about what we want to achieve from a DSS, or what our management wants to achieve from it. It's much easier to meet a project's objectives if we have a clear idea of what they are.

1.5 WHY STUDY DSS?

One reason for studying DSS is that they matter to your future or current employer. You should know about them because you'll probably be working on them soon.

We could stop there. But there are more reasons, perhaps even more important ones, that apply even if you won't be working specifically with DSS in your career.

For one, DSS may be the only type of information system you will be able to pursue in-depth during your course of study. Your DSS course is not, of course, your only information systems course. But your other courses probably encompass several types of information systems. Systems analysis is important for defining and designing any type of system. Programming languages work with any application. Database, networking, and others—all these courses are quite general.

DSS uses all these topics. If you've already studied some or all of them, you'll be able to see how they come together for a specific type of application. If you haven't yet studied these areas in detail, knowing how decision support systems use them will better position you to appreciate them when you get to those courses. In short, studying DSS will help you integrate what you already know, and what you have yet to learn, about MIS and about computers.

A second reason for studying DSS is that virtually every information system has decision support aspects. If you understand DSS, whose primary purpose is decision support, you will be in a better position to work on the decision support side of almost any other information system as well.

A third reason, which applies even if you will not have a career as an MIS professional, is that you will be using computers in your career in any field. Much of your use will be for decision support. You will be expected to develop personal DSS via end-user computing, to be an active contributor to the development of group DSS for your work group, and to provide recommendations for enterprisewide DSS. You will be expected to use such systems, whoever develops them. The more you know about DSS, the more you will be an intelligent and informed DSS consumer—and the better your decisions, made with the help of a DSS whose capabilities and limitations you understand, will also be.

1.6 THE PLAN OF THIS BOOK

The objective of this book is simple: to help you (together with your teacher, your classmates, and your own hard work) truly understand what DSS are all about. At the end of this course, you should be able to look at a corporate decision-making situation and see three things:

- *What* decisions are involved.
- *Where* computers could help.
- *How* computers could help.

You should then be able to make DSS recommendations that fit both the business situation and the technology. You should be able to join a team that is developing a DSS with a good understanding of what that DSS will do for its sponsor—your employer. In short, when it comes to DSS, you should be able to earn your keep.

To help you reach this goal, this book is divided into four major parts. The first part, through Chapter 4, covers DSS in general. You'll learn about how people make decisions, how systems work, and about the characteristics of all decision support systems. You'll see how certain types of DSS fit certain types of decisions, or certain types of decision makers, best.

You'll learn how DSS are developed in Chapters 5 through 7. We'll look at the ways in which information systems can be developed, which fit DSS best, and why. You'll read about the hardware and software technologies that go into DSS. We'll also cover the nontechnical side of putting a DSS into use, including some of the ethical issues that DSS developers may face.

The third part of the book, Chapters 8 through 11, will tell you more about particular types of DSS and important aspects of many DSS. You'll learn about the major kinds of models that are useful for decision support, about systems designed to support decisions made by groups of people, and about systems that follow the reasoning processes of human experts. The first few cases in the appendix will show you some real DSS in use and how the concepts of all the chapters through this point come together in practice.

Chapters 12 through 15 cover **data warehousing.** This growing field deals with storing and organizing large amounts of data, often from a variety of areas, for analysis. This analysis can be guided by the user in a process called **on-line analytical processing (OLAP),** or automatic, referred to as **data mining.** Just as some of the cases in the appendix describe real DSS, the last few cases there describe several real data warehousing applications to enable you to see the contributions they make in business today.

Finally, in Chapter 16, we'll piece the picture together and put you in it as you embark on—or continue—your career.

Most of the chapters conclude with a case that demonstrates the principles of that chapter. These cases involve a fictional department store chain called Fort Lowell Trading Company (FLTC). You'll meet FLTC on page 31 at the end of this chapter. Although you don't have to be a retail sales specialist to understand these cases, by the time you finish the book you may feel like one!

How to Use This Book

Your instructor will decide what chapters you will read in this book, in what order you will read them (which might not be the order in which they are printed), which cases you will study, and which exercises you will work out.

Within those constraints, you can do much to make sure you get the most out of the book and your DSS course. Here are some suggestions. Feel free to modify them to suit your own learning style, but do so consciously with the intent of finding a method that works best for you

- Read the introduction to each chapter. It will prepare you for what is to follow.
- Continue by reading the learning objectives. If you achieve all of them, you will have absorbed the most important points of the chapter. As you read the body of the chapter, you can check off the objectives as you cover the material related to each one.
- Read the body of the chapter carefully. Highlighting or underlining is an individual preference. Certainly if it helps you review the material later, highlight or underline key points as you go.
- Many of the chapters include frameworks for categorizing DSS or some aspect of DSS. For example, in Chapter 4 you'll read about seven major types of decision support systems. These frameworks can provide valuable checklists in your career. When studying them, be sure you understand the factors that make the difference between one category in a framework and another.
- If there are any learning objectives you think you haven't achieved when you finish the chapter, go back and find the appropriate sections or note them as questions to ask your instructor.
- Read the review questions and answer them at least mentally to make sure you have learned the key points, even if they are not assigned as written work.
- Skim all the exercises, including the ones that your instructor did not assign. (There are too many in each chapter for an instructor to assign all of them.) Ask yourself, Could I answer this question if I had to? If an exercise really stumps you, reread the portion of the chapter that covers that material. If an exercise requires using a computer, modify the question you ask yourself to, If I had a computer and a suitable software package, and I knew how to use that software, would I be able to do this exercise?
- Read the Fort Lowell Trading Company case episode for the chapter. Although an episode may not be assigned, your instructor may assign one or more episodes in later chapters. Even though most of the episodes do not build directly on previous ones, it will be easier to analyze the subsequent ones if you are already familiar with the firm and its people. The episode for this chapter contains background information that will be relevant in later chapters. In the few cases in which an episode follows up on something that took place in a previous chapter, this will be mentioned.
- Analyze any cases your instructor has assigned. A case is a summary of a real, or a realistic, business situation. In business, you always have information you don't need, and you usually don't have all the information you could use. So it is in a case situation. Don't expect everything in the case to be important to your analysis or answers; it usually isn't. When information is missing, make any necessary assumptions and state them clearly. Material in your college library may be useful in making realistic assumptions. You saw an example of making an approximate but useful calculation in the section "Why Decision Support Systems Matter" on page 13. Here's another.

Example of Making Realistic Assumptions   You are analyzing a case about a manufacturing firm with annual revenues of $100 million. One part of the case analysis requires you to plan the jobs of the people who staff its information systems department. However, the case doesn't give you any information about those people.

To plan the jobs in this department properly, you must first know how many people are in the department. You could proceed as follows:

1. In your library or on the Web, you learn that a typical manufacturing firm allocates 2 percent of its revenue to information systems. If this firm is typical, you reason, it therefore spends $2 million per year (2 percent of $100 million) on information systems.
2. You know that much of this budget must be used to purchase equipment, software, telecommunication services, supplies, and more. You estimate that about 40 percent of the budget will remain to pay the staff. Staff costs, therefore, total $800,000.
3. You assume that the average IS employee costs the firm, including fringe benefits and employer taxes, about $65,000 per year. The information systems department will, therefore, have $800,000 ÷ $65,000 = 13 people from clerk to director.

This is not a precise calculation. It may be off in either direction. This firm may spend more or less on information systems, per revenue dollar, than the average. The fraction of its IS budget that goes to staff salaries could be on either side of the 40 percent we assumed. Average annual employee cost could be above or below $65,000. But each of these figures is in a reasonable range. If this reasoning led you to conclude that the firm has 13 people in its information systems department, the real number (if this were a real firm) would probably be in the range of 10 to 15. It wouldn't be 5 and it wouldn't be 50. You will not make a big mistake by using 13.

Points to Remember   As you read this book, and throughout your career, remember that *technology is a tool to serve organizational needs.* If it does not serve those needs it is of no value. We must always think about the needs first. Learning about technology is important in business only to the degree that it helps organizations obtain information systems that meet those needs. Only when we understand the needs should we think about the technology to meet them. Reversing these steps will lead to the creation of impressive, but useless, monuments to technology.

Once you have defined a clear business need, remember that *information system development is a team effort.* One person acting alone can put together a spreadsheet to track expenses or a database of sales contact names. Anything much larger takes teamwork. The team will have players in many positions: businesspeople from different functional areas, technical specialists of various types, perhaps representatives of customer or supplier organizations. (You'll read more about the types of people involved in DSS projects in Chapter 7.) All these people must respect the skills of the others, be ready to learn from them, and be ready to acknowledge the value of their contributions. This is the only way major development projects can succeed.

SUMMARY

Decision support systems are information systems whose primary purpose is to provide knowledge workers with information on which to base informed decisions. Decision support systems evolved when managers who used transaction processing system output recognized that it could be of value in decision making. First, they called for this data to be organized in ways that would facilitate its decision-making usage. Later, they called for the development of systems designed explicitly for this purpose. Other types of information systems also have value for decision support but are not as clearly focused on it.

Common characteristics of most or all decision support systems include their use by managers and other knowledge workers, their use of a database, and their use of models. DSS are generally used when a computer cannot be programmed to make a decision for all cases. They support, but do not replace, human decision makers.

As a general rule, DSS are used by people who are higher in the organization than those who use transaction processing systems. Each decision that one of these people makes has more bottom-line impact than does each transaction which a TPS processes. Their use of the system tends to be more sporadic, less steady, than is TPS use.

Decision support systems are designed to provide their sponsoring organizations with certain benefits. These benefits can be categorized as (1) improving personal efficiency, (2) expediting problem solving, (3) facilitating interpersonal communication, (4) promoting learning or training, and (5) increasing organizational control.

KEY TERMS

automatic data processing
database
data mining
data processing (DP)
data warehouse, data warehousing
decision support systems (DSS)
defensive use
effectiveness
efficiency
electronic data processing (EDP)
end-user computing
executive information systems (EIS)
expert systems
facilitating communication (DSS benefit)
groupware

improving personal efficiency (DSS benefit)
improving problem solving (DSS benefit)
increasing organizational control (DSS benefit)
information reporting systems (IRS)
knowledge worker
management information system (MIS)
model (in a DSS)
offensive use
office information systems (OIS)
on-line analytical processing (OLAP)
personal information systems
promoting learning or training (DSS benefit)
strategic information systems (SIS)
transaction processing, transaction processing system (TPS)
workgroup information systems

REVIEW QUESTIONS

1. What is a decision support system?
2. Did decision support systems comprise the first use of electronic computers? If not, what was?
3. What are seven common characteristics of most decision support systems?
4. List eight categories of information systems in addition to decision support systems.
5. Can other types of information systems, besides decision support systems, have value in supporting management decisions? If so, give an example.
6. Are DSS more often used by people at the bottom of an organization or above the bottom?
7. Are the decisions made with the help of DSS of value to the organization? Why or why not?
8. Do DSS generally use most of the organization's computing resources and power?
9. State five potential ways in which DSS can benefit an organization.
10. What is the difference between improving personal efficiency and improving problem solving?
11. In what ways can a decision support system be used to facilitate communication?
12. What do we call a decision support system specifically designed to help the way a group reaches joint decisions?
13. What is one type of decision support system that is well suited to help its users learn how to make the decision on their own?
14. Give three reasons why it is worth your while to study decision support systems.
15. What three things should you be able to see in a decision-making situation after you finish this book (and this course)?

EXERCISES

1. Look at recent issues of information systems–oriented publications such as *Computerworld, Information Week,* or *Datamation,* or general business publications

such as *Business Week* and *Fortune,* for articles that discuss firms using computers to help people make decisions. What decisions are involved in these situations? What are the benefits of these systems to their users? In the absence of the systems discussed in the articles, how would the decisions be made? How (according to the article, which may not be objective) is using the system better than the alternatives?

2. Look at recent issues of information systems–oriented publications such as *Computerworld, Information Week,* or *Datamation* for ads for products intended to help people make decisions. What decisions, or categories of decisions, would these products help make? What are the benefits of these products to their users? In the absence of the advertised product, how would the decisions be made? How (according to the ad, which is probably not objective) is using the advertised product better than the alternatives?

3. Your college probably uses computers to store student records, produce class rosters, produce grade reports, print transcripts, and so forth. (If it doesn't, or if you're not sure, assume it does.) With what decisions could the information it uses for these purposes also help? (Hint: there is at least one decision that you make every term.) Who are the decision makers in these cases? With what information could the computer provide them to help make these decisions?

4. Your firm has budgeted $100,000 to improve the performance of its central corporate computer. Options include augmenting the existing disk drives with additional ones of the same type, replacing the existing disk drives with faster ones, expanding main memory, upgrading the central processor to a faster model, rewriting some time-consuming applications for greater efficiency, adding a front-end communications processor to take some of that load off the main system, getting a stand-alone server to handle some tasks (such as employee e-mail and Web access) that don't require access to the central database, and others. Which of the three example decisions on page 17 does this decision resemble? Would the same solution work? What changes would have to be made in the approach, if any?

5. The decision examples on page 17 were all described as individual decisions. The DSS that went along with them were, correspondingly, designed to support one person making them. Could these be group decisions? If they could, what could a Group DSS do to support the group aspect of making the decision that would not help an individual decision maker?

6. Consider each of the following decisions:
   - Travel agents selecting vacation destinations for clients, based on the clients' expressed interests in vacation activities and the agents' knowledge of what is available in various locations.
   - Individual investors deciding when to buy and sell stocks.
   - A firm's purchasing agent selecting the best supplier for parts on the basis of price quotations and different suppliers' history of quality and on-time delivery.
   - Jet engine mechanics diagnosing engine problems as part of their deciding what repairs to perform.
   - A firm's MIS steering committee deciding which new application projects it will fund, which it will reject, and which it will ask for more information about.

   For each of these five decisions:
   a. Could a computerized DSS help the decision makers make these decisions? If not, why not? If so, how?
   b. State the benefit(s), in terms of the categories of Section 1.4, of each of the DSS you thought would be helpful.

REFERENCES

ALTE80 Alter, Steven L. *Decision Support Systems: Current Practice and Continuing Challenges.* Addison-Wesley, Reading, Mass. (1980).

DAVI88 Davis, Michael W. *Applied Decision Support.* Prentice-Hall, Englewood Cliffs, N.J. (1988).

DRUC88 Drucker, Peter F. "The Coming of the New Organization." *Harvard Business Review* 66, no. 1 (January–February 1988), p. 45.

FREN96 Frenzel, Carroll W. *Management of Information Technology,* 2nd ed. Boyd & Fraser, Danvers, Mass. (1996).

HICK93 Hicks, James. *Management Information Systems,* 3rd ed. Irwin Publishing, Homewood, Ill. (1993).

KANT92 Kanter, Jerome. *Managing with Information,* 4th ed. Prentice-Hall, Englewood Cliffs, N.J. (1992).

KEEN78 Keen, Peter G. W., and Michael S. Scott Morton. *Decision Support Systems: An Organizational Perspective.* Addison-Wesley, Reading, Mass. (1978).

KEEN79 Keen, Peter G. W., and G. R. Wagner. "DSS: An Executive Mind Support System." *Datamation* 25, no. 12 (November 1979), p. 117.

KROE92 Kroenke, David M. *Management Information Systems,* 2nd ed. Mitchell McGraw-Hill, Watsonville, Calif. (1992).

LEIB90 Leibowitz, Jay. *The Dynamics of Decision Support Systems and Expert Systems.* Dryden Press, Orlando, Fla. (1990).

LEIG86 Leigh, William E., and Michael E. Doherty. *Decision Support and Expert Systems.* South-Western Publishing Co., Cincinnati, Ohio (1986).

MILL98 Miller, Burke. "California Daylighting," *Solar Today* 12, no. 6 (November/December 1998), p. 30.

OBRI99 O'Brien, James A. *Management Information Systems,* 4th ed., subtitled *Managing Information Technology in the Internetworked Enterprise.* Irwin McGraw-Hill, Burr Ridge, Ill. (1999).

OMNI97 Omni Healthcare. "Omni Healthcare Uses Decision Support to Help Cut Costs, Streamline Operations, and Reach New Markets," *Data Warehousing: What Works?* 4, The Data Warehousing Institute, Gaithersburg, Md. (1997), p. 2.

OZ98 Oz, Effy. *Management Information Systems.* Course Technology, Cambridge, Mass. (1998).

RATH92 Rathnam, Sukumar; M. R. Arun; Abhijit Chaudhury; and P. R. Shukla. "MUDRAPLAN—A DSS for Media Planning: From Design to Utilization," *Interfaces* 22, no. 2 (March–April 1992), p. 65.

SILV91 Silver, Mark S. *Systems that Support Decision Makers.* John Wiley & Sons, New York (1991).

SPRA80 Sprague, Ralph H. Jr. "A Framework for the Development of Decision Support Systems," *MIS Quarterly* 4, no. 4 (December 1980), p. 1.

SPRA79 Sprague, Ralph H. Jr., and Hugh J. Watson. "BIT-BY-BIT: Toward Decision Support Systems," *California Management Review* 22, no. 1 (Fall 1979), pp. 560–68. Reprinted in *Decision Support Systems: A Data-Based, Model-Oriented, User-Developed Discipline,* William C. House, ed. Petrocelli, New York (1983).

STAI97 Stair, Ralph M., and George W. Reynolds. *Principles of Information Systems: A Managerial Approach.* Course Technology, Cambridge, Mass. (1997).

Fort Lowell Trading Company

Most chapters of this book will let you apply what you learn to the operations of Fort Lowell Trading Company (FLTC), a department store chain based in Tucson, Arizona. Miguel and Elizabeth, seniors majoring in MIS at nearby Sabino Canyon College, met FLTC marketing vice president Lou Giovanelli when he gave a talk to a student group at their college. He invited them to do a term project to study the decision support systems that FLTC uses and help them plan new ones. This chapter gives you some background on the firm and its information systems. This information will help you understand the business issues that FLTC, with Miguel's and Elizabeth's help, will face in the episodes to follow.

Although Fort Lowell Trading Company and Sabino Canyon College are fictional, the historical information on Camp Lowell, Fort Lowell, and Tucson is accurate, as are the Tucson-area features mentioned in the case. Sabino Canyon College is named after a wilderness recreation area in the Santa Catalina Mountains on the northeast outskirts of the city. Pony soldiers from Fort Lowell enjoyed horseback excursions to the canyon in the 1870s. Visitors still enjoy the soldiers' swimming hole.

You can read more about Fort Lowell history on the University of Arizona Web site[7] at http://dizzy.library.arizona.edu/images/diverse/ftlowell/ftlowell.html#buttons.

FLTC HISTORY

Fort Lowell Trading Company was founded by Joshua Hale James as the Camp Lowell Trading Post in 1867 next to Camp Lowell, the name given by the U.S. Army to the old Spanish Presidio in what is now Tucson, Arizona. The army moved to a newly constructed Fort Lowell a few miles to the northeast in 1873, in part to distance soldiers from the temptations of the growing town. By then Tucson had become large enough to support several mercantile establishments, so J. H. James saw no reason to follow the troops. He changed his store's name from Trading Post to Trading Company, befitting its new status as an urban store, and followed the army's lead in upgrading from a camp to a fort, reasoning that soon nobody would remember what "Camp Lowell" had been, but kept it where it was.

The Fort Lowell Trading Company remained a thriving family-owned store through the rest of the 19th century, when Tucson was the largest city in Arizona, and the first half of the 20th. In 1962, Stan James, Jr., a descendant of the founder and son of the then president, convinced his father that the store should expand. Stan Jr. had been back from military service for five years then. He had served in the Korean war, in Europe, and in the eastern United States, before obtaining an

---

[7]This URL was valid in August 1999.

M.B.A. degree from Stanford University. He had worked on the sales floor for a year, been an assistant buyer of men's furnishings, and was then in the marketing and promotions department. He was keenly aware that there were opportunities beyond Tucson and wanted the old family firm to take advantage of them.

After considerable discussion and visiting other multistore operations, Stan Sr. finally agreed but insisted on proceeding cautiously. He wanted only one additional store until the results of this limited expansion could be evaluated. The firm soon opened its second store in the Tucson area, on Broadway east of downtown. Several new shopping centers were opening in that area at around that time. The Jameses realized that their customers would be shopping in those centers. They could follow their customers or lose that part of their business. When this store proved to be a success, Stan Sr. agreed to further expansion: first in Arizona (Phoenix, Flagstaff), then in neighboring states. By 1972, Fort Lowell Trading Company stores were in San Diego, California; Albuquerque, Gallup, and Santa Fe, New Mexico; and El Paso, Texas, as well as three in Tucson: the old downtown store on Fourth Avenue, the first expansion on Broadway, and another on Ina Road north of the city.

In 1973, Stan Jr. became senior vice president of the firm, responsible for all store operations, as his father decided to cut back on active involvement in the business. He continued the policy of gradual expansion into more of Texas as well as a few stores in Colorado and Utah. He felt that people in this part of the country shared enough common characteristics to sell similar merchandise through similar methods. He became executive vice president and chief operating officer in 1979. The following year, he hired Niels Agger, a senior planner from a nationwide department store chain, and the two began to lay plans for expansion outside the Southwest.

Agger and the younger James developed an organizational structure where each region of the country would be managed by a regional vice president with extensive authority over merchandise and merchandising methods within the region. The purchasing power of the entire chain (by then it was truly a chain) would be used to advantage wherever two or more regions wanted the same type of goods, but standardization of products from one region to another was not a requirement.

By 1985, the plan had been implemented and proven successful. Other than a few stores taken over from failing chains in the northeastern United States, all their stores had been built from scratch in new, upscale suburban shopping malls. (The Fourth Avenue store had closed by then.) Their philosophy of "Old-Fashioned Quality and Service with a Modern Touch" caught on with the consumers who shopped at these malls. Stan Jr. was now president and CEO of FLTC while Agger had been promoted to vice president of business development. His parents, following Stan Sr.'s complete retirement, spent their time (and well-earned money) traveling the world to indulge in their hobby of bird-watching. While Stan Sr. was still the largest single FLTC stockholder and retained a seat on its board of directors, he attended meetings only if he happened to be near Tucson at the time (or, occasionally, if his presence was wanted for a specific reason); he took no other part in running the firm.

In 1989, Fort Lowell Trading Company sent out its first mail-order catalogue as an experiment to gauge potential interest in such a venture. (FLTC had sent catalogues to customers before, but only to their own customers and primarily in an effort to attract customers to the stores. Catalogue orders were never treated as a business opportunity in their own right.) They discovered that many consumers outside the Southwest were interested in clothing, jewelry, and housewares with a Southwestern flair—not enough to alter their strategy of customizing each region's merchandise to that region's tastes, but enough to justify a strong catalogue-order effort. They also discovered that many of their catalogue order customers were not, insofar as they knew, customers of their retail stores. Since the only way they could tell who was a retail customer was if a person had an FLTC credit card, their information on this last point was sketchy.

By 1997, Fort Lowell Trading Company was a chain of 185 department stores with annual revenue in the high 10 figures, operating in all regions of the United States and across southern Canada. (Canadian operations used the same localization philosophy as U.S. operations. They were divided into an eastern region, from the Atlantic Ocean west through Ontario, and a western region, from Manitoba to the Pacific.) Catalogue operations accounted for 10 percent of FLTC business by dollar volume but 22 percent of its profits. Catalogue operations included a rapidly growing presence on the World-Wide Web.

FLTC INFORMATION SYSTEMS

Fort Lowell Trading Company leased its first computer, an IBM System/360 Model 40, in 1967 when the Broadway store was in the planning stages. (Most commercial computers were leased, not purchased, in that era.) This was a small mainframe computer that, if purchased, would have cost about $500,000. It operated in batch mode under the DOS[8] operating system. Most files were stored on tape, but the system also had four 10M byte disk drives for system software and a few direct access files. This computer was first used solely for accounting: payroll, accounts payable (a big job in a department store), accounts receivable (primarily the store's own charge card), general ledger, among other accounting functions. Applications were primarily third-party packages written in COBOL. FLTC hired a programmer, Dottie Eastman, to modify the packages when necessary and an operator to run the computer. Eastman reported to the accounting manager, and she, in turn, supervised the operator.

Once the Broadway store had proven to be successful and on the road to further expansion of the chain, was clear, it became obvious that some form of central inventory management would be necessary. The computer was upgraded to a System/370 Model 155 with enough disk storage for the inventory files and for

---

[8]Despite having the same name, IBM's DOS (Disk Operating System) for mainframe computers in the 1960s and 1970s is unrelated to desktop DOS (Microsoft MS-DOS) of the 1980s and 1990s. Later versions of mainframe DOS were named DOS-VSE and are usually called "VSE" to avoid confusion.

future conversion of the accounting system to disk. Because the store couldn't find a suitable package for managing inventory the way they wanted to manage it, they hired another programmer to write the new application. Eastman was given the title of data processing manager and moved up to report to the corporate controller.

The process of gradual evolution and expansion continued. Fort Lowell Trading Company tended not to pioneer with new technologies, preferring to wait until they had been proven by others. They felt that they avoided many mistakes that way and that the advantages of pioneering wouldn't be significant to their business. At the present time they operate two large-scale mainframe computers, an S/390 from IBM and a plug-compatible system from Hitachi Data Systems, connected to each other via parallel Sysplex. These are equipped with a combination of storage devices from these two firms and EMC. Both run under the MVS/390 operating system and support hundreds of terminals. High-speed links connect the central mainframes to each regional headquarters, so staff in the regions can access the central systems as though they were local. This eliminates the need for multiuser computers at the regional level.

In addition, each store has an in-store computer controlling its electronic cash registers and managing its local inventory. These computers send sales and inventory data to the mainframes each night and receive updated central inventory data back. Sales clerks can use them to check local stock on an up-to-the-minute basis, stock at other stores as of the close of business on the previous day, and the on-order status of any item. Customers who want an item that isn't in stock locally can have it delivered from any other store the next day if it is available, via overnight courier service delivery to the requesting store.

FLTC also has personal computers throughout its headquarters operations (both chain and regional) and in the main office of every branch. These are used for typical productivity applications such as word processing, spreadsheets, financial analyses, and so on. The advertising and marketing departments also use them to prepare promotional materials. The firm has a mix of desktop systems, including IBM-compatible computers from four vendors and Macintosh OS systems from two. The IBM-compatible or "Wintel" systems generally run Windows 98. Most Mac OS systems use System 8.6. A few people still use older releases of both, while the central support staff is coming up to speed on more recent ones (and the company braces for the cost of the hardware upgrades that Windows 2000 will require).

FLTC desktop applications are standardized to reduce support costs. Common applications, such as Adobe Photoshop for photo editing or Microsoft Excel for spreadsheets, are used on both the Windows and Mac OS platforms unless a specific need for an exception is demonstrated. The wide availability of cross-platform applications, and the ease of data interchange with them, gives FLTC sufficient compatibility while allowing each knowledge worker to choose Windows or Macintosh as he or she prefers. This approach is also in line with the corporate culture of providing each region or person with the maximum possible autonomy consistent with meeting the firm's needs.

Data is distributed within corporate and regional headquarters on gigabit Ethernet LANs connected to the mainframes via high-speed gateways and a nationwide WAN of T1 and Fractional T1 lines. Many regional buyers and planners use sales data from the corporate database. Their applications run in client/server mode, using the central database but performing most of the work at the desktop. The network is also used for sending electronic mail and other data. Each region's local data is stored on local servers that run Windows 2000. These servers also route electronic mail within the office; via the gateway, to the rest of the organization; or through a security "firewall" system to the rest of the world over the Internet.

Dottie Eastman has stayed with Fort Lowell Trading Company and is now vice president of information services. The firm's total information technology budget—including hardware, software, data communications carrier services, staff salaries, purchased services, supplies, and other incidentals—is about $100 million per year. Though this spending is not all under her direct control, her organization exerts a strong influence on purchases made by other business units. Those units know they will have to call on Dottie's group for support and for integrating their systems with the rest of the organization, so they generally take its recommendations seriously.

In the coming chapters you'll follow Miguel and Elizabeth, two MIS students at Sabino Canyon College in Tucson, as they study Fort Lowell Trading Company's decision support systems. They'll look at the systems that FLTC already uses and consider ways in which the firm could make better use of information technology for decision support.

Fort Lowell Trading Company employees, in the order in which you'll encounter them with the chapter in which they're first mentioned, include:

Lou Giovanelli, Vice President of Marketing (Chap. 1)

Stan James, Sr., retired CEO, member of Board of Directors (Chap. 1)

Stan James, Jr., President and CEO (Chap. 1)

Niels Agger, Vice President of Business Development (Chap. 1)

Dottie Eastman, Vice President of Information Services (Chap. 1)

Ashwin Puri, Director of Application Systems (Chap. 4)

Vanessa McAnaney, lead systems analyst/project leader on new finance system (Chap. 4)

Bob Goldberg, Director of Technology Planning (Chap. 5)

Christopher Demas, Manager of Financial Planning (Chap. 6)

Norma LaRosa, finance department member responsible for cost-of-capital figures (mentioned by Chris Demas, Chap. 7)

Joe Two Crows, Manager, Store Information Systems (Chap. 7)

Leighton Chen, Systems Analyst for Warehouse Simulation (Chap. 8)

Rob Fernandez, Manager, Accounting Information Systems (Chap. 9)

Kareem Davis, Director of Marketing Planning (Chap. 10)

Jim Atcitty, Market Planner on data warehouse pilot project (Chap. 12)

CHAPTER 2

Human Decision-Making Processes

CHAPTER OUTLINE

Introduction

Decision support systems, by definition, exist to help people make decisions. They do not make decisions by themselves. This is why they are called decision *support* systems, not decision-*making* systems. Since DSS must work with human decision makers, they must fit into the way humans work—or, at least, into a way in which the relevant humans can be persuaded to work. If we don't understand decisions and decision making, how can we hope to support them? DSS designers must therefore understand human decision-making processes.

CHAPTER OBJECTIVES

After you have read and studied this chapter, you will be able to:

1. Discuss what a decision is and how decisions are characterized.
2. Describe the phases that every decision goes through.

3. Identify two important ways of categorizing decisions: on the basis of their structure and on the basis of their scope.
4. Outline the nine decision types.
5. Discuss several methods managers use to make decisions.
6. Identify four preferences which determine personality type.
7. Outline the eight stages of the Kepner-Tregoe decision-making method.

2.1 WHAT IS A DECISION?

A **decision** is a reasoned choice among alternatives. We make decisions regularly in our daily lives. Personal decisions include what to have for dinner, which courses to take, whether to do homework or see a movie instead. Business decisions include how much to charge for a product, where to advertise a new service, how to finance construction equipment, which candidate to hire for a job. Business decisions may seem more significant and get more space in the daily paper, but all are part of the same picture.

Making decisions is part of the broader subject of **problem solving.** Problem solving is the overall process of closing the gap between reality and a more desirable situation. To solve a problem, we must first realize that the problem, the gap, exists. We must then conclude that the problem is important enough to do something about. Having done this, we will probably discover that there are obstacles which prevent us from reaching the desired state immediately and effortlessly.

In most interesting cases there is no obvious way to overcome some of these obstacles. Upon reflection, possibly involving a group of people and creativity techniques such as "brainstorming," we will usually uncover several possible approaches. This leads directly to a need for one or more decisions: first in choosing one or more of them, then in refining it. Once those decisions are made, they must be put into action (implemented). The implementation must be monitored to make sure our decisions and the resulting actions do indeed solve the problem. If they do not, we have a new or modified problem. The process then repeats.

Each decision is characterized by a decision statement, a set of alternatives and a set of decision making criteria. These always exist, though we are not always aware of them. Figure 2–1 shows how they relate to each other in the decision context.

The **decision statement** states what we are trying to decide. A clear decision statement is important to intelligent decision making. It keeps our thinking focused clearly on the main subject and away from irrelevant side issues. If a decision is to be made by a group of people, a clear decision statement ensures that all members of the group are trying to decide the same thing. Group decision support tools, which we'll focus on in Chapter 10, can help people in different locations communicate about a joint decision statement.

> If you do not have a clear decision statement, you cannot develop the best system to support people making that decision. Begin every DSS development project by getting—or at least trying to get—a clear understanding of the decision(s) to be made with the help of the proposed system.

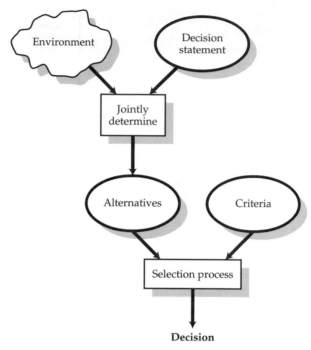

FIGURE 2–1 Relationship Among Decision Statement, Alternatives, and Criteria

The **alternatives** are the possible decisions we can make. Sometimes there are few alternatives: a stadium vendor offers only pizza and hot dogs, or there are only two candidates for a job that must be filled right away. In other situations there are thousands: to pick an investment from all the firms whose stock is traded on major stock exchanges, or to choose the mix of options to be installed in a factory-ordered automobile. For these the decision maker needs to narrow the range down to a reasonable number. Decision support tools such as selective information retrieval systems can help with this task.

Decision-making **criteria**[1] are what we want to optimize in a decision. In making an investment we may be concerned with income, growth, and safety of principal. In choosing a car we care about appearance, comfort, performance, economy of operation, reliability, safety, and initial cost.

It may not be possible to optimize all the decision criteria at the same time. Stocks with above-average growth potential often have above-average risk. Most high-performance cars are not economical to operate. Compromises are called for. Decision makers often cannot define their approach to these compromises in a precise mathematical way. Indeed, they often cannot define their decision-making criteria precisely. However, the criteria and the approaches to compromise exist even if the decision maker cannot specify them.

---

[1]*Criteria* is the plural form of this noun. If there's just one, the singular is *criterion.*

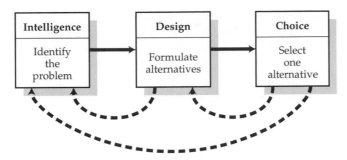

FIGURE 2–2   Flow among Three Decision Phases

Where the selection process among alternatives can be put in numerical terms, computers can help carry out the evaluation. Even where this is not the case, computers can assist in presenting the alternatives in a form that facilitates making a decision.

2.2 THE DECISION PROCESS

Every decision must go through the three phases shown in Figure 2–2. These phases, called **intelligence, design,** and **choice,** were first defined by Herbert Simon in [SIMO60]. Whereas each decision must incorporate each phase at least minimally, the emphasis on each phase, and the relationships among the phases, often differ from one decision to another because of the following:

- Different people may emphasize one phase or another, as we'll see when we discuss preferred styles of behavior on page 59.
- Different decision-making situations call for spending more time in one phase or another.
- We often bounce back and forth among the phases: We may try to select an alternative only to discover we don't know enough to do that yet, so we go back and collect more data. (The dotted lines in Figure 2–2 show this.)

Despite these facts, and despite our not always being consciously aware of what we are doing when we make a decision, all three phases exist in some form in every decision we make. It is important for the prospective developer of a DSS to understand these phases, because computers can support each decision phase in different ways, and the ideal computer support for a decision process depends on the phases that are important for that process.

2.2.1 The Intelligence Phase

The intelligence phase consists of finding, identifying, and formulating the problem or situation that calls for a decision. (This has been called "deciding what to decide.") The intelligence stage may involve, for example, comparing the current status of a project or process with its plan. The end result of the intelligence phase is the decision statement.

Example. We return to our room one evening and find a memo from the dean telling us that next term's courses must be chosen in the next two weeks. We have at this point identified a situation that calls for a decision. The decision statement is simple: What courses should we register for? The intelligence phase for this decision is now complete, and we can proceed to the next phase. (If the decision were less obvious, such as deciding whether to take a year off or whether or not to attend graduate school, the intelligence stage would take longer.)

It is important not to confuse the symptoms of a problem with the underlying problem itself. Suppose a customer calls to complain about late deliveries. If we think in terms of alleviating the symptom, we may arrange for that customer to receive future shipments via overnight air courier service. If the underlying problem is an understaffed shipping department, however, this will merely placate one of many unhappy customers without identifying, let alone dealing with, the real issue. What's more, we can sometimes make a problem worse by dealing with only a symptom. In this example, if we installed a "hot line" for customers to communicate with the shipping department about late deliveries, we would add to the department's workload without enabling it to ship products any more quickly. Since a symptom can often result from any of several causes, it is important to identify its true cause before we try to deal with the problem.

The name of this phase, "intelligence," can be confusing. Intelligence, as we usually use the term informally in talking about decision making, is what we use after we know a decision must be made. Simon borrowed the term from its meaning in espionage or in the military, which involves the gathering of information without always knowing what it will lead to in terms of decisions to be made. In business decision making, we must often collect a great deal of information before we realize that a decision is called for.

Military intelligence can also, of course, be more focused: We might try to determine an enemy's troop distribution in order to concentrate an attack on its weak points. That type of information gathering falls into the next phase of decision making.

2.2.2 The Design Phase

The design phase is where we develop alternatives. This phase may involve a great deal of research into the available options. During the design phase we should also state our objectives for the decision we are to make.

Example: In deciding what courses to take, we know what courses are required for our major, we know that we will have the prerequisites for a subset of these, and we know what courses will be offered next term and at what times. This information enables us to construct a variety of alternative schedules.

2.2.3 The Choice Phase

In the choice phase, we evaluate the alternatives that we developed in the design phase and choose one of them. The end product of this phase is a decision that we can carry out.

The Importance of Creativity

What creative alternatives can you come up with? That's your goal in the design phase of a decision. This classic story helps illustrate what a creative alternative is.

A physics professor asked this question on an exam: How could you use a barometer to find the height of a building? He wanted the standard answer using a barometer's unique capability to measure atmospheric pressure: measure the pressure on the roof, measure it again at ground level, then calculate the height from the difference between the two. He also got these creative (and correct) responses.

- Drop the barometer from the roof. With a stopwatch, time its fall until it crashes on the sidewalk. Use the formula for falling body acceleration under gravity to find the height.
- Tie a long string to the barometer. Lower it from the roof to just above the sidewalk. Swing it from side to side and time its oscillations. Use the formula for oscillation frequency as a function of pendulum length to find the height.
- Walk up the stairs from the ground floor to the roof. Place the barometer against the wall as you go, thus measuring the building in barometer lengths. Then, measure the barometer with a ruler to convert the count to the desired unit of measure.
- Place the barometer in the sun near the building. Measure its shadow and that of the building. Then measure the height of the barometer. Calculate the height of the building from the length of its shadow and the ratio of the barometer's height to the length of the barometer's shadow.

My personal favorite, however, is this:

- Take the barometer to the building superintendent's office. Say to the superintendent, "I have this fine brass and wood barometer. I will give it to you, if you will please look at the plans of this building and tell me how high it is."

Example: In choosing our initial course request, we might consider our personal interests, what we know about the work required in different courses, the reputations of different faculty members, and our preferences for class meeting times. The relative importance of these factors varies from one person to another, and for a given person, from one situation to another. If we want to leave time for an off-campus job, we might opt for classes held only on Mondays and Wednesdays even if this schedule would mean taking an elective we'd rather avoid. Given more scheduling flexibility, we might take a Tuesday, Thursday, and Friday course on a more interesting topic.

The three decision phases are not as separate as this description implies. As Simon points out:

> The cycle of phases is, however, far more complex than the sequence suggests. Each phase in making a particular decision is itself a complex decision making process. The decision phase, for example, may call for new intelligence activities; problems at any given level generate subproblems that in turn have their intelligence, design and choice phases, and so on. There are wheels within wheels.

Thus, decision making is often an iterative process. We start by making a decision. We then proceed to put that decision into effect. At that point we may encounter an unanticipated difficulty: a shortage of parts for our product design, a price tag of

$35,000 on that "cute little BMW," or the fact that all the discount tickets on American Airlines flight 59 to San Francisco have been sold. We return to an earlier stage and consider additional alternatives in light of our new information. We may even revise our decision-making criteria if we realize, having looked at our first choice in more detail, that we left one or more important points out. We may even build iterations into our decision-making process. A common example is in the development of a major information system, where management calls for periodic project reviews. At each review managers decide whether to proceed to the next phase of the project, spend more time in the current phase, back up to an earlier one, or cancel the project entirely.

Knowing the decision phase we are in can help us design the right computer system to support that phase. In the intelligence phase, we may need broad-based information-gathering capabilities. In design, more focused information retrieval or perhaps brainstorming aids could be useful. In the choice phase, optimization tools can help.

2.3 TYPES OF DECISIONS

Decisions can be categorized in several ways. This categorization is useful because decisions of the same type often have common characteristics. They can therefore benefit from similar computer support. If we can categorize a decision while planning a DSS, we will be able to see which DSS have been used to good effect with that type of decision in the past, and can expect similar DSS to help with the problem at hand.

Following Gorry and Scott Morton [GORR71], we can organize decisions along two dimensions: the nature of the decision to be made and the scope of the decision itself. By dividing each dimension into three categories, we obtain nine decision types, as are shown in Figure 2–3. The three categories shown down the left side of Figure 2–3 (from [GORR71]) extend Simon's earlier concept of programmed versus nonprogrammed decisions. Those categories are as follows:

- A **structured decision** is one for which a well-defined decision-making procedure exists. A structured decision could be given over to a computer program, though the economics might not justify developing such a program in every case. More precisely, a structured decision is one for which the inputs, outputs, and internal procedures of all three decision phases (intelligence, design, and choice) can be specified. Each decision phase for which this is true is called a **structured decision phase.** Structured decisions can be left to a clerk with written instructions or to a computer.

FIGURE 2–3 3×3 Decision Type Grid

	Operational	Tactical	Strategic
Structured	1	2	3
Semistructured	4	5	6
Unstructured	7	8	9

A computer system that makes a structured decision by itself isn't a decision support system, as we've defined one, but a decision-*making* system. We include structured decisions here because they complete the picture, because totally structured nontrivial decisions are rare, and because human participation often improves the overall decision-making process even though it might not be strictly necessary.

- An **unstructured decision** is one for which all three decision phases are un-structured. In this case we don't know how to specify at least one aspect of each phase: its inputs, its outputs, or its internal procedures. This may be because the decision is so new or so rare that we haven't studied it carefully. Computers can still help knowledge workers make unstructured decisions, but in different ways and while leaving more of the process to the worker.

- A **semistructured decision** has some structured aspects but cannot be completely structured. This usually means that one or two of its three phases are structured but the other one(s) isn't (aren't). Computers can provide a great deal of specific help with semistructured decisions. Conveniently, most organizational decisions are of this type.

The proper placement of a decision within these categories is not always clear-cut. Sometimes our approach to a problem defines how we think about it. One decision maker may feel that an optimum selling price can be determined by analyzing product costs and price-demand curves. This person would consider the choice phase of this decision to be structured. Another, however, might argue that these curves do not reflect all the factors that affect customer response to price, and that some important factors cannot be quantified. That person would, equally correctly, consider the choice phase of this decision to be unstructured or, at best, semistructured.

The three levels of decision scope across the top of Figure 2–3 (originally from [ANTH65]) are as follows:

- A **strategic decision** is one which will affect the entire organization, or a major part of it, for a long period of time. Strategic decisions affect organizational objectives and policies. Strategic decisions are generally, but not always, made at upper levels of organizational management.

  Example: "We will have an employee cafeteria." Changing this decision could have a substantial impact on the workforce's morale.

- A **tactical decision,** also called a *management control decision,* will affect how a part of the organization does business for a limited time into the future. These decisions generally take place within the context of previous strategic decisions. Tactical decisions are generally made by middle managers: those who are below the top executives who set strategic policies, but high enough to determine how an entire category of future actions will be taken.

  Example: "We will offer a choice of three entrées, one of which will be vegetarian and another of which will be either fish or poultry, each day." This decision is made within the context of the strategic decision—in particular, it assumes there will be an employee cafeteria—and sets guidelines for the next category of decisions.

- An **operational decision** is one that affects a particular activity currently taking place in the organization, but either has little impact on the future or—if it does have an impact—is made within the confines of a controlling policy. Operational decisions relate to activities whose tasks, goals, and resources have already been defined via prior strategic and tactical decisions. Operational decisions are generally made by lower-level managers or by nonmanagerial personnel.

  Example: "Next Tuesday we'll serve vegetarian lasagna, bluefish with mustard sauce, and pot roast." This decision has no impact beyond next Tuesday, except perhaps for some leftover pot roast to use up in a stew on Wednesday. It conforms to the policy established in the previous (tactical) decision.

Decisions of these three types vary in their information requirements: from detailed to aggregated, near-present to future, and so on. Figure 2–4, taken from [KEEN78], shows the key information characteristics of each decision level. If you know the scope of a decision being made, use this table to generate a good idea of the type of data your DSS will require.

The two decision characteristics—structure and scope—are not totally correlated, though they are not unrelated either. As a general rule, operational decisions tend to be more structured. Strategic decisions tend to be less so. Most business decisions tend to fall along the diagonal of Figure 2–3, from the upper left to the lower right corners. Here are examples of the nine decision types to help give you a feel for the categories:

1. *Structured/Operational:* deciding how to cut a log into boards in order to minimize wastage. In most sawmills this decision is not made by computers, though computers have been proven to be good at it; it is usually made by experienced

FIGURE 2–4   Information Characteristics by Decision Scope

Information Characteristic	Operational	Tactical (Management)	Strategic
Accuracy	High	⟵——⟶	Low
Level of detail	Detailed	⟵——⟶	Aggregate
Time horizon	Present	⟵——⟶	Future
Frequency of use	Frequent	⟵——⟶	Infrequent
Source	Internal	⟵——⟶	External
Scope of information	Narrow	⟵——⟶	Wide
Nature of information	Quantitative	⟵——⟶	Qualitative
Age of information	Current	⟵——⟶	Can be older
Flexibility of organizing information*	Can be rigid	⟵——⟶	Must be flexible

*Added to Keen's original figure.

saw operators. The reason for this is it is not practical to measure each log precisely and enter its dimensions—not just the overall length and diameter but all the twists and variations of the log—into a computer quickly enough for the result to be useful. (As of late 1998, however, some pilot projects involving laser beams show promise.)

We can see that this decision is structured by looking at the three decision phases. The intelligence phase is trivial: If a log arrives at the mill, it must be cut. (Can you write an appropriate decision statement?) The design phase is likewise fixed: The products that the mill produces, and hence the acceptable types of cuts, are not within the purview of the saw operator. The operator cannot, on a whim, decide that it would be nice to cut 2-by-5–inch lumber this week instead of the usual 2-by-4 and 2-by-6. The choice phase can be optimized mathematically because the value of each potential board is known from business considerations, and the number of boards that can be obtained via each combination of cuts is a problem in solid geometry.

Inventory reordering also falls into the structured/operational category if the buying organization has a good enough forecast of an item's future use to benefit from the optimization models that have been developed for this field.

2. *Structured/Tactical:* choosing the way in which to depreciate corporate assets. There are many options, including straight-line depreciation and various accelerated depreciation formulas that provide earlier tax benefits than does the straight-line method. Accelerated depreciation, however, may have drawbacks as well, such as making the depreciated asset ineligible for investment tax credits. The issues are complex and vary with every revision of the tax code, but—if the depreciable life of this type of asset is specified by the tax code and the choice can be made on a net-present-value or similar numerical basis—are entirely quantitative and can be dealt with mechanically.

Resource allocation problems that can be solved by linear programming methods are also in this category. As with inventory management, the issue is whether the problem to be solved meets the requirements for this approach.

3. *Structured/Strategic:* This is a rare combination. An example might be a decision that is usually tactical in nature, but which because of its size becomes of the "you bet your company" variety. Deciding whether or not to proceed with an R&D project on the basis of projected ROI might normally be a tactical decision, but if the proposed project will tie up 80 percent of the firm's R&D staff for the next two years it becomes strategic. (If factors other than projected ROI enter into the decision, it might not be structured in the first place.)

A plant location decision could be in this category if the only factors in the decision are quantifiable, such as transportation costs of known raw materials from known locations and of known products to known markets.

4. *Semistructured/Operational:* deciding to accept or reject an applicant to a selective college. Some parts of this decision are quite structured. An applicant with a combined SAT score of 1400 is, all other things being roughly equal, more likely to succeed academically in most colleges than is one with a combined score of 600. Other issues, such as a desire to balance the nonacademic characteristics of an entering class and the degree to which unusual talents,

such as playing second base or double bass, can offset lower-than-desirable grades, cannot be evaluated as quantitatively.

5. *Semistructured/Tactical:* choosing an insurance carrier for an employee health program. Cost per employee is an important and objective factor in this decision. Intangible factors include the acceptability of a carrier to the employee population and the relative importance of different benefits: Is 100 percent hospitalization coverage with a $250 deductible amount better or worse than 80 percent coverage with no deductible? (While actuaries can answer this question on an average statistical basis, the preference of an employee group does not necessarily match the numbers.)

6. *Semistructured/Strategic:* deciding whether or not to enter a new market. Sales projections, marketplace growth data, development cost estimates, and marketing expense forecasts can combine to provide a profit-and-loss forecast. This forecast, however, cannot take into account the myriad of factors that could make it totally worthless. The judgment of experienced managers is needed for that final step.

7. *Unstructured/Operational:* dealing with a machine breakdown. If the machine in question doesn't break down often, there is probably no set procedure for what to do while awaiting repair service. This decision is operational because the way a company deals with one machine failure need not set a precedent for the next.

8. *Unstructured/Tactical:* Hiring decisions typically fall into this area, especially if the job to be filled is above the level where aptitude and ability tests can be relied on as performance indicators. Civil Service procedures have attempted to structure the hiring task for years. The wide use of "escape hatches," such as allowing a police chief to choose the next lieutenant from the three top-scoring sergeants on a promotion exam, testifies eloquently to their lack of complete success.

9. *Unstructured/Strategic:* deciding how to respond to an unfriendly takeover proposal made by a competitor. The actions taken can have a long-term impact on the entire firm. The range of options is so wide, they differ so much from each other, and the issues are so hard to quantify, that direct comparison is all but futile.

Figure 2–5 shows examples of the nine decision types that might come up during your college or university years. Exercise 6 at the end of this chapter asks you to come up with examples of your own for a specific business situation.

FIGURE 2–5 Grid with Examples of Nine Decision Types

	Operational	Tactical	Strategic
Structured	Should I buy another campus meal card?	How should I budget for expenses next month?	What student loans should I take out?
Semistructured	How should I travel to classes today?	Which section of macroeconomics should I ask for?	Which job offer should I take after graduation?
Unstructured	What should I choose for lunch at the cafeteria?	Who should I room with next year?	What should I major in?

2.4 HOW BUSINESSPEOPLE MAKE DECISIONS

Managers' and other knowledge workers' decisions have a great impact on corporate success. The subject of business decision making has therefore been studied intensively for years. (It has also been the subject of a great deal of humor, such as in the *Blondie* and *Dilbert* comic strips.) The many methods by which businesspeople make decisions can be categorized [DEAN91] along three dimensions: rationality, politicality, and flexibility.

Rationality in decision making is the extent to which the decision makers collect and analyze information objectively and choose among the alternatives on the basis of the relationship of these alternatives to predetermined objectives.

Politicality is the extent to which a decision involves competition among decision makers and the extent to which the decision depends on the distribution and use of organizational power.

Flexibility is the extent to which decision makers free themselves from tradition and structure, potentially making choices that "break the mold."

The rationality dimension of this categorization is often used to separate decision-making approaches into two categories: the normative and descriptive models of decision makers' behavior.

In these terms, **normative** models are those that presume a decision maker is objectively optimizing a quantifiable measure of decision quality. (This may be a statistical measure because the future is never completely known.) There is, in other words, a normed scale against which decisions can be measured—and, it is often assumed, unlimited time and resources to devote to analyzing the decision.

Descriptive models, by contrast, attempt to describe the ways people really do make decisions. We don't always have agreed-upon measures of decision quality, we don't usually have unlimited time or resources to analyze a decision, and we often have motivations that can be hard to explain or justify.

It has been said that "normative models describe what we should do, while descriptive models describe what we do." This is not strictly correct. It can be a correct decision, for example, for a manager to make a quick decision even though the decision has not been made as well as possible, if the decision is unimportant and the decision maker's time is better spent on something else. (If our car is running low on fuel and we're in a hurry, we'll probably stop at the first filling station we see rather than search for a less expensive one or a preferred brand.) Many aspects of business in the real world force compromises with theoretical concepts. This is acceptable as long as one knows *what* one is compromising and *why*.

The distinction between normative and descriptive models is important in DSS because DSS both reflect existing decision-making methods and have a goal of improving them. Understanding how people make a given decision today, and seeing how a DSS could fit into that picture, requires a descriptive model. Trying to make that decision as well as possible often requires the system designer to think about a normative model. Both points of view are therefore important.

Example of Normative Versus Descriptive Decision Making   You are considering what to eat for dinner. You have narrowed your options down to two choices:

a green salad with alfalfa sprouts, tofu, and fat-free dressing, or a pepperoni-and-sausage pizza. A normative approach to this decision would consider all the long-term and short-term factors, assign appropriate weights to each, and evaluate each dinner on the basis of those factors. In all likelihood, this approach would recommend the salad as better for you. Nevertheless, many people faced with this decision would opt for the pizza. When we decide by "gut feel" we tend to weigh near-term considerations (taste, in this case) more heavily than we should. We go for instant gratification.[2] As for heartburn and the potentially more serious effects of a high-fat diet over decades—we can worry about those later.

2.4.1 The Rational Manager[3]

Rational management is the classical assumption about how managers make, or are supposed to make, decisions. The rational manager presumably obtains all possible facts, weighs the likelihood of the alternative outcomes, and chooses the one with the highest statistically probable value to the firm. Rational management is a normative model of decision making.

One limit on the applicability of rational management is in the short phrase "highest statistically probable value" in the previous paragraph. This phrase presumes that the decision maker has an objective value scale and that all alternatives can be measured on this scale. This value scale is usually taken to be financial. This can work when all alternatives can be evaluated in financial terms: What is the best depreciation method to use for this piece of equipment? However, many decisions have no such yardstick: Which college should I attend? Which job should I take after graduation? What should I order for dinner? While all three of these decisions do involve financial considerations—colleges cost different amounts of money, jobs differ in salary, and different meals have different prices—they raise other issues as well, which will often outweigh the financial factors.

In terms of the three dimensions previously discussed, the rational manager is clearly high on the rationality scale. This approach can, however, be used in ways that incorporate the other two dimensions as well. As Dean et al. point out, an acceptable decision can be the product of both rational and political factors, perhaps by using rational analysis to select among politically viable options.

A **decision tree**[4] is a useful way to represent the options facing the rational manager. The use of decision trees presumes a sequence of events of the form "If I do A, then X or Y might happen; if Y happens, I can do B or C, in which case R, S, or T might happen," and so forth. They reflect the rational manager's thought process in choosing among those options. Figure 2–6 is an example of a decision tree.

---

[2]"We" here includes this author. While pepperoni and sausage are not his favorite combination, he eats pizza far more often than he has tofu in a salad.

[3]*Rational management* is the traditional term for this decision-making style. We'll use it here and later, partly for this reason and partly because it's shorter than most of the alternatives. You know, of course, that businesspeople in nonmanagement positions make important decisions also.

[4]A different type of decision tree is used to represent a sequence of choices made in arriving at a decision. We'll discuss this type of tree in a data mining context in Section 15.2.1.

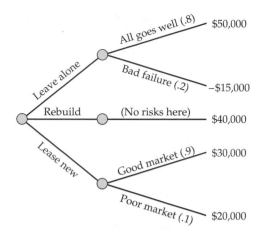

FIGURE 2–6   **Decision Tree for Truck Engine Decision**

This tree has two levels. The first represents the management decision. The second represents the possible outcomes, sometimes called *states of nature,* that can result from choosing each of the options at the first level. A decision tree may have more than two levels but will always have an even number of them. It always starts with a decision, the two types of nodes always alternate, and states of nature are always at the ends of the branches (at the "leaf nodes").

To anticipate briefly a topic we discuss later, the states of nature at the end of the branches aren't always given to us as numbers. In the example of Figure 2–6, we may know the exact cost of rebuilding an engine, but the profit the truck will earn over two years is an estimate. The actual profit will depend on the availability of cargo, future costs of labor and fuel, and whether or not a whole host of possible events actually happen. Decision makers and decision support systems use a variety of models to predict what systems will do in the future. We'll come back to models in general terms in the next chapter. After that, we'll cover some important types in detail in Chapters 8 and 9.

The decision to be made in Figure 2–6 is: Should we rebuild a truck's worn engine, leave it as is, or replace the truck? Leaving it alone costs nothing today, will enable us to make a profit of $50,000 over our 2-year planning horizon with a likelihood of 80 percent, but also presents a 20 percent chance of incurring a $15,000 loss due to unexpected failures. Rebuilding the engine costs $5,000 now and ensures a $45,000 operating profit over the 2 years, for a net profit of $40,000. (We will lose a potential $5,000 in profits while the truck is off the road having its engine rebuilt.) A new truck will cost $50,000 to lease for 2 years, will enable us to earn an $80,000 profit during the 2 years because it will be faster and more economical to operate than our present one, but has a 10 percent probability of a $10,000 charge at the end of the lease if the market for this type of truck is poor at that time.

The decision tree allows us to evaluate the probable payoff of each option. The probable payoff of rebuilding the engine is $40,000, in that we have assumed that

	Profit as function of computer system choice and customer acceptance of firm's services	
Decision alternative	High customer acceptance (30% probable)	Low customer acceptance (70% probable)
Lease large computer system	$200,000	(–$20,000) (loss)
Lease medium computer system	$150,000	$20,000
Lease small computer system	$100,000	$60,000

FIGURE 2–7 Decision Table Example

no chance misfortunes can befall that choice. The probable payoff of letting nature take its course with the engine is $0.8 \times \$50,000 + 0.2 \times (-\$15,000) = \$40,000 - \$3,000 = \$37,000$. A similar calculation, working back from the end nodes and their probabilities, shows that the probable payoff of leasing a new truck is $29,000. Accordingly, the rational manager opts to rebuild the engine.

A tree is not the only possible way to evaluate the possible outcomes of a decision such as this. Other approaches include decision tables[5] and formulas. Figure 2–7 shows a decision table for a business that must choose a small, medium, or large computer, and that may encounter high or low customer acceptance of its services.

Palvia and Gordon compare the three approaches—decision trees, decision tables, and formulas—in [PALV92], from which the example in Figure 2–7 is taken. They found that the table method was preferable overall for the sample task used in their study, but that this varies with the specific task and with the characteristics of the decision maker. The truck engine example previously mentioned is difficult to express as a decision table because the "state of nature" possibilities vary depending on the choice we make. That is, the factors that determine whether an old engine, unrepaired, will fail on the road are not the same factors that determine the resale value of a truck at the end of a lease. Tables work better in situations such as the one in Figure 2–7, where all the choices are subject to the same chance effects. In the example of Figure 2–7, a rational manager who wants to maximize the statistically expected profit would choose the small computer system.

Statistically expected profit is not the only possible decision criterion. At one extreme, a risk-averse manager might want the best possible result if the worst state of nature occurs. That is the $60,000 profit in the bottom right cell of the figure. This manager would make the same choice as the rational manager: Get the small computer. A "high roller," however, might go for the maximum possible payoff if all goes well, even at the risk of high losses if the best state of nature does not occur. This manager would see the $200,000 possible profit in the top row and would get the large computer. Neither of these two philosophies is truly rational in the traditional sense, but they do exist.

---

[5]The term *decision table* can also mean a table that describes how a computer or person should make a fully structured decision. Such a table lists the conditions that affect the decision and the action(s) to be taken for every possible combination of conditions. The two usages are unrelated.

2.4.2 Subjective Utility

Human beings are not, as you have probably noticed by now, entirely rational. Suppose the rebuilding work in the decision tree of Figure 2–6 cost $10,000 rather than $5,000. The expected profit would then be highest if we let nature take its course. The rational manager would instruct the driver to fill the tank, pick up the next load, and hope for the best.

However, many people would view things differently. A manager who recommends a rebuilt engine will probably not be questioned. Nothing much can go wrong if that choice is made. But what if the manager recommends staying with the status quo? At first, he or she can justify that decision on the basis of the numbers and will probably get a small pat on the back for not tying up the truck for repairs. Suppose, though, the engine fails while the truck is halfway between Miami and Vancouver with a perishable, time-critical shipment for the firm's biggest customer. At that point, the manager will be in serious trouble. A year-old decision tree that showed a $3,000-higher statistical profit expectation will not be of much help in his or her defense against charges of professional incompetence. A reasonable (not necessarily rational in the technical sense, but reasonable) person might look at the potential personal gains and losses and make the safer decision to rebuild the engine.

What's happening here is that the manager's **utility curve** is not linear. A person's utility curve defines the relationship between the amount of something that the person has and its value to the person. Most utility curves flatten as the amount of a good that one possesses increases. For example, the value of owning an automobile is, to the typical single, suburban professional, high. The value of having a second automobile is considerably lower (not zero, as there is some incremental value to owning an SUV even if one already has a sports car), that of a third lower yet, and that of a fourth essentially zero. By contrast, a rational manager is presumed to have a linear utility curve: the 10,000th, or the millionth, incremental dollar is worth exactly as much as the first one.

Economists measure utility in units called **utils.** While each of the four automobiles mentioned may be worth the same number of dollars, their value in utils differs. Our suburbanite may decide that the first car is worth more utils than having another $20,000 in the bank, but the second one isn't.

Figure 2–8A shows this person's subjective feelings about the value of owning zero or more cars and of having money in the bank, expressed in utils. The automobile curve, shown as a dashed line, flattens out rapidly after the first one. This is because a second automobile provides much less incremental value to its user than the first one did, and so on, for more automobiles after that.

The money curve, shown as a solid line, is straighter than the automobile curve. This reflects the fact that additional money is potentially useful for other purposes besides buying a lot of cars, whereas a person can use only one car at a time. The straighter money curve also reflects the assumption that our decision maker has more than $80,000, so the part of the money curve we see in Figure 2–8A might reflect the segment between $120,000 and $200,000 of net worth. (If we were looking at the utility value of one's first $20,000, it might well be higher. Few people

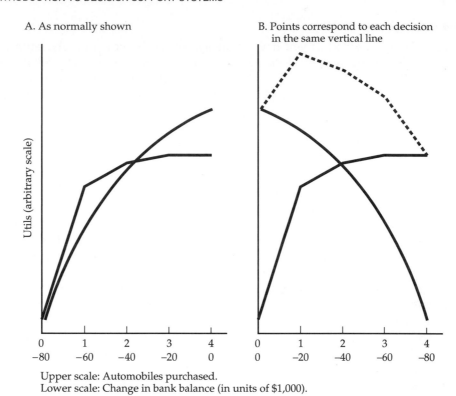

A. As normally shown

B. Points correspond to each decision in the same vertical line

Upper scale: Automobiles purchased.
Lower scale: Change in bank balance (in units of $1,000).

FIGURE 2–8   Cardinal Utility Curves

who have a total of $20,000 to their name would choose to spend every penny of their assets on a car costing that much.)

Figure 2–8B flips the money curve horizontally so the points corresponding to each possible decision line up: no cars and no change to the bank balance, one car and $20,000 less in the bank, and so on through four cars and $80,000 less in the bank. The dotted line near the top of the chart shows the sum of both. We can see that the total is greatest when one car is purchased. That is, therefore, the chosen decision.

Economists call this type of utility theory, which measures utility in terms of an objective yardstick, **cardinal utility.** Some economists, pointing out that none of us has had any real-world exposure to a util, prefer to deal with **ordinal utility.** Ordinal utility theory defines utility in terms of combinations of goods the decision maker considers to be of equivalent value. In terms of ordinal utility, the automobile purchaser might rank the utility of the available options as follows:

1. One automobile, $20,000 less in the bank (highest utility)
2. Two automobiles, $40,000 less in the bank
3. No automobiles, bank balance unchanged

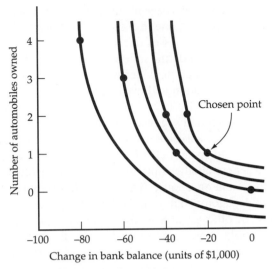

FIGURE 2–9   **Automobile Purchase Indifference Curves**

4. Three automobiles, $60,000 less in the bank
5. Four automobiles, $80,000 less in the bank (lowest utility)

Figure 2–9 shows this decision maker's **indifference curves.** The purchaser con-siders each combination of automobiles and money along a given curve to be of equivalent subjective value. The curves are higher as we move to the upper right of the figure—but, in ordinal utility, there is no measure of their height beyond the ordering from top to bottom. The highest-value curve is the one that passes through the point (one automobile, –$20,000 in the bank). This curve also passes through the point (two automobiles, –$30,000 in the bank). This suggests that if our purchaser could get a second automobile for less than $10,000, he or she would buy it. Continuing upward along the same curve, it indicates that a third car would be purchased if it could be obtained for about $4,000 and that a fourth would have to be practically free.

The third curve passes through (zero automobiles, bank balance unchanged). This curve also passes, approximately, through (one automobile, –$38,000). This suggests that if an acceptable automobile cost up to about $38,000, our buyer would still purchase one. Above that amount, he or she would find alternative means of transportation.

Having made this ranking, or at least the top part of it, our purchaser buys one car for $20,000 and is happy.

In the truck engine example, the positive utility value to an individual salaried manager of a slightly larger corporate profit is small. The negative utility value to this same manager of a loss, where the loss is directly traceable to his or her deci-sion, is enormous. Measured in utils, the –15,000 on the second arm of the deci-sion tree is far too low. A figure of –1,500,000 would be closer to the manager's subjective perception of career disaster if this event should occur. This figure puts the option of leaving the engine alone in a distant third place.

In terms of the three dimensions of decision making, subjective utility is likewise high on rationality—if we define rationality in utils rather than dollars. Since a decision maker's utility function is defined only in the context of his or her views about the future distribution and use of power, it has a clear political aspect as well.

As the heading of this section suggests, utility is a subjective concept. Different people have different utility curves. Given two people each with $100,000 in the bank, one might choose to spend half of it on a BMW 528 and live happily in a studio apartment, whereas another opts to drive a 5-year-old Honda Civic while saving for a down payment on a house. This makes it difficult to incorporate utility concepts into group decision making. Individual utility curves often show up only as "hidden agendas" or other arguments that Dean et al. would put in the political category. If it is possible to get group members to disclose some aspect of their utility curves with respect to a given decision, it will often then be possible to reach a decision that meets all group members' major needs.

For the same reason, subjective utility is a descriptive model of decision making. It provides a mathematical framework which attempts to reflect how people really do make decisions, while still showing that optimization is taking place.

2.4.3 Systematic Decision Making

Several decision-making processes do not yield a decision that is optimal in a mathematical sense, and therefore do not qualify for the rational management label. Nevertheless these processes let a decision maker approach issues in a manner that is free from personal bias.

Systematic decision-making processes in this sense are usually applied to multiattribute decision problems where the alternatives are described by several attributes, and they cannot all be optimized simultaneously. Choosing a car is such a decision: The potential buyer must consider cost, performance, economy, reliability, handling, styling, carrying capacity, convenience of service locations, and more. (Cost often forces a compromise among the other attributes.)

It is often possible to reduce the number of alternatives being considered by determining their **envelope.** The envelope concept allows us to reduce the number of alternatives we must consider. It does this by eliminating all the alternatives that are inferior to some other alternative on all attributes, or, at best, equal on some and inferior on the others. This may not reduce the number of alternatives to one, so it must be followed by something else in order to reach a decision. Still, reducing the number of alternatives to consider can't hurt and is often of considerable benefit.

Suppose we must choose an instructor for a financial accounting course. Published evaluations by previous students rank the five available instructors in terms of the workload each one assigns (which we would like to be low) and how much students felt they learned in the course (which we would like to be high, because we feel that learning financial accounting thoroughly now will give us an easier time in managerial accounting later). The list is as follows, where each factor is ranked from 1 (worst) to 10 (best):

Instructor	Workload (10 = low)	Learning (10 = high)
Kahn	3	9
Keady	9	3
Kilroy	7	7
Kosinski	4	6
Kuchar	6	4

We can plot these rankings as shown in Figure 2–10. The envelope is the line starting at 9 on the workload axis, connecting Keady, Kilroy, and Kahn, and ending at 9 on the learning axis. This method allows us to eliminate Kosinski and Kuchar as options. We could have probably done that more easily in this simple, two-variable case—it's not hard to see that we'll learn more and work less with Kilroy than with either of them—but most practical situations have more than two variables and more than five alternatives. (They are also harder to represent in a graph on two-dimensional paper, but computers take that type of complexity in their stride.) We still have to choose one of the remaining three instructors. That will depend on our feelings about the relative importance of the factors. The systematic decision-making methods that come next in this section help deal with this part of the decision. Others have been proposed in the literature, but this sampling suggests the range of the options.

Lexicographic elimination starts with the most important attribute and keeps the alternative that ranks highest on that score. If two or more are tied, it proceeds to the next, and so on, until either one alternative has been selected or the remaining ones are tied on all attributes. Here, if we decide that learning is the most important attribute in selecting an instructor, the lexicographic elimination method would lead us to sign up for Professor Kahn's section. If a low workload has a higher priority for us, we choose Keady.

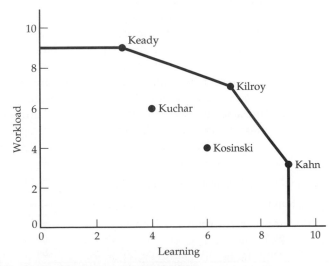

FIGURE 2–10 **Chart of Instructor Choice Options**

The **elimination by aspects** method [TVER72] considers one attribute at a time and compares it against a predetermined minimally acceptable standard. Any alternatives that do not meet this standard are discarded. If we want to learn at least as much as a score of 5 on that scale would indicate, we can eliminate Professor Keady from further consideration. We would then apply the workload standard to try to choose one of the others. If we were willing to work up to an 8, elimination by aspects would leave us with a choice between Professors Kahn and Kilroy. Systematic decision-making methods such as this one often do not narrow the choice down to a single alternative.

Conjunctive decision making [TODD92] applies the same concept as elimination by aspects (comparing attributes against predetermined minimally acceptable levels) but in the reverse order. Instead of comparing the same attribute of all alternatives against its criterion and proceeding through the attributes, it compares all attributes of one alternative against all criteria and proceeds through alternatives. The end result is the same. The amount of work done to get there may differ.

Other methods attempt to integrate the values of all attributes into an overall score for each alternative, based on the importance of each attribute expressed as a numerical weight. The **additive linear model** computes a score for each alternative by multiplying its score on each attribute by a predetermined weight for that attribute. Figure 2–11 applies the additive linear model to the instructor selection problem, assuming that learning has a weight of 10 and low workload has a weight of 6. The entry in each cell is the instructor's rating on the factor in question multiplied by the weight of that factor.

You can see that Kosinski and Kuchar, which were eliminated quickly above by being inside the envelope, have low scores here as well. Keady also does: We value learning more than workload, and we wouldn't learn much in Keady's section. The scores of Kahn and Kilroy are so close that we might choose between them on the basis of schedule, convenience of the classroom where each will meet, or some other factor that we haven't considered yet.

Many other strategies have been proposed as ways to formalize the often-informal process of searching for the best alternative. Twelve are described in [SVEN79]. The implementation effort required for several is discussed in [TODD91].

Systematic decision-making methods rank high in rationality, relatively low in terms of politicality and flexibility—though there are opportunities for both of these to arise in the values set for weights, the ordering of attributes, and the thresholds for rejecting an alternative. It is largely a normative approach to decision making.

FIGURE 2–11 Additive Linear Model of Instructor Choice

	Kahn	Keady	Kilroy	Kosinski	Kuchar
Workload	18	54	42	24	36
Learning	90	30	70	60	40
Total score	118	84	112	84	76

2.4.4 Satisficing

The term **satisficing** was coined by Simon [SIMO60] to describe the actions of a decision maker who wants a decision that's "good enough." If management has set a goal of a 400-pound weight reduction for the rear suspension of a heavy truck and an engineer has reached 415 pounds, there may be little reason to see if yet another design change will raise this figure to 425. As Ackoff and Sasieni put it [ACKO68], "Satisficing appeals to planners who are not willing to stick their necks out."

Satisficing is not always bad. It may be a perfectly sensible thing for a decision maker to do; it is often not possible to discover, let alone investigate, all of the options. Furthermore, the resources that would be expended in looking for further improvements must be taken from some other activity that also has a payoff. Leaving well enough alone in terms of one decision may actually be optimal in a more global sense, by letting a decision maker focus attention on things that really matter. If leaving the above suspension with a 415-pound weight reduction allows the truck company to put the new design into production a week earlier, thereby making it available to customers a week sooner, that may well be better for the business than taking another week to shave off another ten pounds. Or, if it lets the engineer get an earlier start on taking weight out of the front suspension so that both changes will be ready for next year's models, that, too, may be a better use of resources.

The concept of **bounded rationality** is related to satisficing. In making a decision using bounded rationality, the manager recognizes the practical constraints on the decision. Perhaps the organization doesn't want to change quickly. Perhaps the impact of the decision doesn't justify gathering all the information that would be required to make it optimally. Perhaps the marketing vice president will never accept a decision that reduces the size of that department by more than a handful. In all these cases, one is making a rational decision within known or implicit constraints.

Satisficing contains elements of rational and political decision making. It is low on flexibility; in fact, it is often felt to characterize rigid bureaucrats who do well enough to get by but have no interest in achieving the outstanding results that could come from a more flexible approach. The concept of a satisficing decision maker is entirely a descriptive model in the context of a single decision but can take on aspects of normative decision making when the global implications of multiple decisions are taken into account. (Fully normative decision making assumes infinite time and resources, so the reasons for satisficing wouldn't apply to it.)

2.4.5 Organizational and Political Decision Making

The above three approaches to decision making apply largely to an individual decision maker. Many decisions, however, involve more than one person. In those cases the interpersonal aspects of decision making can take on a great deal of importance.

The organizational description of decision making [CYER63] recognizes that organizations consist of people and subunits. Each of these has its own goals, priorities, "rights" (as it perceives them), information which it feels it "owns," and standard operating procedures. Decisions, and the overall decision making process, must reconcile all of these. Where they are in conflict the decision making process can be difficult and painful. Where they are not in conflict, recognizing them permits us to design systems specifically to support the information flow and decision processes of the organization. Such DSS are called *group decision support systems (GDSS);* we'll cover them in detail in Chapter 10.

Viewing decision making as an organizational process combines rationality with politicality. Each unit of the organization (in the limit, each individual) is using a rational process internally in terms of its perception of its own goals. Organizational decision making does not conflict with a rational approach to the overall decision either, as long as the application of this approach does not infringe on what the subunit perceives as its territory. Most models of organizational decision making are largely descriptive, though normative elements may be included in the overall process.

Where the driving factor in arriving at a decision becomes bargaining among the participants, we have what is often called **political decision making.** The word *political* has negative overtones in our society. It calls forth images of hidden, often unethical, decisions made in back rooms by people whose only motivation is their own self-interest. The use of the term in a decision-making context, however, is not necessarily negative. It is the realistic recognition that people may legitimately have different goals, that people committed to a goal can be expected to fight for it, that bargaining is required to reconcile the different goals to a single decision, and that power—interpreted broadly—is an inherent component of any bargaining process.

The nature of the bargaining process depends on the importance of the decision as it is perceived by the decision-making group [KERR92]. The ability, and hence the tendency, of the majority to prevail grows or declines as the importance of the issue grows or declines. So does the tendency of the decision to polarize the group. A management team may almost come to blows over a strategic decision between a new R&D project versus overseas sales expansion, but will probably agree without difficulty on the color of the T-shirts for the company picnic.

However unpleasant it may be to admit that well-intentioned managers can disagree, however difficult it may be to treat disagreement through formal management science optimization methods, the fact is that managers have always disagreed from time to time and probably always will. DSS can help isolate areas of disagreement, articulate common goals, and create a common vision by facilitating the structured, nonjudgmental sharing of information. These capabilities, too, fall under the category of group DSS.

DSS can also help resolve differences through electronic voting or something resembling the Delphi approach. In a truly political environment, though, this type of DSS usage may not be acceptable to the participants. Those who lost the vote may try to overturn the result by going around or above the DSS, negotiating with other group members to change their votes or appealing to higher levels of management.

Politics has been described as the art of the possible. Political decision making is characterized by compromise: "I'll give a little here, if you give a little there." A "win-win" outcome can often be achieved by discovering what issues are truly important to each participant. The DSS developer in a political decision-making environment must be attuned to what is possible, within the organizational culture and power structure, and develop systems that conform to their constraints.

2.5 THE IMPACT OF PSYCHOLOGICAL TYPE ON DECISION MAKING

The pioneering Swiss psychiatrist Carl Jung realized in the 1920s [ISAC88] that individuals have personality traits that remain steady over time. A person's behavior in new situations can be predicted, at least in part, from his or her past behavior in similar situations. Furthermore, people can be placed into categories whose members all tend, as a general rule, to respond similarly to similar situations.

Katharine Briggs and Isabel Briggs Myers [BRIG57] refined Jung's concepts and showed that humans have four key behavioral characteristics. Each of these is characterized by a spectrum ranging from one behavioral tendency to its opposite. Each characteristic reflects an individual tendency, or preference, to use one of two alternative approaches to a given area. Every person is at some point on this spectrum in terms of each of the four characteristics. For example, one person may prefer to evaluate issues logically and objectively, whereas another prefers to evaluate issues subjectively and personally. For convenience, each spectrum is broken down into two halves, giving two possible individual preferences per characteristic. Since there are four characteristics and each can take on either of two preferences, this approach yields a total of $2 \times 2 \times 2 \times 2 = 16$ psychological types. A person's **psychological type** affects his or her behavioral tendencies in many areas, including decision making.

These four preferences, unless they are indulged in when a different behavior is called for, are not "good" or "bad." They reflect a person's mental preferences in the same sense—and with the same lack of inherent value—as a person's physical preference to throw a ball with the left or right hand. Similarly, the 16 categories, called *types,* are not "good" or "bad" either. They are not related to aptitude or to intelligence.

Psychological type is determined by a questionnaire (it is not called a test, as people associate the word *test* with a good or a bad score) of several dozen questions. Each question asks which of two behaviors a person would be more likely to choose in a specified situation. Taken as a whole, and interpreted by a trained professional, the **Myers-Briggs Type Inventory**[6] **(MBTI)**[7] can provide a great deal of insight into one's behavioral preferences. These preferences, in turn, can yield a great deal of insight into the way a person tends to approach decision-making tasks.

---

[6]Myers-Briggs Type Inventory® is a registered trademark of Consulting Psychologists Press, Inc.
[7]MBTI™ is a trademark of Consulting Psychologists Press, Inc.

According to Briggs and Briggs-Myers, the four preferences that determine personality type (summarized primarily from [PROV90]) are **introversion/ extraversion, sensing/intuition, thinking/feeling,** and **judgment/perception.**

1. *Introversion/Extraversion.*[8] This preference suggests whether individuals prefer to direct their energy toward the outer world (E) or the inner world (I). Extraverts understand the world through acting and reacting to it; they need to externalize things to understand them. Introverts understand their world through careful contemplation. They prefer to act or respond after thoughtful consideration of an issue.

2. *Sensing/iNtuition.*[9] This function refers to a person's preferred perception process. It indicates how people take in information and become aware of things, people, events, and ideas. Sensing means finding out about things through the senses and through careful, detailed observation. People who prefer intuition perceive patterns or relationships among ideas, people, and events. Intuitives trust perception based on intuitions and reading between the lines, while Sensors confine their attention to what is real and verifiable.

3. *Thinking/Feeling.* This function refers to a person's preferred judgment process. It describes how people prefer to come to conclusions or make decisions about what they have perceived. Thinking means considering pros and cons or consequences, and coming to a logical choice, decision, or conclusion. Feeling involves weighing personal values and others' reactions: will there be conflict or harmony, approval or disapproval? Those with a Feeling preference often neglect logical reasoning and fail to consider consequences. Those with a Thinking preference often neglect taking other people's reactions—even their own emotional responses—into account.

4. *Judgment/Perception.* This is a "lifestyle" preference. It describes whether one tends to let a Perception process (S/N) or Judgment process (T/F) run one's outer life. People who have a Judging preference want things to be settled, decided, planned, and managed to the plan. They are often seen as decisive and organized, and enjoy working in structured organizations. People with a Perception preference are often seen as flexible, spontaneous, and uncomfortable with much structure and planning. They want to keep plans to a minimum to be able to adapt flexibly to new situations.

One of the two middle functions (S, N, T, or F) is each person's "favorite" function, the one that person prefers to use in his or her preferred world (internal or external). This function is referred to as that person's **dominant function.** For Extraverts, who prefer dealing with the outer (external) world, the dominant function is the one indicated by his or her J/P preference, as that preference indicates which type of process a person tends to use in the outside world. For Introverts, who pre-

---

[8]Personality type workers use this spelling rather than the more common "extroversion." This is not a frivolous idiosyncrasy. The reasons for this usage are spelled out in [BRIG57].

[9]Using the capital letter N to denote the iNtuitive type prevents confusion with I for Introversion. (Chess notation uses N for kNight for the same reason, to prevent confusion with K for King.)

fer dealing with the internal world, the dominant function is the one *not* indicated by the J/P preference. In other words,

If your E/I and J/P preferences are	Then your dominant function is
Extraverted, Judging (EJ)	T or F*
Extraverted, Perceiving (EP)	S or N
Introverted, Judging (IJ)	S or N
Introverted, Perceiving (IP)	T or F

*Whichever is your preference.

As an example of using the dominant function, consider people with type INFP. They tend to let their Perception preference (here iNtuition) run their *outer* lives. However, as they are Introverts, the outer world is not their preferred world. Their dominant function is Feeling, but they use it primarily in their inner world and don't show it easily. They "have a great deal of warmth but may not show it until they know a person well. . . . Although their inner loyalties and ideals govern their lives, they find these hard to talk about. Their deepest feelings are seldom expressed; their inner tenderness is masked by a quiet reserve" [MYER90].

As Provost puts it in [PROV90]:

> It is important to remember that the Myers-Briggs Type Inventory indicates natural preferences—the ways we prefer to be. Often, however, we may act differently from our preferences because the situation demands it or because we are not comfortable with using our preferences. We all express each of these eight preferences at different times in different circumstances, but the MBTI tells us which four we prefer to express most of the time.

The four dimensions create the 16 types shown in Figure 2–12. You can find easily understood descriptions of all 16 types in [HIRS90, ISAC88, KEIR84, MYER90, and PROV90] as well as in several other books.

The impact of personality type on decision-making style is important to the DSS developer because a DSS must reflect the decision-making methods of the people who will use it. Knowing that a DSS user's type is INTJ, for example, suggests that certain types of automated decision support are likely to be useful but that others are not. If a DSS is to be developed for a large user community with members of varying types, it should have features designed to support their varied decision-making preferences. Should that be impractical, management must be alert to the fact that the DSS is not well suited to the decision-making preferences of some staff members. It can then make allowances for this via extra training or alternative approaches to decision support.

The four personality characteristics affect decision making in the following ways:

1. *Introversion/Extraversion:* This preference affects the way in which a decision maker might approach group decisions. An Extravert will prefer to thrash matters out in a group whereas an Introvert will prefer to mull over an issue in private and present fully formed conclusions to the group.

	Sensing (S)	Sensing (S)	Intuitive (N)	Intuitive (N)	
Introverted (I)	ISTJ*	ISFJ	INFJ	INTJ	Judging (J)
Introverted (I)	ISTP	ISFP	INFP	INTP	Perceiving (P)
Extraverted (E)	ESTP	ESFP	ENFP	ENTP	Perceiving (P)
Extraverted (E)	ESTJ	ESFJ	ENFJ	ENTJ	Judging (J)
	Thinking (T)	Feeling (F)	Feeling (F)	Thinking (T)	

*Boldface letters indicate the dominant function of each type.

FIGURE 2–12 Myers-Briggs Personality Type Chart

2. *Sensing/iNtuition:* This preference shows up in the way a decision maker will gather information for a decision, the design stage of the decision-making process. The Sensor will want, in the words of the old *Dragnet* TV show, "just the facts, ma'am"—and all of them. The iNtuitive may need fewer facts, just enough for his or her intuition to put them together and reach a conclusion.

3. *Thinking/Feeling:* This preference impacts the choice stage. The Thinker can be the very model of the classical rational manager, basing decisions on carefully thought-out logic but often ignoring human factors. A person with a Feeling preference will have less use for "management science" approaches.

4. *Judgment/Perception:* This preference influences whether, in working with others, the decision maker will focus on the information-gathering parts of the decision process or on the analysis and decision-making parts. A Judging person may want to rush the information gathering and get right to the choice stage, which he or she considers to be the heart of the matter. A Perceptive will want to postpone the decision as long as possible, extending the design stage and keeping options open while more and more information is collected.

Huitt [HUIT92] summarizes some preferred decision-making techniques of the eight personality types as shown in Figure 2–13. Note that several techniques match more than one personality type. For example, the random word association technique (how can the word *sardine* [selected randomly from a dictionary or suggested by a computer program that is designed to help people generate ideas] relate to this problem?) match both Sensing and Perceiving types. It follows that an individual whose type includes SP would be especially attracted to it.

Psychological type also affects how well people work together.[10] This doesn't mean that all members of a decision-making group should be of the same type or similar types. The varying approaches brought to a group decision by people of different types can improve decision quality dramatically. In this case, it is impor-

---

[10]In some parts of the United States, "personal" ads often state psychological type. Prospective partners can use this information to help gauge their likely compatibility with an advertiser.

Type	Preferred Techniques
Extravert	Brainstorming in group Outcome psychodrama (evaluating scenario through role-playing) Thinking aloud
Introvert	Brainstorming privately Incubation (doing something else as subconscious works on problem)
Sensing	Share personal values, ideas Overload (deliberately considering too many factors to see individually) Inductive reasoning (developing rules from specific instances) Random word technique
Intuitive	Classify, categorize Deductive reasoning (applying rules to specific instances) Challenge assumptions Imaging/visualization Synthesizing
Thinking	Classify, categorize Analysis Network analysis (e.g., Critical Path Method, PERT) Task analysis
Feeling	Share personal values Listen to others' values Values clarification
Judging	Evaluation (comparison to a standard or preestablished norm) Plus-minus-interesting technique (for evaluating alternatives) Backward planning (identify conditions needed to reach goal) Select a single solution
Perceiving	Brainstorming Random word technique Outrageous provocation (absurd statement as bridge to idea) Taking another's perspective

FIGURE 2–13 **Types and Decision-Making Techniques**

tant for the team as a whole to be aware of their varying styles. Team members can then make allowances for the fact that other members, although their styles may differ, can make a significant contribution to the group. Suitably trained managers or human resource professionals in an organization who have psychological type information about employees (with their informed consent and due protection of their privacy) can help plan a good decision-making group. Automated support for deciding group composition is itself a potential DSS application area.

Psychological type is also important in DSS development because certain personality types tend to cluster in certain professions. There's a good chance that a programmer working on a DSS to support a marketing project will have a different personality type from its prospective users. It is important for both to be aware of this so that the programmer can develop the system that its users need—not the system the programmer would have wanted if the programmer had the users' problem.

In Section 4.5, after we've discussed the different kinds of DSS that exist, we'll discuss which are best suited to decision makers of each psychological type.

2.6 THE IMPACT OF CULTURE ON DECISION MAKING

Culture can be defined [RAND87] as "the behaviors and beliefs characteristic of a particular group." Decision making is a behavior. It is often a highly visible behavior and, in group situations, a social behavior as well. We should not be surprised to find that the culture of a group affects the way decisions are made in it. Two aspects of culture influence decision making: **organizational** (corporate) culture and **national** culture.

At the corporate level, some companies (such as Polaroid in the United States are highly centralized. Employees expect all significant decisions to be made at headquarters. Others, such as Hewlett-Packard (also based in the United States are divided into autonomous divisions. An H-P division staff would be surprised, indeed offended, if managers at headquarters involved themselves in decisions the division staff believed were theirs to make. Of course, H-P's headquarters makes some major decisions, and workers at Polaroid have some local decision-making authority, but there is a great middle area where the same decision would be made differently at both firms.

Differences at the national level are even more pronounced. U.S. managers are used to making autonomous decisions, consulting with others only as necessary, and having those decisions carried out without protest. Japanese managers, by contrast, expect decisions to occur only after long periods of discussion among all involved parties. (This is not just random discussion. There are specific times in the process at which new ideas can be suggested, and other times at which existing ideas are to be refined. Foreigners who know little more than "Japanese decision making involves consensus" can make serious business errors.) The net effect tends to be that a decision will be reached more quickly in the United States, but that a comparable decision will be implemented more quickly in Japan because all those concerned are already "on board" with it.[11] Some computer-based DSS, because they lead quickly to a recommended decision without providing time for discussion and consensus building, might not be accepted in Japan, or would make Japanese decision makers uncomfortable if they were forced to use the systems by a foreign corporate management.

Along similar lines, a U.S. manager might appoint a project leader after interviewing several candidates and perhaps consulting with the manager's own peers. Asking the project team members their preferences would be optional, usually done more for morale purposes than to obtain true input, and probably would not weigh heavily in the choice. In Russia, conversely, the opinions of project team members would be the single most important factor in the choice. A manager who attempted to impose a project leader on a group whom the team members did not prefer, or about whom they had not been consulted, would quickly be faced with a major protest. A U.S.-built DSS designed to help select project leaders, therefore, would be unusable in Russia if it did not take this need into account.

---

[11]Debates over which approach leads to the shortest *total* time tend to be emotional and usually do not reach useful conclusions. The most that can be said with certainty is "it depends."

Even the reasoning process people typically use can vary from culture to culture. U.S. managers are typically taught to manage in a top-down fashion, that is, first define one's objectives, then determine how to reach them. The French educational system, by contrast, stresses a form of logical reasoning that French managers follow without conscious thought. They start from the current situation and what facts are known, then determine what future situations can be reached. Both approaches can work but mixing them unconsciously does not. A U.S. manager attempting to justify a decision to a group from France, using U.S. logic, will be unconvincing—and vice versa. A decision support system that was designed in the United States for use by all divisions of a global firm might not be accepted in France for the same reason.

It is therefore important for DSS designers to be aware of both aspects of culture—organizational and national. This is not always easy, for the following reasons.

- The designer of a decision support system (indeed, of any information system) may be new to an organization or may not even be an employee of the organization that the system is to serve. Such a person cannot be expected to understand how the organization's culture affects decision making.
- With the increasing globalization of the economy, decisions are often made by groups composed of a mix of national backgrounds or are made by a group from one background for implementation by people from other backgrounds. Supporting these types of decisions requires an understanding of many cultures. Few people truly understand any culture other than their own.

When you are faced with a DSS design situation, be sure to investigate the cultural aspects of the groups that will use it. This may require you to talk to many people, some of whom will be outside the MIS organization. If national cultures are an issue, you can also benefit from the many books on the subject. (The contrast between the United States and Japan is most frequently discussed, but there are resources on other cultural differences as well.) You don't have to become an expert on worldwide approaches to decision making, but every bit of understanding helps.

2.7 THE KEPNER-TREGOE DECISION-MAKING METHOD

The decision-making method described next was developed by Charles Kepner and Benjamin Tregoe [KEPN73, KEPN81] to improve human decision making before computers became common decision aids. This method helps focus attention on critical issues and get to the crux of the matter without wasted effort. It can also be used in group decision making. Although the method is not the only systematic way to make decisions it is a good one. Its concepts can help DSS developers in two ways: to see where computers can fit into the decision-making process, and to outline a method computers can use to take over some of the decision-making task. The method consists [KEPN73] of the steps shown in Figure 2–14.

In terms of the decision-making approaches discussed in Section 2.4, the **Kepner-Tregoe decision-making method** (K-T) uses the additive linear method

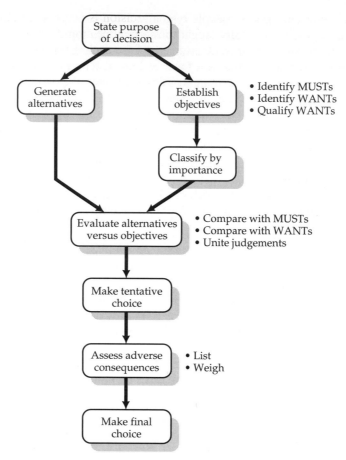

FIGURE 2–14 **Graphical Representation of K-T Steps**

with a few twists. (If you put this fact together with the information in Section 2.5, you may conclude correctly that the K-T method is best suited to decision makers with a Thinking preference.) However, appearances can be deceiving. The K-T method accepts the facts of organizational decision making as well, and in that sense has a political aspect. Furthermore, it is designed not to inhibit flexibility overmuch. It is not well suited to a truly political environment: The "wheeler-dealers" who thrive on that type of decision making may chafe under its constraints and look for ways to sabotage the K-T process if they do not see its outcome tending in a direction they can accept.

2.7.1 State the Purpose of the Decision

The first step in the decision process is preparing a written decision statement. This step corresponds to the intelligence phase of decision making. The Kepner-Tregoe method assumes that the intelligence phase is essentially complete and need only be formalized by obtaining agreement on the decision statement. In other words, we have already realized that a decision is needed, know pretty well what it is, and agree that it's worth spending some time on.

It takes self-control to focus on the purpose of the decision and the evaluation criteria first. Most of us like to think about alternatives, as they are concrete and easy to visualize. (In fact, most of us start to think about alternatives as soon as, or even before, we start to work on a decision.) However, we must resist the impulse to discuss alternatives prematurely. Doing so will get the decision off on the wrong foot by overinflating the factors that favor an attractive alternative, though we might not even realize that this is happening. That, in turn, may impact the quality of the eventual result.

All participants in the decision must agree on this written decision statement. If two managers making a joint decision have different unspoken objectives, they will never agree on a mutually satisfactory solution. By forcing a joint decision statement we make the issues visible and force a compromise set of objectives. A compromise at this stage will be more acceptable than a compromise at the later solution stage because a compromise then is likely to be a "split the difference" decision that leaves neither participant satisfied.

2.7.2 Establish Objectives

The design phase of decision making starts here, at the establishing objectives stage, and continues through the generating alternatives stage (see Section 2.7.4). Just as a decision has a broad purpose, it should also accomplish necessary and desired results. In other words, a certain *output* is expected. Also, certain *input* resources may be available to limit the choice of alternatives. Decision outputs may include, among others,

- People: attitudes, skills, performance, development, health, safety.
- Organization: relationships, communications, responsibilities, coordination.
- Facilities and equipment: space, location, flexibility, adaptability, compatibility.
- Materials: sources, availability, handling, storage.
- Money: costs, expenses, return.
- Production output: quality, quantity, pace, timing.
- Personal: goals, family, strengths, weaknesses.

2.7.3 Classify According to Importance

Not all objectives are of equal importance. Some are essential: Any acceptable solution *must* achieve them. These are called **Must objectives.** You *want* others, but they are not absolutely necessary. Some **Want objectives** are more important than others. In this step you divide the objectives we just determined into these two categories. You then determine the relative values of the Want objectives.

Identify Must Objectives For a result objective to be a Must, you must be able to answer the question, Can you imagine *any acceptable solution at all* that would not meet this result?, with a firm No! With a resource, you must be able to answer No! to Can you imagine any acceptable solution at all that uses more than the upper limit (or less than the lower limit) of this resource? If the applicable question elicits, Well, maybe if . . . , the objective in question is a Want.

To qualify as a Must objective, the target must be measurable, for example, completion in two weeks, absenteeism 10 percent lower within three months, cost not over $10 million. There should be no possible room for disagreement over whether or not an alternative meets a Must objective.

Must objectives are sometimes called **filter criteria.** They are standards by which you will filter out unsatisfactory alternatives.

Identify Want Objectives   Want objectives include those that remain after all the Must objectives have been identified. Want objectives may include: contribute to employee growth (for a programming project), have air-conditioning (for a car), maximum market share in 24 months (for a marketing plan).

Other Want objectives reflect a premium for being better than the Must limit. A personal computer may have an absolute cost limit of $5,000 although, at the same time you might Want to keep the cost lower. Quantitative Must objectives should be checked to see if there is any value in exceeding the filter level.

Not all Want objectives are equally important. Their relative importance must be weighed. While there are many ways to do this (high-medium-low, among others) the most rigorous is assigning a numerical value. Numerical ratings lend themselves to group consensus and to computerization. A scale from 1 to 10 is sufficiently fine to show important differences while not getting bogged down in the meaningless shading that would be involved from 67 to 68.

You now have a decision statement and two lists of objectives: Musts and Wants. The Wants have numerical values. Other people might disagree with your lists or with those of any other decision maker. The important thing is for the lists to reflect the criteria of the people who are making the decision. If bright orange paint is one of your filter criteria for a used car, so be it.

2.7.4 Generate Alternatives

The next step, finding alternatives, should not be a hit-or-miss affair. Only a systematic search can turn up the number of quality alternatives you need to make an appropriate decision. One approach to finding alternatives is to use the Must/Want objectives as your blueprint. Each objective is a tool to open up new possibilities. Thinking of ways to accomplish each objective helps you generate a broader range of alternatives. Suppose one of your Must objectives for a car is bright orange paint. In considering this objective, you will realize that Ideal Auto Body on Littleton Road will paint any car bright orange for $500. You might then broaden your search, adding $500 to the price of cars that are not already bright orange to pay for the paint job.

K-T is not an idea-generating or creativity-boosting method. While it urges the decision maker to search for all possible alternatives, it assumes that he or she can and will do so. It works well with any creativity-oriented technique, such as brainstorming, for generating them, but those approaches are not part of K-T itself.

As you search for alternatives, new objectives may come to mind. If they are valid, add them to your Must/Want lists. Be sure that the new factor, however, is really a desired objective, not just a feature of an emotionally attractive alternative.

2.7.5 Evaluate Alternatives Against Objectives

The choice phase of decision making begins with this step—evaluating alternatives against objectives—and continues through the rest of the process. To evaluate alternatives against objectives we must have the best, most accurate, and most timely information about each alternative. First, we make the evaluation for Musts. Later, we repeat the process for each Want alternative in the order of their importance.

Compare with Must Objectives   The only question that matters here is Does this alternative meet the standard? If it does, keep it for further investigation. If it doesn't, drop it. Borderline values require judgment. Criteria are often set as round numbers, such as "costs no more than $3,000." Alternatives do not always yield round numbers: A desktop computer system, when the prices of its component parts are added, may cost exactly $3,001.29. If you eliminate it, you risk not considering an alternative that meets all the other Musts and compares favorably on the Wants as well. If you accept it, you in effect concede that your Must limit wasn't really a limit after all. Stretch the limit, stretch it a bit more . . . soon the entire decision-making process falls apart. You may want to retain such an alternative while noting it as borderline.

If the Must comparison eliminates all your alternatives, you will either need more alternatives or you will have to relax your criteria. In making this decision, ask Are any standards too tight? Do all reflect absolute requirements? If, on the other hand, no alternatives are eliminated at this stage, it might be well to think through your Must objectives again. Ask Are all the requirements reflected? Are the standards too loose?

Compare with Want Objectives   Now turn to the alternatives that have satisfied all the Musts and search out the best available information on all of them relative to each Want. A brief "key point" summary of information on each alternative may make accurate comparisons easier.

Alternatives may differ in the degree to which they satisfy a Want objective and a way to compare them is needed. Here, again, numbers that reflect your judgments provide a consistent, comparable yardstick. A good approach is to assign a value of 10 to the information describing the alternative that best satisfies each Want objective. The information on each other alternative can then be compared to the best alternative and valued from 10 down to 0 as appropriate. In rating alternatives on each Want, ignore the weight assigned to the importance of that Want objective. Cover it up if necessary.

Unite Separate Judgments   To make an overall judgment you must combine your separate judgments into one evaluation. Here, again, numerical yardsticks show their worth. Multiply the weight assigned to the objective with the score assigned to the information for each alternative. If an objective has a weight of 10 (the maximum) and an alternative was rated as 10 on that objective (also the maximum), the weighted score for that alternative on that objective is $10 \times 10 = 100$.

Now sum the weighted scores for each alternative. The total weighted scores give the relative standing of each alternative and provide a reasoned, visible comparison. The closer two or more alternatives compare, the more necessary it is to double check both the information and your evaluation.

2.7.6 Tentatively, Choose the Best Alternative

You are now ready to make a tentative decision, which will be tested in the next step. Select the alternative, or a very few alternatives, with the highest total weighted scores as your tentative choice(s).

2.7.7 Assess Adverse Consequences

Your tentative selection meets all your Must criteria and best satisfies your Want objectives. The information you used in your analysis is from the past and the present, but your decision will be implemented in the future. Many things can go wrong in the future. Before you commit to a final choice, you must test your chosen alternative by attempting to determine how well it will hold up in the future, how it will respond to changing conditions, and what the impact of overlooking key factors could be. The right decision should yield the best possible result if all goes well. It should also offer reasonable protection against things not going well.

List Possible Adverse Consequences   What could go wrong with your decision? Lots of things! List them all. A used car might fall apart after 200 miles. That fantastic professor you signed up for could become a beach bum in Tahiti and be replaced by an incompetent substitute. You could take a January ski vacation and encounter the warmest weather Vail has seen in decades—or go to Key West and hit a cold snap. The objective categories in Section 2.7.2 are a good checklist for your search.

When we evaluated alternatives, we evaluated all the alternatives against the same set of criteria. The **adverse consequence** lists for each alternative, however, will usually not be the same. One computer system alternative may have the adverse consequence "little third-party software available," while another may suffer from "sales representative is obnoxious."

Weigh the Adverse Consequences   In evaluating the adverse consequences of any alternative, consider these points:

- The likelihood that the consequence will occur. This is its **probability.** Probability is a score here, not a mathematical probability from 0 to 1.
- The impact if the consequence happens. This is its **seriousness.**

Assign the probability of each adverse consequence a value of 10 (virtually certain to occur) to 1 (highly unlikely to occur). Similarly, evaluate its seriousness on a scale of 10 (catastrophic) to 1 (a mild annoyance). A 10-10 rating means we are certain of disaster. Obviously, any alternative with such a consequence is unsatisfactory. A 1-10 rating means that disaster is remotely possible. The obnoxious computer salesperson might be a 10-1: We know it will happen, but we can live with it.

All actions carry risks. Looking at the probability and seriousness of adverse consequences is intended to put risk into perspective, not to panic everyone into inaction (sometimes referred to as the "paralysis through analysis" syndrome). Think of it as a tool for (1) identifying alternatives that are clearly unsatisfactory, and (2) helping minimize what goes wrong with the alternative that is eventually chosen by alerting you to the need for contingency planning.

2.7.8 Make a Final Choice

If your tentatively chosen alternative has no significant adverse consequences, or if you can see how to deal with those that it has, make the choice.

If you are not satisfied with its level of risk, consider the alternative that next best satisfied your Want objectives and test its consequences.

If two or more alternatives are close, review each closely to

- Assess the degree to which each consequence is both probable and serious for each alternative.
- Judge (sum) the total impact of all consequences for each alternative.

If one alternative has a low total impact and no 10-10 consequences, make this choice (10-10 consequence in this context is a shorthand term that includes any consequences that rank high on both probability and seriousness: 10-9, 8-10, and so on).

If two are close on total impact but one has no 10-10 consequences, make this choice.

If one has a somewhat higher total impact but no 10-10 consequences, whereas the other has a lower total impact but does have 10-10 consequences, choose the one with the higher total impact.

If all have a high total impact and one or more 10-10 consequences, think carefully about considering more alternatives. If you can't come up with some acceptable ones, your plans will have to include provisions for reducing the likelihood or the seriousness of the adverse consequences. Preventive actions and contingency plans cost money, but it is often money well spent. The process of assessing adverse consequences, by alerting you to the need for such plans and actions before disaster strikes, will help prevent disasters from happening.

Using The Kepner-Tregoe Method

This is a brief example of how the Kepner-Tregoe decision-making method could be applied in a practical situation. The number by each step indicates the section of the text in which that step is discussed.

DECISION PURPOSE (2.7.1)
To pick a speaker for the next dinner meeting of our civic organization.

(continued)

Using The Kepner-Tregoe Method—Continued

OBJECTIVES (2.7.2)

To find a speaker who will speak at no charge, will inform meeting attendees about a topic of current interest, will entertain them, will motivate guests attending the meeting to join the organization by showing them how valuable its programs are, and will provide material for a good newspaper report on the meeting.

IMPORTANCE (2.7.3)

Must: speak at no charge.

Want: Inform   10

Motivate   8

Article   6

Entertain   4

ALTERNATIVES (2.7.4)

President of our organization

Town high school principal

U.S. representative in Congress from our district

Executive from local biotechnology firm

EVALUATION AGAINST OBJECTIVES (2.7.5)

Musts: all Yes except representative in Congress, Maybe

Wants:	Our Pres.	HS Prin.	US Rep.	Biotech
Inform	4	6	10	8
Motivate	6	6	8	10
Article	2	4	10	6
Entertain	10	8	2	4

UNITE SEPARATE JUDGMENTS

Multiplying each of the above scores by the weights we derived earlier, the candidates rank as follows:

1. U.S. representative: 232
2. Biotechnology executive: 212 (a close second)
3. High school principal: 164
4. Our president: 140 (Amusing, but otherwise not suitable)

CHOOSE BEST ALTERNATIVE TENTATIVELY (2.7.6)

We opt to invite our district's representative in Congress.

ASSESS ADVERSE CONSEQUENCES (2.7.7)

- May turn us down (probability 6; seriousness 10)
- Having accepted, may cancel at last minute (1-10)
- May turn out to be a dud as a speaker (5-5)

MAKE A FINAL CHOICE (2.7.8)

The key to accepting the tentative first choice is our ability to deal with its highest-scoring adverse consequence, that the representative may turn down our invitation. We plan to deal with this by asking for an early answer. If it is negative, we will turn to the biotechnology executive. We believe we will be able to get the biotech executive with six weeks' notice. Accordingly, we direct our corresponding secretary to invite the representative and to obtain an answer at least six weeks in advance of the meeting. Knowing that members of Congress typically schedule speaking engagements at least this far in advance, we think this is reasonable.

SUMMARY

A decision is a choice among alternatives. Each decision is characterized by a decision statement, a set of alternatives, and decision-making criteria.

Decision makers go through intelligence, design, and choice phases in the process of reaching a decision. In the intelligence phase, the need for a decision is determined. In the design phase, alternatives are developed and researched. In the choice phase, the alternatives are evaluated and one of them is chosen.

Decisions can be categorized according to their degree of structure: structured, semistructured, or unstructured. They can also be categorized on the basis of their organizational impact: strategic, tactical (managerial control), and operational.

Managers make decisions with varying degrees of rationality, politicality, and flexibility. Common combinations of these attributes yield the decision approaches of rational management (seldom found in its pure form), rational management based on subjective utility, "satisficing," and organizational or political decision making.

The way in which people approach decisions, and the decision-making phases on which they prefer to focus, depends on their personality type. Personality types can be characterized in terms of four preferences: introversion/extraversion, sensing/intuition, feeling/thinking, and judgment/perception. These preferences yield a total of 16 personality types. Knowing the personality type of a decision maker will help design appropriate tools to support that person.

A systematic decision-making process helps ensure that all aspects of decision making receive proper consideration and lends itself, at least in part, to computerized support. One such process, the Kepner-Tregoe process, goes through the stages of (1) stating the decision purpose, (2) establishing objectives, (3) classifying the objectives by their importance, (4) generating alternatives, (5) evaluating the alternatives against the objectives, (6) making a tentative choice, (7) assessing its potential adverse consequences, and (8) making a final choice.

KEY TERMS

additive linear model (for multiattribute decision problems)
adverse consequences
alternatives
bounded rationality
cardinal utility
choice phase (of decision making)
conjunctive decision making (for multiattribute decision problems)
criteria (singular: criterion)
decision
decision statement
decision tree
descriptive (approaches to decision making)
design phase (of decision making)
dominant function

elimination by aspects (for multiattribute decision problems)
envelope
extraversion (psychological type)
feeling (psychological type)
filter criteria
flexibility
indifference curve
intelligence phase (of decision making)
introversion (psychological type)
intuition (psychological type)
judgment (psychological type)
Kepner-Tregoe method
lexicographic elimination (for multiattribute decision problems)
Must objectives
Myers-Briggs Type Inventory (MBTI)
normative (approaches to decision making)
operational decision
ordinal utility
organizational decision making
perception (psychological type)
political decision making
politicality
probability (of an adverse consequence)
problem solving
psychological type
rationality
rational management
satisficing
semistructured decision
sensing (psychological type)
seriousness (of an adverse consequence)
strategic decision
structured decision
structured decision phase
tactical decision
thinking (psychological type)
unstructured decision
util
utility curve
Want objectives

REVIEW QUESTIONS

1. What is a decision? Give three examples.
2. Define the three elements of a decision.
3. Define the three phases of decision making.

4. What is a structured decision? A semistructured decision? An unstructured decision?
5. What are the three levels of decision scope? Define each.
6. Describe three dimensions along which managers differ in the ways they make decisions.
7. Why do managers seldom make purely rational decisions?
8. What is "satisficing"? Do you ever make decisions that way?
9. Give an example of political decision making.
10. What are the four preferences that determine one's psychological type?
11. How will an Introvert and an Extravert differ in their preferred decision-making style? a Judging person versus a Perceiving person?
12. List the stages of the Kepner-Tregoe decision-making process. Describe each in a line or two.

EXERCISES

1. A-Plus Manufacturing is a $1.6 billion per year firm with four plants and a nationwide distribution network. The product moves through 38 branch offices and 312 distributors, all of which maintain some inventory. Distributors generate 37 percent of the orders but only 24 percent of the dollar volume. A-Plus products are classified into 176 groups representing 12,000 finished goods listed in the catalog. Of these, 3,600 are carried in inventory (in one or more of the 350+ possible locations) and 8,400 are made to order. About 1,500 new items enter the product line annually. A similar number are discontinued. A-Plus can deliver 90 percent of orders according to customer requests if they are consistent with lead times stated in the catalog, with no delays or adjustment of dates. They hope to improve this service level to 95 percent with a new computer system, giving them a competitive advantage.
   a. What, precisely, is the decision they must make here? Write a clear, concise decision statement.
   b. Where does this decision fall in the grid of Figure 2–3?
   c. Do you expect this decision to be made rationally? Why or why not?
2. What is wrong with each of the following decision statements? Give a corrected decision statement for each case.
   a. For a college admissions office DSS, which predicts the academic success of applicants on the basis of their secondary school records and their standardized exam scores: to predict how well applicants will do at our college.
   b. For a fast-food chain DSS, which determines the likely revenue of new restaurants based on characteristics of their location: to build our next restaurant where it will generate the most revenue.
3. Write down three decisions you made within the past week. Place each of them in the appropriate box of Figure 2–3.
4. Call or speak to a manager or executive (a businessperson you know, the dean of your school, a town official). Ask this person about a recent decision that he or she made on the job. Answer Exercise 1, parts *a, b,* and *c,* for that decision.
5. What do the intelligence, design, and choice phases consist of for the following decisions?
   a. Buying a car.
   b. Applying to graduate school.
   c. Deciding which of three proposed, nonoverlapping information systems projects to undertake, if your budget can only accommodate one of them.

6. Assume you own an automobile dealership. State one decision you or your employees would make that fits in each box of Figure 2–3. Put your answers on a grid in the form of Figure 2–3.

7. Page 41 has a box on creative alternatives for finding the height of a building by using a barometer. What is the characteristic of a barometer that makes it useful in each of the alternative methods of finding the height of the building? What other object (there are many; just name one) has each of these properties? What criteria would you use for choosing one of these methods to find the height of the building using the barometer?

8. Write a decision statement for each of the decision examples on pages 44–46 (the different categories in the grid of Figure 2–3). The first one, deciding how to cut a log at a sawmill, has been done for you.

9. Draw a decision tree (see Section 2.4.1) for the following situations:
   a. You are considering buying a car. One alternative is a new car. It costs $11,000 and will last for the four years you plan to keep it. It will be worth $6,000 at the end of that time unless it has been in a major accident, which you think is 25 percent likely, in which case it will be worth $4,000. Your other choice is a used car that costs $6,000. It has a 50 percent chance of lasting the four years and being worth $3,000 at that point. It also has a 50 percent chance of needing major repairs, becoming worthless, and forcing you to another expense estimated at $6,000 to buy a second used car during this period. This second used car will be worth $4,000 at the end of the period. Ignoring the time value of money, which should you purchase?
   b. (This is a multilevel decision tree.) You think a bit more about what might happen to your used car in exercise 9a. If it needs major repairs, you can carry them out for $4,000. They will last the rest of the planning period and the car will again be worth $3,000 when you go to sell it. You still have the option of buying a second used car as in 9a. You can also, if you're feeling rich at that time, lease a new car for the remaining (estimated) two years of your planning period at $2,000 per year. Again ignoring the time value of money, what should you do?

10. On page 50, we said "a rational manager [faced with the decision in Figure 2–7] who wants to maximize the statistically expected profit would choose the small computer system." Justify this statement.

11. On pages 51–52, we said "few people who have a total of $20,000 to their name would choose to spend every penny of their net worth on a car." Suppose alternatives to the $20,000 new car are (a) a late-model used car, with a 2-year dealer warranty, for $10,000 and (b) an older car with no warranty for $5,000. How would the person with a net worth of $20,000 evaluate the four options (including purchasing no car at all) in terms of utils?

12. Talk to a counselor trained in the MBTI. Obtain his or her opinions about the ways in which different personality types approach decision making. Compare these with the comments in the text. (Since we are talking about general tendencies and because there is a great deal of variation among individuals, you should expect some minor differences.) What does he or she suggest a decision maker should do (a) to recognize when his or her preferences do not match the needs of a decision-making situation, and (b) to deal with this mismatch?

13. Apply the Kepner-Tregoe decision-making method (Section 2.7) to
   a. Buying a new (new to you, if not newly manufactured) car.
   b. Choosing an advertising program for Baa-Bits ("The only sheep food that sheep ask for by name").
   c. Choosing a college major.

14. Apply the Kepner-Tregoe decision-making method *by yourself* to decide where to locate a warehouse for Baa-Bits (see exercise 13b) and Moo-Bits (its bovine

equivalent). Then use the method in a group of three or four students and reach a *group decision.* Assess (a) the time it took to reach an individual versus a group decision, (b) how easy it was, and (c) the quality of the result.

15. Apply the Kepner-Tregoe evaluation method (just that part of the overall K-T process) to selecting a site for a new health club and senior citizen recreation center in a metropolitan area. There are three candidate sites, one of which will be chosen. The weights in this case have been chosen to add up to 100 percent, rather than being set independently from 1 to 10, and the individual scores are given on a 1 to 5 scale rather than a 1 to 10 scale, but the way these are applied to the decision is exactly the same.

Location factor	Weight	Score Site (a)	Score Site (b)	Score Site (c)
Total client-miles driven per month	25	4	2	5
Facility utilization	20	3	3	4
Accessibility by public transportation	20	3	2	4
Expressway accessibility	15	4	2	3
Land and construction costs	10	1	5	1
Employee preference/convenience	10	5	3	3

16. Your employer, a computer vendor, is to participate in a trade show 2,000 miles from your headquarters. You have developed a project plan to build a booth, ship a new prototype computer to the show, write demonstration programs, staff the booth, and provide enough literature for the expected demand. List at least six things that could go wrong with your plan (the adverse consequences). Assess the probability and seriousness of each. State three on which you would concentrate for either preventive action or a contingency plan.

17. For each of the eight steps of the Kepner-Tregoe decision-making process, state how a computer could be used to support
    a. an individual decision maker
    b. a group decision

18. Discuss which psychological preferences might affect a person's effectiveness in carrying out each step of the Kepner-Tregoe decision-making process. What does this suggest about the composition of a group formed to carry out this process for a joint decision?

19. You are driving in summer in Northern Canada and see a sign that says "Gas station and restaurant 2 km, next stop 100 km." What decisions do you have to make? What information do you need in order to make them?

REFERENCES

ACKO68   Ackoff, R. L., and M. W. Sasieni. *Fundamentals of Operations Research.* Wiley, New York (1968).

ANTH65   Anthony, Robert N. *Planning and Control Systems: A Framework for Analysis.* Studies in Management Control, Harvard University Graduate School of Business Administration, Cambridge, Mass. (1965).

BRIG57   Briggs-Myers, Isabel, and Katharine C. Briggs. *The Myers-Briggs Type Indicator.* Educational Testing Service, Princeton, N.J. (1957).

CYER63   Cyert, R. M., and J. G. March. *A Behavioral Theory of the Firm.* Prentice-Hall, Englewood Cliffs, N.J. (1963).

DEAN91 Dean, James W. Jr., Mark P. Sharfman, and Cameron M. Ford. "Strategic Decision-Making: A Multiple-Context Framework." In *Advances in Information Processing in Organizations,* vol. 4. (James R. Meindl, Robert L. Cardy, and Sheila M. Puffer, eds., JAI Press Inc., Greenwich, Conn. (1991), pp. 77–110.

GORR71 Gorry, G. Anthony, and Michael S. Scott Morton. "A Framework for Management Information Systems." *Sloan Management Review* 13, no. 1 (Fall 1971), pp. 55–70.

HIRS90 Hirsh, Sandra Krebs, and Jean M. Kummerow. *Introduction to Type in Organizations,* 2nd ed. Consulting Psychologists Press, Palo Alto, Calif. (1990).

HUIT92 Huitt, William G. "Problem Solving and Decision Making: Consideration of Individual Differences Using the Myers-Briggs Type Indicator." *Journal of Psychological Type* 24 (1992), pp. 33–44.

ISAC88 Isachsen, Olaf, and Linda V. Berens. *Working Together: A Personality Centered Approach to Management.* Neworld Management Press, Coronado, Calif. (1988).

KEEN78 Keen, Peter G. W., and Michael S. Scott Morton. *Decision Support Systems: An Organizational Perspective.* Addison-Wesley, Reading, Mass. (1978).

KEIR84 Keirsey, David, and Marilyn Bates. *Please Understand Me: Character and Temperament Types.* Prometheus Nemesis Book Co., Del Mar, Calif. (1984).

KEPN73 Kepner-Tregoe Inc. *Problem Analysis and Decision Making.* Kepner-Tregoe Inc., Princeton, N.J. (1973).

KEPN81 Kepner, Charles H., and Benjamin B. Tregoe. *The New Rational Manager.* Princeton Research Press., Princeton, N.J. (1981).

KERR92 Kerr, Norbert L. "Issue Importance and Decision Making." In *Group Process and Productivity.* Stephen Worchel, Wendy Wood, and Jeffry A. Simpson, eds. SAGE Publications Inc., Newbury Park, Calif. (1992).

MYER90 Myers, Isabel Briggs. *Introduction to Type.* Consulting Psychologists Press, Palo Alto, Calif. (1990).

PALV92 Palvia, Shailendra, and Steven R. Gordon. "Tables, Trees and Formulas in Decision Analysis." *Communications of the ACM* 35, no. 10 (October 1992), pp. 104–113.

PROV90 Provost, Judith A. *Work, Play, and Type.* Consulting Psychologists Press, Palo Alto, Calif. (1990).

RAND87 *The Random House Dictionary of the English Language,* unabridged 2nd edition. Random House, New York (1987).

SIMO60 Simon, Herbert A. *The New Science of Decision Making.* Harper & Row, New York (1960).

SVEN79 Svenson, O. "Process Descriptions of Decision Making." *Organizational Behavior and Human Decision Processes* 23, no. 1 (1979), pp. 86–112.

TODD91 Todd, Peter, and Izak Benbasat. "An Experimental Investigation of the Impact of Computer Based Decision Aids on Decision Making Processes." *Information Systems Research* 2, no. 2 (June 1991), pp. 87–115.

TODD92 Todd, Peter, and Izak Benbasat. "The Use of Information in Decision Making: An Experimental Investigation of the Impact of Computer-Based Decision Aids." *MIS Quarterly* 16, no. 3 (September 1992), pp. 373–393.

TVER69 Tversky, Amos. "Intransitivity of Preferences." *Psychological Review* 76, no. 1 (January 1969), pp. 31–48.

Fort Lowell Trading Company: The First Meeting

Elizabeth and Miguel couldn't help feeling a bit nervous as they signed in at the Fort Lowell Trading Company headquarters lobby for their first meeting with Dottie Eastman. Lou Giovanelli had set up the meeting and they had confirmed it with Ms. Eastman's secretary, but they still felt tense. They knew this project was critical to their MIS program at Sabino Canyon College, and they knew that her help and support would be vital to it. Also, the two had little experience working with senior officers of major corporations and were a bit in awe of her status.

As soon as she walked into the lobby, though, the two felt at ease. Far from being the ogre they had feared, she greeted them warmly with "You must be Elizabeth and Miguel. Lou said some very nice things about you. I'm looking forward to seeing you both around a lot over the next few months."

With that she signed the "escort" column of the visitor register, pressed her employee badge against a reader by a double door, and opened it when a buzzer sounded. The three moved into the IS office area and down a corridor toward a corner of the building. They arrived at a large office with a conference table near the door. In addition to pads of paper and pens at each seat, an insulated pitcher and several glasses stood in the middle of the table.

Dottie waved the two students into the office ahead of her, saying "Make yourselves comfortable. There's ice water in that pitcher, in case you're still warm from outside. I want to dig out a couple of things from my files that we might want later."

As soon as the two were settled in and had filled their glasses, Dottie continued, "I should probably start by telling you something about the information systems organization here. Most companies have pretty similar computer systems, once you allow for being in different business and all, but the way they organize their people is all over the place. We're set up in a way that works for us, but it might not be like anything you found in your textbooks."

With that she took out one of the pieces of paper she had fished out of a file drawer (Figure 2–15) and placed it on the table where all three could see it. "This is our paper organization chart," she explained. "We don't always work this way but at least it tells everyone who has to approve their raises."

"We have four basic categories of computers at Fort Lowell," she began. "We've got the corporate mainframes, right down the hall from here toward the center of the building. These are connected to local servers all over the company via a high-speed network. The servers, in turn, support whatever mix of client systems a department needs. That's three. The fourth category is the store computers. They run the POS terminals and track the store's own inventory. They're on our network, too."

"Excuse me, Ms. Eastman, but what's POS? Is that the company that made them?" Miguel asked.

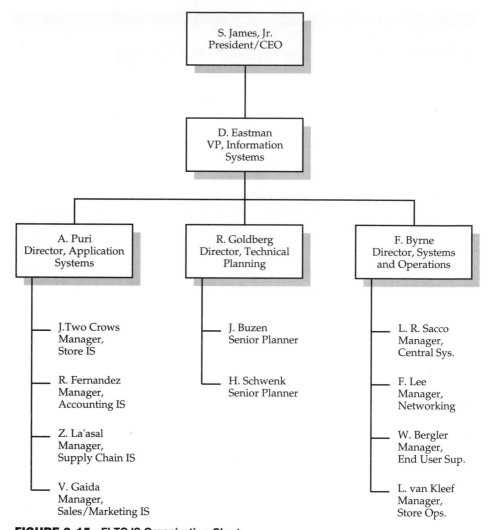

FIGURE 2–15   **FLTC IS Organization Chart**

"Sorry about that, and please call me Dottie," Dottie smiled. "We get so caught up in store jargon that we forget it's not standard English. POS means 'point of sale.' A POS terminal, or a point-of-sale terminal, is basically an electronic cash register. And please keep interrupting if there's anything else you have questions about. Anyhow," she continued, "we spend about $100 million on information systems each year. That sounds like a lot of money but by the time you split it up into all the pieces it doesn't go as far as we'd like. About a quarter of that, or $25 million, goes to people. That, in turn, gives us about 300 information systems professionals throughout the whole company.

"About two-thirds of those people are in my organization. Fortunately, that doesn't mean they're all in this building, or we'd run out of space! That includes all the people who deal with our mainframes or our networks. It includes the people who work on the store computers, since those are 99 percent standardized from one of our stores to the next. It also includes a small crew of 'rocket scientists' who set our technology standards and watch for new technologies we might be able to use.

"My group also includes our microcomputer help desk. We centralized that so we could develop some real expertise for tough problems and offer people more of a career path than they could get working in a division. Most of its people are located across the company but they all report into here," she said as she indicated a box on the right side of the chart.

"The business analysts who plan new information systems, though," she continued, "are mostly part of the different functional groups. We might not have done that 10 years ago, but today marketing people or anybody else have to know a lot about information systems. Since that's the case, we figure it makes sense to have marketing people plan marketing systems and so on. Then they work with our system designers and programmers to make them happen.

"Each group also has its own specialists in its own applications. For instance, our PageMaker experts are in the groups that do graphic design. When somebody else has a question, say someone in human resources is doing an employee newsletter and hits a snag, that's where they go. They usually call the main help desk first, because they don't always know who supports what, but the help desk people know where all the resources are."

"Where do your decision support systems get developed?" Elizabeth asked.

"Part of the reason you're here is that we don't think enough of them do get developed," Dottie laughed. "In theory, a business analyst in, say, finance, would come up with an idea and sketch it out. If it runs on our central systems, or if it's a good-sized client/server project, our central staff would schedule the project and put the system together. If it's smaller, the business analysis group in that department would do it, with help from the micro support people.

"Problem is, that's just the theory. A lot of the business analysts don't see chances for decision support systems as often as they should. They just don't come up with the ideas. And our mainframe programmers are sitting here, reading *Computerworld* articles about what someone else is doing, and they wonder 'how come we don't do anything like that?' No organization is perfect. I think you just hit on a problem with ours."

"So, is that what you'd like us to do?" asked Miguel. "Come up with some new ideas for decision support systems?"

"Sure is," Dottie replied. "If you can even come up with one or two, it will be worth all the time we're spending with you for the entire semester."

"Sounds good," Miguel continued. "When and how can we start?"

"One good place might be with Niels Agger in business development. I'll call Niels and alert him that you'll be in touch. Then you can call to set up a meeting. On second thought, he travels a good deal and I know he's in today. If you're not in a hurry, can you meet with Niels now if he's not tied up? Yes? Great! I'll give him a call!"

EXERCISES

Consider these Fort Lowell Trading Company decisions:

- FLTC is trying to decide where to locate a new store. Many new shopping malls are being built all across North America. (This evaluation does not include potential locations outside North America, since they operate only in North America today and overseas expansion would be a separate, major strategic decision.) As a well-known company with a good reputation for quality, FLTC is an attractive tenant, so mall developers seek it out and try to persuade it to locate a new store in their malls. FLTC cannot accept all these offers so it must select the few that it wants to pursue in detail.
- FLTC has decided to build a new store in the Cincinnati, Ohio, area. Three new malls are being planned there: one on the north side of the city, one west of the city near the Ohio River, and one across the Ohio in northern Kentucky. While there are other options—for instance, they could build a free-standing store or work with a mall developer to develop a fourth new mall—they have, for the time being, decided that their new store will be in one of these three malls. They must choose one.
- FLTC is screening résumés for a regional marketing and promotion manager for the northeastern United States. The good news is that they are an attractive employer, so they are flooded with applications for this position. The bad news is that good retail marketing people are rare but people who think they would be are not, so few of the applicants are qualified. They believe they may have to hire someone with a retail sales management background who can learn enough about marketing to create effective programs, or a person with little experience who they think can grow into the job.

For each of the above decisions, answer the following questions:

1. What do the intelligence, design, and choice phases consist of for this decision? Write a clear decision statement for each.
2. Where does the decision fall in the grid of Figure 2–3?
3. How do you feel this decision will be made, in terms of the approaches listed in Section 2.4?
4. Suppose the key decision maker's personality type is ENFJ. What does this tell you about his or her probable preferred approach to this decision?
5. Suppose this person must make the decision together with another, whose personality type is INTP. What does this tell you about this person's probable preferred approach to this decision? What conflicts might arise because of the differences between the two personality types?
6. Would the Kepner-Tregoe decision-making method help with this decision? Why or why not?
7. Apply the Kepner-Tregoe decision-making method to those decisions that you think it could help with or to those decisions specified by your instructor. Make up any numbers you need, but try to make them reasonable.
8. Describe, in general terms, a decision support system that could help make this decision. Discuss what it would do in terms of supporting the decision, not how it would work technically.

CHAPTER 3

Systems, Information Quality, and Models

CHAPTER OUTLINE

Introduction

The third word in decision support systems is *systems*. It is not there by accident. A decision support system is a particular type of system. We must therefore understand systems if we hope to understand DSS.

If a decision support system is to provide us with useful assistance, its output must be of sufficient quality for the decision we are about to make. Information quality has several aspects, which all affect the usability of a DSS. You'll read about them in this chapter as well.

Finally, as you saw in the sample definitions of DSS in Chapter 1, many DSS contain models. For that reason we must also understand something about models before we get further into the types of DSS in the next chapter. Since a model is a representation of a system, this chapter will introduce you to models as well.

CHAPTER OBJECTIVES

After you have read and studied this chapter, you will be able to:

1. Define a system and describe its characteristics.
2. Define an information system.
3. Read and understand data flow diagrams used to represent systems.
4. Explain how decision support systems fit into the overall category of information systems.
5. Evaluate the quality of information available to help make a decision.
6. Explain why we use models in decision support systems.
7. Understand the value of models in DSS.

3.1 ABOUT SYSTEMS

You probably have an informal, intuitive idea of a system. Chances are that you use the word in daily conversation: the school system, the nervous system, your old car's @#$%&*%!! electrical system. In order to study systems properly, we need a more precise definition that will allow us to know exactly what we mean when we refer to one:

A **system** is a group of interacting components with a purpose.

The key words in this definition are

- *Group.* A system must consist of more than one item. A piece of paper, unless one cares about its molecular structure, is not a system.
- *Interacting.* The components must operate in some relationship to each other. A collection of components that are not connected to each other, such as a piece of paper in one room and a pencil in another, is not a system. These same components would comprise a writing system, however, if they were brought together.
- *Components.* The components may be elementary items, incapable of (for our purposes) further subdivision. Alternatively, they may be systems in their own right: smaller systems, to be sure, but systems nonetheless. Small systems that are components of a larger system are called **subsystems** of the larger system.
- *Purpose.* Without getting into metaphysics or religion—does the earth, as an ecological system, have a purpose? Does the solar system have one? Do we? We note here that the systems discussed in this book all have a purpose. Knowing the purpose of a system helps us understand it or redesign it to carry out this purpose better.

Every system also has a **boundary.** The boundary of a system separates the components of that system, which are inside it, from the rest of the world (its **environment**), which is outside the system. Objects or information can cross the boundary of most systems: inward, outward, or in both directions. If nothing crosses the boundary of a system in either direction, that system is called a **closed system.** Otherwise, it is called an **open system.** Figure 3–1 shows both types.

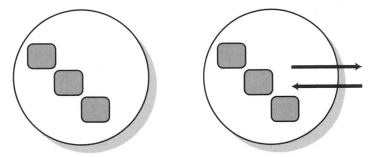

FIGURE 3–1 Closed (Left) and Open (Right) Systems

Completely closed systems are rare in the real world. It is, however, sometimes useful to simplify the analysis of a system by treating it as closed. For example, we might study the performance of an automobile by running it on a closed track. In the real world, it would make a series of trips over public roads between a variety of origins and destinations. Also in the real world, it would take on and discharge passengers and packages, but a closed-track evaluation is easier to control and allows us to eliminate extraneous variables that might affect the results differently from one test to another.

Systems can be of many types. Consider a few from everyday life:

- *Your body.* Figure 3–2 depicts the human body with some of its systems. These components include the circulatory system, the skeletal system, the digestive system, the respiratory system, the nervous system, the immune system, and several more you can find in anatomy books. Each of these, as its name suggests, is itself a system: for example, your circulatory system consists of your heart, veins, arteries, and capillaries. Your body's systems interact in many ways: the digestive system puts nutrients into the circulatory system, the nervous system sends out electrical signals that control the other systems, and so on. The purpose of the system, again avoiding metaphysics and religion, is to sustain its existence and to perpetuate the species. Its boundary is your skin. Air, food, and drink cross the boundary of the system in the inward direction; used air, digestive waste, and occasional flakes of dry skin cross it outward. Information enters the system via your senses and leaves it via your voice and actions.

- *A metropolitan area transportation system.* Its components are roads, cars, trucks, buses, railroad lines, trains, signals, drivers, traffic control officers, passengers, and more. They interact by intersecting in space (as at a road crossing), by exchanging passengers, by giving information to each other (traffic officer to driver, signal to train engineer, bus driver to passenger), and in several other ways. Its boundary depends on the purpose for which we are studying the system: for some purposes we would include railroad station buildings in the system, for other purposes we might not. It also has a geographic boundary that determines which roads and railroad tracks are part of our system and which are not. Passengers, vehicles, and so on cross the system's boundary in both

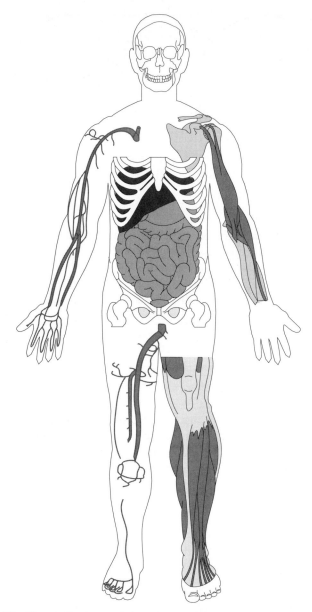

FIGURE 3–2 **The Human Body and Some of Its Systems**

directions. So does information, as in a radio traffic report giving information about conditions in the area to drivers outside it. The purpose of this system is to move goods and people within the defined area.

As with the human body system, each important component of the transportation system is itself a system. Figure 3–3 shows some of its levels. Some people are concerned only with the rail component of the transportation system.

National transportation philosophy

Regional transportation policy

Regional rail transportation plans

Railroad schedules

Train 402

Engine 5516 pulling train 402

The diesel motor of Engine 5516

The fuel system of Engine 5516's diesel motor

The injectors controlling the air–fuel ratio inside the motor's cylinders

The chemical reactions between the air and fuel in the cylinder

The atomic structure of fuel molecules

The structure of carbon, etc., atoms in terms of elementary particles

FIGURE 3–3 **Hierarchy of Transportation Subsystems**

At a lower level, people who work for a locomotive manufacturer might consider the locomotive to be their system, and let others worry about the trains that it might later pull. The locomotive's diesel engine is a complex system in its own right, but it is a single component to the locomotive designer. To another person the fuel system of that locomotive is the system. Moving down further, a combustion chemist might be concerned with a small aspect of the fuel system. The breakdown doesn't stop until we reach elementary particles in the domain of the nuclear physicist. Studying combustion chemistry or nuclear physics is of little on-the-job value to a regional transportation planner.

As these examples suggest, the ways in which the components and boundary of a particular system are defined are largely up to the person studying it. The value of a system study depends vitally on studying the right system: not too much and not too little, not in too great detail or at too high a level of generalization. The officer controlling traffic at an intersection can't worry about subway schedules or the fuel injection system of every passing car. He or she must focus on movements of vehicles that are within a few hundred feet of the intersection and moving toward it. This type of focus is intuitive to all traffic control officers who survive their first day on the job. The equivalent focus in an information system is not nearly as intuitive but is just as important for the career survival of information system professionals.

Systems often incorporate feedback. **Feedback** is output from a system component that becomes, perhaps after additional processing, input to a system component. When you press a button in an elevator, it activates a motor to change the

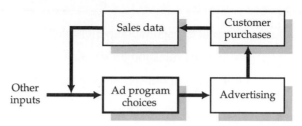

FIGURE 3–4 Advertising Program Selection System with Feedback

position of the elevator. Elevator position information is *fed back* into the system via sensors along the elevator shaft. The elevator's control circuits, in turn, use this information to determine when to stop the motor in order to align the elevator with the requested floor. Systems that use feedback to adjust their outputs, based on how well the result of those outputs matches the desired result, are called **closed loop systems.** Those that do not use feedback to adjust their outputs are called **open loop systems.**

Feedback can be **internal** to a system, as in this elevator example, or **external** to it. In many DSS, the important feedback is a function of the system's environment and is thus external to the system. The system diagrammed in Figure 3–4 is an example of external feedback. The choice of an advertising program has an effect on customer purchases, which, in turn, influence our future choices of advertising programs. This effect takes place through customer reactions and sales data. Since customers are outside our advertising selection system, this system has external feedback.

The study of systems in general and the (often unexpected) ways they behave is the subject of *general systems theory.* You can read more about general systems theory in books such as [RAPO86], [VONB68], [WILS90], or any of several others that your library probably has indexed under that subject heading.

3.2 INFORMATION SYSTEMS

An **information system** is a system whose purpose is to store, process, and communicate information.

In the 1990s we associate information systems with computers. Many information systems, and virtually all large ones, use computers today. Yet an information system need not use computers. Computers first became widely available in the 1950s. They were initially too expensive for all but the largest businesses and government agencies. People stored, processed and transmitted information for centuries before then, however. They used a variety of devices—paper and pencil, abaci, and more—to store data, to calculate with it, and to communicate it to other people. Some of these devices are still in use and may still be the best way to deal with an information-handling task. Part of an information system de-

Precomputer Information System Technology

Information systems technology is not a new concept, but it has just changed a bit over the years.

Centuries ago, the Incas of Peru used an accounting system based on string technology [MENN69]. It was totally solid state, required no electricity, and was proof against most natural disasters except fire. To guard against that eventuality, they used what we would call a replicated database, with important records copied to widely separated geographic locations on a schedule based on the communication technologies in use. (This also facilitated local database access by distributed users, another reason we use distributed databases today.)

The Inca system, called *quipu,* used horizontal ropes about 1 foot 8 inches (50 cm) long from which hung 48 secondary cords, each about 1 foot 4 inches (40 cm) long. These cords were colored to designate the various areas of government: tribute, land, economic productivity such as crops and herds, wars, religious rituals. Each cord had three knots. The knot closest to the main rope designated hundreds, the next one down designated tens, and the third one designated individual units. One style of knot represented the digit *1,* whereas another type of knot with two to nine loops represented those digits.

Several of the cords hanging from the main rope could be grouped with a loop of string. A head string was then added to the loop, containing the sum of the entries on the individual strings. (In today's terminology, they entered the total as a separate database record: usually a poor idea, but reasonable for historical data when calculation times are long compared to record retrieval times. Data warehouses often precalculate category summaries for precisely that reason.) In this way, individual villages could send their crop counts to the regional capital. A regional official would tie the village cords to the regional quipu and create a head string representing the crop count of the entire region. A duplicate head string was forwarded to the national capital in Cuzco. There, it became one of many regional quipu, which were in turn totaled to give national crop data.

Each Inca village had four official quipu keepers called *camayocs.* Much as we use multiprocessors today, this provided increased computing power compared to one camayoc, and redundancy for continued system operation in case one dies or is otherwise unavailable. In addition, regional commanders and officials at Cuzco—military commanders, judges, the heads of noble families—used the system. Just as information processing and today's computers influence our thought patterns, quipu influenced those of the Inca. Early European visitors to South America reported that the Inca made efforts to translate everything they were told to quipu-based numerical terms. They had a great deal of difficulty understanding concepts that did not translate properly into those terms.

signer's job is to determine which parts of an information processing task are best done by computers and which, conversely, should be done by humans or by "low-tech" methods.

The payroll system diagrammed in Figure 3–5 is a typical information system, albeit not a DSS. Its components include people (payroll clerks), a variety of paper forms, checks, and a computer. Information enters the system via forms and exits via check stubs and reports. Information is also transmitted among the components of the system, in part via forms and in part electronically. Data are stored partly on paper forms, partly in computer files. Processing is done largely in the computer.

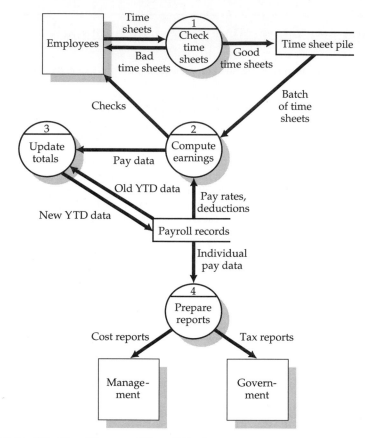

FIGURE 3–5 Data Flow Diagram of Payroll System

3.3 DATA FLOW DIAGRAMS

Figure 3–5 represents the payroll system as a **data flow[1] diagram (DFD).** A DFD is a popular way to describe an information system. A DFD shows the components of the system: **processes,** shown as rounded rectangles in the DFD, and **data stores** (computer or paper files), shown as open-ended rectangles.[2] Where a component of a system is itself a system, it can be described in a *lower-level DFD.* A DFD shows interactions among the components in the form of data flows among the processes and data stores. It shows the boundary of the system implicitly: the

---

[1]Some authors use *dataflow* as one word. Expect to see both forms used.
[2]If you've studied systems analysis, you may have used either Gane-Sarson DFDs like this one or Yourdon-DeMarco DFDs, which use slightly different symbols. Both work the same way. Their differences are cosmetic.

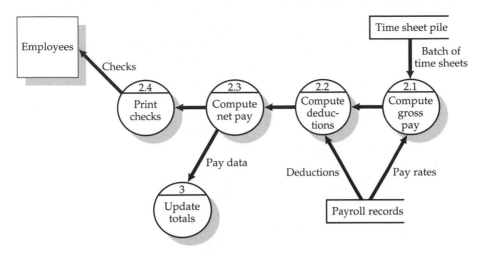

FIGURE 3-6 DFD of Earnings Computation

processes and data stores are inside the system, whereas the square boxes represent **external entities** that communicate with the system.

A data flow diagram is not a complete description of a system. It doesn't show, among other things, the purpose of the system. Fortunately, we can usually infer a system's purpose from other information sources. A DFD also does not show the timing relationships among the processes in the system.[3] The DFD in Figure 3–5, for example, does not tell us if paychecks are produced daily, weekly, monthly, or at some other interval. As with the purpose of the system, we must find this information elsewhere.

Data flow diagrams are important because they help people communicate about what the components of a system are, how the system works, and what it does. They are more precise than normal English for this purpose. They communicate a great deal of information via a few easily understood pictures. When a system becomes too complex to show in one DFD, we can use a layered set of data flow diagrams: one like Figure 3–5 to show the overall system, and additional ones to show how its components work internally. Figure 3–6 amplifies payroll Process 2, Compute Earnings. The processes in Figure 3–6 are all numbered 2.*n* to show that they are parts of Process 2, Compute Earnings, in the top-level data flow diagram of the payroll system.

We'll use DFDs to describe systems through the rest of this book. If you haven't already studied data flow diagrams in an introductory MIS course, you can learn about them in a systems analysis course.

---

[3]Suggestions such as [FRIE95] have been made to expand the information content of DFDs, adding timing information among other items, but none have caught on widely.

3.4 DSS AS INFORMATION SYSTEMS

A decision support system is a specific type of information system. If we know that an information system is a DSS, we can infer some conclusions about it that do not apply to all types of information systems:

- A DSS usually uses one or more data stores (databases or sets of files) that provide information to support the decision. Some of these may be maintained by the DSS itself. Some may be maintained within the organization that uses the DSS. A DSS can also use external (often public) information sources, such as stock market price data or business credit ratings.
- The DSS does not update the databases that it uses as external information sources. They are updated by suitable transaction processing systems, either within the organization using the DSS or outside it.
- The DSS communicates with the decision maker. Depending on the situation, we may depict the decision maker as an external entity or as part of the system. The choice will often depend on whether we are studying an entire decision process or a system to support the way decisions are already being made.
- In all likelihood, the decision maker supplies the DSS with specific information defining the decision to be made within the general category of decisions with which the DSS can help. That information tells the DSS what data to extract from its data stores.

A general schematic of a DSS that conforms to this description is shown in Figure 3–7. This figure is not tied to a specific DSS application. It applies equally to a loan approval system or to a system that selects media for an advertising

FIGURE 3–7 **Data Flow Diagram of Generic DSS**

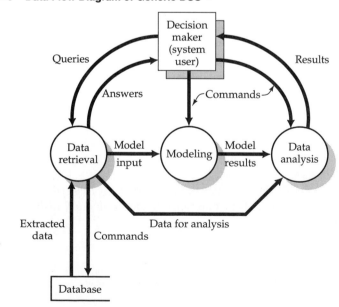

campaign. In the case of a specific system, we would replace the generic component names with names that reflect the specific components of that system. For example, the component shown as "database" in Figure 3–7 might be labeled "credit history database" for a loan approval system. The emphasis on each component of a DSS, and the specific lower level components into which we could break down each higher level element, also vary widely from one DSS to another.

Before embarking on the design of any DSS, whether in this course or on the job, you should start by defining it as a system. There are two ways to view the overall system you will design: as a decision support system or as a decision-making system. In the former case, illustrated in Figure 3–8, the decision maker is outside the system you are studying. In the latter case, illustrated in Figure 3–9, the decision maker is inside the overall system though still outside its DSS component. (If the computer part of the system could make decisions all by itself, it would be a decision-*making* system, not a decision *support* system.) The design choices that are open to you depend in part on the point of view you choose.

To start designing your DSS, ask yourself these questions:

- What is the purpose of your DSS, in terms of the decision being made and the outputs it must supply? (Be as specific as you can.)
- What are the external entities (decision makers, information sources) with which the DSS communicates? What are the data flows to and from these external entities?

FIGURE 3–8 **Context Diagram of DSS as System**

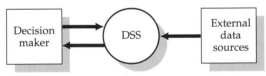

FIGURE 3–9 **Decision-Making System Incorporating DSS as Component**

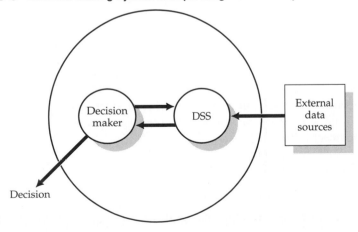

- What internal data files does the DSS use? Where do they get their information? If they get it from outside the system, what are the external entities that provide it?
- What are the major processes in the DSS? What are the data flows among them?

You may not be able to answer all these questions when you start to define a system. The exercise of trying to take a "first cut" at them will still pay off, both in terms of increasing your understanding of the system and in telling you what you don't yet know and must therefore make an effort to find out. Just remember that the first cut *is* a first cut. Don't get so attached to it that you can't see its flaws later on.

If you can answer these questions, you will understand your DSS as a system. One test of this understanding is being able to draw it as a data flow diagram. Success in diagramming your system means you are well on your way to its successful design.

3.5 INFORMATION AND INFORMATION QUALITY

3.5.1 Information versus Data

Information is anything that reduces uncertainty. Therefore, the greater the reduction in uncertainty, the more information we have:[4]

- Picking the winner of next year's NCAA Division I men's basketball tournament from all eligible colleges conveys more information than picking it from the two teams in the final game.
- Saying "Jane received an A in English 201" conveys more information than saying "Jane passed English."
- Telling a customer "We'll deliver your stove next Thursday between 1 and 3 p.m." conveys more information than "We'll deliver your stove toward the end of next week."

The value information provides to knowledge workers in an organization is also in reducing uncertainty. Information is vital to decision making in many areas. For example,

- You are trying to decide whether to go to the movies tonight after dinner. Your decision depends on when the show starts.
- As the marketing head of a consumer electronics firm, you need to decide whether or not to approve the development of a new CD player for motorcycles. Your decision depends on development costs, production costs, the number you expect to sell, the price you will be able to charge, and the availability and cost of development funds.
- As an investor, you want to decide which of several stocks to buy. Your choice depends on their future price changes and the dividends each will pay.

---

[4]Engineers formalize this concept in their definition of a *bit* as a measure of uncertainty reduction.

In each of these cases you need information: when the movie starts, how many motorcycle CD players you will be able to sell, stock price and dividend payouts. Without the required information you are unable to make these decisions. Furthermore, with poor information, you are likely to make poor decisions.

Let's see what information you *really* need for these decisions. To choose a movie, you may think you need to know when it starts. But what really matters is not when it starts but when it starts *relative to other events in your day.* If a movie starts before 7:15, you won't have time to finish dinner. If it starts after 8:30, it may end later than you want to be out for the evening. On other days, in other situations, however, your availability for a 7:00 movie might be quite different. Hence, the real question you need answered is Does the movie start between 7:15 and 8:30, or not? Given that information, you can decide whether to see the movie or not. If you decide to see it, then—and only then—will you need its actual starting time in order to schedule your departure.

The process is similar for our other sample decisions. To decide whether or not to develop the motorcycle CD player, you do not need to know the individual data elements comprising its business plan. What you need to know is the plan's projected return on investment (ROI) in relationship to your firm's requirements, and how this plan compares with other projects competing for the same funds. You might be interested in the supporting details, and knowing them might even increase your confidence in the ROI numbers, but that's not the same as *needing* to know them.

Before investing in the stock market, you compare the risks and returns of different stocks with each other, and with alternative investments such as bank CDs and lottery tickets, in the context of your future plans. (A 70-year-old retiree, 45-year-old lawyer, and 20-year-old college student have different financial needs.) There is, as many investors learn to their sorrow, no surefire formula for predicting future stock prices. Still, reducing your uncertainty is of value. The more you can reduce your uncertainty, the greater the value of your information.

In short, decisions are seldom made on the basis of raw data. Decisions are made on the basis of data that has been processed, evaluated, compared, and considered in the context of other data. That processed data is *information.* As Barry Devlin puts it in [DEVL97],

> Data is what the information systems department creates, stores and provides. Information—data in its business context—is what the business needs.

Several data elements, suitably processed and placed in their business context, create useful information for decision making.

Creating Information from Data   The preceding examples showed two ways of processing data into information:

1. *Comparing one data element with another.* We compare the starting time of a movie with our earliest possible arrival, the projected rate of return on developing motorcycle CD players with our firm's requirements, the dividend yield of one stock with another's.

2. *Performing calculations on data.* We calculate our earliest possible arrival time at the movie theater from the ending time of dinner and expected travel time. We compute the expected profitability of the motorcycle CD player from projected costs and revenues. We combine expected rates of return with risk levels in estimating the desirability of different stocks.

Calculations and comparisons are the two basic operations that computers or people do with data. They are often intertwined. If we want to calculate the after-tax return of an investment, we must deal with income tax rates that vary with income level. Figuring the tax requires comparing income data with the income levels at which tax rates change before we can carry out the correct computations.

Some of the data used in the preceding decisions comes from sources inside the decision maker's organization, whereas other data is internal to it.

- Movie times originate with the theater, perhaps reaching you via an ad in the daily newspaper. You know, or can estimate, when you will finish dinner, how long it takes to reach the theater, and when you want to get back home.
- One group of employees prepared a sales forecast for the motorcycle CD player, another estimated development time and cost, and a third determined the cost of building each unit. Other groups did likewise for other projects that compete, within the firm, for the same R&D funding. Banks can provide the cost of borrowing capital. Financial advisors can estimate how much the firm could raise by offering new stock.
- Stock price data originates (for major firms) with stock exchanges. It is available in newspapers and electronically. Historical data can be obtained from several public sources. Financial analysts develop estimates of future growth, which are reported in the press. The investor knows his or her own personal objectives.

Each of these decisions requires a mix of internal and external data. Individual data elements are of little use for decision making until someone puts them together. This is a general principle: *The information systems that provide the greatest value are those that link people and organizations via shared data.*

What Can Go Wrong in the Process   Let's see what can happen if we make the wrong decision in each of these cases.

- You get to the movie after it starts, or you stay out later than you wanted to.
- You authorize the motorcycle CD player and it flops. Or, you reject the project, and the project you approve in its place turns out to be a disaster. A competitor's motorcycle CD player is a runaway success in the marketplace.
- You pick a stock that goes down and you lose a lot of money.

Each of these outcomes is the result of imperfect information. However, imperfect information is sometimes unavoidable. A fall in the stock price of a logging company, for example, might result from a volcano eruption near its forests. As of now there is no way to predict such a rare event and its impact well enough to help investors.

In other cases, extra effort put into data gathering can improve the quality of our information. Market research into motorcycle CD players can vary in thoroughness, in timeliness, and in how well its sample represents potential customers. All of these factors are under the control of the managers who authorize the research.

Higher quality information, clearly, leads to better decisions. But improving the quality of information costs money. We must analyze the impact that lower quality information can have on a decision—that decision's sensitivity to information quality—in order to decide if the higher quality information is worth its cost.

It is sometimes, but not always, possible to calculate the value of high quality information. Reconsider the engine rebuilding decision example on page 49. If we could determine ahead of time whether or not the engine would fail, we would rebuild it 20 percent of the time and leave it alone 80 percent of the time. The expected profit from the truck over the 2-year planning period would be $48,000. The value of perfect information, compared with what we now have, is $8,000. This sort of calculation can be used to decide if better information is worth paying for.

Because information quality is so critical to decision making and therefore to DSS, we'll discuss its elements next. Whenever you develop a DSS, evaluate the quality of its inputs in terms of these factors so you can determine if they are sufficient for the decisions that your system will support.

3.5.2 Information Quality

Every good or service has an associated *quality level:* its degree of excellence in the context of its intended use. Information is no exception. Just as we can state the factors that determine the quality of a bicycle or a pizza, we can state the factors that determine the quality of information. Understanding these factors is the key to obtaining high quality, high value information.

The degree to which information can contribute to a decision, and hence the value of that information for decision-making purposes, depends on its quality. High quality information enables its users to make good decisions quickly. Lower quality information leads to poor decisions and wastes decision makers' time. As Larry English writes in [ENGL98]—specifically about data warehouses, since he was writing for a readership interested in that subject, but with applicability to all DSS:

> Data warehousing projects fail for a variety of reasons. All of the reasons can be traced to a single element: non-quality. Poor data architecture, inconsistently defined departmental data, inability to relate data from different data sources, missing and inaccurate data values, inconsistent uses of data fields, unacceptable query performance (timeliness of data), lack of a business sponsor (no data warehouse customer), etc., are all components of non-quality data. . . .
>
> Management can no longer afford the luxury of the excessive costs of nonquality data. In the information age a quality, shared information resource is the differentiator. Lack of quality information is to the next decade what product quality was to the 1980s.

The quality of information is the value of that information for its intended purpose. If we need to find out how fast we are driving, a needle pointing at a dial marked every 5 miles per hour, accurate to within 2 or 3 miles per hour, is of sufficient quality. That same way of presenting a firm's annual revenues would be woefully inadequate. But a nine-digit number, displayed on a car's instrument panel in tiny type, would not help us see quickly if we are exceeding the speed limit. We must know the purpose for which information will be used before we can judge its quality.

The positive impact of computers on information quality is generally obvious: faster, easier, cheaper, and so forth. This is why people use computers to process information. They usually achieve these objectives, or computers wouldn't be used as widely as they are. Yet using computers has a downside as well. The information systems world is becoming increasingly aware of information (or data) quality issues and their impact on decision making. Indeed, the February 1998 issue of leading computer science journal *Communications of the ACM* devoted a 29-page special section to this very topic. One article [REDM98; the others are listed in the references to this chapter as well] states:

> Poor data quality compromises decision making. . . . Decisions are no better than the data on which they are based. And since any decision of consequence depends on thousands of pieces of data, the chance that a decision is based only on good data is extremely small.
>
> The slightest suspicion of poor data quality often hinders managers from reaching any decision. One executive explained it to me this way: "We spend about half our (decision-making) time just arguing about whose data is better!"
>
> While all decisions involve some amount of uncertainty, it is clear that decisions based on the most relevant, complete, accurate and timely data have a better chance of advancing the organization's goals.

DSS developers must be aware of information quality issues and the impact of computers on information quality. They must guard against the dangers of negative computer impacts—especially because of a common tendency, as one gets caught up in the technical aspects of information processing, not to see the business picture and therefore to be unaware of the business implications of what one is doing. As you encounter each information quality factor in the next section, be sure you understand the potential negative impacts of computer processing on information quality so you can minimize them on the job.

3.5.3 Information Quality Factors

Information quality can be analyzed in terms of 11 factors, shown in Figure 3–10. The information must be of sufficient quality for its purpose in terms of each factor if it is to be of adequate decision support quality overall. Cost is at the center of Figure 3–10 because it must be balanced against other factors. This is typical of most business trade-offs: the benefits of an improvement in any aspect of the organization must be balanced against its cost.

Relevance   Information is **relevant** if it applies to the task being performed—in our context, to making a decision. Its degree of relevance depends on how

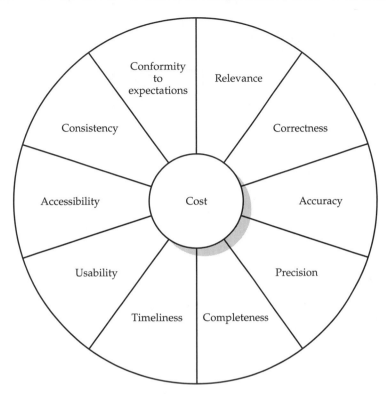

FIGURE 3–10 Eleven Information Quality Factors

much of the information being supplied is related, and how much is not related, to that task.

Information must be relevant if it is to be of any value at all. The relevance of information, that is, the quality of information in terms of this factor, varies from one situation to another. Knowing the price of AT&T stock on the New York Stock Exchange could be quite relevant for an investment decision. It would be totally irrelevant to choosing an advertising program for cat food or for optimizing the production setup of a wheelbarrow factory.

Relevance is not an all or nothing situation. There are many data elements on a stereo amplifier specification sheet. Some readers care if the amplifier can drive 8-ohm speakers: they own such speakers, so this is a Must criterion in their decision. Others do not care about this because they are buying a complete new system. If they like this amplifier they will buy speakers that it can drive. The relevance of the whole package, to most readers, is lower than a custom-tailored list containing only what that reader wants to know, but is generally acceptable. Most business-people, having faced such situations for years, can screen out unnecessary parts, but doing so takes time and effort that could be better applied to the task at hand. Figure 3–11 illustrates this sorting process.

Knowing what information is relevant in a particular situation requires understanding the business. Is the average customer discount relevant to setting the list

I don't care . . .

dimensions

weight

color of case

power consumption

I care . . .

price

output power

distortion

8-ohm speakers

FIGURE 3–11 Information Bombards a Person Who Sorts It Mentally Into "I Care" and "I Don't Care" Streams

price of a new product? Only the marketing staff knows. A guess on the part of the MIS staff members developing a DSS is just that—a guess, no matter how well intentioned and intelligent those people are. Information systems professionals are no more likely to understand all the data requirements for a decision support system than they are to understand all the data requirements for a Web-based customs brokerage system for international commerce or any other complex business process. A data requirements study should be one of the first parts of any DSS project even if the analysts are sure they know what is needed. If nothing else, such a study provides valuable protection against human error.

In cases where there's a possibility that information might be relevant but we can't be sure, it's best to err on the side of gathering and storing too much supporting data as long as the cost of doing so isn't prohibitive. Needs change over time. So does the relevance of data. Someone, at some time, may need or want this borderline item. At that point it is nice if that piece of information, though not currently on a computer screen, can be derived from data in the system.

Whether or not to display any extra information is a separate question. Too much information on a screen clutters it and makes it harder to focus on important items. One solution is to have a way for users to get the details behind an initial display. The development approach of *prototyping,* where users evaluate sample screens while a new information system can be changed easily, is a good way to determine what is needed in situations like this. You'll read about prototyping on page 261.

Impact of Computers on Information Relevance   On the surface, computers do not affect information relevance. What a manager needs to know to make a decision is the same with or without the computer. However, computers make it easy to present huge masses of data—some relevant, some not. (When people complain about drowning in information, they're more likely to be drowning in data.)

Therefore, DSS developers must analyze what information is needed and present only that. This is harder than displaying everything, leaving users to sort out what is important from the clutter. But it's necessary to do this if information is to be of the highest quality, and hence of the highest value, to decision makers and to the organization.

Correctness   In addition to being relevant, high quality information must be correct. Incorrect information can lead to poor management decisions, dissatisfied customers, and worse. The **correctness** of a data element means that it is based on the right part of the "real world." If we were to look at the real world, what we would find would be consistent with what the data element led us to expect. In Figure 3–12, the data element *A* can describe the location of any of the 11 black dots in the circle. If it is derived from the location of the one we want to identify, *B,* it is correct even if (as we'll soon see) it's a bit off—in fact, even if errors in determining it made it closer to one of the other 10.

The terms *correct, accurate,* and *precise* (the next two information quality factors) are often used with somewhat overlapping meanings. We don't always mean exactly the same thing by them each time we use them in informal conversation. Here we're using them with precise meanings that may not correspond entirely to the way one might use them informally.

Some correctness situations are absolute, where the data elements have no error tolerance. A telephone number is either correct or it isn't. If it isn't, it's useless. A catalogue number either refers to size 9B black dress shoes or it doesn't. If it doesn't, using it to order those shoes will yield unpredictable results.

Other data elements are still correct, that is to say, they refer to the right item in the real world, if they are somewhat off from their actual value. Approximate values are good enough for much numerical data. In fact, the question is often not whether numeric data are exact, because they can't be, but whether they are close enough. Stating that $\pi = 3.14159$ is correct (and accurate to six significant digits). As long as we take the possible error in our data into account when we use it, approximate data are not incorrect. Whether approximate data are of sufficiently high quality is the subject of the next quality factor, accuracy.

Nonnumeric data can also be nearly correct. My name is often misspelled. Informally, one might say that the spelling "Efram Mallack" is incorrect. As we use the terms here, it is correct—it does, after all, refer to me—but it is inaccurate. It is of sufficient quality for me to receive my paper mail, but not of sufficient quality to deliver e-mail or to persuade me that the writer is a close personal friend.

Impact of Computers on Information Correctness   The correctness of information depends on the correctness of the inputs and their processing. (Some processing errors, such as using inconsistent data elements, have their own headings later in this section.)

A: Data in a computer

B: Real-world data point A is intended to represent. A is correct
   if its value was derived from this data point.

C: Another real-world data point. A is incorrect if its value was,
   by mistake, derived from this data point.

FIGURE 3–12   Circle Diagram Showing Correctness

The major reason for incorrect input data is incorrect human input. Computers are quite willing to accept incorrect input and to use it, whereas a human clerk would catch many obvious errors instantly. Incorrect inputs cannot lead to correct outputs.

A well-designed information system incorporates data validation procedures to minimize the amount of incorrect data introduced into storage. These validation procedures can be divided into several categories [BRAC96]. All types can be enforced automatically in some fashion, though different features of the database management system, the data-entry process, and the application program may be required in each case. The designer of any application that incorporates a data-entry process should include checks from each category, or verify conclusively that the category does not apply. These checks can include the following:

1. *Data value integrity*—ensures that the value of a field is from an appropriate domain. This domain can be specified either as a list of allowable values (MARITAL_STATUS must be one of S, M, D, or W) or rules to be checked (employee birth year must not exceed the current year minus 15).
2. *Conditional data value integrity*—specifies the domain as a function of the value of some other data element. Here again, it can be expressed as a list of allowable values (for shoes in U.S. sizing, if SIZE > 11 then WIDTH must be B, C, or D) or as rules (if MONTH is 1, 3, 5, 7, 8, 10, or 12, DAY must be a positive integer less than or equal to 31).
3. *Data structure integrity*—specifies relationships that must hold among data elements in the database. The most common case of data structure integrity is *referential integrity,* where something in one record must match something in another record. The CUSTOMER_NUMBER field of an invoice record may be required to match the CUSTOMER_NUMBER field of a customer record, and the customer record may not be deleted if any matching invoice records remain. Other types of data structure integrity may state that a match must *not* exist: one person may not be both a student in, and an applicant for admission to, the same academic program.

   Data structure integrity may be conditional. In a student database, a person whose status is ENROLLED, ON_LEAVE, or GRADUATED may need to have a transcript record, but one whose status is APPLICANT may not need one.

   Maintaining data structure integrity often requires taking actions that affect a database in a specific order. It may be convenient to enter order data before entering data about a new customer, but (unless provisions are made to defer the check until the operator has finished entering the entire order, including customer data) doing so would fail the referential integrity test.

Data-validation checks can never completely eliminate the possibility of errors. Knowing that a data element is from the allowable domain is helpful but does not assure us that it is the right element of that domain. (September 20, 1946, is a valid birthday, but happens not to be this author's.) Additional checks, up to and including double entry of the data by different people, may be required. Automating as much as possible of the data-entry process will reduce human error, though other error sources (such as smudged bar codes) can still cause errors to creep in.

Out-of-date data are often incorrect. Addresses in databases are often not updated until some event, such as an invoice being returned as undeliverable, forces them to be. In the meantime, analyses by postal zone can provide bad information. How much difference does this make? That depends on the decision, on its sensitivity to the geographic distribution of customers (or whatever), and on how much of the database is incorrect.

Incorrect formulas can create errors even when the input data are correct. In the late 1980s, a construction firm used the Lotus 1-2-3 spreadsheet program to calculate bid prices. As a result of bad output, it lost a bid that, it stated, it would otherwise have won. The firm then sued Lotus Development Corporation, claiming that an error in their software had caused the bad output. The case was dropped when it was found that a construction company employee had used an incorrect range in a spreadsheet formula, but only after a great deal of time, expense, aggravation, and negative publicity on both sides.

The faith many people put in computer output raises the possibility of the deliberate use of incorrect data to achieve one's ends through unethical means. This is especially apt to happen when individual workers have control over their own information-processing resources. (It is less likely, though never impossible, when reports or screen displays are produced centrally by a staff of information system professionals with no vested interest in their content.) Although the vast majority of people in any organization are ethical and would not "fudge" data, managers must always be alert to this possibility. When important business decisions are based on computer output produced by one individual, especially when he or she has a stake in the outcome, that output should be audited carefully for correctness. If this is always done as a standard policy, honest employees will not regard it as a suspicion of wrongdoing but as a policy of protecting them from possible wrongdoing by others.

Accuracy   The **accuracy** of a data element is a measure of how close it is to its real world value. This measure of information quality applies to items that have some error tolerance. These include most numerical quantities, unless they are used as identifiers such as a student ID number. It also includes many text strings that are long enough for people to derive meaning despite errors, and many pictures. Figure 3–13 shows the accuracy of a data element as its distance from the actual location of the point we want to identify. Note that accuracy is meaningful only if a data element is correct. If a data element is incorrect the concept of accuracy is not meaningful for it.

The term *accuracy* can also apply statistically to a group of data elements or to an individual sample from that group. For instance, we might say that a particular data element—about which we know nothing beyond the statistics of the group to which it belongs—has a 90 percent chance of being within $100 of its actual value.

High quality information is close enough to its true value for the use or uses to which it will be put.

The accuracy information quality factor allows for some errors in the underlying data. Note the following:

- It is often not practical or necessary to track down all the minor elements that contribute to a summary data value. Figures on business plans can usually be rounded to three or four significant figures. Planners don't try to predict how many pencils a project team will use per month. They make a reasonable estimate for the overall category of office supplies and let it go at that, or just assume that the corporate overhead rate will cover these items.
- Knowing the outdoor temperature to within 5 degrees Fahrenheit (3 degrees Centigrade) or so is sufficient to guide our choice of clothing.
- Most automobile odometers are accurate to about 2 percent. That's close enough to remind us to change the oil when we ought to.

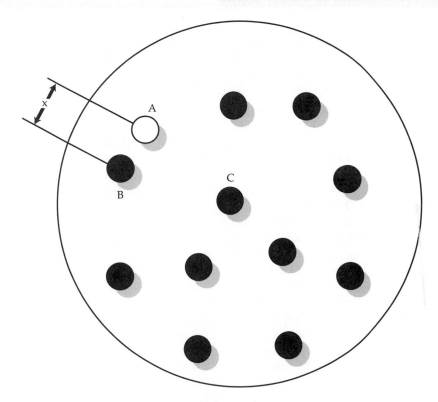

x: The accuracy of point A, given that it is correct

FIGURE 3–13   Circle Diagram Showing Accuracy (Sense 1)

It is possible to prepare a business plan or budget to the penny, to measure temperature to a fraction of a degree, and to calibrate an odometer to within 1 percent (taxis must do this), but these are not necessary for the stated purposes. This accuracy would cost money. Most people, faced with these trade-offs between accuracy and cost, make the above choices.

When assessing the accuracy of information, keep the following two principles in mind:

First, *the accuracy of a numeric information item is a function of the accuracy of the data elements that made the most important contributions to it.* Suppose we are considering investing corporate funds in several R&D projects. The internal rate of return[5] (IRR) of one of them has been forecasted as 21.623 percent per year. However, this figure was almost certainly based on estimates of such items as future sales and inflation rates, which are not known to nearly five significant digits. If key inputs to a calculation are not this accurate, its output can't be.

---

[5]You have probably studied, or will study, the concept of internal rate of return (IRR) in a finance course. For now, it's a measure of project profitability. Higher numbers are better.

If computations leading to a result are complex, it may not be easy to see the effect of inaccurate input on the output. In that case, we can carry out a *sensitivity test*. To do this, we vary the input to a computation over its range to see what happens to the output. If the project's IRR turns out to vary over about 0.1 percent for any reasonable rate of inflation, we can conclude that the IRR figure is accurate to one decimal digit as regards that particular source of error.

Second, *the difference between two data elements may be more accurate than either one is by itself.* This happens when both are calculated in the same way from the same assumptions. We do this informally when we look at a photograph and say "Jim is about an inch (about 2.5 cm) taller than John." We'll probably be within a quarter of an inch (or about 5 mm) of their height difference, though we can only estimate their absolute heights to the nearest 4 inches (10 cm) or so.

In the R&D project selection situation, suppose the internal rates of return of two projects have been forecast as 21.623 percent and 22.487 percent per year. We may disagree with the estimates of inflation or other factors that went into these calculations and recalculate the IRRs based on our own assumptions. If we did so, we would probably get almost the same difference between the two IRR figures even though the figures themselves could be quite different from the original two. This will be so when the impact of different assumptions affects both projects the same way. The question you must ask is: What is the real information here? In this case, it may not be the IRRs themselves but their difference.

Sensitivity testing can be valuable here as well. We would vary the inputs a reasonable range to see what happens to the difference between two IRR figures. If the second project turns out to be about 0.85 percent better than the first for any reasonable rate of inflation, we can conclude that inflation rate does not affect the choice of one project over the other.

Nonnumeric data can also be inaccurate though correct. Spelling my name "Efram Mallack" is an example of correct, but inaccurate, data.

Impact of Computers on Information Accuracy   Input data may be inaccurate. This is true whether or not its processing will involve computers. Computers can introduce additional inaccuracy in several ways.

First, most computers store numbers with a finite quantity of digits.[6] This quantity may be determined by the hardware, by the programming language (with most hardware), or by the programmer (with most languages). In either case, input digits beyond this limit are discarded. When a computer must discard high-order digits (for example, attempting to store a $1 million annual salary in a storage area which allows only six digits), it usually provides some internal notification of this. Whether or not this notification reaches the user, and what (if anything) the user is

---

[6]You may have read about the Y2K problem, which resulted from the fact that some older computer programs and databases were originally designed to store only the last two digits of the year. This made it impossible to distinguish the 21st century from the 20th.

then able to do about it, depends on the programmer. When a computer is forced to discard low-order digits (storing 1.3912 as 1.39, because there is room for only two digits to the right of the decimal point), there is usually no notification. The digits are lost.

Second, round-off errors in processing can create inaccurate results from accurate input. Dividing the integer 2 by the integer 3, and representing the result by a finite number of decimal digits as in 0.666, creates inaccuracy. Whereas most computers do not use the decimal system internally, the same principle applies. In a lengthy calculation these errors accumulate and can become significant. There are ways to estimate and minimize round-off errors, but programmers don't always take the trouble to learn and use them.

Finally, there is a remote possibility of a computer design flaw leading to wrong answers. In mid-1994, a user of Intel's then-new Pentium processor discovered that, for certain inputs, a division quotient that was supposed to have 15 accurate significant digits was off in the sixth. While this flaw received far more publicity than its importance to most users justified—in part due to inept handling of the problem by Intel—it did point out that computers are not perfect.

Computers can introduce inaccuracy to nonnumeric data as well. Pictures require very large amounts of storage. Programs that work with pictures often use compression techniques that sacrifice small details to save storage space. The resulting images are not fully faithful to the originals but suffice for their intended uses. If a picture is intended for posting on a Web site, this inaccuracy would be acceptable since its effect on the intended use of the picture is small. Introducing it allows the system to improve other, more important, information quality factors. If the picture were being used for scientific analysis of the Martian surface, the same loss of quality would be unacceptable.

Precision The **precision** of a data element is the maximum accuracy that can be represented by the way a data element is stored in a computer or presented to its users.

We can visualize precision as a grid overlaid on the world, either internally to an information storage system (computer, pad of paper, calculator, or abacus) or externally when data are presented to their users. Figure 3–14 shows precision in this sense. Excess precision raises two problems. It may not reflect the underlying data properly, and it may make the data hard to use.

The precision with which one presents data sends a message about its accuracy. Precision exceeding accuracy is useless and can be misleading. If we are told that one advertising plan has a projected brand awareness increase of 36.717 percent and a second of only 35.941 percent, we may be tempted to choose the first. If we know that both figures are at best accurate to within 4 percent or so, we will consider the plans equivalent on this score. Presenting these figures as 37 percent and 36 percent would have been less misleading. Presenting them as 33–41 percent and 32–40 percent, or as 37±4 percent and 36±4 percent, would have made the situation crystal clear.

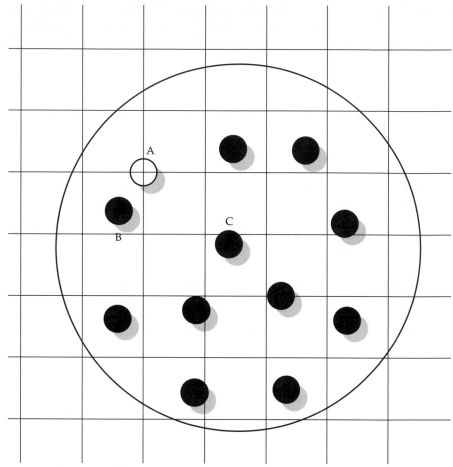

Precision: only points at the intersections of the grid lines can
be represented precisely by the computer. All other points must
be approximated, more or less accurately.

FIGURE 3–14 **Circle Diagram Showing Precision**

Since computers make it easy to calculate with high precision, it is tempting to print results with a large number of digits. (This tendency is occasionally referred to as the disease of "spreadsheetitis.") Printouts with six digits after the decimal point look impressive. Before choosing an output format, however, one should always examine the accuracy of the input data. Never give more precision than the accuracy of a result justifies. The use of excessive significant digits, to create the appearance of accuracy that isn't there, can be unethical if it is done to obtain an advantage that the real information does not justify.

This issue, excessive precision, tends not to arise in school. If you are given a figure of $103,229 in accounting homework, you know it's precisely $103,229—

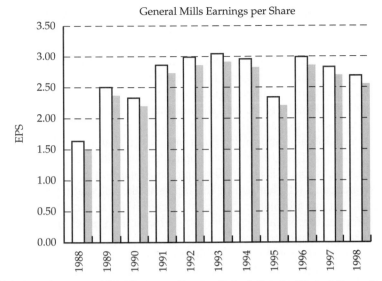

FIGURE 3–15 **Corporate EPS Shown as Precise Calculation, to Nearest Penny in Annual Report, and on Graph**
(*Source:* 1998 Annual Report of General Mills, Inc.)
Calculation: EPS = Profits ÷ average number of outstanding shares
$421.8 million ÷ 158 million = $2.66962 per share
Reported data: $2.67 per share

not one penny more, not one penny less. You don't have to worry about where that figure came from or possible inaccuracies in the data that led up to it. If you round it to $103,230, let alone $103,000, you get the wrong answer and a poor grade. Real business situations are seldom, if ever, that precise.

It may be appropriate to provide *less* precision than the accuracy of the available data could justify. Consider these instances.

1. Corporate earnings per share (EPS) are usually stated to the nearest cent, even when the input data can provide correct tenths or hundredths of a cent (see Figure 3–15). Cents are precise enough to evaluate profitability trends and to compare different firms' stock, and they are easier to deal with.
2. Graphs are often the best way to convey relationships among data, yet graphs are seldom highly precise. Where high precision must be combined with the convenience of graphs, the graphs can be backed up by tables to provide more precision than the graph offers. The graph in Figure 3–15 conveys the history of General Mills's earnings per share over a decade far more quickly than a table ever could, with precision sufficient for most purposes.
3. Color coding generally requires classifying data into a few ranges such as green for OK, yellow for marginal, and red for problem. Like graphs, color displays can be backed up by numeric data—or color can be used to highlight specific numbers, which the user can then choose to read.

Impact of Computers on Information Precision Whereas computers tend to reduce accuracy, they tend to increase apparent precision by providing more output digits than accuracy justifies. For instance, suppose we read that the area of the United States is 3.618770 million square miles, presumably accurate to at least four or five significant digits, and know its population is about 300 million. A computer can divide one of these figures by the other and tell us that its population density is 82.90109623 people per square mile. However, our population figure was a rough guess. This guess is accurate to one significant digit (the U.S. population is between 250 and 350 million) but not two (it is not, in 1999, between 295 and 305 million). All we really know about the population density of the United States, therefore, is that it is about 80 people per square mile.

A computer can't tell that one of the inputs to the calculation was a rough approximation, but an information-literate user can. It's that person's ethical responsibility to format the output appropriately before others infer from the precision that it is correspondingly accurate.

Don't provide more significant digits than the accuracy of your data justify. Printing the U.S. population density as 82.9011 people per square mile implies accuracy of at least five, probably six, significant digits. If a number with six-digit accuracy happens to be exactly 80, printing it as 80.0000 will carry the correct message. What about a number like 20,000? Does it have one significant digit of accuracy, five, or somewhere in between? In technical fields, where people pay attention to accuracy and precision issues, its accuracy could be conveyed by writing the number as 2×10^4 if it has one significant digit of accuracy, as 2.000×10^4 if it has four, and so on. In business, where readers are unlikely to be familiar with scientific notation, it's hard to convey the accuracy message when a number happens to end with several zeros. If the number appears with other numbers, readers can infer its accuracy from the others, as in Figure 3–16.

An information system developer may have a choice between numerical representations with different levels of precision. Some of these can be expressed as a certain number of decimal places, such as representing financial quantities to the penny (in the United States), whether the figures represent the cost of a pencil or the annual revenue of IBM. Others can be expressed as a certain number of significant digits with a scale factor, the computer storage equivalent of scientific notation. It is often helpful to carry more significance internally than the final result of a computation warrants.

Completeness High quality information must be complete. **Completeness** means that it includes all the necessary elements for the decision that is to be

FIGURE 3–16 Three Columns of Numbers with Different Accuracies

One Significant Digit	Three Significant Digits	Five Significant Digits
20000	20000	20000
30000	36100	36122
+40000	+42700	+42749
90000	98800	98871

made, and that each element is based on all relevant factors. The value of the *Official Airline Guide* would decrease if it listed only some scheduled airlines. If it omitted one or two minor regional carriers, some travelers might still find it useful. However, if it left out American and United, it would be useless to nearly every potential reader.

Sometimes incompleteness is obvious. Omitting a company's biggest product line from next year's sales forecast will be spotted instantly. But omitting a new product would be less obvious, as readers may not know when it is to be introduced. Likewise, an experienced traveler would notice if American Airlines were left out of the *OAG* but might not notice if Sam's Air Shuttle and Pizza Delivery were missing.

Incompleteness can also mean that an item of information is not based on all the data elements that should contribute to it. If an annual sales figure does not reflect returned products, it is incomplete and therefore of lower quality than it might be. Is this important? That depends on its purpose. As with any other good or service, the need for highest quality (here, most complete) information varies. It may be a good business decision to trade off one information quality factor for other advantages. Less completeness can often be traded for better timeliness or lower cost. Only a person who is familiar with the intended use of the information can make these trade-offs properly.

Impact of Computers on Information Completeness   Computers don't, by themselves, make information less than complete. What they do is *mask* possible incompleteness from those who use the information.

Computers are perfectly willing to add up all the branch sales figures of a firm, without realizing that a zero for Chicago sales means that Chicago hasn't reported sales yet. To the computer, zero is just another number. Any junior clerk would see the omission and write "Missing Chicago!" by the total, but computers aren't that insightful. They can be programmed to check for this sort of thing, but often aren't. Numbers that come out of computers tend to be taken at face value. People don't ask the same questions that they would ask of a person supplying the same number.

Timeliness   The **timeliness** of an information element refers to relationships among three items:

1. The time that information is needed.
2. The time that information is made available.
3. The time that its underlying data was obtained.

Information timeliness has two characteristics.

First, *information must be available in time for its intended use.* This reflects the relationship between the time information is needed and the time it is made available. A 48-hour weather forecast that takes 49 hours to produce merely confirms what happened outside an hour ago. Information value often deteriorates with time. Many business decisions are worth more if made earlier.

Second, *information must reflect up-to-date data.* This reflects the relationship between the time information is made available and the times its underlying data was obtained. A chart of stock prices that ends a month ago will be of little use to investors who trade on small price changes, though it may help one who invests for the long term. A teller machine that authorizes withdrawals on the basis of week-old account balances is useless. Inventory, price, and production schedule data must be current for most of their uses.

Impact of Computers on Information Timeliness   Computers and telecommunication networks generally have a positive effect on the timely availability of data. However, they also increase people's expectations regarding this timeliness.

This can be a problem because fast computer networks don't always mean instant information. All they can do instantly is communicate information that is already in a computer to which they are connected. A network can be pointless without corresponding data gathering, storage, and processing capabilities.

As an example, several companies give customers and distributors instant access to product data that they previously obtained on paper. Some had good results. Others had disappointing reactions. That is because only a small part of the time it takes to get a document into readers' hands is printing and distribution time. The rest goes to writing, editing, reviewing, and approving it. Instant access to the result cannot shorten those tasks. When people receive documents by mail, they at least subconsciously understand that the documents are a few days or weeks old when received. But when people receive documents from a computer, they don't make the same allowances, even though most of the document preparation process hasn't changed. Unless the overall process time can be shortened, readers—who tend to think of computer networks as providing "instant information"—may be disappointed.

The issue, then, is not that computer networks harm the timeliness of information in an absolute sense. It is that they can increase people's expectations of timeliness more than they improve the timeliness itself. To develop effective information systems—and not just merely efficient computers and networks—we must view the entire information-processing cycle, from gathering the source data to delivery of the final output, at the overall system level, and to manage user expectations within that overall context.

Usability   The **usability** of information is how quickly and easily its intended users can figure out what they need to know from what they see. Information presented so that they can complete tasks without extra effort is usable. Information that forces them to extra effort to interpret it is not equally usable.

High quality information is presented in a usable format. Format includes good table design, which involves presenting related items so that relationships are immediately apparent. It includes appropriate use of color and graphs, and choosing appropriate graphs for each purpose. Format also includes choice of fonts, letter sizes, italics, boldface, shading, borders, and so forth, though these can be overdone to a point where visual clutter detracts from usability.

The best format for presenting information depends on the people who will use the information and how they will use it. It is often helpful to present information in more than one way, or to give its users a choice of formats. When employees can load corporate data into a spreadsheet program, they can organize and format it to their own needs.

International organizations must consider language differences. Information presented in a language that its reader does not understand is not highly usable. If it is simply necessary to label columns on a report or areas on a graph, it is usually possible to provide multiple versions in all necessary languages. In other situations, matters are more complex. For example,

- Consider a customer list in alphabetical order. "Llama" traditionally followed "Lugarno" in Spanish, since Ll was considered a separate letter between L and M until 1994. "Haakon" comes after "Huldre" in Norwegian because aa is considered a single letter (actually, an alternative way of writing å) that comes after Z at the end of the alphabet. A system designer who follows the sorting practices of one language may lead users in other countries to think that some data elements are missing.
- Many programs provide on-screen *menus:* lists of actions the computer can perform. Users can often choose a menu item by typing its first letter or an underlined letter. It may be difficult to find translations that start with, or include, the letters that are used in English. (It may even be impossible. There's no Y in Italian.)[7] Changing a program to respond to different letters can be more difficult than merely translating some text.

Impact of Computers on Information Usability Computers can improve information usability. For example, they can create graphs in a fraction of a second. A production supervisor can try many types of quality control graphs and choose the best. To experiment with hand-drawn graphs, where each takes several minutes to create, would not be practical. Computers can reorganize information in an instant to the best order for each of several different uses, provide boldface or italics to highlight information, check spelling, and more. Properly used, computer-processed information can be much more usable than a manually produced version.

Again, the danger here is in going overboard and creating visual clutter. Too much fussing with typefaces and formats, while it can be fun, detracts from the usability of the information presented. Unless you are a professional graphic designer, let simplicity and clarity be your guide.

Computers can also detract from usability, as we saw in the discussion of precision. Many people have set aside digital watches in favor of the old-fashioned clockface type because hands make it easier to check time at a glance or see How long until 3 o'clock? Digital watches, however, are better for timing laps on a track. The designer of a computer application must understand users' needs and provide information in the format, or formats, that best meet those needs.

---

[7]This refers to native words in that language. The letter *Y* is present on keyboards used in Italy, and some words borrowed from foreign languages use it.

Accessibility   Information of high quality is **accessible.** This means that authorized people can obtain it quickly, with an acceptable level of effort, from the places in which they are expected to be when they need it.

The accessibility of computer-based information requires an investment in equipment and networks. If these are underpowered, data will arrive at users' screens slowly, and accessibility, as they perceive it, will be poor. Accessibility requires authorization tools that do not create an undue barrier while providing sufficient security. And it may require programs that translate among the internal data storage formats of different computer systems.

Impact of Computers on Information Accessibility   In principle, computers should improve the accessibility of information. With networks linking desktops to shared databases, the contents of those databases ought to be available where needed, when needed. Whereas this principle is technologically correct, it ignores the human factor. Computers are not necessarily user friendly. The need to navigate through networks, remember passwords and authorization codes, and enter confusing commands is a powerful deterrent to computer use. People who are in a position to do so will often just ask an assistant to "please get this." Others may do without the information they can use, or waste time in retrieving it.

Much can be done in system design to minimize or eliminate this issue. Modern user interfaces make information more accessible than it was a decade ago. The interface of any new computer system must reflect the needs of the people from various fields who will use it—not those who will develop it, who may be computer experts.

Consistency   **Consistency** means that all data elements that contribute to an information item, or to a set of related items, are based on the same assumptions, definitions, time period, and other factors. Consistency is an attribute of information, or processed data, that does not apply to individual data elements.

Suppose a sales manager wishes to calculate the productivity of a firm's sales force to compare it with industry averages. The manager might ask the computer to divide last year's sales by the size of the firm's sales force and display the result—only to be severely disappointed. The manager thought the firm hired good salespeople and trained them well, and that they were at least as productive as the average firm's, but the computer says they're far worse. What's going on here?

Perhaps the inputs were inconsistent, as shown in Figure 3–17. When asked for the size of the sales force, the typical information retrieval program would give its size as of the moment of the request. If a firm is growing, its sales force is bigger at the time of the request than its average for the previous year. To get a meaningful result, the sales manager must ask for the average size of the sales force over a period corresponding to the sales data.

Information consistency is usually a more important consideration in decision support applications (in the above example, the sales manager was presumably preparing for some sort of decision with respect to sales personnel) than in transaction processing. In transaction processing, one typically deals with one record,

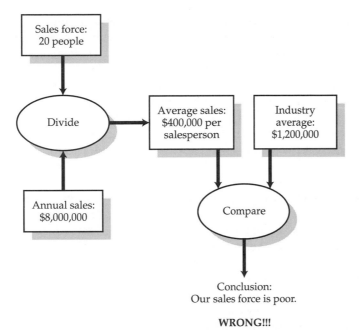

FIGURE 3–17 Informal Flow Diagram of Using Inconsistent Data

or at most a small number of records, relating to one business entity: the number of seats left on Flight 355, the bank accounts belonging to Jane Q. Jones. Decision makers, by contrast, must often bring together many data elements from a variety of sources or consolidate thousands of records from a database.

Information collected at different times is often inconsistent because business definitions change. This can be a problem in analyzing trends, computing growth rates, or identifying problems. For instance, suppose sales records show a substantial drop in dollar volume for the Southeast U.S. region in the first quarter of this year. This might have happened because the state of Virginia was moved into the Mid-Atlantic region before the year started, perhaps to equalize sales potential among regions. A computer wouldn't know this. It would report the drop as a fact without providing any interpretation. If the person viewing the data didn't know of (or didn't happen to remember) the change, he or she might become concerned for no reason or take ill-advised action.

Information consistency issues can be serious in an international context. The same term can mean different things in different countries. Some differences are due to cultural misunderstandings. Some are due to differences in business practices, legislation, or quasi-legislative regulations such as accounting practices. The definition of a depreciable asset, for example, may differ from one country to another, as can the time at which a sale is recognized for revenue purposes. The sum of financial figures from different countries, if not adjusted for these differences, will not be meaningful in terms of any one country's practice. If the differences are small, this becomes an accuracy issue. Some loss of accuracy may be acceptable for the purpose for which the figures are used, such as overall strategic planning. If they are large, the figures may be useless or misleading.

Impact of Computers on Information Consistency   Computers can hurt or help the consistency of information depending on how they are used.

The first part of this section gave an example of how computers can hurt information consistency. However, if information-literate people develop a system, they will be aware of the need for consistency and will apply checks as necessary. Ensuring information consistency is thus an issue for any information system designer or developer.

The catch is that any manager or professional may design and develop a personal DSS to support his or her own decisions. The sales manager in a preceding example didn't go to a programmer to compare sales force productivity with the industry average. The manager was sufficiently *computer*-literate to put the question directly to the computer but not sufficiently *information*-literate to understand the pitfalls. Technical professionals cannot prevent people from misusing computers and the information in them, in this and similar ways.

Conformity to Expectations   Information must conform to the expectations of the person who will use it. **Conformity to expectations** is how well the information's processing, timeliness, and so on match what this person expects. If several people will use the information, their expectations must be consistent with each other. That can also be a problem, but it's an organizational problem, not an information quality problem. (One way of dealing with that problem is to provide the information to different people in different ways.)

Consider a request to provide last year's dollar volume. This request is open to multiple interpretations, such as the following:

- Is "last year" the most recently ended calendar year, the most recent calendar year for which we have complete data, the most recent fiscal year (which may not follow the calendar), the most recent four quarters, 12 months, or something else?
- Does the term *dollar volume* refer to what customers ordered, what we shipped to them, what they accepted, or what they paid for?
- What should we do about items shipped during the year but returned after it? Shipped before the year, returned during it? Ordered during the year, canceled after it? Ordered before the year, canceled during it?
- Should we include the value of all the multiple-year agreements (such as subscriptions) sold during the year, that of the fraction of their term within the year, or something else?

Each of these questions may have one right answer for tax accounting, another for managerial accounting, a third for commission payments, and a fourth for customer-preference trend analysis. Each of these may be important for decision making at different times. What is important is that *the information system must provide an answer that matches the needs and expectations of the person who will use it.*

Computers have made this problem worse. Prior to their use, an assistant would have answered requests such as "get me last year's dollar volume." This person would have asked the requester many of the questions we raised above. Other questions would have come up during the process of getting the data, since getting data involves talking to other people who would have asked their own questions. Computers, however, may produce whatever a programmer thought last year's dollar volume ought to mean. To make matters worse, by the time managers realize there might be misunderstandings, that programmer will have probably left the company.

International issues arise here much as they did with the consistency factor. All users will expect computer output to conform to their country's concepts. In a multinational organization it may be impossible to satisfy everyone in this respect. If it is impossible to meet everyone's expectations for this reason, it may be necessary to modify their expectations through training, meetings, or explanations built into the computer output.

Expectations do not relate only to the content or composition of an information item. Users also have expectations with regard to accuracy, timeliness, and other information quality factors. For example, a company might require a monthly report from each sales office by the third business day of the next month. People might get upset if it is late even if they don't really need it that quickly.

Impact of Computers on Information Conformity to Expectations   Computers have no direct effect on the conformity of information to users' expectations. They do, however, have an indirect negative effect.

This effect occurs because the development and use of large computer-based information systems calls for people with skills that are not required for manual information systems: programmers, software designers, computer operators, and more. A computer presents the result of their work. This can affect its conformity to expectations in two ways, neither good:

- Whenever more people are involved in anything there are opportunities for misunderstandings. The specifications of a complex computer system are filled with tiny details. An error or misunderstanding about any of them can impact the result.
- People who go into programming may differ from those who gravitate toward business positions. (Studies have shown, for example, that the most common personality types in information systems departments and in marketing departments are quite different.) When a precomputer executive asked a staff assistant to collect data, chances are the assistant's educational background and business perspective resembled the executive's, allowing for age and experience. Those of a programmer working on the same request may be quite different. Many programmers do not have the intuitive grasp of business concepts that businesspeople get in college or early in their careers.

There are several ways to deal with this. Awareness of potential problems can go a long way toward avoiding them. Training programmers in business can help. So can the trend toward hybrid business-technical jobs. Finally, for simple (especially individual, sometimes work group) DSS, end-user computing guarantees that the output will conform to the user's expectations, because in end-user computing, the user determines what the system will do.

Cost The **cost** of anything is a measure of the resources, translated into financial terms, that an organization must expend to obtain it. This definition applies to information as well.

Ideally, information should be free or nearly so. The ideal is hardly ever realized. Even when an organization doesn't have to pay for its raw data, costs are associated with collecting it, storing it, processing it, and sending results to their destinations. These costs can and should be minimized.

The cost of obtaining information is important because we must often justify an information system by analyzing its cost and benefits. Costs are comparatively easy to calculate when a new system is being developed from the ground up. Often, however, firms add new capabilities to existing systems. In these cases, it is necessary to compare the costs and benefits of the newly added capabilities.

When a computer is purchased or a network is installed for several purposes, how much of its cost should be allotted to any one of them? In some cases a percentage allocation is appropriate. In others, only the incremental cost—the cost incurred for this one purpose, that would not be incurred in its absence—is the appropriate figure to use. This is a problem in managerial accounting, not in DSS development, but you should be aware of it in this context.

There is often a trade-off between cost and other factors. Timely availability of input data can often be improved by automated data entry or telecommunication networks. Attractive information presentation may require new printers. Increased accuracy may require a new computer to perform the now-lengthier calculations in acceptable time. Accessibility may involve network upgrades to improve response times. Are these investments worthwhile? That question can only be answered by considering the costs and benefits involved. Increasingly, such investments are deemed desirable. The need for up-to-date, accurate information is increasing as the pace of competition quickens. The costs of obtaining it are dropping year by year.

Impact of Computers on Information Cost Computers, as noted earlier, are not free. Costs are associated with purchasing them, servicing them, and providing them with space, electricity, and supplies. Other costs are associated with purchasing or developing programs to tell the computers what to do. More costs are associated with installing and operating the networks that link computers, and thus organizational units or entire organizations. Finally, there are the salaries of those whose job it is to tend these computers and these networks and help people use them.

These costs are visible. They are easy to identify and, in most cases, to quantify. Yet these are often not the most significant costs associated with obtaining and using computer-based information. They pale in comparison to the cost of the time of those who use the information: the production coordinators, travel agents, marketing managers, financial analysts, and salespeople whose job involves making decisions with information.

People made these decisions before computers. They used essentially the same information. Obtaining that information through computers can save their time or waste it. It can make them more productive or less. Which will it be? The answer depends on information quality. High quality information will save their time and make them more productive. Low quality information will waste their time and lower their productivity.

Another cost factor associated with using computers is this: Computers encourage the tendency of some people to fiddle with their data far beyond the point of diminishing returns. Computers make it so easy to try one more budget option, to rearrange the wording of a sentence, that people get carried away with these activities when they should be concentrating on the content of what they do. It is important to recognize when the value of this fine-tuning justifies the effort—and when it has become junk computing that must be controlled.

3.6 MODELS

Now that we understand what a system is we are in a position to deal with the concept of a **model:** a replica of a real system or object. This definition applies to all types of models: model trains, design models used by automobile stylists, and model legislation that is intended to be adopted with local variations by several states. People use models to capture important aspects of the real item, while simplifying their work by eliminating other aspects that are irrelevant to a particular situation or make the model more elaborate than necessary for its purpose. For instance,

- A model railroad lets hobbyists capture the appearance, much of the atmosphere, and the operating challenge of a real railroad. However, it does not require an area the size of a small state, several dozen permits from assorted regulatory bodies, and a budget measured in tens of millions of dollars.
- A styling model (traditionally made of clay, today on computer screens in all but the final stages) lets people see how an automobile design will look. It does not require investing in tooling for shaped metal parts, or assembling mechanical and interior components that do not affect the external appearance of the finished car.
- Model legislation lets experts debate the merits of an issue without becoming embroiled in the political issues and bargaining that arise in any real legislature, and without having to answer to constituents or special-interest groups for having cast an unpopular vote.

Models often have advantages over the real thing for their specific purposes. A model railroad lets its designer determine landscape features that the planner of a real railroad, constrained by nature, cannot alter. If a deep gorge provides dramatic scenery or an opportunity to use an intricate model of a wooden trestle, in it goes. A clay or CAD mockup can be changed more easily—to round a fender, to lower a headlamp—than a production vehicle. Their deficiencies (neither a model railroad nor an automobile styling mock-up can haul passengers or cargo) are not significant for their users' purposes. Eliminating that requirement allows us to develop models more quickly and easily than the actual item could be developed.

In decision support systems, we use models to predict the outcome of decision choices we might make. Models have several advantages over the real thing for this purpose.

One advantage of models is ease of *access* and *manipulation.* It is often impractical to test business alternatives in practice. A firm choosing among six factory equipment layouts could not set up six factories, one with each layout, to compare their operating costs. Yet that firm may be able to develop computer models of the six layouts, using methods we'll discuss in Chapter 8, and choose the best.

In some cases it is literally impossible to compare all the alternatives, even without cost constraints, since trying one alternative changes the conditions. For example, the U.S. Federal Reserve Board cannot set the rate of interest it charges to member banks, watch the national economy for six months to see the results, and then pick a different rate retroactively if it doesn't like the effects of its first choice. With a computer model, the Federal Reserve Board can try several possibilities. It can reset the starting conditions of its model to today's economic situation before each experiment and predict what the impact of each possible interest rate is likely to be. Although the result of this process is seldom perfect, it's better than guessing.

As a second advantage, it is often easier to *collect data* from a computer model than from the actual system. To understand the production bottlenecks in a real factory we would have to station an observer at each work station, to note and record where work in process builds up and where equipment or people are idle. A computer can collect this data easily as a by-product of running a model.

Third, a model can *compress time* and yield results more quickly than the real world can. Decision makers can see the expected results of a year of production, or several years of economic policy, in minutes. This contributes to the practicality of evaluating several decision options via computer models.

There are many different types of models. Because of the importance of models in DSS, Chapter 8 is devoted to discussing those types and investigating a few commonly used ones in more detail.

SUMMARY

A decision support system is a system. More specifically, it is an information system.

A system is a group of interacting components with a purpose. In addition to its components and its purpose, every system has a boundary that separates the components of the system from the world outside the system. A system may incorporate feedback. Feedback can occur within the system or outside it.

An information system is a system whose purpose is storing, communicating, and processing information. Most large information systems in business today incorporate computers, but many important information systems do not. It is important to consider noncomputerized information-processing methods as solutions to business problems.

Data flow diagrams are a convenient and widely accepted way to record and communicate (1) the processes and data stores that comprise a system and (2) the information flows among them and between them and the outside world. Data flow diagrams do not, however, show the timing relationships among system activities, the conditions under which certain activities occur, or the reasons why they occur. For this reason they must be augmented by other system description methods.

Decision support systems, as information systems, use data stores that are created and updated by other systems. They communicate their results, not to other information systems, but to human decision makers.

Information is whatever reduces our uncertainty about something we didn't know or were unsure of. The more the information reduces our uncertainty, the more information we have. Information is derived from data by comparing two data elements, by performing computations on several data elements, or by a combination of these.

Information is the basis for nearly every organizational decision. High quality information causes these decisions to be made correctly. Low quality information can cause them to be made incorrectly, harming the organization. The ability of information to contribute to the goals of the organization depends on the quality of that information, which can be described in terms of 11 factors:

Relevance—the degree to which it applies to the task being performed. Computers can provide so much information to their user that the relevance of the information is reduced.

Correctness—whether or not the information matches reality. Computers can produce correct information only if their inputs are correct and the processing of those inputs has been specified correctly.

Accuracy—a measure of the difference, if any, between an information item and the reality it represents. Computers can introduce inaccuracy through computational processes. Reduced accuracy may be acceptable if it permits improving information quality in other respects.

Precision—the potential accuracy conveyed by internal or external data representations. Computers allow high precision, but the underlying accuracy of the data does not always justify it.

Completeness—the inclusion of all relevant data in arriving at information. Whereas computers do not generally affect completeness directly, they may hide its absence.

Timeliness—includes two aspects: the availability of information in time for its intended use, and the currency of the information as of the time of that use. Computers can improve the timeliness of information, but the cost of their doing so must be weighed against the value.

Usability—the ease of using the information for its intended purpose. Computers can increase information usability by formatting it appropriately, but this can be overdone.

Accessibility—the degree to which information is available to users when and where needed. Computers generally improve accessibility, but poor performance, a poor user interface, or obtrusive security procedures may impair it.

Conformity to expectations—measures how closely the creation of an information item matches the expectations of the person or people who will use it. Ensuring that computer-derived information conforms to expectations raises concerns that do not arise with manually developed information.

Consistency—an information item based on data elements that refer to the same time frame, organizational entity, and assumptions. The impact of computers on consistency depends on the degree to which system designers took this factor into account.

Cost of information—refers to both the costs of the computers, networks, and more, that are used to obtain that information, and the cost of the time users spend working with that information. Cost can usually be traded off against other information quality factors.

A model is a simplified representation of a real system or object. Models are used in decision support systems because (1) they are easier to manipulate than the real systems whose behavior we want to study, (2) it is easier to extract data from them, and (3) they generate results more quickly. For a model to be useful we must be sure not to simplify the description of the real system so far that the usefulness of the model is lost.

KEY TERMS

accessibility (information quality factor)
accuracy (information quality factor)
boundary (of a system)
closed loop system
closed system
completeness (information quality factor)
conformity to expectations (information quality factor)
consistency (information quality factor)
correctness (information quality factor)
cost (information quality factor)
data flow diagram (DFD)
data store (in a DFD)
environment (of a system)
external entity (in a DFD, of a system)
external feedback
feedback
general systems theory
information system
internal feedback
model

open loop system
open system
precision (information quality factor)
process (in a DFD or system)
relevance (information quality factor)
sensitivity test
subsystem
system
timeliness (information quality factor)
usability (information quality factor)

REVIEW QUESTIONS

1. What is a system? What are the key characteristics of a system?
2. Give one example of a system with internal feedback, and one example of a system with external feedback, other than the ones in this chapter.
3. How does an information system differ from a system in general?
4. What does a data flow diagram show? What doesn't it show?
5. How does a decision support system differ from an information system in general?
6. Give an example of the difference between data and information.
7. What are the two fundamental operations involved in turning data into information?
8. List the 11 factors that define information quality.
9. State how computers affect each of the 11 factors that define information quality.
10. What is a model? Give two examples of noncomputer models, other than the ones in this chapter. For each, state one feature it shares with the real system that it models and one feature it does not share with the real system.
11. What are three reasons to use computer models to support decision making?

EXERCISES

1. Draw the boundary of the payroll system of Figure 3–5 on a photocopy or sketch of that figure.
2. Consider your DSS course as a system. What is its purpose? What are its inputs? Its outputs? Its major processes?
3. Describe your college or university registration system as a system. Specify its purpose, its components, and their interactions. (If you have recently transferred from another institution and are more familiar with its registration process, diagram its process with a note to your instructor explaining what you have done.)
4. Draw a data flow diagram for the registration system in exercise 3.
5. Consider a corporate photocopying center. Employees who need copies of documents come to the center with the original document. They fill out a form stating the number of copies required; requirements such as stapling, binding, three-hole punching, or colored paper; the requestor's name; and the project number to be charged for the job. The job is ready for pickup some time later: within two hours for short jobs (up to 20 original pages, up to 25 copies, no binding, unstapled or single staple in top-left corner, white paper without holes), during the next half day for medium-sized jobs (a less limiting definition), and within 24 hours, not counting weekends and holidays, for large jobs or those with unusual requirements. These are upper time limits that the center

commits to meet under any circumstances short of a natural disaster or extended power outage. Most jobs are ready much sooner.

   a. Describe the photocopying center as a system. What parts of the above description didn't you need for this purpose?

   b. Draw a data flow diagram of this system.

   c. A manager asks a secretary for copies of a report. The manager's secretary takes the originals to the photocopying center and, at a later time, returns to pick up the finished copies and bring them to the manager. Is the secretary part of the system? Why or why not?

6. Insurance companies hire people to evaluate claims and decide how much, if anything, the company should pay. The decision process includes determining if the claim is allowable under the policy, examining the terms of the policy to determine how much of the claim should be paid, and evaluating the amount of damage or some other measure of how much money the claimant might be due. Each of these parts can be quite complex. Low-skilled personnel can deal with simple situations that involve small amounts of money, such as reimbursement for standard prescription drugs under a medical insurance policy, in minutes. Complex situations involving larger amounts of money, such as a permanent disability claim for a 35 year old injured at work, may require months of investigation by skilled medical, rehabilitation, and legal professionals.

   a. Pick a specific insurance situation of your choice. Draw a data flow diagram for its claim processing.

   b. In part (*a*) you put the claimant either inside or outside the system. Justify your choice.

   c. Expand one of the processes in your DFD into a lower level DFD.

7. The value of information is a function of its quality. For each of the following decisions,

   • Give an example of low information quality in terms of the 11 information quality factors.

   • State how that low information quality could affect the decision.

   • State how you would avoid that type of low information quality.

   Example: incorrect information (the second quality factor) on the first decision could be an inaccurate statement of the applicant's college GPA. That could lead the firm to choose a less qualified applicant over another who did not overstate his or her GPA. This could be avoided by careful checking of the applicant's college transcript. (Some quality factors may have no impact on some of the decisions.)

   You will have to choose a specific information item to use with each information quality example. In the above example, the information item chosen was the applicant's GPA. You will therefore need 11 information items for each of the following parts (*a*), (*b*), and (*c*). You can use the same one 11 times, use 11 different items once each, or anywhere in between (such as four items, each used with two or three information quality factors).

   a. Choose an applicant for a financial analyst position from a pool of six new college graduates.

   b. Decide how to allocate a $250,000 advertising budget among specific media.

   c. Select a warehouse location to serve the western United States. Assume that all the firm's customers have been served from its headquarters location in Rhode Island, and that business in the West has grown enough to justify a second distribution center.

8. Consider the following alternative versions of the author's name as they might appear in the "To:" field of a business memo. In which information quality factors, if any, is each one deficient?

a. Efrem G. Mallach

b. Efrem Mallach

c. Ephraim Malik

d. Remy Mallach (a childhood nickname)

e. E. Mallach

f. Efrem Mall (truncated to fit the available space, which is too short)

g. John Henley

h. Efrem M.

9. You plan to deposit $1,000 in a bank for a term of five years and must choose between variable-rate certificates of deposit offered by two banks. The interest rate paid by each certificate is adjusted each year based on a published interest rate index. The one offered by Adams Bank pays the index rate for the following year. The one offered by Baytex Bank pays 1 percent less, but at the end of the period Baytex gives you $75 for having left your money on deposit for the entire period. Baytex claims that, using their forecasted index rate of 7 percent, you will do better with their certificate (which will, if that is the index value, pay 6 percent). You are certain that the index will be between 5 percent and 10 percent during this entire period. Using a spreadsheet program, set up a formula for the value of each certificate after five years and see if their claim is sensitive to interest rates within this range.

10. You are staying at the Hilton National Olympia hotel in London. You wish to travel to a meeting by Underground (known as the subway to North Americans). Your hotel is a 2-minute walk from the Kensington Olympia station and a 12-minute walk from the next closest station, High Street Kensington. However, the desk clerk has told you that service from Kensington Olympia is not as frequent at times that there is no exhibit in the adjacent exhibit halls. Consider the following factors:

• Trains from Kensington Olympia do not start running until 7:30 A.M. (vs. 6:00 A.M. from High Street Kensington) and stop at 8:45 P.M. (vs. midnight).

• Kensington Olympia is served only by a minor branch of the District Line. It is necessary to transfer at least once to get to any location of significant interest to most travelers, often twice. High Street Kensington is served by the Circle Line, which stops at many important points and has direct transfers to all other lines, and by a more useful subset of District Line trains as well.

• Kensington Olympia trains run every 16 to 17 minutes during most of the day. Specific departure times of Kensington Olympia trains are posted at the station and are available by telephone. Trains from High Street Kensington are over twice as frequent on each line in each direction. (Because the District and Circle lines share trackage for part of their routes, about 15 stations are served by both. This effectively doubles the frequency of trains to those stops from High Street Kensington.)

• The fare from Kensington Olympia to most of London is slightly higher than from High Street Kensington (£1.60 vs. £1.30, about $2.60 vs. $2.10, to anywhere in the central area).

You also know that you can take a bus from your hotel to High Street Kensington for £1, with frequent service and a trip time of about 5 minutes, or a taxi for about £3 and about 3 minutes travel time. (There are usually taxis waiting outside your hotel. The nearest bus stop is less than a minute away.) The time it would take to reach your destination by bus would be too long, and the taxi fare too high, to consider either of those for the entire trip.

You are considering a DSS to help decide which of these two stations to use.

a. Place this DSS in the appropriate square of Figure 2–3. State clearly any assumptions you made. If you think either of your two axis placements is not obvious, justify it.

b. List five information items that will have to be input into your DSS each time it is used. (For example: Is there currently an exhibit at the Olympia exhibit hall? List five *other* items, not including this example.)

c. For each of your five information items, give an information quality problem it could have. State what you could do to improve that item's quality. (You will have a total of five potential information quality problems and proposed solutions.)

d. Intuitively, do you think developing this DSS is a good idea? Why or why not?

REFERENCES

BRAC96   Brackett, Michael H. *The Data Warehouse Challenge: Taming Data Chaos.* Wiley, New York (1996).

DEVL97   Devlin, Barry. *Data Warehouse from Architecture to Implementation.* Addison Wesley Longman, Reading, Mass. (1997).

ENGL98   English, Larry. "The High Costs of Low Quality Data," *DM Review* 8, no. 1 (January 1998), p. 38.

FRIE95   Friedman, William H. "Enhancing Dataflow Diagrams," *Journal of Computer Information Systems* (Spring 1995).

GORD78   Gordon, Geoffrey. *System Simulation,* 2nd ed. Prentice-Hall, Englewood Cliffs, N.J. (1978).

MENN69   Menninger, Karl. *Number Words and Number Symbols: A Cultural History of Numbers,* English translation: MIT Press, Cambridge, Mass. (1969); German original: Vandenhoek & Ruprecht, Göttingen (1958).

RAPO86   Rapoport, Anatol. *General Systems Theory: Essential Concepts and Applications.* Abacus Press, Cambridge, Mass. (1986).

VONB68   von Bertalanffy, Ludwig. *General Systems Theory: Foundations, Development, Applications.* Braziller, New York (1968).

WILS90   Wilson, Brian. *Systems: Concepts, Methodologies, and Applications.* John Wiley & Sons, New York (1990).

Papers from the February 1998 Special Edition of *Communications of the ACM* on Data Quality

KAPL98   Kaplan, David, Ramayya Krishnan, Rema Padman, and James Peters. "Assessing Data Quality in Accounting Information Systems," *Communications of the ACM,* 41, no. 2 (February 1998), p. 72.

ORR98   Orr, Ken. "Data Quality and Systems Theory," *Communications of the ACM,* 41, no. 2 (February 1998), p. 66.

REDM98   Redman, Thomas C. "The Impact of Poor Data Quality on the Typical Enterprise," *Communications of the ACM,* 41, no. 2 (February 1998), p. 79.

TAYI98   Tayi, Giri Kuman, and Donald P. Ballou. "Examining Data Quality" (introduction to special section on that subject), *Communications of the ACM,* 41, no. 2 (February 1998), p. 54.

WANG98 Wang, Richard Y. "A Product Perspective on Total Data Quality Management," *Communications of the ACM,* 41, no. 2 (February 1998), p. 58.

CASE

Fort Lowell Trading Company: Niels Agger and the FLTC Web Site

Inasmuch as Niels didn't have any meetings scheduled for that afternoon, he was available to meet with Elizabeth and Miguel. Dottie walked them from the information systems office area over to business development, on the same floor but on the other side of the building.[8] She ushered them into his office. In contrast to her own neat workspace, this one was a model of clutter. Niels, a tall, thin man with shaggy hair and mustache, sat behind a desk covered with memos, brochures, and drafts of catalogue pages, with an open laptop computer off to one side displaying what appeared to be a Web page showing furniture.

"Believe it or not, he can actually find things in here," Dottie said to the two. "Niels, these are Miguel and Elizabeth from Sabino Canyon College. I'm glad you were able to free up some time for them this afternoon."

"Happy to, really," Niels replied. "Pleased to meet you. Come on in—if you can find room!"

"Thank you," said Miguel, as Dottie headed back to her office. After the two were seated, he continued with "Dottie said she picked me because she thinks some of the decisions in my area could use some computer help. Is that what she told you too?"

"We did hear her end of the conversation when she called you," Elizabeth answered. "Please remember that she didn't say we'd be able to help, though. We're college juniors taking a decision support course, not professionals with 10 years on the job!"

"OK, then. You haven't made any promises. Still, let's talk about some of the decisions we make here. Maybe two fresh minds will come up with something we haven't thought of before.

"What we're supposed to do here in Business Development is, in a nutshell, to develop the business. When I first came here, nearly 20 years ago, that meant opening our first store outside the Southwest. Then it was other things, and then it was catalogues. We're still working on those, there's a lot to do, but now it's the

---

[8]This episode continues where the Chapter 2 episode left off.

Web. We have a Web site and we get orders from it, but it's really just our catalogue on a screen instead of on paper."

"Are people ordering from your Web site?" asked Miguel.

"Quite a few are, and we can document that each Web order costs less to process than a telephone or mail order. Still, this raises as many questions as it answers. One, we don't know how many of them would have ordered from our catalogue if we didn't give them the Web option. In fact, they might have even ordered more. Our phone order people are good at asking 'Would you like a matching scarf with that coat?' but the Web site can't do that, at least not yet. Going the other way, we don't know how many people might try the Web site and like it if they had a reason to."

"Have you tried giving them a reason? I've read about companies that give Web customers special incentives. In fact, a friend of mine was making phone calls with a calling card he got for looking at a Toyota a while back. He had to bring the dealer a coupon that he could only get off their Web site. Interesting way to get people to look at cars and at the same time see who was visiting their site."

"We've thought about it—things like a coupon for $10 off their next order after that, or free shipping, or pick one of these three free gifts. But, again, we don't know if the information we'd get is worth whatever we'd give away. We wouldn't know how many of the people who placed orders would have placed them without the incentive. We have to try something pretty soon, though. We don't know if we should expand our Web site, close it down, or what."

EXERCISES

1. Write a clear decision statement for the decision Niels Agger and FLTC face as described at the end of this episode.
2. Would the Kepner-Tregoe decision-making method (see Chapter 2) be useful in helping to make this decision? Why or why not?
3. Assume someone said, "We think the Web site is profitable because we got $X of orders from it, so we made a profit of $Y, and it only cost $Z to put it up so we made $Z minus $Y." (Of course, a person saying this would use real numbers for X, Y, and Z.) Evaluate this profitability figure in terms of the 11 information quality factors in this chapter. Do you think the quality of this information item is high enough to base a decision on the future of the FLTC Web site on?
4. Suppose FLTC offers buyers a $10 credit toward their order if they (a) order from the Web site and (b) provide some demographic information, which will be kept confidential. How good would this information be, in terms of the information quality factors covered in this chapter, in the context of making the decision about what to do with the Web site?
5. What could you use a model of to help Niels make this decision? In terms of the three reasons for using models in Section 3.6 (ease of manipulation, ease of data collection, time compression), what would be the justification for using it?
6. Find a Web site that offers visitors an incentive to buy a company's products or services via the site rather than via some other distribution channel. (For example, an airline that offers travelers bonus credit in its Frequent Flyer program for flights they book on the Web.) How much is the incentive you found worth, in dollar (or other currency) terms? Would that incentive persuade you to order from the Web rather than another channel, assuming you wanted this company's product or service in the first place? Do you think it will be effective with many other people? In general, is it a good idea? Discuss.

CHAPTER 4

Types of Decision Support Systems

CHAPTER OUTLINE

4.1 **The DSS Hierarchy**

4.2 **Generalizing the DSS Categories**

4.3 **Matching DSS to the Decision Type**

4.4 **Individual and Group DSS**

4.5 **Matching Benefits to the DSS User Community**

4.6 **Matching DSS to the Decision Maker's Psychological Type**

4.7 **Usage Modes**

4.8 **Institutional versus Ad Hoc DSS**

Introduction

The variety of decision support systems is overwhelming. As we've seen, a DSS can range from a spreadsheet on a desktop microcomputer to a custom-written system for hundreds of users, accessing a multi-terabyte database, running on large servers costing millions of dollars supporting a worldwide network of client systems. DSS differ in their scope, the decisions they support, the people who use them, and what they do for those people.

Fortunately, we can place decision support systems into categories. This is helpful for the same reason people place anything into categories: Categories help us generalize from our experience. We can learn what tools, techniques, and approaches have worked in each category. Then, when we face a new situation, we can begin by deciding what categories that situation fits. Approaches and techniques that have worked in those categories before have a good chance of working in the new situation as well.

CHAPTER OBJECTIVES

After you have read and studied this chapter, you will be able to:

1. Describe the seven basic types of DSS and apply each type conceptually to a real decision-making situation.
2. Identify how the seven basic types can be grouped into broader categories.
3. Explain why each type of decision support system is best suited to different types of decisions.
4. Define individual, multi-individual, and group DSS, and explain how each type tends to provide different benefits.
5. Discuss how different types of DSS match the needs of decision makers of different psychological types.
6. Describe the usage modes of DSS, the types of people they involve, and how they have changed with technology types.
7. Explain how and why an institutional DSS and an ad hoc DSS differ.

4.1 THE DSS HIERARCHY

4.1.1 Overview of the DSS Hierarchy

We can categorize decision support systems into the seven levels shown in Figure 4–1. This hierarchy, originally from [ALTE80], is based on what a DSS does, not how it's built. Since people and business decisions haven't changed much in the past 20 years, it still fits well even though the technologies underneath DSS have changed dramatically. While the categories don't fit every system that exists, and while there are gray areas between some adjacent categories, they are an excellent place to start.

From the bottom to the top, the seven DSS types and Alter's original definitions are

- **File drawer systems** allow immediate access to data items.
- **Data analysis systems** allow the manipulation of data by means of operators tailored to the task and settings or operators of a general nature.

FIGURE 4–1   DSS Hierarchy from [ALTE80]

Top	Suggestion Systems
	Optimization Systems
	Representational Models
	Accounting Models
	Analysis Information Systems
	Data Analysis Systems
Bottom	File Drawer Systems

- **Analysis information systems** provide access to a series of databases and small models.
- **Accounting models** calculate the consequences of planned actions on the basis of accounting definitions.
- **Representational models** estimate the consequences of actions on the basis of models that are partially nondefinitional.
- **Optimization systems** provide guidelines for action by generating the optimal solution consistent with a set of constraints.
- **Suggestion systems** perform mechanical work leading to a specific suggested decision for a fairly structured task.

4.1.2 The Seven DSS Types

In this section we'll look at the seven DSS types in a bit more detail. We'll cover them in the order given above. However, even though they are in a sequence, don't think of the higher levels as being somehow "better" than the lower ones. They are more complex, and they carry out more of the decision-making process on their own, but they may not match a given decision situation as well as a simpler type of DSS would.

In general, the first categories—the lower ones—are better suited to less structured problems. The latter ones are better for more structured decisions, or for decisions that recur often enough for people to have developed good ways to deal with them.

File Drawer Systems   These are the simplest DSS, yet they can often be of value. Retrieving a desired piece of information can help reach decisions. When an ATM prints your account balance, when a travel agent or a Web-based reservation system informs you that there are no seats left on a flight about which you inquired, when an order entry operator tells you that your credit card's limit will not cover the goods you're trying to order, they are all using file drawer systems. In each case you are then in a position to make a decision and to take suitable action: to move funds from one account to another, to choose an earlier or later flight, to reduce your order or use a different method of payment.

Business decisions are also often based on a single data item. When a supplier says, "Sorry, we can't ship you any half-horsepower electric motors until a week from Tuesday," a purchasing agent can decide to respond "OK, we'll take them then;" to ask about three-quarter-horsepower or one-third-horsepower motors; or to check with another supplier.

The statement that business decisions are often based on a single data item is not in conflict with what you read in the last chapter: that decisions are based on data that has been processed, via calculations and comparisons, into information. In this case, the calculations and comparisons are done intuitively by the decision maker based on his or her business knowledge and experience. The purchasing agent's response of "OK" to the delay in receiving ordered electric motors is based on the agent's comparing the date on which the motors are needed with the available date—a week from Tuesday. The decision is also based on knowing how motors of different sizes would or would not fit the company's product.

Data Analysis Systems   It is a rare data management system today that cannot also carry out operations such as conditional retrieval of records and elementary arithmetic summaries of selected data. In the early 2000s pure file drawer systems (that is, file drawer systems that can't do more if the need arises) are found only in dedicated end-user applications such as checking a bank balance at an ATM or the inventory status of a product at a supplier's Web site. Almost all software packages and systems used as file drawer systems also have some data analysis capability. Any SQL-based relational database management system can find the sum and average of the data it retrieves. These operations are built into the lowest level of the SQL standard.[1] The airline reservation system that displays "no more seats on that flight" can also display a list of alternate flights to the same destination at about the same time. If one is working with such tools, then, rather than with a finished application, one is not likely to encounter file drawer systems.

Integrated software packages that combine a spreadsheet with data management capability create useful data analysis systems for desktop microcomputers, though spreadsheet programs have modeling and analysis capabilities beyond what this category of DSS requires.[2] Where their data management capabilities do not suffice, most spreadsheet packages can import files from other data or database management software. Setting up the transfer may require some technical skills, especially if the files in question reside on another system (usually called a *server;* see page 209) connected to the user's computer via a network. Once a person with the requisite skills has set up the connection and the importing procedures, importing the latest data for local analysis does not tax the typical end user.

Analysis Information Systems   Alter's name for this category could cause confusion. If the second category is called "data analysis systems," shouldn't this one be "information analysis systems?" The emphasis in this category name, however, is on the "analysis." The last two words are to be taken as a single phrase, "information systems." They mean that an information system carries out the analysis.

The key distinguishing feature between the preceding DSS category and this one is that we are now combining information from several files. In other words, we have what is in effect a true database, though we might not use what a computer scientist would consider database technology. An analysis information system could let a user compare the sales growth trend of one firm's products, calculated from its internal sales data, with industrywide data from an external source.

Analysis information systems have become increasingly popular since the mid-1990s, though few of their users would recognize that name. Instead, the current term, which you've heard before, is *data warehouse.* This is far from the first time

---

[1]Structured Query Language, a standard way to access data in relational databases.
[2]While many microcomputer users refer to this capability as "database" management, MIS professionals and users of larger systems reserve the term *database* for software that can associate data from several files. We will retain the historically precise usage and insist that a database manager must have multifile capability. You should not, however, expect all end users to make this distinction.

that a concept has been "reinvented," given a new name and using new technologies, in the information systems field—often to succeed in its new incarnation far beyond its acceptance the first time around. Because of the critical role that data warehouses play in decision support today, Chapters 12 through 15 of this book are about them.

Accounting Models   The term *accounting model* refers to a model with no uncertainty and where the calculations in each time period depend only on other data from that time period. Such models arise frequently in accounting. Balance sheets and income statements are accounting models, where certain calculations must be performed in order to yield the correct results. Double-entry bookkeeping is an accounting model that allows the owners of a business to know how much the business is worth without checking its bank balances, outstanding invoices, inventories, and so on.

The most common tool used to represent accounting models is the spreadsheet program. It was invented by two business school students to automate accounting calculations for their case analyses. Other tools can also be used, especially if the accounting model is a small part of a larger DSS.

Material Requirements Planning (MRP) systems, a basic component of most manufacturing software, incorporate accounting models. The bill of materials (BOM) for a product states what components, and how many of each, go into that product. If the BOM of a desk calls for 4 legs, precisely 4 legs are needed: not 3, not 3.5, not a statistical distribution with a mean of 4 and standard deviation of 0.3. There is no uncertainty in the calculations to be performed with this number. If the MRP system is used to help make production planning or shipment scheduling decisions, it would be part of an accounting model DSS.

Whereas an accounting model itself cannot incorporate any uncertainty, its inputs may not be known precisely. For instance, [ALTE80] discusses a model used by a shipping firm to calculate its costs, in order to decide on the prices it will offer to people who want to charter its ocean freighters. Two factors in this calculation are fuel consumption and the unit cost of fuel at the time of the voyage. Both are subject to uncertainty, though historical data for a given ship allow the firm to estimate its fuel consumption closely and fuel price forecasts are available from several petroleum industry sources. Once the firm has estimated those, the model itself behaves as if the figures were known precisely and does not take their uncertainty into account. The model in this DSS is therefore an accounting model. Similarly, a budget forecast that uses an estimated future inflation rate and estimates of future revenues and expenses, or any such model, is an accounting model in the context of these seven DSS categories.

Representational Models   Representational models reflect uncertainty, often in individual or collective human behavior, or represent the dynamic behavior of systems over time—where what a system in the model does at one instant depends on what happened before.

Representational models are widely used to forecast the future effect of a decision: the productivity of one factory setup versus another, the stockout frequency of one ordering policy versus another, the response time of one computer system configuration versus another. By representing how we expect a real-world system to respond to certain inputs, we can consider different decisions (system inputs) and choose among them on the basis of their predicted results (system outputs). We'll cover several types of representational models in Chapters 8 and 9.

Optimization Systems   Given a suitable model, we can estimate the effect of various decision alternatives. If the alternatives can be enumerated or laid out along mathematical axes, a program can choose the one that yields the best results. Although the best mathematical forecast is not always the only basis for decision making—using it alone corresponds to the "rational manager" concept of Chapter 2—it often helps a decision maker to have this information. A system that selects the best of several alternatives on a numerical basis is called an optimization system. We'll discuss optimization methods in Chapter 9.

Suggestion Systems   It is often a short step from determining an optimal decision to suggesting that the decision maker should make that decision. When decisions are highly structured it may be practical for a DSS to make such a suggestion. Such DSS are called, appropriately, suggestion systems.

Another type of suggestion system codifies the decision-making process into a number of rules. These rules can mimic the decision-making process that a human expert would use, providing a descriptive model of the decision-making process. Alternatively, they can describe the correct way to make a decision when this can be defined, which is a normative model. Either way, the system then suggests that the user make the same decision that these rules would yield. This approach works well where human expertise or the desired decision-making process can be codified into a reasonable number of rules. The technology of expert systems is often used to construct this type of suggestion system. You'll read about expert systems in Chapter 11.

4.1.3 Applying the DSS Types to Airline Yield Management[3]

A concrete example will help clarify the distinctions among these seven DSS types. Yield management is a business problem that is simple enough to understand (not really simple: real business problems seldom are) yet complex enough to need computer support. The first industry to practice deliberate yield management as a profit-maximizing strategy was the airline industry. Industries that can use yield management are generally characterized by high fixed costs, low variable costs, a product or service that loses value rapidly if not used, and several types of customers with different characteristics who use what is essentially the

---

[3]The author is grateful to Professor Peter Belobaba, of the M.I.T. Department of Aeronautics and Astronautics, for his constructive comments on an earlier version of this section.

same product or service. (You may have run into the term *price discrimination* when you discussed these concepts in your economics course.)

The Yield Management Problem   Most airlines offer a variety of fares on a given flight segment. It is often said that an airline can fill a flight with no two passengers paying the same fare with precisely the same terms and conditions. Airlines expend a great deal of effort on **yield management** (also called *revenue management*): deciding what conditions will apply to each discount fare, how large a discount to offer potential passengers who meet those conditions, and how many seats will be available at each discount level.

Suppose, to simplify reality a bit, a flight has two coach class fares. The higher fare is called *full coach fare.* It is available until the plane takes off, and is refundable in full at any time—even after the flight, if the ticket was not used for any reason. A full coach fare ticket can be rewritten for any other flight to the same destination, even if the price has gone up in the meantime.

The lower SuperSaver fare, by contrast, has several restrictions. One possible set of restrictions is that SuperSaver tickets must be purchased at least 30 days before the flight, are available only for round-trips that include a Saturday night stay at the destination, can be reissued for a different flight only for a substantial additional charge, and are not refundable if not used or reissued before the flight leaves.

Many vacationers plan their trips more than a month ahead, stay at their destination at least one Saturday night, and are willing to plan around specific flights in return for substantial savings. Most business travelers plan trips on shorter notice, want to return home as soon as their meetings are over, and need flexibility to deal with unforeseen events. Therefore, many vacationers can qualify for SuperSaver fares, but most business travelers cannot.

The airline's dilemma is this: It doesn't have enough business travelers to fill a plane. It can, however, find enough vacationers to fill one by setting the discount fare low enough. If it sets a low SuperSaver price and allows vacationers to fill the plane, the flight will be full a month before it takes off. The airline will then have no seats left for business travelers who need them at the last minute. Since business travelers pay a higher fare, the airline's profits will be less than they might be. In addition, besides paying more for their tickets, business travelers fly more than most vacationers and are therefore any airline's most desirable customers. They will be unhappy if they can't get seats and may transfer their allegiance to another carrier.

To avoid these problems airlines limit the number of seats they sell at discount fares. For example, an airline may decide that only 40 of 100 coach seats can be sold at the SuperSaver price. If a 41st traveler requests this fare, it will not be offered—even if the traveler meets the conditions of advance notice and a Saturday night stay.

The decision the airline must make is how many SuperSaver tickets to sell. If the limit is too high, business travelers will be turned away because the plane is full of low-fare vacationers. If it is too low, the plane will take off with empty seats that could have held vacationers with SuperSaver tickets. SuperSaver tickets may be less profitable than full-fare tickets, but they are more profitable than empty seats.

Suppose full-fare sales form a normal distribution with a mean of 40.5 full-fare ticket sales in a 100-seat airplane. Half the time, the airline sells 41 or more full-fare seats; the other half of the time, the airline sells 40 or fewer. Suppose the airline could fill the plane with SuperSaver travelers, if they allow that to happen. How many SuperSaver seats should the airline sell?

The answer depends on the ratio between the two price levels.[4] If SuperSaver fare is exactly half full coach fare, the airline should sell 59 or 60 SuperSaver seats; it doesn't matter which. (That is, the 100-seat capacity of the plane less the 40 or 41 full-fare seats typically sold.) When the limit is changed from 60 to 59, they give up a sure SuperSaver sale in return for a 50 percent chance of a full-fare sale. Given the 2:1 price ratio between the two fares, the two revenue streams are statistically equivalent and will even out in the long run.

Suppose they make more than 60 SuperSaver seats available. Because the airline has a better than even chance of selling 40 full-fare seats, they are giving up (statistically) more than 50 percent of a full-fare sale for a half-fare sale. That's a bad deal. If they offer fewer than 59 SuperSaver seats, they would give up (again statistically) half-fare seats for a less-than-50 percent chance of full-fare sale. That's a bad deal, too.

If a SuperSaver ticket cost two-thirds of the full-fare price, the airline would raise the limit. They would now want a two-thirds chance of filling all the full-fare seats. For a normal distribution, the two-thirds point is about 0.43 standard deviations above the mean. They would reserve 0.43 standard deviations fewer tickets for full-fare passengers. If full-fare sales, which we already know have a mean of 40.5, have a standard deviation of 14, the airline would offer 65 or 66 SuperSaver seats. They have thereby increased the probability that some potential full-fare passengers won't find room from 0.50 to 0.67. They accept this because selling a SuperSaver ticket is now, at two-thirds of full coach fare, relatively more desirable to the airline than when it cost only half of full coach fare. That makes the airline willing to sacrifice a statistically larger fraction of a full-fare sale to get the sure SuperSaver sale.

Conversely, if the SuperSaver price were one-third full coach fare, they would lower the limit to give a one-third chance of filling the plane. For the preceding distribution, the airline would make only 53 or 54 SuperSaver seats available. The company accepts a higher probability of taking off with empty seats because SuperSaver seat sales are, at this lower price, less desirable than before. All these situations can be visualized in terms of the decision tree of Figure 4–2. It is clear

---

[4]More precisely, it depends on *profit* levels: price less variable costs such as meals and extra fuel, plus average profit on drinks, headsets, etc. Since these are small compared to either price or the flight's share of fixed costs, using price is close enough for practical purposes.

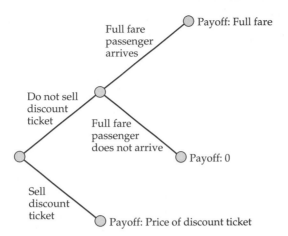

FIGURE 4–2   **Airline Discount Ticket Seat Quota Decision Tree**

from the decision tree that the correct decision is to keep the seat empty if the price of a full-fare ticket, times the probability that a full-fare passenger will arrive (or that a traveler who can't get a discount ticket will agree to pay the full fare) exceeds the price of a SuperSaver ticket.

The yield management process is complicated in practice by the existence of far more than two coach fares. In addition to full fares and SuperSaver fares, there may be 14-day, 7-day, and 3-day advance purchase fares with fewer or no restrictions. There are discounts for passengers above and below certain ages, for those accompanying a full-fare passenger, for those willing to leave after a certain hour at night, for those connecting via a certain city. There are discounts for people attending conventions that have agreed to feature the airline in their publicity materials. There are free tickets for travelers who have flown a certain number of miles on the airline and earned this reward. Tickets are given to travelers who were "bumped" from an oversold flight, or to travel agents to let them sample the airline's service firsthand. Each has its own limits and special considerations. The decision tree for this situation is considerably more complex, as it must reflect all the fares and their probabilities.

Yield managers can manipulate three variables for each fare:

1. *The number of seats the airline will sell at a given fare level.* This can be adjusted at any time. Airlines adjust the number of discount seats available daily or even more frequently. If high-priced seats are selling more quickly than expected, the number of discount seats is reduced, and vice versa.

   Airlines *nest* seat quotas. This means the number of seats available at one fare is never greater than the number available at any higher fare. If a fare is sold out, so are all the less expensive fares. If a fare is available, so are all the more expensive fares.

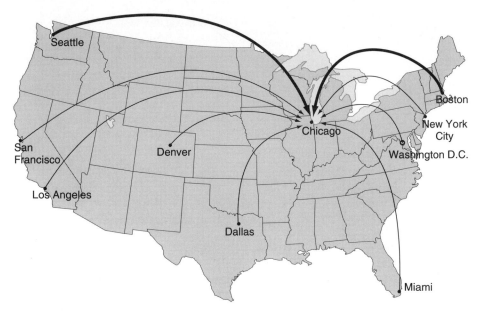

FIGURE 4–3 **American Airlines Route Map Focusing on Chicago Hub**

2. *Price.* All airline fares are subject to change without notice. Full fares and most discount fares can change daily. Some discount fares are harder to fine-tune via minor adjustments due to competitive pressures and widespread advertising.

3. *The restrictions that apply to discount tickets.* These are somewhat flexible, but the travel industry is used to certain types of restrictions (e.g., a Saturday night stay as a requirement for the lowest fares) and too much originality might confuse travel agents or encounter resistance.

Matters become more complicated when we consider the entire route structure of an airline. Consider, for example, American Airlines' 3:45 P.M. Flight 1631 from Boston, Massachusetts, to Chicago, Illinois.[5] This flight, whose route is highlighted in Figure 4–3, is part of American's "hub" system. Westbound flights from several eastern U.S. cities converge on Chicago within a half-hour period. They stay on the ground for an hour or so, allowing passengers to move from one plane to another. They then take off at about the same time to various West Coast destinations. Soon after, the process repeats in the eastbound direction. The hub approach is quite popular. Different airlines use different cities: United Airlines shares Chicago with American, TWA's major east–west hub is in St. Louis; Delta uses Cincinnati and Salt Lake City. The concept is not limited to North America:

---

[5]The flights in this example existed in late 1998. American's schedules may have changed since then, but the concepts have not.

Sabena's eastbound trans-Atlantic flights all converge on Brussels at about the same time each morning, after which other flights fan out to destinations throughout Europe. Northwest and KLM do the same cooperatively in Amsterdam. The same principles apply to all.

Some of Flight 1631's passengers want to go to Chicago. A few will stay on the plane as it continues to Calgary. Most will transfer to other flights: American's westbound flights to Los Angeles, San Francisco, Seattle, and others; commuter flights to smaller cities throughout the midwestern United States; or flights on other airlines. American can, if it wishes, collect passenger preference data in this regard.

Suppose a traveler wants a SuperSaver ticket from Boston to Seattle and back. The Boston–Chicago segment has no more SuperSaver seats available, but the Chicago–Seattle segment (whose Flight 1073 originated in Syracuse, New York) does, as do the desired return flights. Should American sell this SuperSaver ticket or not? If it sells the ticket, it loses the statistically expected additional profit on a full-fare seat sale for the Boston–Chicago segment. If it does not sell the ticket, thus keeping the Boston–Chicago seat open for the statistically expected full-fare passenger, it runs the risk of letting the Chicago–Seattle flight and both return flights take off emptier than they have to be. There's no simple answer to this question. It is complicated, in this case, by the fact that the Boston–Chicago segment is short, and hence inexpensive, whereas the sum of the Chicago–Seattle segment and the two return flights is longer and hence more expensive. To complicate things still further, the Boston–Chicago segment could be critical to the overall itinerary of a full-fare passenger who could arrive at the last minute, corporate credit card at the ready.

Current industry practice is not to sell a discount ticket if the fare is sold out on any of the flight segments involved. That rule is simple to state and to administer, but probably not optimal. Some airlines are developing *origin–destination yield management systems* to make this decision on the basis of a traveler's entire itinerary.

Travelers' schedule flexibility adds yet another dimension of complexity. A Boston business traveler with a morning appointment in Dallas may not be willing to leave before mid-afternoon of the previous day. A vacationing couple who finds the most deeply discounted fares sold out on their first choice of flights, a month or more in the future, can adjust their plans with little or no inconvenience. Yield management thus has the desirable (to the airline) effect of pushing low-fare travelers toward flights that are less popular with business travelers. This evens out demand over time of day and day of the week—leading, in turn, to better utilization of aircraft, facilities, and personnel.

Applying DSS to Yield Management   Yield management analysts can use decision support systems to help set the capacity limits of the various fares. Corresponding to the seven levels of the DSS hierarchy, some DSS they could use are the following:

- *File drawer system.* Yield management analysts could find out how many seats were sold on a given flight at a given fare with a given set of restrictions. Using

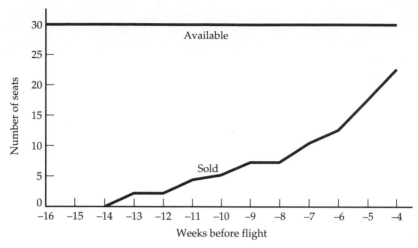

FIGURE 4–4   **Graph 1 of Ticket Bookings over Time (SuperSaver Tickets Generally Do Not Sell Out by Cutoff Date)**

this information, they could (manually or with another information system) set or modify prices, conditions, and capacity limits for future flights.

- *Data analysis system.* Such a system would simplify extracting the historical data from the database. It could calculate averages, trends, and similar aggregates from the raw data.
- *Analysis information system.* An AIS (or, as it would more likely be referred to today, a data warehouse) could present historical average booking data for a given type of ticket at a given fare in the form of a graph, such as Figure 4–4. This tells us that, historically, the SuperSaver fare did not sell out by its purchase deadline (which, for purposes of this example, is four weeks before the flight). If this flight generally takes off with empty seats, we should consider lowering our SuperSaver price further, reducing the four-week advance purchase requirement, or creating other incentives. Suppose, however, the curve looked like Figure 4–5. In this case, SuperSaver tickets typically sell out before the cutoff date. Some customers for this type of ticket, who arrived before the deadline but after the capacity limit was reached, were presumably turned away. This suggests that we could make the tickets less attractive and still sell out by the deadline. One way to do this is to raise the fare for such tickets—say, from half to 60 percent of full coach fare. Or, we could tighten the conditions: perhaps keep the current fare for 45-day advance purchase, which history tells us would usually sell out, and institute a slightly higher fare with more available seats for 30-day advance purchase.
- *Accounting model.* An accounting model could calculate the expected revenue for a given seat allocation. Figure 4–6 depicts how an analyst might expect to sell seats. An accounting model could calculate the expected revenue, as shown at the bottom of the rightmost column in the figure, and the corresponding

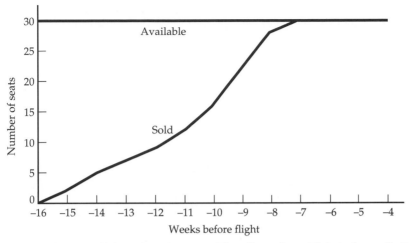

FIGURE 4–5 **Graph 2 of Ticket Bookings over Time (SuperSaver Tickets Generally Sell Out Well Before Cutoff Date)**

Fare type	Price	Quantity	Revenue
Unrestricted coach	$800	30	$24,000
3-day advance purchase, refundable	750	20	15,000
7-day advance purchase, refundable	650	20	13,000
14-day advance purchase, $100 cancellation penalty, $50 charge to change flights	500	20	10,000
30-day advance purchase, nonrefundable, $50 charge to change flights, Saturday night stay required	350	20	7,000
		Total	$69,000

FIGURE 4–6 **Accounting Model for Expected Flight Revenue**

profit. A spreadsheet program is well suited to such calculations. (Of course, the result of such a calculation can be no better than what is input, in particular the quantity of seats that will be sold at each price level. The pricing analyst would have to obtain those numbers from another source. A spreadsheet by itself can't provide that information. This is an example of a situation where the spreadsheet seems to provide totally accurate information. Its user must be aware that its inputs may not be as accurate as its output appears.)

- *Representational model.* Here we start to consider human behavior. The usual method of considering human behavior in a situation such as this is via the price–demand elasticity curve of classical economics. If we reduce a particular fare by $50, what will happen to demand? Airline managers have vast amounts of historical data that describe the shape of elasticity curves. Given one or two points on the actual curve for a particular fare and flight segment, they can estimate the complete curve well enough for practical purposes.

By combining representational and accounting models, we could estimate the revenue that will accrue from any mix of restrictions (among those for which our data warehouse contains historical data), prices, and capacity limits. Such a model would allow analysts to choose a set and evaluate its effect. Based on this evaluation they could make another, hopefully better, set of choices. They could repeat this process until they feel that more changes will not improve the result. This mini-example shows how a real decision support system often incorporates more than one of the capabilities defined by these categories.

- *Optimization system.* The variables under our control are few in number, at least on any given flight segment, and known precisely. It is relatively easy to program a computer to evaluate them over the range of interest and return the "best" answer. This process, however, would be limited to a single flight segment. When several flight segments interact with each other, a solution requires the application of complex network optimization algorithms. (It also requires origin/destination passenger data that most airlines, as a practical matter, do not have.)

- *Suggestion system.* This type of system could cope with the issues that arise when several flight segments interact. An expert system, with rules that describe what managers do in the situations that normally arise, might be able to help with the systemwide optimization problem. It couldn't do anything that managers couldn't also do in principle, given enough time, but its ability to process large amounts of data quickly might allow it to produce recommendations while they are still useful.

  The expert system would have a large number of rules and an even larger number of data points with which to deal. It would utilize a historical data warehouse covering hundreds of tickets on each of hundreds of flights per day over several months. It would be expected to recommend capacity limits for every fare type for a given flight on the different days of the week. Such a system would be a major undertaking but could confer a significant strategic advantage on the airline that developed it.

  Airlines also use expert systems in a more limited way to make capacity decisions on an ongoing basis. Systems with a few simple rules repeatedly check the rate at which tickets are being purchased for every flight and adjust the number of discount seats available based on the most recent data available. These decision-making (not decision support) systems address the clerical, structured aspect of yield management.

Yield management has been called the most significant strategic airline information system application after reservation systems. In 1999, every airline of significance[6] is listed on every major reservation system, so the use of such a

---

[6]With the exception of a few discount airlines whose marketing strategy is based on minimum cost for passengers who are willing to do a little extra work.

system no longer confers a strategic advantage on the airline that sponsors it. Yield management is thus perhaps the most important strategic information system an airline can have today. It ties in directly to the mainstream operations of the firm. Its impact goes directly to the bottom line. It is not surprising that airlines use DSS to help make yield management decisions. (You can read more about yield management in [GROS97], about American Airlines' DINAMO yield management DSS in [SMIT92], and about Hertz's use of the concept on the Web at http://www.dfi.com/txt/p01_3.htm.)

4.2 GENERALIZING THE DSS CATEGORIES

We can collapse the seven DSS categories into two broader categories. As Alter points out in [ALTE80], this simplification loses some information, but it is still helpful in taking a first look at a new system.

The bottom three levels of the hierarchy focus almost entirely on a database. Above the file drawer level they have some analysis capabilities, but these capabilities do not involve a detailed model of a system or a business situation and do not dominate what the system does. We refer to these and similar DSS as **data-oriented. Data warehouses** are the primary example of data-oriented DSS today.

The upper levels concentrate more on the model of a business system, less on the database. The database component may still be present, and may even be as large as it is in one of the first three types, but is relatively less important as the modeling components dominate this type of DSS. Such a DSS is called **model-oriented.** Databases in model-oriented DSS are often small, self-contained, and constructed solely for use by the model. Analysis information systems are in a gray area between data-oriented and model-oriented DSS.

The models at the fourth and fifth levels of the hierarchy, accounting and representational, are system models. They model what goes on inside the r e a l - w o r l d system about which a decision must be made. Because they do not address how a decision should be made, the concept of normative versus descriptive models does not apply to them. Those at the top two levels, optimization and suggestion models, often also reflect the process a decision maker would use (a descriptive decision model) or should use (a normative model) in dealing with the decision in question. It is sometimes convenient to refer to a DSS based only on a model of the decision process as a **process-oriented DSS.** This focuses our attention on the way such a DSS mimics the real or idealized human decision-making process.

4.3 MATCHING DSS TO THE DECISION TYPE

DSS can be categorized according to the type of decision they help with: structured, semistructured, or unstructured.

Fully structured decisions may be below the level at which DSS is useful. They can be programmed into a computer and made without human assistance. A data-oriented DSS can be useful if the data on which to base the decision are not known in advance and must be determined by people before the decision can be made.

Where people must review a fully structured decision, a suggestion model can suggest the right course of action with its recommendation either confirmed (normally) or overridden (occasionally) by the person.

Semistructured decisions lend themselves to model-oriented DSS. These will most often use system models. Such a model can predict the effect of choosing alternatives, but the human must still assess the unstructured factors, or deal with the unstructured decision phases, and make the final decision.

Unstructured decisions are the realm of data-oriented DSS. Where a decision has no structure, we cannot build a model of the system underlying that decision. This is because such a model, by its nature, is based on what we know of a system's structure. All a DSS can do in an unstructured situation is to present the available information to decision makers in the format they want and with as much predigestion as the circumstances permit. A DSS that follows a human expert's decision-making process may also be helpful here, to help ensure that necessary factors are considered and necessary decision-making steps are taken.

4.4 INDIVIDUAL AND GROUP DSS

Decision support systems can also be categorized on the basis of the type of group, if any, that they support. Certain DSS are used by individuals making **individual decisions.** A marketing manager deciding on next year's ad budget is in that situation. This person wants to pick the ideal advertising budget for his or her firm. The final decision is made by the marketing manager alone, though people in that type of situation often discuss options with colleagues and seek their advice.

At the lowest level, a data-oriented DSS that provides information on the cost, reach, and likely impact of different media choices can help this person make an informed decision. An analysis information system could automate some simple calculations on these data. Moving up from there, an accounting model could consolidate the data and calculate the total exposure of an overall advertising program: seven half-page black-and-white ads in *Time,* a one-minute commercial every week for a month on major league baseball's "Game of the Week," . . . Such a model could provide a chart that tells the marketing manager how many people will see one of the ads, how many will see two ads, and so on. A representational model could predict the impact of these impressions on purchase decisions over time, providing guidance not only in selecting the right advertising program but also in making sure enough stock is in stores to satisfy the anticipated demand.

Other DSS are used by individuals in making decisions that are made by many people across an organization, where consistency is required. A bank may want to make sure that all its loan officers apply certain criteria to the applications they review, even though the loan officers make each decision individually. We call such DSS **multi-individual DSS.**

Finally, some DSS support decisions that are inherently made by a group as a whole. Such **group DSS** must take into account not only the models and data of the decision, but also the dynamics of the group decision-making process. Soft-

Model-oriented			
Data-oriented			
	Individual	Multi-individual	Group

FIGURE 4–7 Two-dimensional Grid of DSS Types

ware designed to support the work of a group is often called *groupware.* This term includes both group DSS and other packages, such as electronic mail or meeting scheduling, that are inherently group-oriented but which are not usually considered decision-support systems as such. We'll discuss group DSS in Chapter 10.

An individual or multi-individual DSS takes on some group DSS characteristics if the individuals' managers review and comment on the decisions in question. A department manager may use a spreadsheet program to develop a budget for the department. For that purpose the spreadsheet—or the model built with its help—is an individual DSS. If the budget is subject to review and approval by the division manager, however, the decision is a group decision; it may be a small group, since it consists of only two people, but a group nonetheless. Any tool used to help make that decision therefore has aspects of a group DSS.

The expectation of using an essentially individual DSS in this fashion may affect its design. The department manager mentioned previously may format and label the budget spreadsheet beyond his or her own informational needs. This is done with a view to showing the spreadsheet to the division manager, justifying its contents, and possibly vying with other department managers for a share of the divisional resources.

The classification of DSS into data-oriented and model-oriented DSS, and classification into individual, multi-individual, and group DSS, are separate issues. Both dimensions can be visualized as shown in Figure 4–7. In the figure, the vertical axis shows the way the DSS supports the decision-making task: data-oriented or model-oriented. The horizontal axis reflects the individual, multi-individual, or group nature of the decision. We'll revisit this two-dimensional approach to classifying DSS in more detail in Chapter 10, where we'll also look at some of the kinds of DSS that could go into the (currently empty) boxes of the figure.

4.5 MATCHING BENEFITS TO THE DSS USER COMMUNITY

There is a strong relationship between the type of people who use a DSS and the benefits, as discussed in Section 1.4, that the DSS provides. As a rule—which, like all other rules, is subject to many exceptions—the overall tendencies are shown in Figure 4–8. An *H* in this table, for *high applicability,* means that the benefit listed at the left is a common primary benefit for DSS intended for this type of use, often the main intent of the system as a whole. An *M* (*moderate*) means that it is usually an incidental benefit but is not uncommon and may be reflected in system design.

	Individual	Multi-individual	Group
Improving personal efficiency	H	H	L
Expediting problem solving	L	M	H
Facilitating interpersonal communication	L	L	H
Promoting learning or training	M	H	H
Increasing organizational control	L	H	M

FIGURE 4–8   **Relationship between DSS Users and DSS Benefits**

An *L* (*low*) means that this benefit does not usually apply to the type of use indicated at the head of the column.

The first row indicates that improving personal efficiency generally applies to individual and multi-individual DSS. The focus of most group DSS is on the decision-making process of the group as a whole, not on the personal productivity of any one of its members.

Improved problem-solving can apply to individual, multi-individual, or group DSS. Speed and objective quality improvements apply to all three. Consistency improvements relate primarily to multi-individual DSS.

Interpersonal communication is primarily a factor in group situations, so improved interpersonal communication applies most strongly to group DSS. It may also be a factor in multi-individual DSS. Where it applies to individual DSS, it is usually because the output of the DSS is used as a "convincer."

Improved learning applies primarily to individual and multi-individual DSS. Multi-individual DSS are often designed to promote some form of organizational uniformity. Learning about organizational norms—the spread between a high raise and a low one, the sentences usually given to first offenders convicted of motor vehicle theft—is part of this process.

Improved organizational control is often a major motivating factor in the development of multi-individual DSS. It can also apply to group DSS, as management can define the decision-making process that the DSS supports. The group will then be forced to use that process. For example, a group DSS can make sure that insurance applications above a certain amount of coverage are reviewed and approved by an underwriter before being returned to the agency that submitted them.

4.6 MATCHING DSS TO THE DECISION MAKER'S PSYCHOLOGICAL TYPE

In Section 2.5 we discussed psychological type and its impact on decision-making style. Because decision-making styles differ, and DSS are intended to support human decision-making styles, DSS must reflect these differences. It should not come as a surprise, then, to learn that people of different psychological types are best served by different types of DSS. This is a good place to look at this issue since you already know about psychological types and you've just read about types of DSS. You will be able to relate this information to most of what you read later in this book.

Sometimes a decision maker must use a DSS best suited to a person of a different psychological type. This may be for reasons of corporate standardization or because a better-suited DSS is not available. In this case he or she should be aware that using this DSS calls for using nonpreferred behavioral styles. Since, as we noted on page 61 in a quotation from [PROV90], the styles are preferences—not behavioral dictators—and using a nonpreferred style is always possible. It may call for a conscious effort, though, particularly if an individual preference is strong.

In organizations that use psychological type as a team-building tool, a manager will often be aware of his or her subordinates' types. This knowledge, properly applied, can help managers match DSS characteristics to employees' preferred working styles.

Our discussion of the impact of the four psychological preferences on DSS usage discusses each type in isolation. A more complete discussion would cover individually each of the 16 four-letter types that were shown in Figure 2–12. Such a discussion can be found in several sources, such as [HIRS90] and [PROV90].

4.6.1 Introversion/Extraversion

As we noted in Section 2.5, the characteristic of Introversion/Extraversion does not affect a person's decision making directly. It does, however, affect the type of interaction a person tends to prefer during the decision-making process.

The Extraverted (E) type enjoys discussing ideas and options with other people and is productive in this freewheeling mode of interaction. If he or she uses electronic meeting aids, for example, those aids would ideally provide for concurrent use by several people interacting at one time, such as an Internet chat system.

The Introverted (I) type tends to be less comfortable with immediate interaction. This person prefers to mull over a decision and reach a position before discussing it with others. Delayed electronic interaction, such as in electronic discussion groups where replies are posted after a time delay, may be more comfortable to such a person.

When a group decision is to be made, it is not possible to customize the DSS to the needs of an individual. In that case, it may be desirable to develop a DSS that can be used in different ways. Here we might provide an electronic town meeting capability for interactive discussion and allow other group members to review the dialogue and add their comments at a later time.

4.6.2 Sensing/Intuition

A person with a preference for Sensing (S) may want a large number of facts and may therefore tend to be well served by a data-oriented DSS or by complete, detailed models. One with an iNtuitive (N) preference will tend to reach a conclusion on the basis of hunches that require less in the way of data. The type of model needed to support this person's intuitive approach may not have to be as detailed or exhaustive as the one that the person who prefers Sensing may like to use. However, the iNtuitive who reaches a conclusion on the basis of simplified models and "gut feel" may have trouble justifying this conclusion to others of a more Sensing preference.

4.6.3 Thinking/Feeling

As you read on page 62, the Thinkers (T) base decisions on carefully thought-out logic but sometimes ignore human factors and values. They approach the concept of the rational manager in this regard. Thinkers may opt to make a decision solely on the basis of an optimization or suggestion model DSS.

People with a Feeling (F) preference, on the other hand, may focus on people in their decision making. Left on their own, they would gravitate less toward this type of DSS. They will find decision support tools that support interaction among people, including groupware tools such as those discussed in Chapter 10, to be useful. This is true even for individual decisions, since these people are concerned with how others will react to any decision they make.

People with both preferences can benefit from an optimization or suggestion model DSS, but the way in which they use that system may differ. The Thinking decision maker may tend to give the DSS output too much weight, whereas the Feeling decision maker may give it too little. By being aware of these tendencies, decision makers and managers can use the combined strengths of both types to reach decisions that satisfy both numerical and human criteria.

4.6.4 Judgment/Perception

The person with a Judging (J) style prefers to reach closure on a subject quickly, gathering only as much data as he or she feels necessary for this purpose. Model-oriented DSS suit this personality type well. The danger here is that this type of person may tend to make a decision even when the timing is not urgent and deferring the decision could allow gathering additional useful information.

The Perceptive (P) has the opposite tendency: to gather as much information as possible while keeping the decision options open. These types like data-oriented DSS; however, their information-gathering tendency may mean putting off the decision itself as long as possible. Perceptives are often seen as procrastinators by their judgment-oriented colleagues.

A process-oriented DSS that automates a decision-making process such as that of Kepner-Tregoe, which we discussed in Section 2.5, can help both types by forcing both to spend enough time—but not too much time—on both the information-gathering and decision-making parts of the process.

4.6.5 Combinations of Preferences

Huitt [HUIT92] has studied the types of assistance that are required by people having different combinations of types, or **temperaments** [KEIR84]. For Huitt, when it comes to problem solving the S-N dimension is the key variable, but the second variable is different for Ss and Ns. For Sensing types, the J-P preference is the second to be considered: Should the existing data be organized and structured (the J tendency) or should additional data be gathered (the P tendency)? For iNtuitives, the second dimension to consider is T-F: Is the tendency to make the decision on the basis of logic or impact on people? Figure 4–9 shows the relationships he described.

Temperament	Needs help in . . .
S-P	Coherence of plan
	Following selected solution
S-J	Categorizing and classifying
	Generating creative alternatives
N-T	Attending to facts and details
	Looking at impact on people
N-F	Attending to facts and details
	Developing realistic alternatives
	Monitoring implementation carefully

FIGURE 4–9 **Relationship between Temperament and Decision Support Needs (from [HUIT92])**

We can use this information to select the most appropriate types of decision support systems for a group if we know something about the personality types of its members. For example, if the group consists primarily of S-Js, it will most likely need help in generating creative alternatives (the design stage of the decision-making process). Support for brainstorming techniques, as provided by electronic meeting systems (see a discussion of these systems on page 399) can be useful here. If it consists largely of the more visionary and idealistic NFs, however, there will be plenty of creative alternatives. The issue will then be which ones can realistically be implemented (the choice stage). Brainstorming support will be of little use in answering this question. Software that helps evaluate potential difficulties and adverse consequences will be more to the point.

4.7 USAGE MODES

Different DSS are used in different ways by the people whom they support. This is important to understand, since the ideal user interface for a DSS depends on how it is going to be used.

Alter identified four major usage modes for DSS [ALTE80]; these modes are quite general. Today's DSS still fall into these modes, although their shares of DSS usage have shifted since Alter's work. He called these four modes subscription mode, terminal mode, clerk mode, and intermediary mode.

Subscription mode refers to situations where a decision maker receives DSS output on a regular basis. This term originally referred to piles of paper arriving on decision makers' desks at regular intervals. That usage mode has not disappeared but has become rarer, as more managers have desktop microcomputers linked directly to their firms' databases.

Another form of subscription mode arose in the 1980s. This form consists of preprocessing data into reports and charts, which remain in a computer's file system for access when needed. They may be distributed to servers throughout an organization for local access. The reports and charts can then be retrieved without delay when they are needed for decision making. The preprocessing (and distribution, if used) can take place at night when computer workload is low, with digested data available to managers in the form of summaries and graphs the following morning. Many executive information systems, which we'll discuss on page 476, work this way.

Terminal mode refers to direct use of the computer by the decision maker. The word *terminal* implies a decision maker using a terminal to interact with a multiuser computer. Today's interaction is as likely to be with a microcomputer located on the decision maker's desk. The interaction is the same in either case, as one cannot determine from the interaction whether a desktop microcomputer or a remote system is driving the screen, keyboard, and mouse. Terminal mode is increasing in popularity, at the expense of both the preceding and the following modes of operation.

Clerk mode means that a decision maker fills out a form to specify the information to be retrieved, or the operations to be performed, by the DSS. A clerk then enters the data into the computer, directly or via an off-line device such as the once-ubiquitous keypunch machine. After the DSS performs its operations its output is delivered to the decision maker.

Clerk mode is seldom encountered now that personal computers permeate the workplace from the shop floor or checkout counter to the executive suite. Decision makers may still need professional assistance with a DSS, but that is not the same as needing clerical help. Professional help falls under the next heading.

Intermediary mode refers to situations where a decision maker uses the DSS via a professional assistant, who contributes actively to posing the problem to the DSS. This contribution involves the assistant's intelligence and professional skills, not just keying in the content of a filled-out paper form. Decision makers use intermediaries in three roles. These may at times be combined in one individual:

- **Staff assistants** are general helpers to top executives. They perform tasks that the executive could also perform, but which do not demand his or her unique talents. A staff assistant's job is to save the executive's valuable time. An office assistant often falls into this category.
- **Technical support staff** have specific skills in the computer aspects of using a decision support system. For instance, retrieving information from a database may require mastering a query language. If a busy manager does not use this query language often, it may be more cost effective for the manager to explain the need to a specialist who already knows the language, and then let that person interact with the DSS.
- **Business analysts** are people with specific skills in management science, operations research, production planning, financial analysis, or other fields. They assist decision makers by figuring out exactly what question should be posed to the DSS, by designing simulation models, by carrying out linear programming optimizations, and more. Many managers know what these tools are and, in a general way, how they can be of value, but do not have the specialized knowledge to use them themselves.

The skills of several individuals may be needed to solve a problem or reach a decision. This is especially true of strategic decisions that are made rarely but have far-ranging impact, such as choosing the location of a new factory. A given type of system can work in a combination of usage modes. A university registration system may have aspects of all four modes: subscription, terminal, clerk, and intermediary.

Subscription Mode   Students receive schedule sheets before every term and grade reports after it ends. Faculty members receive class rosters for their courses when the course starts, after the period for course changes ends, and before grades are due. These documents appear automatically; students and teachers don't have to specifically ask for them.

Terminal Mode   Administrators can access the system directly from their offices when they need information. Students can often also use it directly: to verify their enrollment status, or to register for an upcoming term—using Touch-tone telephones, conveniently located registration terminals on the campus, or by visiting a registration page in their institution's Web site.

Clerk Mode   Where students do not have direct access to terminals, they can check their registration status by asking a clerk in the registrar's office. This clerk does not perform any operations that are beyond the capabilities of a student (the clerk often *is* in fact a student in a work-study job) but adds a measure of security when a registration system lacks safeguards against one person's accessing information about another.

Intermediary Mode   In choosing courses, students often consult faculty advisors who analyze the students' records to suggest courses they might take next. Faculty advisors correspond to the "business analyst" intermediary role above: they are chosen for expertise in advising students, not for expertise in using a computer.

Obtaining registration status information from a staff member of the registrar's office may have aspects of intermediary mode if using the system requires a great deal of technical training or practice. The staff member in this case performs a technical support intermediary role.

The staff assistant role generally does not apply to student registration systems. The purpose of a staff assistant is to save the decision maker's time. Colleges and universities seldom provide students with this type of staff support.

4.8 INSTITUTIONAL VERSUS AD HOC DSS

An important characterization of decision support systems, which will affect how you go about developing and implementing them, is between **institutional** and **ad hoc DSS.**

An institutional DSS is one that is part of the fabric of an organization. It is used regularly, usually by more than one person. Using an institutional DSS becomes part of the way a particular decision is made, and its users cannot usually imagine doing business without it. For example, a system that advertising agency staff members use to compare the cost per exposure of several potential ad media, within a target group defined by age, sex, and income level, would usually be an institutional DSS.

An ad hoc DSS is developed for one-time use, often by a single individual, with the expectation that it will be discarded after the need for it has gone away. Many managers develop such "mini-DSS" using spreadsheet or data management packages.

A system initially developed as an ad hoc DSS may turn out to have a life far beyond its developer's initial expectations. As a personal example, the author of this book developed an ad hoc DSS using a spreadsheet to calculate course grades on the basis of homework, exam, and term project grades. (This is a decision support system, not a decision-making system, as I adjust its preliminary recommendations to reflect class participation and other nonquantifiable factors before submitting grades to the registrar.) I found myself re-creating an essentially identical spreadsheet the following term and eventually developed a template that could be customized to the number of homework assignments, exam weights, and other factors of a given course. I now use this template as a starting point for grading each course. If my colleagues make copies of the template and begin to use it, it will have evolved fully from an ad hoc to an institutional DSS. At that point, all the perils of widespread distribution of any "quick and dirty" software will begin, such as lack of documentation, minimal input validation, poor or nonexistent error messages, and the potential vulnerability of other users to my unplanned departure.

Some DSS have institutional and ad hoc aspects. For example, an organization may create a decision-making database, referred to as a data warehouse in the terminology we'll start using in Chapter 12. It would be an institutional component of a DSS. Individual users might create and save specific queries to that database that they use on a regular basis in their jobs. These would be ad hoc DSS components. The important thing is to understand how each part is used and therefore what its requirements are, not to put the entire system into a pigeonhole.

SUMMARY

Knowing the different types of decision support systems is useful because it enables us to zero in quickly on types of tools and techniques that are likely to be useful with a new problem. DSS can be divided into categories in several ways.

One basic set of categories divides DSS into seven major categories: file drawer systems, data analysis systems, analysis information systems, accounting models, representational models, optimization systems, and suggestion systems.

We can then group these seven DSS categories into three major categories: data-oriented, model-oriented, and process-oriented. Data-oriented DSS include file drawer systems, data analysis systems, and analysis information systems. Model-oriented DSS include accounting models, representational models, optimization systems, and suggestion systems. Optimization and suggestion systems, whose recommendations are based on a human decision-making process rather than on an analysis of an underlying system, are process-oriented DSS.

Different DSS categories help make different types of decisions. Suggestion systems are often well matched to structured decisions. Other types of model-oriented DSS usually fit semistructured decisions well. Data-oriented DSS are most useful with unstructured decisions.

DSS can also be categorized according to whether they support decisions made by one individual, by several individuals whose decisions must show some consistency (multi-individual decisions), or by groups operating as a whole. The benefits to be derived from a DSS depend in large part on its usage modes in this sense.

Different types of DSS suit the needs of people having different personality types. An Introverted person may prefer a group DSS that allows for thinking before responding whereas an Extravert would lean toward interactive discussion. A Sensing person will want greater amounts of data than an intuitive. Both Thinking and Feeling people can use model-oriented DSS, but the Thinker will tend to rely more on its output. Judgment-oriented people will tend to use a data-oriented DSS for a long time, while Perception-oriented people will generally close off its use and make their decision sooner. A further breakdown by combinations of types, or temperaments, can also be valuable in choosing appropriate decision support tools.

Decision support systems can be used in four modes: subscription, terminal, clerk, and intermediary. Intermediary mode may involve staff assistants, technical support staff, and business analysts. Clerk mode is little seen today, but the other three are all appropriate to some decision makers and decision-making situations.

Finally, decision support systems can be designed for one-time (ad hoc) use or for regular, repeated (institutional) use. The expected usage affects the documentation, error handling, user interface, training, and technical support that the DSS must have.

KEY TERMS

accounting model
ad hoc DSS
analysis information system
business analyst
clerk mode (usage)
data analysis system
data-oriented DSS
data warehouse
file drawer system
group DSS
individual DSS
institutional DSS
intermediary mode (usage)
model-oriented DSS
multi-individual DSS
optimization system

process-oriented DSS
representational model
staff assistant
subscription mode (usage)
suggestion system
technical support staff
temperament
terminal mode (usage)
yield management

REVIEW QUESTIONS

1. What are the seven basic DSS categories?
2. Which categories of DSS are considered data-oriented? Which are considered model-oriented?
3. To which type of DSS, in terms of these categories, does the modern concept of a data warehouse correspond?
4. What is a process-oriented DSS? To which DSS categories do they correspond?
5. Which types of DSS are most helpful with structured decisions? With semistructured decisions? With unstructured decisions?
6. Define individual, multi-individual, and group decisions.
7. What DSS benefits are most often associated with individual DSS? With multi-individual DSS? With group DSS?
8. How would the difference between introverted and extroverted personality types affect DSS usage?
9. How would the difference between sensing and intuitive personality types affect DSS usage?
10. How would the difference between thinking and feeling personality types affect DSS usage?
11. How would the difference between judging and perceiving personality types affect DSS usage?
12. What are the four basic DSS usage modes? Give examples, other than the university registration example on page 151.
13. What are the three types of DSS usage intermediaries? What is the benefit of using each?
14. What is the difference between an institutional and an ad hoc DSS? Why does this difference matter?

EXERCISES

1. Consider the examples of DSS in the boxes in Chapter 1. Place each of those examples in the appropriate category per each of Sections 4.1, 4.2, 4.4, 4.7, and 4.8.
2. You work in the admissions office of a selective university. Each year, you and your colleagues have three months (from a mid-January application deadline to mid-April, when applicants are notified) to review about 12,000 application folders and make about 3,000 offers of admission. Each applicant may be accepted, rejected, or deferred (placed on a waiting list for possible acceptance later if fewer students than expected accept the university's offer of admission). Each applicant's folder contains test scores,

secondary school transcript(s), letters of recommendation, applicant essays, lists of activities and honors, and perhaps additional information.

Two admissions officers first read each folder. If they agree, their decision is forwarded to the director. If they disagree, a third reader breaks the tie—and a fourth, if necessary. The director personally reviews, and may reverse, all rejections and deferrals of alumni children, recruited athletes, and applicants from certain ethnic minorities. The director also reviews a random sample of other decisions to check the consistency of decision making by staff members. Suggest how (*a*) a data-oriented DSS, (*b*) a system-model-oriented DSS, and (*c*) a process-oriented DSS could be used to help your office in its work. In each of your three answers—that is, answers to parts (*a*), (*b*), and (*c*)—also state whether your suggested system would be an individual, multi-individual, or group DSS. (It is not necessary to have one DSS from each of these last three categories.)

3. Describe a specific DSS that the admissions office of exercise 2 could use. State which psychological types might tend to work well with that system and which might not. Keep in mind that people of all preferences *can* learn to use the system.

4. Quantify the benefits of each DSS type discussed in the airline yield management example (beginning on page 134) as much as possible. Express your answer in terms of quantities that an airline would be expected to know, such as the number of flights per day, the total salary of its yield management analysts, total revenue on the flights in question, and so on.

5. On page 139 we said that a policy of refusing to sell a low-fare ticket on a multisegment route, if the quota of such tickets has been sold on any of the segments involved, is "probably not optimal." Do you agree? Can you think of a better decision rule? How could your rule be administered with the aid of computer-based DSS?

6. In terms of the DSS benefits listed in Section 1.4, what is the benefit of each step up the DSS hierarchy with the airline yield management DSS beginning on page 134? Does each step contribute to reduced cost, lead to more effective decisions, improve communications, or provide some other benefit?

7. Carry out a literature search, preferably using an automated document retrieval system or a Web search engine, for articles about yield management DSS. How do the systems you found fit into the frameworks discussed in this chapter?

8. Describe how you could apply yield management concepts to promotional rates in the hotel industry.

9. Colleges and universities use yield management in several ways, though they may not call it that. For example, they offer above-normal financial aid—in effect, a lower price—to students who plan to major in unpopular fields, can contribute to athletic success, or have other desirable attributes. Define a DSS that a college financial aid office could use to optimize its allocation of scholarship funds in this sense.

10. You are driving along the road from Newbury to Reading in England when you notice a turnoff to the left indicating the road to Upper Bucklebury. You and your travel companions pull out of traffic to decide whether or not it's worth going to visit that village.
   a. What is the decision statement here?
   b. You probably wouldn't build a DSS to deal with this decision alone, but someone might build one to help with its general category. What is the "general category" of decisions that includes this one and that someone could conceivably build a DSS to help with? What sort of organization do you think might be motivated to develop such as DSS? Why?

     c. List five data elements that will affect your decision. For example, one might be "How much spare time do we have before we have to be somewhere?" (That one doesn't count. List five *more*. You will now have a total of six.)

     d. Describe three possible DSS at three different levels in Alter's hierarchy, not including more than one of the first three levels, that could help with this decision. For each DSS, specify precisely what inputs it would require and what outputs it would provide to its users.

11. Describe how each of the four usage modes (page 149) could apply to a DSS used by the admissions office of exercise 2. For intermediary mode, answer for each of the three types of intermediaries. (All told, you will have six answers.)

12. Reread your answer to exercise 6 of Chapter 1. Then

     a. State if each of the systems you described in your answer to 6(*a*) is an individual, multi-individual, or group DSS.

     b. Draw a copy of Figure 4–8 without the letters in the cells. For each benefit you identified in part (*b*) of that exercise, put a check mark in the cell in the benefit row and the DSS type column. See how closely your pattern of check marks matches the high-moderate-low relationships shown in the figure.

REFERENCES

ALTE80   Alter, Steven L. *Decision Support Systems: Current Practice and Continuing Challenges.* Addison-Wesley, Reading, Mass. (1980).

CORR91   Correa, Arlene. "On-Line Conference," *Digital Review* 8, no. 19 (May 13, 1991), p. 16.

GROS97   Gross, Robert G. *Revenue Management: Hard-Core Tactics for Market Domination.* Broadway Books, BDD, New York (1997).

HIRS90   Hirsh, Sandra Krebs, and Jean M. Kummerow. *Introduction to Type in Organizations.* Consulting Psychologists Press, Palo Alto, Calif. (1990).

HUIT92   Huitt, William G. "Problem Solving and Decision Making: Consideration of Individual Differences Using the Myers-Briggs Type Indicator," *Journal of Psychological Type* 24 (1992), pp. 33–44.

KEIR84   Keirsey, David, and Marilyn Bates. *Please Understand Me: Character and Temperament Types.* Prometheus Nemesis Book Co., Del Mar, Calif. (1984).

PROV90   Provost, Judith A. *Work, Play, and Type.* Consulting Psychologists Press, Palo Alto, Calif. (1990).

SMIT92   Smith, Barry C., John F. Leimkuhler, and Ross M. Darrow. "Yield Management at American Airlines," *Interfaces* 22, no. 1 (January–February 1992), pp. 8–31.

CASE

Fort Lowell Trading Company
Introducing the Finance System to Its Users

Elizabeth and Miguel wore their interview suits to the Fort Lowell Trading Company headquarters the following Tuesday. Ashwin Puri, Director of Application Systems, had invited them to sit in on a meeting between several MIS managers and the corporate finance department. Although they didn't expect to say much, they did want to look their best. They entered the conference room with about a dozen other people, nodded to a few they recognized from earlier meetings, and took seats along the rear wall.

Ashwin opened the meeting, "Thanks to all of you for coming over this afternoon. We're getting ready for a total redesign of the systems that support our finance operations, and we'd like as many people to be involved as possible so we can hear all the viewpoints. We can't promise to satisfy all the requests, of course, but at least we'll listen."

"Sure you will. That's what you said four years ago with the capital planning decision system, and we never did get it!" came an angry voice from the left side of the conference table.

"I didn't say that," he responded calmly. "Four years ago I was implementing our store inventory systems. I didn't have anything to do with the capital planning decision system, or with any other choices in finance systems."

"Yeah, yeah," came the same voice. "You MIS types always change jobs just in time to avoid getting blamed for anything. If someone doesn't like your store inventory system today, whoever's running it now is probably saying, 'I didn't have anything to do with that, I was doing finance systems when they built it.' Your name will never come up. Nobody ever takes any responsibility for a darn thing!"

The two students looked at each other in astonishment. What had they gotten into? Fortunately, the unidentified voice continued in a less angry tone: "OK, I guess it isn't really your fault, but I'm so frustrated. We have to make all these decisions; we know computers can help us make them, but we don't get diddly."

"That's why we're here today," Ashwin responded in a conciliatory tone. "We know we didn't do much for finance as we went through a bunch of other things: the store systems, the Web site, that Year 2000 audit. We didn't have any choice about Year 2000. The calendar forced that one on us. We would have been perfectly happy to stay in the 20th century for a few more years!"

"Now we want to make sure you get a lot more than diddly with your new system. In fact, we even brought in some outside witnesses. I'd like you all to meet two decision support systems students from Sabino Canyon College, Elizabeth and Miguel. They're here to learn what we're doing, not tell us what to do, but they wouldn't be at this meeting if I didn't think we'd be giving you some good decision support tools. That's them at the back of the room."

After pausing to allow a brief glance back by most of the attendees, he continued. "Basically, we're thinking in terms of an integrated system for budgeting and cash flow planning. We'd like to agree on a general concept this afternoon and then flesh it out in individual meetings with a bunch of people over the next couple of weeks. Once we have a fairly good idea of what it would do, we'll be able to attach cost and schedule estimates to it and plan the project."

"What if the cost is too high or the schedule is too long?" asked the same voice that had spoken up earlier, followed by "Yeah, what then?" or the equivalent from several others.

"That's theoretically possible but we don't think it will happen," Ashwin answered. "We checked with three other companies that have databases, systems, and networks pretty much like ours and developed systems like this. Even though they're not department store chains, they all painted a consistent picture of what it took. If we come in anywhere near their figures, we're OK.

"Anyhow," he continued, "I'd like to introduce Vanessa McAnaney. She's going to be the lead systems analyst on this system and the project leader when it gets to that stage—that's *when,* not *if!* Vanessa just joined us from Macy's, where she worked on a system very much like what we have in mind. I can promise you this: if we weren't serious about building this system, we wouldn't have hired her and paid for her move to Tucson."

"Thank you, Ashwin," said Vanessa as she took his place by the overhead projector at the head of the table. "I'd like to start with the decision support aspects of the new system, since it seems that's what you're most interested in. We can talk about the budgeting, the database, and all the other parts later. OK?"

As several people nodded or mumbled agreement, Vanessa put an overhead slide [Figure 4–10] on the projector.

FIGURE 4–10 FLTC's Finance DSS

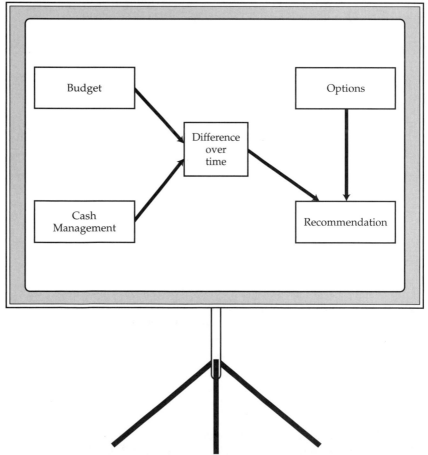

"The key decision we're concerned with is raising cash. The budgeting subsystem, which runs both an accrual budget and a cash budget in parallel, tells us what we need and what we expect to take in from operations. The cash management subsystem tells us what we have. Actually, calling it a 'cash management' subsystem is selling it a bit short; it can track any kind of financial asset. It just has to know how long it takes to turn the asset into cash and how much we should allow for value fluctuations. I mean, if we wanted to treat this building as a possible source of funds for operations, the system could do it.

"So," she continued, "the system will tell us how much cash we need and when. If it looks like we'll come up short, it lets us look at the options. You know, the usual ones: draw down our line of credit, etc., etc. Issuing new stock isn't an option because we're not publicly traded. On the other hand, we can do things because we're a store that some other types of companies can't do. For instance, we can run a special sale and turn some inventory into cash in a hurry. That has its downside, like the goods might sell for more if we held onto them for a while, but it's on the list."

"At the concept level, that sounds like what we need," said one of the participants from finance. "Of course, we'll have to see more of it. I do have a question: Where does it get its data about sources of cash?"

"In the first pass we'll have to input them by hand," Vanessa conceded. "We're building in hooks to pull prime rates off the 'Net and get current rates from each bank we've got a line of credit with, but that's down the road. We don't want to have to check out all those links for the first time with a brand-new system."

"Now," she continued as she pointed to the underlined word at the bottom right of the overhead, "this is how the decision support system ties into the budgeting part. To go into a bit more detail, here's how that's going to work." She paused briefly as she changed overheads on the projector.

About an hour later, as the meeting was breaking up, Ashwin brought Vanessa over to where Elizabeth and Miguel were seated. "Vanessa," he said, "you'll probably be spending some time with these two good people over the next few months, so it might be a good idea to meet them now."

"Thank you, Ashwin," she said. "Very pleased to meet both of you. Tell me, what did you think of our session today?"

The two students hesitated. Finally Miguel broke the silence with "Parts of it were a bit different from what we expected."

"I bet they were!" she agreed. "I was warned before I took the job—Ashwin and Dottie were totally open with me that way. It must have caught you by surprise, though. We need the system, but it might have been put off a year if those folks didn't scream as loud as they did. Real decisions are a lot more impacted by personal issues than the average business school textbook lets on."

EXERCISES

1. Write a clear decision statement for one important decision with which the new system will help.

2. Define, briefly, five DSS that could help FLTC make this decision. Put each into one of the seven DSS categories. If you don't have one in at least every other category—that is, if two adjacent categories are both empty—define another DSS for one of them. (You don't have to be an expert on finance to answer this question, though you should use the material from your introductory courses in it.)

3. Which of the DSS in your answer to exercise 2 do you think would be the most useful to FTLC in practice? Why? For this DSS,
   • Would this be an individual, multi-individual, or group DSS (page 144)?
   • What would be its usage mode (page 149)?
   • What would be its major benefits (page 145)?

4. At the end of this episode Vanessa stated that the real world is more influenced by personal factors, such as the anger and frustration of the anonymous complainer in this episode, than business school courses suggest. Do you agree? Why or why not?

PART II

BUILDING AND IMPLEMENTING DECISION SUPPORT SYSTEMS

CHAPTER 5

DSS Architecture, Hardware, and Operating System Platforms

Introduction

Computer applications run in an environment that includes hardware and an operating system. Decision support systems are no exception. If you will be involved in planning a DSS, you will have to choose the environment in which it will run. At the overall level, this means defining its architecture. Within the architecture, you will have to choose among mainframes, minicomputers, and microcomputers plus several other options. Your choices will differ in their hardware and in the operating systems they use. You will also have to consider different approaches to linking several computers and to sharing the workload. Each choice has its pros and cons. Picking the right one combination can help make your DSS more responsive and successful. Picking the wrong one can help it fail.

Even if you will be using a DSS planned and developed by others, it helps to know what you can expect from its architecture and the resulting hardware/operating system/networking environment. This chapter will tell you about the major environments in which DSS run.

CHAPTER OBJECTIVES

After you have read and studied this chapter, you will be able to:

1. Explain the importance of an information systems architecture.
2. Describe the DSS architecture and identify the factors you should consider in planning it.
3. Describe the types of hardware environments used for decision support systems.
4. Outline the advantages and disadvantages of each type of hardware environment.
5. Explain what a data warehouse is and why it is useful in DSS.
6. Explain why client/server computing is popular.
7. Describe why the use of open systems is increasing.
8. Explain why DSS are often the reason an organization moves to open systems.
9. Discuss how downsizing figures in the choice of hardware/software platforms.
10. Outline several factors to consider in selecting a hardware/software environment for a decision support system.

5.1 DEFINING THE DSS ARCHITECTURE

An important issue to consider before planning individual systems is developing an overall enterprise **information systems architecture.** The **architecture** of an information system refers to the way its pieces are laid out, what types of tasks are allocated to each piece, how the pieces interact with each other, and how they interact with the outside world.

Information system architecture is a high-level concept. The architecture does not specify that a Compaq Model XYZ will be installed in each purchasing agent's office, that the manufacturing local area network (LAN) will support 17 users, or that a market planning model will become operational in June 2002. The following definition of an information systems architecture, from [MART91], applies well to DSS:

> A written expression of the desired future for information use and management in an organization, that creates the context within which people can make consistent decisions.

The intent of an information systems architecture, whether for decision support systems or for any other information systems, is to achieve the following:

- Interoperability of systems, so that information can be brought to the point of use quickly and easily.
- Compatibility of systems, so that resources can be shared easily and leveraged across the organization.

• Expandability of systems, so that limited single-function components do not create bottlenecks that obstruct the growth of the organization.

An information system architecture corresponds to a city master plan. The plan estimates future needs and builds on those estimates. It lays out areas for homes, shopping, and industry; indicates what type of roadways will be needed and approximately where; and suggests when infrastructure elements such as sewage treatment facilities will need expansion. But it does not state that a two-family house will be built next September at 120 Elm Street or that parking along Oak Street will be limited to one hour on weekdays from 9 A.M. to 6 P.M. A city plan could, however, specify that Elm Street is zoned for single-family homes on plots of not less than 10,000 square feet (about 1,000 square meters). Such a zoning law forces the building at No. 17 to fit into an appropriate framework without constraining its details. This is what an information systems architecture is supposed to do.

For city zoning to work, it must reflect the needs of all segments of the city. It is possible to restrict certain parts of a city to single-family homes on 10,000 square feet (about 1,000 square meters) or more. However, it is not practical to limit an entire city to such buildings. Modern life requires stores, factories, offices, and (though perhaps not within the city) farms. Reality tells us that many people cannot afford that type of residence. Similarly, an information systems architecture must reflect the needs of all users in the organization. It must balance the desire for instant access to every byte of data with financial realities. It must be practical for today's technology without unduly constraining the future. It must be specific enough to guide system developers, yet flexible enough to meet needs not yet foreseen and adapt to technologies not yet predicted. All in all, a tall order.

Having a well-defined and well-communicated decision support system architecture provides an organization with significant benefits. Nontechnical benefits include the ability to create a common vision that keeps all project participants working in tandem, the ability to communicate system concepts to management (leading to a greater likelihood that their expectations will be met), the ability to communicate needs to potential vendors, and the ability of other groups to implement systems that must work with this DSS. Technical benefits of a DSS architecture include the ability to plan systems in an effective and coordinated fashion and to evaluate technology options within a context of how they will work rather than abstractly. Achieving all these benefits requires that both IS professionals and prospective system users—who, after all, are the ones who understand the problems that the system is to help solve—must cooperate closely in developing the architecture.

The overall architecture of a DSS should be laid out and understood before specific hardware and software selection decisions are made. The nature of this architecture depends on the DSS. Mini-DSS developed by individuals for their own use do not justify an architectural planning effort, though the overall IS architecture of the organization may determine some aspects of how and where they fit into the picture. Enterprisewide DSS do require careful advance planning if they are to succeed.

To lay out a DSS architecture you must consider the spectrum of DSS that your organization will use. To do this systematically, you should consider:

- Strategic, tactical (management control), and operational decisions.
- Unstructured, semistructured, and structured decisions.
- All levels of management and knowledge workers in the organization.
- All major functional, product or line of business, and geographic divisions of the organization.

If your DSS architecture allows for needs in all these categories, it will be sufficiently comprehensive and robust to stand the test of time. Your DSS architecture must reflect the following elements:

- Its database or databases, including any existing databases, internal or external to the organization, and any databases that are created specifically for DSS use. The architecture should state who is responsible for different types of databases—at the personal, departmental, and enterprise levels—for ensuring their accuracy, currency, and security.
- Its model or models, including information about their sources of data, the organizational responsibility for maintaining them, limits on access to them, and so forth. It may not be practical to specify every individual model at the initial stages, but it should be possible to define the major categories.
- Its users, including any assumptions about their locations, jobs, levels of education, and any other factor that may affect their use of the DSS. "Location" in this context means both geographic location, type of working environment (office, factory, construction site, home, truck cab, and so on) and any other factors that will affect the delivery of decision support system services to those users.
- Software tools through which the users access the database and the models. Some of these, especially for simple database queries, may be provided by the database package itself. Others may be developed or obtained separately. One major category of software tool that will require careful consideration is on-line analytical processing software for accessing a data warehouse. We'll discuss this type of software in detail in Section 13.1.
- Software tools through which system administrators manage the database and the models, again over and above those provided by their underlying platforms.
- Hardware and operating system platforms, at a generic level, on which the databases and models reside, on which the programs run, and through which users access the DSS. Any constraints, such as a policy to standardize on products of a given vendor or products that use a given operating system, should be stated here, with due allowance for upgrades to both hardware and software as technology evolves.
- Networking and communication capabilities through which these platforms are interconnected. These must reflect individual needs to connect to one or more servers and databases, workgroup needs to communicate within each group, and enterprise needs to link workgroups to each other, to shared data, and perhaps to

customers or to external databases. If it is the intent to standardize on one or two of several alternative technologies—for example, in high-speed LAN connections to the desktop—this should be specified here.

In many DSS situations the interconnection mechanism will simply be the corporate network, either an existing one or one that is planned within an overall corporate information systems architecture. Should this be the case it must be examined to make sure it meets present and future DSS needs, because those may not have been foreseen when the network concepts were first defined.

- The culture of the organization that will use the DSS. If its culture is centralized, it may be acceptable (or even desirable) to have a central database, a central library for models with central control over its contents, and systemwide standardization on one or a few software packages of each major type. If its culture is decentralized, it may be more appropriate to give each part of the organization control over its own information resources, with provision for sharing or merging where this is called for. Similar considerations apply to user versus MIS control of these resources and of the uses to which they are put.

The content of the information technology architecture is deepening with time because more and more capabilities are being included in the platforms upon which applications are built. In the early days of computers one bought bare hardware. Then computers were sold with operating systems, but users were still responsible for programming their own data management capabilities. Packages have handled that need since the 1980s, but now computers come with built-in or added-on capabilities for networking, electronic mail, three-dimensional graphics, and other features. The amount of application software is not decreasing because new types of applications are always being developed, but the number and complexity of the functions that are considered part of the architecture is increasing steadily.

Figure 5–1 shows a generic view of a DSS architecture. Figure 5–2 shows a specific DSS architecture. Both diagrams must, of course, be supplemented by a great deal of explanatory text. The general elements of Figure 5–1 have become more specific in Figure 5–2, though not to the point of constraining the designers of specific DSS unduly or limiting the use of as-yet-unknown technologies and products. If this architecture meets the needs of its sponsoring organization, we can conclude certain things about that organization: for example, it has a centralized culture; it exercises a great deal of management control. It is, however, open to new technologies, since it has standardized on some fairly recent ones. This is typical: no one DSS will have all the elements of a "standard" DSS in precisely the average proportions.

Developing an overall DSS architecture is not the work of a few minutes, or even a few hours. The architecture must be specific enough to guide future system design but flexible enough to accommodate new technologies. It must accommodate today's needs and tomorrow's as well. It may take many weeks of work on the part of many people to come up with it. Once it is defined, additional effort may be required to modify or replace (over time) existing systems that are inconsistent with the new concepts.

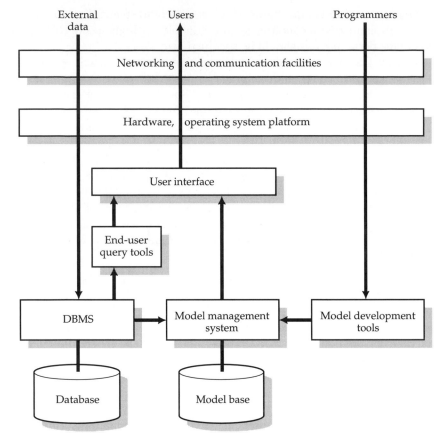

FIGURE 5–1   **Conceptual DSS Architecture**

The rest of this chapter discusses some of the major architectural options as they apply to decision support systems—first in general, then in more detail

5.2 THE MAJOR OPTIONS

The term **platform** refers to the combined hardware/operating system environment that supports the applications, which for our purposes are decision support systems. DSS can run on several types of platforms.

1. The central corporate system.
2. The central system linked to other computers on users' desktops via a network—an internal corporate network, the Internet, or an intranet (an internal network using Internet-based user interfaces).
3. A separate system that obtains data from the central system and provides it to users, again usually over a network.
4. A freestanding system at the user's desk.
5. A combination of the above.

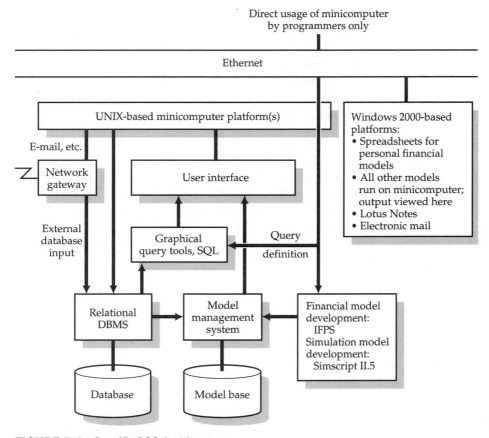

FIGURE 5-2 Specific DSS Architecture

Each approach has several possible variations, and each also has its advantages and disadvantages. The following sections discuss the major approaches. In reading them, keep in mind that there are gray areas between any of the approaches. Systems that follow any of them cleanly, purely, and totally are the exception.

5.3 DSS ON THE CENTRAL CORPORATE SYSTEM

Virtually every medium-sized or larger organization, and every major division of large organizations, has a central computer system. These systems run operational transaction-based applications such as accounting, order entry, and time billing. They also often run strategic applications such as electronic data interchange with customers or facilities for rapid inquiry into the status of critical orders. Such central multiuser systems usually use an integrated database management system for the organization's important information.

The hardware platform of a central multiuser system is usually a mainframe or a large minicomputer. Transaction processing users usually access the system through terminals or via desktop microcomputers equipped with a terminal emulation package. (Accessing it via microcomputers, which function as computers in their own right, and handle part of the application, is called *client/server computing*. This is a separate topic we will cover on page 171.)

Given that the central shared system already exists, it is tempting to put new applications on it. This is therefore where most new corporate applications are expected to run. **Capacity planners** monitor the central system's load as new applications are developed and as the user community grows. They watch items such as its response time statistics, the amount of disk storage space remaining available for future use, and communication line usage. Using mathematical tools (based on concepts we'll discuss in Chapters 8 and 9), they predict how the system will perform as its load increases. When they see that response time or capacity will become inadequate, they decide how best to improve the system. The required changes may be as simple as adding another disk drive or more main memory. They may be as inexpensive as swapping files among drives in order to balance those drives' loads more evenly. At the other extreme, it may be time for a complete system replacement.

Where total replacement is called for, the new system chosen is usually a larger model of the same family as the old. Exceptions arise when the system being outgrown is the largest model of its product line (so no larger model exists), where the product line has become obsolete, where changes in the nature of the workload make it no longer suitable, or where new and more desirable types of systems have come into use since it was originally selected. As soon as the system expansion, upgrade, or replacement is complete, the load-monitoring process resumes until the new system itself becomes inadequate.

If corporate applications are generally put on the central system, and if this mode of regular load increases and upgrades are considered normal, a new DSS can be put on the central system as well. Doing so has both advantages and disadvantages.

Advantages of Using the Central System

1. MIS staff members are already familiar with the system.
2. Many users already know how the system works. (All users are not created equal. Even when a system is used widely within an organization, this point is irrelevant unless the individuals who are to use the proposed DSS are familiar with it.)
3. The necessary hardware (terminals, communication links) to use the system is already in place in the organization. (As with the previous point, being in the organization overall is less important than being available to the specific managers and professionals who will use the proposed DSS.)
4. DSS applications can access the central database directly for up-to-date information, as they reside on the same system and run in the same programming environment.
5. The processing power of a large system can run complex DSS, such as large simulation models, thousand-rule expert systems, or massive information retrieval tasks, in acceptable elapsed times. (The rapidly increasing power of

desktop computers, which you can read about in the daily newspaper and probably studied in your introductory MIS course, makes this less of an issue every year [or week].)

6. Most large systems have a variety of available DSS tools such as 4GLs, database managers, simulation packages, expert system shells, and EIS (executive information system; see page 476) software.

Disadvantages of Using the Central System

1. The central system was probably not originally selected for DSS applications and may not be well suited to them. This applies to the hardware and to the systems software, including the operating system, database manager, and so forth. Mainframe operating systems are often optimized for efficiency and throughput where DSS need interactivity and responsiveness.

2. The cost of additional resources to run a DSS may exceed the cost of smaller computers to handle the same task. Much of the cost of a mainframe goes to its ability to move massive amounts of data quickly and to be shared effectively by many users. These capabilities are vital to transaction processing but are often of marginal value to DSS.

3. There may be a tendency to force unsuitable software tools into DSS use, rather than getting suitable ones, because they are already there. This is especially true of database management systems. Many central corporate systems today use either hierarchical or network database structures. As we'll see in the next chapter, these are less suitable for DSS than other, more modern, database structures.

4. DSS responsiveness may be impacted by other loads on the system. It may be organizationally unacceptable to give the DSS users a high enough priority for system resources to avoid this problem, because doing so could degrade the system's responsiveness on the applications that justified buying it in the first place.

5. DSS users may have to wait in line behind other application development efforts. As with the previous point, this is in principle under management control, but the reality of the situation may put other projects first.

6. The user interface of most large systems is not as easy for nontechnical people to use ("user-friendly," in the vernacular of the 1990s) as that of most smaller systems. The operating system tends to be command-oriented and designed for close control of the system by a professional programmer. Graphical user interfaces, such as many desktop systems offer, are often nonexistent or do not provide full access to the system's capabilities.

7. Support for graphics may be poor. Even if an application can handle graphics, existing terminals may be alphanumeric, and existing communication links may not be up to the increased load of graphs and images.

5.4 DSS AND CLIENT/SERVER COMPUTING

Many organizations deal with the aforementioned disadvantages by providing individual users, via their desktop computers, with access to data on the central computer. The desktop computers then handle the computations and other processes of a DSS. These processes usually include supporting the usual elements of today's easy-to-use graphical user interfaces, such as windows, pull-down menus, and the use of a mouse or other pointing device.

This approach is referred to as **client/server computing.**[1] The system storing the database is called a **server.** The server system, in this example, acts as a data repository. The **client** system, typically on the user's desktop, runs the application using data from the server. The result is a close matching of each partner's capabilities to its role in the overall system.

The term *client/server* describes any situation in which an application is partitioned to run on two or more systems of different capabilities, using each to best advantage. Many people are familiar with small LAN versions of client/server: Using a print server to share a color laser printer among several client PCs, or using a file server to eliminate the need for each PC to have its own copy of all application programs are examples.[2] The variations of client/server computing, most of which can be useful in DSS, fall along the spectrum of Figure 5–3.

Using a LAN doesn't necessarily indicate client/server computing. For instance, the server (here called a **file server**) could be used essentially as a large, shared disk drive. It sends, or downloads, files on request to the individual user systems on the network. Those systems carry out all the processing. If they have modified the file, they send the modified version back to the server when they are done. (This requires some coordination, either at the server or via suitable user procedures, to make sure one user's changes don't overwrite another's.) Although useful systems can be built to operate in this mode, they don't qualify as client/server; these systems fall above the top of the bracket that defines client/server computing in Figure 5–3 because the desktop system is responsible for the entire application. This approach doesn't incorporate task sharing, which is the hallmark of true client/server computing.

If we were to draw a picture of almost any information system as a system, we would put the database at one end and the user interface at the other. Every approach to client/server computing stores the data in the server and provides the user interface via the client. The rest of the application, which lies between user interaction on the one hand and physical access to disk records on the other, can be on either computer. At one extreme, the application logic is on the server and the client does little more than display results on a screen. At the other extreme, the client could ask for individual file records as it needs them and carry out all the processing itself. Most approaches to client/server computing fall between these two extremes. The precise point at which to divide a job depends on the following major factors:

---

[1]The term *client/server* is always written with a slash—not a hyphen, space, or other separator.
[2]This statement refers to physical copies of the software, which occupy disk space, must be upgraded when a new release comes out, etc. Firms must usually purchase a license for each concurrent user, or a "site license" for all users at a given location, even if one physical copy is installed on a server and shared via a LAN. Software vendors offer a variety of licensing plans to meet the needs of different types and sizes of organizations.

Free-standing personal computers

Disk server provides shared mass
storage managed by client systems

File server transfers shared files to
client systems on request

Database server transfers selected
records to clients on request

Client/
server
computing
can be
any of
these

Database server processes requests,
returns selected records to clients

Cooperative application processing:
server sends intermediate results to
clients

Server carries out calculations, sends
results to clients to format and present

Server formats results and sends
screen description to client to display

"Dumb" terminals on shared,
multiuser computer

FIGURE 5–3 Client/Server Computing Spectrum

- *The computing power relationship between the two systems.* If the server is a microcomputer much like the clients, it is probably desirable to push as much work as possible onto the clients. If the server is a powerful minicomputer, a multiprocessor "supermicro," or a mainframe, and the clients are low-end desktop machines, it is probably appropriate for the server to handle most of the work unless it is burdened by supporting a very large number of client systems. The increasing power of desktop systems, mentioned previously as a decreasing advantage of central systems, affects this decision factor as well.
- *The load pattern.* If DSS usage is frequent and regular throughout the day, it is a good idea to give each user sufficient power for his or her needs. If it is more sporadic, putting the bulk of the computation on a shared central system can yield savings without impacting system responsiveness. That will give each user access to the power of the server when needed without having expensive high-end systems sit idle on users' desktops during long periods of inactivity. (There will be occasional slowdowns, when several users attempt to run a complex query at the same time, but these will be statistically rare.)

• *Minimizing communication needs.* The time it takes to communicate requests and responses between the client and the server is a common bottleneck in client/server systems. The most efficient division of labor is often the one that minimizes the need to communicate between the two parts. Thus, approaches that send an entire file to the desktop of a person who wishes to access it, although simple to program at the server end, may not be as efficient as approaches in which the server selects the records of interest and sends only them.

Client/server approaches where the client does most of the work, relying on the server only to supply it with raw data, are often referred to as **fat client** approaches. In the other direction, a client system that does little more than provide a user interface to results provided by the server is often called a **thin client.** These terms can be used to describe either the way an application is designed to work or the capability of a client, in terms of processing power, RAM size, and other measures, to take on more than the user interface of a task.

Clients and servers need not be in a one-to-one relationship. Servers are usually designed to provide one, or a limited number, of services. They offer these services to many clients. Clients, on their side, can request service from many different servers. Figure 5–4 shows a system with several clients making requests and several servers, located on two local area networks, satisfying them.

We began this section as a transition from mainframe computing by suggesting that the mainframe need not do all the work—that microcomputers connected to it could do much of it themselves. The server need not, however, be a mainframe. Indeed, one of the prime attractions of client/server computing is the savings in hardware cost that can be achieved if a mainframe is replaced by a much less expensive computer. Even if desktop computers aren't in place for any other reason, the savings obtained by replacing a mainframe by one or more small servers can more than make up for the cost of replacing all the terminals with desktop systems and the cost of installing LANs. In today's environment, when desktop computers and LANs are a "given" in most firms, the savings that can be achieved by using them fully are even greater. (Before spending these savings, though, read the drawbacks of client/server computing later in this section.)

Client/server computing describes the way software works, not the hardware on which the software runs. You can't go out and buy a "client/server computer" in the same way that you can buy a microcomputer or a workstation. You can buy the hardware elements of a client/server system, of course. You can even buy a system designed with the expectation that it will be used as a server, optimized for that use, and having the word *server* in its name. But this system isn't a server until it is connected to clients. No law of physics, logic, or computing restricts the server role to computers so designed and designated by their manufacturers, or that prevents computers designed and designated as servers from being used for something else. The term *client/server* refers to the way computers cooperate to get a job done overall. By contrast, a supercomputer (for example) is a supercomputer no matter how it's used or what it's used for.

By analogy, you can't buy a taxicab from a car dealer. You can buy the hardware elements of a taxicab, of course. You can even buy a car designed with the

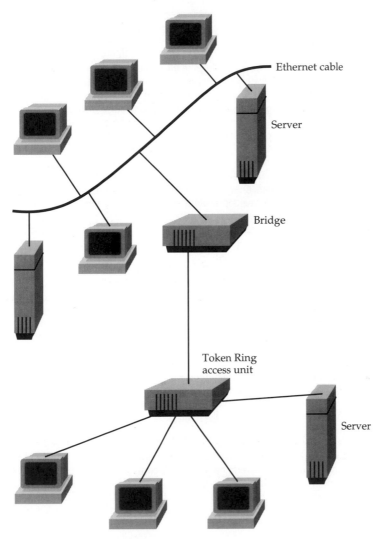

FIGURE 5–4 Client/Server Network

expectation that it will be used as a taxicab, optimized for that use, and having the words *taxi package* in its option list. But this car isn't a taxicab until it is licensed by local authorities and made available to the public for hire. No law of physics, logic, or motor vehicle usage restricts the taxicab role to cars so designed and designated by their manufacturers, or that prevents cars designed and designated as taxis from being used for something else. The term *taxi* refers to the way a car is used to provide transportation services for hire. By contrast, a minivan, for example, is a minivan no matter how it's used or what it's used for.

D&B Goes Client/Server

Dun & Bradstreet (D & B) Software is a large (over $500 million revenue per year) supplier of mainframe software for manufacturing, financial, and human resource applications, and has been part of Geac Computer Corporation since 1996. Under this name and the previous names of its constituent organizations, McCormack & Dodge and Management Science America, D&B Software earned the reputation of a "mainframe only" firm. Yet they responded to the trend to client/server computing by announcing a set of products of this type. These products work by downloading data to a relational database server on a local area network. Users at client workstations can then access this database for decision support purposes.

The D&B package includes three components: Financial Stream Analysis, InterQ, and SmartStream. Financial Stream Analysis is, as its name suggests, a tool for analyzing financial data. It runs on the client desktop system and lets users compile data into a variety of graph, bar, and pie charts for analysis.

At the other end of the application, InterQ creates links between the server and the central database that supports the client/server tools. Part of InterQ runs on the server, part on the IBM or compatible mainframe system.

Between the two, SmartStream is a workflow automation tool, which allows users to collect data from several sources automatically for their analysis. SmartStream can obtain data from D&B's mainframe financial and accounting applications, from other mainframe databases, and from public information services such as Dow Jones and CompuServe, forwarding the collection to users when it is complete. SmartStream can be programmed to compile and deliver data at preset times or after specific events. SmartStream is not restricted to supporting Financial Stream Analysis: Users can also opt to enter its data into their own server-based or client-based application software.

The client/server approach has several benefits in this application. It augments the financial data managed by the mainframe application by adding data from complementary sources, it reduces the mainframe cycles required to access this data, it improves query response time to users, and it makes it possible to analyze the data via well-known and easy-to-use microcomputer-based tools.

A complete package of all three tools to support 10 users is priced at $99,000. Additional services such as planning and training could increase this figure substantially. The SmartStream server can use any of several network operating systems that use Intel 80X86-family hardware. The initial client software supports MS-DOS/Windows. D&B is extending the software package to additional servers, additional clients, and additional application areas.

Advantages of Using a Client/Server System

1. Client/server computing allows each part of an overall application to run in a hardware/software environment optimized for that part and that part alone, whether it demands a large database, high-speed computing, or high-resolution color graphics. This optimization tends to minimize the overall cost of the system.
2. Potential cost savings in hardware are possible with this approach because many small computers cost less than one large computer and terminals to support the same user community.
3. The modular nature of the system simplifies expansion. Clients can be added to the network or upgraded independently of the server(s). The server(s) can be upgraded without affecting the clients.

4. Because the client/server approach is increasingly popular, many applications and software development tools are designed to run in a client/server environment. Organizations can often reduce development time and cost by using these.

Disadvantages of Using a Client/Server System

1. The complexities of application development and management are much greater in a client/server system than they are on a single computer.
2. The tools to support system administration, security, resource accounting, and other management control aspects of client/server computing are not, as of 1999, as fully developed as those for large-scale multiuser computers—though this situation is improving rapidly and is far better than it was even a few years ago.
3. The MIS staff must be familiar with two systems. (This means expertise in both must exist in the organization. It does not mean that individual staff members must know both.) In addition, some staff members may need a third set of skills to link the two.
4. Security becomes a major concern. Whenever users access critical corporate data over a network, system developers must be sensitive to the possibility of unwanted access as well. Security features, perhaps including firewalls to limit access from outside the organization, are an added level of complexity. These features also increase the overall cost in several ways: the cost of the security software, the cost of people to install it and manage its use, and the cost of additional hardware resources to run it.
5. Hardware savings tend to be eaten up in higher end-user support costs arising from the fact that the client environment is more varied and more complex than the terminal environment of a multiuser computer. In total, most adopters of client/server computing find that it is not significantly less expensive—if at all—than the centralized environment it replaced. Indeed, since that central environment was usually several years old at the time of the replacement, it is often possible to save as much or more simply by modernizing it.

5.5 THE INTERNET AND CLIENT/SERVER COMPUTING IN DSS

As you know, the **Internet** is a giant worldwide information source. The **World Wide Web,** especially, provides easy access to information on a wealth of topics. Much of this information can be useful for decision making. It is possible to take this same technology and this same interface and use them to access a corporate DSS. The Web architecture, the **HyperText Markup Language (HTML)** for developing Web pages, the **Java** language that most browsers can interpret, the **JavaScript** language for commands added to HTML, and the standards that Web browsers must follow define, in effect, a **platform** for applications. DSS can use this platform so that any user with a Web browser can access those DSS easily.

Of course, one doesn't always want any user with a Web browser to access a corporate DSS. MacDonald's doesn't want Wendy's or Burger King—or real estate speculators—to access the systems it uses to select desirable restaurant sites, either to learn what they are planning or to plant spurious data. General Motors likewise doesn't want Ford or Daimler Chrysler accessing the customer survey data it uses to choose next year's color choices. To prevent this from happening, Web sites can be protected via lists of authorized users and passwords. Another technology that can help here is an **intranet:** an internal corporate network, not accessible from outside the firm's internal communication net, which uses the familiar Web interfaces in presenting its data and programs to end users.

A **network computer (NC)** is the limiting step in the direction of thin clients (see page 174). A network computer amounts to a single-function computer that can access the Internet (and specifically the World Wide Web), can run programs written in Java or another Internet-based language that it downloads from the 'Net, but has no freestanding computing capability of its own. Network computers provide many of the same advantages as terminals on multiuser computers—low hardware cost, central control over applications, reduced end-user support costs—with the widely familiar and easy-to-use Web browser user interface. The suitability of a network computer for decision support applications depends on the same factors (see the bulleted list on pages 173–174) that determine the suitability of a thin client for the application.

Advantages of Using the Web as a Server

1. One need not be at one's office to use the Web. It is accessible from anywhere in the industrialized world. Travelers at hotel rooms, headquarters personnel visiting a branch office or vice versa, salespeople at customer sites—even vacationers who stop into an "Internet café"—can access the application as if they were at their desk.
2. The Web can be accessed via any type of hardware one happens to have. If some members of an organization prefer Windows on their desktop, others opt for the Mac OS, and still others want UNIX, Linux, or a home TV set attachment, all can still share the same applications.
3. End users know how to use the Web. Every U.S. college student studying business, most U.S. high school students studying anything, and millions of library visitors have used it for many different reasons. Putting a DSS application on the Web requires little or no training in the computer aspects of that application. (The need for training in the DSS itself has little to do with the platform it's on, and may still be required.)

Disadvantages of Using the Web as a Server

1. Web access can be slow, especially over standard modems and telephone lines. The hardware and communication links needed to provide fast access may be more expensive than local area networks for use within an office complex.
2. Web site design and DSS design are separate skills. Both are required for an effective Web-based DSS. Graphics, frequently added to Web pages to improve their appearance, can take a long time to load without contributing meaningfully to application content. Web site developers, who access development pages on

fast workstations over speedy local links or directly from disk files, often do not realize how long it takes those same pages to load in the typical user environment. (Some Web development tools provide a running update of typical Web page loading time on the screen as the page is being laid out, but seeing "24 seconds" in a corner of a screen does not have the same impact as waiting for those 24 seconds to go by when one would rather get on with one's work.)

3. Many Web users pay for access by the minute, making regular or repeated access expensive. Even when users enjoy flat-rate pricing or (in the corporate environment) effectively zero incremental cost for additional usage, heavy use can load down internal networks and access points, impacting everyone's response times and forcing expensive system upgrades.

4. Serving a given number of users with a Web-based or Weblike application requires a more powerful (hence more expensive) server than would be required to provide those same users with the data they need to run a conventional client/server equivalent.

5. Java, the most common language for developing applications to run on Web clients, does not provide good performance. For one thing, it is usually interpreted (in order to run on multiple platforms) rather than compiled into machine code. For another, the standardization of arithmetic results under Java requires interpreters to avoid the built-in scientific processors of modern desktop computers, performing those operations in software instead to reach what is usually, for all practical purposes, the same answer.

5.6 DSS USING SHARED DATA ON A SEPARATE SYSTEM

It is not necessary for the server in a client/server system to be the central corporate computer that stores the live, operational database. It is often a good idea to extract meaningful decision support data from the operational database and load it into a different computer. That second computer can then be accessed directly via terminals, or can act as a server in the client/server computing model.

The new system can range from a microcomputer to a "supermini." The choice depends on the required capacity, the required software tools, and the number of concurrent users. If the DSS is to be used by more than one person, minicomputers or multiprocessor servers are popular choices.

The linked-system approach is effective when the application allows for a decision support database that is separate from the firm's transaction-processing database. As you know, such a database is often called a **data warehouse**—a subject you'll read about in more detail starting in Chapter 12. There are several reasons why an organization might want to separate its decision support data from its transaction data. These include

- To use a database structure that is well suited for decision support applications, whereas its corporate database is in a different one for transaction processing.
- To consolidate data from two or more existing databases, when it would be too difficult to merge them into a single database. (Perhaps each supports a separate set of existing applications, which would require conversion to use a common database.)

- Along the same lines, to incorporate external data into the DSS database.
- To avoid overloading the computer that houses the existing database with the incremental DSS workload.
- To accommodate different security requirements for accessing the two types.
- To take a "snapshot" of the operational database to use as a common basis for decision making while the operational database continues to change.

Using two databases doesn't have to mean using two computers. Of the preceding six reasons, only the fourth argues for a second computer. A firm can put two DBMS on its central computer, and transfer data within that computer from the transaction processing database to the data warehouse database. However, the additional resources—RAM, disk space, processing power, and so forth—that the central system would require in order to accommodate both databases, the DSS application, and its users often cost more than a smaller dedicated computer with the required capacity. Organizations in this situation therefore often opt for a separate computer to hold their data warehouse or other DSS database. They update the data warehouse by downloading selected portions of the operational database from the central computer to the DSS computer every day, week, or month, according to the type of data and users' information needs. Communication links are normally used for this transfer, though in some situations magnetic tape is a suitable medium. The data warehouse then makes this data available to the DSS. Figure 5–5 shows this approach.

When a data warehouse combines data from two or more sources located on different computers—the second of the preceding six reasons—it can't possibly reside on the same computer as all of them. Since there's no real advantage to being on the same computer as one of them (procedures for data transfer among systems will still be needed for all the others), it usually makes more sense to use a separate data warehouse server in that case as well.

Client systems at the users' desks then access the data warehouse on that server. The clients carry out much of the data analysis and other processing. Major suppliers of relational database management systems and of data warehousing products (which we'll discuss in more depth later in this book) all support a client/server split between the back end of their products, which manages the database itself, and their various 4GL, query, analysis, and report writer front ends. The client part of the application, running on the user's desktop, accepts users' requests for information or analysis. It converts the requests, if necessary, to a form in which the server can understand them, and transmits them to the server system. The server responds by sending only the necessary data to the client. The client then carries out any further processing that the application requires.

Because corporate data warehouses tend to be large—tens of gigabytes up to several terabytes—the servers required are correspondingly large. Multiprocessors, which harness the power of two to several dozen processors to a single overall task, are useful here because they increase the computing power of a system beyond that of a single processor without requiring the expensive technologies used in mainframes or supercomputers. Some multiprocessors are general-purpose machines, originally developed as extensions of desktop product lines or as larger

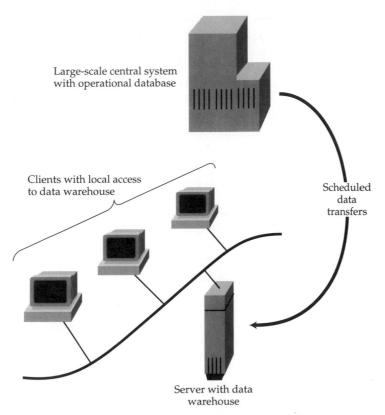

Large-scale central system
with operational database

Clients with local access
to data warehouse

Scheduled
data
transfers

Server with data
warehouse

FIGURE 5–5 Three-tier System with Operational Database, Data Warehouse, and Clients

systems. Others are designed as specialized **database computers.** These function
in effect as very large, fast, and intelligent disk drives, and must be used in conjunction with a general-purpose computer to create a complete server or information system. A smaller "data mart," by contrast, could run on a smaller server,
often a high-end microcomputer equipped with server software.

A data warehouse is a read-only database. Its users cannot update the "live" organizational information. (They can update the contents of the data warehouse, if
application software permits them to do so, but updating the data warehouse does
not affect the central database or future transaction processing.) That limits the use
of a data warehouse to situations where decision makers access corporate information but do not change it. If an application running in this environment must update the main database, it must be done in some other way. One approach is to
have DSS computer mimic a transaction processing user and submit transactions.

Advantages of Using a Data Warehouse (or Other Separate DSS Database)
1. The DSS hardware can be optimized for that purpose and that purpose alone.
2. DSS hardware need not be shared with other applications, so DSS response
time is preserved no matter what is going on elsewhere in the organization.

3. The cost of upgrading the central corporate system to run DSS applications is avoided. While this saving is offset by the cost of the new computer, the economics of different technologies and markets will often make that computer less expensive than the required central system upgrade would be.

4. Compared to full-blown client/server computing, in which the applications can update the server database, the unidirectional data warehouse environment is simpler and less prone to errors.

5. Most servers and microcomputers are user-friendly or can be made so by an available graphical user interface package. It is not usually possible to replace a central computer's operating system just to cater to decision makers' desires for interface friendliness.

Disadvantages of Using a Data Warehouse (or Other Separate DSS Database)

1. The need to transfer data between two systems, to create the data warehouse and keep it up to date, is an additional workload on the central system. Unless this work can take place totally during times of light system use it will add to the central system load, though hopefully it will add less than running the full DSS would.

2. The MIS staff must be familiar with two systems. (This means expertise in both must exist in the organization. It does not mean that individual staff members must know both.) In addition, some staff members may need a third set of skills to link the two. (This is the same drawback of client/server computing that we noted on page 177.)

3. The total user community will use two systems. Some users, of course, will access just one or the other: If order entry operators use the transaction processing system and sales promotion planners use the data warehouse system, each needs to learn only one. Even in this case, the user support organization will have to deal with both.

4. Users who access both systems may need two types of terminals or may have to follow complex network log-on procedures to access the correct one. Switching from one to the other may be time consuming.

5. Decision support data are only as current as the most recent down load to the data warehouse. This may suffice, especially if the downloading is done at least every 24 hours. (This can be an advantage because it ensures that everyone uses the same data.)

6. Re-creating the data warehouse may take several hours, and the DSS system may not be available for use during this time. If the update is performed outside normal working hours, perhaps in the early morning, it may involve operator inconvenience and overtime pay. Unattended operation is an attractive way to avoid these problems but leaves the process vulnerable to mishaps that can only be corrected by an on-site operator.

5.7 DSS ON A STAND-ALONE SYSTEM

Many decision support systems do not access a central database. Some run models whose input, consisting of only a few numbers, comes entirely from its user's knowledge or from external sources and can be keyed in easily for each run. A budgeting system may take all its input from its user, eventually creating a spreadsheet that can be carried to another system on diskette or sent to it over a network for consolidation. DSS that helps real estate agents choose houses to show a potential buyer, or a system in a new car showroom helping buyers select the options they want, need only the answers to some simple questions.

DSS that do not access a large central database are typically model-oriented or process-oriented. Whereas some of them use databases that are developed and maintained locally by their individual users, such databases are unlikely to be large or complex. A "real" data-oriented DSS normally requires some form of link to an existing or external database. Its hardware would therefore usually fall into one of the previous categories.

DSS that do not access a large central database are candidates for stand-alone systems. A stand-alone DSS can be run on a computer dedicated to the DSS task or on a multiple-user computer used in time-sharing mode. In the former case, the computer is usually a desktop microcomputer[3] or a high-performance workstation. In this latter case, many users may be sharing the hardware, but each is using a stand-alone application in a self-contained software "cocoon."

Being "stand-alone" is a matter of degree. The absolutely, totally, 100 percent stand-alone system is almost as rare as the unicorn. Even users of nominally stand-alone systems exchange files via diskette or send electronic mail via a dial-up modem link. What the term really means here is that the operation of the decision support system doesn't depend on a regular connection to another computer. Such a connection probably does exist and can be used for DSS-related purposes, such as sending its results to a colleague for review and comment.

Advantages of Using a Stand-Alone System

1. The system can be totally optimized for DSS. Compatibility considerations may, if desired, be ignored completely.
2. The complexity of sharing a resource with other users is avoided.
3. The complexity of integrating a two-system application is avoided.
4. There is no overhead in communicating with other systems.
5. The person or department "owning" the system has complete control over it. While not a technical factor, this is often psychologically and/or politically important.

Disadvantages of Using a Stand-Alone System

1. Any data the system requires must be provided by its user. This is why stand-alone systems are not well suited to data-oriented DSS.
2. Sharing the results with other users, or using a shared database, may be more difficult than it would be if the system were designed to operate in a shared-data environment.

---

[3]These are often called personal computers or PCs. Since many people associate these terms solely with Intel-based Windows systems, we are using an alternative term that does not have that association.

3. The individual user or department responsible for the stand-alone system must usually deal with its own system administration needs, such as installing new software releases and backing up files regularly. Most end users are not well disciplined in this regard. They often learn about the need for regular backups through the agonizing personal experience of not having one when it could have saved the day.[4]

4. It may be difficult to integrate a stand-alone system with corporate applications at a later date if no thought was given to compatibility in the planning stages. MIS staffers, upset at having been ignored during planning, may understandably take an all-too-human "I told you so" or "stew in your own juices" attitude to bailing the user out at this point.

5.8 OPEN SYSTEMS AND DSS

You may have heard or read the term **open systems.** You may have heard the UNIX operating system, mentioned briefly above, discussed in this context. With more and more organizations moving toward open systems, there's a good chance that your employer (now or after graduation) will be one of them. Furthermore, and importantly for the purposes of this book, open systems and DSS have a close relationship.

Open systems[5] are systems whose interfaces are not under the control of any single hardware or software supplier. Rather, they are defined by neutral bodies through an open process in which all parties can, if they choose, participate. (While vendors tend to have the most to gain or lose as a result of these discussions, and therefore supply most of the discussants, user organizations can and do participate.) Once they are agreed upon, both the interface specifications and the right to produce systems that conform to those specifications are available on equal, and equitable, terms to all firms.

The advantage of open systems to users is that they permit a user organization to mix and match hardware and software products from several suppliers, choosing the "best of breed" product of each type, with a high degree of assurance that the resulting collection will work together. The advantage to vendors is that they can produce a product of one type—a workstation, a network component, a database management system, or a query tool—and have it work with complementary products from many sources. Open systems thus create a level playing field, in which small vendors can compete with larger ones on an approximately equal basis.

Open systems are not all positive. The standards-making process is long and laborious. The standards eventually arrived at are often compromises, lacking the clear vision and pure focus that a single-vendor product can have. Dominant vendors,

---

[4] It has been said, not entirely in jest, that there are two kinds of computer users: those who have lost files due to a hardware or software failure, and those who will. (This author falls into the first group.)

[5] Not to be confused with the same term as used in Chapter 3, a system that exchanges information with its environment. Both usages are too entrenched to change, but the context should always make it clear which is meant.

whose market shares may be threatened by increased competition, have historically opposed open standards through a variety of subtle and not-so-subtle tactics. And standards, while they go a long way toward providing compatibility of products from different sources, are seldom complete enough to make coordinated operation an effortless "nonevent." Despite these drawbacks, the adoption of standards-based computing is increasing.

System openness encompasses multiple aspects. The first aspect is system interconnection, or networking. Openness in this sense means that systems from different sources can exchange data as the user organization requires. Systems that conform to a vendor-independent set of data communication and networking standards are open in this sense. In wide area networking, this type of openness usually means conforming to the Open System Interconnection (OSI) standard of the International Standards Organization or the TCP/IP set of protocols used on the Internet, though other standards exist as well. Network computers, which follow the standards used on the World Wide Web, are open in this sense.

The second aspect of openness is the way individual computers operate. Openness here means that one set of programs, including both programming tools and user-developed applications, runs in the same way, with essentially the same commands and user interfaces, on computers obtained from several sources. The key ingredient in this type of openness is the operating system, as it defines the environment in which all other software runs. Network computers fall down a little in this regard, as some languages used for Web-based applications, such as Microsoft's ActiveX, are to a degree under their originators' control.

The primary multiuser open operating system is **UNIX.**[6] UNIX is independent of hardware architecture. It has been adapted, or "ported," to systems based on nearly every type of processor and having nearly every instruction set of commercial significance. Whereas the history of UNIX is complex and had periods of contention, there are today consistent standards for UNIX or UNIX-derived software environments. There is no manufacturer of computers above the desktop level in the United States today that does not support a UNIX-based operating system on at least one of its product lines. Most commercial software packages have been written to support it, including both applications and supporting components such as networking tools and database managers. All UNIX variants, including the free Linux system that is popular at the microcomputer level, present nearly identical interfaces to their users and to the application programs that run under them. As a result, user organizations can move programs between UNIX-based systems without a great deal of difficulty.

Another multiuser, independent standardization activity is called **POSIX.** This U.S. government–endorsed standard is based on UNIX but standardizes its interfaces at a higher level. As a result, non-UNIX operating systems can add an intermediate "shell" to run POSIX-compliant software by converting POSIX calls to

---

[6] For historical, legal, and competitive reasons, many computer system vendors do not refer to their UNIX-derived operating systems by the name *UNIX*. Thus, if you want UNIX on a Hewlett-Packard computer, you ask for HP/UX; on an IBM computer, for AIX; on Sun, for Solaris; and so on.

Downsizing for Decision Support

Many firms are moving mainframe-based applications to minis or micros: at times as part of an overall system redesign, but often just for decision support or other tasks to which the mainframe is poorly suited. This process is usually called **downsizing**.[7] Some proponents prefer the term **rightsizing**: They feel it connotes that the smaller size is the right size, not just smaller for the (currently popular) sake of being smaller.

Open systems often play a key role in downsizing programs. A mainframe application can seldom be moved lock, stock, and barrel to one smaller system: It just won't fit. Rather, its size and scope require it to be split over several cooperating smaller systems. The ability of those smaller systems to cooperate depends on their all conforming to a suitable set of standards. These will often be open systems standards.

One firm that downsized a key decision support application was American Airlines Decision Technologies of Fort Worth, Texas [GILL92]. It uses complex mathematical models to schedule its parent firm's crews, equipment, and flights. It originally used the corporate mainframe for this purpose; however, this created several problems.

For one thing, the IBM mainframe took too long to process the work. Analysts "had to wait in line with everybody else," said vice president of computing resources Chip Steinmitz. Worse yet, work fell behind: With the delay in starting to run the models, they began running out of time to complete them.

American Airlines Decision Technologies considered expanding its mainframe. However, that would not have fit the analysts' work patterns. "The individual analyst needs to have an interactive type of computing environment," says Steinmitz. "Even though it takes a third longer to run a job on a workstation, an analyst can get more runs through in 24 hours." The MVS mainframe was replaced by a client/server network using a mix of hardware. (The mainframe itself remained in place to be used for other tasks.) Workstations were UNIX-based, from four vendors, and microcomputers. The firm spent $4 million on new equipment in 1991 and saved that much in mainframe usage charges during the network's first year.

Was it all gravy? Hardly. "We encountered unanticipated costs dealing with network complexity and LAN administration," Steinmitz points out. "We had to configure the network with

---

[7]This term is also used in a general business context to refer to reducing the overall size of an organization by cutting staff. The two meanings are distinct, though it is not always clear which is meant.

their equivalent under another operating system. This strategy permits some suppliers of proprietary systems to claim a degree of openness, but adds a layer of overhead and inefficiency to their systems when they use this shell.

At the desktop level, Microsoft Windows has many characteristics of an open system. It is under the unilateral control of Microsoft, but Microsoft does not sell computer hardware. Microsoft therefore makes Windows available to all hardware vendors. Most versions of Windows run only on microprocessors compatible with the Intel Pentium family, but several semiconductor firms (in addition to Intel) make these. (Some versions can run on other instruction sets but have not enjoyed market success on non-Intel architectures.) Furthermore, Microsoft publishes the Windows interface specifications, so any software firm can write programs that will run under Windows on anyone's hardware.

Downsizing for Decision Support (continued)

shared file servers that anyone can get at. Networking them all together was more expensive than we anticipated." They also had to develop system and network management tools for their multivendor environment. Finally, their application programmers, who were used to support a systems programming staff in the mainframe environment, found that they had to take on its responsibilities as well. Still, they are well satisfied with their decision.

Avis Rent-A-Car Systems, Inc., of Garden City, New York, had a data access problem [MORA92]. Accessing either of the two databases on their IBM 3090 600E mainframe meant either using a complex mainframe tool or writing a COBOL program to extract the data. To make life easier for their business planners they installed Apple Macintosh microcomputers equipped with Apple's Data Access Language (DAL). They now use DAL Client, part of Apple's operating system for the Macintosh, to access mainframe databases. They also use DAL Server for UNIX, from Pacer Software, Inc., to connect to Informix and Sybase relational databases on Sun and Hewlett-Packard equipment via the same user interface. Like American Airlines Decision Technologies, Avis did not replace its mainframe but was able to forestall upgrades by moving some of its workload to the smaller platforms.

Avis has used its Mac-based query tools for critical decisions in human resources, marketing, and fleet management. "Today, programmers can take query tools and get an answer in an afternoon that would have taken six months of development time," says Peter Tittler, Avis networks and technology vice president. Furthermore, some of the applications devoured so many mainframe computing cycles that Avis couldn't afford to use them as extensively as they otherwise would have. "Using the Mac has allowed us to answer business questions that we would not have attempted in the past," adds Tittler.

A third firm, Miller Brewing Company of Milwaukee, Wisconsin, has also decided to downsize its information systems environment [APPL92]. They currently use a mainframe for transaction processing and paper for decision support, addressing questions such as how best to stack beer in a shipping container.

Miller is starting small, with a pilot application to process beer export orders using local networks and client/server computing. This pilot will involve only 8 to 10 users and an investment in the low five figures. The next step will allow employees to access sales and marketing data via easy-to-use microcomputer-based tools and LANs rather than the cumbersome mainframe. Their eventual network will, as with the previous two systems, retain the mainframe as a server. Clients will be Apple Macintoshes and IBM personal computers.

Network computers have no visible operating system (they need a rudimentary one to coordinate their resources internally, but the user doesn't see it) so this issue does not arise for them.

Some of the more popular proprietary operating systems have enough market share that many software products are available to run under them and with each other: IBM mainframe MVS, VMS for Compaq's (previously Digital's) VAX, the Mac OS. Because of the size of these systems' user communities and of the industries that have grown up around them, their developers cannot make arbitrary changes to their interfaces on a whim any more than Microsoft can arbitrarily make major changes to Windows. Their "owners" can and do, however, decide their future roadmaps on their own and do not welcome outside attempts to influence their direction.

A third aspect of openness is hardware interface openness. Hardware interfaces to many microcomputers and minicomputers are in the public domain or can be licensed. Anyone can build components to plug into those buses; in some cases, anyone can also build computers to accept such components. The interfaces to other systems are more tightly controlled by their owners. Hardware openness, while important to system designers, does not raise any issues that are unique to DSS.

DSS has accelerated the growth of open systems. The reason: the arrival of DSS injected a second component into what had been, historically, single-purpose transaction processing systems. Let's follow one possible scenario for this evolution:

1. The transaction processing systems of Company X run on its central mainframe. Because most of its transaction processing systems are related to each other and share a database, one vendor can satisfy all of Company X's shared computing needs with one product line. Company X has therefore standardized on one vendor's computer line for its transaction processing applications and is satisfied with it.

2. DSS arrives. Company X's first DSS are implemented on its existing computer—not because it is the best choice, but because it is the only choice.

3. DSS users are not fully satisfied with the central computing environment. They feel that it and its staff are not always responsive to their needs—not unreasonably, since DSS usage accounts for a mere 5 percent of the mainframe's workload. They are also unhappy with their charges for computing resources, having heard that microcomputers and client/server computing are more cost effective for DSS applications.

4. These users put their DSS on a microcomputer or a server with at least partial success. They soon find that parts of their application, such as a database that must be shared or that is too large for a small computer's disk capacity, are better left where they are. They also realize, however, that it is technically difficult to leave them where they are and access them there because of incompatibilities between their small system and the large central system. This, in turn, constrains their ability to do their jobs on the system of their choice. They press the firm's MIS organization to enable them to access corporate data.

5. The MIS department realizes, perhaps after some resistance and top management pressure, that these requests are reasonable—even important to the business. They see a need for systems of various sizes exchanging information: perhaps among separate applications in a traditional network, perhaps among parts of one application in a client/server architecture. They also realize that their current proprietary architecture does not permit this. They see that a solution must involve several different types of computers and move toward open systems as the most practical way to have these computers cooperate. (An alternative outcome, in which the MIS department does not realize that these requests are reasonable, may have an unplanned career impact on MIS managers.)

5.9. CHOOSING A DSS HARDWARE ENVIRONMENT

Here is a list of questions you can ask to help make your choice among the previously listed options. None of them, except possibly the first, will give you a hard-and-fast direction that you can follow without further thought. As a group, though, their answers will help point out the right DSS hardware approach.

1. Are there any corporate policies that you must follow? If there are, they may narrow your choice by mandating one option, or by eliminating some options.
2. How large and widespread will the DSS user community be? If it is large and widespread, will its members use exactly the same application, variations on one application, or different applications? When they use the same application, do they use it independently, or must their usage be coordinated through a shared database or in any other way? The more similarity, the more sharing, the more you should look toward shared systems and LANs with high-end servers. The less sharing and similarity, the more power probably belongs on individual desktops.
3. Are most of the prospective users already using a particular system? If so, see if it can be used as is or with modifications such as a modest upgrade or interconnection via a LAN.
4. Is there a corporate mainframe with sufficient capacity, or to which sufficient capacity can be added at reasonable cost? (It may have sufficient capacity now, but normal load growth may mean that it won't in the future. Adding the DSS may hasten the need for an upgrade. Exercise 2 on page 192 addresses this issue.)
5. Is another powerful server system available, linked to that mainframe or not, with sufficient capacity?
6. Do prospective users already have microcomputers or workstations that can handle the application?
7. If new systems are required, will the existing central system be able to share data with them? to shoulder an application jointly with them?
8. Do the necessary development tools exist for any of those systems? Are they already within the organization, available from the system vendor, or available from third parties?
9. With which of these systems and tools, if any, are the prospective DSS developers already familiar?
10. Does the application require access to a database? If so, does that database already exist? If not, is it to be derived from corporate data or from a separate source? If from corporate data, how up to date should the database be for the application to function (to the minute, as of the end of the last business day, etc.)?
11. Does the application's use of the corporate database require only the ability to read the data, or must it also be able to update the data?
12. How much processing power does the application require? How much data storage capacity?
13. Are prospective users capable of performing (and willing to perform) basic system administration tasks, such as installing software and backing up data files?

SUMMARY

Before embarking on the development of any major decision support system, you should have a clear idea of both its architecture and the overall DSS architecture of your organization. Knowing these will help you communicate your DSS vision to management and will help you plan systems that will continue to meet user needs in the future.

Decision support systems can run on a variety of different platforms. Each type has both advantages and disadvantages, which often make one better than another in a specific situation.

An existing multiuser computer (typically a mainframe) may be suitable when it has adequate capacity (not always the case!), prospective DSS users are already using it, and rapid access to central corporate data is required.

The approach of client/server computing allows a shared computer such as this to provide decision support data and handle other aspects of the task to which it is well suited, while allowing more economical and easier-to-use desktop computers to provide the user interface and handle other parts of the overall job. A *thin client* is a desktop computer designed with limited capabilities to handle only the user interface, while the server does the rest of the job.

The World Wide Web can also be used to supply decision support data to users. This has the advantages of universal accessibility and familiarity. A *network computer* is a desktop system that can access the Web but has no stand-alone computing capability. An *intranet* is an internal network that uses Web protocols to control data transfer.

It is not necessary to provide decision support data directly from the live database. Instead, the necessary data can be consolidated into a specialized decision support database, often called a *data warehouse*. While this is not absolutely necessary, data warehouses are often housed on separate systems from the operational database. In other situations, model-oriented or process-oriented DSS often do not need a database at all. In these cases a stand-alone decision support system, usually running on the user's desktop system with no active connections to the outside world, may be the best solution.

Many of these approaches involve combining several computers into one system in order to accomplish the overall task. Open systems provide a good basis for developing applications that require cooperation among systems of several different types.

KEY TERMS

architecture
capacity planners
client
client/server computing
data warehouse
database computer
downsizing

fat client
file server
HyperText Markup Language (HTML)
information systems architecture
Internet
intranet
Java
JavaScript
mainframe computer
minicomputer
multiprocessing, multiprocessor
network computer (NC)
open system, open software environment
platform
POSIX
proprietary operating system, proprietary software environment
rightsizing
server
thin client
time sharing
UNIX
World Wide Web

REVIEW QUESTIONS

1. What is an information systems architecture?
2. Why is it good to have an information systems architecture?
3. How does a DSS architecture differ from an overall corporate information systems architecture?
4. Give eight factors that a DSS architecture must take into account or reflect.
5. What are the major DSS hardware environments?
6. State the advantages and disadvantages of running a decision support system on the central corporate computer.
7. Define client/server computing.
8. In client/server computing, is it possible to have many clients sharing many servers?
9. When are microcomputers on a LAN likely to be more economical than a shared system with terminals for decision support usage?
10. What are fat clients? Thin clients? Network computers? An intranet?
11. What are three reasons that DSS accessed over the Web may be slow?
12. What is a data warehouse? Can it be updated by its users?
13. What is multiprocessing? Why is it helpful?
14. What is the difference between a stand-alone application and a stand-alone hardware system?
15. Define *open systems.*
16. What is the most widely used multiuser open operating system? Which vendors offer hardware on which it can run?
17. Is there a relationship between DSS and open systems? If so, what is it?

18. How might corporate policies influence your choice of a DSS hardware/software environment?

19. State several technical factors that would influence your choice of a DSS hardware/software environment.

20. State several nontechnical factors that would influence your choice of a DSS hardware/software environment.

EXERCISES

1. Develop a DSS architecture for a retail clothing chain's marketing department. It must include at least three databases:
- Sales information from all stores.
- Product availability and pricing information from warehouses and suppliers.
- Industry market share and trend information from an external public information supplier.

Its models will include at least
- An advertising response model.
- A financial model for ordering clothing that considers the need to dispose of unsold merchandise via end-of-season sales or by selling it to discounters.
- A model that compares the income to be gained by selling the firm's mailing list with the lost profits if the customers buy from competitors who bought the list.

The chain's stores are located throughout the United States and Canada. Its suppliers are located all over the world. Its marketing staff is located primarily in Terre Haute, Indiana. Its advertising agency is located in New York, as is a small marketing staff to deal with that agency and with the many clothing suppliers based there. Include all the elements discussed in the text, not just those that appear in Figures 5–1 and 5–2.

2. The second drawback of using the central corporate system for DSS (page 171) reads in part, "The cost of additional resources to run a DSS may exceed the cost of smaller computers to handle the same task." What if the central system has sufficient excess capacity to handle the DSS load without an upgrade? Does this statement still apply? If it applies some of the time, but not all of the time, when does it and when doesn't it?

3. The seventh drawback of using the central corporate system for DSS (page 171) reads in part, "existing communication links may not be up to the increased load of graphs and images." A typical alphanumeric monitor displays 25 lines of 80 characters each. A typical microcomputer graphics monitor displays 800 dots horizontally by 600 dots vertically. A typical link from a computer to a terminal can transmit data at 56 Mbps. Assuming nonstop one-directional transmission without pause or error, which is optimistic, calculate how long it would take to transmit

a. A screenful of alphanumeric data.

b. A screenful of black-and-white graphics.

c. A screenful of 256-color graphics.

(Your answers will be, fortunately, a worst case. There are many ways of compressing screen descriptions. These take advantage of different character frequencies in character strings, the use of common geometric shapes such as rectangles, and repeated dots or areas of one color for shapes that are hard to describe geometrically. A desktop micro-computer can perform simple decompression without visibly degrading response time.)

4. Consider the client/server computing spectrum as shown in Figure 5–3. Assume an application calls for selecting and retrieving about 100 customer records out of a 100,000-record file, and graphing some data found in those records. Assume each record is 2,000 bytes long. This application could be partitioned in (at least) three ways:

- Transmit the 100,000-record file from a file server to the client system. The client then retrieves the desired records and displays the graph.
- Using a database server, retrieve the desired 100 records and transmit them to the client system. The client then creates and displays the graph.
- Retrieve the records and create the graph on a powerful central system. Transmit the description of the graph as in part *(c)* of exercise 3 above to the client, which displays the colored dots it receives.

Calculate the number of bits that must be transmitted over the client/server link for all three of these cases. How long would the communication process take

a. If 33.6 Mbps modems are used?

b. If a 10 Mbps LAN is used?

c. If a 1,000 Mbps gigabit Ethernet LAN, such as Fort Lowell Trading Company has, is used?

Assume all connections can transmit data at one-third of their theoretical maximum rate, which is approximately correct.

5. Consider the two applications in the box on downsizing on page 186. Where would you put them in the spectrum of client/server approaches shown in Figure 5–3?
6. Using the Web search engine of your choice, find five software products that claim to have some decision support capability. List the hardware/operating system platforms on which they run. (Many products run on more than one platform.)

REFERENCES

APPL92   Appleby, Chuck. "Client/Server on Tap," *InformationWeek* no. 366 (March 30, 1992), pp. 92–93.

GILL92   Gill, Philip J. "The Challenges of Downsizing," *Open Systems Today* (March 2, 1992), pp. 70–78.

MART91   Martin, E. Wainwright, Daniel W. DeHayes, Jeffrey A. Hoffer, and William C. Perkins. *Managing Information Technology: What Managers Need to Know.* Macmillan, New York (1991).

MORA92   Moran, Robert. "The Drive for Easier Access," *InformationWeek* no. 362 (March 2, 1992), p. 44.

CASE

Fort Lowell Trading Company
The Hardware

Miguel and Elizabeth had devoted their last few meetings with Fort Lowell Trading Company to the general subject of applications. They thought a broader picture of FLTC's systems might be helpful before getting into the applications in more detail. Dottie Eastman agreed, so she arranged for them to meet with Bob Goldberg, the firm's director of technology planning in the FLTC information systems group. As a member of Dottie's top-level staff, he participated in all major decisions affecting its systems. In addition, he and a small group of technical specialists were responsible for planning and selecting new hardware and system software for the central corporate site and the nationwide FLTC WAN. They were also responsible for monitoring new technologies that could be of value to FLTC and ensuring that appropriate business managers were aware of them. They did not, however, get involved with store computers—the store information systems department was responsible for them—or with desktop equipment.

Bob was already in the lobby when the two students arrived, having been warned by Vanessa McAnaney that they tended to be on time or early. He welcomed them warmly and led them into the now-familiar MIS office area.

"Wouldn't it be simpler if we could just come in here by ourselves?" asked Miguel.

"Probably," agreed Bob, "but we get paranoid about security. Not every ID badge will unlock those double doors—just the ones that belong to people who have a reason to be here. Everyone else has to be let in. I don't think even Stan James's badge would let him in, though he could probably get his name put on the access list if he really wanted to."

"Was there a problem that led you to tighten up on this?" Miguel continued.

"No, fortunately. Reading about other folks' problems in *Computerworld* is as close as we want to come to things like that. It's not just someone deliberately messing things up. That's pretty unlikely. It's mostly that once lots of people start wandering through here it's only a matter of time until someone trips and pulls out a network cable, or spills soda into a disk drive, or something like that."

With that the group reached Bob's office and went in. The two students' eyes were immediately drawn to a picture of a dramatic sunset with birds flying in front of bright red-orange clouds. "Where did you get that sunset photo?" Elizabeth asked. "It's gorgeous!"

"Thank you," Bob smiled, "because I didn't get it—I took it. And it's a sunrise, not a sunset. It's off the Outer Banks in North Carolina. One of the side benefits of hurricane season in late summer is cloud formations that make some of the most incredible sunrises on the planet. You just have to get up early and point your lens east. And," he laughed, "you both know that August is not a bad time to get away from Tucson!"

With that, the three sat down around a small round conference table. Bob opened their discussion, "I pulled this diagram out before you came to show you our basic hardware setup. This is just the top-level diagram, of course. There are others showing the software, how the regional headquarters are set up, and so on. We can get to those later this afternoon if you'd like."

"Most of our operational data processing gets done here," Bob continued, pointing to the center of the figure. "These two systems—he indicated the IBM and HDS mainframes—are linked so they can share a database, share workloads, and back each other up if either of them fails. I'm happy to say we've never been down because of a hardware failure at the central site.

"We have these T-1 lines coming out of Tucson," Bob continued, "going to our regional headquarters. These are fast enough that people out there can use the mainframe complex as if it were local, so we don't have much by way of computers at the regional sites. One of the issues we're grappling with, by the way, is whether this is still the way to go. It made a lot of sense when we were just sending character data back and forth. Pictures are starting to slow it down a bit. Once we get into some of the data warehousing things people are talking about we may have to do a lot of rethinking. That's probably my group's single biggest project for next year. We just don't know whether the regions will want to share one set of data, or they'll have different data, or they'll share the same data but they'll each want to have their own copy. We also don't know how much usage the data warehouse will get from the regions, how much network traffic that will mean . . . you get the idea. We'll probably start by keeping the network we've got, but we'll watch it carefully to see how it goes."

"What about hardware for running other decision support software?" Elizabeth asked.

"We've never broken that out as a separate item," Bob confessed. "We don't do a lot with DSS at the corporate level. That has to change, of course. That's a big part of why you two are here. But that's how it's been so far. When anybody wants to use a computer for decision support, they just use whatever computer they have or have access to. The load on the central systems has been small enough not to affect things much. And, if they use their own PCs, of course, that doesn't show up in the system workload data."

FIGURE 5–6 Overall FLTC System Architecture

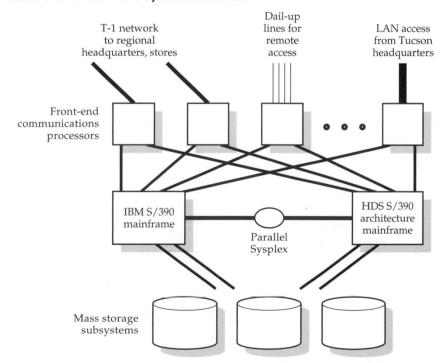

EXERCISES

1. Which of the modes of operation listed in this chapter does FLTC seem to be using? Which is it not using? (You may want to review the introductory material on the FLTC information systems, page 33, before answering this question.)

2. Suppose FLTC decides to put a database for sales trend analysis (a data warehouse) at the central site, with users accessing it over the existing networks. (Whether or not it runs on the central mainframe complex or on some other computer is a separate issue and is not part of this question. You may assume that any computer it runs on is many times more powerful than a typical desktop computer.) This would be a form of client/server computing. Suppose marketing planners in the regions will access and analyze this database to help decide what products to order, in what styles, colors, sizes, etc. Using the criteria on pages 173–174 for dividing a job in the client/server environment, which parts of the job would you recommend be done centrally; which on the user's desktop? State any assumptions you make clearly.

3. Do you think Bob's last statement, that he hasn't had to worry about DSS until now because it has been such a small fraction of the overall system load, is reasonable? Why or why not?

4. In the architecture diagram (Figure 5–6), the central systems are labeled as HDS S/390 architecture mainframe and IBM S/390 mainframe.

   a. It would have been possible to be either more specific or less specific in this description. Give an example of both a more specific description and a less specific description.

   b. Which of the three descriptions—the one in the diagram and the two in your answer to part (a) of this question—do you feel is best for a corporate information systems architecture definition? Why?

   c. Why is the IBM mainframe referred to in the diagram as a S/390 whereas that from HDS is referred to as S/390 architecture?

DSS Software Tools

Introduction

A decision support system is an information system. It uses the same building blocks as any other information system. However, it uses them in specialized ways that the DSS builder must be aware of. This chapter covers what you have to know about software for DSS, with emphasis on the types of software and the user interface issues that are especially useful for decision support purposes, without trying to repeat what you already know from your introductory MIS course.

CHAPTER OBJECTIVES

After you have read and studied this chapter, you will be able to:

1. Outline four methods of obtaining a DSS, and explain how the choice among them depends on organization size and problem uniqueness.
2. Identify the types of database management systems and their usefulness in decision support applications.

3. Discuss how Structured Query Language (SQL) can be used to retrieve information for decision support.
4. Describe the types of specialized languages used to build decision support models, to perform statistical analyses, to forecast future values of important business variables, and more.
5. Identify what programming languages are used for DSS, and why fourth-generation languages are popular for this purpose.
6. Briefly explain how programs written in one leading 4GL look and work.
7. Discuss several types of operating system and decision support system user interfaces.
8. Identify factors to consider and steps to take in defining the user interface of a decision support system.
9. Understand the guidelines for using color in your user interface.
10. Summarize several emerging technologies that will help you design decision support system user interfaces during your career.

6.1 DSS SOFTWARE CATEGORIES

There are four fundamental ways to obtain any software capability: to purchase a turnkey package, to customize a package, to use specialized tools or "generators" designed for the task at hand, or to write the necessary programs from scratch. Since a decision support system is software, these approaches apply to DSS as well. The choice between packages (customized or not) and custom software usually depends on two factors:

1. *The degree to which your needs resemble those of many other organizations.* This determines the likelihood that software developers will have found the market for the capability you need attractive enough to develop packages for resale.
2. *The financial impact of the application,* which determines the value of getting exactly the capability you want versus what you can get in a standard package. The size of the organization is a factor here. A system that cost $300,000 and could increase the profits of General Motors by 1 percent of gross sales would be a wise investment. The same $300,000 investment would not be advisable if the result was a 1 percent-of-sales increase in the profits of Sid's and Suzie's Sandwich and Soda Shoppe (S&SS&SS).

   The reason size is a factor is that the cost of developing a computer program is only loosely related to the size of the organization which will use it. If S&SS&SS has gross sales of $100,000 a year, then General Motors is around 1 million times its size by that measure. GM's inventory and other business functions are more complex than Sid's and Suzie's, but not a million times more complex. (Managing their inventory is probably about 100 times more complex, since GM has more types of parts used in more types of products, more suppliers, and more locations.) The ratio of application benefit to cost therefore goes up with the size of the organization.

   As another example of this phenomenon, consider the Authorizer's Assistant system which American Express uses to help staff members decide whether or not to authorize a credit purchase. It cost hundreds of thousands of dollars, perhaps millions, to develop this system. But this development expense was justified in terms of the enormous annual credit volume, and proportionate potential losses, of the American Express credit card business. The annual credit losses of Allen's Hardware on its store charge accounts, even if such a computer system could eliminate all of them, wouldn't justify the same expenditure.

General Motors will need thousands of terminals, workstations, or microcomputers to handle a corporate application, whereas S&SS&SS probably has one microcomputer to accommodate all its needs. However, the cost of deploying an application—hardware, communication links, system administration, user support—has little to do with how that application was originally obtained. These costs must be incurred whether the application was purchased, customwritten, or anything else. Therefore, they are not a consideration in choosing how to obtain a DSS.

These factors, and the areas where each approach is usually applicable, are shown graphically in Figure 6–1. This suggests that you should look toward standard packages and tools where your application is common to many firms or where your firm is small. If your application is unique and your organization is large, consider custom development. Below that part of the graph, in medium-sized organizations and for applications with some standard features, customized packages play a part. As examples, Figure 6–2 shows where General Motors' word processing needs would fall on the graph (standard application, large company) versus the sales forecasting needs of Pat's Pretzel Pushcart (unusual application, small company). If your application is unique and your firm is small, you may

FIGURE 6–1   Application Uniqueness versus Company Size

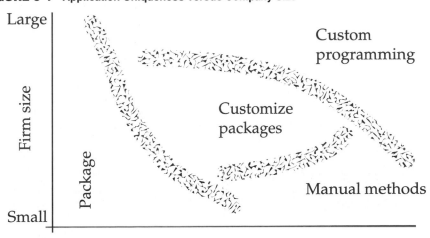

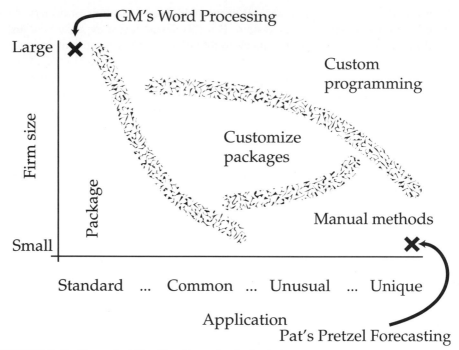

FIGURE 6–2   Figure 6–1 Plus Two Examples Indicated

have to forego an application-specific DSS unless you can find a creative way to reduce its cost. (You can still probably do useful work with a spreadsheet or similar general-purpose package, of course.) Possible cost-reduction measures include:

- Developing a system for future resale to other firms with similar needs. The Mrs. Fields' chain of cookie stores developed software to forecast demand as a function of time of day, day of week, weather, holidays, type of store location (business street, shopping mall), and other factors that affect cookie sales. It then recouped much of the cost by going into the software business.
- Sharing the cost with similar firms that do not compete directly with yours, either because their lines of business are not quite the same, because they serve a different geographic sales territory, or some other reason.
- Finding IS students who will develop your system as a term project. A small family-owned ice cream shop on Cape Cod has a sophisticated, customized demand forecasting and supply ordering program of which any large firm would be proud—because its owners' son needed a senior project for his operations management major.
- Finding a software developer—perhaps a start-up firm—in need of user assistance in developing a new program or penetrating a new market, which will, in turn, work with you to apply that program to your needs.
- Persuading one of your suppliers to develop the program or to fund its development for later licensing to you and to their other customers.

This list barely scratches the surface. The moral: don't let lack of money deter you from obtaining computer-based decision support capabilities without trying to brainstorm a creative way out of your difficulties.

6.2 STANDARD PACKAGES

Standard packages to help make specific decisions have been developed for a few common decisions.

Scan the back pages of any microcomputer magazine. You're sure to find several ads for investment software. This software can generally dial up an on-line information service on a schedule you specify (usually daily), put the current prices of stocks you're interested in into its database, create a variety of performance charts, and recommend what you should buy or sell. Such programs follow the *technical approach* to stock price prediction: They predict future price behavior from past trading patterns. The logic behind this approach is that trading patterns are clues to investor feelings, so the patterns that preceded certain types of price changes in the past are likely to do so again. (The *fundamentals approach,* figuring out what a stock ought to be worth and comparing that value with its current price, requires analyses that are less amenable to automation.)

The characteristics of this decision that make it attractive to package suppliers are

- Many people make these decisions, so the potential market is large.
- The decision has financial importance to many of these potential users.
- The underlying factors are the same for all of them. (Individual investors vary in the importance they attach to different performance measures and in the set of stocks of potential interest, but a price-volume chart is a price-volume chart to everyone.)
- The support infrastructure—public databases that can provide the necessary data to anyone, free or for a small fee—already exists.

Decisions having these characteristics are, unfortunately, rare, and especially so in the business world. Where they exist, and where companies have developed DSS to help with them, these companies often do not want to give away their secrets to their competitors. The likelihood of your finding a ready-to-use package that will give you meaningful help with a business decision is next to zero. What you *can* find is a large number of tools, which you can combine so as to create the decision support capability you need. We therefore turn to those next.

6.3 SPECIALIZED TOOLS AND GENERATORS

Although few decision support applications are sufficiently general to justify the development of packages that do nothing else, many DSS applications do have common features. **DSS tools** and **DSS generators** allow DSS developers to utilize standardized "building blocks," which support these common features, to develop their own custom applications. As a potential DSS developer, you should be aware of the tools that are available so you can choose the best one for your needs on each project.

The terms *DSS tool* and *DSS generator,* both quite common in the DSS literature, create a great deal of confusion. As Sprague originally conceived them [SPRA80, SPRA82; discussed in SILV91, pp. 201ff], DSS tools would generally be used to create DSS generators, which in turn would generate the specific DSS used by decision makers. He associates the use of DSS tools in this sense with the toolsmith role discussed on page 267. The use of DSS generators is associated with the higher level, more business-oriented, roles.

The proliferation of customizable packages such as spreadsheet programs has made this approach less popular than it once was. (It wasn't universal in 1980 either. Part of Sprague's message was that, given the software technologies of the time, it should have been.) Adapting Sprague's concepts to the late 1990s, we can say that a DSS generator will usually have the capability to become or to create an entire DSS. The software that supports a financial modeling programming language, such as the IFPS language, which we discuss on page 216, would be a generator. A blank spreadsheet package, before we insert formulas and macros, would usually be considered a generator as well. A DSS tool deals with part of the DSS but not all of it. A graphing package to graph data from some other source, which is useless without such a source, would be a DSS tool. So would database management systems, if we consider them as tools for organizing and accessing data without the higher level capabilities, such as end-user query packages, that are often sold along with them. You'll see more examples of DSS tools and generators in Chapters 13 and 14 when we discuss the software components of a data warehouse.

The major categories of specialized software used to assist DSS development are

1. Database management packages.
2. Information retrieval (query and reporting) packages.
3. Specialized modeling packages (including spreadsheets) and languages.
4. Statistical data analysis packages.
5. Forecasting packages.
6. Graphing packages

These are described in the following sections.

6.3.1 Database Management Systems

A **database management system** [BRAD87, COUR88, and many other books] allows users to store data in an organized form and retrieve it on the basis of specified selection criteria. Products within this broad category range from less than $100 to more than $100,000, with a correspondingly wide range of features and capabilities. However, "more expensive" does not always mean "better for the purpose at hand."

The simplest so-called "database managers" do not, according to computer scientists, deserve this name. To a database expert, a critical defining characteristic of a true database is its ability to integrate several types of data, typically stored in several files: for example, pulling out lists of students with unpaid bills from one file, their schedules from another, their instructors' office addresses from a third,

The Knowledge Gourd

The Hawai'ian language evolved from Polynesian roots centuries before computers were developed. Driven in part by a desire to preserve the ancient Hawai'ian cultural legacy, the language has been updated to encompass modern technology. The newly coined Hawai'ian term for a database, for example, is *hokeo 'ikepili.* It is derived from three words:

Hokeo—a container for storing things, originally a gourd.

'Ike—knowledge.

Pili—relationships.

Hokeo 'ikepili, therefore, translates to "container of related knowledge." Although its English form is a bit long for everyday use, it is probably a more appropriate term than "database"!

in order to send notices to the students' instructors alerting them to the situation. Many microcomputer-based packages can deal with only one file at a time. In the interests of technical accuracy we will call such one-file-at-a-time programs **file managers** or **data managers.** You should expect to hear many end users refer to these programs as database managers, however, especially those whose computing experience has been primarily with desktop machines.

Data managers can be quite useful as personal filing systems, allowing a decision maker to recall data quickly when it is needed to make a decision. In the DSS spectrum on page 130, data managers are file drawer systems. The more capable ones can calculate totals, averages, trends, and more on selected data elements from a file. These capabilities bring them up to the category of data analysis systems.

Data managers can also serve as a "back end" to a system in a higher category. For example, a data manager could supply input to a model that calculates the results to be expected from a new marketing program aimed at selected customers from a list. When the data manipulation requirements of such a DSS are modest, data managers provide an easy way to meet them. If one is willing to get involved in custom programming, it is perfectly practical to process data from multiple files even if one's data accessing package can work with only one at a time. In most cases, however, if the application calls for integrating data from more than one file, it's a good idea to start with a tool designed to handle the job.

Moving up from data managers, we come to full-fledged database managers that can associate records from several files with each other. Using such a system, a decision maker could, for example, see what percentages of the motors in vacuum cleaners returned for warranty repair last year came from each supplier, versus the percentage of motors that each supplier provided overall. If one vendor supplied only 5 percent of all vacuum cleaner motors, but its motors were responsible for 30 percent of the warranty claims, a purchasing manager might decide to insist on documented quality improvements before buying any more motors from that vendor.

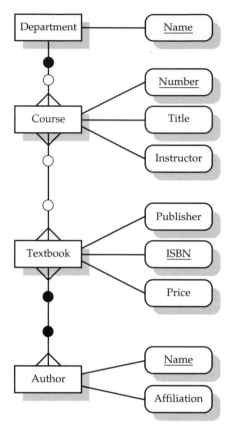

FIGURE 6–3 College Bookstore Entity-Relationship Diagram

Any database reflects a conceptual **data model.** The data model specifies the entities about which the database contains data and the ways in which these entities are related. The data model is often illustrated as an **entity-relationship diagram.** Figure 6–3 shows such a diagram for part of a college bookstore database. According to this diagram, the database contains data on courses, textbooks, and authors. The crow's-feet and circles at the ends of the line describe the nature of the relationships among the entities.

- Each department offers zero or more courses. (We allow zero as a possibility because some "departments" may be administrative conveniences that do not offer courses, or some very small ones may skip a semester now and then.)
- Each course is offered by one department. (Our database design does not allow for joint course offerings. In some colleges joint offerings are common, so the database would have to allow for them. One reason for developing an entity-relationship diagram is that it makes this type of assumption explicit and visible.)
- Each course has zero or more textbooks. (This covers all the possibilities.)

- Each textbook is used for zero or more courses. (Zero is allowed here so we can store data on texts used in the recent past, even though they're not used now, so we'll have the data on hand in case they are used again in the future.)
- Each textbook has one or more authors. (This is an assumption. It may not always be correct.)
- Each author wrote one or more textbooks. (We do not store data on potential authors or on authors of books in which we have no interest, so we have no authors with zero books to their names.)

The entity-relationship diagram also shows the attributes of each entity. The example in Figure 6–3 shows a few of these attributes. Attributes that identify the entity, also called **keys** or **key attributes,** are underlined.

The ERD of the entire database would be far more complex—courses are divided into sections, each section has an instructor, courses are taught during terms (important because BIO 301 may have different instructors and textbooks in different terms), and so on. However, the same concepts apply as the diagram expands to include these complexities.

You will encounter data models in (at least) these ways as a DSS developer. They are listed in increasing order of the technical demands they place on you.

1. Data models describe the relationships among business data independently of how the data might be stored in a computer [FINK89, SCHE92]. Using them will help you understand the business data that your DSS will use. For this purpose you need not be precise about the formal, technical aspects of entity-relationship diagramming. However, as we saw in the previous example, it is important to be quite precise about the business relationships it conveys.
2. Your DSS uses an existing database. Examining its data model, presuming it exists (it should!) is a good way to understand what it contains and how its elements are interrelated.
3. Your DSS must present its users with different views of an existing database. Drawing their ERDs is a good way to understand what data must be extracted from the database and to communicate this understanding to your system's users.
4. You must design a database for your DSS. Database design should always begin with a conceptual data model, usually expressed as an ERD. Database management courses and books can teach you what you have to know for this purpose.

Database managers are categorized according to the way in which they organize their data. There are four basic database structures: hierarchical, network (or CODASYL), relational, and multidimensional. We'll discuss the first three of these next. Inasmuch as multidimensional databases are used primarily with data warehouses (in a DSS context), we'll cover them in Chapter 13.

A **hierarchical database** manager links records of different types in a strict hierarchy from top to bottom, as shown in Figure 6–4. Each record, except those at the top level, is associated with a specific parent record. Each parent record can

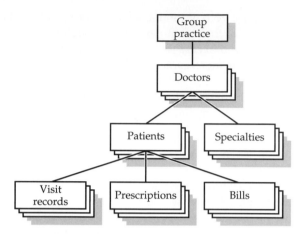

FIGURE 6–4   Hierarchical Database Example

have several child records. These may be of different types, and there may be multiple records of each type.

Linkages among records in a hierarchical database are made via pointer fields in the records. The pointer fields are defined as part of each record when the database is defined. (While they occupy storage and hence must be considered in calculating database space requirements, they do not appear as part of the user-visible record format.) Records can only be linked where predefined pointers exist. In the example of Figure 6–4, it would be difficult to find a doctor with a given specialty who lives in the same town as a particular patient.

The earliest database management systems (DBMS) followed the hierarchical model. Most popular low-end microcomputer database managers are of this type as well. A hierarchical structure is well suited to representing simple data structures, such as customer/invoice/line item. It is weaker in handling more complex relationships, such as many-to-many relationships. In the example of Figure 6–4, a hierarchical database could not deal easily with a situation in which each doctor can have several patients (as in the figure) and each patient can also have several doctors (not in the figure).

A **network database** structure provides more flexibility in the way different files are linked. The use of the term *network* here to describe a database structure does not refer to data communication networks. A database whose parts are spread over a communication network is called a distributed database, not a network database.

Figure 6–5 shows an example of a network database structure. A product is associated with several higher level entities: the invoice on which it was sold, the warehouse in which it was stored, and the supplier from which it was obtained. Several of these relationships can be many-to-many: a warehouse contains multiple products, and a widely used product can be stored in several warehouses. An invoice can be for several products, and a product may appear on more than one invoice. A supplier can supply several products, and a product may come from more than one supplier. The diagram uses the common convention of an arrowhead to indicate the "many" end of a relationship. The only single-valued relation-

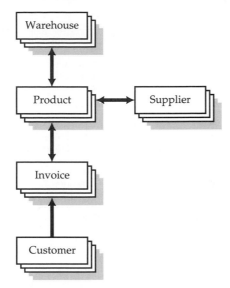

FIGURE 6–5 Network DBMS Example

ship here is that from invoices to customers. Each invoice is associated with one, and only one, customer.

Compared with hierarchical DBMS, network DBMS software is more complicated because it must be able to represent more complex data structures. A large-scale network DBMS usually requires a full-time database administrator. Most mainframe DBMS in use today are of this type. Many network DBMS follow the **CODASYL** (COnference on DAta SYstems Languages) standard. Such databases are often referred to as CODASYL databases.

A **relational DBMS** stores its data in the form of two-dimensional tables as shown in Figure 6–6.[1] There are no pointers in the records of a relational database. (They may exist behind the scenes to improve performance, but users can ignore them.) Rather, the database management software links records from several tables by matching corresponding fields. This is the greatest strength and the greatest weakness of the relational model: a strength because information retrieval is not constrained to predefined links, a weakness because the links must be created (at least in theory) each time they are used. In this example, if a night telephone operator responding to a call from Wilson needs a cardiologist who lives in Wilson's hometown, Dr. Kelly's name can be found easily—without having to find out where Wilson lives and then search the database for cardiologists living in Fremont.

---

[1]Many people, especially those whose computing experience is only with microcomputers, think the word *relational* comes from the ability of a database to relate files, so any database that can deal with multiple files is relational. This is incorrect. This term comes from the mathematical concept of a *relation*. In essence, it means that all data elements in a record relate to the same real-world entity. This error is found in DBMS ads and sales literature, perhaps because "relational" is a good marketing buzzword. Even some otherwise knowledgeable authors have fallen into this trap.

DOCTOR TABLE

Name	Specialty	Hometown	Phone Number
Jones	hematology	San Jose	408-555-9876
Kelly	cardiology	Fremont	510-555-1234

PATIENT TABLE

Name	Insurance	Hometown	Complaint
Smith	Blue Goose	Mountain View	sniffles
Wilson	Improvident	Fremont	heartburn
Davis	None	Santa Clara	tonsillitis

FIGURE 6–6   Relational DBMS Example

If you've studied database management, you may be thinking at this point, But the DBMS has to find out where Wilson lives and scan the database, doesn't it? Of course it does, internally. However, because it's done inside the DBMS, the user (or application program) doesn't see it and doesn't have to deal with it. Perhaps more importantly, because it's done inside the DBMS, it can easily be done inside a server even when an entire application program resides on a client system. This makes relational DBMS, with their high degree of autonomy in responding to complex queries, well suited to a client/server environment.

Relational DBMS were developed after the other two types; they came into commercial use in the 1980s though they had been actively researched since 1970. Minicomputers also came into commercial use at about this time, and high-performance workstations became popular. Most minicomputer and workstation DBMS therefore follow the relational model today. Relational DBMS were slow to catch on with microcomputers, because early microcomputers lacked the processing power to handle them with acceptable response times. As microprocessors became more powerful, relational DBMS came into use at the desktop. At the mainframe level, users' decades of investment in network DBMS prevent rapid conversion to the relational approach, but mainframe users are moving in their direction.

Relational DBMS are better suited to DSS applications than the other types. This is because their records do not contain predefined links to associated records in other files. This provides them with greater flexibility in retrieving data based on previously unplanned criteria. If a market planner wants a list of all customers located in cities that have a warehouse in them, a relational database can satisfy the query easily. Answering the same query with a hierarchical or network database would require either predefined links from warehouse records to customer records—not likely, if the requirement wasn't foreseen—or a special program, which is not within the capability of the typical end user. Relational databases can therefore provide, as you'll read in Chapter 13, a good foundation for a data warehouse designed to respond to unplanned queries.

A second advantage of relational DBMS is that their retrieval operations return the set of all records satisfying a given set of conditions. Other DBMS return one record and require programming to get more than one, though some DBMS packages include query capabilities that handle this programming for common cases. Since many decisions involve looking at or summarizing many records, the set orientation of a relational DBMS is helpful. This, too, is an asset in the data warehouse environment where most analyses require looking at all the records that satisfy certain criteria.

A final advantage of relational DBMS is interface standardization. **Structured Query Language (SQL,** often pronounced "sequel") [AGEL88] is used by all major RDBMS. Although SQL is not fully standardized, and while existing SQL standards do not address all aspects of database manipulation, partial standardization is better than none. Translators (sometimes called **middleware**) allow applications written for one relational DBMS to access others. This is possible only because all SQL variants share the same fundamental underlying concepts. Since DSS often obtain and correlate data from several preexisting systems, this ability to access a variety of different DBMS is important.

Data Retrieval for Decision Support Using SQL

Suppose we have two tables in our employee database. One gives employee names, numbers, and hometowns. The second gives employee numbers and the languages (besides English) the employee speaks.

EMPDATA Table

EMPNO	Name	Town
101	Abel	Arlington
102	Baker	Bedford
103	Chan	Concord
104	Dinsmore	Dracut
105	Exley	Everett

EMPLANG Table

EMPNO	Language
101	French
101	Spanish
102	German
103	Chinese
103	Russian
104	Italian
104	French

(continued)

Data Retrieval for Decision Support Using SQL (continued)

Getting an employee list with addresses is simple:

```
SELECT NAME, TOWN FROM EMPDATA
```

To get the same list, alphabetically by employee name:

```
SELECT NAME, TOWN FROM EMPDATA ORDER BY NAME
```

Finding out how many different towns our employees live in is a bit more complex:

```
SELECT COUNT (DISTINCT TOWN) FROM EMPDATA
```

We can combine, or **join** in relational terminology, two tables to learn which of our employees speak, say, French. This might be helpful in picking someone for an overseas assignment, or, perhaps less interestingly, to escort a French visitor through our factory:

```
SELECT NAME FROM EMPDATA, EMPLANG
WHERE EMPLANG.LANGUAGE = 'FRENCH'
AND EMPDATA.EMPNO = EMPLANG.EMPNO
```

The second line specifies that we want only the numbers of those employees who speak French. The third line joins the two tables, using their common employee number field, to give us the names corresponding to those employee numbers: Abel and Dinsmore.

As a final example, suppose we want to find out which of our employees speaks more than one language:

```
SELECT NAME FROM EMPDATA, EMPLANG
WHERE EMPDATA.EMPNO = EMPLANG.EMPNO
AND EMPNO = (SELECT DISTINCT EMPNO
  FROM EMPLANG FIRST
  WHERE EXISTS SELECT *
    FROM EMPLANG SECOND
    WHERE FIRST.EMPNO = SECOND.EMPNO
    AND FIRST.LANG NOT = SECOND.LANG)
```

This query goes through the EMPLANG table twice for each entry in the table. In the outer loop, it goes through the table once and finds the employee number and language. It then executes the inner loop for each row of the table. In the inner loop, it scans the entire table for instances of the same employee number (next-to-last line) with a different language (last line). It records all it finds, eliminating (because of the keyword DISTINCT on the third line) duplicate employee numbers. Once it has the desired list of employee numbers, it uses the EMPDATA table to translate them to names: Abel, Chan, and Dinsmore.

You can see how SQL, deceptively simple in these easy examples, gets difficult quickly for complex queries such as the last example. It is easy to make an error in a complex query, perhaps retrieving something other than what was wanted and not being able to tell by examining the result. Queries that are not carefully planned can also run for a very long time. The execution time of this last example grows with the square of the EMPLANG table. If this table has 1,000 rows, the DBMS will make a million comparisons. That's not too bad, but "industrial-strength" DBMS may have many millions of rows. Queries that perform trillions of comparisons are best avoided. A "back of the envelope" execution time estimate, done by a trained analyst in a few seconds or minutes, should be undertaken whenever an end-user query runs for what seems to be a long time without results. Quite often, it will show that the results would not appear for another month, or before the user retires. If the query is important, proper planning and database organization—again a task for a trained professional—can usually make its execution time acceptable.

A fourth type of database management system, which is entering commercial use in the late 1990s, is the **multidimensional** (or dimensional) DBMS. This type is particularly useful in data warehouses, so we'll discuss them in Chapter 12.

6.3.2 Information Retrieval Packages

Most **information retrieval packages** are designed to pull user-specified data out of a file or database. The user might type the computer equivalent of "Get me our sales history for Acme, Inc." or "Show me bran muffin shipments, by month and region, for the past year." The database will respond with the requested data—or with "I don't understand what you want" or "I don't have that data." Most packages give the user some flexibility in obtaining the information as a table or a graph, with control over formatting as well.

Such information-retrieval capabilities can be either included as part of a DBMS-based system or sold as separate packages. DBMS suppliers, mindful of the difficulties inherent in end-user attempts to access a database via SQL, vie with each other for the best offering in this area. Many information-retrieval packages combine both capabilities: They incorporate their own database management capability but can access data stored by other DBMS as well.

The strength of a good information-retrieval package lies in its combination of power and ease of use. Power, in this context, refers to the ability to specify complex queries. Ease of use means that end users can master the package, or enough of the package to obtain the results they need, without getting a graduate degree in computer science. As we just saw, SQL provides power in the hands of a trained professional, but not ease of use. Simple microcomputer-based packages provide ease of use but not power. The challenge to the developer of an information-retrieval package lies in combining the two. Since vendors of specialized information-retrieval packages compete with the query capabilities offered by DBMS vendors, they must offer more than DBMS vendors offer in at least one of those two areas if they are to find a market.

In 1999, an increasing fraction of knowledge workers' information-retrieval needs are met through data warehouses. For that reason, we discuss information-retrieval packages in that context—specifically, in the first half of Chapter 14, under the heading of On-Line Analytical Processing (OLAP). There are, of course, other packages that retrieve information from other files or databases. The capabilities described there apply to those packages as well.

A different type of information-retrieval package finds information by searching for words in a text database. You may have used such systems in a library, looking for articles on a given topic, or in searching the World Wide Web. You type in a list of words related to the subject of your search. If you wanted to find articles or Web pages on the meeting between King Richard Lion-Heart and Robin Hood in Sherwood Forest, you might type: Richard Hood Sherwood. The system would respond with articles that contain these words and which are, therefore, hopefully on the subject of your interest. Such systems can be viewed as dividing everything in the database into four categories as shown in Figure 6–7.

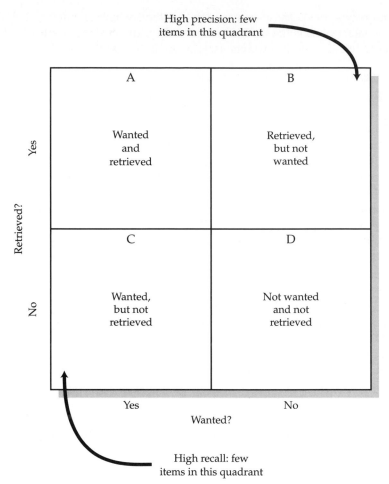

FIGURE 6–7 Two-by-Two Information-Retrieval Grid

The ideal information-retrieval system of this type will retrieve all the items of interest and none of the others—everything in the database will end up in either the top-left quadrant (you wanted it and you got it) or the bottom-right quadrant (you didn't want it and you didn't get it) of the figure. Unfortunately, this is usually not what happens. The typical system will miss some articles you would have wanted to see. Perhaps they refer to King Richard as Lion-Heart instead of using his name, or perhaps they call Robin Hood "Robin of Locksley." They will also return references to articles you don't care about that happen to include the same words. You might, for example, get a children's story about the day Richard Jones wore a new jacket with a red hood to the Sherwood Elementary School.

Systems that retrieve few irrelevant items are said to have high **precision.** Such systems have few articles in Quadrant B (the top right) of Figure 6–7 (retrieved but not wanted). This is often achieved by being highly selective and therefore missing many desired items as well. On the other side of the coin, systems that miss few relevant items are said to have high **recall.** Such systems have few entries in the Quadrant C (the bottom left) of the grid: wanted but not retrieved. Unfortunately, high recall is often achieved by being less selective in what is retrieved, thus creating low precision.

One way to improve recall and precision is to have either document authors or information-retrieval professionals attach a list of keywords to each document. This is effective but demands additional work before a document can be searched for. Research aimed at improving precision and recall simultaneously is going forward. In the meantime, successful results depend on proper phrasing of each query. If the first set of results seems to be too small, try including additional keywords that might lead to more hits. If it is too broad, try to see if there is a pattern to the irrelevant items retrieved. You will often be able to exclude them by telling the system *not* to return items that contain a given word or phrase. For instance, if you're looking for articles about RICO, the U.S. Racketeering In Corrupt Organizations act, including the specification

AND NOT "PUERTO"

in your request (the syntax may vary, depending on the system you are using) will prevent it from burying the desired items under thousands that discuss Puerto Rico. As with many other skills, practice, while it may not make perfect, leads to improvement.

6.3.3 Specialized Modeling Languages

As we noted earlier, many DSS incorporate models of various types. Models of a given type tend to have many characteristics in common. For that reason, standard packages have been developed to deal with many popular types of models. These packages do not incorporate any models themselves. They simply make it easier for the user to define the characteristics of his or her model to the computer. This section deals with languages used for financial, or accounting, models. We'll discuss dynamic discrete-event models, including examples of two specialized languages for this type of modeling, in Chapter 8.

The term **accounting model,** which we introduced in Chapter 4, refers to a static model with no uncertainty. As we mentioned there, the familiar **spreadsheet** is the standard tool with which most knowledge workers and managers manipulate accounting models.

A spreadsheet, in its basic form, looks like a two-dimensional grid of cells. Each cell can contain a number, a formula that uses the contents of other cells to yield a result, or text for annotation. Figure 6–8 shows a simple example. Cells A1, A2, A3, and A4 in this spreadsheet contain labels. (In most spreadsheet packages, a label too long to fit into one cell spills over into adjacent ones if they are blank. That is why the label in cell A1 seems to be in cells B1 and C1 as well.) Cells B2 and B3 contain constants (numbers). Cell B4 contains the formula B2 − B3. The spreadsheet program carries out the specified computation and displays the result in the cell. The formula itself can be inspected by switching the

	A	B	C	D
1	INCOME STATEMENT FORECAST			
2	INCOME	$10,000		
3	EXPENSES	$9,000		
4	PROFIT	$1,000		
5				

FIGURE 6–8 Spreadsheet Example

spreadsheet to "display formulas" mode or by selecting cell B4, which causes its formula to be displayed in a box at the top of the screen.

Most modern spreadsheets can do more than this. They include dozens, often hundreds, of built-in functions for mathematical and business computations: loan amortization, net present value calculations, statistics, and more. They have conditional computation capabilities where different calculations can be carried out depending on the result of a formula. They can create several kinds of graphs automatically from the data they calculate. They may extend the two-dimensional grid to three or more dimensions. They can treat their content as a simple database, with form-based data entry, sorting, and retrieval. They provide macro-instructions or simple programming languages to automate repetitive procedures. They may have enough formatting capability—font choices, sizes, borders, character attributes, and color—to create finished presentation materials. But the basic concept— an array of cells that contain numbers, text, or formulas—remains as it has been since the 1970s.

As the spreadsheet is essentially an electronic reproduction of an accountant's and financial analyst's paper-and-pencil tool, it fits a financial analyst's needs well. However, spreadsheets have several disadvantages for this purpose. Consider, for example, the spreadsheet in Figure 6–9. This spreadsheet has one change from that of Figure 6–8: Profits are given as $2,000, not as $1,000. The error could have been introduced in either of two ways: via an error in the formula used to calculate cell B4, or by simply typing the figure $2,000 directly into that cell. The first could result from an honest error. A malicious user might do the latter, knowing that most spreadsheet readers would assume that a number next to such a label was calculated from a suitable formula. (Whereas a person is unlikely to introduce a deliberate error into a spreadsheet meant only for his or her use, many spreadsheets are used to suggest or justify decisions to other people.) There is no way to tell by looking at Figure 6–9 how this error was introduced.

In the spreadsheet of Figure 6–9, which has three data cells, round numbers, and a concept that most people understand, nearly any manager would spot this error in a few seconds. In a spreadsheet with 186 rows and 55 columns, full of ar-

	A	B	C	D
1	INCOME STATEMENT FORECAST			
2	INCOME	$10,000		
3	EXPENSES	$9,000		
4	PROFIT	$2,000		
5				

FIGURE 6–9   Spreadsheet Example with Error

cane formulas and complex calculations leading to a nonobvious answer at the bottom right, an equally serious error would not be nearly as noticeable. Spreadsheet packages, however, provide little protection against either human error or malice. Specifically, spreadsheets have (at least!) the following drawbacks:

- Because each cell is independent of every other cell, formulas that are supposed to be identical in several cells are independent of each other. While all spreadsheets provide a copy or replicate capability to eliminate repetitive typing, the potential for error still exists. This capability does nothing to ensure that the correct formula was copied into the correct cells or that the formulas remain identical thereafter. A formula may be correct in one cell but incorrect in an adjacent one that supposedly carries out the same calculation. Modifications made to a spreadsheet after it has been in use for a while are especially likely to cause such errors. People selecting a range of cells to modify, whether with cursor keys or with a mouse, are prone to going one cell too far or stopping one cell short of the correct position.
- Because formulas are normally hidden from the user and are scattered all over a spreadsheet, it is difficult to ascertain just what is "inside" a spreadsheet by inspecting it. Moreover, data references in a spreadsheet are often in cryptic row-column format, where the referenced cells themselves contain the results of calculations involving yet other cells. Most spreadsheet packages let their users name ranges and thereafter use the range name rather than a row-column reference, but spreadsheet developers often find it easier to select a desired range by dragging the mouse than to go through the range-naming process.
- For both of these reasons, spreadsheets are susceptible to malicious change by anyone with an ax to grind and few ethical scruples about how he or she grinds it.
- The limitations of the basic spreadsheet paradigm, cells containing formulas that carry out calculations on data in other cells, are too confining for some applications.

The rest of this section discusses approaches that have been developed to bypass these constraints. To alleviate the first and second of the above problems, many

```
Columns 1993 .. 1996
Revenues = Price * Units Sold
Price = 150, previous * 1.05
Units Sold = 1000, previous * 1.15
Cost of Goods Sold = Units Sold * Unit Cost
Unit Cost = 100, previous *1.05
Gross Margin = Revenues - Cost of Goods Sold
Utilities = 4950, previous * 1.05
Overhead = 8250, previous * 1.1
Depreciation = 3025
Selling Expenses = .10 * Revenues
Gen and Admin = .115 * Revenues
EBIT = Gross Margin - sum (Utilities thru Gen and Admin)
Interest Expense = Annual Rate * Debt
Annual Rate = .11
Profit Before Tax = EBIT - Interest Expense
Tax = .46 * Profit Before Tax
Net Profit = Profit Before Tax - Tax
```

FIGURE 6–10   IFPS Model

	1993	1994	1995	1996
Revenues	150000.00	181125.00	218708.44	264090.44
Price	150.00	157.50	165.38	173.64
Units Sold	1000	1150	1323	1521
Cost of Goods Sold	100000.00	120750.00	145805.63	176060.29
Unit Cost	100.00	105.00	110.25	115.76
Gross Margin	50000.00	60375.00	72902.81	88030.15
Utilities	4950.00	5197.50	5457.38	5730.24
Overhead	8250.00	9075.00	9982.50	10980.75
Depreciation	3025.00	3025.00	3025.00	3025.00
Selling Expenses	15000.00	18112.50	21870.84	26409.04
Gen and Admin	17250.00	20829.38	25151.47	30370.40
EBIT	1525.00	4135.63	7415.62	11514.71
Tax	701.50	1902.39	3411.19	5296.77
Net Profit	823.50	2233.24	4004.44	6217.94

FIGURE 6–11   IFPS Financial Model Output Example

firms have turned to software that was developed specifically for **financial modeling.** The most widely used package of this type is IFPS from Execucom. IFPS runs on computing platforms from mainframe to desktop. The IFPS model in Figure 6–10 shows a corporate income forecast for four years. Figure 6–11 shows the output of this model. It resembles a spreadsheet on the surface. The difference is that the model exists as a separate, easily visible, and easily auditable entity. For example, the last line of the model ensures that every element in the output line labeled "Net Profit" will be calculated from the same formula, and shows us what that formula is. It is not possible, by accidental slip of a finger on cursor key or mouse, to copy a revised formula up to but not including the last cell of its intended range. It is also not possible to alter deliberately a formula in one out-of-the-way cell. When the model is listed, there are no out-of-the-way cells.

This IFPS model shows some of the basic features of IFPS:

- Output cells are referred to by row and column names. Cryptic letter-and-number cell references do not exist.
- Formulas apply to an entire row unless stated otherwise. Formulas can be applied to part of a row, but this must be stated explicitly in the model. For example, the Total column is computed differently from the others.
- A backward reference uses the word *previous* instead of an obscure cell reference. If the element taken from the previous column is not on the same row, this must be stated explicitly.

Consider line 4 of Figure 6–10. In English, it instructs IFPS to set the first year's sales to 1,000 units and each subsequent year's sales to 1.15 times the prior year's value. Had a spreadsheet user entered 1.25 rather than 1.15 here, by mistake or by malice, the error would have been hidden in the formulas underlying the output and would have been hard to see in the output alone. (If first quarter sales were 1,458 units rather than a nice, round 1,000, nobody would notice.) In the IFPS model, by contrast, the 1.15 is clearly visible. Any attempt to override it for one column—say, to nudge predicted 1996 gross margin over $90,000, or to improve an R&D project's standing in a competitive corporate ranking process—would jump out at a glance.

IFPS capabilities include goal-seeking, "what if?" testing of alternatives, and a full set of financial and mathematical functions. Modern spreadsheet programs include these as well. The major difference between financial modeling programs and spreadsheet programs is the way in which the model is set up.

How widespread are spreadsheet errors? Several studies have shown that spreadsheets in regular business use often contain inadvertent errors. Davies and Ikin [DAVI87] examined 19 Lotus 1-2-3 spreadsheets and found that four of them had major errors. Simkin [SIMK87] cites a consultant for an accounting firm who found 128 errors in the spreadsheets of only four clients. Some of these spreadsheets were used to make multibillion-dollar decisions. He also cites the case (referred to earlier on page 103) of a manager in a Florida construction firm who forgot to adjust the endpoint of an @SUM formula range when he inserted a new row into a spreadsheet, so the cost element in that row wasn't added into the total cost of the project. His firm's bid on a project was more than $250,000 lower than it should have been. The firm won the bid but wished it hadn't. Panko [PANK98] examined 20 published reports of field audits, development experiments and code inspection experiments. The error frequencies reported are, to put it mildly, alarming—even in models that have been in regular business use for six months or more.[2]

Auditing packages, which are available for the major spreadsheets, help find both accidental and malicious errors in standard spreadsheets. For example, The Cambridge Spreadsheet Analyst (Intex Solutions, Needham Heights, Mass.) display all the formulas of a spreadsheet, highlighting items that appear to violate the

---

[2]Prof. Panko maintains a Web site at http://www.cba.hawaii.edu/panko/ssr with information on spreadsheet errors, including lists of articles and papers on the subject.

rules of logic that most correct spreadsheet models follow. They provide a global view of patterns, showing exactly how far a particular formula was replicated: If all the formulas for the year 1999 were replicated through 2003 except for the one in the Units Sold row, this will be immediately evident. They check for circular references: situations where the formula in one cell uses data in a second cell, whose formula in turn uses the data in the first cell (perhaps with more steps along the way). This is occasionally a useful modeling technique but is usually a mistake. They can provide cross-references between cells and formulas in other cells that refer to them: a **trace**, which lists the sources of input to a given cell, and a **probe**, which lists cells that use a given cell's output. Spreadsheet auditing package users report that they uncover many previously unsuspected errors, almost universally due to human error and often potentially costly.

Figure 6–12A shows a simple spreadsheet. Unit sales were supposed to grow 5 percent per year from 2001 through 2004. In order to predict higher profits in 2004, someone removed the formula from the 2004 column of the Unit Sales row, where it would have forecasted sales of 1,159 units, and replaced it with the constant 1,200. An auditing package, in this case the Worksheet Auditor macro bundled with Excel, produced the worksheet map shown in Figure 6–12B. It is instantly obvious that cell E5 differs from its predecessors in row E: It contains a numeric constant, not a formula. (A clever person bent on deception, if he or she knew that only this check would be done, could enter a formula precalculated to yield 1,200 rather than a constant. Other spreadsheet auditing packages, however, will flag formulas that differ from those in the cells to their left.)

The fourth spreadsheet problem noted on page 215—that its fundamental paradigm does not suit all requirements—is the reason other types of software exist.

6.3.4 Statistical Data Analysis Packages

Virtually every decision involves an attempt to predict what will happen in the future if a given course of action is chosen. Will I like this restaurant's mustard sauce, or will their Hollandaise taste better? How much will sales increase if we cut our prices by 10 percent?

A fundamental premise of decision making is that the future depends, in part, on factors we control. By determining how a system—be it our taste buds or a business system—has reacted to these factors in the past, we hope to estimate how it will react in the future and thus gauge the likely outcome of our decisions. These relationships are often statistical. Specialized **statistical software** helps us deal with the statistics.

The simplest type of prediction is based on regression calculations, which you may have studied in a statistics class. Consider Figure 6–13A. It plots U.S. Government fuel economy data (average of city and highway) versus weight, both from [ROAD99], for 100 cars and small vans.[3] There is clearly a relationship:

---

[3]The first 100 gasoline-powered vehicles alphabetically in the list, from Acura CL through Nissan Altima.

	2001	2002	2003	2004
Unit Sales	1000	1050	1103	1200
Unit Price	$1.00	$1.00	$1.10	$1.10
Net Sales	$1,000.00	$1,050.00	$1,212.75	$1,320.00
Expenses	$900.00	$1,000.00	$1,100.00	$1,200.00
Profit	$100.00	$50.00	$112.75	$120.00

FIGURE 6–12A Spreadsheet with Deliberate Error

Map of Worksheet1

	A	B	C	D	E
1					
2					
3		9	9	9	9
4					
5	T	9	F	F	9
6	T	9	9	9	9
7	T	F	F	F	F
8	T	9	9	9	9
9	T	F	F	F	F

LEGEND	
T	Text
F	Formula
9	Number
L	Logical
#	Error

FIGURE 6–12B Audit Map

Heavier vehicles tend to get worse mileage. At the same time, the data points do not all fall on a perfectly straight line, so other factors must be at work as well. Most adults of the early 21st century are sufficiently familiar with automobiles to guess what some of these might be. (The car at the bottom center, with average weight and the worst fuel economy on the chart, is the Lamborghini Diablo.) By calculating the "best fit" line through the given points we can accomplish two things:

1. We can develop a formula (in this case the equation of a straight line, but a more complex shape if the data or our knowledge of the underlying system suggest one) to predict, approximately, what highway mileage an unknown car of a given weight will obtain. Figure 6–13B shows the same data as Figure 6–13A,

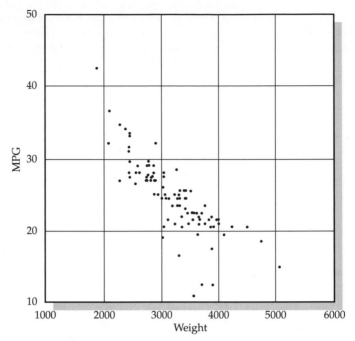

FIGURE 6–13A SYSTAT Plot of Vehicle Mileage versus Weight

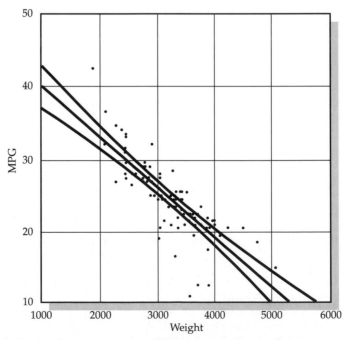

FIGURE 6–13B SYSTAT Plot of Vehicle Mileage versus Weight with Best Linear Fit and 95 percent Confidence Intervals

with the best linear fit and 95 percent confidence bands added.[4] (Both are print-outs from SYSTAT by SYSTAT, Inc., Evanston, Ill.) We can conclude from this chart that an unknown car weighing 3,500 pounds is likely to get about 22.5 miles per gallon, while a 2,500-pound vehicle is likely to achieve about 29.5 miles per gallon.

2. We can determine the **correlation** between this estimating formula and the actual mileage figures. That, in turn, tells us statistically how much of the mileage variation from one vehicle to the next is explained by vehicle weight and how much of it must be due to other factors. The correlation between vehicle weight and gasoline mileage, as determined by the Pearson correlation formula, is −0.864. In other words, vehicle weight appears to account for about 86 percent of the variation in fuel consumption, whereas other factors explain the other 14 percent. The negative sign indicates that fuel economy goes up as weight goes down.

This calculation, by the way, points out an important consideration in using statistical software. SYSTAT provides a number of correlation tools—Pearson, Spearman, Kendall Tau-B, and more—which can produce different results. (Pearson correlation calculations, for example, can be more susceptible to influence by a few outlying points than are Spearman.) And correlation calculations are one of the simpler statistical analyses. The moral: Be sure you know what you're doing with statistics before you use one of these packages. They enable a novice to create impressive garbage in seconds. If you're incorporating this type of software into a larger decision support system for users who may not be trained in statistics, be sure to provide guidance in what calculations to perform and how far to trust their results.

As an example of the potential of drawing unwarranted conclusions from data, consider the aforementioned statement: Weight appears to account for about 86 percent of the variation in fuel consumption. The words *appears to* were deliberate. Vehicle weight is highly correlated with engine size (heavier cars need larger engines to achieve acceptable performance; larger engines use more fuel to overcome internal friction and move their own weight), aerodynamic drag (heavier cars tend to be larger and therefore have more air resistance), and rolling resistance (heavier cars tend to have larger tires with more contact area). The danger lies in assuming that statistical correlation implies cause and effect. We do not know from the given data how much of the difference in fuel consumption is due to weight, how much to other factors that tend to go along with weight. If we took a 3,500-pound car that got 22.5 miles per gallon, and by use of exotic lightweight graphite and titanium cut its weight to 2,500 pounds without changing its engine, size, shape, or tires, would we get 29.5 miles per gallon? We don't know.

---

[4]These bands indicate the interval in which the true mean from which these samples were taken has a 95 percent likelihood of being, not the interval in which 95 percent of the data are expected to be. (You can see that well over 5 percent of the data points lie outside the lines.) This is an example of how the "obvious" interpretation of a statistical concept, to a person who never studied statistics, can be misleading.

An automobile executive who ordered a weight reduction program based on these data, expecting that result, would be on shaky ground.[5]

SYSTAT and many competing packages run on most popular microcomputer and larger systems. Most statistical packages allow a decision maker to deal with more than one dependent variable at a time, though it is difficult to show more than one—and impossible to show more than two—via standard graphical output on a two-dimensional computer screen or sheet of paper.

Statistics packages have other capabilities as well. They can create cross-tabulations to analyze data from market research questionnaires as a basis for marketing decisions: how, for example, does pizza consumption vary by age group? Other forms of statistical analysis allow decision makers to identify clusters in data: What types of people buy purple refrigerators? What eating patterns are associated with a particular medical problem? They also allow users to delve more deeply into aspects of the data that appeal to them. For example, a SYSTAT user can point at the highest-mileage point at the top left of Figure 6–13 (A or B) with the mouse. Upon doing so, the data list will scroll to show the Chevrolet Metro, rated at 41 miles per gallon in the city and 44 on the highway, at the top. (It's also the lightest car in the sample.) The same process works on any desired group of data points by selecting a "rope" tool and drawing a line around the points in question. All will be highlighted in the data list. The specifics of this operation differ in other packages, but the concept of being able to identify points of interest is the same.

As with so many other types of software, many packages that were originally meant for statistical analysis have evolved well beyond that. The SAS System, with roots that go back for decades and which runs on a variety of platforms from several vendors, is an example. Its name was originally an acronym for "Statistical Analysis System," but (like NCR Corporation, which once stood for "National Cash Register") it kept the initials while removing their original, literal meaning. The SAS System still incorporates advanced statistical tools, forecasting methods, time-series analysis, regression and variance analyses, multivariate analysis, spectral analysis, tools for econometric modeling, and optimization methods for operations management. It includes the variety of graphical output methods that one would expect from a dedicated statistics package. However, it has been extended to include data access capability for many popular DBMS, the ability to create easy menu-driven access, and an end-user report generation tool. The result is a package that can be of use to people whose DSS needs include statistical analysis but are not necessarily limited to it.

A common management application of statistical data analysis is in **statistical quality control,** or **SQC** as it is commonly called. This field provides management with information they need to determine if a production process is behaving

---

[5]We also don't know, for that matter, that a correlation isn't due to chance. Out of every 20 statistical correlations that each have less than a 5 percent chance of being due to chance, one, on the average, *will* be due to chance alone. We can improve the odds by insisting on a higher certainty factor, or as in this case by using a large number of data points, but we can never eliminate chance as a possible cause of statistical correlation.

properly.[6] Managers typically want to know four things about the statistics of process output:

1. Is its mean where it should be? If not, some part of the process is out of adjustment.
2. Is its spread what it should be? If the spread is too large, too many defective items may be produced. If it is too small, excessive costs may be incurred.
3. Is its shape what it should be? If not, some part of the process is out of adjustment.
4. Are the trends of these three items stable over time? If not, a process that is in control now may be on its way out of control in the foreseeable future.

Figure 6–14 shows statistical distributions representing the results of trying to cut lumber to a length of six feet with allowable error of one-quarter inch in

FIGURE 6–14 **Statistical Process Control Diagrams**

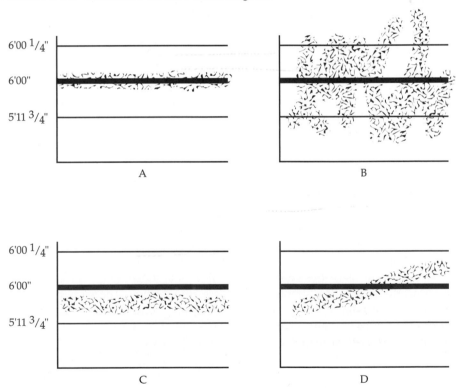

---

[6]The term *production* is used in a general sense here. "Producing" insurance policies, mortgage loan application approvals or rejections, or any other repetitive tangible item would qualify.

either direction. Figure 6–14A shows a process that is in control, though its spread is smaller than necessary. Part B shows a process that is not in control; Part C shows a process that is off the desired mean even though tight error control keeps the outputs within the allowable limits, and Part D shows a process that is in control with the desired mean but is veering out of control toward the high side. Production managers use a variety of specialized charts for statistical quality control in addition to the general diagrams of Figure 6–14. They often also use specialized SQC software packages to create these charts and analyze them further.

6.3.5 Forecasting Packages

Forecasting can be defined as predicting the future based on facts known at the present. The word is used to mean two different things in business:

- One type of forecast is a pure prediction of a phenomenon that will take place in the future. This includes a variety of activities, including customer order forecasting and lottery number forecasting (which, according to most experts, doesn't work). This type of forecast is usually based on some type of historical data and statistical trend analysis.
- Another type of forecast is derived from a model of how known (or, perhaps, statistically predictable) factors influence other factors that cannot be predicted as easily.

You can find good descriptions of all types of forecasting commonly used by business managers in any of several books such as [ELLI90], [WEBS86], [WILL87], or [WILS90] or others your library has indexed under that topic. A good source of up-to-date information on forecasting, including real-world case studies, is the quarterly *Journal of Business Forecasting Methods and Systems*.

A common forecasting problem is time-series forecasting, also called time-series analysis. **Time-series analysis** extrapolates a trend based solely on its historical changes with no reference to any underlying mechanism that may be responsible for that trend or to a possible relationship between the forecasted item and some other variable. There are three basic approaches to time-series analysis: extrapolation, moving average, and exponential smoothing.

Extrapolation takes the available data, fits a curve to them, and extends the curve into the future. The simplest curve is a straight line. The straight line that best fits a set of points $\{x, y\}$, based on the common criterion of minimizing the sum of the squares of the vertical distances from the line to each of the points (referred to as a **least-mean-squares (LMS)** fit) can be written as

$$y = a + bx$$

where a and b are the solutions to the pair of linear equations

$$\begin{pmatrix} n & \Sigma x_i \\ \Sigma x_i & \Sigma x_i^2 \end{pmatrix} \begin{pmatrix} a \\ b \end{pmatrix} = \begin{pmatrix} \Sigma y_i \\ \Sigma x_i y_i \end{pmatrix}$$

where n is the number of data points and the summations are carried out over all the points. Their solution is given by

$$a = \frac{\sum x_i^2 \sum y_i - \sum x_i \sum x_i y_i}{\Delta}$$

$$b = \frac{n \sum x_i y_i - \sum x_i \sum y_i}{\Delta}$$

where Δ is the determinant of the equations, or

$$d = n \sum x_i^2 - \left(\sum x_i\right)^2$$

Figure 6–15 shows an LMS fit to a set of monthly data, extrapolated another two months in the future. It is also possible to fit other curves to the data if there is reason to believe that a straight line is not appropriate. For example, the data may reflect market penetration of a product, which is inherently limited to 100 percent. A decaying exponential curve may be a good choice to represent the remaining customer base of a disappearing product.

The mathematics of LMS fitting are not difficult as long as the curve can be described by an equation with a small number of parameters. Figure 6–16 shows an example of fitting a decaying exponential curve.

Moving average extrapolation uses only the most recent data as a basis for the forecast. One may, for instance, use the last six months. As new data become available older data are discarded. This method can be used, for example, for

FIGURE 6–15 **Least-Mean-Square Fit to Time-Series Data**

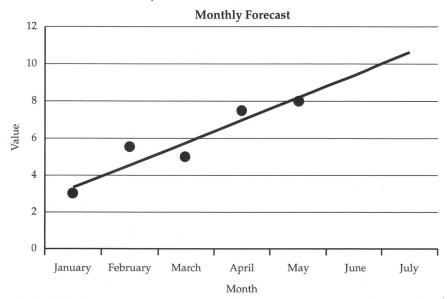

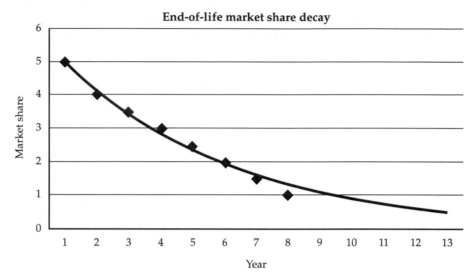

FIGURE 6–16 Decaying Exponential Fit to Time-Series Data

gauging the fitness of an endurance athlete. The athlete's performances over the past few months are more important for this purpose than earlier data. Any of the above methods can be applied to a moving average.

Exponential smoothing is based on the same philosophy as the moving average—newer data are more relevant than older—but does not apply a sharp cut-off. Where the moving average method considers all data points equal up to a point and worthless beyond that point, exponential smoothing reduces their value gradually as they recede into the past. For example, last month's data may be weighted at 100 percent in the forecast, the previous month's at 90 percent, the month before that at 90 percent of *that* or 81 percent, and so on through 72.9 percent, 65.6 percent, etc. This method is used in space navigation, where new data update the current position estimate. (It used to be used in earth-based navigation as well, but GPS satellites have turned older navigation methods into topics for historians and hobbyists.)

An advantage of exponential smoothing is that it isn't necessary to keep all the old data around. One need only keep the weighted sum. As each new data element arrives, the weighted sum of the earlier data is reduced to 90 percent of its previous value (or any desired weighting factor) and the new element added in. The process repeats indefinitely.

Many phenomena reflect two (or more) underlying trends over time: a long-term, or **secular trend,** and one or more periodic cycles. Demand for skis, for instance, is seasonal and also responds to long-term rise or fall in the popularity of skiing over several years or decades. Demand for restaurant tables is affected by the time of day, day of week, and, in locales with seasonal activity trends such as ski resorts, by the season as well.

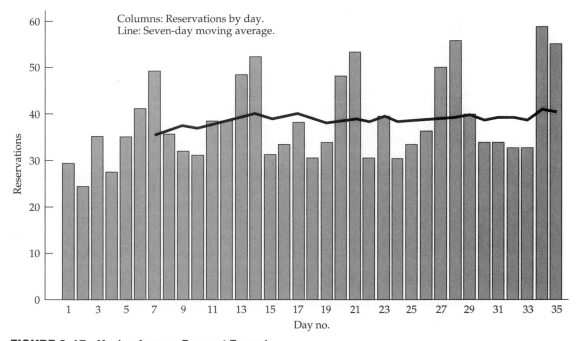

FIGURE 6–17 **Moving Average Forecast Example**
Note: This graph might correspond to a newly opened restaurant. A restaurant that had been in business for more than a few months would probably not show much change over a five-week period unless seasonal factors were at work.

Developing a time-series forecast involves three steps:

1. Determine the periodic cycles of the phenomenon. Some phenomena react to more than one cycle: perhaps a weekly cycle, a seasonal cycle, plus some sensitivity to overall business cycles. In this case, it is necessary to identify all the major cycles to which the phenomenon is sensitive.
2. Determine the secular trend of the phenomenon. The secular trend can often be found, or at least visualized, by averaging several periodic cycles of a phenomenon. Figure 6–17 shows a seven-day moving average of table reservations at a restaurant, hour by hour. While individual days vary greatly, smoothing out the daily variations by averaging over a week shows longer-term trends clearly.
3. Determine how much of the historical variation in the phenomenon can be explained by these two factors, and hence how much remains to be explained by other factors. This corresponds to the correlation step in static statistical analysis.

It can be dangerous to trust the output of a forecasting package too much. All forecasts assume that nothing of importance is going to change from the base period to the period being forecasted. Economic factors have caused drops in nearly every measure of economic importance from time to time. No pure time-series forecast based on previous years could have predicted these. A forecast that attempted to consider economic conditions would have been at the mercy of economic forecasters. Although their predictions are far from perfect, to the dismay of managers, politicians, and investors everywhere, they are usually better than nothing.

6.3.6 Graphing Packages

Most people assimilate data most readily in the form of a picture. While graphs cannot convey differences among numbers smaller than about 1 percent of their full scale, higher precision is usually wasted in decision support applications. (DSS differ in this respect from transaction processing applications. An accounts payable program that generated supplier checks whose amounts were accurate to within 1 percent or so would not be acceptable. This is a case of differing *information quality requirements.*) Most decisions are based on trends or differences that are clearly apparent on a graph.

Today's spreadsheet and statistical data analysis packages include built-in graphing capabilities that suffice for most users' everyday needs. Stand-alone **graphing software packages** offer more options for visual data analysis to those whose needs are more complex. Using such a package is not much harder than using a spreadsheet with its own graphing capability, since these packages are all designed to import data in common spreadsheet formats. Getting data from the spreadsheet to the graph requires, at most, switching from one program to another and using a system-supplied "clipboard" or an intermediate data file. It may even be easier if the graphic package is designed to take advantage of the linking capabilities built into most contemporary operating systems.

Competition has led to rapid improvement in microcomputer spreadsheet package graphing capabilities. The more graphically oriented Microsoft Excel forced Lotus to upgrade the capabilities of Lotus 1-2-3 in this area. Then, Lotus's better integration of graphs with the spreadsheet on which they are based forced a Microsoft response. Meanwhile, other competitors tout graphics features as advantages over the market leaders. The need for specialized graphing packages is not likely to disappear when the utmost in flexibility and graphical appeal is needed, as you can see in Figure 6–18 (created by DeltaGraph 4.5 from SPSS, Inc.). However, their applicability will continue to narrow as spreadsheet and statistics packages become better able to satisfy nearly all requirements.

Graphing packages, by the way, should not be confused with *graphics packages.* (Some people use the term **charting packages** for what we have called graphing packages to reduce the potential confusion.) There are many software packages that create attractive or useful drawings for advertising, publications (such as many of the illustrations in this book), architecture, engineering, training, enhancing the appearance of Web pages,—among other purposes. Whereas graphics packages are important to business, they do not usually have a major role in DSS.

6.4 PROGRAMMING LANGUAGES FOR DSS

The final approach to DSS development is to write the necessary software from scratch. "From scratch" is a bit of a misnomer here, since true from scratch software development is a rarity today. Few if any DSS would not take advantage of at

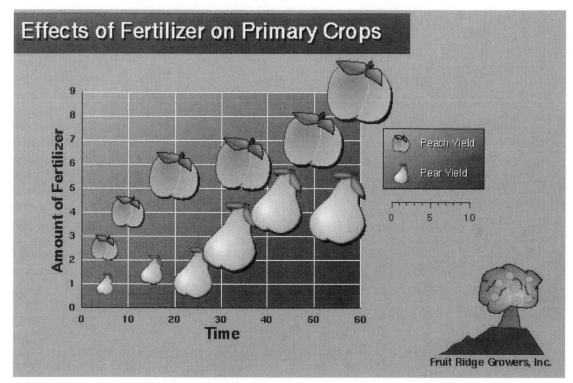

FIGURE 6–18   Output of Graphing Package
Source: Copyright 1999 SPSS, Inc. Used with permission.

least some capabilities listed in the previous section. However, important components of many DSS cannot be satisfied by standard tools and are still written in a programming language of some type.

6.4.1 Third-Generation Programming Languages

While so-called experts have been predicting their demise for decades, **third-generation languages (3GLs)** such as Pascal and C—even the older COBOL, which dates from the early 1960s—remain the mainstay of system developers as the 21st century opens. Despite substantial progress in more advanced languages and standard software packages, most programmers still work at the procedural (3GL) level. New languages such as Java, designed for developing Web-based applications, are unquestionably in the traditional 3GL mold.

Third-generation languages have the advantage of standardization. Chances are you have been, or will be, exposed to at least one popular 3GL during your academic career. You will then be able to use that language, with a bare minimum of additional system-specific training, on any hardware platform and under any operating system you encounter. In addition, the concepts underlying most 3GLs are close to one another. An experienced Pascal programmer has a big head start on learning C.

Compilers for popular 3GLs have been refined over the years and produce code that utilizes hardware efficiently. If one is writing a program that will be used regularly by many people over an extended period of time, so the hardware resources needed to support the application are significant to the organization, hardware resource utilization considerations usually make a 3GL the approach of choice. High-volume transaction processing programs fall into this category.

Efficiency is less of a consideration with most DSS. DSS are usually used less intensely. A manager will examine a forecast, think about it, discuss it with a colleague, change a parameter, and then request the computer to generate another forecast. This is quite different from the work of an order entry clerk who does nothing but enter orders all day long. Furthermore, an organization is likely to have fewer managers who use a DSS than it has employees in computer-intensive jobs. While this doesn't mean a DSS developer should take a "hardware efficiency be damned" attitude, it is less likely, as a rule, for hardware usage efficiency to be a major factor in the overall cost of a DSS.

The bottom-line impact of DSS usage on the firm is also more substantial than is the impact of most transaction processing applications. No customer will choose a particular supplier because it processes its accounts payable especially well. The value of having a new accounts payable (A/P) or payroll program running a month earlier is therefore relatively small. The value of having a new decision-making tool running a month earlier, by contrast, can be enormous.

The net effect of these considerations is to justify an attitude of "let it be inefficient, just get it to me right away!" on the part of managers who need a DSS. There are exceptions, of course, but they tend to be exceptions. In most cases, the added value of having the DSS available quickly more than makes up for any inefficiencies in how it uses the hardware. For these reasons fourth-generation languages, or 4GLs, are often the approach of choice for DSS development.

6.4.2 Fourth-Generation Programming Languages

The defining characteristic of a **fourth-generation language (4GL)** is that its user specifies *what* the computer is to do, not *how* the computer is to do it. Do you need a sales report by region for the past three years? List the items to be reported on, how you want them organized and totaled, and let the 4GL do the work. A 3GL programmer, by contrast, must specify in detail how the program should cycle through the regions and the years, and must write the necessary statements to accumulate the desired totals. This process is labor intensive, time consuming, and error prone. Logic mistakes, such as omitting the first or the last item on a list from a total, are often detected only after a program has been in use for months or years. By this time many decisions will have been based on its output.

This example serves to point out the key differences between 3GLs and 4GLs. A 4GL user trades flexibility and run-time efficiency for speed of development. Where the built-in capabilities of the 4GL suffice, and where the utmost in machine utilization efficiency is not required, a 4GL can cut application development time by an order of magnitude.

If we evaluate these characteristics in the context of DSS, we find that

- The flexibility of a modern 4GL is usually sufficient for most database extraction, analysis, and reporting tasks. Most current 4GLs offer nearly all the flexibility of their COBOL counterparts. Programmers can use complex commands where necessary and still take advantage of 4GL conciseness throughout the vast majority of their code.
- The greater hardware resource utilization of most 4GLs is usually not a major issue with DSS, as they tend to be used by a small user community making decisions that have a big financial impact on the organization.
- Quicker application development time is often an important 4GL advantage with DSS. Time spent waiting for the DSS to become available is time during which the best decisions are not being made. It is also often necessary to modify DSS quickly to react to changing conditions. Modifications to transaction processing systems, to respond to changes such as a modification to the tax code, new accounting standards, or the introduction of the Euro, generally allow more lead time.

For these reasons 4GLs are usually a better DSS development tool than 3GLs where they meet the need. The most widely used 4GL today is FOCUS, from Information Builders, Inc., of New York City. FOCUS runs on the most popular computing platforms: Windows and Macintosh at the desktop, UNIX, VMS, and AS/400 in the mid range, and IBM MVS at the mainframe level. Many other 4GLs exist. Some are offered by computer system vendors (MAPPER and LINC from Unisys); some from database management system suppliers such as Oracle, Informix, and Progress to work with their DBMS; and some, like Mark IV from Informatics, originally developed as data extraction and reporting tools and have been substantially enhanced over the years.

Figure 6–19 is an example of a program in the 4GL FOCUS. Figure 6–20 shows its output. This program reads a file SALES and organizes it by store code (called STORE_CODE). For each store it first prints out an informative heading. It then prints a list by product giving the product code, units sold, units rejected

FIGURE 6–19 FOCUS Program Example

```
TABLE FILE SALES
HEADING
"PRODUCT SALES REPORT"
" "
SUM UNIT_SOLD
COMPUTE
TOT_REJ = RETURNS + DAMAGED;
PCT_REJ/D5.2 = TOT_REJ/UNIT_SOLD * 100;
BY STORE_CODE
BY DATE
BY PROD_CODE
ON STORE_CODE RECOMPUTE PAGE-BREAK
END
```

```
PRODUCT SALES REPORT

STORE_CODE      DATE      PROD_CODE      UNIT_SOLD      TOT_REJ      PCT_REJ
..................    ........    ..................    ..................    ..............    ..............

14Z             10/3      B10            30             5.00         16.67
                          B17            20             3.00         15.00
                          B20            15             1.00          6.67
                          C17            12              .00           .00
                          D12            20             5.00         25.00
                          E1             30            11.00         36.67
                          E3             35             6.00         17.14

*TOTAL STORE_CODE 14Z                    162           31.00        19.14
```

FIGURE 6–20   One Page of Output Produced by FOCUS Program Example

(damaged units plus returned units), and percentage of units sold that rejects represent. The rejection percentage is printed in a five-character field with two places to the right of the decimal point, as specified after the first slash on line 8 of the program. The other fields, whose formats are not explicitly specified in the program, will be printed in their (wider) standard formats. The program finally prints the total of UNITS_SOLD because it is so directed in the SUM command, and carries out the reject computations for the total line as well. It repeats the process for each store until there are no stores left.

Many introductory MIS texts show such a 4GL program with its COBOL equivalent, one or two pages long. The intent is to convince the reader that 4GL programs are shorter than equivalent 3GL programs. Most people find this side-by-side comparison quite convincing.

A program such as the one in Figure 6–19 is still a program. It must follow precise rules of statement order and statement formation. Consider the first line, TABLE FILE SALES. It means that the program is to create a TABLE (as opposed to, say, a graph) using data from a FILE called SALES. While this line is easy to understand when it is explained, a novice can hardly intuit that a FOCUS program ought to start this way. Whereas businesspeople can learn a 4GL in a one-week workshop, they will forget all they have learned in a month or two unless they use it regularly on the job. This explains why you may encounter people with similar backgrounds who hold widely differing opinions on the value of 4GLs to end users.

Because of this natural tendency to forget the details of programming language syntax, most modern 4GLs offer a graphical development interface that handles these nit-picking details via menus and graphical screen painting. Via these development tools, FOCUS under MS-DOS (known as PC/FOCUS) lets you perform the following:

- Define a new database, including field names and characteristics. Figure 6–21 shows a database being defined. The user is now choosing a specific format for the field named DATE, which has the alias (alternative name) DTE and has already (in the box you can partially see under the "Select a date format" box) been specified to contain a date. This box appears automatically as soon as the Date option is chosen for the content of this field. You can see how the various

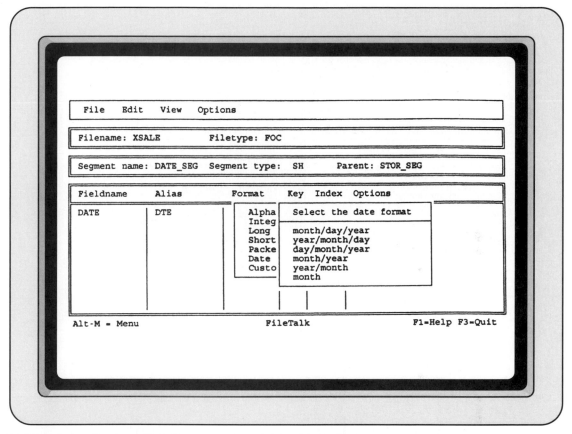

FIGURE 6–21   Database Field Characteristic Definition Screen Shot
Source: PC/FOCUS Getting Started (manual), p. 5-20. Copyright 1993 Information Builders, Inc. Used with permission.

options for date formats are all displayed for the user to choose from. The database definition step is not necessary if an existing database will be used, as FOCUS can read the data dictionaries of most popular DBMS packages.

- Design attractive data entry screens, including data validation (numerical values within a range, values on a list, values included in another named file) and context-sensitive help for the operator.
- Create complex database queries via the TableTalk facility. As a query is formulated, FOCUS displays the actual FOCUS code (as in Figure 6–19 being created in a window at the bottom of the screen. A manager can use this code as a learning aid, modify it if the query is beyond TableTalk's limits, or ignore it. Figure 6–22 shows a user composing a query. At this point the user has identified the file to be used—the same file, SALES, as in the previous example—and is about to specify what is to be printed (actually a generic term for output, as "printing" can go to the user's screen) in the first column of the requested report. The list of options in the left window is longer than what is shown, as indicated by the downward pointing arrow in its top-right corner. Options change as the report definition progresses. TableTalk can define reports that join data from several files, sort data, calculate

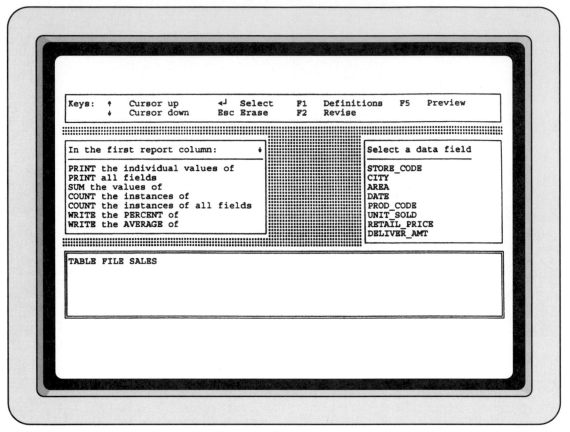

FIGURE 6–22 **Screen Shot of Query Composition**
Source: PC/FOCUS Getting Started (manual), p. 10-25. Copyright 1993 Information Builders, Inc. Used with permission.

aggregates (sum, count, average, etc.), put in control breaks when a sort variable changes, incorporate page headers and footers, and have any desired format.
- Plot data as a line chart, vertical or horizontal bar chart, scatter diagram or pie chart.
- Enter data into the FOCALC spreadsheet component of the FOCUS system, which provides the capabilities of popular spreadsheet packages.
- Define menus that let another user enter any of several different modules. This capability is useful to MIS professionals developing a multimodule application for end users.

The need to interface to one or more existing databases and to modules written in a 3GL are often important factors in 4GL choice (or, indeed, the decision to use one in the first place). Most 4GL packages, even those that incorporate their own database management capability, can access the most widely used third-party databases. Below the top few database formats, however, the need for database access may narrow your choices. So it is with 3GLs: interfaces to C and COBOL are common, those to other languages are less so. Be sure to check these requirements before you get too far into 4GL selection. When in doubt, assume your DSS will have to access every conceivably relevant database in sight. It is better to eliminate a 4GL with potentially useful features than to discover, six months into a development project, that accessing the manufacturing database has become a DSS requirement—and your chosen 4GL can't read it.

If 4GLs are so wonderful, why aren't they more widely used? For several reasons.

- Most existing mainframe-based transaction systems are written in COBOL. It is easiest to modify and extend these in COBOL, rather than restructure them to incorporate 4GL and COBOL modules.
- 4GLs are designed primarily for applications such as summary reports, not complex data manipulation. There are some jobs where they just won't do, or where they must be twisted to fit where a 3GL would slide in smoothly. Fear that a job may turn out to be in this category may motivate people to choose a 3GL in the first place even when its capabilities are not required.
- There are more trained and experienced 3GL programmers than there are trained and experienced 4GL programmers. People tend to use the tools that they know.
- 4GLs are not standardized, whereas most 3GLs are. A FOCUS user must learn Progress, MAPPER, or Delphi almost from scratch, whereas a Windows Pascal programmer can adapt easily to Pascal under Solaris (based on UNIX) on a Sun workstation.
- Force of habit and 3GL "snobbism" in some quarters (4GL users aren't "real" programmers; 4GL research is not "academically deep"). These reasons may not be defensible, but they do exist.
- The continued concern of many veteran IS managers with run-time efficiency. This may influence their decisions even when objective analysis suggests it shouldn't.
- The cost of the 4GL and its supporting software. These can easily reach six figures for a mainframe-and-micro client/server installation. Managers looking at such sums to support a few users will often say "let's keep using the languages we've already got," as it would take a great deal of saved programmer time to make up this cost.

Despite these factors, 4GL use is increasing. The business advantages, especially in a DSS context, are too great to ignore.

6.5 DSS USER INTERFACES

Since decision support systems are intended to work closely with human decision makers in carrying out their tasks, a DSS can only be as effective as its interface with those humans permits. Compared to the clerical and administrative workers who are the primary users of transaction processing and information reporting systems, the knowledge workers and managers who use DSS tend to have the following characteristics:

- They use DSS for only a fraction of their working day. They spend the rest of their time performing other tasks, many of which do not require a computer.

- They are chosen for their positions for reasons other than computing skills. These skills, or even their attitude toward computers, may not be considered in hiring.
- Their tasks are less standardized.
- Each execution of their tasks has greater impact on organizational performance.
- They exercise more individual judgment as to the best way to perform their tasks.
- Their high pay makes it cost-effective to accommodate their personal preferences at the expense of additional system development effort or computer resources.
- Their relatively high organizational status (compared to, say, order entry operators) conditions them to expect organizational accommodation of their individual needs.

These factors make it important to give a DSS the proper interface to its users. While DSS **user interfaces** are often determined or at least constrained by the software packages used in the DSS, developers often have considerable latitude in customizing these or in writing other parts of the system. This makes it essential for DSS designers to understand interface considerations.

6.5.1 Factors to Consider in User Interface Design

All the above user characteristics affect desired DSS user interface. Larson [LARS82] points out the following DSS factors that are determined or affected by its user interface:

- *Time.* How long does it take the user to perform his or her task?

    Some fraction of task time is determined by DSS execution time. Execution time is not an interface issue. Proper interface design can, however, minimize *wasted* time.
- *Learning.* How long does it take a novice to learn the system?

    Nobody over a week old is a true novice at everything. Proper design must consider what the user already knows and how this knowledge fits together in the user's mind.
- *Recall.* How easy is it for a user to recall how to use the system after he or she has not used it for some time?

    This is more important for DSS than for most transaction systems because people often return to DSS after long intervals of non-use. Some DSS, for example, help with annual decisions. An interface that facilitates recall will reduce the time it takes to "get back up to speed" each year.
- *Versatility.* Can the system be used to perform a variety of end-user tasks?

    A DSS must be versatile enough to accommodate the full range of tasks for which decision makers will want to use it. Once a system becomes widely used, tasks related to its original purpose, but distinct from it, will often arise. New tasks may require new development work, but it should be possible to incorporate them into the existing user interface framework.
- *Errors.* How many errors does the user make, and how serious are those errors?

The most serious errors lead to wrong decisions. Following closely behind are errors that corrupt a corporate database. Then come errors that bring down ("crash") the computer, followed finally by errors that waste the user's time but have no other ill effects. Fortunately, most DSS user errors are in the last category. Proper interface design can minimize the wasted time that results. Don't make users reenter a whole series of 70 numbers from the beginning if they miskey the 67th!

Understanding the users' usual decision-making process can help minimize errors. If they are used to entering dates in the sequence month-day-year, don't require them as year-month-day, even if that's how a computer stores them internally. If a system is to be used by people scattered across the globe, DSS planners must accommodate the major differences. In the case of dates, for instance, they should provide a choice between a month-day-year or day-month-year sequence.

It is possible to instrument a system to track user errors so that common ones can be identified and dealt with through interface improvements. If a DSS doesn't justify this level of effort, it may still be feasible to watch users exercise a system prototype. If they have problems with one area, don't argue with them or show them the documentation they should have read more carefully. Change the system to make the error less likely, or at least to make recovering from it as easy, quick, and painless as possible.

• *Help.* Does the system provide help when the user has trouble?

On-line help facilities are becoming the norm for all software, including "industrial-strength" DSS. Modern development tools make it easy to incorporate on-line help into a system. Wherever possible, help should be *context sensitive:* The help facility should recognize what the user is trying to do, or at least what screen the user is on, and provide help that is tailored as closely as possible to the current need.

On-line help should be meaningful. The on-line help for an order entry field clearly labeled "Telephone Number" should say more than

```
Enter telephone number here
```

It could usefully read

```
Enter customer's daytime telephone number, area code first. To be
called if there are questions about the order. If not available, or
if customer declines to provide it, enter ten zeros and continue.
```

Writing helpful error messages takes more effort than mindlessly plugging in "content-free" ones, but it's important to system usability.

Expert systems have unique requirements in this area, since they are often expected to explain to users why they want a particular data item or how they reached a conclusion. We'll discuss the user interface of expert systems in Chapter 11.

- *Adaptability.* Does the system adjust to the user's level of competence as he or she becomes more experienced? Does it tailor itself to different users?

  It may be difficult or impractical for a system to be truly self-tailoring. It is easier, and may be sufficient, to let experienced users select an "expert" mode in which prompts are minimized. In a graphical user interface environment, you can provide keyboard equivalents for commonly used menu commands, as some users like to use mice (or trackballs, trackpads, joysticks, etc.) and others don't.

- *Concentration.* How many things must a user keep in mind while using the system?

  Most people have difficulty keeping more than six or seven active facts in mind at any one time. One way to reduce the memory load is to label screens and output with the parameters of the current scenario: "Profit Projection: 6% inflation, 10% sales growth, Model 47 shipments start April 2001. . . ."

- *Fatigue.* How quickly does the user tire while using the system?

  Physical fatigue—or, more seriously, repetitive strain injuries such as carpal tunnel syndrome—is seldom a factor with DSS because usage frequency is not high enough to cause them. Mental fatigue can arise, however. Minimize it by keeping the necessary concentration within reason (see the previous point) and by asking for information in the sequence in which users normally think of it.

- *Uniformity.* Are the commands of this system identical to equivalent commands of other systems?

  People can learn any interface if they want to. What is difficult is learning two, three, or more interfaces, no matter how simple each one is, and switching frequently among them. A DSS developer must therefore be aware of other systems with which the intended DSS users are familiar. If any standards control some of their user interfaces, such as those for Windows or the Mac OS, developers should conform to these if possible.

- *Fun.* Does the user enjoy the system?

  This does not mean cute error messages or jokes on the screen. Those are hard to do well, nearly impossible to make amusing to all users (especially for an international or multicultural user community) and grow stale quickly. It means keeping users informed about what the system is doing, warning of time-consuming operations, providing progress displays or reports as long operations are carried out, and generally minimizing the frustrations of using an uncooperative system.

Another user-interface issue, unique to DSS and often not adequately considered, is the type and amount of guidance that a DSS provides its users in the decision-making process [SILV91a]. This guidance can be inadvertent: Users tend, all other things being equal, to select the first or last items from menus, which can influence their choice of a statistical analysis method or graph type. Providing a default selection has the same effect.

Consider the chart types available in your spreadsheet program. If you select a column graph, you will be offered a choice of column graph formats. Some will have lines across the columns, some won't, and so on. One will be highlighted when the gallery is displayed. Most of the time, most people click "OK" and accept that format. A chart format is easy to change if you don't like the result, but a poor decision made because an inappropriate statistical analysis method happened to be first on a list can have far-reaching implications.

Decisional guidance can also be built into a system after determining that a particular approach or process is better than what many users, unaided, would chance upon by themselves. This is distinct from on-line help. On-line help assumes that the user knows what to do but not how to do it.

Some DSS offer more of an opportunity for decisional guidance than others. A DSS that does not provide for many discretionary user judgments cannot benefit greatly from it. A DSS that lets users choose among several decision methods, alternative models, ways to cross-tabulate a set of data, forecasting techniques, and other details provides rich opportunities for decisional guidance. Most DSS developers today do not take full advantage of them. Silver [SILV91a] suggests areas to look at, with several concrete examples.

The following sequence of steps for developing a DSS user interface has been suggested. There is room for decisional guidance (at least) in steps 3 to 5, 8, and 9.

1. Determine who your user is.
2. Determine what the user will use the system for.
3. Determine what sequence of steps the user must follow to accomplish a task.
4. Diagram the steps in item 3 and the decision tree involved. Review them with the user.
5. Determine which of these steps require interaction with the system.
6. Determine information and decision requirements for each interaction.
7. Select the categories of dialogue (menus, prompts, forms, etc.).
8. Diagram the flow of dialogue, showing all decisions and their information requirements. Review these with the user.
9. Design screens.
10. Try it, analyze it, simplify it, change it, try it . . .
11. Update the decision diagrams.
12. Bulletproof the dialogue (i.e., what if the user does something unexpected?)

Even if you will develop a DSS via prototyping (see next chapter) or some other method that simplifies the formal development steps, you must still understand who your user is, what the user will use the system for, what sequence of steps he or she will follow, and so on. You may be able to skip over some of the formal diagramming steps, such as steps 4, 8, and 11, but you should understand them nonetheless.

A Cautionary Note   Color is often recommended for enhancing user interface design. Color can call attention to exceptional data, help users distinguish items on a chart, and convey information at a glance. Blue creates a sense of trust, green means go or all clear, red indicates danger.

However, system developers must remember that about 4 percent of people of European ancestry have significant color vision deficiency. Its most common form is inability to distinguish between red and green. In total color blindness, all colors appear as shades of gray. Color vision deficiencies are somewhat sex-linked: about 1 man in 12 suffers from this problem, but only about 1 in 200 women.

As a result, always follow these two guidelines for your use of color:

1. *Never allow color to be the only way a system conveys any information.* Augment it by other cues for people who do not see the color difference. Include numerical values in addition to color codes, provide cross-hatching on top of color, use blinking characters, or choose colors that are perceived as substantially lighter or darker than each other. (Canary yellow is perceived as lighter than, hence different from, navy blue even by a person who cannot tell "yellowness" from "blueness.") Standard formulas exist for computing shades of gray from a color's three color components. (They are used in preparing color images for monochrome displays or printers.) Colors that are well separated by these formulas are perceived as different by people with no color perception. Or, just set your display to gray-scale mode and make sure you can use the system without difficulty.

2. *Where your underlying hardware and software permit, allow the user to customize an application's use of color.* Some color vision deficiencies can be compensated for (as they affect ability to use an application) by changing, for example, red to blue, so that a user who cannot distinguish red from green can tell the two colors apart. In some systems, colors that cover an area, such as a region on a map, can be replaced by monochrome patterns such as dots, stripes, and cross-hatching.

A third guideline for the use of color, unrelated to color perception, is that light colors create fewer annoying screen reflections than dark ones. This is especially true in an office environment with fluorescent lights. As a result, use light colors to cover large areas of the screen. Reserve darker ones for smaller spot usage.

6.5.2 User Interface Styles

There are four general ways to control computers: command-line interfaces, graphical interfaces, menus, and question-and-answer dialogues. Each has its place in the DSS user interface picture. They can often be combined usefully in a single application or set of related applications.

Command-line interfaces are the oldest form of computer control, dating back to the days in which each command was entered on a punched card. They still underlie several operating systems, such as the complex job control languages of mainframe systems.

With command-line interfaces, it is the user's responsibility to know what commands are available and how to enter them with their parameters. Such interfaces can be quite powerful, giving users detailed control over a system, but they are hard to learn. Most people who are not primarily computer professionals never learn more than a fraction of any command set and make frequent mistakes in command entry. Although such mistakes can usually be corrected, they exact a cost in time and frustrate users trying to deal with an unforgiving, detail-ridden system.

Graphical user interfaces (GUIs) dominate at the desktop level and are increasingly popular on larger systems. Figure 6–23 shows a GUI screen display. Each small picture, called an **icon,** represents a program or a data file. A pointing

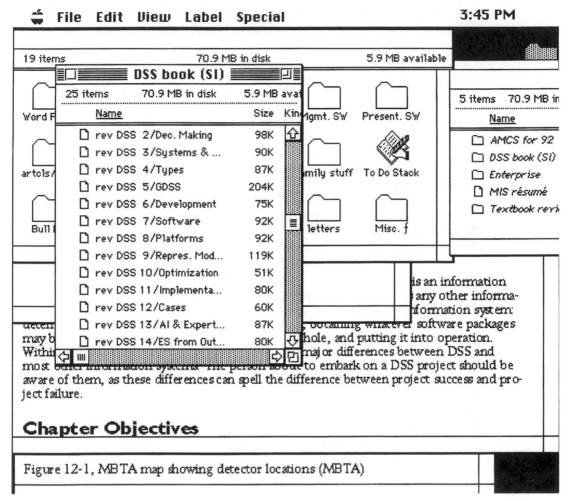

FIGURE 6–23 GUI Screen Shot

device (typically a **mouse** but possibly a trackball, joystick, or one of several other possibilities) allows the user to select one or more of them. The **menu bar** or **action bar** at the top of the screen lists operations that can be performed on programs and files. To run a program, the user points at the program's icon, clicks a button on the mouse to select that program, points at a menu, moves the mouse to point at an entry on the menu that drops down from the menu bar, and releases the button. (This takes far less time than it took you to read about it. In addition, most GUIs provide **keyboard shortcuts,** multiple mouse buttons or multiple button-clicking patterns which allow users to perform common operations without accessing a menu.) The specifics of button clicking vary from one GUI to the next, but the principles are common to all.

The fundamental psychological principle underlying GUIs is that *recognizing a command is easier than recalling it.* If a user forgets which menu has the Print command, he or she simply pulls down a few until it appears. There is no way to make a mistake in the command format, to type the wrong letter, to omit a parameter, or to enter them in the wrong order. The use of a GUI environment affects the application in two ways:

1. Application programs that are meant to run under a GUI are expected to conform to standards set by its designers. Conformance is important if a GUI is to fulfill one of its promises: that all applications in its environment work the same way, reducing learning time and facilitating training. A GUI-conformant application should use windows, menus, and a pointing device as decreed by the standards of that GUI. Developing an application for this environment is more difficult than developing one whose commands are keyed in when the application decides to ask for them.
2. Developers of applications with a graphical user interface benefit from the facilities provided by a GUI-oriented operating system. GUIs provide commands to create, move, and resize windows, create menus, create dialogue boxes, detect and respond to mouse clicks, and handle all the other minutiae of the GUI environment. Creating the same interface functionality from scratch is more difficult.

If your DSS is to run under a GUI you must decide whether conforming to its standards is worth the added development effort. If you are developing a DSS package for commercial sale, you have no practical choice but to conform. If your system will be used only within one firm, you need not do so. In this case, your decision will often be guided by the availability of programmers who have experience in developing applications for that GUI or your use of a package that provides this interface as an automatic by-product. If neither is available, don't delay deploying a valuable DSS while its developers learn the niceties of a new interface style. Get the basic system working with a simpler interface, let the company derive its benefits, and then enhance its user interface for full GUI conformance.

Commands can be entered into a DSS from **menus,** which the application displays on the screen. Such menus differ from GUI menus because the latter are always present. A GUI user can always invoke a menu entry, and the system must always be ready to respond to it. Option menus displayed on the screen, however, are shown only when the application program decides that its user should make a choice. The real difference is not the cosmetic one of whether menus drop down from the top of the screen or are displayed in a window. It is the deeper, conceptual difference of whether system or user decides what to do next.

Question-and-answer dialogues are appropriate when the user must specify data values or other parameters before the system can carry out a desired operation. A DSS used to plan a retirement financial plan, for example, might ask for the age of the individual for which the plan is to be developed, his or her marital status, ages of any children being supported, annual income, and so forth. The user responds to each question by typing the appropriate answer.

In the GUI environment, question-and-answer dialogues are usually presented via dialogue boxes such as the one in Figure 6–24, which was created with Microsoft

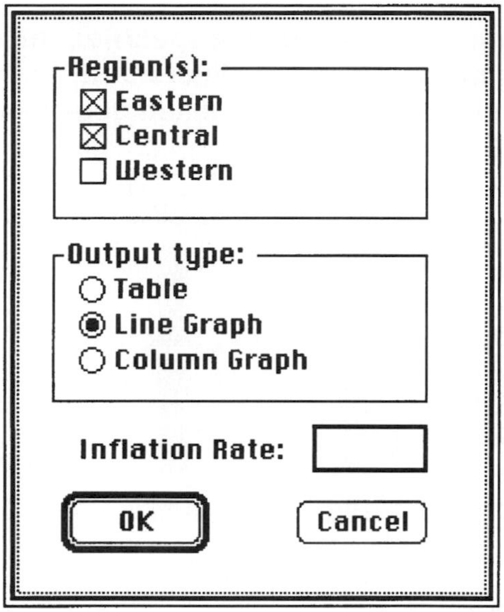

FIGURE 6-24 GUI Dialogue Box

Excel. The user can enter data in any order by clicking on the appropriate box and typing: selecting regions before output type, vice versa, or even mixed—first selecting Eastern region, then choosing a line graph, then deciding that the Central region ought to be on the graph, too. The user can even click "OK" before entering all the values. The system must incorporate error checking to handle this situation (the user in the figure has specified the desired regions and output type, but not the inflation rate) as well as every error a user could make in typing the individual entries.

Each user interface style suits certain situations. Several modes can be combined in one DSS; for example, a menu that lists available calculation options, followed by a question-and-answer dialogue to enter the parameters that apply to the chosen one. A DSS that operates under a GUI can still display dialogue boxes in which a user may make choices or answer a question. A new DSS is unlikely to use a command line interface style today unless it incorporates an existing program that uses this style.

Animation is an increasingly popular part of DSS user interfaces. Animation is widely used to show how a system evolves over time for a given set of parameters. Users can see how waiting lines build up, how materials move through a factory or warehouse, how congestion slows traffic at an intersection. Animation can enhance a user's sense of realism as he or she navigates a set of decision alternatives. When it comes to designing the most effective animation for a decision support task, González and Kasper [GONZ97] report that

1. Animation is an increasingly popular DSS user interface style.
2. Animation, rather than just a creative way to display a decision situation, can affect decision quality.
3. Little is known about how to design animation to improve decision effectiveness.

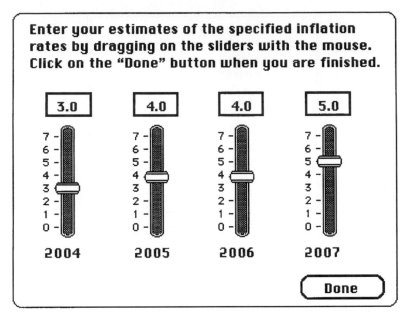

FIGURE 6–25 Application Interface with Slider

They suggest using realistic images and gradual transitions wherever possible, but concede that more research remains to be done before general guidelines for DSS animation design will be known.

Most user data entry is via a keyboard. Some GUI-based applications use graphical "sliders" to enter numerical data, as shown in Figure 6–25. The user points at the slider bar with the mouse (or other pointing device), holds down the mouse button, moves the mouse, watches the slider move on the screen, and releases the mouse when it is in the right place. A numeric display, as shown above each slider in Figure 6–25, can confirm the current slider position and offer users the option of entering a numeric value via the keyboard. A series of such sliders might represent a decision maker's estimate of the growth rates of several markets, of the relative importance of several product design factors, or, as in the figure, of expected inflation rates over the next few years.

In accepting keyboard data, any application should provide as much error checking as possible. This is especially important for DSS, whose users are not generally experienced typists and are therefore likely to make keying errors. Menus of choices are better than blanks to fill in. If there is no alternative to free entry, the program should perform reasonableness and validation checks on input data. The temperature of a living human, for example, can be checked to be between 85 degrees and 110 degrees Fahrenheit (30 degrees to 45 degrees Celsius). If your DSS must allow an occasional unusual data item, it should at least ask, "Do you *really* mean that?"

Data entry methods are evolving. Pen-based computers (which use a special stylus, not a pen with ink) are in use today. They are well suited for applications

New England

The six New England states are located in the northeast corner of the <u>United States</u>. They were among the first parts of <u>North America</u> to be settled by <u>Europeans</u> in the <u>seventeenth century</u>. New England states include <u>Connecticut</u>, <u>Maine</u>, <u>Massachusetts</u>, <u>New Hampshire</u>, <u>Rhode Island</u>, and <u>Vermont</u>.

Click on any part of the map or on any underlined word for more information.

FIGURE 6–26   Hypertext Screen with Map and Text

that require an easily carried computer and do not call for entering large amounts of data. For example, United Parcel Service (UPS) personnel use pen-based computers to enter package delivery information. Despite recent advances in handwritten character recognition, however, the keyboard remains the most practical way to enter long character strings with speed and reliability.

Voice recognition is likely to be the step after pen-based computing. It may limit the future of pen computers to environments in which speech is unacceptable, such as taking meeting notes or retrieving information while speaking on the phone. Potential voice recognition users include (among others) businesspeople who can't, or won't, type. This includes many DSS users.

6.5.3 Hypertext/Hypermedia

Hypertext refers to an electronic document whose parts are electronically linked to avoid the limitations of traditional linear media such as bound books. (Many Web sites work this way.) **Hypermedia** extends hypertext by adding text, graphics, animation, and sound to the electronic "document." Together, hypertext and hypermedia allow users to access information as required by their needs rather than by the structure of a database or the limitations of a computer program. A user faced with the hypertext screen shown in Figure 6–26 can click on any of the highlighted words to get another screen with more information about that topic. Alternatively, he or she could click on any part of the map to get more information about that state—perhaps including photographs of its cities and scenery, the sound of its name spoken correctly, or a summary of any articles about it that appeared in yesterday's *New York Times*. Each screen can have hypertext links to other screens, which can be linked to others, which are linked to others. . . . The

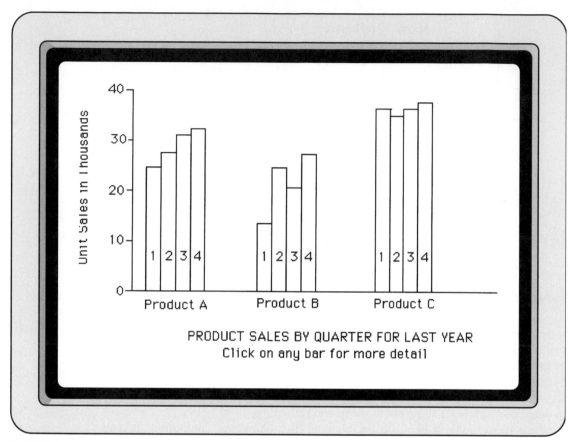

FIGURE 6–27   Screen Shot of Hypertext Sales Graph

process is limited only by the range of available screens, the content of the available databases to support drilling down for more and more detail, and the imagination of the developer.

Information retrieval is a natural match to hypertext. A system might show a column graph of sales by product as shown in Figure 6–27. If its user clicks on a column in the graph—in this case one that shows a drop in sales—the system might display Figure 6–28. Clicking on one of the three buttons in that dialogue box would lead the system to display the requested sales breakdown or cancel the request. (It is especially important to let users cancel a request if it will take a long time to execute, make irreversible changes to a database, or lead the user to a part of the system from which it will be difficult to return.) The chosen column is highlighted on the underlying graph so the user can verify visually that he or she clicked in the right place. If the wrong column is highlighted, usually due to clicking in the wrong place but perhaps reflecting an error in the program that calculates columns from mouse coordinates, the user can cancel the request and click again.

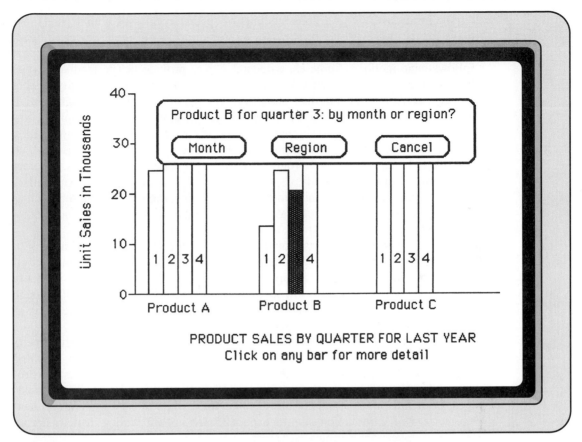

FIGURE 6–28 Same Screen as Figure 6–27 with Superimposed Dialogue Box

Research, such as that reported by Ramarapu et al. in [RAMA97], indicates that nonlinear systems such as hypertext lead to faster problem solving, more accurate problem solving, and higher user satisfaction than do linear systems. Fortunately, hypertext is becoming common in a variety of contexts. You are probably familiar with it as the standard navigational approach of the World Wide Web. It is supported by a wide range of products at the mainframe, minicomputer, and microcomputer levels. These allow hypertext and hypermedia systems to be built without using the Web, or an in-house Weblike system, as the infrastructure.

Virtual Reality   Another emerging way of interacting with computers is **virtual reality (VR).** Virtual reality uses hardware and software to give an impression that a computer-created environment exists. VR is a step beyond animation.

The most highly publicized type of virtual reality is **immersive virtual reality,** sometimes referred to as goggles and gloves VR. Immersive VR attempts to give the user a sense of inhabiting a computer-created space with the ability to manipulate objects in that space.

The immersive VR user dons a helmet or special eyeglasses with separate displays for the two eyes. He or she uses a three-dimensional input device: a hand-held controller, gloves equipped with finger position sensors, or a TV camera that follows hand motions. Some experimental gloves provide tactile feedback when the user presses against a virtual "object." Using immersive virtual reality, a store manager could evaluate alternate store floor layouts by "walking" through them to get a feel for how they would look if built. He or she could push a display a few feet to one side, lengthen or shorten a counter, and move the customer information booth. The result of these manipulations could be stored in a database, which could later be input to a CAD program to produce architectural drawings. A somewhat more limited application, for custom kitchen design, is described in [BYLI91]. Immersive VR can be intense and draining, though applications such as store layout design or statistical data visualization are unlikely to have much emotional impact.

A level below what experts would call true VR are the functions of turning to see different views of a scene, zooming in and out, and similarly adjusting a computer's "window" on a real or computer-generated image. This capability is widely used in games, for example, allowing players to move about the bridge of Starship Enterprise or, at one public Web site, the *Titanic*. It has business applications as well, especially where the more complex types of VR are not required.

Virtual reality is in use today for specialized purposes including entertainment. Its full incarnation is not yet a reality in DSS. One reason is that, today, anything more than flat, cartoonlike images requires a major investment in custom programming. Yet graphical user interfaces and hypertext were laboratory technologies, or dreams in the minds of a few visionaries, when today's mid-career managers were in school. You should expect to see virtual reality in mainstream business applications during your career.

SUMMARY

Decision support systems can be obtained as a complete package, as a customized package, or as custom software. Totally turnkey packages are not usually available. Custom software is appropriate for large firms solving important problems, though smaller firms can often find creative ways of reducing its cost. Customized packages or systems that use a great deal of "canned" software are common.

Types of software that you can use in DSS development include database management packages, information retrieval (query and reporting) packages, specialized modeling packages (including spreadsheets) and languages, statistical data analysis packages, forecasting packages, and graphics packages.

Database management packages support one of three database structures: hierarchical, network, or relational. The hierarchical structure is most common on desktop microcomputers, the network structure on mainframes, and the relational structure on minicomputers and workstations. The relational structure offers more flexibility in responding to unforeseen information retrieval requests than do the others. This makes it more suitable for most decision support system uses. Fortunately, relational DBMS are moving down to the microcomputer level.

Most relational databases are accessed via queries in Structured Query Language, or SQL. While SQL is not fully standardized, its variants are sufficiently similar for a person who knows one of them to learn another quickly. Unfortunately, complex queries are difficult to express in SQL and can take a long time to run. Most relational DBMS vendors therefore also offer end-user query packages that make it easier to access their databases.

In addition to the information retrieval capabilities built into many DBMS, one can buy a separate information retrieval package. These tend to be either more powerful than those offered with the DBMS, easier to use, more general (in the sense of accessing more than one type of database), or, in a few cases, less expensive.

Of several types of financial modeling tools, the simplest is the spreadsheet, which consists of an array of cells. Each cell can contain text, a number, or a formula. Formulas operate on the contents of other cells and produce, in most cases, numbers. These numbers can be used as input to other formulas. The results can be displayed in numerical form or graphed.

Spreadsheets are prone to error for several reasons, thereby creating the need for two other types of software: spreadsheet auditing packages, which help detect (accidental or intentional) spreadsheet errors, and financial modeling languages such as IFPS, which formalize the "loose" spreadsheet approach to defining a financial model.

Statistical data analysis packages automate standard statistical operations: finding means, spreads, patterns, and correlations; determining statistical confidence levels, creating cross-tabulations, and more. While a package cannot tell you to use statistical methods, it can help you use them once you determine the need.

Forecasting is the application of statistical techniques to predict the future value of some variable based on its past behavior. The need for sophisticated forecasting methods, combined with the fact that the same methods are used by managers in every industry, has led to wide availability of packages that perform this task.

Most spreadsheet, statistical, and forecasting packages can produce graphic output. Yet their basic purpose is not graphics, so their capabilities are often limited in this regard. Specialized graphing packages can take their output, in a number of standardized data interchange formats, and create a wider variety of charts and graphs with it than the original package could. The need for graphing packages is dropping as the graphing capabilities of other types of software improve.

Where programming is necessary to develop a decision support system, one can use either a third-generation language or a fourth-generation language. Third-generation languages are widely known to programmers and reasonably well standardized. However, they involve a long and error-prone programming process. Fourth generation languages, while not quite as flexible and somewhat less efficient in their use of computer time, permit faster application development. Their capabilities are normally sufficient for DSS needs and their computer usage inefficiency is not normally a barrier in a DSS application. They are therefore usually better suited to DSS development than are 3GLs. Many 4GLs include end-user facilities through which a non-technical person can retrieve information from a database, sort it, tabulate it, and generate simple reports to support his or her decision-making needs.

Planning the user interface is an important part of planning any DSS, perhaps more so than with most other types of information systems. DSS users have more sporadic and more varied needs than do most other IS users, and their activities tend to have higher organizational impact. Factors to be considered in planning the DSS user interface include minimizing task performance time, minimizing learning and recall time, maximizing system versatility, minimizing errors (and making it as easy as possible to recover from those that do occur), and adapting to different user needs, including the availability of help for those who need it. Additional factors to take into account are the user's ability to keep several things in mind, user fatigue, and command consistency with other systems with which the users are familiar.

Color can often enhance a user interface but must be used with due consideration for those users who cannot see a difference among the developer's color choices.

The four most common user interface styles are commands typed by the user, menus of choices for the user, blanks for the user to fill in, and graphical user interfaces. Each of these applies both to the DSS itself and to the operating system under which the DSS runs. While there is no forced connection between the two, the user interface of the operating system has an indirect impact on that of the DSS: it creates expectations as to how the DSS will operate, and it provides capabilities within which the DSS must exist or that the DSS can use. Developing an application that conforms fully to the standards of a GUI is, despite the availability of operating system facilities, more difficult than developing a comparable application that operates via menus and typed-in commands.

User interface technology is evolving. Pen input is practical today, especially if the user is willing to print uppercase characters with reasonable care. Voice recognition is usable for disconnected speech (with pauses between words) for constrained subject areas. Hypertext and hypermedia, as ways of combining different types of information and letting the user navigate flexibly through the resulting "information universe," are also proving useful. Virtual reality, in which the computer creates the illusion that the user is actually manipulating the system under study, is still in the laboratory but shows great promise.

KEY TERMS

accounting model
action bar
animation
auditing package (for spreadsheets)
charting software package
CODASYL database standard
command-line interface
correlation
data management, data manager
data model
database

database management, database management system
DSS generator
DSS tool
entity-relationship diagram
exponential smoothing
extrapolation
file manager
financial modeling software
forecasting, forecasting software
fourth-generation (programming) language (4GL)
graphical user interface (GUI)
graphing software package
hierarchical database
hypermedia
hypertext
icon
immersive virtual reality
information retrieval package
join (in a relational database)
keyboard shortcut
keys, key attributes
least-mean-squares (LMS) fit
menu (interface)
menu bar
middleware
mouse
moving average
multidimensional (dimensional) database
network database
precision
probe (in spreadsheet auditing context)
query
question-and-answer dialogue
recall
regression
relational database
secular trend
spreadsheet
statistical quality control (SQC)
statistical software
Structured Query Language (SQL)
third-generation programming language (3GL)
time-series analysis
trace (in spreadsheet auditing context)
user interface
virtual reality (VR)

REVIEW QUESTIONS

1. What are the four ways to obtain any software capability?
2. Why are most custom DSS developed by large companies?
3. If you are not in a large company, should you assume you can't develop a custom DSS? Why or why not?
4. Why are standard packages to support many business decisions not widely available?
5. Contrast a DSS tool with a DSS generator.
6. In a full-text information retrieval system, what is the difference between *precision* and *recall?*
7. What are the three basic database structures?
8. What is the essential difference between the hierarchical and network database structures on the one hand, and the relational database structure on the other?
9. Why are relational databases better suited to decision support than the other types?
10. What is SQL? What types of databases is it meant to work with?
11. What noncomputerized object does a spreadsheet screen resemble?
12. What are some disadvantages of using spreadsheets for business planning?
13. What are two approaches to overcoming some of these disadvantages?
14. What do statistics packages do?
15. What are the basic steps in developing a time-series forecast?
16. Why are graphing packages losing importance?
17. What are some popular third-generation programming languages?
18. What is the essential difference between a 3GL and a 4GL?
19. Give two factors that make 4GLs undesirable for high-volume transaction processing applications but which are less serious drawbacks for most decision support applications.
20. What factors make the user interface design issues of a decision support system different from the user interface design issues that arise with transaction processing systems?
21. Give at least 10 factors to consider in DSS user interface design.
22. Why should you not rely exclusively on color to convey information to a DSS user?
23. What are the four basic user interface styles?
24. How does the use of a graphical user interface by the operating system influence the use of a GUI by a DSS application?
25. Name two alternatives to keyboard data entry.
26. What is hypertext?

EXERCISES

1. You work for a car rental firm that wants to develop a decision support database with information on its rental offices, fleet, customers, and rentals. Draw entity-relationship diagrams for the following three cases:
   a. All cars "belong" to one rental office, are always rented at that office, and are always returned to that office. (If a customer returns one to another office it is returned "home" immediately, empty if necessary.)
   b. All cars belong to one rental office but may be returned elsewhere. They may remain away from their home for a considerable time.
   c. Cars do not belong to a particular office.
2. Sketch four relational tables for question 1*a.*

3. Using a spreadsheet package, decide if you should take the investment credit given the following information. Assume that your tax rate does not change from year to year. (The rate itself is unimportant.)
   - Your internal rate of return requirement is 15 percent per year.
   - The asset has a depreciable life of 5 years and has no salvage value at the end of that period.
   - If you take straight-line depreciation, you are eligible for a 10 percent investment credit in the first year. (That is, your taxes are reduced by 10 percent of its purchase price.)
   - If you forego the investment credit, you can take sum-of-digits accelerated depreciation: 5/15 of purchase price in the first year, 4/15 in the second, 3/15 in the third, 2/15 in the fourth, and 1/15 in the fifth year.
4. Obtain population data for your state at 10-year (U.S. federal census) intervals going back 50 years. (If you don't live in the United States, use comparable data for your country or region.) Fit a straight line to them—using a forecasting package if you have one, otherwise a spreadsheet package if yours has the necessary functions, or by hand—to predict what the population will be 10 years from your last data point. Do you think this forecast will be accurate? Give two reasons why it might not be.
5. In Section 6.3.5 we took the moving average over precisely one cycle, which was seven days for the restaurant example of Figure 6–17. What would have happened if we had taken a different period, say five days or eight days? Would any period other than seven days give meaningful results?
6. Find a review of a 4GL, or a comparative review of several 4GLs, in a newspaper, magazine, or reference service volume. What characteristics did the writer consider important? What features of the package did the writer like or dislike? Did the system reviewed provide graphical end-user development tools like those of PC/FOCUS? For what applications did the writer recommend using the 4GL or 4GLs?
7. Interview a programmer who has used both at least one 3GL and at least one 4GL in his or her work. Find out how easy it is, in his or her opinion, to develop systems, to debug them, and to modify them when requirements change. What advantages and disadvantages does this person see to the two types of languages? Which does he or she prefer? Why?
8. Why is it important to determine who your user is before designing a user interface? As an example, consider a student course selection advising system to be used by
   a. students.
   b. faculty advisors.
   c. professional counselors who spend about a third of their time advising students on course selection and the rest counseling them on other issues.
   How would the ideal user interfaces differ for these three types of users?
9. Create a written description of the screen display in Figure 6–27 and its behavior, using no pictures. Comment on how well you feel this description conveys what the screen will look like compared to
   a. Figure 6–27 plus a written description of its behavior.
   b. Figures 6–27 and 6–28 together, plus text.
   c. seeing it on a computer screen.
10. Find and read one or more articles on virtual reality. Suggest some potential applications for this technology in managerial decision making. Don't use trivial variations on the architectural design examples on page 248.

REFERENCES

AGEL88   Ageloff, Roy. *A Primer on SQL.* Times Mirror/Mosby, St. Louis, Mo. (1988).

BRAD87   Bradley, James. *Introduction to Database Management in Business* (2nd ed.). Holt, Rinehart and Winston, New York (1987).

BYLI91   Bylinsky, Gene. "The Marvels of 'Virtual Reality,' " *Fortune* 123, no. 11 (June 3, 1991), pp. 138–150.

COUR88   Courtney, James F., Jr., and David B. Paradice. *Database Systems for Management.* Times Mirror/Mosby, St. Louis, Mo. (1988).

DAVI87   Davies, N., and C. Ikin. "Auditing Spreadsheets," *Australian Accountant* (December 1987), pp. 54–56.

ELLI90   Ellis, Dennis, and Jay Nathan. *A Managerial Guide to Business Forecasting.* Graceway Publishing Co., Flushing, N.Y. (1990).

FINK89   Finkelstein, Clive. *An Introduction to Information Engineering.* Addison-Wesley, Reading, Mass. (1989).

FRID90   Fridlund, Alan J. "Number-Crunching Statistics Software," *Infoworld* 12, no. 9 (February 26, 1990), pp. 59–69.

GONZ97   González, Cleotilde, and George M. Kasper. "Animation in User Interfaces Designed for Decision Support Systems: The Effects of Image Abstraction, Transition and Interactivity on Decision Quality," *Decision Sciences* 28, no. 4 (Fall 1997), p. 793.

KEAT89   Keating, Barry. "Statistics Software for Economists: Macintosh," *Business Economics* 24, no. 3 (August 1989), pp. 54–57.

LARS82   Larson, James A. *End User Facilities in the Nineteen Eighties.* IEEE Computer Society, Los Alamitos, Calif. (1982).

PANK98   Panko, Raymond. "What We Know About Spreadsheet Errors," *Journal of End User Computing* 10, no. 2 (Spring 1998), p. 15.

RAMA97   Ramarapu, Narender K., Mark N. Frolick, Ronald B. Wilkes, and James C. Wetherbe. "The Emergence of Hypertext and Problem Solving: An Experimental Investigation of Accessing and Using Information from Linear Versus Nonlinear Systems," *Decision Sciences* 28, no. 4 (Fall 1997), p. 825.

ROAD99   *Road and Track '99 Car Buyer's Guide.* Hachette Fillipacchi Magazines, New York (1999).

SCHE92   Scheer, August-Wilhelm, and Alexander Hars. "Extending Data Modeling to Cover the Whole Enterprise," *Communications of the ACM* 35, no. 9 (September 1992), pp. 166–172.

SILV91   Silver, Mark S. *Systems that Support Decision Makers.* John Wiley & Sons, New York (1991).

SILV91a   Silver, Mark S. "Decisional Guidance for Computer-Based Decision Support," *MIS Quarterly* 15, no. 1 (March 1991), pp. 105–122.

SIMK87   Simkin, M. G. "How to Validate Spreadsheets," *Journal of Accountancy* (November 1987), pp. 130–138.

SPRA80   Sprague, Ralph H., Jr. "A Framework for the Development of Decision Support Systems," *MIS Quarterly* 4, no. 4 (December 1980), pp. 1–26.

SPRA82   Sprague, Ralph H., Jr., and Eric D. Carlson. *Building Effective Decision Support Systems.* Prentice-Hall, Englewood Cliffs, N.J. (1982).

WEBS86   Webster, Charles E. *The Executive's Guide to Business and Economic Forecasting.* Probus, Chicago (1986).

WILL87   Willis, Raymond E. *A Guide to Forecasting for Planners and Managers.* Prentice-Hall, Englewood Cliffs, N.J. (1987).

WILS90   Wilson, J. Holton, and Barry Keating. *Business Forecasting.* Richard D. Irwin, Homewood, Ill. (1990).

CASE

Fort Lowell Trading Company
Software Packages

Chris Demas was waiting for Miguel and Elizabeth when they arrived at Fort Lowell Trading Company headquarters the following Monday afternoon. "How were your weekends?" he asked.

"We both had a Finance exam this morning," Elizabeth responded. "Spent all yesterday studying for it. Too bad you couldn't have taken it for us!"

"I'm not sure that would have helped," laughed Chris. "My book learning is getting old, and a lot has probably changed. I know the part I work with pretty well, because I have to keep up, but there's more to finance than that."

"What's the part you work with the most?" asked Miguel.

"As the financial planning manager," Chris answered as they reached his office, "I'm concerned mostly with where we'll get enough funds for our operations. As you already know, almost every business has to pay for things long before they generate income. A dress could stay on one of our racks for months until it's finally sold, but the company we got it from won't wait that long to get paid. So we need to get working capital to tide us over until we finally sell the dress. The more we grow, the more working capital we need. So I have to keep looking for money."

"What are some of your options?" Miguel continued. "I mean, we've studied some of them, but I'd like to hear how it *really* works!"

"For starters," Chris responded, "one of the standard ones doesn't work for us. We're not publicly traded, so we can't just go out and sell more stock to anyone who will buy it. We don't want to change that, because we don't want to get caught up in the Wall Street game of quarterly earnings and we don't want to have to keep pumping up the stock price to stop some corporate raider or some huge mega-chain from taking us over. . . . Do I sound too intense about this?" he finally asked with a laugh.

"You did get a certain gleam in your eye," Elizabeth answered candidly. "I suppose a lot of people here feel strongly about that?"

"Yes, we do. It might sound hokey but it's true. Anyhow, that still leaves us with a load of financing options. Every bank in the country would love to lend us money because we're the next surest thing to the U.S. Treasury for paying it back. But their terms are all a little bit different. One will give us a line of credit for

X percent. Another will give it to us for X minus something but we have to draw down so much of it right away. A third will give us a straight loan for two years for some other percent, and a fourth will give us the same loan for a higher rate but guarantee renewal for another 2 years at, say, not over a 2 percent rate increase. And the rates may vary depending on what we put up as collateral, including no collateral at all. How on earth do you compare them? And that's just bank loans! Then there's bonds, commercial paper, and lots of other options. We haven't seriously considered factoring our accounts receivable yet, but just about anything else is fair game."

"In terms of our project," Miguel said in bringing the discussion back to the reason for the meeting, "how do you use computers to help make this decision?"

"Right now we do some basic things. I've worked up some spreadsheets that compare one bank loan or line of credit with another, making some assumptions about how much money we're going to need and when we're going to need it. I plug in a cost-of-capital figure I get from Norma LaRosa down the hall and do net-present-value calculations on the cost of each loan or line of credit. There's some guesswork involved here, because I have to guess what we'll be able to borrow at when the shorter loans have to be repaid, but it seems to work."

"What sort of results have you been getting out of it?" Elizabeth asked.

"Some interesting ones," Chris replied. "There really are differences in the cost of different loans depending on when we're going to need the funds. The banks cost them out based on their assumptions and how they raise money themselves. If the pattern of our need for cash is way off from what they assumed, two arrangements that look similar on the surface could turn out to be quite different in what they mean to us. It's saved us a lot of money by clueing us into those situations before we sign on the line, not after."

"And have you run into any problems with it?" she continued.

"Just one, now that you mention it. Early on, right after I put it together, I used it to compare two banks' lines of credit. It came back and told me that one was a lot better than the other. Good thing they came out looking that different, because it clued me in that there was something funny going on. In the real world two banks are never that far apart on this sort of thing. It turned out I had mistyped a ratio for one of the compensating balances, you know, how much money we have to keep on deposit with them in return for their extending the line of credit to us. I fixed that, and the thing has been solid ever since. I hate to think what would have happened if I hadn't caught that, though."

EXERCISES

1. What is "factoring accounts receivable"? Why don't you think Fort Lowell Trading Company considers it a viable option for raising capital?
2. Write a decision statement for the decision Chris uses his spreadsheet to help with.
3. Chris says his bank loan comparison spreadsheet requires him to make "some assumptions about how much money we're going to need and when we're going to need it." These assumptions are just that. They could turn out to be off in either direction. It might be more appropriate for him to couch them in statistical terms: the amount of

capital he expects the firm will need in a given period plus the standard deviation (or other measure[s] of dispersion, depending on the distribution) associated with his confidence in that expectation. If he did this, how could he then use a package such as Crystal Ball (see page 330) to help compare bank loans? Specifically, what items would he produce as output graphs?

4. Nothing Chris said about his loan comparison spreadsheet suggests that he applied any sort of auditing package to it. Of course, he may have done it but just didn't think it was worth mentioning in this discussion. In any case, should he apply one? Why or why not?

5. Could proper software development discipline have caught the error Chris discussed in the last paragraph, the wrong ratio for the compensating balance? If so, how? (Do not include spreadsheet auditing packages in your answer to this question.)

6. How do you think a financial modeling package such as IFPS would compare with a spreadsheet program for Chris's purpose here: better, worse, or the same? Justify your answer. (Assume the financial modeling package has all the necessary functions, such as NPV calculations, built into it, so neither program has an edge on that basis.)

CHAPTER 7

Building and Implementing Decision Support Systems

CHAPTER OUTLINE

Introduction

By now you should have a good conceptual understanding of decision support systems, what they do, and how they do it. But as you probably already realize, conceptual understanding is of little value unless it is put to use. In this chapter you'll learn about the nuts-and-bolts issues—both the technical and the nontechnical—of putting a DSS to use in a real-world environment—including the types of people a DSS project will require, the approaches it might take to the development process, and the "people issues" involved in taking it from a working system to day-to-day use.

At the conceptual level, many of these issues are the same as the issues that arise for the development and implementation of any other information system. After all, a decision support system *is* an information system. Just as it uses the same fundamental software building blocks as any other information system, it is built through the same conceptual steps as any other information system: determining user requirements, choosing hardware, obtaining whatever software packages may be of use, programming the rest, testing the whole, and putting it into operation. Within this general framework, however, there are major differences between DSS and most other information systems. The person about to embark on a DSS project should be aware of them, as these differences can spell the difference between project success and project failure.

CHAPTER OBJECTIVES

After you have read and studied this chapter, you will be able to:

1. Describe the traditional system development life cycle and discuss its advantages and disadvantages in decision support system development.
2. Describe two approaches to prototyping and how well each matches decision support system development needs.
3. Identify how and when end-user development matches DSS development requirements.
4. State who the participants are in any DSS development project, and what they do.
5. Describe the implementation stage of a decision support system and explain how it fits into the overall decision support system life cycle.
6. Describe the activities that take place during the DSS implementation stage and state why each is important.
7. Summarize four basic approaches to system conversion, and explain how they apply to DSS as opposed to the way they usually apply to other types of information systems.
8. Explain why potential DSS users resist change and how this resistance can be overcome.
9. Describe technical and user-related issues that arise in DSS implementation, and how you can use your knowledge of the issues that arise to help ensure a successful implementation.
10. Discuss the ethical issues that arise in implementing decision support systems.
    - How you can use your knowledge of the issues that arise to help ensure a successful implementation of your DSS.
    - Ethical issues that arise in implementing decision support systems, and how you can approach them in your work.

7.1 THE DSS DEVELOPMENT PROCESS

Three approaches to information system development are commonly used:

1. The traditional system development life cycle (SDLC) approach.[1]
2. The prototyping approach, with two major variations.
3. End-user development, often with professional support.

---

[1]As used here, SDLC is not to be confused with the other common meaning of this acronym: Synchronous Data Link Control, a data communication protocol.

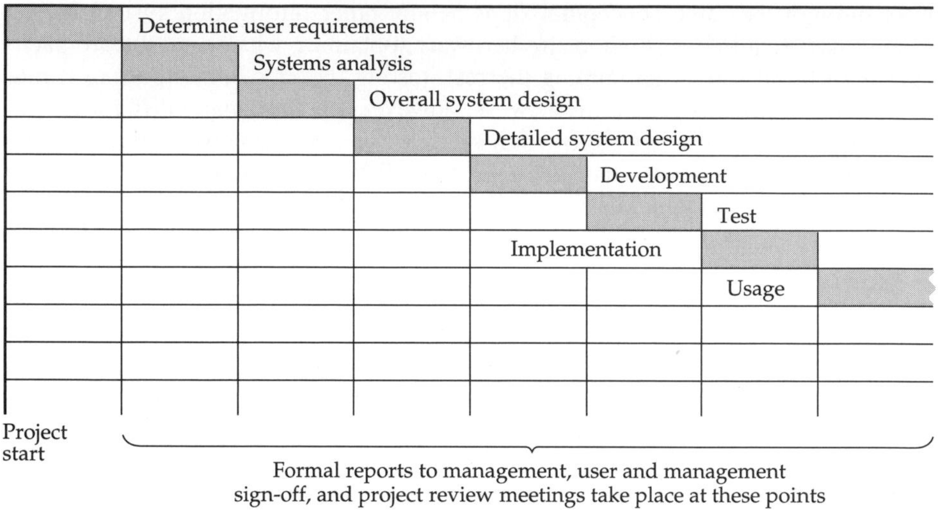

	Determine user requirements							
		Systems analysis						
			Overall system design					
				Detailed system design				
					Development			
						Test		
					Implementation			
							Usage	

Project start

Formal reports to management, user and management
sign-off, and project review meetings take place at these points

FIGURE 7–1   **Typical SDLC Stages**

7.1.1 The SDLC Approach

The **system development life cycle (SDLC)** approach is based on a series of formal steps. Figure 7–1 shows a typical series of steps. You may have seen a slightly different version in your introductory MIS course or a course in systems analysis and design. Different versions of SDLC vary in the precise number of steps and in their detailed definitions, but all follow this general pattern.

Each SDLC step culminates in a written document which must be reviewed and approved before the next step can begin. Reviewers include both prospective users of the system, who verify that the documented functionality and external interfaces meet their needs, and its developers, who verify that the system's internal interfaces are consistently defined and meet all technical requirements. User involvement is greatest at the early stages of the process, when system functionality is defined, and at the end, to verify that the system meets the users' needs. It drops off in the middle, when activity consists primarily of more technical tasks such as programming and database development.

Advantages of SDLC   When the SDLC approach was first formalized in the late 1970s, it was a clear improvement over the then-common state of anarchy. System development was commonly practiced as a "black art" with little or no management control. The idea of a standardized series of steps, with formal documents and formal procedures for proceeding from each step to the next, was traditional in engineering disciplines but revolutionary in programming.

The SDLC approach did indeed provide important discipline to system developers. It was soon adopted for transaction processing systems, which were the norm in that era. It is still widely used for this purpose. It has the advantage that using it ensures that no important area has been overlooked. It is especially common today when a formal contractual relationship exists between the developers of an application system and its eventual users, as it provides written evidence that can be used to arbitrate any disputes.

Drawbacks of SDLC   The SDLC approach is too rigid for systems whose requirements change rapidly. User requirements, agreed upon at the first stage of the process, are frozen forevermore. A change forces nearly a complete restart of the entire development cycle, as subsequent documents are based on the originally agreed-upon user needs. Changes are therefore not often attempted; in fact, SDLC can be described as a means of preventing change rather than a way of dealing with it and accommodating it. When a system emerges at the end of the SDLC development cycle, months or years later, it may meet user needs as originally defined, but those needs might no longer exist or might have changed beyond recognition.

Another drawback of the SDLC approach is that specification documents are poor user-developer communication vehicles. Users have a hard time articulating what they need in a system. Responses to "What would you like to have?" tend to be of two varieties: either incremental improvements over the present system, to correct known deficiencies without extending it significantly, or "blue sky" wish lists that cannot be satisfied outside a science-fiction novel. The useful middle ground, which is the systems analyst's goal, is hard to elicit. If a systems analyst perseveres and defines a meaningful new system, its 200-page technical description is not likely to be read and reviewed in any case.

These disadvantages are more telling in a DSS context than they are in a transaction processing context. As a result, the SDLC approach is usually less appropriate than one of the following approaches for DSS development. The SDLC approach may still make sense for large DSS projects that will be used by many people. Such DSS are generally used for operational, occasionally for tactical, decisions.

7.1.2 Prototyping

Prototyping, which follows either the steps shown in Figure 7–2 or those shown in Figure 7–3, evolved in response to the deficiencies of the SDLC. In the prototyping approach, systems analysts sit down with potential users and develop a system that appears to work—on the surface—approximately the way the eventual system will work. They use tools such as 4GLs that support rapid development, if necessary at the expense of efficient computer utilization. They omit (only for now!) error checking, access to a real database, connection to a real network, help screens, little-used options, and all the other minutia that account for the overwhelming majority of development time. The result is something that users can try out, react to, comment on, and eventually approve with the confidence that it meets their needs. Missing features will be added later, once users are satisfied with the way the prototype works.

Once approved, the prototype can be used in either of two ways. In one scenario, a prototype is used as a surrogate specification. This specification is turned

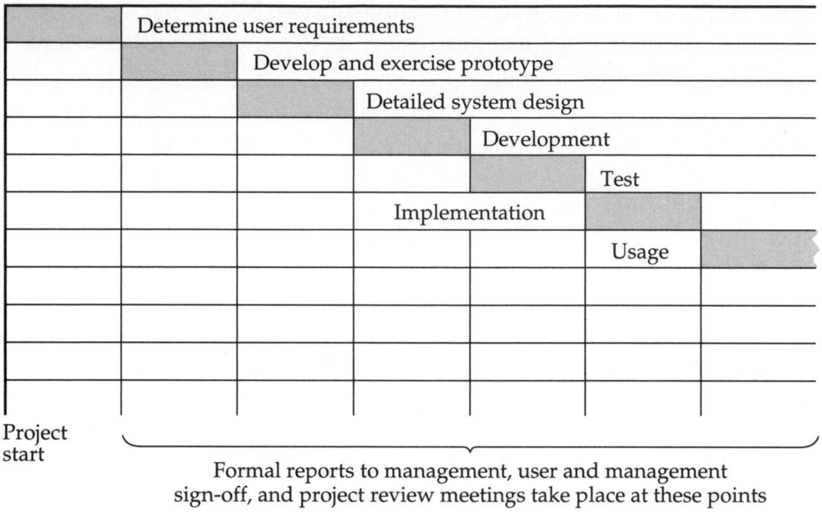

Determine user requirements

Develop and exercise prototype

Detailed system design

Development

Test

Implementation

Usage

Project start

Formal reports to management, user and management sign-off, and project review meetings take place at these points

FIGURE 7–2 Typical "Throwaway" Prototyping Stages

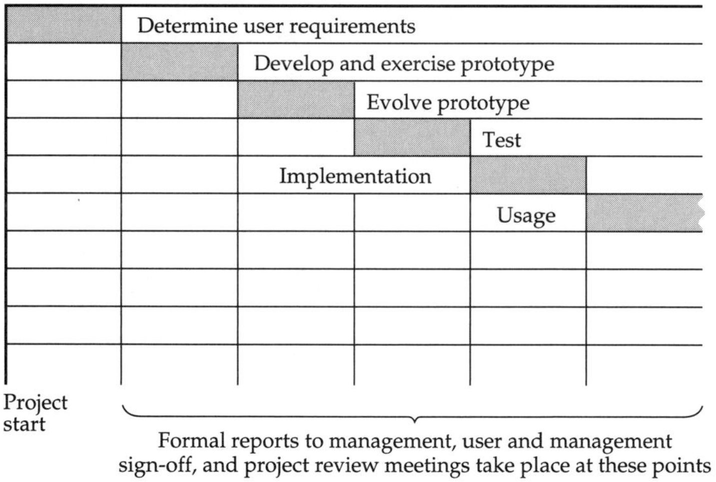

Determine user requirements

Develop and exercise prototype

Evolve prototype

Test

Implementation

Usage

Project start

Formal reports to management, user and management sign-off, and project review meetings take place at these points

FIGURE 7–3 Typical "Evolutionary" Prototyping Stages

into an operational system using the same tools that would be used had the specification been written on paper. In the other approach to prototyping, the prototype evolves directly into the finished product. It is attached to a live database and features are added to it, but it remains written in the 4GL or other high-level tools originally used.

The first approach, often called **throwaway prototyping** (Figure 7–2), picks up the SDLC stages midway through the development process. It is well suited to transaction processing applications. Such systems are used heavily by many people to process large volumes of data. Efficient application execution is therefore paramount. The run-time inefficiencies and hardware resource requirements of 4GLs and other high-level development tools, while far smaller than they once were, may be unacceptable in that environment.

Throwaway prototyping is less well suited to DSS because DSS typically have different usage patterns. Most DSS are used by fewer people than are most TPS and are used less regularly. If run on an individual decision maker's desktop computer, or on a dedicated system purchased to host a data warehouse, inefficiency is irrelevant unless it calls for an expensive upgrade or creates unacceptably long run times. If run on the corporate mainframe, DSS usually account for only a small fraction of its load. The impact of inefficient hardware usage is thus far smaller than it would be for a TPS. The value of DSS to the organization, and hence the value of having them available quickly, exceeds the cost of a little hardware. These factors usually make the second approach (Figure 7–3), called **evolutionary prototyping** or **rapid application development,** better suited to DSS. Keeping the prototype as the foundation of the application, and continuing to use its high-level development tools, speeds the programming process.

Evolutionary prototyping is especially appropriate for what is often called a **quick-hit DSS** [SPRA82]. This is a DSS developed for a one-time situation where there is a recognized need and a high potential payoff. The drawbacks of limited DSS applicability and inefficient hardware usage are nearly irrelevant in this situation. The importance of having the DSS as soon as possible is paramount.

Evolutionary prototyping is also often appropriate for data warehouses, as it is not difficult to demonstrate a variety of end-user interfaces before the various data sources have been fully integrated with the system. You'll read more about developing data warehouses in Chapter 15.

Advantages of Prototyping Compared to the SDLC approach, prototyping improves user-developer communication. It introduces flexibility and responsiveness to the development process. Change is no longer something to be avoided—it is built into the process and encouraged. The system that is developed is more likely to meet user needs than is a system developed through SDLC.

Disadvantages of Prototyping Prototyping can extend the development schedule if it is improperly used. The inclination to tinker with systems—to make minute changes that do not improve the usefulness of the finished product—is always tempting. Users and developers must control their all-too-human tendencies in this regard in order to obtain a useful system within their lifetimes.

Prototyping raises the possibility of using the wrong tools, or using the right tools in the wrong way. Developers, especially, must understand the limitations of screen forms packages, 4GLs, and other rapid prototyping tools.

Finally, and most importantly, the nearly finished appearance and interface of a prototype may mislead users into thinking the system itself is nearly done. They may have unreasonable expectations about the time required to turn a prototype into a functional product. A prototype resembles the visible tip of an iceberg (Figure 7–4): most of the system is below the surface and not visible to its users but must still be developed if the system is to work.

FIGURE 7–4 Iceberg

User education is the best solution to this problem. Developers must take the time to describe the missing features, point out that they are more complex than the visible ones and take more time to work out, and explain what would happen if they were skipped.

7.1.3 End-User Development

In prototyping there is a cooperative relationship between users and developers, but the developers are ultimately responsible for creating a working system. **End-user development** gives the responsibility for creating a DSS to the decision makers themselves.[2]

End-user computing is often associated with desktop microcomputers. Affordable personal computers were, without a doubt, the key factor in its rapid spread during the 1980s. They remain the most popular end-user computing platform today. However, there is no inherent connection between the two. Today's minicomputer and mainframe software, much of it developed in the mold of popular microcomputer tools, provides a suitable environment for end-user computing as well. Many end-user–oriented packages are available in microcomputer, minicomputer, and sometimes mainframe versions. Some of these originated in the microcomputer world and were "ported" to larger systems. Others originated at the large system level and were brought down to micros as the latter became powerful enough to support them. In either case the end-user computing tool, and hence the

---

[2]An *end user* is an individual with a business problem that a DSS is meant to help solve. This term is used to distinguish such people from MIS professionals, whose job is to develop systems to help solve other people's problems. This term is usually written with a hyphen when used as an adjective, as in "end-user computing," but without it when used as a noun, as in "We must train end users."

ability to do end-user computing, is available on both small single-user and large multi-user computers.

The lowly spreadsheet is a common end-user development tool. Using a spreadsheet program, a manager can analyze the impact of different budget options and select one that best meets a department's needs. Market analysts can study different breakdowns of a market into segments, while making sure that all segments sum to the right overall totals and show the correct trends. With today's permeation of personal computers into nearly every organization, with "spreadsheet literacy" a requirement of every college business curriculum, managers and professionals are generally expected to be able to carry out such analyses on their own. More advanced packages, such as Crystal Ball, which you'll read about in the next chapter, are also often written to be usable by end users.

More complex end-user projects can be carried out with the aid of professional support. Many firms have a department in the MIS group whose task it is to provide such support. (This group is often called an **information center,** a term that originated in IBM Canada in the 1970s.) With the help of this support staff, managers can explore the use of database accessing tools such as 4GLs to satisfy their own information needs. Most information centers provide training classes, telephone help, and walk-in or by-appointment consultation for users with information processing needs. Many also set organizational standards for essential hardware and software components of personal information systems. Such standards help ensure compatibility among personal systems developed throughout the firm, make it possible for a central group to provide support without having to know about many different packages that meet similar user needs, and may enable the firm to negotiate substantial volume purchase discounts with suppliers.

An end user developing any DSS beyond the most trivial could benefit by considering the formal stages of the SDLC. Each is there for a reason. Each has been found to provide a benefit, even if that benefit is not immediately apparent. While it isn't necessary for the user/developer to go through the full detail of every SDLC step, every major topic deserves thought. The developer should think about objectives before starting, consider costs and benefits, plan how the system will eventually be tested, and so forth.

Today's managers and professionals are, in historical terms, in the most difficult situation that ever existed or will exist regarding end-user system development. Knowledge workers of the past were not expected to be able to develop their own systems. Those of the future will have tools we can only dream of to make the job easier. The managers and professionals of today—you, on the job in the next few years—are often expected to develop their own systems, but they must know a good deal about computers to do it well.[3]

---

[3]The situation resembles that of automobile drivers around 1920. A generation earlier, automobiles were not a factor in most people's lives; it was not assumed that a typical adult could drive one. A generation later, automatic transmissions and electric starters had made the driver's job far easier. The driver of 1920 was caught in the middle. The pace of change in computing is, of course, far faster.

Advantages of End-User Computing for DSS Development   The greatest advantage of end-user development is that the person with the problem feels, *and is,* in control of its solution. This control manifests itself in several ways: physical control over the hardware (if a desktop microcomputer is being used), lack of conflict with other projects for developer time, and the understanding that comes with having put the DSS together from the ground up.

There can also be significant time and cost savings associated with end-user development. Instead of explaining a problem to a programmer—or, worse, explaining it to a systems analyst, who in turn attempts to explain it to a programmer, who is then expected to program it—the user programs it directly. The time that would be taken up by communication is eliminated and can be used for more productive purposes. Misunderstandings and errors introduced in the communication process, that must be removed at the cost of more user and developer time, are likewise eliminated.

Disadvantages of End-User Computing for DSS Development   Users may get carried away with the computer aspects of a problem, at the expense of their primary jobs. A $95,000-per-year marketing director should not do work that a $40,000-per-year programmer could do—and probably do better. Small end-user development projects save money because the need to communicate with system developers is eliminated. Large ones may waste money because people are working outside their professional field and are therefore not working cost effectively.

A second danger is that most professionals and managers are not trained in, or even aware of, system development discipline. They usually do not test systems thoroughly or document them carefully. They tend to be casual about backing up files and ensuring adequate data security. Some of these attitudes may be acceptable in a system developed for one-time use over a short period by one individual. Unfortunately, many systems planned for one-time, one-person use turn out to be more widely used, and for longer periods than their developers could possibly have foreseen. Problems that result from lax development attitudes and incomplete testing can cost more in the long run than proper development discipline, with the involvement of information systems professionals, would have cost in the first place.

A third danger, which you may have already encountered in your school career, is that some end users get carried away "playing graphic designer." They spend time trying out fancy fonts, putting borders around spreadsheet cells and shading behind paragraphs, finding cute clip art on the Web, and generally tinkering with the appearance of a report or screen instead of concentrating on its content. Sadly, businesspeople all too often overestimate their graphic design abilities and create distracting visual clutter when straightforward output would be better.

7.2 DSS DEVELOPMENT PROJECT PARTICIPANTS

Any DSS development project requires the use of several complementary skills. In all but the most trivial cases, it will not be possible to find these skills in one person. Instead, it is necessary to assemble the right mix of contributors in the DSS project team. The key DSS development roles, as originally put forth in [SPRA80], are listed below in order of increasing technical expertise, and decreasing business expertise, required for each job.

When Sprague originally described these roles, he assumed an approach to DSS development that made sense for the technology of that era. As you'll see in the next section, that approach is not always appropriate today. The descriptions of each role that follow adjust Sprague's original concepts, which remain valid, to today's technology.

The user (or users). This is the person or group responsible for solving the problem that the DSS is to help with. Users are generally nontechnical people in functional areas of the business, such as marketing or finance.

The intermediary. This is the individual who will help the user or users of the DSS. Using an intermediary implies the intermediary usage mode discussed on page 150, where we listed three common types of intermediaries. If the DSS is to be used in a different mode, the intermediary role does not apply.

The DSS builder or facilitator. This is the technical expert who will make technical decisions about the hardware platform(s) to use (see Chapter 5), the software tool(s) to use (see Chapter 6), the models and/or databases to incorporate into the DSS, and how they will be integrated with each other. This is generally a person with a great deal of experience who understands both the business problem and the available technologies.

The technical support person. This is the programmer who integrates existing packages into one overall system and carries out custom programming that contributes directly to DSS functionality. His or her responsibility begins with the packages that comprise part of the DSS and ends with a functional DSS for the user.

The toolsmith. This person focuses on the tools that will be used in constructing the DSS and the packages that will be combined into it. He or she is an expert on these tools and packages and their effective use. This is the person who creates underlying capabilities, often not visible to the user, but required for the technical support personnel to carry out their more user-oriented jobs effectively.

A large DSS project may involve several people in some of these roles. For instance, the technical support *person* may become a technical support *team*. A small project may have one person covering several roles. An example is when users with sufficient computer literacy create their own spreadsheet models via end-user computing. When they do this, they are filling the role of technical support person or intermediary with respect to the DSS in question.

Before embarking on a DSS development project, review the list of roles in this section and make sure that they are all adequately covered—or that you have good reason to believe that the roles which are not covered do not apply to this project.

7.3 THE IMPLEMENTATION STAGE

You've already read about the development process for decision support systems. The discussion so far has taken us to the point of a working program: If the proper inputs go in, the proper outputs will come out. A working program—even a working system—is not the end of the process, however, unless its developer is to be its only user. As you probably learned in a systems analysis course, the program or system has to be rolled out to its user community. This part of the system life cycle is called **implementation.** A typical definition of implementation is "the process of assuring that the information system is operational and then allowing users to take over its operation for use and evaluation" [KEND88]. Figure 7–5 shows graphically the place of implementation in the overall system development process, along with some of its major subtasks. The phases are shown as overlapping because they do. The lines indicating the ends of the phases slope because implementation phases may continue for some parts of the system or the database after they have finished for others.

Definitions of implementation differ. Your introductory MIS textbook (or instructor) may not have agreed with your systems analysis textbook (or instructor). Specifically, some people include part or all of the system design and development process under this heading. This usage is particularly common within the software vendor community, since their programmers' job is done when the software is sold to the user organization.[4] In this book we'll take the usual user-side view. We'll use the word *implementation* to include everything that takes place from the moment that system developers determine that their system is technically ready to be placed in the hands of its intended users, until the system is fulfilling its purpose for members of the organization.

If a DSS is developed using end-user computing tools and will not be made available to a large user community, implementation may be trivial: Its developer starts using it, and that's that. However, many DSS are developed via either the

FIGURE 7–5 Implementation Stage of System Development Process

---

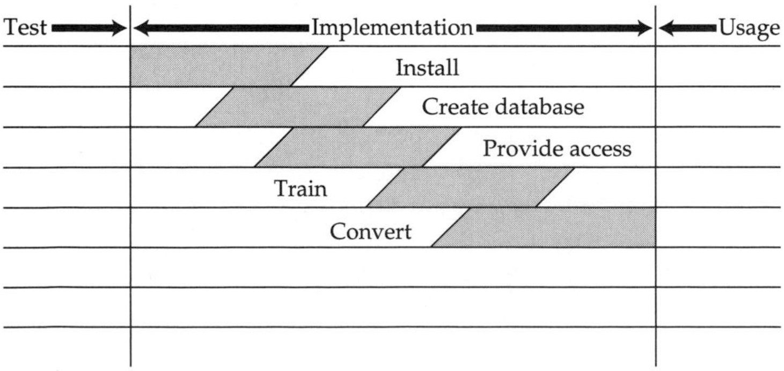

[4]This is not meant to suggest that vendors ignore or neglect their support responsibilities, only that the activities which users consider to be implementation aren't part of the vendor's job.

traditional SDLC or a prototyping approach. In these cases, implementation is critical: "There are no prizes for plowing a straight furrow if the crops don't come up!" Most of the discussion that follows applies to such systems. As we noted on page 265, though, systems developed via end-user computing can also benefit from systematic thought about these issues, even if they do not require a full-blown version of every step in the process.

Implementation includes the following activities. All must be included in the overall DSS project plan, with the necessary resources allocated to each. You can see that the complexity of each activity can vary dramatically from one DSS to another. A DSS that is simple in one aspect of its implementation will often be complex in another.

- *Obtaining and installing the DSS hardware.* This does not apply if the intended user community is already using the required hardware for other purposes. However, a new DSS often involves upgraded central systems, new LANs, new servers, new or upgraded desktop hardware, new networking connections, and perhaps more. These must be installed and fully operational before the next step can begin.
- *Installing the DSS and making it run on its intended hardware.* This will be trivial if the system was developed on the same computer on which it is intended to run in production use. In that case it is already installed, and its users need only be made aware of how to invoke it. Installation is more of an issue if a system must be installed in multiple computers throughout an organization, or if it was developed on a dedicated "software factory" computer and must now be transferred to its production environment.
- *Providing user access to the system.* This is trivial if the system is installed in microcomputers on the users' desks. In more complex situations, providing user access may require installing networks, extensive new wiring, and either terminals or a terminal emulation hardware/software package in the users' microcomputers. It may also require registration of the users on the system, including passwords, creation of electronic "mailboxes," assignment to groups, granting of priority levels, allocation of disk storage, and more.
- *Creating and updating the database.* Again, this activity can be trivial or nonexistent if an existing database is to be accessed without modification. In many situations, though, a specialized DSS database (or data warehouse; see the next part of the book) must be created, perhaps combining existing corporate files and databases with data from external databases. In a data warehouse, creating the database is often the single most complex part of the entire project. You'll read about this activity in Chapters 13 and 15.

    The DSS database may also have to be distributed to a number of computers or LAN servers. This should have been done at least once during system testing. Now it is necessary to make the procedure a regular, and hopefully automated, activity.
- *Training the users on the new system.* People who don't know how to use a system can hardly be expected to use it willingly or to obtain the maximum benefit from it. Training should not be left to programmers, who are often impatient

with nontechnical end users. A systems analyst with good people skills can be used in a pinch, but trained trainers are the ideal.

In a mainframe or minicomputer environment, or if multiple microcomputers, servers, and LANs are involved, it may also be necessary to train system operators, administrators, and other support personnel on the operational aspects of the new system.

- *Documenting the system for its users and for those who will be responsible for maintaining it in the future.* Ideally, much documentation will have been written as the DSS was developed. Reality, however, suggests, otherwise. Pressure to get the system working, and the common reluctance of many programmers to write documentation, combine to make this an afterthought. The implementation process is not complete until all the required types of system documentation have been written and are known to be satisfactory.
- *Making arrangements to support the users as the system is used.* This is especially important for DSS, whose users often use the system infrequently (thus forgetting details from one session to the next), use it in different ways each time (thus using different commands, options, etc.) and, as managers or senior professionals, may expect better support in all aspects of their work than their clerical colleagues do.
- *Transferring ongoing responsibility for the system from its developers to the operations or maintenance part of the MIS group.* Specifics will depend on how the organization's MIS group is organized.
- *Switching over to the new system from previous methods of making decisions or obtaining information to make them.* This topic is so important that we've devoted Section 7.4 to it.
- *Evaluating the operation and use of the system.* This is the only way management can determine if it is receiving the benefits it expected when it commissioned the DSS—and, if not, why not. Whether the answer to this question is in the affirmative or in the negative, this answer is important for the future of DSS in the organization. The evaluation must include objective assessments such as usage frequency, subjective assessments of user satisfaction, and an attempt to determine the impact of the system on the quality of decisions made and on the time it takes to make them. Adelman covers this subject in detail in [ADEL92].

These steps, at the topic level, resemble the implementation steps you studied for information systems in general in your introductory MIS course. However, there are some differences in their application to DSS. The key difference, other than items specifically noted previously and later in this chapter, is that the user community is likely to be higher in the organizational hierarchy than the users of other types of information systems. It will therefore be less accepting of demands that seem arbitrary. You will have to accommodate their schedules and other requirements more than you might for other types of information systems.

The implementation process will also differ slightly depending on whether SDLC, prototyping, or end-user computing was used to develop a DSS. As noted above, implementation of end-user–developed systems will be trivial if their developers are also their users. With prototyping, all the implementation steps must be followed. The biggest difference you will see is that the users you worked with in developing the prototype have probably become evangelists for the system within their own organizations. If they are well respected within those organizations, their support will reduce organizational resistance (see Section 7.5) to the new system.

7.4 SYSTEM CONVERSION

The most visible component of the implementation process is the system **conversion** itself. Palvia et al. discuss several conversion strategies in [PALV91]. The four basic strategies, which you probably learned in your introductory MIS or systems analysis course, are direct cutover, parallel conversion, pilot conversion, and phased conversion. Here's how these four basic conversion strategies apply to decision support systems:

1. In **direct conversion** or **direct cutover,** the entire organization stops using its old system and starts using the new one at the same time. This is a high-risk conversion strategy for transaction processing systems, as the impact of any problems is felt throughout the organization. It may be suitable for DSS, however. Since DSS usually access, but do not modify, the database they use, reverting to the previous decision-making methods (the previous computer system or use of manual methods) is often feasible. This differs from the typical transaction processing case, where the older system may have been designed for an older set of data files, and the data in these files are no longer current—or where an error can corrupt the operational database, making it unsuitable for further processing.

   In order to minimize the risk of direct conversion, it is necessary to keep the old programs, database updating methods, hardware (if applicable), and everything else needed for the older methods intact until the new system is known to work.

2. **Parallel conversion** involves running both the old and the new systems and comparing their results. The new system is accepted after the results have matched for an acceptable period. This is not a workable strategy for on-line transaction processing systems, as it requires users to enter all their transactions twice. (It can be used if the old system is manual and sometimes if it is batch-oriented, but those situations grow rarer every year.) If the system in question supports a large number of regular users, running two versions may also impose unacceptable hardware resource requirements. Finally, differences in the internal processing sequences of the old and new systems, or timing-dependent interactions among several people modifying the same database at the same time, may cause two on-line systems to give different answers even if both are operating perfectly. Either set of answers would be acceptable by itself, but they're different.

   In the case of data-oriented DSS, parallel operation is pointless: Why display the same data twice? For high-level DSS, especially suggestion systems that require little user input and perform complex optimizations, parallel conversion may be a reasonable approach. Furthermore, the user community of such systems tends to be small, though exceptions exist. In this case, the hardware resource impact of parallel conversion is probably acceptable. Timing-dependent differences are unlikely to cause a problem because DSS read, but do not modify, their databases.

The only difference between parallel conversion and direct cutover for DSS is an operational one, since the old methods must be kept around and usable in either case. The questions are, Are users able to access the old methods, and do they use them? If they do, at least as a check on the new system, it's parallel conversion. If they don't, it's direct cutover.

3. **Pilot conversion** means introducing a system to a small part of the organization, expanding its use once it is known to operate properly there. Eventually it will be in use by the entire organization. This is a good approach for single-user or multi-user DSS, as it limits conversion risk and allows system developers to concentrate any problem-resolution efforts on a small number of users and locations. It may not be feasible for a group DSS, since the very nature of a group DSS requires it to be in wide use within the decision-making group. If the pilot conversion strategy is used for group DSS, the pilot group must be large enough to provide a meaningful user community. If the GDSS is intended to support people at different locations, as a video teleconferencing system, the pilot group must encompass multiple geographic sites. In addition, the bottom-line benefits of many DSS argue for rolling it out on a wide basis as quickly as possible. These factors combine to make pilot conversion, which is usually the most desirable approach for transaction processing systems, less than ideal for DSS.

4. **Phased conversion** means introducing a system in stages, one component or module at a time, waiting until that one is operating properly before introducing the next. Eventually all the modules will have been introduced. This is an appropriate strategy for a DSS that can be divided into several modules, each providing new and visible benefits to its users. This is often the case with group DSS, for which pilot conversion may not be appropriate. For example, it might be possible to introduce a groupware package (see Chapter 10 for more on groupware) for communication within an organization and, once it is performing well in this role, add the capability to scan external databases for *Wall Street Journal* articles containing specific keywords. If the first modules of a DSS do not provide some visible benefit to users, they will create a negative attitude toward the system that will increase user resistance to the remaining— presumably more beneficial—modules.

Ideally, a phased conversion will begin with the most important modules and proceed through the less important ones. In some cases this will not be possible. If data flow serially through the modules, the only practical phasing strategy may be to start with one end of the system and proceed to the other. If your system relies on a data warehouse, the first conversion phase will have to be the creation of this data warehouse. You may then have some flexibility in sequencing the other phases.

	Viability of Conversion Method for	
	Transaction Processing Systems	Decision Support Systems
Direct cutover	Usually unacceptable risk	Usually acceptable risk
Parallel conversion	Usually Impractical	Usually practical
Pilot conversion	Generally first choice	May raise operational issues
Phased conversion	Usually requires large effort to interface two databases	Good choice for read-only systems such as most DSS

FIGURE 7–6   Conversion Strategy Desirability Comparison Chart

Figure 7–6 shows how the desirability of each conversion strategy for DSS compares with its desirability in other types of information systems. Many practical conversion situations call for a combination of these basic strategies. For example, a system may initially be implemented on a phased basis in part of the organization. Once it is running in its entirety for that user community, it can be rolled out to the entire firm. This would be a pilot approach with phased conversion within the pilot. Or each module can be rolled out to the entire organization as the next one is introduced to the pilot group. This would be a phased approach with pilot conversion within each phase.

7.5 OVERCOMING RESISTANCE TO CHANGE

Change is inherent in the implementation of any new system. Change is, however, uncomfortable to those who undergo it. Niccolò Machiavelli knew this centuries ago, when he wrote [MACH32], "there is nothing more difficult to take in hand, more perilous to conduct, or more uncertain in its success, than to take the lead in the introduction of a new order of things." He went on to explain that few people will stand to gain much from a change, so the change will have but few and lukewarm defenders. Many will stand to lose a great deal from it and will therefore fight it tooth and nail.

The prospective DSS implementer must therefore be keenly aware of the personal and organizational impact of a change.

> The design and implementation of a DSS is an example of planned technological change. The success or failure of a proposed DSS depends on how well this change process is managed. [CHER90]

Managing change is not a technical issue. It has nothing to do with megabytes of disk space, programming languages, or client/server networks. It deals with *people.* This is often an uncomfortable situation for MIS staffers, who may have chosen their field in part because it put less emphasis on interpersonal relationships than other careers might. (This is not true of everyone in MIS, but it is why some people gravitate toward working with computers.) Yet managing change is a necessary task.

Organizational culture is a key consideration in planning any change. Some organizations welcome change. Others say, in effect, "we've always done it this

Introducing Automation:
The Social Security Administration

In the late 1970s, the U.S. Social Security Administration developed a minicomputer-based system via which claims representatives in its field offices could access individual Social Security records. The purpose of this system, which had many aspects of a "file drawer" DSS, was to eliminate the laborious paper-based process of obtaining information about a claimant's entitlement to Social Security benefits, the history of a claim, and other such information. Much of the necessary data were in computer files at Social Security Administration headquarters in Baltimore, Maryland. Prior to the development of this system, those files could not be accessed on-line from the field offices.

The initial attempt to implement this system in a small number of pilot field offices was a disastrous failure. The reasons were totally nontechnical. Many of the claims representatives had previously held clerical and secretarial positions. They had been promoted from those jobs to their current professional positions and were proud of their new status. The visible symbol of their promotion was that they no longer had a typewriter—a device with a keyboard—on their desks. Now the MIS group was trying to put a terminal—not exactly a typewriter, but still a device that requires keyboard skills for effective use—on their desks again. "What are they trying to tell me here?" they thought. "What is the real message in this computer thing? Will I be a secretary, in fact if not in title, again?"

Once the problem was recognized, the MIS group removed the unwanted terminals from the offices where they had been placed and replanned the implementation. They began in a new set of pilot offices by installing one terminal on the manager's desk and training the manager to use it. From time to time claims representatives, in the normal course of their work, would ask their manager a question about a case. The manager would say "Let's look that up" and enter a query into the terminal. The answer appeared in seconds rather than weeks. Soon the claims representatives were asking "How can I get one of those terminals?" The answer was, of course, "How soon would you like it?" Once the terminals were installed, the claims representatives became enthusiastic users of the system.

Nothing about the system changed between the first attempt at a pilot implementation and the second. Nor did anything change in the claims representatives' backgrounds. What changed was their image of a terminal: from a symbol of a clerical position to a symbol of a managerial position. Once they had seen the terminal on their managers' desks, claims representatives no longer focused on its keyboard and therefore no longer associated the device with clerical work.

The specifics of this situation would be different today. Today we are used to seeing terminals and computers on the desks of professionals and managers. The lesson, however, is timeless: The culture and symbols of an organization are as important as, and perhaps more important than, technical factors in introducing new computer technology to end users.

way" and resist change. Once you have been with an organization for a while you'll probably have a good idea what its culture is and how easily changes are likely to go over. If you're new to an organization, or haven't been exposed to situations that would permit you to evaluate its receptivity to change, ask more experienced colleagues. The better ones will be impressed with how perceptive you are about the need to take cultural factors into account.

Change can be thought of as taking place in a three-stage process. This process was first put forth by Lewin [LEWI47, LEWI47a, also most books on organizational behavior] and is now generally known as the Lewin-Schein Theory of

Change. These stages are unfreezing, moving, and refreezing. **Unfreezing** creates the conditions and attitudes that are necessary before meaningful change can take place. **Moving** constitutes the change itself: putting the new system into operation to replace the old. **Refreezing** involves making the new system as much a part of the organizational fabric as the old one ever was.

The need to manage change in this sense applies, of course, primarily to *institutional* DSS in the sense of Section 4.7. An ad hoc DSS, intended for one-time use and discarded as soon as the need for it goes away, does not become part of the organizational fabric and therefore does not need the level of acceptance that an institutional DSS requires. If an ad hoc DSS is useful for its intended purpose, it will be used. If not, it won't be. In either case it will soon be gone.

7.5.1 Unfreezing

In the unfreezing stage it is important to create a strong motivation for change. If the present system is generally felt to be unsatisfactory, that may be sufficient motivation by itself. If not, it is necessary to create a vision of how much better things could be and to show how the proposed system will help make them better. The content of these preparatory activities can be based on the justification that was developed before management approved the DSS project, but the benefits must now be made clear to the prospective users of the system. They, not only the managers who hold the purse strings, must be able to visualize its benefits.

In creating this vision, it is important to focus on improvements that the user perceives as beneficial to himself or herself. This incentive need not be as crass as "Use the new system and get a 10 percent raise." However, benefits such as improved decision making, faster response time, and others are often more important to top management or to the corporate bottom line than they are to the individuals in question. It is necessary to translate these to those individuals' perspective, showing them how they will personally benefit by using the new system. If some system benefits don't lend themselves to this translation, they should be ignored or downplayed at this stage, though they may have been crucial to obtaining management approval for the new system.

There are three ways in which people can be unfrozen from their present position:

1. By increasing the forces that motivate them to change. If the current release of the corporate standard word processing package isn't enough better than the package people are already using to be worth the conversion effort, perhaps the next one will show enough new features to make them want to switch.
2. By reducing the forces that motivate them to resist change. Education can be a powerful change agent in this sense, since fear of the unknown is a big reason that people resist change.
3. By adjusting an existing force so that it becomes a force for, rather than against, change. If a compensation plan based on this quarter's profits is changed to a deferred compensation plan based partly on next year's profits, people will be more likely to make investments that will pay off in the future.

Favorable	Unfavorable
Top and unit managers felt the problem was important to the company	Unit managers could not state their problems clearly
Top managers became involved	Top managers felt the problem was too big
Unit managers recognized a need for change	Unit managers did not recognize need for change
Top managers initiated the study	Unit managers felt threatened by the project
Top and unit managers were open and candid	Unit managers resented the study
Unit managers revised some of their assumptions	Unit managers lacked confidence in the DSS implementers
	Unit managers felt they could do the study alone

FIGURE 7–7 Favorable and Unfavorable Factors for Unfreezing Stage

Some unfreezing activity can take place before system implementation. As soon as systems analysts start studying the need for a new system, they are finding areas that could be improved and thus creating a vision of a better way of working. However, this work may not have involved the entire user community, may have been undertaken before it was certain that the new system would be developed, almost certainly did not explicitly focus on changing user attitudes, and may have taken place several months before system implementation starts. It is therefore necessary to revisit the unfreezing issue now, to make sure that user attitudes as a whole are ready for change and to prepare them if they are not.

The administrative side of system implementation must also be looked to at this time. Though this is conceptually distinct from unfreezing, it tends to occur at about the same time because it must also be done before the implementation proper can begin. Here the implementers or their manager must develop a complete project plan for the implementation process, describing the people who will participate in this process, their respective roles, and milestones by which the progress of the implementation can be measured against its plan.

Several favorable and unfavorable forces that can influence the likelihood of success are given in [ZAND75]. The ones that affect the unfreezing stage are listed in Figure 7–7. Here, and in the two subsequent figures from that source, we have substituted "DSS implementers" for the original "management scientists."

7.5.2 Moving

The most visible component of the moving stage is the actual conversion, or cutover, from the old (perhaps manual) decision-making methods to the new DSS. The technical aspects of conversion are sufficiently important that we devoted Section 7.4 above entirely to them.

Training that takes place during the conversion process must be matched to the conversion strategy. If pilot conversion is to be used, for example, the training must first be provided to the pilot department. If parallel conversion is to be used, the trainers must deal with any expected differences between the outputs of the old and new systems. The specific training requirements that the chosen conversion strategy imposes must be taken into account in the project plan developed during the unfreezing stage.

Favorable	Unfavorable
Unit managers and DSS implementers gathered data jointly	DSS implementers could not educate the unit managers
Relevant data were accessible and available	Needed data were not made available
New alternatives were devised	Unit managers did not help develop a solution
Unit managers reviewed and evaluated alternatives	Unit managers did not understand the solution of the DSS implementers
Top managers were advised of options	DSS implementers felt the study was concluded too quickly
Top managers helped develop a solution	
Proposals were improved sequentially	

FIGURE 7–8   **Favorable and Unfavorable Factors for Moving Stage**

During the moving stage the project leader must continually monitor project progress against plan. This monitoring has two purposes: to determine that project milestones are being met on schedule and to determine, by speaking with both MIS staff members and system users, that they are being met with the required quality. If either of these is not the case, corrective action must be instituted. If adverse consequences were properly considered while the plan was being developed, as described on page 70, the necessary corrective action(s) will usually have been identified in advance. Favorable and unfavorable factors for the moving stage, again from [ZAND75], are listed in Figure 7–8.

7.5.3 Refreezing

Refreezing makes sure that the users of the new system have the necessary internal commitment to using it on an ongoing basis. This is particularly important in DSS, as most DSS are used when the user decides to use them. This is different from transaction processing systems: An order entry operator, for example, must enter an order when it comes in no matter how he or she feels about doing so. By contrast, if the users of a DSS think they can make decisions adequately without the new system, they will ignore the system once its developers leave the users' offices or will resent being forced to use it against their will. In either case, the desired system benefits will not be fully achieved.

Chervany and Palvia [CHER90] found that three factors have positive effects on all stages of the change process. According to their research, you will increase the likelihood of successful DSS implementation if you

- Have a strong project "**champion**" in the form of a highly placed executive who supports the project visibly.
- Allow sufficient time for each stage of change to take place.
- Make sure each stage of change is successful before moving to the next.

They also found that the ability to reverse the change, which is often felt to reduce the pressure associated with a change and therefore to facilitate it, has the opposite effect in the moving and refreezing stages. One possible explanation is that users, once "unfrozen" from their previous state, can go in either direction. If they know a change is reversible, they will not have the emotional commitment to the new system that will make it succeed. The lesson for DSS developers is that the ability

Favorable	Unfavorable
Unit managers tried the solution	DSS implementers did not try to support new managerial behavior after the solution was used
Utilization showed the superiority of the new solution	DSS implementers did not try to reestablish stability after solution was used
DSS implementers initiated positive feedback after early use	Results were difficult to measure
Solution was widely accepted after initial success	Standards for evaluating the result were lacking
Unit managers were satisfied	Top managers ignored the solution recommended by the DSS implementers
Solution was used in other areas	Solution was incompatible with the needs and resources of the unit
The change improved the performance of the unit	Top managers did not encourage other units to use the solution

FIGURE 7–9   **Favorable and Unfavorable Factors for Refreezing Stage**

	Technical	User Related
Things to watch out for (negatives)		
Things to do (positives)		

FIGURE 7–10   **Two-by-Two DSS Implementation Grid**

to try out a system (via prototyping, end-user development, or a 30-day free trial of a package) can be helpful in the development and unfreezing stages, but the commitment to change should be absolute thereafter.

This need for commitment is a reason not to use the parallel conversion strategy beyond an initial time period. The same holds for direct cutover if the old system remains available to users, a mouse-click away, with nothing but a management directive preventing them from accessing it. If the old system must be kept around as an insurance policy, it should be made as unavailable as possible by removing it from users' desktop computers, archiving it on the central mainframe, or some other means. Figure 7–9 shows Zand and Sorensen's favorable and unfavorable factors for the refreezing stage.

7.6 DSS IMPLEMENTATION ISSUES

You probably studied the area of system implementation in your more general MIS courses. Our goal here is to take what you already know and to focus it specifically on DSS implementation issues. DSS implementation differs from the implementation of other types of applications for both technical and user-related reasons. Each type is important. Furthermore, each type of reason can be divided into causes of failure and strategies for success. These two two-way splits can be visualized as in Figure 7–10.

7.6.1 Technical DSS Implementation Issues

Technical factors in DSS implementation include making sure that the DSS operates as it is supposed to, with adequate performance and reliability, and yields accurate (as accuracy is defined for the system in question) results. Specific factors to watch for in the technical area include the following issues.

Unfamiliarity with This Type of System   Clearly, the more familiar the developers are with the type of system they are designing and programming, the more likely they are to have a smooth development process. However, familiarity extends to the implementation stage as well. Developers who are unfamiliar with a particular class of system are more likely to follow a specification without fully understanding what it is about, less likely to intuit user needs, less likely to design useful interfaces, less likely to provide support that truly meets the unspoken questions, than those to whom this type of DSS is second nature. The best way to deal with the issue of unfamiliarity is to bring it out into the open, discuss it, and make sure that the developers pay special attention to understanding the true user requirements.

Unfamiliarity is not exactly the same as incompetence, though the results of the two are often similar. Unfamiliarity creates specialized, often temporary, incompetence which should not be seen as a personal reflection on the people in question. This makes it possible to deal with unfamiliarity frankly and openly, without the negative connotations that calling people "incompetent" would carry.

Response Time   Users get frustrated quickly when activities which they perceive as "simple" take a long time. Response time can and should be evaluated during testing, of course. However, developers who are aware of the internal complexity of a particular operation may be more tolerant of long execution times than are users, who see only the end result of each computational process. Furthermore, developers may have been using a lightly loaded system or high-performance workstations. The general user community may have to contend with a heavier load on the server, slower microcomputers, networks bogged down by transaction traffic, or a full-scale database instead of the small one that was put together to test the software.

Response time, if inadequate, can be improved by faster hardware (a "brute force" approach which, though potentially expensive, usually works), by program tuning, and by database and network optimization. The nontechnical side of response time, user expectation, is also important. It is discussed on page 281.

Reliability and Availability   A system that crashes unpredictably at frequent intervals, that must be brought down during working hours for database reorganization and updating, that is subject to network failures which make it unusable, or which can only be accessed via an insufficient number of specialized terminals is not available to its users when and where they need it.

Poor Data Quality   As the old saying goes, "garbage in, garbage out." The output of a system can only be as good as its inputs. This can be a serious problem when data are collected from several sources, some of them external, for aggregation as in a data warehouse. The information quality factors you read about in Chapter 3 come into play here. The data must be monitored carefully for accuracy and timeliness. Another issue mentioned there, which is especially important in DSS (and, within DSS, especially important in data warehouses) arises when combining data from multiple sources: data *consistency*. Each of several individual data elements may be accurate, but combining them may create nonsense if they apply to different time periods or use different definitions for some of their underlying concepts. A decision based on inconsistent data will be little better than a random guess.

7.6.2 User-Related DSS Implementation Issues

The user-related issues in DSS implementation are often more complex than the technical ones. They may also be more difficult for the typical MIS professional to deal with. Some user concerns about a new DSS must be addressed before the project reaches its implementation stage, of course. Far earlier, when the new system was being defined, systems analysts worked with its prospective users to determine their requirements. At that point it was necessary to develop a good relationship with the users, establish the credibility of the design team, and lay the foundation for a smooth implementation later on. If this preparatory groundwork was not properly done, the implementation will be much more difficult than it has to be.

Specific user-related implementation concerns with which DSS implementers must deal at this time include the issues that follow.

User and Management Support   If a system's prospective users don't support it, they will at best use it sullenly. At worst, they may sabotage it openly. If management doesn't support the system, the users themselves never will. Systems that are initiated by users, or that have active user participation in their development, are more likely to have user support than those that do not.

Users and managers who are not truly committed to a new system can draw upon a wide variety of "game-playing" techniques to obstruct its implementation without appearing to oppose it overtly. Such games include "passing the buck" regarding the responsibility for a particular aspect of a system, appropriating its budget for "emergencies," slowing down progress while appearing to work hard, and more. Grover et al. discuss several such "games" in [GROV88].

As previously noted, much of the groundwork for this support should have been laid well before a new system is ready to be implemented. Whether or not this was done, the project team must now make sure that both users and their managers understand why the new system was developed and how it will help them. A memo from a highly placed and personally respected member of management, timed to arrive shortly before user-visible implementation activities begin, is often helpful here. The visible attendance of one or more managers in a user training class, assuming that classroom training is to be used, can also convey a strong message to the overall user community.

Unstable User Community   The stability of the user community is closely tied to the previous factor. If users disappear or change frequently, it will be difficult to enlist their consistent support. No sooner will the DSS implementers have created a vision of the new system with one group of users but those users will be gone and another group will have taken their place. This leads to several difficulties: The group that must ultimately use the system may not be the same as the one whose needs it was developed to meet. The new group may have different backgrounds, different problem-solving styles, or different views of technology. The purpose, the usage pattern, even the very decision statement that was so carefully worked out several months ago may turn out to be worth little.

There is little a DSS implementer can do to increase the stability of a user organization. However, the astute implementer can and must be aware of it. DSS design strategies that maximize flexibility in system usage modes, inputs, and outputs will help keep the system adaptable to any new group. If the changes take place one person at a time, regular meetings with the group as the system is being developed will help maintain the attitude that the new system is welcome and will be of value.

Response Time   This is another way to look at the second technical issue discussed in the previous section (page 279). It is a nontechnical issue as well because it is neither "wrong" nor "right." Response time can only be considered adequate or inadequate relative to user expectations.

Several studies have shown that users will accept response times for as long as several minutes if they perceive a system to be carrying out a complex, time-consuming task on their behalf. Conversely, they will become frustrated in as short a time as one second if they perceive a task as trivial. Unfortunately, the complexity of a task to a computer is not always the same as its apparent complexity to a nontechnical end user. Proper management of user expectations can make a slow system adequate. Improper management of this factor can make a far faster system inadequate. Steps a DSS developer can take to help manage user expectations include the following:

1. Training and documentation can explain to users what goes on behind a seemingly simple operation, so users will understand why a command does not yield an immediate answer. This is especially applicable to database operations that involve comparing entries in one table against those in another, or where data (invisibly to users) must be obtained from remote sources.
2. An estimate of completion time before an operation starts, a periodically updated "working" message displaying a completion percentage or an estimate of remaining time to completion, a graphical progress bar, or another indication that the system has not "crashed" gives users a sense of security that a long response time is normal. The Windows hourglass and Macintosh wrist-watch are examples of operating system developers using this technique.
3. When system load is expected to increase and thus slow response times in the future, a **speed governor** can be applied to a program to prevent users from subconsciously developing expectations that will not be sustained when the entire

user community is active. A speed governor consists of an idle loop that is invoked as part of each user command. The number of times the loop is executed is under system administrator control, and is reduced to maintain consistent response times as the number of system users increases. Palvia et al. mention the use of such a governor for this purpose at Polaroid Corporation's distribution division in [PALV91]. Since this approach uses processor cycles, it is acceptable only in a system which is dedicated to a particular application or which has excess capacity. Were other applications, besides Polaroid's distribution system, running on the same computer, the governor could have impacted their response times as well and would therefore probably have been unacceptable.

Training   Types of training include classroom training, one-on-one tutoring at the user's office, self-teaching training vehicles such as books and videotapes, and computer-based instruction, increasingly including multimedia. The choice among these depends on the number of people to be trained, their locations, the time frame within which the training must take place, and the available resources. Figure 7–11 compares the resource requirements of four training methods. The time availability of the trainees must also be taken into account. The more resource-intensive methods, such as one-on-one training, may be appropriate when the user community includes top executives or others whose time is considered, rightly or wrongly, much more valuable than that of the trainer. Classroom-based training is feasible only when it is practical to assemble a sufficiently large number of users at the same time and in the same place and when the required facilities, such as a computer or terminal for at least every pair of trainees, are available.

   Although system design is not, strictly speaking, a training method, good user interface design can minimize the need for training. A prompting or menu-driven interface requires far less training of its users than a command-line interface would call for. There are trade-offs here too, of course: Training is a one-time expense for each system user, whereas many easy-to-use interface styles such as GUIs exact an ongoing cost in hardware resource usage.

FIGURE 7–11   Relative Resource Requirements of Different Training Methods

		Type of Instruction			
		Classroom	**One-on-one**	**Books, Manuals**	**Videotape, Multimedia**
	Human resources to develop	Medium	Low	High	Very High
Resource Requirements	Human resources to deliver	Medium	High	Very low	Very low
	Other resource requirements	Computer-equipped classroom	None	None	VCR, CD-ROM-equipped workstation, etc., per chosen medium

Trainers must take the users' existing point of view as a departure point for any training. As pointed out in [MALL91], the trainer must not only know about the new system but also a great deal about how its prospective users solved the same problem before the new system was available. They have undoubtedly developed mental models of how the world works, may have a specialized vocabulary to deal with it, and have acquired a set of habits that reflect their traditional way of reaching the decision in question. A trainer who does not know about these, or does not take them into account in the training, will lose much of his or her audience during the first five minutes.

Availability of Support   No formal training class, no user manual, no on-line help facility can answer all the questions that could possibly arise. Some questions will have to be answered by knowledgeable people as they come up. Providing a support **hotline** ensures that these questions will go to the right person or group of people. Such a support facility may already exist within an end-user computing support group or information center. If not, it will have to be set up. The degree of formality depends on the DSS user community. If the user community is small and geographically centralized, giving users the name and telephone extension of the responsible systems analyst may suffice. If it consists of several hundred people spread over two or three continents, a more permanent **help desk** structure should be established.

Such a help desk is a visible line item on someone's budget, but it is not an added expense to the organization as a whole. Users will have questions about a new system whether a help desk exists or not. If the organization does not provide a standard way for users with questions to obtain answers, one of two things will happen: Either the users will obtain an answer through any available informal channel or the questions will go unanswered.

- In the first case, the organization is still absorbing the cost of answering the question. Indeed, it is probably answering the question less efficiently, and hence at greater cost, than if a standard channel existed.
- In the second case, the organization will not obtain the benefits it was counting on its new DSS to provide. That is penny wise and pound foolish.

Voluntary or Mandatory Use?   The use of transaction processing systems is seldom voluntary. If the only way an airline issues boarding passes is through a computer printer, its reservation clerks will have to use the computer; they have no choice. With DSS, the option to make a decision without computer input is always there. An advertising manager who thinks computer-based demographic data on magazine readership will not help choose a better ad schedule will not use a DSS that provides demographic data. Will the ad schedule such a person chooses be better than he or she could have chosen with the computer? Probably not, but that's not the issue.

Should such people be forced to use the computer? There is no single right answer to this question. In the case of group DSS (see Chapter 10) mandatory use, or a high degree of pressure, may be appropriate because only a "critical mass" of users can make a group system viable. In other cases, especially where the system meets a visible, felt need, the carrot of better job performance may be more effective than the stick. Even there some motivation and exhortation is a good idea: Relying solely on exposure is generally ineffective.

In one situation, which Alter called "Connoisseur Foods" in [ALTE80], a food company developed a customer response model to help brand managers plan and manage their merchandising activities more effectively. Some of the newer brand managers took to the system like ducks to water and were soon using it to advantage. Others, including "people-oriented" brand managers who had come up through the sales ranks, resisted. The management policy in this case was to permit voluntary use of the system, though their manager of marketing services was reported as saying that, were he in charge, "no brand plan [could] be produced or changed without explicit evaluation based on a brand model. Furthermore, brand managers would have to submit printouts annotated with their own comments and analysis." Upper management overruled him.

In this case the system became generally accepted over a few years. One reason was that management did not stress its use in helping brand managers make their plans. Rather, they focused on how well the results of those plans matched the predictions of the model. Since the model was known to be accurate within a few percent as long as nothing changed in the external environment or the competitive picture, major deviations signaled such changes. This warned Connoisseur Foods management of such changes more quickly than they would have otherwise found out, thus enabling them to respond before it was too late.

7.7 USING THE LISTS OF ISSUES

At this point you are probably thinking, "Now that I've read long lists of things to worry about, what on earth do I do with them?" Here's one suggestion: The lists break down two ways—things to watch out for (negatives, unfavorable factors) versus things to do (positives, favorable factors), and technical versus user-related issues. Those two breakdowns gave us the grid you've already seen as Figure 7–10.

When you plan a DSS project, go over the lists in the preceding sections and try to pick issues for each quadrant of this grid: potential technical pitfalls for the top-left square, and so on for the other three.

One entry in each quadrant of the grid is a good target to shoot for. However, this is not a rigidly fixed rule. If you rack your brain for days and can't find an entry for one of the quadrants, so be it. Don't lose any more sleep trying to find something that isn't there. Chances are that quadrant of the grid is under control. Conversely, if you go through the list and find two or three important issues that all belong in the same quadrant, put them all in. The grid is a planning tool. You should control it; it shouldn't control you. Its purpose is to give you a structured way to whittle all these lists down to a manageable size. Used this way, it can be quite helpful.

This process will give you a situation-specific short list of critical factors. Plan for and watch them. That will give you enough to keep you busy and will pick up the most critical issues for your particular project. You might end up with a filled-in grid that looks like Figure 7–12.

	Technical	User Related
Things to watch out for (negatives)	Slow response time due to need to scan the entire database to answer common queries	Concern that local database on LAN server will not be up to date
Things to do (positives)	Verify that all prospective users have at least a Pentium II microprocessor and 32MB of RAM in their system	Make sure trainers have used the existing mainframe based query system and know how the new query syntax differs from the old one

FIGURE 7–12 Filled-in DSS Implementation Grid

7.8 ETHICAL ISSUES IN DSS IMPLEMENTATION

DSS professionals must do more than just apply their technical skills to DSS development and implementation. They have a professional obligation to use these skills in an ethical manner. Unfortunately, this is not always easy. The temptation of what has been called "a deal with the Devil" [CHRI90] is ever present. The DSS developer who knows in advance what temptations may arise, and has thought about how he or she might respond if they do, will be better equipped to withstand them. In the long run this ability will pay off.

Ethical issues arise throughout the life cycle of any information system, including DSS. The implementation stage is where they come into clearest focus. Until then, the DSS is being developed in a laboratory. It is in actual usage where it might potentially invade people's privacy, contribute to unethical management decisions, and more. That's why we're discussing the subject of ethics in a DSS context in this chapter. However, ethical behavior cannot be put into sealed compartments, separated from the rest of one's professional life. Ethical considerations apply to all stages of DSS development from the beginning. The sooner they are addressed in a system, the more likely they are to come to a satisfactory resolution for all concerned. If you wait until the implementation stage to raise an issue that has existed since the system was defined conceptually, management can well ask, "If that bothers you, how come you didn't say anything for the past eight months?" Even if the issue is ultimately resolved in an ethical fashion, resources will have been wasted, and hard feelings that could have been avoided will have been created.

Consider this scenario: You are developing a decision support system to help bank loan officers process second mortgage and home improvement loan applications. Bank executives know that members of certain groups have less access to credit than other members of the community. For lack of alternatives, members of these groups, once they find a bank that will grant them a loan, will pay higher interest rates than others would accept before taking their business elsewhere. Bank executives also realize that members of these groups tend to cluster in certain neighborhoods, which can be defined by street names and numbers. You have been told to add 0.25 percent to the system's recommended interest rate on loan applications from those addresses. What do you do?

This is a relatively straightforward example of a deal with the Devil. The bank's actions are clearly unethical and probably illegal. You should refuse to participate in such an activity. But even this open-and-shut scenario raises some of the key issues that arise in any ethical consideration. Some of the critical topics [CASH92] are as follows:

Storage of Information One commonly applied test here is this: If the information stored in your system were itemized on the front page of tomorrow's paper, would you be embarrassed? Is there any information, the storing of which invades someone's (or some organization's) privacy? Is there any information there that belongs to someone else (or to some other organization) which was not obtained through appropriate channels?

In the case of this scenario, applicant's privacy is being invaded through the implicit association of their address with their ethnic background. The information may be stored as tables within program code rather than as the content of a traditional file or database, but the ethical issue is the same.

Use of Information Here you must assure yourself that information, openly collected, is being used for the purposes for which those who provided it believed it would be used—or, at least, is being used in ways that they would approve if they knew about them. A few people will provide information even though they believe it will be used for unethical purposes. Fortunately, most won't. Therefore, adhering to this guideline also provides some protection against unethical uses of the information.

In the preceding scenario, loan applicants presumably believe that they are providing address information so the bank can verify the nature of the property on which it is being asked to grant a loan, record a security interest in the property until the loan is paid off, mail bills and other notices to the correct place, and similar aboveboard purposes. They do not expect it to be used as a criterion for discriminatory rate setting.

Sharing of Information Information has value, and property of value can be sold. Information is unusual in this respect: After it is sold, the original owner still has it! Yet sharing one's information with others is a form of information usage. The same criterion applies: Did those who provided the information believe, or expect, that it would be shared? If they didn't, would they approve?

Electronic information sharing is common in this day and age. Most periodicals sell their mailing lists: Subscribers to *Field and Stream* are excellent candidates for direct mail campaigns by fishing rod manufacturers. One can obtain a list of *Computerworld* subscribers who are MIS managers in manufacturing organizations with more than 50 employees, plan to buy 3Com networking equipment next year, and work in Iowa. Many mail-order marketers sell their lists as well. Yet because of public pressure, most people who collect names for their own business purposes allow the people whose names are collected to indicate "do not sell." Lotus Marketplace's home edition, a CD-ROM which would have provided demographic data on millions of residential units in the United States, was withdrawn from sale in 1991 (before it was shipped) after a massive public outcry—and 30,000 written requests to be removed from its database. And there are laws against the U.S. Census Bureau sharing individual information, even with other agencies of the federal government.

The bank scenario previously mentioned does not raise any sharing issues, but it could. Were the system described in the scenario to be implemented, the bank could record which customers took out loans at an above-market rate. Sharing this list, for example, with a personal loan firm would compound the unethicality of developing this system in the first place.

Human Judgment This category refers to whether human judgment is being used properly in the overall decision process. The appropriate use of DSS can both help and hurt here. In particular, it is important to allow humans to review system recommendations that are not totally structured: in other words, to have a decision *support* system rather than a decision-*making* system.

The bank scenario falls down badly on this score. It is designed to support human judgment being applied in an unethical (in this case, discriminatory) manner. Participating in developing a system designed for this purpose is unethical even if one could argue, as in this case, that the system is simply carrying out a calculation based on certain objective data elements and parameters.

Combining Information Where information is concerned the whole can be greater than the sum of its parts. The U.S. military has recognized this for decades: A file drawer can be classified Top Secret even though no single piece of paper in it is classified above Secret, if there are enough such pieces of paper. So have criminals: The announcement that Mr. Doe and Ms. Roe will honeymoon in Hawai'i (obtained from the local paper) and their addresses (from the phone book), combined, are an invitation to "case the joint." The prospect of having everyone who knows something about a person pool their information to create a detailed profile is, to many, not pleasant. The process of having this done quickly, automatically, and with little effort on the part of those creating the profile is even less pleasant—since, with manual information processing, the level of effort required to collect and combine information was a barrier to widespread attempts to do so. The bank scenario, because it deals with a self-contained system, does not raise the issue of combining information from multiple sources.

Error Detection and Correction Information systems should always incorporate procedures for preventing errors, for verifying the information in them, and for correcting errors that are detected. This is especially important in DSS, where the information in a database is usually trusted by its users and is relied on for far-reaching decisions. There are, for example, U.S. laws that require a credit bureau to provide individuals with copies of their credit reports on request, to correct errors brought to its attention, and, in case of an unresolvable disagreement over whether an item is an error, to include the individual's statement about the item with any report sent out in the future.

Ethics in Software Testing

The following message was posted to the Internet newsgroup misc.business.consulting, which discusses issues that consultants face in their work, on April 8, 1996. The consultant who posted it gave it the subject line, "Lesson learned—Don't give in to client's rush tactics." The lessons he learned aren't just for consultants but for everyone with any influence on software testing. It is presented here precisely as posted, with no editing.

This past week, I learned a valuable lesson, and am posting this so that perhaps it can help someone else avoid falling into the same trap.

One of my company's clients was having their computer system switched over to a new system, and was in a great hurry to have the conversion completed. My advice to this client was to thoroughly test the system, which is using their special purpose application software (not supported by my company—supported by the vendor, who provides very little information about the software) before the conversion. The client did some testing, but refused to keep careful logs (actually, they kept no log!) of what did, and didn't, work, as I advised them to do, and I suspect that they didn't do a very thorough job of the testing that they did do. Instead of the client being patient with the testing process, the client was impatient and in a big hurry to have their data files transferred to the new system.

I did something that I never usually do, and won't do again: give in to a hurried client and move ahead with a project faster than I think that it should proceed. Some of their equipment still hadn't been tested with the new hardware, as the client didn't want the inconvenience of not using a few pieces of equipment for a short period of time with the old system while it was to be tested with the new system. Unfortunately, after the data files were transferred, the client needed to begin using the new system (vital to their business—point of sale) almost immediately. It turned out that everything *almost* worked.

The special application software on the client's system needed to have an initialization program run with root privileges (a definite no-no in my opinion, but the vendor insisted), which made some minor changes to some various system files that it didn't really need to change, which caused some problems.[5] Furthermore, it turned out that a parallel printer

---

[5] A program with root privileges refers to a program that can bypass the normal operating system protections against modifying critical system files. This is occasionally necessary, for purposes such as changing a user's password, but its use must be controlled carefully to make sure that such programs don't cause errors.

A loan approval DSS, even if conceived in an ethical fashion, could recommend rejecting an application because of a data entry error: an annual income of $5,000 rather than $50,000, or monthly rent payments of $5,000 rather than $500. An ethically implemented DSS would give the applicant the reason for rejection, allow errors such as these to be corrected, and reprocess the application without prejudice due to the prior rejection once the errors are corrected.

Taking the concepts a step further, such a DSS might incorporate "reasonableness checks" on the data to catch as many such errors as possible before the application is processed: The likelihood of a person earning $50,000 per year paying $5,000 per month in rent is, to say the least, small. You may never be able to make your database totally free of errors—survey after survey have found that most

Ethics in Software Testing (continued)

board which worked in their old system refuses to work properly in their new system, so they're now quite unhappy about going a few days without one of their printers (they have other ones to use, but that's not enough for them, and they're screaming quite loudly, and may attempt to damage my company's reputation).

Oh what fun . . .

Lesson learned: never, ever, allow yourself, or others working for you, to be rushed by a client against your better judgment. Please don't let them rush you! If a client doesn't want to wait, and won't cooperate with necessary testing, tell them that you're not going to proceed until you are confident that it's been proven safe to do so. Let them be the one to break the contract if they aren't happy with how fast things are moving along. Giving in isn't worth the headaches that follow.

Has anyone else here fallen into this sort of trap, and did they manage to escape from it unscathed?

QUESTIONS

1. Replies to this posting, besides expressing sympathy for the consultant who found himself in this situation, generally endorsed the suggestion in the next-to-last paragraph: leaving the engagement, if necessary, rather than giving in to time pressure. Is this always practical? What are some of the difficulties?
2. What if the person trying to get the organization to slow down isn't a consultant, but is an employee, and was clearly told by his or her management to put the system into use by a specific date? What should someone do in that situation? What are some of the obstacles to doing the "right" thing?
3. Do you think employees of a firm, or nonemployees under contract to a firm, are more likely to be subjected to this type of pressure? What precautions can either type of person take *before* the fact to prevent it or minimize its impact?

databases contain a substantial number of errors—but you might be surprised to realize how many errors can be caught if checking is carefully thought out.

Several codes of ethics have been proposed for information systems practitioners. Most professional societies have one to which their members are expected to adhere and which provides penalties for violating them. (These penalties typically involve expulsion from the society, as a professional association can't do much more.) The codes of ethics of the Data Processing Management Association, the Institute for Certification of Computer Professionals, the Association for Computing Machinery, the Canadian Information Processing Society, and the British Computer Society are compared in [OZ92]. He points out that, while all the codes are similar, they are sometimes in conflict. For example, one requires its members to obey all laws, whereas another requires its members to violate laws that they consider unethical. Clearly, a member of both societies (a common situation, since many people join these societies to obtain their publications at the lowest rates) can be faced with a quandary.

SUMMARY

Systems can be built by the MIS department on the basis of a fixed user specification, by the MIS department on the basis of a user-approved prototype, or by the end users themselves with professional help and support. If a prototype is used, it can either be used as a machine-executable specification or evolved into the finished application. The first approach usually yields higher performance and may be more appropriate to transaction processing applications. The second often produces the application more quickly and therefore may suit DSS better.

You should also have a clear idea of who will fill each development role on the project, or be certain that the role does not apply. The roles to consider are user, intermediary, DSS builder (or facilitator), technical support person, and toolsmith.

The implementation stage of any information system is the process of taking it from its developers and bringing it to production use. DSS implementation, which begins when the DSS developers determine that their system is ready for its users, includes the technical activities of purchasing and installing hardware and software packages, installing the DSS, connecting systems and networks to the users' desktops, and creating the DSS database. Nontechnical implementation activities include training, documentation, support, and transferring the system formally from its developers to those who will maintain it. The importance of each of these implementation activities varies from one DSS to another.

The actual conversion from previous decision-making methods to the new DSS is an important part of the implementation process. There are four basic approaches to conversion: direct cutover, parallel operation, pilot conversion, and phased conversion. Phased conversion is often the most appropriate way to convert to a new DSS. Direct cutover and parallel operation are also appropriate if the previous decision-making methods were manual. Pilot conversion, generally the ideal approach for transaction processing systems, does not stand out as strongly for DSS. In any case, a combination of methods may be useful.

Conversion to any new system involves change. People resist change. This resistance must be managed effectively if the new system is to succeed. The way to manage it depends on organizational culture and the existing attitudes of prospective system users.

Change is most effectively handled in three stages: unfreezing, moving, and refreezing. In the unfreezing stage, prospective users must be shown how a new system can make the relevant aspect of their life easier. In the moving stage, they are trained on the new system and encouraged to use it. In the refreezing stage, their commitment to the new system is reinforced. Active management support is mandatory during all three of these stages.

The DSS implementer must be on the alert for several factors that can interfere with a successful implementation effort. Technical factors include user unfamiliarity with the type of system in question, unacceptable system response times, inadequate system reliability and availability, and poor data quality. Nontechnical factors include the existence of active management support, changes in the user community, user expectations of response time, training, support, and usage policies (voluntary or mandatory). These categories suggest areas to focus on for successful management of the implementation process.

Ethical issues are important with any DSS. They come to a head at the implementation stage since a DSS raises ethical concerns only when it is used. However, they must often be addressed before that stage in order not to waste effort developing a system whose usage would be unethical. Ethical issues in a DSS context usually relate to the DSS database and to decisions made on the basis of its content. The DSS must only store information that was obtained through ethical channels, share it with those with whom its supplier would agree it may be shared, and combine it only with information that does not create an overall invasion of privacy. It must provide means to detect as many errors as feasible and to correct those that are detected. Data should only be used for the purposes for which they were supplied, humans should review any recommended decisions that have the potential to reflect inappropriate use of the data, and the decision-making methods supported by the DSS should always be consistent with ethical principles.

KEY TERMS

builder (see DSS builder)
champion
change
conversion
cutover
direct conversion
DSS builder (development role)
end-user development
evolutionary prototyping
facilitator (development role)
help desk
hot line
implementation
information center
installation
intermediary (development role)
managing change
moving
overcoming resistance
parallel conversion
phased conversion
pilot conversion
prototyping
quick-hit DSS
rapid application development
refreezing
speed governor
system development life cycle (SDLC)
technical support person (development role)

throwaway prototyping
toolsmith (development role)
training
unfreezing
user (development role)

REVIEW QUESTIONS

1. What are the three basic methods of developing an information system?
2. For what types of DSS is the SDLC approach best suited?
3. What is a prototype?
4. What are the two basic approaches to prototyping? Which is usually better suited to DSS development?
5. Who is responsible for creating the DSS when end-user development is used?
6. What is an information center? What does it do?
7. What are three dangers in end-user computing?
8. Explain the five major DSS development roles.
9. What is implementation? Does the definition in this book agree with that in your introductory MIS and systems analysis textbooks (if you had them)?
10. What stages does implementation follow in the SDLC? In the prototyping approach to system development?
11. Describe at least six activities that are part of the implementation process.
12. State the four basic system conversion strategies.
13. What would it mean to combine (a) parallel operation with pilot conversion, (b) pilot conversion with phased conversion?
14. Why is it important to overcome resistance to change in implementing a DSS?
15. What are the three stages of overcoming change?
16. What three factors can contribute to making all three stages of the change process successful?
17. In which stages of the change process does it help the change process if DSS users can return to previous decision-making methods? In which does it impede successful change?
18. List three technical and three nontechnical issues that can impact DSS success.
19. Is system response time a technical or a nontechnical issue? Explain.
20. When in the life cycle of a DSS should ethical issues be considered?
21. What ethical factors might constrain the type of information to be stored in a DSS database?
22. State at least two ways of detecting erroneous data entered by a user into a DSS database.

EXERCISES

1. You have been asked to develop a DSS to help the staff of a large credit card company decide how to deal with overdue accounts. They become involved in the process only when an account is 90 days overdue, since for the first two months the computer automatically appends a note (friendly the first time, firmer the second) and adds a finance charge to the monthly bill. They have access to information about the

cardholder, his or her credit history, and any other information they could reasonably expect to have under the circumstances. Their options include simply letting finance charges accumulate, calling the cardholder, writing a letter to the cardholder, informing credit reporting bureaus, cutting off credit temporarily, canceling the account, turning it over to a collection agency, garnishing the cardholder's wages, instituting legal action, and various combinations of these. What development approach would you choose for this DSS? Why?

2. It has been suggested that end-user development might be good for ad hoc DSS but not for institutional DSS. Suggest one argument in favor of this position and one against it.

3. Read Case 5, "A Whole New Ball Game (sort of)," in the Appendix. Then pick one implementation issue for this case to go in each quadrant of Figure 7–10.

4. How would you handle training needs, and why, for each of the following DSS? (It's basically the same DSS but applied to three different user communities.)

   a. A system for faculty advisers to use that will help them recommend appropriate courses for the students they advise to take during the next term.

   b. A system for students to use that will help them choose appropriate courses to take during the next term.

   c. A system for the college academic counseling center, which has two counselors on its staff to work with students of all majors, to use in suggesting appropriate courses for students to take in the next term.

5. In the Connoisseur Foods case mentioned on page 284, top management overruled the manager of marketing services and made use of the brand model system voluntary. Do you agree with their decision? Why or why not? Can you suggest an intermediate approach: less than mandatory, but with more direct motivation than what is described there?

6. (This question is adapted from an example in [CHRI90].) The manager of your firm's marketing department has been asked by the chairman to present an analysis of the company's customer base at the executive summit meeting in three days. The data are located on five different application systems with a different file or database structure in each. Additionally, a given customer may be on more than one of the five systems, but there is no common identifier to link the customer in one system with the same customer in another. Due to the complexity of the data structures and the incompatibilities among the systems, it will take a week of work (with maximum pressure and overtime) to do the requested analysis.

   The basic conception of this information usage is fundamentally ethical: nobody questions the right of a firm to analyze its own customer data for internal purposes, and nobody has suggested that either the marketing manager or the chairman plans any unethical use of the data. Ethical considerations still affect your response. What ethical issues, if any, are being raised here? What should you do?

7. In 1998, Image Data LLC of Nashua, N.H., proposed to create a database of drivers' photographs that would be available to subscribers for a fee. Thus, stores who were offered a driver's license as check-cashing identification could verify that the person offering the license was the person to whom the license had originally been issued, even if the photograph on the license had been altered since then. This system depended on their ability to purchase files of digitized driver photographs from enough states to make the system useful. As this book goes to press in 1999, the state of South Carolina has reversed its earlier position after a massive outcry and is canceling its contract to sell its drivers' photos to Image Data. In a prepared statement, Governor Jim Hodges said he expected the state to be sued but felt that this was a "fight worth fighting."

a. What is the decision statement for a decision this DSS could help with? Who makes this decision?

b. Use the on-line information retrieval system of your choice to find out what happened to this project since early 1999.

c. Is the Image Data system ethical, in terms of the factors listed in Section 7.8?

d. Do you know if your photograph is available on-line to stores and other interested parties, through this or a similar system? If it is, how do you feel about this? If it is not or you don't know, how would you feel about its being available?

REFERENCES

ADEL92   Adelman, Leonard *Evaluating Decision Support and Expert Systems.* John Wiley & Sons, New York (1992).

ALTE80   Alter, Steven L. *Decision Support Systems: Current Practice and Continuing Challenges.* Addison-Wesley, Reading, Mass. (1980).

CASH92   Cash, James I., Jr., F. Warren McFarlan, and James L. McKenney. *Corporate Information Systems Management* (3rd ed.). Richard D. Irwin, Homewood, Ill. (1992).

CHER90   Chervany, Norman L., and Shailendra Palvia. "An Experimental Investigation of Factors Influencing Predicted Success in DSS Implementation," Working Paper MISRC-WP-91-04, Management Information Systems Research Center, Curtis L. Carlson School of Management, University of Minnesota, Minneapolis, MN 55455 (1990).

CHRI90   Christoff, Kurt. *Managing the Information Center.* Scott Foresman and Co., Glenview, Ill. (1990).

GROV88   Grover, Varun, Albert L. Lederer, and Rajiv Sabherwal. "Recognizing the Politics of MIS," *Information and Management* 14, no. 3 (March 1988), p. 145.

KEND88   Kendall, Kenneth E., and Julie E. Kendall. *Systems Analysis and Design.* Prentice-Hall, Englewood Cliffs, N.J. (1988).

LEWI47   Lewin, Kurt. "Group Decision and Social Change," in *Readings in Social Psychology* (T. M. Newcombe and E. L. Hartley, eds.). Henry Holt and Co., New York (1947).

LEWI47a   Lewin, Kurt. "Frontiers in Group Dynamics," *Human Relations* 1 (1947), p. 5.

MACH32   Machiavelli, Niccolò. *The Prince* (1532), translated by W. K. Marriott.

MALL91   Mallach, Efrem G. "Training Paradigms," *Managing End-User Computing* 4, no. 9 (April 1991), p. 5.

OZ92   Oz, Effy. "Ethical Standards for Information Systems Professionals: A Case for a Unified Code," *MIS Quarterly* 16, no. 4 (December 1992), p. 423.

PALV91   Palvia, Shailendra, Efrem G. Mallach, and Prashant Palvia. "Strategies for Converting from One IT Environment to Another," *Journal of Systems Management* 42, no. 10 (October 1991), p. 23.

SPRA80   Sprague, Ralph H., Jr. "A Framework for the Development of Decision Support Systems," *MIS Quarterly* 4, no. 4 (December 1980), p. 1.

SPRA82   Sprague, Ralph H., Jr., and Eric D. Carlson. *Building Effective Decision Support Systems.* Prentice-Hall, Englewood Cliffs, N.J. (1982).

ZAND75   Zand, D. E., and R. E. Sorensen. "Theory of Change and the Effective Use of Management Science," *Administrative Science Quarterly* 20, no. 4 (December 1975), p. 532.

CASE

Fort Lowell Trading Company
Implementing ROSCOE

"The ROSCOE system? What's that?" asked Miguel when Joe Two Crows, FLTC's manager of store information systems, said that the firm's sales department was hoping to implement it in all of its stores.

"Well," said Joe as he leaned back in his chair, "I might as well start with the name. ROSCOE stands for 'Rating Our Sales Clerks On Everything.' The idea is that we want to measure their performance as fully, and as objectively, as we can. That way we can figure out who should get raises and promotions, who should get help and training, and so on."

"How do you rate salespeople today?" asked Elizabeth.

"Mostly two ways," answered Joe. "In some departments we pay commissions. We keep track of who sells how much. The people who sell the most, in the long run, are the ones we figure are doing the best job—because, after all, selling is what a store is about. The other way is by the manager's evaluation.

"Neither of these is perfect, though," he continued. "First, commissions only measure one part of what salespeople do. It's an important part, but so much of what we're about is built on customer service. Say someone spends an hour helping a customer plan an outfit. That customer may end up just buying a belt, maybe not even that. But she'll love us, and come back, and buy lots of stuff in the future from some other salesperson. The first one doesn't get credit for that but the store benefits. Besides, some departments don't work on a commission basis. Second, managers' evaluations can be way off in so many ways. If your manager doesn't like you, for whatever silly reason, you can be the best in the world but it won't matter.

"So, ROSCOE is supposed to let us measure the things that really make a salesperson effective. It's supposed to give us a handle on what they really do all day long. It will do statistical sampling—ask people at random times what they've just been doing, put it into a bunch of meaningful categories, and produce reports. The idea is that it could be way off for a given day, because it will only have a few data points for that day, but ought to be real close over a quarter or a year."

"Sounds like a good idea to me, Joe," agreed Miguel. "But what does it have to do with us?"

"The thing is, I'm a bit worried about this one. Not about the software—we know it works. It's everything else, the people stuff. How will the clerks on the floor react to this? Will they think we're snooping? Will they give it straight answers, especially if they think that lying will improve their report? In short, is it worth the effort or are we trying to do something that's doomed from the start? I just don't know! I mean, I'm a technical guy. I got involved in computers at our community Web site in Taos, learned to program at ASU, got a master's in computer science, the whole bit, but I've never been involved in anything like this before."

EXERCISES

1. What decision would ROSCOE help make? Write a clear decision statement for that decision. Is this decision structured, semistructured, or unstructured? Strategic, operational (managerial control), or tactical?

2. Ideally, what should have been done before ROSCOE got to this stage in order to answer Joe's questions? When should each of the items in your list have been done?

3. What actions should FLTC take to unfreeze its salespeople from their present position prior to moving to ROSCOE?

4. Try to put an issue for FLTC's implementation of ROSCOE in each quadrant of the grid in Figure 7–10.

5. What conversion method would you recommend that FLTC use to implement ROSCOE? Why?

6. Does ROSCOE raise any ethical issues? If not, why not? If so, what are they, and should Joe Two Crows be concerned with them?

Models in Decision Support Systems

Introduction

All DSS above the simplest data-oriented ones are based on models. Their purpose, usually, is to allow a DSS, and hence the decision maker who is using it, to predict what would happen in the real world if certain choices were made. This enables the decision maker to evaluate alternative actions without trying them out in practice—obviously saving in time, expense, and overall hassle, to say nothing of reducing the likelihood of a seriously wrong decision that could do major damage to an organization.

This chapter discusses the basic types of models that a DSS developer should know about. It then focuses on the most important type of representational model in DSS: simulation models. Simulation follows a system of interest through the changes it would experience in the real world in order to predict where it would end up. On the way, a simulation model can tell decision makers what ups and downs the system experiences, where it works well, and where it can be improved. The result provides insight that is difficult or impossible to obtain via any other means.

Other types of models are discussed elsewhere in this book. You will read about expert systems, which model a decision-making process, in Chapter 11. Chapter 9 will introduce you to two types of mathematical system models that can be a useful alternative to, or used in conjunction with, simulation. But simulation remains the backbone of many DSS. Understanding its principles will benefit you often during your career.

CHAPTER OBJECTIVES

After you have read and studied this chapter, you will be able to:

1. Explain why models are used in DSS.
2. Describe the basic types of models.
3. Discuss what a discrete-event simulation model is, how it works, and why it can be a useful component of a decision support system.
4. Clarify the difference between simulation and a simulation model.
5. Explain what "system state" is and what it means.
6. Plan specific steps to take when designing a discrete-event simulation model.
7. Describe what is involved in planning and running a complete simulation study.
8. Explain why pseudo-random numbers are important in simulation and describe some "low-tech" methods of generating them.
9. Discuss when a static simulation model might be useful.

8.1 TYPES OF MODELS

You learned in Chapter 3 that a model is a representation of an actual system. Models embody system characteristics that are important to the model's users. At the same time, models simplify reality by eliminating other characteristics that are not important for their purposes, though these characteristics may be quite important in other contexts. Here's a more formal description of this concept:

> The central idea in structure-mapping is that an analogy is a mapping of knowledge from one domain (the base) to another (the target) which conveys that a system of relations that holds among the base objects also holds among the target objects. Thus an analogy is a way of focusing on the relational commonalities independently of the objects in which those relations are embedded. [GERT89]

In simpler language, the central idea of a model is that important relationships that apply to the system being modeled also apply to the model. For example, suppose that increasing the speed of a conveyor belt by 10 percent results in a 5 percent increase in factory production in a model. If the model is accurate, the same relationship should hold in the real factory. Other aspects of the original, which relate mainly to the way the relationships are realized in practice (gears and pulleys versus bits in a computer's RAM) do not apply to the model.

Most management decisions are based on information about the real world rather than on physical characteristics of something in the real world. For example, if a factory manager is told that Plan A will produce 10 percent more dishwashers per shift than Plan B with the same equipment and only 2 percent more workers, that manager can choose Plan A without actually seeing the finished products appear.

Therefore, if a model can provide decision makers with the same information that observation of the real world would provide, while at the same time offering advantages over observing the real world, that model will be a useful tool. That is the essence of model usage in DSS.

8.1.1 Model Types

Basic types of system models include graphical models, narrative models, physical models, mathematical models, and symbolic or information-based models.

- We saw examples of a **graphical model** on page 90 in the description of the data flow diagram. A map is another, familiar type of graphical model. Relationships such as "York is north of London," "San Francisco is about three times as far from Boston as Chicago is," or "A van can reach Route 10 from Main Street by driving south on Elm" hold on the map as in reality. We can reason about locations and distances using maps, without losing sleep over the fact that they are merely pieces of paper or images on a display screen.
- A **narrative model** describes a system in a natural language such as English. The definition of a DSS on page 12 is a highly simplified narrative model of a decision support system. (One could also say that the above definition of a model is a narrative model of a model.)
- A **physical model** is a smaller or idealized representation of the real system, such as a model railroad or an architectural model of a building being designed.

These three types of models, while often useful, are generally not part of decision support systems. (You might use a graphical model or a narrative model to describe a decision support system, but describing a DSS isn't the same as being part of a DSS.) Figure 8–1 shows several types of models.

Since decision support systems are information systems, the models used in DSS represent reality by information about reality. (Strictly speaking, they represent reality by data, which we, or computers, can process into or interpret as information.) This type of model is often called a **symbolic model.** The term **information-based model** is more accurate, though it is not used as widely because it is a bit more cumbersome.

The data elements in an information-based model can be of any of the data types that computers and computer programs can deal with. These include

- *True/false or yes/no values:* that an investor should, or alternatively should not, invest in common stocks. (Such data elements are often called *Boolean variables,* after the mathematician George Boole who studied their properties in the mid-nineteenth century.)
- *Character strings:* that this investor might consider a common stock represented by the letters GM, GE, or IBM.
- *Numerical values:* that this investor should purchase 200 shares, or should buy if the price per share drops to $35. The mathematical aspect of the model, where the DSS has one, usually emphasizes its numerical data elements.

Models incorporate **procedures** and **formulas** to manipulate their data elements. These procedures and formulas derive new data element values from values of

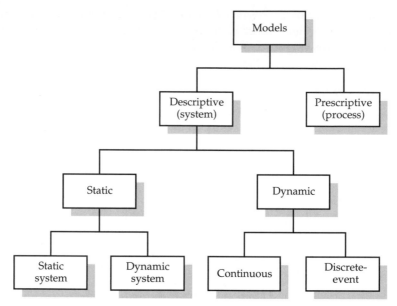

FIGURE 8–1   "Family Tree" of Model Types

other data elements in the model and from external values entered into the model. External values can come from the user, from a database, from a device such as a product inspection system, or over a communication link from another organization such as a customer or a stock exchange. A procedure that accessed suitable information sources could derive a per-share price of $62.50 and an annual dividend payment of $1.32 from the character string "T," the New York Stock Exchange symbol for AT&T common stock. A formula could then determine the annual yield of this stock to be 2.11 percent.

A useful characteristic of most models, which applies even to this mini-example, is that the model remains valid when the data change. That allows us to change one or more variables and see the effect of the change(s).

In other models, the procedure may enable a model to reflect the passage of time. In a business model, the closing inventory of one day may become the opening inventory of the next. In a factory production model, a component that enters a painting process at a given time may emerge, a half hour later, painted and ready for the next step. Within a computer, the progress of this component may be represented by a numeric variable changing from 6 to 7. In many software tools that are used to develop this type of model, these internal values are hidden from the user, but they always exist in some form behind the scenes.

8.1.2 Model Types Used in DSS

A DSS can incorporate several different types of mathematical models. The next few pages cover the major categories. We'll then focus on some important types of DSS models in more detail in the rest of this chapter and the beginning of Chapter 9.

System versus Process Models: What Are We Modeling?   A mathematical model, as we mentioned previously, is an information-based representation of an actual system. In the case of decision support systems we want to use this model to help us make decisions. Two types of models can help us toward this goal. One type of model, called a **system model,** models the system that we wish to study. The other type, called a **process model,** models the process that humans follow in making a decision about a system. (Process models are also called *prescriptive models,* because they prescribe what a decision maker ought to do. They can, as you read in Chapter 2, be *normative* or *descriptive.*) System and process models have different strengths and weaknesses, and correspondingly have different areas of application to DSS.

To understand the distinction between these two types of models better, consider a decision support system that corporate tax planners will use in deciding how to depreciate business assets. Options include accelerated depreciation, with several allowable variations, or straight-line depreciation plus (sometimes) an investment tax credit. A system model would incorporate the tax formulas for each case and a financial present-value algorithm. A process model would incorporate rules of thumb used by experienced tax planners or derived from careful analysis of the alternatives, such as "If the depreciable life of the asset is 10 years or greater, and the asset is eligible for investment tax credit, use straight-line depreciation and take the ITC."

When its rules apply, the process model can be more efficient. It reaches the same conclusion—to take the ITC or not—with far fewer steps. However, a process model does not incorporate the "deep knowledge" of a system that would let it adapt easily to unforeseen circumstances. If the hurdle rate used in present value calculations changes, if the corporate tax rate changes, or if the tax codes allow a new type of accelerated depreciation, the process model would be utterly lost. A system model could simply plug in a new hurdle rate, new tax rates, or new depreciation formulas and obtain the correct answer for the new situation.

Process models form the basis of most expert systems, which we will fit into the DSS picture in Chapter 11. Group decision support systems that bring people together electronically to help them reach a decision, which we discuss in Chapter 10, often also incorporate models of a decision process.

Mathematical models are an important subset of system models. A mathematical model describes the relationships among elements of the system being modeled in the form of equations. The familiar mathematical model

$$e = mc^2$$

describes the relationship between the mass of an object and the energy that will be produced if that mass is converted entirely to energy, or the similar-looking

$$d = at^2$$

describes the distance that an object has traveled during time t, starting at zero velocity, and with acceleration a. With a mathematical model, one substitutes numbers for variables in the model, solves the equations of the model (not always possible, let alone within the skill of the person trying to solve them), and has the answer. We'll discuss several types of mathematical models that are useful to DSS in Chapter 9. The rest of this chapter is devoted to models of systems that cannot be completely described by equations—usually because the interactions among their components are too complex.

Static versus Dynamic Models: Cause and Effect Over Time   An important distinction between two types of system models is the distinction between *static models* and *dynamic models*. As Gordon puts it [GORD78]: "Static models show the values that system attributes take when the system is in balance. Dynamic models follow the changes over time that result from system activities." A static model of a pendulum would show it hanging, vertical and motionless. A dynamic model would describe it swinging to and fro. The dynamic model could track its frequency, amplitude, and rate of decay.

A static model can model either a static system or a dynamic system. A **static system** is one in which the passage of time does not play a part. In a **dynamic system,** the passage of time, with cause-and-effect relationships connecting one time period to the next, is essential to system behavior. The static model, by showing when a system is in balance, can tell decision makers how the system will eventually stabilize even if it does not show them how it gets to that point. This information is often useful by itself. Because it involves much less data, it can be easier for a decision maker to analyze. A static model may also be able to provide results more quickly than a dynamic one, allowing decision makers to consider more options in a given amount of time. For example, a static model of a toll plaza can tell a planner that the average waiting line, under certain specified traffic conditions, is 5.4 cars long with a standard deviation of 2.3 cars about this value. The planner can use this information to decide if the toll plaza and its staffing are adequate for those conditions.

For a static model to apply to a dynamic system, that system must be in equilibrium (in balance), often referred to as being in its **steady state.** Over a period of time, the number of cars arriving at the above toll plaza must equal the number of cars that leave it. If we have appropriate formulas relating these factors we can calculate average statistics on line length without actually following the progress of individual vehicles or even how the line grows and shrinks over time. Many of the mathematical models you'll read about in Chapter 9 work this way.

In a dynamic model, which can only be of a dynamic system, the flow of time is inherent in the modeling process. Data values change over time. An assembly line model works this way as it tracks products through a manufacturing process. When a subassembly finishes one step of the process, the next step can begin. Variables inside the model change to reflect this event. A model of traffic flow at an intersection, which we might use to minimize delays by adjusting the signal timing, works this way as well. A model of consumer response to advertising could relate the impact of one ad on a consumer's product awareness to the number of prior ads for the same product to which the consumer has already been exposed. We can look into the system at any instant (in model time) and see just what the model says is going on then: which subassemblies are at what stage of the process, how many

	A	B	C	D	E
1	Kitson Corporation Summary Financial Forecast ($MIL)				
2		1999	2000	2001	2002
3	Revenue	2.00	2.20	2.42	2.66
4	R&D Costs	0.25	0.30	0.35	0.40
5	Advertising Costs	0.10	0.12	0.14	0.16
6	Cost of Goods Sold	0.80	0.87	0.95	1.04
7	General & Admin.	0.45	0.50	0.55	0.60
8	Total Costs	1.60	1.79	1.99	2.20
9	Profit Before Tax	0.40	0.41	0.43	0.46

FIGURE 8–2 Corporate Budget Spreadsheet

cars are waiting in each lane of the intersection, how many consumers have been exposed to different numbers of advertising messages. In these and other dynamic models, what happens at one instant affects the modeled system at future instants. The way this influence takes place is a major part of any dynamic model.

The distinction between static and dynamic models can be confusing, because a collection of static models can appear to show a quantity varying over time. Consider three spreadsheet models of a corporate budget, each showing the major revenue and expense categories for the years 1999–2002. Each looks exactly like Figure 8–2; they vary only in their formulas, which the figure doesn't show.

- If all four data columns are independent of each other, this is a static model (really a set of four independent static models in adjacent columns) even though it shows how profits are predicted to vary over the four years. Each of the four 1-year models is separate from the others. No relationships among the years are built into the numbers. We may infer a relationship from our knowledge of the business context, our interpretation of the column headings as referring to successive years, and our experience with similar tables, but that's all in our heads. Our inferring a relationship from a printout or a screen display doesn't create a relationship in the model.
- If the spreadsheet used a formula to enter revenue increases of 10 percent per year, it is still a collection of four static models. We can use a formula in cells C3, D3, and E3 to simplify data entry and make it easier to evaluate different assumptions about revenue growth, but that does not affect the models themselves.[1] Row 3 provides input to the models but doesn't participate in the modeling process. Each column still models one year in isolation. There is nothing in the system being modeled, or in our understanding of how that system works, that

---

[1] A well-designed spreadsheet that took this approach would put the 10 percent assumed annual revenue growth rate in a clearly labeled cell at the top rather than hiding it in a formula that is replicated across a row.

relates one year's revenue to that of the previous year. The assumption that each year's revenue will be 110 percent of the previous year's is external to our model of how the business works, even though it is internal to the spreadsheet (because of how spreadsheets work).[2]

- If a spreadsheet formula relates one year's R&D and advertising revenues to the next year's sales revenues, it becomes a dynamic model. Such a model might, for example, say

$$\$ \text{ revenue (year } n + 1) = 0.5 \times \text{revenue (year } n) + 8 \times \text{R\&D (year } n)$$

Here we are modeling *cause-and-effect relationships*. The formula says that next year's sales will equal half of this year's sales plus eight times this year's R&D spending. This means we'll still get some revenue from selling and supporting our current products, but if we don't develop new products our firm will sink rapidly into bankruptcy. Increased R&D spending leads to better products in the future, hence higher sales and higher profits then, but also costs money, hence lowering profits in the near term. Advertising (not shown in the example formula) leads to increased customer awareness, hence to higher sales in the future (though not as distant a future as for R&D expenditures), but also costs money today. This cause-and-effect relationship between events in one time period and outcomes in succeeding ones is the essence of a dynamic model. Using this and similar relationships, we can decide how much to spend on R&D, advertising, and other activities in order to optimize the overall picture.

Continuous versus Discrete-Event Models: How Do Quantities Vary in the System? Dynamic system models mimic the behavior of a real dynamic system over time. They allow us to examine this behavior and thus observe, learn about, or optimize the system. The system being modeled can be a physical system: We might want to study blood pressure in an artery, temperature in an engine combustion chamber, or the trajectory of a space vehicle as it passes through the gravitational fields of Jupiter's moons. It can be a socioeconomic system, where we are interested in income, population, and resource consumption trends. In business, it might be a manufacturing system where we must choose among factory arrangements or equipment.

Dynamic system models can be divided into two categories: continuous-system models and discrete-event models. **Continuous-system simulation models** describe physical or economic processes in which the numbers that describe the system vary continuously. For example, blood pressure varies continuously over time. It does not jump instantaneously from one value to another. Rather, there are processes that cause it to rise or to fall at given rates. (There may be events, such as stress, that cause it to change rapidly, but the pressure curve is still continuous.) For

---

[2]This assumption may not be totally plucked out of thin air. It may be based on some other model, such as an economic model that shows a growing market for our products, but that model isn't in this spreadsheet.

every time interval, no matter how small, there may be a change in pressure. When blood pressure changes from one value to another, it passes through every intermediate value on the way. The same is true of the location of a train along a track, the position of a piston in an engine, the temperature at a given point on a jet engine turbine blade, the weight of a growing infant, and other physical phenomena.

Simple continuous systems can be studied via calculus and differential equations. The differential equations that describe complex systems are usually too complex to solve in closed form; that is, too complex to get the answer in the form of a formula that we can evaluate by plugging in numbers. Those equations can, however, be solved numerically.

By contrast, **discrete-event models** deal with systems in which individual **events** occur at identifiable points in time and change the state of the system instantaneously from one value to a different one. For example, the arrival of an order at a valve manufacturer may change the state of the system from "2 Model 100 valves on order" to "3 Model 100 valves on order." The system does not go through an intermediate state of "2.5 Model 100 valves on order," whereas a continuous system would progress through all values between 2 and 3 before settling at its new level. We treat the arrival of the order for the third valve as an instantaneous event. No matter how finely we divide time, there is a precise instant at which we say this order arrives. There are exactly two orders on hand before this event occurs, and exactly three on or after that instant.

Business systems are usually characterized by identifiable events that cause instantaneous change in the system: An order arrives, a product is shipped. This is in some sense a simplification. If one were to look at the actual shipping process, one would see a warehouse worker take a product off a shelf, put it in a shipping area, load it onto a truck (where there is an instant at which the carton is, for example, two-thirds on the truck and one-third not yet on) and so on. From a business planning point of view, these stages are irrelevant. Modeling them increases the model's complexity without increasing its usefulness. Business simulations therefore usually don't use continuous models. Socioeconomic planners use continuous models, but their work, while undeniably important, is not in the mainstream of corporate DSS. Since discrete-event models suit most business planning needs, they are the most common type of dynamic system model found in real DSS. They are therefore the only type of dynamic system model we will discuss further in this book.

Deterministic versus Stochastic Models: Statistical Uncertainty   Another categorization of system models involves our confidence that the relationships in the models hold true in the real world. Some models reflect certainty. Others involve uncertainty or risk. There is no uncertainty only when every relationship in a model is true by definition or by decree.

Most models have elements of certainty and uncertainty. A corporate business model may reflect certainty in the accounting relationships among its variables, but there will be some uncertainty in its estimates of future sales. A manufacturing model may reflect fixed relationships among production quantities and parts inventory withdrawals, but there is some statistical variability in the time it takes a worker to assemble a product. A traffic control model may use a formula with no uncertainty to represent the timing intervals between signal changes but may incorporate some uncertainty in its description of the arrival rate of cars at an intersection.

A model is **deterministic** if its outputs are fixed for a given set of inputs, **stochastic** if they reflect an element of uncertainty. We must define this uncertainty statistically if the model is to be of practical use. A deterministic model of a three-step assembly process might indicate that each step takes exactly one hour, so the entire process takes three hours. A stochastic model of the same assembly process might have the duration of each step vary around the one-hour average, with a normal distribution having a standard deviation of ten minutes. This is more realistic, because most physical processes and nearly all human activities have some variability from one instance to the next.

The stochastic model's output will therefore vary randomly over a range of possible outcomes. If we run this model many times we will obtain many different answers, clustered around three hours. The distribution of total assembly time around its mean will depend on how the duration of each step varies around its one-hour mean and on how the steps in the process interact with each other.

A deterministic model, in this sense, corresponds closely to the *accounting model* category of DSS you read about in Chapter 4. Stochastic models, by contrast, fall into what we called the *representational model* category of DSS there.

We can deal with uncertainty by describing the statistics of a data element: its mean and its variance (or standard deviation) if it follows a normal distribution, its cumulative distribution function for continuous distributions in general, or the discrete probabilities that the data element will take on each value in a set of possible individual values. However we describe the statistics of a random variable, there are two ways a model can use its statistical description:

- One is to carry the statistical description through the model and produce the answer in the form of a statistical description at the end. We could tell a model, for instance, that next year's estimated revenues are expected to have a normal distribution with a mean of $1.5 million and a standard deviation of $0.2 million. Based on this input, a model might tell us that next year's net profits before tax will also have a normal distribution, with a mean of $150,000 and a standard deviation of $100,000.
- Another approach is to choose a value from the distribution of each statistically described variable, every time it is needed, and use this chosen value in the model. To do this in the same situation as the previous example we would start by picking a value at random from the given distribution of next year's revenue. Say we assume it will be $1,546,873. We would carry this figure through the model and obtain, for that specific revenue, a profit figure of $173,436. We would then repeat the process: Our second try might pick $1,412,890 for revenue and obtain $106,445 as the corresponding profit. After a large number of samples we would have a large number of predicted profit figures. We could then analyze or graph these figures, which represent the expected profit distribution.

If the models are equivalent and we do our job properly, we will find that the graph has a mean of about $150,000 and a standard deviation of about $100,000. We would be unlikely to find an exact match because the output in this second case depends on which random values we happened to pick. If we repeat the process with a different set of random values, we will get a slightly different graph, but if we did our job correctly both will have similar statistics. The more values we use, the smoother the graph will be, and the closer to the "true" output distribution.

With the second approach we must exercise our model many times to get an accurate statistical picture of its predictions. This increases the computer time required to get a useful result, often substantially. However, the second approach always works. In modeling complex systems, it is often impossible to use the first approach—that is, to carry the statistics of all the distributions through to the final result.

It is important to distinguish between uncertainty in a model and uncertainty in its inputs. Consider a financial model in which next year's revenue is estimated statistically. The model that translates revenue into profits is deterministic. All its relationships are true by accounting definitions. This model, though, is a component of a larger model of the overall business. The larger model incorporates uncertainty in estimated revenue. Our decision to characterize a model as deterministic or stochastic depends on what we put inside the model and what we put outside it. In this case the overall business model is stochastic but its financial portion is deterministic—an accounting model, in the sense of Chapter 4.

This little example, by the way, points out the need to agree on the boundary of a system. If one person considers the uncertainty in revenue forecast to be inside the system and another considers this uncertainty to be outside the system, the two might argue endlessly over the validity of this model in predicting the future of the business, without realizing that their disagreement revolves about where each one draws the boundary of the model.

The familiar spreadsheet is a useful tool in dealing with deterministic models.[3] Financial planning software can also be used for this purpose. Sophisticated financial planning packages and some state-of-the-art spreadsheet packages can deal with uncertainty in the inputs to the accounting model as well. You saw an example of a financial planning package on page 216.

8.1.3 Simplification in Models

All models simplify the real world. Even accounting models, which at first glance seem totally precise, use simplifications. For example, no firm calculates depreciation on individual pencils. This simplification is sanctioned by tax codes (after all, an income tax return is itself a model of the real world) and by generally accepted

---

[3]The ability of some spreadsheet packages to deal with uncertainty in input data, sometimes referred to as "scenarios" or "data tables," creates multiple models with different user-specified input values rather than incorporating uncertainty into one model. This is often useful, but each model is still deterministic.

accounting practices, so it's not much of a simplification. If the purpose of our model is to predict how a tax return will look, it isn't one. Yet, conceptually, ignoring depreciation on a 29¢ pencil does simplify the reality of what assets the business purchased and how long each one is expected to retain some economic value.

A modeler must, in developing a model for decision support, determine which simplifications are acceptable and which are not. Some simplification is essential to make models practical. Too much simplification, such as ignoring depreciation on a $4 million airplane, can make a model useless. Guidelines for builders of most business models are usually not as clear cut as the tax code definition of a depreciable asset.[4]

As another example, consider a model of a traffic intersection. Transportation planners use such models to determine how to optimize traffic flow: how long to make each part of the light cycle, whether or not to use dedicated left turn lanes and/or left turn light cycles, whether allowing right turns on red lights will improve vehicle flow, and so on. A complete model of a four-way intersection is quite complex, and even it is likely to be incomplete. Signals at other nearby intersections are likely to affect the arrival rates of cars at the intersection we are studying, dooming a model that treats one intersection in isolation to inaccuracy, if not total irrelevance, before we start. Yet traffic planners do use single-intersection models successfully. They can improve traffic flow by following the recommendations of simple models. Even a model of the simplest possible intersection, two one-lane, one-way streets, can be useful because

- Building a simple model teaches us a great deal about how to model the type of system we wish to study. A simple model is therefore a useful starting point even if we plan to move on to more complex models of our system.
- Many complex models can use simple models as components. If we can build a good model of how a disk drive behaves in a large computer system, we can then incorporate this model into a more complex model of an eight-drive subsystem or of the computer system as a whole.
- Examining a simple model may show general principles of how the system in question behaves. This might be hidden behind the mass of detail we would get from a more complex (or more complete) model. For instance, a model of the simplest two-one-way-streets intersection will show us that total motorist waiting time is minimized if the light turns yellow in each direction as soon as all the waiting cars (including those that join the line after it begins to move) have passed through. Once this rule is known, it can be used to optimize complex intersections as well. (Question: If a DSS uses this rule of thumb to advise traffic planners on the best settings for traffic lights, what kind of model is that DSS using?)

The assumption of individual, discrete events taking place in a business, while central to many models, may also be a simplification of reality. On page 305 we saw how a model could simplify the reality that shipping a product takes place

---

[4]As your accounting instructor can confirm, the U.S. tax code is not usually considered an example of clarity.

over several minutes. The assumption of discrete, instantaneous events is among the most widely accepted, and acceptable, simplifications used in modeling any kind of business operation.

8.2 DISCRETE-EVENT SIMULATION MODELS

A **simulation model** is, for our purposes, a dynamic, usually stochastic, discrete-event model that allows us to predict the behavior of a business system by modeling the expected behaviors and interactions of its components over time. This is useful because we often know how each system component behaves, but we are unable to assess the impact of their interactions on the behavior of the overall system.

To recap some concepts from earlier in this chapter:

- A dynamic model is one which explicitly reflects changes in the system over time.
- A stochastic model is one whose output reflects statistically defined uncertainties in system behavior.
- A discrete-event model is one in which changes in the system are taken as occurring at instants in time, rather than extending over a finite interval.

The terms *simulation, model,* and (in combination) *simulation model* are often used interchangeably or nearly so. This usually doesn't cause problems but there *is* a difference. The **model** is the description of the system, usually in the form of a computer program. We call it a simulation model when we want to make it clear that we're not discussing some other type of model or some other use of a model. **Simulation** is the process of using this model to study a system. A model is a thing. Simulation is a process. Simulation can't exist without a suitable model, and a model meant for use in simulation may be useless for anything else, but the concepts are different.

8.2.1 The Concept of Discrete-Event Simulation

The basic concepts of discrete-event simulation are simple, though a discrete-event simulation model of a complex system is full of complex detail. The model represents the state of the system by the values of data elements (*variables*) in the computer. The values of these variables change as events occur in the system. If we know how often different types of events occur, we can know when and how the variables change. The changes in the values of these variables reflect what would happen to the system in the real world.

For instance, the arrival of a car at a filling station may change the state of one pump and the attendant from "idle" to "busy." This would be represented in the model by variables going from "idle" to "busy," from "false" to "true," or from 0 to 1, depending on how a programmer, working within the constraints of a specific programming language, chose to represent them.[5] Subsequently, running the programs that implement the model will (again via the values of suitable variables)

---

[5]If the model developer is using a specialized simulation language or package, this decision will have been made by the programmer who originally wrote that software tool.

reduce the amount of fuel in the station's storage tank, increase the amount of money in its cash register, update a simulated clock to reflect the passage of (modeled) time, and finally allow the pump and attendant to rest again—unless another car has arrived in the meantime and must be taken care of. Simulation programs are usually also designed to gather helpful information about system behavior: the fraction of time that the attendant is busy, the amount of money taken in for the day, the amount of time cars have to wait, and the average length of the waiting line, whether it is unavailability of a pump or of an attendant that causes them to wait, and other data elements.

Most discrete-event simulations are stochastic, or probabilistic. This is because we often know a great deal about the statistical behavior of a given process, but we can't predict the future behavior of any one instance of that process precisely. For example, we may know how many cars arrive at the gas station in a typical hour and what the statistical distribution of this quantity is. We do *not* know that a car will arrive at precisely 10:23:38 next Thursday morning, will take 8.38 gallons of premium unleaded fuel, will pay by credit card, and will depart at 10:31:05. The computer determines the times at which events occur and their exact nature—Does this car use regular fuel, premium fuel, or diesel? How many gallons? Does the driver pay by cash or credit card?—by generating pseudo-random numbers. We use them to sample from the statistical distributions that the modeler specified. If the statistics of our distributions match the real world well, the overall set of computer choices will be representative of what would happen in reality. While one day's simulation run will not match any single day in the real gas station, the statistics of 50 days of simulation runs should match the statistics of 50 days' operation closely. Since we are trying to make business decisions that will apply to the expected future, such a statistical match is what we want. Finding an exact event-by-event match would be as unlikely as having a monkey at a keyboard type an award-winning novel.

We gather data to help make decisions by tracking what happens over time in the model. The owner of a filling station can figure out the optimum frequency for fuel deliveries from a supplier by running a simulation model, such as the one discussed above, for several possible choices and selecting the one for which the model predicted the best results. The same approach can help choose the right number of pump attendants to hire, or whether or not to offer discounts for cash payment. The accuracy of the decisions depends on the accuracy of the model: how well its processes represent what goes on in a filling station, and on how well its statistics represent how customers, attendants, vehicles, and equipment behave.

The key to understanding how discrete-event simulations work is the **future events queue.** This is a list of events that are scheduled to take place in the system, together with the time that each will occur. For example, suppose the car at pump 3 starts fueling at 10:23 A.M. We calculate, based on statistics for fueling time, that fueling this car will take two minutes. It will therefore be ready to pay two minutes past 10:23, or at 10:25. We put an event into the future events queue for 10:25, labeled "car at pump 3 ready to pay." After we've processed all the events that take place between 10:23 and 10:25, this will be the next event in the system, and we can process it.

Strictly speaking, updating the clock to the next event in a future events queue isn't absolutely necessary. It is also possible to use a fixed time step: checking every minute, for example, to see if something ought to happen then. This is seldom done with business simulations because it's not nearly as efficient as using a future events queue. In other types of simulations, especially where things happen more frequently relative to the time scale of the model, it's a fine approach. You may have encountered it in the context of adventure or war games—which are, after all, a type of simulation.

Processing an event such as this means updating the variables (data elements) in the model to reflect what happens when the event occurs. The specifics, in this case, depend on whether or not there is a free attendant at that moment. Assuming there is, we note that the attendant is now busy, calculate how long payment will take (based on our statistics for the payment process and the values of still more pseudo-random numbers) and put a "car at pump 3 finishes paying" event in the future events queue for, say, 10:30. This cycle of processing events and scheduling new ones repeats until the run is over. A simulation run consists of nothing more than placing events in the future events queue, taking them out when their turn arrives, and processing them to update the values of variables, while recording what happened for future analysis.

8.2.2 A Discrete-Event Simulation Example

You don't need a computer to construct a simple simulation model and run experiments with it. Let's say we want to model the operation of a barbershop to determine how many barbers we should hire. We can't hire more than three barbers, because there are only three chairs in the shop. The lower limit on the number of barbers is one (or zero, if closing the business is an option). Let's assume that, at this time of day, customers arrive at an average rate of one every 10 minutes. Let's also assume that a haircut always takes exactly 25 minutes. In simulation terminology, these parameters are called the **interarrival time** and **service time,** respectively.

We plan to do our first "run" with two barbers on duty. If they seem to be busy most of the time, we'll try three. If they're usually idle, we'll try one. (This is how interactive simulation studies usually work. Alternatively, we could instruct a computer to try all the possibilities, then come back later to inspect the results.) Figure 8–3 illustrates this barbershop.

We can use a piece of paper to record our data, much as a computer would use locations in its RAM. We mark off six columns on a large piece of paper: one for the status of each of the two barbers we'll have in this run, one for each of the three seats in the waiting area, and one for the future events queue. Figure 8–4 shows how this might look. We'll also need a way to generate random customer arrivals. A standard six-sided die is a simple choice that works well in this case. Since we want an average arrival rate of a customer every 10 minutes, we can assign the six sides of the die to 5, 7, 9, 11, 13, and 15 minutes as shown in Figure 8–5. Those values will give us our desired average. So would several other choices, but this set will do nicely. It gives us a uniform distribution of interarrival times. (In a real study, we'd record barbershop customer arrival times for several hours and base the distribution we use on the statistics of the data we record.)

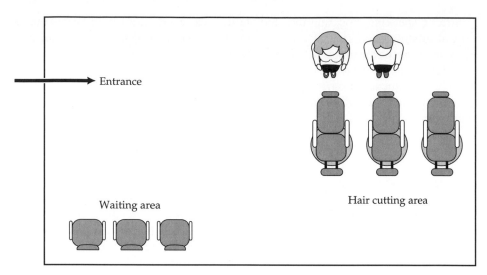

FIGURE 8–3   Schematic of a Barbershop

Barber #1	Barber #2	Seat #1	Seat #2	Seat #3	Fut. events Q
Busy 8:07–8:32	Busy 8:18–8:43	Busy at 8:27			8:07, ~~Cust. arrives~~ 8:32, Barber #1 Customer leaves 8:18, ~~Cust. arrives~~ 8:27, ~~Cust. arrives~~

FIGURE 8–4   Sheet of Paper with Simulation Model of Barbershop

When the barbershop doors open at 8:00 A.M., the shop is empty. We roll the die to find out when the first customer will arrive. Suppose we roll a 2. That corresponds to 7 minutes (why?) so the first customer will show up at 8:07. We write "8:07: customer arrives" as the initial entry in the future events queue. Now we are ready to start the simulation cycle.

Die roll	Interarrival time (minutes)
 ⚁	5
 ⚂	7
 ⚃	9
 ⚃	11
 ⚄	13
 ⚅	15

FIGURE 8–5 Correspondence Between Die Faces and Interarrival Times

The first—and, for now, the only—event in the future events queue is the customer arrival at 8:07. We advance our mental clock to 8:07 to process it. We will schedule two future events as part of this processing: the completion of the first customer's haircut and the arrival of the second customer. To process the haircut, we write "Busy 8:07–8:32" in the column corresponding to barber 1. This is for the purpose of collecting statistics. (Why 8:32?) We also enter "8:32: barber 1 customer leaves" into the future events queue.

Now, we roll the die again for the next arrival. We roll a 4, which corresponds to 11 minutes. The second customer will arrive 11 minutes from now, at 8:18. We enter "8:18: customer arrives" in the future events queue. This completes the handling of the 8:07 event, so we cross it off.

The next event in the future events queue is now the 8:18 arrival of the second customer. We write "Busy 8:18–8:43" in the second barber's column, and roll the die for the next arrival. We roll a 3, corresponding to 9 minutes between arrivals. The next customer will arrive at 8:27. We enter this event in the future events queue. We can now cross off the 8:18 event as having been fully processed and take care of the next one. Our future events queue tells us that the next event is the next arrival, at 8:27.

There are no available barbers when the third customer arrives at 8:27. We write "Busy at 8:27" on the first seat in the waiting area. We do not yet know how long that seat will be busy, because waiting time (unlike hair cutting time) is not fixed in the description of the model. Waiting is not something we designed into the system. Rather, it is a byproduct of the other things we designed into the system. We find out what it is as a result of running the model. We now roll the die again to schedule the next arrival: a 5, corresponding to a time of 13 minutes. We enter an 8:40 arrival into the future events queue and cross off the 8:27 entry.

The next customer will arrive at 8:40. However, something else will happen before then. The next entry in the future events queue is now "8:32: barber 1 customer leaves." The first barber can now take the waiting customer. We write "Free at 8:32" on that seat and "Busy 8:32–8:57" on the first barber's chair. We then enter the 8:57 haircut completion time into the future events queue and cross off the 8:32 entry. Now we can deal with the fourth customer, who arrives at 8:40, by putting him in the waiting room.

You can see that there is not necessarily a 1-to-1 relationship between processing events and scheduling new ones. Some events, such as the arrival of a customer when there is a barber available to cut his hair, result in the entry of two new events in the future events queue: completion of the haircut (25 minutes in the future) and arrival of the next customer (5 to 15 minutes in the future). Other events, such as the departure of a customer when there are no waiting customers, do not result in any new events being scheduled. In the long run, insertions into the future events queue and removals from it must balance, but the insertions and removals resulting from a single event may not.

This model is complex enough to show you why "industrial-strength" simulation models need a well-organized and efficiently processed future events queue. Future events queue entries are not created in chronological order: We made an entry for 8:27 after we had already made an entry for 8:32. Having the events listed in order makes it unnecessary to remember, or to scan the sheet of paper, for the next event. We can handle a three-seat barbershop without a formal queue, but not much more than that. The best way to organize future event queues in a computer has been a subject of considerable research for years.

You can also see how a fixed-time-step approach would be less efficient here. Something of interest happens in the barbershop once every 10 minutes or so. Using a fixed time step, we'd have to check (on the average, more or less) nine times at which nothing happens for every time at which something happens. It's much more efficient to organize matters so we can jump directly to the next event and skip all that checking.

This process can continue indefinitely. When we're done, we will be able to figure out how many customers were served, how many were turned away because there was no space in the waiting area (what assumption did we just make?) and, if we know how much barbers are paid and how much a haircut costs, the shop's profit for the day. The same model, with a different set of variations, can also tell us if it's worth buying another chair for the waiting area, taking two chairs out of the waiting area to accommodate a fourth barber, or converting the shop to a cappuccino-and-latte bar.

Three things should be clear from this example:

1. The fundamental process of simulation, and the calculations involved, are simple.
2. The recordkeeping, even for a simple model such as this, gets tedious quickly.
3. The concepts are suitable for far more complex systems than this barbershop, though we wouldn't want to keep track of everything by hand in such systems. They can be applied to nearly any business process where resources are limited, activities take time, and there are known relationships among resources, activities, and some output of business interest.

That makes simulation a natural for computers: They excel at repeating tedious calculations over and over again, they don't make careless mistakes, and they do this sort of thing a lot faster than people can.

8.2.3 Designing a Discrete-Event Simulation Model

Now that you understand how a discrete-event simulation model works, we can look at the process of designing one. This process consists of the following steps:

1. *Determine the objective of the model.* What decision are we trying to make? What must we optimize or find out in order to make that decision? What information must the model give us if we are to learn what we must know? Without a clear understanding of these issues we cannot determine what output our model must provide or what simplifications are appropriate for it.

2. *Define the system itself.* What is inside it; what is not? What are its components? We often want to study a range of similar systems that vary in a few parameters of interest, such as the number of attendants at a gasoline station or the length of an aisle in a warehouse. If the system depends on such **parameters,** called **controllable variables,** we must specify what they are now. In the barbershop example, the only controllable variable was the number of barbers on duty. If we weren't dealing with an existing shop layout, we might have chosen to make the number of seats in the waiting area a controllable variable as well.

3. *Define the state of the system in terms of a set of state variables or uncontrollable variables.* Choosing the state variables simplifies reality because every system has levels of detail that are unimportant to a given planning task. The position at which a car stops in a filling station is unimportant for business planning, but the type and amount of fuel it purchases do matter. In the barbershop model, we care about when the customers arrive, not how long their hair is. Understanding the purpose of the model is essential to determining the proper set of state variables.

   The concept of a **state variable** or **uncontrollable variable** (meaning that it is not controlled directly by the person running the simulation, but rather changes on its own as the simulation runs according to the rules of how the simulated system behaves) can be difficult. The uncontrollable variables are those characteristics of a system that vary during its operation. In our barbershop model, the number of barbers on duty is not a state variable as it does not change while the shop is open. It is a parameter of the model, a controllable variable, because the person running the simulation controls it—sets it to one, two, or whatever. The number of barbers who are busy at any given moment *is* an uncontrollable, or state, variable: We do not enter it into the computer but rather let the simulation process determine what it is at any moment. Its value, which ranges from zero to the number of barbers on duty, rises and falls as customers come into the shop and as haircuts are completed. We saw another uncontrollable variable when we ran the simulation model: the number of customers waiting at any moment.

   If we wanted to evaluate the impact of alternative coffee break policies on barbershop productivity, we might make the number of *working barbers* a state

The Concept of "System State"

The concept of "the state of a system" is fundamental to all representational models.

Definition: The **state of a system** is the set of information stored in that system that changes during system operation as events occur and affects system response to future inputs. It is this information that lets us know what a system is doing at any instant. The system state consists of all the information we must know in order to reproduce a situation in its entirety, and no more than that. Consider a bakery. When a customer walks in to buy a loaf of dark rye bread, one of three things can happen:

1. The customer buys the bread, leaving with bread in hand and a lighter wallet.
2. The bakery is out of dark rye bread. The customer leaves without making a purchase.
3. All clerks are busy. The customer waits for service.

To determine which of these outcomes will occur, we must know at least two things about the current situation in the bakery: whether or not there are any free clerks and whether or not there is any dark rye bread available. Both of these change during system operation, and both affect system response to the customer. Both are therefore part of the system state.

In a real bakery, the information about the availability of dark rye bread is in physical form. A clerk checks the bin where dark rye is stored. If there isn't any bread there, the clerk informs the customer. In a computer model, system state information is stored as values of data elements in computer memory.

The individual items that combine to define the state of the system are called *state variables.* In the bakery model, one state variable reflects the inventory of dark rye bread. Another reflects what the clerks are doing. The way we define the state variables depends on the rest of the model. Knowing whether there is or is not a loaf of dark rye on hand will tell us how to handle this customer. We could represent this state variable by a Boolean, or yes/no, variable. That representation would not prepare us for the next customer, however, because we would have no way to know if there are any more loaves left after the first customer departs. It is better to store our dark rye inventory data as a number, decrementing its value as purchases are made and incrementing it as fresh loaves emerge from the oven.

There are also different ways to deal with the salesclerks. We could treat them as identical units and keep track of how many of them are busy at any moment, or we could treat them as individuals and keep track of which ones are busy at any moment. The first approach makes it easier to vary their number. The second makes it easier to model different capabilities, such as processing special cake orders or authorizing refunds. A third approach, using a pool of clerks for each possible combination of capabilities, would give maximum flexibility but would complicate the model. Knowing the model's purpose helps us choose from among these options.

variable. This new variable's value would change as barbers go on break and return. This possibility points out the importance of knowing a model's purpose before we define its details.

4. *Define the events that can affect the state of the system and the impact of each event on each state variable.* Some are **exogenous events;** they originate outside the system. Their occurrence is not affected by the state of the system, though they affect its state. Customer arrival is an exogenous event: It happens no matter what is going on within the system at any moment. **Endogenous events,** on the other hand, originate inside the system. Their occurrence may depend on the state of the system: A car that isn't being fueled can't finish the

fueling process, a person whose hair isn't being cut can't finish his or her haircut, a disk drive that isn't broken can't be repaired.

5. *Choose the time units which the simulation will use.* A fine time scale lends itself to precise output, but this precision may not be justified by the accuracy of the model itself, and a fine time scale may waste computer time. A coarse time scale may reduce computer time requirements but, if taken to extremes, may limit the usefulness of the results.

   The correct time scale depends on the rate at which the process being modeled occurs and the purpose of the study. To model activity in a gasoline station accurately we need a time scale of seconds or tenths of a minute. However, if our fuel station owner only wants to schedule fuel deliveries, we may care only about the total sales volume per hour or per day. In that case, a coarser time scale could be used. Most computer systems, simulation packages, and programming languages can work with fractional time units, so the key issue here is choosing a time unit that is convenient for the humans who will use the output.

6. *Define, statistically, the rate at which each event occurs.* This means defining the statistical distribution of processing times at each processing step as a customer or other unit progresses through the system. This lets us define the time of event occurrence relative to preceding events. If we know how long it takes (statistically) to fuel a car, then the time at which a car finishes the fueling process is defined, again statistically, relative to the time at which it starts fueling. This approach of defining the duration of each step in a series of operations lets us model a complex process by combining models of simpler subprocesses.

7. *Determine the statistics you would like to obtain from your simulation and what data you need in order to obtain them.* If you want to know, for example, the distribution of waiting times after a product is fully assembled until it can be painted, the program will need a table for the different time intervals of interest and must make an entry in this table for each unit that is assembled and painted. Some simulation packages collect some system statistics automatically, but it is still important to analyze the user's decision-making needs to know if you must specify or program additional ones.

8. *Define the initial (starting) state of the system.* The **initial state** includes what customers are present, what they are doing, what machines are busy, what inventory levels exist, and what orders have been placed. It is common to start with an empty system such as a store when it opens for the day. We may have to run the model for a while until it settles down into a state that reflects typical operation. It's often a good idea to then save this state, so we can restart from a consistent, known point for any desired combination of controllable variables.

Having made these eight decisions, we describe the model to a computer in the form of a program. This program must reflect all the events that can take place in the system, their occurrence statistics, and their impact on the state variables. It begins by setting the state variables to their initial values. It then generates random numbers from the specified occurrence rate distributions to determine event occurrence times. Events are placed in the future events queue as the program schedules them. The simulation program takes the first event from this queue, changes the state variables to reflect its occurrence, and may enter new events into the future events queue as a result of its having taken place. This process repeats until the run is ended by a user-specified criterion, such as the passage of a certain (simulated) elapsed time or processing a certain quantity of simulated transactions.

Simulation programs can be written in general-purpose programming languages such as C or Pascal. Most simulation professionals in business, however, use special-purpose simulation languages such as **GPSS, SLAM,** or **Simscript.** These languages and their run-time support packages have several advantages:

- They handle simulation "housekeeping" tasks such as keeping the future events queue in order and searching it for the next event. While it is not difficult to program a simple future events queue, programming an efficient one is a substantial undertaking. Developers of commercial simulation packages put a great deal of effort into this area and generally do a good job.
- Simulation concepts and terminology are built into them, easing the translation of reality to "computerese."
- They provide easy ways of generating the statistical distributions required to describe system activity. Several common ones are usually built in.
- They provide basic statistical analyses of each simulation run, including percentage of busy times and waiting line lengths, with no additional programming effort.

The user of such a language can develop a simulation in far less time than an equally competent programmer working from scratch with general-purpose tools. General-purpose programming languages may still be used when a special-purpose tool is not available, when a simulation model is a minor part of a larger DSS, or when a simulation model is small and its developer already knows a general-purpose language well. As a compromise approach, subroutine packages for simulation have been written for several popular programming languages. The **GASP** package for FORTRAN is one example. C and C++ users have a wide range of choices also, including C++SIM, SIM++, and CSIM18.

Part of the above gasoline station model, which deals with cars arriving, being fueled, paying, and leaving, is shown programmed in GPSS and in SLAM II in Figure 8–6A and B.[6] The differences between the two models are cosmetic: The use of the verb "create" or "generate," separating operands from the verb by spaces or a comma, how two numbers are used to define the range of a uniform distribution. That is because the models were deliberately written in a parallel fashion to stress the underlying similarities between the two ways of expressing the concepts. Both languages allow the same model to be described in many other ways, with SLAM II allowing more variation in this respect than GPSS. Some ways of writing this model in one language wouldn't look nearly this similar to a model written in the other one.

---

[6]Gasoline stations in which operators fuel customers' cars are admittedly nearly extinct in many locales.

GENERATE	120, 60	(uniformly distributed arrivals, 60–180 seconds)
ENTER	PUMP	(take any available pump, else wait)
ENTER	OPER	(take any available operator, else wait)
ADVANCE	15, 5	(10–20 seconds time, uniform distribution, to start fueling)
LEAVE	OPER	(operator goes about other duties)
ADVANCE	90, 30	(60–120 seconds, uniform distribution, to fuel car)
ENTER	OPER	(need not be same operator)
ADVANCE	60, 30	(30–90 seconds, uniform distribution, to finish and pay)
LEAVE	OPER	(operator done, car still at pump)
ADVANCE	10, 5	(5–15 seconds, uniform distribution, to move away from pump)
LEAVE	PUMP	
TERMINATE	100	(transaction leaves system; run for 100 cars)
PUMP	STORAGE 2	(two pumps specified for this run)
OPER	STORAGE 1	(one operator specified for this run)

FIGURE 8–6A Partial GPSS Model of Gas Station Fueling Process

NETWORK;	(start of network statements)
CREATE, UNFRM (60.,180., 1);	(uniformly distributed arrivals, 60–180 seconds)
AWAIT, PUMP;	(take any available pump, else wait)
AWAIT, OPER;	(take any available operator, else wait)
ACTIVITY, UNFRM (10, 20);	(10–20 seconds time, uniform distribution, to start fueling)
FREE, OPER;	(operator goes about other duties)
ACTIVITY, UNFRM (60, 120);	(60–120 seconds, uniform distribution, to fuel car)
AWAIT, OPER;	(need not be same operator)
ACTIVITY, UNFRM (30, 90);	(30–90 seconds, uniform distribution, to finish and pay)
FREE, OPER;	(operator done, car still at pump)
ACTIVITY, UNFRM (5, 15);	(5–15 seconds, uniform distribution, to move away from pump)
FREE, PUMP;	
TERMINATE, 100;	(transaction leaves system; run for 100 cars)
RESOURCE/PUMP (2);	(two pumps specified for this run)
RESOURCE/OPER (1);	(one operator specified for this run)

FIGURE 8–6B Partial SLAM II Model of Gas Station Fueling Process

The same model in Simscript would be longer and more complex, since Simscript doesn't make as many assumptions as either GPSS or SLAM II about what is being modeled. On the one hand, that forces the programmer to do more work in specifying this information. On the other, it allows one to model systems that differ from the standard mold.

A corresponding GASP model would look like a FORTRAN program with calls to subroutines with names such as SCHDL to schedule future events. The GASP user must already be familiar with FORTRAN. If one knows and likes FORTRAN, and especially if the simulation must be linked with other programs in that language, GASP can be a good choice. (GASP routines can also be accessed from other programming languages if the user prefers, but they are written in FORTRAN and therefore interface most easily with programs in that language.)

The program segments of Figure 8–6 do not include commands to gather statistics about system behavior. Most simulation languages automatically collect a great deal of such information. An analyst for whom this standard output is not sufficient can specify additional, optional tabular or graphic output. If the facilities of the language do not provide enough flexibility, models written in languages such as SLAM II and GPSS can be linked to routines written in any of several general-purpose 3GLs. Simscript, since it is as powerful as any other 3GL, won't pose this problem. Since GASP II models are already in FORTRAN, the problem can't arise there either.

A more specialized tool for developing simulation models is called a **simulator** [BANK91]. Simulators are generally intended to be used in simulating only one type of system, such as (commonly) a manufacturing plant. A simulator has built-in building blocks for elements common to systems of this type. A manufacturing simulator, for instance, would have built-in building blocks for conveyor belts (where transport time depends on the distance to be covered), palletizers (that swing into operation as soon as, but not before, the required number of products has accumulated), and more. Simulators often incorporate animated displays of the "factory" in addition to numerical output. Several simulator packages, such as ManSim/X, SIMFACTORY (itself written in Simscript), ProModel, SiMPLE++ (written, as one might guess, in C++), and Witness, run on desktop microcomputers. These packages are all designed to simulate production and logistics operations. ServiceModel, from ProModel Corp., is (as you probably figured out from its name) for modeling service operations.

Figure 8–7 shows a screen shot from Witness. The upper portion of the screen is a schematic diagram of a factory floor with a conveyor belt. To its right, a clock shows the progress of simulated factory time. Below them is an animated picture of the conveyor belt carrying automobile bodies.

8.2.4 Another Simulation Example

Here's how we might apply the eight simulation development steps to a model of a supermarket. The decision maker, who will use this model, hopes to decide how many checkout counters to open and how many baggers to hire for optimum profit. This manager wants to hire the least-cost combination of checkout clerks and baggers that keeps the checkout line below a predetermined length 95 percent of the time.

As you read through the supermarket example, see where the model simplifies reality. Some, but not all, of the simplifications are pointed out. (Exercise 9a at the end of this chapter asks you to find others.)

1. Given our objective as stated above, we need to know the 95th percentile figure for the checkout line length distribution. We may decide that an overall statistical picture of line length distribution would be useful so we can modify the decision criterion in the future.
2. The system consists of the supermarket from the entrance door to the end of the checkout process. We will not study the parking lot or anything else that goes on before customers walk in the door. We also assume that customers whose orders have been bagged proceed out the door with no delay or important congestion.

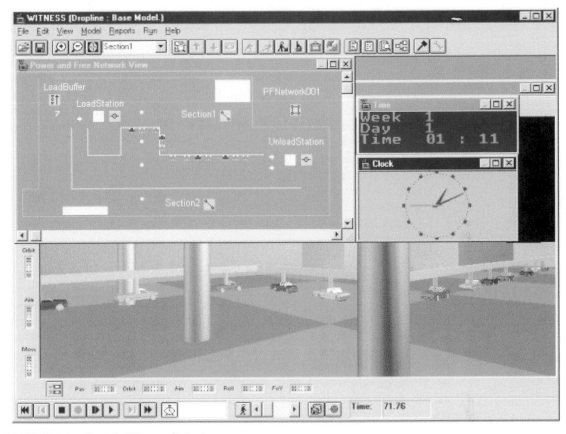

FIGURE 8–7 Sample Witness Output

Our controllable variables here are the number of open checkout counters and the number of baggers. The number of open counters is an integer from 1 to the number of counters built into the store. (Remodeling the store for additional checkout counters is not an option for this model, though it could be in other situations.) The number of baggers is an integer from 0 to the number of open counters.

3. The state variables are the number of shoppers in the store and the number of shoppers at each open checkout counter. All are nonnegative integers.

4. The state of the system changes when

- A shopper enters the store. This is the only exogenous event in our system.
- A shopper finishes shopping and enters the checkout line. This is an endogenous event. Its occurrence rate depends on the number of shoppers in the store and possibly, depending on our model, on how long they've been there. In a common approach to programming simulation models, the time at which each shopper will enter the checkout line is calculated and placed in the future events queue when the shopper enters the store. This corresponds to calculating the time at which a haircut will be over when the customer sits down in the barber's chair.

To model this event we must determine how shoppers decide which check-out line to enter. A simple model could choose randomly. More realistically, our model might choose the counter with the shortest line, picking randomly among all counters having this line length if there are several. Introducing an express counter for shoppers with few items would make the model more complicated but might be important for accuracy. The number of express counters and the upper limit on the size of order that can go through an express counter might be controllable (user-specified) variables, though that would go beyond the stated objectives of this particular study.

- A shopper finishes checking out and leaves the system. (We assume that a clerk does not start checking out the next shopper until the bagger, if any, has finished the current one. See Exercise 5*b* at the end of this chapter about relaxing this assumption.) This, too, is an endogenous event. Its time can be calculated and the event entered into the future events queue when the customer begins the checkout process. A shopper's checkout can't start until all shoppers in line ahead of him or her have finished.

5. We need the 95th percentile of checkout line lengths. There are several ways to obtain this. One is to sample the system every so often. If we take 100 samples, the 95th-largest is our answer. Another is record the total number of customers in line between each pair of events. (Question: Why can't this number change between events?) We would then create a table showing the total time for which the average line length was 0 customers, 0.1 customers, 0.2 customers (Question: How many checkout counters do these choices imply we have?) and so on. There are other possibilities as well. If we are using a simulation package, it may include one or more built-in statistics gathering capabilities and we might opt for the most suitable of these.

6. An appropriate time scale for supermarkets would be seconds if we want to use integers. If our software allows fractional time units, we might prefer to deal with minutes or hours. This system need not be modeled to the microsecond. Supermarket shopping processes do not take months or years.

7. We can obtain arrival rate statistics by counting shoppers during a period similar to the one we are modeling, be it a weekday afternoon or Saturday morning. We can time shoppers as they move through the store to get statistics on the distribution of shopping times. We can similarly time the checkout process to learn (statistically) how long it takes and how it is affected by the presence of a bagger. If we wish, we could also track individual shoppers to determine the correlation between the length of time a shopper spends shopping and the length of time it takes that same shopper to check out—and, if we want to model that aspect of the store, their eligibility to use an express counter. (Shoppers who spend more time in the store tend to purchase more items and therefore tend to take longer to check out, though the correlations among shopping time, number of items purchased, and checkout time are less than 100 percent.)

8. The initial state of the system might be an empty store. As previously mentioned, we could run the model for a few "hours," record its state, and use that as the initial state for subsequent runs having the same parameters.

STORAGE	CAPACITY	AVERAGE CONTENTS	TOTAL ENTRIES	AVERAGE TIME/TRANS.	AVERAGE UTILIZ.
CLERKS	4	2.713	1085	1.607	0.678
BAGGERS	2	1.902	761	1.293	0.951

FIGURE 8–8 Sample Supermarket Simulation Output

The output of this model could be a graph such as Figure 8–8. It shows that, for the set of parameters evaluated and the set of pseudo-random numbers chosen by the computer, the average shopper waited in line for about three minutes. The overwhelming majority of shoppers waited from one minute to six minutes. Whether or not these times are acceptable depends on the decision maker. What is acceptable in one store, that stresses low prices and attracts shoppers willing to put up with some annoyance to get them, might not be acceptable to another store that stresses service and charges higher prices for it.

8.2.5 Complete Simulation Studies

One simulation run tells us how the simulated system behaves for one choice of controllable variables and one set of pseudo-random numbers. That is not enough for management decisions. A full-scale **simulation study** runs the simulation several times for each set of controllable variables to give us a distribution of results. If the model is valid, this distribution resembles the distribution of results we would see in reality. Repeating the process for each choice of controllable variables lets us evaluate the effect of changing the controllable variables and helps us choose the best set.

Instead of running the model several times, we might consider one long run covering a period of time equal to the sum of the shorter individual runs. For example, the computer could run the model once for 20 hours of simulated supermarket activity or 10 times for two hours each. (A real supermarket would experience time-of-day usage peaks and valleys over 20 hours, but that isn't a problem in a computer model.) In general, one long run is not as good as the same total time divided into several shorter ones. The reason is a phenomenon called autocorrelation. **Autocorrelation** means that what happens later in a run depends on what happened previously in the same run. If the supermarket, because of an unusual but statistically possible choice of pseudo-random numbers, gets unusually crowded, the effects of this crowding will linger for a long time and will affect the results of one long run. If we use several short runs that start from the same initial conditions but use different pseudo-random number sequences, the overcrowding will affect only one of the runs and will not have much impact on the final results.

We might choose to run the supermarket model 50 times for each set of controllable variables (number of open counters and number of baggers). We could plot the results, as in Figure 8–9, or tabulate them as in Figure 8–10. Either form lets us decide how many clerks and baggers to hire for the given shopper arrival rate.

If the supermarket we are studying has 10 checkout counters, there are 65 possible combinations of checkout clerks and baggers. (Why?) We could start the

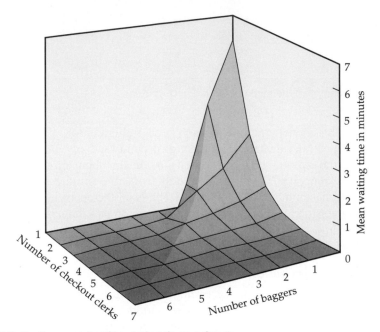

FIGURE 8–9 **Supermarket Simulation Output Graph**

Baggers	Checkout Clerks						
	1	2	3	4	5	6	7
0	6.12	2.63	0.95	0.31	0.09	0.03	0.01
1	3.81	1.61	0.63	0.18	0.06	0.02	0.01
2		0.87	0.38	0.11	0.03	0.01	0.00
3			0.22	0.07	0.02	0.01	0.00
4				0.03	0.01	0.00	0.00
5					0.01	0.00	0.00
6						0.00	0.00
7							0.00

Mean Customer Waiting Time as Function of Number of Checkout Clerks and Baggers

FIGURE 8–10 **Typical Tabular Simulation Results Display**

computer on its task of $65 \times 50 = 3,250$ runs. Each run might cover two simulated hours, hence about 2,000 simulated shoppers, and hence about 10,000 simulated events. If a computer takes a millisecond to simulate each event, it takes 10 seconds for each run, or 32,500 seconds—about nine hours—for the whole study. We would have to come back a long time later to get our results. This might make sense if we can leave an overnight or weekend job, or use a more powerful computer on which it would take far less computer time.

In interactive usage, we could look at one set of results and then plan the next test. If six open counters can't handle the load, there is no sense in trying five or fewer. Or, if six open counters keep the line length far below its upper limit, we might try two or three next. With this approach, each set of 50 runs would take under 10 minutes. We could also save time in this situation by trying just a few runs for the first few conditions, saving the full set of 50 runs per condition (with correspondingly greater statistical validity) for zeroing in on the best answer after we have identified its approximate location. Using our knowledge of supermarkets and our intuition to choose the conditions for each set of runs, we could probably find the best set in well under an hour. Of course, we would be tied to our computer for the entire time. With a batch run we could go home, and later spend a few minutes examining the results.

We could get the best of both worlds by programming the computer to follow a "hill-climbing" optimization approach as described in the next chapter. With this scheme, the computer would run the model for a few choices of controllable variables, decide the direction in which results improve, and try more choices in that direction. It could then find the best combination after trying far fewer than all 65. The drawback is that someone would have to program the searching and optimization process.

8.3 RANDOM NUMBERS, PSEUDO-RANDOM NUMBERS, AND STATISTICAL DISTRIBUTIONS

The behavior of a simulation model depends on the numbers that determine when each event occurs. Ideally, these numbers should be chosen at random from the specified distributions of interevent or **service times.**

There are many ways to generate **random numbers.** Rolling dice, tossing coins, and drawing a card from a well-shuffled deck don't require fancy technology and work well. (Simulation models that use random numbers are often called **Monte Carlo simulations** after the casino in Monaco. It uses a variety of physical random number generators in its business.) Special dice with more or fewer than the usual six sides exist. They are used in noncomputer simulations such as "Dungeons and Dragons" or war games. Opening a phone book to an arbitrary page with your eyes closed, and choosing the digit on which your finger lands, is another method. Tables of random numbers have been published. (There may be one in the back of your statistics textbook.) Operations researchers used these tables before digital computers became widely available.

A practical low-tech way to generate random decimal digits uses this book, or any other reasonably thick one. Open the book to a random page. The tens digit of the page number is your random digit. Only the tens digit works: you influence the hundreds digit when you decide where to open the book, and the units digit depends on your choice of the left or right page. To get a random number from 00 to 99, repeat the process a second time.

It is possible to equip a computer with a physical random number generator. A microphone can pick up random background noise in the room where the computer is located. Its voltage can then be converted to digital form. The low-order bits in the digital representation of the background noise are truly random. Another method is to use the low-order digits of a high-resolution system clock, if it ticks so often during the processing of an event that its low-order digits are for all practical purposes random.

Using truly random numbers has the disadvantage that their sequence is not repeatable. It is easier to check out a computer program when the same input sequence can be repeated for testing. For that reason, virtually all simulation models use **pseudo-random numbers.** These are numbers generated by a repeatable formula, which behave statistically as if they were truly random. Most such formulas generate uniformly distributed integers from 0 to the largest positive integer that the computer in question can conveniently represent. If your computer uses 32-bit signed integer data, this would be about 2,147,500,000.

All simulation packages and most programming languages have built-in functions that return uniformly distributed pseudo-random numbers over a more useful range. The output of these functions ranges from 0 to 1 (more precisely, from 0 to the largest fraction less than 1, 0.99999 . . . , which the computer can represent) or from 0 to a user-specified figure. The RAND or @RAND function in your spreadsheet package works this way. This range is created by scaling the output of an integer pseudo-random number generator.

The built-in random number generators of most systems are not perfect. Computer science journals regularly critique popular ones and suggest improvements. A common criticism is that a generator produces numbers that repeat themselves after a far shorter period than the computer's word length requires. Built-in generators improve as their developers become aware of new research and new versions of software supplant older ones. Meanwhile, they are widely used and suffice for most decision support tasks. A modeler about to embark on a simulation study that will determine the fate of civilization as we know it, or even the fate of a corporation, should make an effort to verify that his or her pseudo-random number generator passes the randomness tests in the computer science literature—and replace it if it does not.

From a Pseudo-random Number to a Simulation Value   Users of such functions who want a nonuniform distribution must convert the output of the built-in function to a number from the desired distribution. This is done via a **cumulative distribution function (CDF)** as shown in Figure 8–11. The curve in the figure corresponds roughly to the normal distribution with which you're familiar from your statistics course work. The way a distribution and a pseudo-random number generator combine to create a sample from the distribution is shown in Figure 8–12. This figure shows the same CDF as in Figure 8–10, with numbers added to the horizontal axis. (The scale of the vertical axis, from 0 to 1, is inherent in the concept of a CDF.) Let's say our pseudo-random number generator has returned a value of 0.6, as shown by the left end of the heavy horizontal line. We go to the CDF curve at a y value of 0.6 and take the corresponding x value. In this case, it's about 1.37.

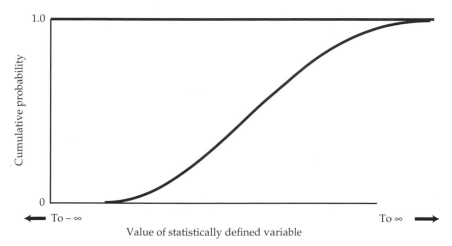

FIGURE 8–11 **Cumulative Distribution Function**

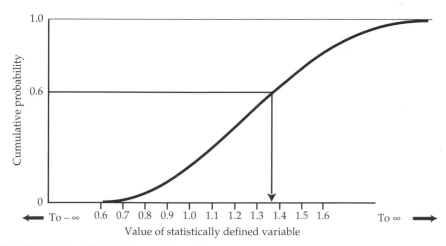

FIGURE 8–12 **CDF with Usage Example**

You can see from this example how a steeper CDF, such as the one in Figure 8–13, will yield samples that cluster more closely about its midpoint—about 1.25 here. A CDF such as the one in Figure 8–14 describes a bimodal distribution, where a process tends to take either a short time (around 0.8 to 0.9 time units) or a long time (about 1.5 to 1.6), but seldom anything in between. Many business processes work like this, such as paying in cash (short) or by check (long) at a supermarket, or leaving an airport with hand luggage only (short) or after waiting for checked baggage to be unloaded (long).

Programming the process of taking a sample from a CDF, given a pseudo-random number, is not difficult if the CDF is approximated by a series of straight-line segments represented by their endpoints in the form of an array or table. The program

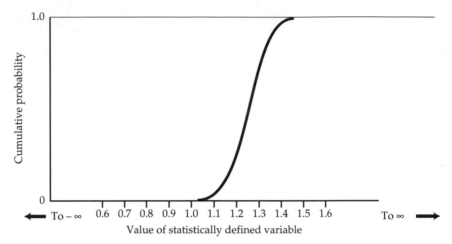

FIGURE 8–13 CDF with Narrow Distribution

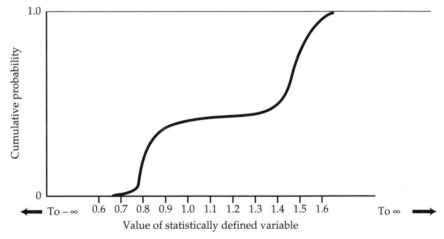

FIGURE 8–14 CDF with Bimodal Distribution

need only locate the segment within which the given pseudo-random number falls, and then use the equation of a straight line to obtain the desired value. Twelve segments are sufficient to approximate the normal distribution well enough for all practical purposes. Using a set of straight-line approximations in this way also enables the model builder to prevent a normal distribution from producing negative numbers for inherently nonnegative quantities such as service or interarrival times. With a true normal distribution these are always theoretically possible, since the tails of the normal distribution extend indefinitely, though they may be extremely unlikely.

One particularly useful distribution is the exponential distribution, where knowing how much time has gone by since the last occurrence of an event is of no statistical value in helping us predict when the next event will take place. (By contrast, if the time of a given process has a normal distribution with a mean of 10 minutes and a standard deviation of 1 minute, and 12 minutes have gone by since the process started, we can be sure it will end pretty soon.) Because exponential distributions are especially important to some of the mathematical models we take up in the next chapter, you'll read about them there.

Simulation packages include a set of common distributions, such as the normal and exponential distributions, along with easy ways for the programmer to define other distributions. General-purpose programming languages may not.

8.4 STATIC SIMULATION MODELS

We stated earlier that simulation models are dynamic. This is true 99 percent of the time, which is why we covered dynamic simulation models first. There are also static situations where we can apply the same idea of using pseudo-random numbers to drive a system model. Here's an example:

Suppose a manager wants to estimate next year's profits. One way is to develop an accounting model that will calculate profits as a function of sales volume for each of the firm's five products. We don't generally know, however, what next year's sales will be. The best we can do is to estimate them statistically.

If we have estimated sales distributions for each of the five products, we can pick a random member of each distribution and get a possible outcome of next year's business activities. We can then pick another set of five possible sales volumes and get another possible outcome. After repeating this process a number of times, we will get a picture of next year's probable profit distribution, on the assumption that our sales distributions and our profitability formula were accurate.

To run through this process, suppose we have five products numbered 1 through 5. Conveniently, each sale of product 1 yields a profit of $1, each sale of product 2 yields a profit of $2, and so on. We must also cover fixed costs of $10,000. Our profits therefore depend on the sales of our five products according to this formula, with all quantities in dollars:

$$\text{Profit} = (\text{product 1 unit sales}) + 2 \times (\text{product 2 unit sales})$$
$$+ 3 \times (\text{product 3 unit sales}) + 4 \times (\text{product 4 unit sales})$$
$$+ 5 \times (\text{product 5 unit sales}) - 10{,}000$$

Suppose we estimate that the probable sales of each product are uniformly distributed within the following limits. That is, for product 1, any unit volume from 800 to 1,200 units is equally likely, and sales below 800 units or above 1,200 units will not (according to our estimate) occur under any circumstances.

Product 1: 800 to 1,200 units
Product 2: 700 to 1,100
Product 3: 600 to 1,000
Product 4: 500 to 900
Product 5: 400 to 800

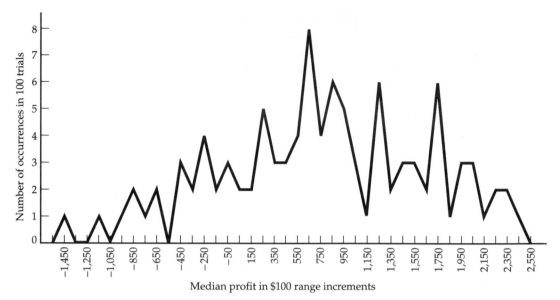

FIGURE 8–15 **Chart of Estimated Profit Probabilities**

One choice of pseudo-random numbers might give us these estimated sales of the five products for next year:

Product 1: 1,120 units
Product 2: 785
Product 3: 660
Product 4: 845
Product 5: 610

For this set of estimated sales, profit is forecasted to be

$$(1,120) + 2(785) + 3(660) + 4(845) + 5(610) - 10,000 = \$1,100$$

Other possible estimated sales volumes would result in higher profits, lower profits, or a loss. A hundred different choices of sales volumes from these distributions gave the estimated profit distribution shown in Figure 8–15. It matches the basic parameters you could figure out from the problem description: All the trials yielded profit figures between –$2,000 and $4,000, and the peak was somewhere around the expected mean of $1,000. Yet many managers would not have guessed the approximate shape. A different hundred trials would, of course, have yielded a different chart. Many more trials would have yielded a smoother curve.

Packages are available to help decision makers use static, stochastic, simulation models such as these. These packages often build on the spreadsheet metaphor, which most late-1990s managers are comfortable with. Crystal Ball (Decisioneering, Inc., Denver, Colorado) is such a package. Crystal Ball, which is available for Microsoft Windows® and Apple Macintosh®, takes a model from any popular

	A	B	C
1	*Sales Forecast Example*		
2	*Product No.*	*Units*	*Price*
3	1	1000	$1.00
4	2	900	$2.00
5	3	800	$3.00
6	4	700	$4.00
7	5	600	$5.00
8	Profit	$1,000	
9			

FIGURE 8–16 Spreadsheet with Profit Model

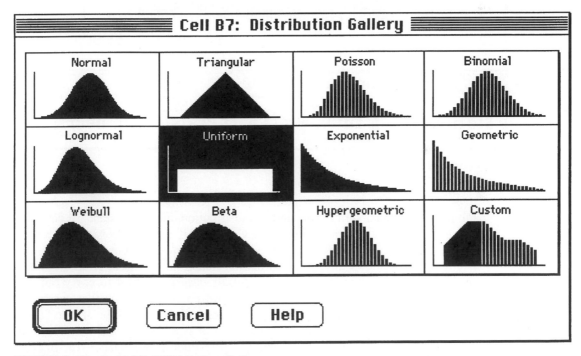

FIGURE 8–17 Crystal Ball Distribution Gallery

spreadsheet package that has been saved in any of several standardized spreadsheet file formats. Figure 8–16 shows the aforementioned simple model in a spreadsheet. It then allows the decision maker to define any cell containing a constant as an "assumption cell" subject to a user-specified statistical distribution. These distributions are chosen from the "gallery" of Figure 8–17. The uniform distribution is highlighted in the figure because that is the distribution we plan to use in our simulation. Each distribution, once chosen, is further specified by appropriate parameters:

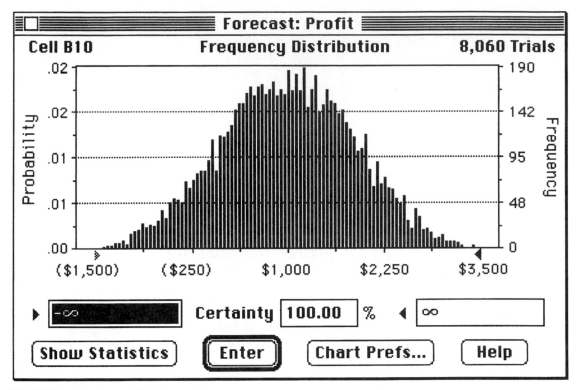

FIGURE 8–18 Crystal Ball Output Graph

minimum and maximum for the uniform distribution, mean and standard deviation for the normal distribution, and so forth. Crystal Ball also lets decision makers define custom distributions if none of the standard ones meet their needs.

Figure 8–18 shows the profit distribution that results from running the model just over 8,000 times. Because Crystal Ball is programmed to carry out this process efficiently, rather than being a general-purpose package that can be instructed to carry out many different types of processes and must be able to handle them all, those 8,000 runs take only a minute or two on even a slow microcomputer with no math coprocessor. If you compare Figures 8–15 and 8–18, you will see that the additional runs have smoothed out the jagged peaks of Figure 8–15 considerably. The mean and range of the distribution are, of course, about the same in both.

The advantages of using a package such as Crystal Ball, rather than programming one's own distributions into a spreadsheet (as the author did in creating Figure 8–15) or using any other "home-grown" approach, are substantial:

• It is easy to add statistically defined variability to the deterministic model of Figure 8–16. Defining all five uniform distributions, once the underlying spreadsheet was written and loaded into Crystal Ball, was the work of about a minute.

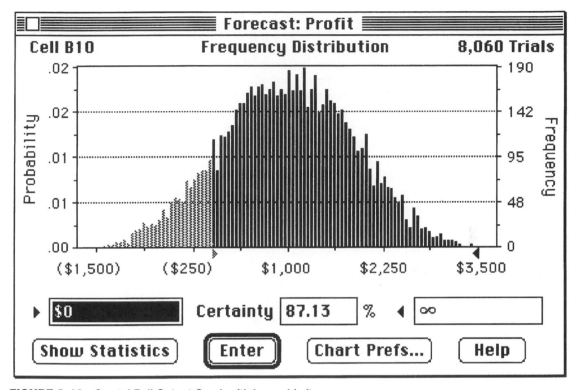

FIGURE 8–19 Crystal Ball Output Graph with Lower Limit

- A wide variety of statistical distributions is available, many of which would be quite difficult for a decision maker (even one who is an expert programmer) to define directly.
- The parameters of the distributions, indeed the distributions themselves, are easy to change.
- The output facilities exceed what spreadsheet packages offer for this type of problem. In Figure 8–18, the user can (for example) move the triangular "grabbers" at either end of the *x* axis from their current positions, or type new values into the boxes representing the limits of the interval of interest, to see what percentage of the runs yielded results with a particular range. Figure 8–19 shows how this works if the lower limit is raised to $0. The highlighted box under the center of the graph now shows that 87.13 percent of the runs yielded a profit.

Their major disadvantage is the need to use two packages: one to define the model and one to run it as a simulation. This is not a serious issue and should not deter a decision maker from using this type of tool. Facilities such as Dynamic Data Exchange or Object Linking and Embedding under Microsoft Windows, or Publish and Subscribe under the Mac OS, can cause two programs to behave much like a single one. Over time, you can expect to see high-end spreadsheet packages enhanced to incorporate some, if not all, of the capabilities that now call for specialized software.

Demand elasticity curves play a key role in many static representational models. These include the economist's price elasticity curve, which tells us how the quantity of an item that customers purchase varies as its price changes. There are, however, many other curves that relate the demand for a product to some external, and (hopefully) predictable or controllable, factor: the demand for skis as a function of weather, the demand for cameras as a function of advertising, the demand for a new car model as a function of the gasoline mileage its designers are able to achieve. All of these and more figure in many useful DSS. Crystal Ball and similar packages can deal with many such situations by defining **correlated variables.** In the above sales and profit forecast, for example, we might have specified that the sales volume of product 5 has a 0.5 correlation with the sales volume of product 1. (Perhaps product 1 is house paint and product 5 is stepladders.) More complex cases call for custom programming.

SUMMARY

Many decision support systems use representational models to predict the impact of possible decisions. These models maintain the relationships among important items that a decision maker must know while being much simpler to develop, change, and use than the real system in question would be.

Models are of several types. The highest-level categories are system and process models. System models can be static or dynamic. Static models can be of static or dynamic systems. Dynamic models, which must inherently be of dynamic systems, can be continuous or discrete-event.

Simulation is the process of using a simulation model to study a dynamic system. Simulation models as used in business are, in almost all cases, dynamic, discrete-event, and stochastic models. They model what happens in a system over time by tracking the individual events that take place in the system. Running a simulation consists of repeating a simple cycle over and over again. Each repetition consists of (a) taking the next event off the future events queue, (b) updating the model's representation of the system to reflect the occurrence of that event, (c) recording any data we will need for later statistical analysis of system behavior, and (d) entering any new events it triggers into the future events queue. This process, while conceptually simple, involves a great deal of tedious bookkeeping and is therefore well suited to computers.

To design a discrete-event simulation model, you must determine its objectives, define the system to be modeled, define the state variables that describe what the system is doing at any instant, define the events that will change their values, choose the simulation time scale, define (in terms of that time scale) the statistics of each event type, and define the initial state of the system. Having established these parameters of your model, you can now program it in a special-purpose language such as GPSS or Simscript, or in a general-purpose language such as C. Simulation languages generally include capabilities that will allow you to develop your model more quickly.

Running a stochastic simulation requires the use of random numbers to choose elements of statistical distributions. Truly random numbers are rarely used because they are not repeatable and therefore make it difficult to check out a computer program. The most common approach is to use formulas that generate pseudo-random numbers: numbers that behave statistically as though they were random.

In order to obtain values for the simulation, pseudo-random numbers are used together with the cumulative distribution functions of the statistical distributions that apply to the system being modeled. In practice, CDFs are usually approximated by a small number of straight-line segments. Simulation packages include a set of standard CDFs for common distributions. Simulation models must be exercised for long enough for fluctuations due to specific choices of random variables to die down. Several runs of moderate length are generally better for this purpose than one long run of the same aggregate length.

Static simulation models also exist, though they are less common than dynamic simulation models. Since a static model represents a system in rest at a single point in time, such a model can be used to study the statistics of where a system comes to rest for statistically described inputs.

KEY TERMS

autocorrelation
continuous-system simulation model
controllable variable
correlated variables
cumulative distribution function (CDF)
deterministic model
discrete-event simulation model
dynamic model
dynamic system
endogenous event
event
exogenous event
formula
future events queue
GASP (set of simulation subroutines for the FORTRAN programming language)
GPSS (simulation programming language)
graphical model
information-based model
initial state
interarrival time
mathematical model
model
Monte Carlo simulation
narrative model

parameter
physical model
procedure
process model
pseudo-random number
random number
service time
Simscript (simulation programming language)
simulation
simulation study
simulator
SLAM (simulation programming language)
state (of a system)
state variable
static model
static system
steady state
stochastic model
symbolic model
system model
uncontrollable variable

REVIEW QUESTIONS

1. What is a model?
2. Why do decision support systems use models?
3. What are the major types of models?
4. Why are continuous models generally not used in business?
5. What two basic types of representational models are used for decision support?
6. What is the future events queue? What is it used for?
7. What steps does the basic simulation processing cycle consist of?
8. What are the first two steps you must take in defining a simulation model?
9. What is the *state* of a system?
10. Why are specialized simulation languages often used to develop simulation models?
11. In what two ways does a simulation study differ from a single run of a simulation model?
12. What are pseudo-random numbers? Why are they useful in simulation models? How are they created?
13. What is a static simulation model? Give an example of where one might be useful.

EXERCISES

1. You have prepared a spreadsheet outlining how you plan to spend your advertising budget for each of the 12 months of next year: so much on each of several TV programs, so much on direct mail, so much on magazines of various types, etc. Your spreadsheet shows totals by category and the grand total for each month.
   a. Is this a static or a dynamic model? Why?

b. You enhance your spreadsheet to show the number of people who will be exposed to your message each month and, for each month, the number of people who will have been exposed to your message a given number of times from January 1 to the end of that month. Is your spreadsheet now a static or a dynamic model? Why?

2. You have been hired by an airline to model the effects of last-minute gate changes for aircraft at an airport. "Last-minute" means that people are already at the gate at which the aircraft was originally supposed to park, either to greet arriving passengers or to board the next flight. (Such changes are usually the result of an aircraft already at the gate being unable to leave, due to a mechanical problem or some other reason.) If the gate assignment is changed these people must go to the new gate. Your model is to predict the time it takes them to reach the new gate so that the airline can determine if the switch will impact its flight schedule. The purpose of doing this is to allow the airline to consider different gate changes and choose the one with the smallest impact. Define three different ways you could model the walking time of individual passengers, with different degrees of simplification, that you could use in a simulation model for this problem. State which is the simplest approach that you think would give useful results for airline planners to use.

3. At Bender College 40 percent of current undergraduates are freshmen, 30 percent are sophomores, 20 percent are juniors, and the remaining 10 percent are seniors. Draw the cumulative distribution function for this distribution. Then determine the classes of 20 students by generating 20 random digits (via the page-of-a-book method on page 325, using the random number generation function of a spreadsheet, or with a table of random digits) and using your distribution. How closely did your results match the "official" statistics?

4. Environmental engineering firms use simulation, among other places, to model movement of pollution through the air. For instance, if a fire at a chemical plant releases toxic fumes, simulation can indicate which residential areas should be evacuated in time for their residents to gather up their belongings and leave in an orderly fashion before the pollution arrives.
    a. Would this be a discrete-event or a continuous simulation? Why?
    b. What are some of the statistically defined parameters that such a simulation would require?

5. Your TV store makes a profit of $50 on each set it sells. If a customer wants a set and you don't have any, you lose this profit. However, it costs $4 to keep a set in stock for a day or part of a day, and it costs $100 to place and process each order. This cost per order is independent of how many sets you order. Orders are placed at the end of the day. They also arrive at the end of the day, five business days after being placed.

    Assume there is an equal probability of customers wanting to buy 1, 2, 3, 4, 5, or 6 sets per day. Assume you start with 30 sets in inventory. Start your study by simulating the following ordering strategies for 20 business days each:
    a. Order 20 sets when stock plus sets already on order total 20 or below at the end of the day.
    b. Order 30 sets when stock plus sets already on order total 20 or below at the end of the day.
    c. Order 30 sets when stock plus sets already on order total 30 or below at the end of the day.

    Lay your work out in the form of a table with a column for each day and rows as shown. Use a six-sided die to determine customer demand for each day. (Roll the die 20 times to obtain a series of orders for the 20 days and use that series for all strategies.) Use your ordering strategy to determine orders placed each day. Enter the amount of each order placed in the "orders received" cell five columns to the right.

Item	Day 1	Day 2	Etc.
Opening inventory	(30 for first day, then copy prior day's close)		
Demand	(Random, 1 to 6, from die toss)		
Unit sales	(Smaller of demand or opening inventory)		
Orders received	(Orders placed five days earlier)		
Closing inventory	(Copy to next day's opening inventory)		
Orders placed	(Based on strategy being modeled)		
Operating profit	(Unit sales × $50)		
Carrying costs	(Opening inventory × $3)		
Ordering costs	($100 if an order was placed, else $0)		
Today's profit or loss	(Algebraic sum of above three items)		
Cumulative profit or loss	(Previous day's cumulative profit or loss, plus today's profit or minus today's loss)		

Your results won't be exactly the same as your classmates', since you will have different random number sequences. Different sequences will favor different strategies; for example, a run of heavy orders will cause ordering many sets to look better than it should. However, a pattern should appear when you compare your conclusions across the class.

Which of the three strategies yields the highest profit? Based on your results, think of a strategy that you feel might yield still higher profits. Try it and compare it with the best of the three given ones.

6. Your factory, located on Phobos in the year 2027, produces elbats in two stages. First they are encabulated. This takes a uniformly distributed time from 6 to 24 minutes. The encabulator has a capacity of one elbat and can start on the next one as soon as a finished one leaves it. (Your factory never runs out of raw materials.) Next they are fluxicated, which takes a similar time. The encabulation and fluxication times of an elbat are not correlated; that is, knowing how long it took to encabulate a given elbat does not imply anything about how long it will take to fluxicate that elbat. If the fluxicator is busy, elbats which have been encabulated are placed in a fopper until the fluxicator can start work on them. If the fopper is full, the encabulator stops until the fluxicator finishes the elbat it's working on and takes a new one from the fopper. At that point the just-encabulated elbat can be moved from the encabulator to the fopper, freeing the encabulator to start on a new elbat. (See Figure 8–20.)

The fopper costs 500 Phobos Credits for each elbat it can fop (for example, a fopper with a capacity of 3 elbats would cost PC1,500) and wears out in 30 working days. Each elbat produced earns a profit of PC3. If the fopper is too small, you will lose money because production will drop every time the encabulator must stop due to a full fopper. If it is too large, you will have wasted money by buying too large a fopper. You wish to determine the optimal fopper capacity.

Simulate this system with a computer or by hand. If you use a computer, simulate foppers of capacities from 1 to 5 elbats. Simulate 1 eight-hour working day per run. Carry out 10 runs per capacity and average them.

If you do not have access to a simulation or a general-purpose programming language (or want to learn how to use one), you can simulate this system with a spreadsheet. First, put the fopper capacity in a visible cell near the top of your

FIGURE 8–20 **Flow Diagram of Elbat Production**

spreadsheet so the formulas can refer to it and adapt correctly when you modify it. Fopper capacity is the key controllable variable, or parameter, of this model. Be sure to make all references to this parameter absolute references so they are not modified as you copy your formulas down the spreadsheet. Below that, each row corresponds to producing 1 elbat. You will need the following columns for your simulation:

- Serial numbers starting at 1, so you can count elbat production easily.
- The time the elbat finishes encabulation. This is the time the previous elbat left the encabulator plus a random number evenly distributed from 6 to 24. Since most spreadsheet pseudo-random number generators return numbers that are uniformly distributed from 0 to (for all practical purposes) 1, you will have to scale its output to get the desired range of 6 to 24.
- The time the elbat leaves the encabulator. This is the later of (*a*) the time it finishes encabulation or (*b*) the time the fopper has room for another elbat. You will have to determine when the fopper has room for another elbat by checking if the *n*th earlier elbat has entered the fluxicator, where *n* is the fopper capacity. Getting this calculation right is the trickiest part of developing the spreadsheet model. Check it using fopper capacities of 0 and 1, where you can verify correct operation by inspecting the data yourself. If it works correctly for both of these, it is likely (but not certain) to work correctly for other capacities as well.
- The time the elbat enters the fluxicator. This is the later of (*a*) the time it leaves the encabulator and (*b*) the time the previous elbat leaves the fluxicator.

- The time the elbat leaves the fluxicator. This is a random number evenly distributed from 6 to 24 plus the greater of (*a*) the time the previous elbat left the fluxicator or (*b*) the time this elbat left the encabulator.

 Depending on how you set up your model, you may need additional rows above the first elbat production row; in this way formulas that check on earlier elbats to see if they can proceed into the fopper or fluxicator will have something to refer to. If you don't do this, you will need either to make the formulas in the first few rows of elbat production different from those further down or to use conditional tests (the IF function) to see if a reference to an earlier elbat is valid. All three of these approaches can work.

 The serial number of the last elbat that leaves the fluxicator before 8 hours (480 minutes, if that is your time unit) have elapsed is that day's production.

 Once you have the right formula in each column, you can copy that row down for as many rows as you think you will need. There is no harm in using extra rows, though in a complex simulation the extra computing time could become significant. (How many elbats is it theoretically possible to produce in 8 hours under optimal conditions?)

 A fully instrumented simulation would have additional columns for collecting statistics on encabulation times, fopping times, fluxication times, and waiting time for the fopper to have room. It would also keep track of how the number of elbats in the fopper varies over time, with distributions showing how much of the time the fopper was empty, how much of the time it contained 1 elbat, etc. Adding some of these items to your simulation may help you verify that it is operating properly.

 If you do this exercise by hand, use a generator of decimal digits such as the page-of-a book method on page 325, to determine encabulation and fluxication times. Assign each digit to 6, 8, 10, . . . , 24-minute encabulation or fluxication times. Simulate one 4-hour half-day with a two-elbat fopper, using a paper-and-pencil method such as you saw in the barbershop example on page 311. On the basis of your results, decide whether to try a larger or smaller fopper next. Try one other fopper size for four simulated hours and state which is better.

 Now think about the limiting cases of the above exercise. How many elbats can your factory produce per day if fopper capacity is infinite? If it is zero?

7. You have a simulation model of a gasoline station. The owner wants to know if offering discounts for cash payment with exact change would be profitable. What additional items of information (that is, over and above what you already had to know to develop the basic model) do you need to know, or assume, in order to test this proposal? How do you think you could find or estimate each one? What would the key controllable variable (parameter) of this simulation be?

8. Your bakery sells dark rye bread in a normal distribution with a mean of 100 loaves per day and a standard deviation of 15 loaves per day. Each loaf costs 25¢ to bake and sells for $2.00. Unsold loaves are donated to charity at the end of the day.
   a. How many loaves of dark rye bread should you bake for each day?
   b. After answering part *a*, but before calculating the answer to part *c*, determine upper and lower bounds on the answer to part *c*.
   c. Your bakery sells both dark and light rye bread with daily demand statistics for each as given for dark rye in part *a*. Customers who want one type of bread have a 50 percent likelihood of buying the other if their desired shade of rye bread is not available but the other shade is. (They are probably less willing to accept a prune tart as a substitute, but that's not the issue.) How many loaves of each type of bread should you bake now?

9. This question refers to the supermarket model on page 320.
    a. List at least three simplifications that were made in that model but were not mentioned there.
    b. The states and events of the supermarket model were defined on the assumption that a clerk cannot start checking out a shopper until the bagger, if there is one, has finished bagging the purchases of the previous shopper. Suppose we allowed a bagger to finish one shopper while the clerk was processing the next. How would this change affect the state variables and events of our model?

10. Jacki operates a pet grooming establishment having these characteristics:
- Customer interarrival time is uniformly distributed over 5 to 15 minutes.
- Jacki charges by 30-minute service units, with a fraction of a unit counting as a full unit. Fifty percent of the pets require 30 minutes of service, 50 percent require 60 minutes.
- Ninety percent of the pets require one groomer, 10 percent require two groomers. This is a function of pet size and is not correlated with service time.
- Customers who arrive when all groomers are busy, or whose pets require two groomers and arrive when only one is available, leave and do not return.
- Customers pay $15 per 30 minutes, per groomer. The cost of a grooming therefore ranges from $15 (one groomer, 30 minutes) to $60 (two groomers, 60 minutes).
- Groomers on duty are paid $15 per hour whether they are busy or idle. (This includes all employment costs including employer taxes, fringe benefits, etc.)

    a. Prior to running the simulation in the next step, use the information in the first three bulleted points above to determine, roughly, how many groomers typically will be busy.
    b. Determine the optimum number of groomers by simulating Jacki's business on a computer.
    c. Discussion question: How close was this optimum number to your answer to part *a?* If they differed, why do you think they did?
    d. Jacki's Grooming has become famous because the pets it grooms consistently win prizes in pet shows. It is therefore in great demand and can charge more for its services than other pet grooming establishments charge. Rerun your simulation for a price of $50 per 30 minutes per groomer, assuming the groomers' pay does not change. Has the optimum number of groomers changed? If so, why?

11. We stated on page 330 that the minimum, maximum, and expected profits from the five-product example are, respectively, –$2,000, $4,000, and $1,000. Justify these figures.

REFERENCES

On Simulation

BANK84 Banks, Jerry, and J. S. Carson. *Discrete-Event System Simulation.* Prentice-Hall, Englewood Cliffs, N.J. (1984).

BANK91 Banks, Jerry, Eduardo Aviles, James R. McLaughlin, and Robert C. Yuan. "The Simulator: New Member of the Simulation Family." *Interfaces* 21, no. 2 (March–April 1991), pp. 76–86.

BRAT87 Bratley, Paul, Bennett Fox, and Linus Schrage. *A Guide to Simulation* (2nd ed.). Springer-Verlag, Berlin and New York (1987).

GERT89   Gertner, D. "The Mechanisms of Analogical Learning," in *Similarity and Analogical Reasoning,* eds. S. Vosniadou and A. Ortony. Cambridge University Press, New York (1989), p. 201.

GORD78   Gordon, Geoffrey. *System Simulation* (2nd ed.). Prentice-Hall, Englewood Cliffs, N. J. (1978).

KARI90   Karian, Zaven A., and Edward Dudewicz. *Modern Statistical Systems and GPSS Simulation: The First Course.* W. H. Freeman & Co., New York (1990).

LAW91   Law, Averill M., and W. David Kelton. *Simulation Modeling and Analysis* (2nd ed.). McGraw-Hill, New York (1991).

PEGD80   Pegden, C. D., R. E. Shannon, and R. P. Sadowsky. *Introduction to SIMAN.* System Modeling Corporation, Sewickley, Pa. (1990).

POWE92   Power, Michael, and Elizabeth Jewkes. "Simulating Natural Gas Discoveries." *Interfaces* 22, no. 2 (March–April 1992), pp. 38–51.

PRIT86   Pritzker, A. Alan B. *Introduction to Simulation and SLAM.* John Wiley & Sons, New York (1986).

ROSS90   Ross, Sheldon M. *A Course in Simulation.* MacMillan, New York (1990).

RUBI81   Rubinstein, Reuven Y. *Simulation and the Monte Carlo Method.* John Wiley & Sons, New York (1981).

RUSS83   Russell, E. C. *Building Simulation Models with Simscript II.5.* CACI, Los Angeles (1983).

On Pseudo-random Numbers

ANDE90   Anderson, Stuart L. "Random Number Generators on Vector Supercomputers and Other Advanced Architectures." *SIAM Review* 32, no. 2 (June 1990), pp. 221–251.

CART90   Carta, David G. "Two Fast Implementations of the 'Minimal Standard' Random Number Generator," *Communications of the ACM* 33, no. 1 (January 1990), pp. 87–88.

KNUT81   Knuth, Donald. *Computer Programming: Seminumerical Algorithms* (vol. 2, chap. 3). Addison-Wesley, Reading, Mass. (1981).

RIPL90   Ripley, B. D. "Thoughts on Pseudo-Random Number Generators." *Journal of Computational and Applied Mathematics* 31, no. 1 (July 24, 1990), p. 153.

CASE

Fort Lowell Trading Company
Using Simulation

Tucson was having a bit of much-needed rainfall the following Wednesday when Elizabeth and Miguel returned to Fort Lowell Trading Company headquarters. They signed the now-familiar visitor register and asked the receptionist to let Niels Agger know that they were here.

"Does this rain remind you of home?" Elizabeth asked as soon as Niels had signed them in and placed his ID badge against the reader by the double doors.

"A bit, though it wouldn't be quite as warm there this time of year," he smiled. Looking pensive, he continued, "Actually, what we're going to talk about today has a lot to do with the place I grew up. It might even give me a business reason to go back and visit Aunt Lynne and Uncle Brendan."

"That was somewhere in Canada, wasn't it?" asked Miguel.

"Yes, in Calgary. About two hours east of some of the most beautiful scenery in the world. Not that Tucson isn't, of course. It's just different. We're a bit short of glaciers around these parts."

"That we are," Miguel agreed. "Come to think of it, I've never seen one outside a geography book. But what does Calgary have to do with our decision support systems?"

"I don't know if anyone ever mentioned this to you, but Calgary happens to be the headquarters of our western Canada region. Our sales are really growing there. There's a lot of oil money coming into the city and the region, and something about our stores strike a chord with the customers there. Maybe it's the southwestern aspect—this part of the United States has a lot in common with western Canada, except for the temperature. You probably know that most North American department store chains are from the East, the Midwest, or the northern West Coast. Most of the big stores in Calgary are Canadian chains like Eaton's, but they're all based in eastern Canada. We're probably the only U.S. chain to do well there. We have a separate subsidiary to operate there, of course. It's a Canadian corporation, but it operates like part of the same company.

"Anyhow, our Canadian sales have reached the point where we need a new warehouse to handle the business. We've decided to put it in Calgary because it's our regional HQ, it's easy to reach from here by air, it's in the same time zone we're in or an hour off when they go on Daylight Savings, it's closer to our Asian suppliers than an eastern location would be, and there's good space to be had near the airport north of the city at very reasonable prices."

With that the three reached Niels's office. His usual clutter had been pushed off to one side to make space at the table. A young man was already seated there. He got up as the three entered the room. "Leighton, these are Elizabeth and Miguel, the two Sabino Canyon College students I told you about," Niels introduced them. "This is Leighton Chen, a systems analyst who'll be planning the Calgary warehouse I was just telling you about."

"Delighted to meet you," said Leighton, smiling. "Niels said you know everything and have the solutions to all our problems."

"He did, did he?" laughed Miguel as Niels muttered, "Well, not exactly *all* our problems, but they do seem to know something about this decision support stuff."

"In that case," Leighton continued, "let me tell you about what we're doing. Niels said he'd fill you in on the general background as you walked over here, so I'll skip that part. What we're basically trying to do is design a warehouse that will handle all our Canadian operations for the next 10 years, allowing for adding things like more turret trucks within that period, and will be expandable by adding onto the building beyond that. This means the size of the building, the number of aisles, the kind of equipment, the number of truck doors, the size of the staff—everything. 'Ten years' assumes a certain growth rate, of course. We're really designing for business volume, not for calendar time.

"We have lots of statistics about what the warehouse will have to do. We know how often orders come in and how often shipments go out. We know what kinds of things tend to come in the same shipment—one kind of clothing, for instance, in all sizes and colors—and we figure that isn't going to change much. And we have lots of data about the kinds of things that people tend to order at the same time. So we're in pretty good shape that way."

"This isn't a new problem, of course," he continued. "People have been building warehouses since the Egyptians—remember Joseph telling Pharaoh to store enough grain for seven lean years? Which means people have known about design issues for almost that long. I don't suppose they used automatic palletizers and robotic conveyor belts back then, but their problems were probably just as important to them as today's problems are to us. Either of you ever hear of the Warehousing Education and Research Council?"

"Well, no, not exactly," Elizabeth answered, blushing slightly.

"Not to worry. I hadn't either until I got this project two weeks ago. Their purpose in life is to help people like me. You wouldn't believe how many books they have on designing and running a warehouse. I got a few and they blew me away.

"So, there are several centuries' worth of rules of thumb that tell you how to design a warehouse. But these don't tell you exactly what you need to know.

"We're also not the first people to think about using simulation to try out different layouts. That's not the problem. We know it works. We just don't know how to apply it to our situation right now.

"Our biggest concern is that this warehouse isn't like most others. One difference is that we bring in a lot of things that have to be cleared through Canadian customs. We also have to time a lot of outgoing shipments to catch the last flight of the day to wherever a customer is. Mostly, that's somewhere in Ontario, so today that would be either Air Canada's 5:30 flight or Canadian's at 6. This means a big push toward the end of the day. If we get a shipment that cleared Customs in mid-afternoon and the trucker wants to get home for dinner, it's a problem.

"What this comes down to is that we're looking at a lot of options. We could take a programming language designed for simulations like these, say SIMAN or SiMPLE++, and write it ourselves. There are some packages out there but they tend to be limited. Or, we could just go to a company that's done it before and work with them to do what we need."

EXERCISES

1. Do you feel that using simulation to compare alternatives is a good approach to designing FLTC's Calgary warehouse?

2. How would you define the system to be simulated in this case? Be specific as to what is inside it, what is not. Draw a diagram that shows the boundary clearly and shows what crosses the boundary in both directions. (It may help if you start with items that are obviously either inside or outside the system and work from those ends to the middle. For example, a conveyor belt in the warehouse definitely is in the system, whereas Canadian Airlines' 6 P.M. Flight 978 from Calgary to Toronto definitely is not. Somewhere between being taken off the conveyor belt and being put on that plane, an outgoing shipment leaves the system to be simulated. Where? Of course, you have to deal with the incoming side as well.)

3. What would be three state variables you would use to define the state of this system? (You will have to make some assumptions to answer this question. As part of your assumptions, draw a block diagram of a possible warehouse indicating its major components.)

4. List three events that take place in this system, which affect the values of the above state variables.

5. Chen mentioned several rules of thumb to (hopefully) help a designer come up with an efficient warehouse. Using the Web search engine of your choice, try to find such rules on the Web.

6. Would you recommend that Chen develop the warehouse simulation himself, contract with an outside firm to develop it, or do something else? (Assume he has a bachelor's degree in business with two operations courses and has worked in logistics for FLTC for two years, so he knows more about warehouse operations than the dialogue indicates, and that he's quite comfortable using a variety of computer-based tools in his work, but that he's never developed a simulation model after a simple one in college.) Justify your answer.

CHAPTER 9

Mathematical Models and Optimization

CHAPTER OUTLINE

Introduction

Decision making involves, as you know, choosing a course of action that will benefit an organization (or a person) more than any other course of action could. "More" in this sentence is a mathematical concept: The benefits of the chosen course, however they are measured, must be greater than those of other courses that could be followed. Because the choice process involves (explicitly or implicitly) numerical comparisons, it is not surprising that mathematical methods have a place in decision support systems. Not every DSS uses them, to be sure. Some DSS are used primarily to place information in front of a decision maker who will then choose the best on the basis of experience and intuition. But others do, so it is important for the DSS student to at least be aware of the basic methods they might use.

This chapter will introduce you to several ways that DSS use mathematical methods. Some use mathematics as an alternative to simulation in modeling a system. Where these methods can be used—and they do have their limitations—they can provide answers more quickly, and of more general applicability, than simulation can.

Other mathematical methods are used for optimization. Optimization is the act or the process of choosing the best of several alternatives. Using this term implies that there is a mathematical way to compare alternatives and to decide, objectively, which of them is "best." The function whose value we are evaluating and comparing is called the **objective function** of the optimization process. Optimization figures directly in the sixth category of DSS, Optimization Systems. It also figures in some DSS in the seventh category, Suggestion Systems. There, one good basis for suggesting an alternative is to compare it with others and find them wanting. Even when optimization isn't built in to a DSS, it is often part of the overall decision process that includes the DSS. An example of this would be a complete simulation study to which a DSS provides input via a model. The DSS builder must, for all these reasons, be familiar with basic optimization methods.

This chapter discusses some optimization methods used in DSS. It is not designed to make you an expert on them. Courses in operations analysis can take you in that direction if it matches your interest. Our objective is more modest: to make you aware of the methods that exist and what they can do. When you encounter an optimization problem on the job, you will then know what to look for and will be in a position to deal with the basic issues. Many software packages support one or more optimization methods, but it will be up to you to realize when they might be useful and which one(s) to use. If the system you're working on calls for programming an optimization method from scratch—not the usual situation, but it does come up—you will be able to learn more at that point or have an intelligent discussion with an expert about what is needed.

CHAPTER OBJECTIVES

After you have read and studied this chapter, you will be able to:

1. Describe how the mathematical approaches of queuing theory and Markov process analysis work and what they can contribute to DSS.
2. Summarize how simulation studies, queuing theory, and Markov process analysis compare, and how they can be used together to study a business system.
3. Understand what optimization is and why it is important to many decision support systems.
4. Describe the complete enumeration method, where it applies, and what its limitations are.
5. Identify how calculus can be used in optimization and when it cannot.
6. Discuss the linear programming method, including the difference between linear programming and a linear programming model.
7. Explain how the simplex method can solve linear programming problems.
8. Discuss how the numerical optimization approach of hill-climbing works.
9. Use Box's method for numerical optimization.

9.1 QUEUING MODELS

Simulation, which you read about in the last chapter, carries the system under study step by step through its activities. Its user can then derive statistically valid conclusions from a sufficiently large sample of those activities. **Queuing models,** on the other hand, obtain the statistics of system behavior directly, without following individual events. Where the simplifications that queuing theory requires are acceptable, it determines the average behavior of a system faster than simulation. This is a static model of a dynamic system, as it describes the steady state in which a system settles down rather than how the system behaves minute by minute.

Furthermore, queuing models describe system behavior by formulas that can be evaluated for any desired set of system parameters (controllable variables), rather than as numbers that are calculated for one set of parameters and must be recalculated from scratch for any other set. These characteristics make queuing models a useful adjunct to simulation, especially in DSS used to plan complex systems.

9.1.1 Queuing Theory Concepts

The basic concepts of queuing theory are:

1. The possible states of the system are determined by studying the system, the variables that define its state (its state variables), and their possible combinations.
2. The rates at which each state changes to each other state—that is, the rates of each possible **state transition**—are determined as functions of transaction arrival rates into the system and service times of system processes. These are, in turn, determined by studying the system and its environment. These rates are called **state transition rates.**
3. If the system is in a stable situation (referred to as being in its **steady state**) the average transition rate *into* each state must necessarily equal the average transition rate *out of* that state. This condition on the state probabilities yields equations from which the state probabilities themselves can be found.
4. Solving these equations yields the state probabilities themselves. From these we can determine other statistics of interest, such as average customer waiting times or average queue lengths.

9.1.2 A Queuing Theory Example

Consider a building with a pay phone on each floor. People who want to make telephone calls, and who find it available when they arrive, use it. Those who find the phone in use wait for it to become free. Those who find it in use with someone else already waiting go to a phone on another floor.[1]

The phone therefore has three states: idle, in use with nobody waiting, and in use with a person waiting. Possible state transitions are shown in Figure 9–1. No transitions are shown from state 1 directly to state 3. That is because two customers never arrive at precisely the same instant: There is always an interval, however short, between their arrivals. This can be shown to be true in the limit for random arrivals, though it would not hold for a simulation that chops time into finite steps.

---

[1]We have made assumptions about caller behavior here. These are not the only possible assumptions, of course, but they are simple and we had to assume something. Any model that reflects human behavior must incorporate some such descriptions of it, whether they are based on the model-builder's intuition or extensive observation.

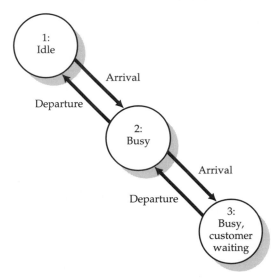

FIGURE 9–1   Pay Phone State Diagram

Suppose the average telephone conversation lasts five minutes. (Phone companies keep statistics on things like this.) Therefore, if a conversation is taking place, there is a 20 percent chance that it will finish in the next minute. In terms of state transitions, transitions from state 2 (phone busy, nobody waiting) to state 1 (phone idle) occur at an average rate of 0.2 per minute, but only if the system was in state 2 to begin with, or else the transition can't occur at all. Therefore, the overall average rate of this transition is 0.2 per minute times the likelihood that the system was in state 2, or P_2. Similarly, 3→2 transitions occur at an average rate of 0.2 per minute times P_3.

We also need the average customer arrival rate, which we can learn by watching the phone. Suppose the average interval between arrivals is ten minutes, for an average arrival rate of 0.1 customers per minute. That means there is a 10 percent chance of a customer arriving in the next minute. Again putting this in terms of state transitions, transitions from state 1 to state 2 occur at an average rate of 0.1 times P_1, and 2→3 transitions take place at an average rate of 0.1 times P_2. These transition rates are shown in Figure 9–2, which is otherwise the same as Figure 9–1.

Now comes the crucial step (see the concept in point 3 on page 348). If the system is in its steady state, *the rate of transition into each state must equal the rate of transition out of it.* The reason for this is that if these rates are at all different, the state probabilities are changing and the system hasn't settled down. (Consider a tub where the rate at which water comes in from the faucet doesn't equal the rate at which water leaves via the drain. The water level in the tub must be rising or falling. If it's not doing either, the two rates must be equal.) Therefore, the rate of transition into state 1 must equal the rate of transition out of state 1, the rate of transition into state 2 must equal the rate of transition out of state 2, and the rate of transition into state 3 must equal the rate of transition out of state 3.

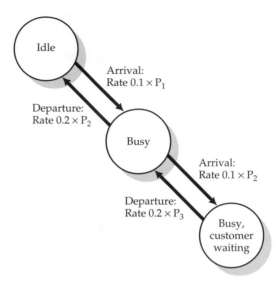

FIGURE 9–2 Pay Phone State Diagram with Transition Rates

In the case of state 1, there is only one type of transition into it, the 2→1 transition, and only one out of it, the 1→2 transition. We can write the condition of equal transition rates as follows, in what is called the **equation of balance** for state 1:

$$0.2\,P_2 = 0.1\,P_1$$

Similarly, we can write the equation of balance for state 2:

$$0.1\,P_1 + 0.2\,P_3 = 0.1\,P_2 + 0.2\,P_2$$

which we can simplify, by combining the two terms on the right side, to

$$0.1\,P_1 + 0.2\,P_3 = 0.3\,P_2$$

and for state 3:

$$0.1\,P_2 = 0.2\,P_3$$

These three equations have three unknowns, the three P_i. Unfortunately, they are linearly dependent on each other (the first and third, added algebraically, yield the second) so there are only two independent equations in three unknowns. This is true of all queuing theory models: If a system has n states there are always n equations of balance in the P_i, which are equivalent to $n - 1$ linearly independent equations. Since we need n independent equations to find n unknowns, we need a third independent equation here to find the P_i. This third equation comes from the fact that the system is always in one of its three states (why?), so the three state probabilities must sum to 1:

$$P_1 + P_2 + P_3 = 1$$

We can now solve these equations to obtain the state probabilities for the telephone as $P_1 = 4/7$, $P_2 = 2/7$ and $P_3 = 1/7$. What do these numbers mean?

- Since $P_1 = 4/7$, the phone is idle 4/7 of the time. Conversely, it is busy $P_2 + P_3 = 3/7$ of the time. This might suggest the income to expect from the telephone, which would help us decide if it is worth installing one.
- If potential customers arrive every 10 minutes and leave after 5, we would expect the phone to be busy exactly half the time. Lower usage must be due to customers seeing a line and leaving, "balking" in operations research terminology. Since the usage ratio of 3/7 is 6/7 of what we would expect in the absence of departures, we know that 1/7 of its potential customers went elsewhere. This information can help decide whether or not to install a second phone near the existing one.
- Someone is waiting by the phone 1/7 of the time, about eight-and-a-half minutes out of every hour or over an hour during the working day. This might suggest installing a soda machine nearby.
- The average customer who does not go away immediately waits for one minute, 40 seconds to use the phone. (We won't go through the math here, since the purpose is simply to show you the kinds of information this method can provide, but it's in any book on queuing theory and many on operations analysis.) Managers can use average waiting time information to decide if the level of service being provided is satisfactory.

9.1.3 Generalizing the Solution

Decision makers often want to investigate the effect of different arrival and service times on their conclusions: What would happen if the average conversation were to last four minutes, or six? What would happen if we removed one of the five pay phones in the building, increasing the arrival rate at the remaining ones? To study several alternatives, it helps to represent the state transition rates by algebraic symbols. Operations researchers use the lowercase Greek letters λ (lambda) for mean interarrival time and μ (mu) for mean service time. With these symbols, the equations of balance (only two of which, as you recall, are independent) are

$$\mu P_2 = \lambda P_1$$

$$\lambda P_1 + \mu P_3 = (\mu + \lambda) P_2$$

$$\lambda P_2 = \mu P_3$$

To solve these, it is convenient to define the **utilization ratio** $\rho = \lambda/\mu$, which is 0.5 with the numbers used earlier. In terms of ρ (lowercase Greek rho) the equations become

$$P_2 = \rho P_1$$

$$\rho P_1 + P_3 = (1 + \rho) P_2$$

$$\rho P_2 = P_3$$

Solving these yields

$$P_1 = 1 / (1 + \rho + \rho^2)$$
$$P_2 = \rho / (1 + \rho + \rho^2)$$
$$P_3 = \rho^2 / (1 + \rho + \rho^2)$$

We can insert any value for ρ into these formulas and obtain the state probabilities directly. For example, if conversations average 6 minutes and arrivals still average 10 minutes apart, $\rho = 0.6$. This yields $P_1 = 0.510$, $P_2 = 0.306$ and $P_3 = 0.184$. Of an additional 10 percent potential utilization, 6.1 percent went into actual utilization. (The idle time dropped from 57.1 percent to 51.0 percent, so the busy time went from 43.9 percent to 49.0 percent. We could also obtain the busy time by adding P_2 and P_3.) The remaining 3.9 percent is reflected in a higher level of balking. It means that, because people make longer calls, more potential customers will find the phone busy with someone waiting and will walk away.

9.1.4 Arrival and Departure Time Distributions

We made, but did not state, an important mathematical assumption in the above example: that interarrival and service times have the given means but are otherwise totally random. If they were not totally random, the results would have been different.

Suppose, for instance, that interarrival times were constant. One potential telephone user arrives precisely on the hour, another at 10 minutes past, a third at 20 minutes past, and so on. Suppose also that all conversations took precisely five minutes. These "distributions" have the same means as our earlier ones, but the results are quite different. In this idealized situation nobody would ever wait to use the phone, let alone find another person waiting. The more regular the arrival and service times, the better most systems behave in minimizing waiting times and maximizing resource utilization. (This is why doctors and many other professionals see clients by appointment instead of waiting around their offices in case a patient or client shows up.)

The assumption of random interarrival and service times corresponds to an **exponential distribution** of these times as shown in Figure 9–3. This distribution has a high probability of short times. It allows for long times with decreasing likelihood. An important characteristic of the exponential distribution is that *knowing the elapsed time since the last event does not help predict the next one.* For example, knowing that a telephone conversation has already lasted an hour does not help predict whether or not it will end in the next minute. (Human phone conversations behave this way, though some data transmission situations do not. The increase in data traffic over the past decade or so has forced telephone companies to discard many time-honored assumptions.) This is an important underpinning of queuing theory, since it means that the mean transition rate from one state to another is a constant. Arrivals usually behave similarly: In the absence of a controlling factor such as a congested parking lot entrance, knowing that nobody has entered a supermarket for 10 minutes does not affect the statistical likelihood that a

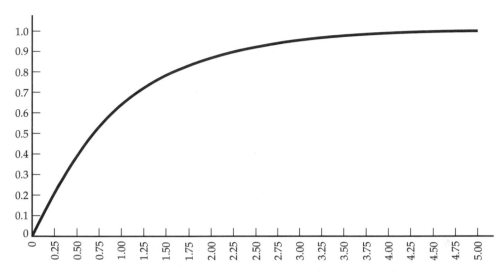

FIGURE 9–3 Cumulative Distribution Function of Exponential Distribution

shopper will show up in the next five seconds. The concept of an event being "due to happen," simply because it hasn't happened for a while, is intuitively attractive but does not match most real situations.

Queuing models can be solved only for exponentially distributed transaction arrivals and service times. Fortunately, this is not as restrictive as it might seem. Passing a customer through two processes, each with mean service time of one minute, creates a composite process with mean service time of two minutes but smaller variance than a single exponentially distributed process with a two-minute mean would have. Using more subprocesses reduces the variance still further and can approximate a normal service time distribution. Using several processes in a model in this way does not imply that the system itself consists of a series of processes. It is just a mathematical trick to allow us to model some types of reality more closely than an exponential distribution would.

Such multistage distributions are called **Erlang distributions,** after a Danish telephone engineer who pioneered queuing theory in the early 1900s. They are useful in modeling processes where a given step takes a relatively constant time with small variation, such as the access time of a computer disk drive. Their disadvantage is that they increase the number of states in the model, and hence the number of equations of balance and the work of solving them in closed form. Figure 9–4 shows a two-stage Erlang distribution (a "2-Erlang" distribution for short) and a 10-Erlang distribution alongside the exponential distribution. You can see how the Erlang distributions start out flatter, indicating fewer very short activity times; get steeper and cross the exponential, indicating more activity times toward the middle; and then flatten out again as activity times rise far above the mean.

We can also create distributions with *greater* variance than the exponential distribution. This is done by replacing a real process with two parallel exponential

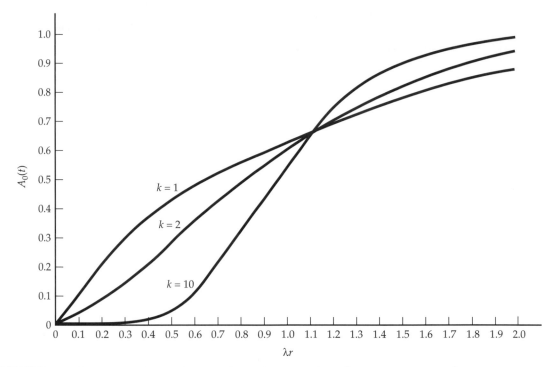

FIGURE 9–4 Cumulative Distribution Functions of Exponential, 2-Stage Erlang, and 10-Stage Erlang Distributions

processes in the model, one of which has a much smaller mean time than the other, and sending transactions at random to one or the other. The resulting distribution is called **hyperexponential.** Hyperexponential distributions are good for modeling some data communication connection times or the execution times of user commands to a computer. Here, too, there is no implication that the system itself puts transactions through one of two processes, either a "long" one or a "short" one. The two processes that we have created are a mathematical fiction designed to create a desired service or arrival time distribution from a combination of exponential ones.

9.1.5 Queuing Theory on a Computer

Because queuing theory is basically a mathematical technique that does not depend on a computer to formulate or solve its equations, the first requisite for using it in a DSS is sufficient mathematical brainpower to carry out those steps. Although the DSS developer need not have this brainpower personally, it must be available to his or her organization.

The equations, once they have been developed, are simple (sometimes trivial) to put into a computer. If the overall DSS lends itself to the spreadsheet paradigm, the formula capability of any spreadsheet program is fully sufficient for queuing theory calculations. So are the computation capabilities of data management programs, even low-end ones such as Microsoft Access or Claris FileMaker. If the

DSS uses custom programming, adding a few statements to handle queuing theory calculations should not tax its programmer.

You may encounter a reference to simulation or spreadsheet models of queues. It's important to read these carefully as the term *queue* does not always imply queuing theory. A queue, in operations terminology, is a waiting line for anything.[2] Queuing theory is one way to analyze queues. Simulation is another. You don't necessarily have queuing theory just because you have a queue.

9.2 MARKOV PROCESS MODELS

9.2.1 The Markov Process Model Concept

A **Markov process** is a system that progresses from one state to another over time, where the likelihood of its being in a given state at any time step depends only on its previous state and not on its prior history.

Consider, for example, the weather model in Figure 9–5. This model tells us that if we know today's weather, we have a better-than-random chance at guessing tomorrow's. If it's sunny now, there's a 60 percent chance of sun tomorrow, and so on.

Given an initial state (the weather on day x), we can determine the probabilities of the next state (the weather on day $x + 1$) from the transition probabilities shown in the diagram. A matrix notation is convenient for this purpose. The **state transition matrix** corresponding to Figure 9–5 is

$$T = \begin{pmatrix} 0.6 & 0.4 & 0.1 \\ 0.3 & 0.2 & 0.5 \\ 0.1 & 0.4 & 0.4 \end{pmatrix}$$

FIGURE 9–5 State Diagram of Weather System

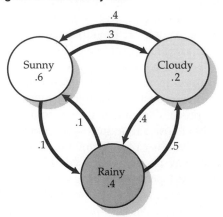

---

[2]Or in English as spoken in Great Britain. There, people use *queue* where a North American would say *line*. You'll hear them refer to a bus queue—or, using the term as a verb, "queuing up for a bus."

Each entry in this matrix represents the probability of a transition from the state corresponding to the entry's column, to the state corresponding to its row, in one time period. For instance, the 0.4 in the center of the top row represents the probability of a transition from state 2 (cloudy) to state 1 (sunny). Since the system must always go to some state, the sum of all the entries in a column must always be 1.

To use this matrix, we express the current state of the system as a vector. We represent the state "today is sunny" as (1,0,0). If we're not sure what the weather is (or will be), there is more than one nonzero entry in the state vector. Since the weather is always one of those three, **state vector** elements must always sum to 1.

To get tomorrow's probabilities, we multiply today's state vector by the transition matrix:

$$x_{k+1} = Tx_k$$

For this weather example, that becomes

$$\bar{x}_{k+1} = \begin{pmatrix} 0.6 & 0.4 & 0.1 \\ 0.3 & 0.2 & 0.5 \\ 0.1 & 0.4 & 0.4 \end{pmatrix} \begin{pmatrix} 1 \\ 0 \\ 0 \end{pmatrix} = \begin{pmatrix} 0.6 \\ 0.3 \\ 0.1 \end{pmatrix}$$

For the day after tomorrow, we repeat the multiplication:

$$x_{k+2} = Tx_{k+1}$$

which in this case yields state (weather) probabilities of (0.49, 0.29, 0.22).

Eventually this process converges and we reach the steady-state system probabilities. In the case of weather, this means we have gone far enough into the future that knowing today's weather is of no predictive value. (Theoretically, it will never be of no value at all, but its value will shrink into insignificance.) In general, this means we have gone far enough into the future that knowing the initial state of the system we are studying is of no (or insignificant) predictive value.

The weather model lends itself perfectly to this formalism because a time scale is inherent in its description. People are used to discussing weather in a time frame of days. To formulate the pay phone example of Section 9.1 as a Markov process, we must choose a time period between steps. From a theoretical point of view state transition rates apply only to infinitely small time steps, since for a finite time step there is a nonzero probability of two events occurring in one interval. Fortunately, the Markov process equations always converge to the correct answer despite this. We must only choose a time step short enough to leave, for every state of the system, a positive probability of remaining in that state.

Consider state 1 of the pay phone, where it is idle. Transitions out of state 1 occur at an average rate of 0.1 per minute. There is about a 1 percent probability of two customers arriving during the same minute, and about a 0.1 percent probability of three showing up. For a Markov process approach we ignore these. We can use a one-minute time step, as it would give a 90 percent probability of remaining in state 1. We can also use a five-minute time step. A 10-minute time step would reduce the probability of staying in state 1 to zero and would therefore not work, nor would a larger step. We could use a nine-minute time step, but it approaches the limit and our calculations would converge slowly. (Exercise 7 considers transitions into and out of all three states.)

A Markov process analysis of the pay phone problem will, if we make no errors, give the same answer as queuing theory did. As long as we define states in the same way and use the same transition rates, the two formulations are equivalent because both assume exponential distributions of service and interarrival times.

9.2.2 Computer Calculations for Markov Processes

Because of its apparent simplicity, programming a Markov model on a computer doesn't seem a daunting task. It's just one matrix multiplication after another! Specialized packages for Markov process calculations hardly exist. Two points are worth noting before you embark on programming one, though.

1. Realistic Markov transition matrices are quite sparse. That is, most of their elements are zero. A full-size model may have hundreds of states. However, each state can only go to a few other states because only a few events can occur in each state. A $4,000 \times 4,000$ transition matrix in 32-bit floating-point form (about six significant decimal digits) occupies 64MB of computer storage. This would fill the entire RAM of most 1999-era desktop computers, without allowing space for the resident portion of the operating system and an application to manipulate the matrix, and would tax some larger ones. However, this is a **sparse matrix:** Almost all of those 64MB will contain zeros. The locations and contents of the nonzero matrix elements can be stored in far less space. Still more space can be saved if need be, because Markov transition matrices usually contain identical values repeated many times in systematically related locations. Software packages that manipulate sparse matrices efficiently exist and are worth investigating.

2. Because of round-off errors in computing, the sum of the state probability vector elements will drift away from 1.000000 . . . after many iterations. The vector must be renormalized after every hundred iterations or so. **Renormalization** involves summing the elements of the probability vector and dividing every element of the vector by this sum. For example, if they add up to 1.005, dividing every vector element by 1.005 will restore their sum to 1.000. Repeating this renormalization from time to time will squash round-off errors before they get out of control.

9.3 SIMULATION, QUEUING THEORY, AND MARKOV PROCESSES COMPARED

All three of the approaches we have described for modeling dynamic systems—simulation in the previous chapter, queuing theory and Markov processes in this—have advantages and disadvantages in decision support applications.

One perspective on their relationship is that simulation provides a dynamic model of a dynamic system, whereas the other two approaches provide static models of a dynamic system after it has settled down to its steady state behavior. Simulation tracks what goes on inside a system and forces us to infer its characteristics by summarizing a large number of observations. The others tell us these characteristics but do not give us the same visibility into its innards.

Queuing theory provides the most general solution to a given problem and often the fastest as well. Simulation model results are the least general and usually take the longest time to obtain—because of both programming time and computer execution time. Markov process analyses are intermediate on both counts. Therefore, at first glance one should prefer queuing theory to a Markov process analysis and the Markov process approach to simulation. This is true as long as all three methods are feasible. This is not always the case. Specific points to consider are:

1. Can the system in question be modeled with sufficient realism by a reasonably small (that is, solvable) number of states?
2. Do exponential distributions of interevent times, or distributions that can be derived from the exponential without a great deal of added complexity, fit the actual distributions acceptably well?
3. Does the DSS developer have enough comfort with the mathematics, or have access to skilled mathematicians, to develop a queuing model of the system and solve it, in closed form or numerically?
4. Can the necessary decision-making information be obtained from the limited data that queuing theory and Markov process analyses yield?

These questions will often lead the analyst to simulation as a practical matter. It has often been said, "When all else fails, try simulation." However, the choice is not always either-or. The methods are complementary. A useful approach may include a simulation model for detailed insight into a system, coupled with one or both mathematical approaches. The mathematical models indicate the overall trends to be expected in system behavior and, applied to limiting cases, serve as a check on simulation results. A mathematical check on limiting cases is often a valuable DSS development aid even if the eventual DSS will incorporate only a simulation model.

9.4 OPTIMIZATION

The purpose of any DSS is to help decision makers choose the best course of action for an organization. Sometimes "best" can be interpreted numerically: the highest return on investment, the lowest cost for a required capacity, the highest score on a weighted combination of factors. In such situations, computers can often help people find the course of action that leads to the highest, or lowest, numerical score. The term **optimization methods** encompasses the techniques they use to do this.

9.4.1 Complete Enumeration

The simplest optimization method is to evaluate all the possible choices, compare their merits using a suitable yardstick, and pick the best. As its name implies, that's what **complete enumeration** does. The Kepner-Tregoe decision-making method, which you read about in Section 2.7, works this way.

Complete enumeration is feasible only when the options or the decision parameters are discrete and few in number. It might be a reasonable optimization approach for choosing among four alternative leasing plans, five building sites, or six applicants for a job. In the supermarket example of the previous chapter, 65 possible combinations of checkout clerks and baggers could be used. Complete enumeration can deal with this problem, but only because the nature of the problem lends itself to a clear, two-dimensional presentation and then only if enough computer time is available. One or two hundred combinations push the limit for complete enumeration. A real analyst faced with the supermarket problem should also consider other methods, especially if the analysis is to be repeated regularly: perhaps for several supermarkets, perhaps over and over again for one store under different conditions and for an extended period of time.

Complete enumeration is not possible in theory when the decision parameters are continuous. When parameters are continuous, they can theoretically take on an infinite number of values over any range of interest. We can't evaluate an infinite number of possibilities in a finite time. The same applies in practice to parameters that are "nearly continuous," such as a price that can theoretically vary over a million-dollar range by 1¢ steps.

However, we can often apply complete enumeration to continuous or nearly continuous problems by choosing a reasonable number of points spaced over the interval of interest. Suppose we want to choose the best price for a new aircraft based on our predicted production cost and estimated price-demand curve. If we know that it will sell for somewhere in the range of $2 to $3 million, we could predict profit at prices ranging from $2 million to $3 million by steps of $50,000, a total of 21 different prices. Once we have narrowed the optimum price down to an interval of $50,000 or $100,000 by this method, we could try steps of $1,000 or $5,000 within that interval. This process can continue until we have sufficient precision for the question at hand. For aircraft prices, the nearest $500 is surely sufficient. The nearest $10,000 may well suffice, given the approximate nature of price-demand curves, the common practice of setting such prices at round numbers, and the fact that prices in this range are often just the starting point for negotiations anyhow.

Complete enumeration can also be used as part of a larger optimization process. Suppose some of the controllable variables (another term for decision parameters) have a few discrete values each and others don't. We can enumerate the possible combinations of the discrete variables. Each combination defines a smaller problem, in which only the remaining (continuous) variables change. We can then use one of the other techniques of this chapter to optimize the solution for that combination of the discrete variables, a much simpler process than optimizing the entire set of variables at once. After thus obtaining the optimum solution for each combination of the discrete variables, we can use complete enumeration to compare them and get the optimum solution to the problem as a whole.

From a computer point of view, programming complete enumeration is a "brute force" approach that relies on computer time instead of prior analysis or more sophisticated search techniques. The programming aspect is usually trivial, involving nested loops around a kernel that evaluates each alternative. The choice between computer time and thinking time is highly situational: If computer time is readily available, and the expertise to program a less resource-intensive method harder to come by, complete enumeration may be the best approach from the overall business point of view.

Decision trees, which we discussed on page 48, support the complete enumeration approach to optimizing a decision. If the states of nature at the ends of the branches of a decision tree are represented by continuous distributions, calculus can be used to compare them [MALL75]. The use of calculus here is subject to the limitations discussed in Section 9.4.3.

9.4.2 Random Search

A related method to complete enumeration is random search. In **random search** the analyst does not try to evaluate the objective function for all possible combinations of the controllable variables. Rather, the analyst (or the analyst's computer program) chooses several, perhaps a few hundred, random combinations of the controllable variables. After a large number of runs (the term *large* is not precisely defined, but after a while additional runs will not improve the result) the highest output is taken as the best estimate of the optimum.

We might use random search in a business optimization problem such as choosing an advertising schedule. There are simply too many advertising media to be able to try all possible combinations. Advertisers use rules of thumb—"Don't run ads for fishing rods in *Vegetarian Times*"—to cut the options down to a reasonable amount but can never really be sure that these rules did not eliminate some good possibilities. A computer program that tried a few hundred or a few thousand randomly chosen combinations to see if it could improve matters might be a good idea.

As another example, random search can be used to pick common stocks for investment purposes. Suppose you have developed a model that predicts stock prices on the basis of historical day-to-day price changes and the corresponding trading volumes on each day. (Such models are actually used, based on the idea that a price change associated with high trading volume is more likely to indicate a trend than a price change which took place with low volume.) You cannot, given your available computing resources, apply your model to every stock on all possible markets. You can, however, pick 100 stocks at random and use it on them. In doing so, you would assume that those 100 stocks are likely to include some good investments. Even though it might miss the best ones, the difference between the ones it picks and the best is likely to be less than the inaccuracy of your model.

The random search technique cannot guarantee convergence. Its results cannot be proven optimal in a mathematical sense but are usually quite acceptable for business decision making.

Random search is often a good way to optimize a system for which you have developed a simulation model. Applying random search to the output of a simulation study raises this question: Is it better to use several runs at one point, thus getting a better estimate of the function value at that point, or to expend the same computer time in trying more random points? The jury is out on this issue. As a practical suggestion, use enough runs at each point to estimate the function value at that point to within the accuracy to which you want to find the optimum. Less accuracy than this in estimating the function value at one point may lead to choosing the wrong point. More will be a waste of your time and the computer's, especially if you could have tried more points instead.

9.4.3 The Calculus Approach

We learned in freshman differential **calculus** that the **derivative** of a function is zero when value of the function is at its maximum.[3] We learned that we can find the maximum of a function by finding its derivative, equating this derivative to zero, and solving for the value of the unknown variable, which is usually called x.

In using this method, we must watch out for points at which the derivative is zero but which are not the maximum we seek. Figure 9–6 shows the maximum of a function (indicated by the letter A) and the three ways we can go wrong.

1. The derivative of the function is also zero at a minimum (B).
2. If the function has one or more inflection points, its derivative is zero there as well (C).
3. If the function has several local maxima (D), only one is the global maximum.

The same conceptual approach works with more than one unknown as well. Suppose we have a function z of x and y, written $z(x,y)$. Geometrically, this function describes a surface (such as the one in Figure 9–7) whose height above the x-y

FIGURE 9–6 Points at Which the Derivative of a Function Equals Zero

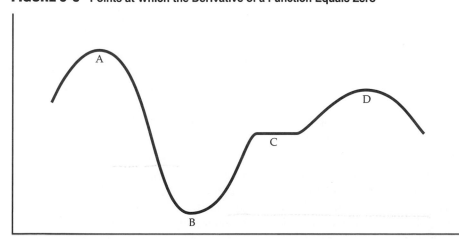

---

[3]This discussion assumes we are trying to maximize the objective function. You should be able to apply it to the reverse situation—that is, minimizing the objective function—easily.

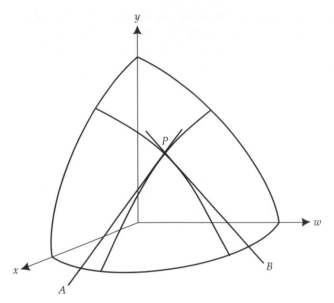

FIGURE 9–7 Surface Showing Partial Derivatives

plane is the value of the function z. By treating y as a constant and differentiating z with respect to x, we obtain the **partial derivative** of z with respect to x. This partial derivative is written $\partial z/\partial x$ where ∂ is the Cyrillic (the alphabet used with Russian and some other Slavic languages) equivalent of the lowercase d used in differential calculus. Similarly, by holding x constant and differentiating z with respect to y, we obtain $\partial z/\partial y$. We can now set both partial derivatives equal to zero and get two equations in the two unknowns x and y. Solving these equations gives the values of x and y that correspond to the maximum value of the function z. If the equations have several solutions, complete enumeration of z at each solution pair tells us which (x, y) pair truly gives the maximum. The same approach works with functions of more than two variables, though we can't visualize their geometric representation.

Behind this facile paragraph lies a world of complexities that make calculus less useful for optimization than one might hope. Among its chief limitations are

1. The variable we are trying to optimize must be <u>continuous.</u> We can't move by infinitesimal steps from "Buy a Grumman Gulfstream" to "Buy a Learjet," or from "install one lathe" to "install two lathes."
2. We <u>must have a mathematical expression</u> for the function we are trying to optimize. If its value can only be obtained numerically, perhaps by simulation or by a Markov process approach, we cannot differentiate it even if it is continuous.
3. The functions we must optimize may be so complex that differentiating them, and solving the resulting equations for the values that make the partial derivatives equal to zero, are beyond the ability of the people charged with the task.

4. The mathematical optimum may lie in a region of the surface which, due to **constraints** on the problem (limits on the values of one or more variables), is not a feasible solution. Basic calculus methods do not handle constraints well or at all. Linear programming, discussed in the next section, can solve some problems in which constraints are a factor.

Calculus remains a useful tool in economic problems that deal with market elasticities, fixed and variable costs, and desired price and production levels. The optimal order quantity problem, which you may have studied (or may study in the future) in operations analysis, is an example of such an application area. There, calculus is used to balance the cost of carrying inventory over time, given the cost of capital, against the cost of placing many small orders. Calculus can also sometimes be applied to a simplified version of a problem to gain insight and provide a general feel for the issues, even if other methods then have to be used to solve the problem in all its complex detail. (This is similar to how one might apply queuing theory to a simplified model of a dynamic system, gaining insight into its behavior and providing a check on simulation study results.) The limitations of this method keep it from wider use in business decision making.

9.4.4 Linear Programming (LP)

Linear programming (LP) is an optimization technique for problems that satisfy three conditions:

1. The objective function (what we're trying to maximize or minimize) is a linear function of system outputs. That is, it is of the form

$$y = a_1x_1 + a_2x_2 + a_3x_3 + \ldots$$

2. Each system output is a (nonnegative) linear combination of system inputs.
3. Some or all quantities of system inputs are constrained to be above or below certain known values.

The typical application of linear programming is resource allocation. For example, suppose our firm sells red cubes, orange cubes, and unpainted cubes. We know that

- Red and orange cubes are produced from unpainted cubes and paint.
- Producing a red cube requires an unpainted cube and one ounce of red paint. Producing an orange cube requires an unpainted cube, half an ounce of red paint, and half an ounce of yellow paint.
- We make a profit of $2 per orange cube, $1.50 per red cube, and $1 per unpainted cube. These figures reflect selling prices and all costs associated with painting orange and red cubes.
- We have on hand 100 unpainted cubes, 20 ounces of red paint, and 10 ounces of yellow paint.
- Leftover paint is of no value.

One feasible solution would be to leave the paint on the shelf and sell the 100 unpainted cubes. Our profit would be $100 \times \$1 = \$100$. Since we have the paint, however, we can do better if we use it. If we paint 20 cubes red, using up all our red paint, our profit is $80 \times \$1 + 20 \times \$1.50 = \$80 + \$30 = \$110$. The best solution, as found by linear programming, is to use all the yellow paint and half the red paint to produce 20 orange cubes, and the remaining 10 ounces of red paint to produce 10 red cubes. Our profit is then $115.

In this example the optimal solution to the problem used all our resources. We had no unpainted cubes, red paint, or yellow paint left over when we were done. In general this will not be the case; some resources are usually left over. Here, if we had more yellow paint than red paint, we would have had no use for the excess yellow paint unless we could find a new market for yellow cubes. That sort of strategic planning, while within the province of corporate management, is beyond what linear programming (or any other numerical optimization method) can do.

We can visualize a linear programming problem in two variables on a graph such as Figure 9–8. It shows a plant that produces a mix of two products, A and B. Product A, which yields a profit of $2 per unit produced, requires two units of input S and one unit of input T. Product B reverses the proportions, using one unit of S and two units of T, and yields a profit of $3 per unit produced. We have 100 units of each input on hand.

In mathematical notation, our objective function is $2A + 3B$. It is related to the inputs by the equations $A = 2S + T$ and $B = S + 2T$, and is subject to the constraints $S \leq 100$ and $T \leq 100$.

FIGURE 9–8   Two-Resource LP Diagram

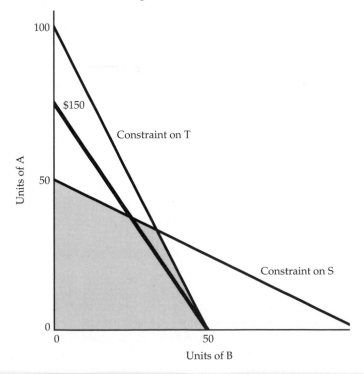

The axes in Figure 9–8 represent the amounts of product A and product B we choose to produce. The lines forming the shaded four-sided polygon outline the **feasible region** for this problem. The axes bound the region from the left and below, since we cannot produce a negative amount of A or B. The steeper of the two diagonal lines represents what we can produce with 100 units of T: for each two units of A we produce, using one unit of T each, we can produce one less unit of B. The other diagonal line represents the S constraint in a similar fashion.

The heavy line in Figure 9–8 represents one of the parallel lines of equal profit, specifically that for $150. One of its ends represents producing 75 units of B only for a profit of $2 each. We can't do this, because we don't have enough T on hand, but the point serves to anchor one end of the line. Its other end represents producing 50 units of A only at a profit of $3 each (which we could do). Any choice along a given line represents the same profit and is therefore equally desirable. The highest-profit solution is on the line parallel to the $150 line, which passes through the point where the S and T constraint lines cross. There we produce 33 1/3 units each of A and B, use all our inputs, and earn a profit of $166.66 and 2/3 of a cent.

You may ask, How can we produce a third of a unit of a product? A continuous production process can produce fractional units of output. A paper mill can produce any desired length of paper. Its output need not be an exact multiple of our unit of measure, which is after all arbitrary. (An integer number of feet is unlikely to be an integer number of meters.) Other production processes deal in discrete units: A motorcycle factory cannot ship half a motorcycle if it has an odd number of tires in its inventory. In this case, the linear programming solution guides us to the vicinity of the optimal choice. We can then test the integer solutions adjacent to the LP solution by complete enumeration. In our example we might inspect the four options shown in Figure 9–9:

- 30 units of A and 35 of B, for a $165 profit (and 5 units of S left over).
- 32 units of A and 34 of B, for a $166 profit (and 2 units of S left over).
- 33 units each of A and B, for a $165 profit (and 1 unit each of S and T left over).
- 34 units of A and 32 of B, for a $164 profit (and 2 units of T left over).

Being rational managers in the sense of Chapter 2, we choose the second option to maximize our profits. This assumes that leftover resources have no value, like the paint in the previous example. If they did, we could add this value into the objective function as a new type of output that has the specified value and uses one unit of the specified resource. This would complicate the equations somewhat but is quite compatible with linear programming concepts. In this example, if leftover units of S are worth at least 34¢, we would select the first option over the second. (Why?)

This example shows many of the characteristics of all LP problems, though we can't visualize them physically once they get beyond three outputs:

- There is a feasible region bounded by the constraints.
- The constraints are straight lines in two dimensions, planes in three dimensions, hyperplanes in four or more. They are never curved because, by definition, LP only deals with linear equations.

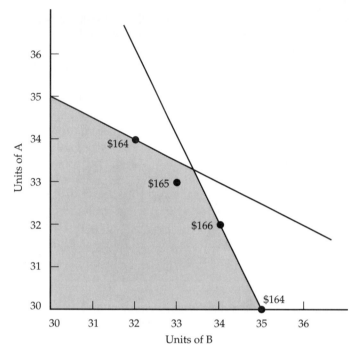

FIGURE 9–9 **Four Decision Options in LP Problem**

- The optimal solution is typically at a corner of the feasible region, or at a nearby point that yields an integer solution if one is required. For some combinations of resource usages and profit figures an entire edge of the feasible region may be optimal. In the above example, if the profit from selling a unit of B were twice that from a unit of A, the equal-profit lines would have the same slope as the T constraint. Any point along that constraint line would then be an optimal solution.

You may hear people refer to a linear programming *model.* The model here is the mathematical model of the production system: that each unit of output uses a linear combination of input quantities, that each unit of output has a value and that input quantities are constrained. The equation $y = . . .$ on page 363 is a linear programming model. To the degree that some characteristics of the real production system are not linear, or are not included in the model, the model simplifies reality. The major—some might say the only—use of a linear programming *model* is in the linear programming solution *process.*

The most common method for solving linear programming problems is called the **simplex method.**[4] It was introduced by George B. Dantzig shortly after World

---

[4]The name comes from the mathematical concept of a *simplex,* an *n*-dimensional structure with $n + 1$ data points. A one-dimensional simplex is a line segment. A two-dimensional simplex is a triangle. A three-dimentional simplex is a pyramid with a triangular base (a tetrahedron). The term does not imply that the method is "simple." It isn't.

War II. The simplex method starts at any corner (or vertex) of the feasible region. It then determines whether profit increases or decreases as one moves from that vertex to an adjacent vertex. This process continues until the optimal solution has been found. The simplex method always converges to the solution if one exists, although it may take a great deal of time for large problems.

Despite its intuitive appeal and the sound of its name, programming the simplex method is far from simple. Determining where vertices lie, given a set of linear constraint equations, is far from a trivial task. Fortunately, many software packages (often referred to as linear programming *codes* in professional literature) have been written to solve linear programming problems. They can run on virtually any computer you are likely to encounter. A DSS developer must be aware of the linear programming concept and its areas of applicability but does not have to be able to program its solution methods from scratch.

Several packages are available for solving LP programs on personal computers. The April 1997 issue of *OR/MS Today* summarized the characteristics of 40 of them. (They revisit this topic every two or three years, so you may be able to find a more recent version of their study as you read this.) They found that most of the packages use the same algorithms and run on the same or similar platforms (nearly everything runs under Windows, with many also supporting UNIX, Mac OS, and a few other environments) but that there are significant differences among them. The most important functional difference was between **solvers,** which simply provide a numerical solution to a problem already formulated for linear programming, and **modelers,** which offer a more complete environment for dealing with linear allocation problems. They also found a wide price range, with some products available at any of several price points depending on the size of the problem one wishes to solve. Comparative reviews are also published from time to time in this and other journals.

The message here is not that you should necessarily get the best package according to any review. Most reviews find no single "best" package by all criteria. It is that

- Many linear programming packages exist.
- All have pros and cons.
- Different strengths and weaknesses matter in different situations and to different people.

When you are faced with an on-the-job problem that LP seems to address, you will have to check out the software available to you at that time and compare its capabilities with *your* needs.

The major drawback of linear programming as an optimization method follows from the three conditions at the start of this section. Many real-world optimization problems do not produce outputs that are linear functions of their inputs. Advertising exposures, for example, may (if we ignore quantity discounts, which happen to be significant in the ad business) be a linear function of advertising expenditures in various media—but the effect of multiple exposures on consumer mind-share is far from linear, and it's that effect that really matters. Nonlinear programming methods exist but are not as well-developed as the linear ones. If the conditions of the start of this section apply to your decision support problem, try LP. If not, look further.

An adjunct to any of these methods, which is useful in solving linear programming problems where the solutions and resources are constrained to integer values, is the **branch-and-bound approach** [NEMH88, SCHR86, and other sources your school library undoubtedly has]. With this approach, the problem is first solved *without* the restriction to integer values, much as we first did in the given example. Then we proceed in this way:

1. We can create a series of subproblems from the original problem by assigning the values on either side of the fractional value in the solution to one of the variables. For instance, we could define subproblems in the given problem in which we produced 32, 33, and 34 units of A. This is the *branching* part of branch-and-bound.
2. The optimum solution to the entire problem must be the optimum solution to one (or, unusually but possibly, more than one) of these subproblems. Therefore, we solve each of them—again for the optimum without integer constraints, though at least one of the variables must be an integer because of the way the subproblems were defined. In solving them, we use the simplex method or any other approach we prefer.
3. We continue to do this, defining subsubproblems for each subproblem and so on, until we've checked out all the possibilities. Fortunately, we don't have to actually evaluate them all. If the optimal solution to a subproblem *without* integer constraints is no better than the best integer solution found so far, we can discard that entire subtree of the problem. This is the *bounding* part of the method. In practice, we will only have to evaluate a small number of branches all the way down. Furthermore, since each level down a branch simplifies the problem by eliminating one variable from the evaluation, the subproblem evaluations become simpler and simpler as we go.

9.4.5 Numerical Methods

This section is at the end of this chapter because the analyst is reduced to **numerical optimization methods** when all else fails: when there are too many alternatives for complete enumeration, calculus won't work, and the problem does not meet the conditions for linear programming. Numerical methods are especially valuable in providing guidance to a simulation study by determining the set of decision variables to be tried next. We mentioned this concept briefly when we discussed a complete study using the supermarket simulation on page 323. You still need to be able to evaluate the objective function for any given set of decision variable values, but that's all.

Some numerical methods are little more than guesswork that has been given the fancy title of **heuristics** or the more down-to-earth name "rules of thumb." Such rules are the foundation of expert systems, a key technology for descriptive decision models in DSS which you will read about in Chapter 11. Optimization, however, is a normative concept which can benefit from a more formal, structured approach. There are well-founded approaches that yield an optimum solution to most practical problems, to any desired degree of accuracy, with reasonable expenditures of human and computer time.

A few common numerical methods are described in this section to make you aware of what is possible and, in general terms, how these methods work. An analyst who wishes to try any of them in a real system can find full descriptions in applied math texts. Your college or university may offer courses that go into optimization in more depth, in either its mathematics or its operations analysis curricula. Applied mathematics graduate students and faculty members at local colleges and universities can often provide expert advice and assistance to those who are not themselves experts, usually on short notice and at reasonable cost.

Hill Climbing **Hill-climbing** methods are an attempt to apply the concepts of calculus to situations in which derivatives are unavailable or useless. We first evaluate the objective function for an arbitrary choice of controllable variable values. (The choice is seldom totally arbitrary but is based on the knowledge and intuition of an analyst or decision maker.) We then also evaluate it for small changes of each such variable in both directions from the initial choice. On the basis of these evaluations we construct a local approximation to the function surface mathematically, in effect calculating derivatives numerically because we can't get them by differentiating the objective function. For the simplest possible case, two points x_1 and x_2 along an axis, the slope of the approximation to the derivative is given by the straight line

$$\frac{\Delta f(x)}{\Delta x} = \frac{f(x_1) - f(x_2)}{x_1 - x_2}$$

where $f(x)$ is the function whose derivative we are approximating.

If we have more than two points along an axis, we can fit more complex (but still easily differentiable) curves to the surface. A parabola, which requires three points, is a popular choice.

Having approximated the derivative along the directions of all the decision variables, we choose a new set of values for these variables, in the direction in which the surface seems to be increasing most rapidly, and repeat the process. Figure 9–10 illustrates hill climbing for an objective function of two variables. As the slope of the surface decreases, or as we pass the peak, we reduce the step size to avoid overshooting the peak too much. If we have approximated the derivatives via a parabola

FIGURE 9–10 **Illustration of Hill Climbing**

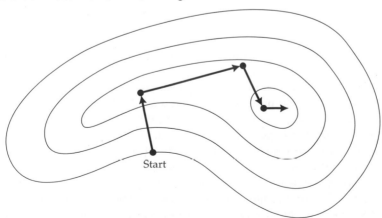

Start

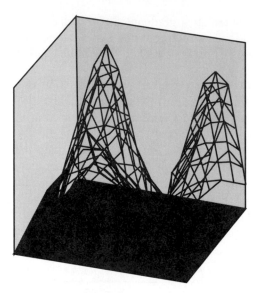

FIGURE 9–11 **Surface with Local Maxima**

or higher order curve, we can determine the maximum of that curve analytically and use the distance to this maximum as the step size. The peak is reached when a small change in the value of any decision variable reduces the value of the objective function.

Hill-climbing methods can be useful when the objective function is continuous, so we would use calculus if we could, but it is nonlinear, so we can't use linear programming. Consider, for example, a standard linear programming problem with a twist: using linear combinations of resources to produce several possible products, where profits per unit are not a constant. Instead, unit costs go down as we produce more of each product. That violates linear programming condition 1. Yet as long as we know what the unit costs are for all possible production volumes of each product, it's easy to evaluate the profits for a given combination of outputs. To use hillclimbing, we would start by picking one feasible solution. We then vary it a bit in each possible direction: more of product 1, more of product 2, and so forth. Eventually we arrive at the correct allocation of resources to products for maximum profit.

The biggest problem with hill-climbing methods is their tendency to zero in on local maxima and not find the global maximum, as illustrated in Figure 9–11. (This would not happen in the resource allocation example of the previous paragraph unless some of the cost-volume relationships were "bumpy." This is the problem we noted with the calculus approach on page 361—it finds all local maxima—but it's worse with hill climbing because it doesn't give us a complete list of all possible solutions. We can often foil this tendency by repeating the hill-climbing process several times with different initial values for the decision variables. Starting at different points, and hence climbing different slopes, should find different local maxima if several exist. After finding each identified local maximum several times, there is good assurance (though never certainty) that all local maxima have been found. The highest of these is taken as the global maximum.

Another occasional difficulty with these methods is their tendency to overshoot the maximum repeatedly and thus oscillate around it without ever converging to it. Proper step size management can handle this problem.

Box's Method   One of several methods that avoids the need to create even a local approximation to a function surface, and which is therefore suitable for objective functions that are found via simulation or similar methods, is due to M. J. Box [BOX65; see RICH73 and SHER74 regarding computer programming of the method]. While it is old in terms of the computer age, it is easy to visualize and still works well. It works as follows:

1. Evaluate the function for at least $n + 1$ randomly chosen sets of decision variable values where there are n decision variables. (A set of decision variable values corresponds to a point in a multidimensional space, each dimension of which corresponds to one of the decision variables. In plain English, it's picking a value for each of the decision variables.) If more than $n + 1$ points are used, the structure is called a complex, by analogy to the simplex structure used in linear programming. **Box's method** is therefore also known as the **complex method.** (Ironically, it's simpler to program than the simplex method.)

2. Find the **centroid** of these points. This is done by finding the arithmetic mean of each dimension (decision variable) independently.

3. Reflect the point corresponding to the lowest function value across the centroid to its other side. (Using the lowest function value for this reflection assumes we are maximizing the objective function. Were we minimizing it, we would reflect the point corresponding to the highest value.) See Figure 9–12 for the process thus far. The figure shows two decision variables and four data points.

4. Evaluate the function at this new point. If the new point is not the lowest-valued point, repeat steps 2 and 3. Since every time we repeat these two steps raises the lowest value to be higher than at least one other value, the net effect is to keep raising the average value of the objective function at the collection of points. In other words, the points are getting closer to the maximum of the function.

5. If the reflected point is still the lowest valued, it was probably reflected across a maximum and down the function surface on its other side. Move this point halfway back to the centroid. This has the effect of making the pattern smaller as the maximum is approached. Calculate the new centroid and repeat the process from step 2, continuing until convergence has been achieved; that is, all the points in the complex are sufficiently close to each other so that the value of the objective function value does not change, within your tolerance limits, from one to another.

This basic approach must be modified to work in practice. The reflection process may try to take one or more decision variables outside their allowable range, especially if (as often happens) the objective function reaches its maximum at one or

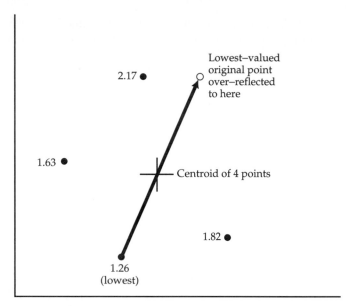

FIGURE 9–12   Initial Steps of Box's Method

more of the constraints. If this occurs, these decision variables must be set to a suitable value just inside the boundary. (If they are set to values on the boundary, the set of points may in time flatten itself against the boundary and be unable to leave it.) This occasional "under-reflection" has the effect of shrinking the pattern even though it is not approaching a maximum. To counteract this effect, unconstrained reflections must "over-reflect." Instead of choosing the new point precisely opposite the old one from the centroid, it is chosen across from the old point but 1.2 or 1.3 times as far from the centroid.

Box's method is better than hill climbing at avoiding local maxima, since it tends to find the global maximum if any of the widely dispersed initial points or any of the early, wide-ranging reflections is near it. However, it can be fooled also. It's a good idea here, too, to try several runs with different initial sets of points. A few trials will usually confirm the first maximum that was found. It can then be taken as the global maximum.

SUMMARY

A second category of representational models consists of mathematical models. The two mathematical approaches that are most often used to study dynamic systems are queuing theory and Markov process analysis. Both are based on the concept of defining the states in which the system can be, the possible transitions among those states, and the rates at which those transitions take place.

In queuing theory, balancing transitions into and out of a state yields equations that can be solved for the probability that the system is in each state. These state probabilities, in turn, give us statistical information about system performance. If the equations are solved in terms of symbolic variables for the state transition rates, their solution describes system behavior as a set of equations. We can substitute any transition rates we wish into these equations and obtain the corresponding system behavior.

In Markov process analysis, the state transition rates are used numerically to track the system from its initial state until state probabilities stabilize. These probabilities are then used as they would be in queuing theory to obtain information about system behavior. Markov process calculations consist of repeated vector-matrix multiplication.

Both queuing theory and Markov process analysis assume exponential distributions of interarrival and service times. Other distributions can be modeled by introducing additional states (and hence additional complexity) into the model.

Queuing theory analysis yields the most general answers of the three approaches to system representation, but is the most limited in its applicability. Simulation "always works," but its answers describe only one situation with one set of random number choices. Markov process analysis is between the other two. Two or more methods can often usefully be used in combination.

Optimization, choosing one of several numerically compared alternatives to maximize (or minimize) the objective function, is an important part of many decision support systems. Approaches to optimization include complete enumeration, random search, calculus, linear programming, hill climbing, and a variety of other numerical methods.

Complete enumeration means trying all possible choices and picking the one that produces the best predicted results. Random search is related. The difference is that in random search, we do not try all possible choices but rather a randomly selected subset of them.

Calculus can optimize continuous, differentiable functions of the decision variables. This limits its usefulness to situations in which the objective function meets these requirements and we can solve the often-complex equations that are involved.

Linear programming can optimize systems in which the objective function depends linearly on how resources are allocated to alternative uses and where this allocation is subject to constraints, such as the available quantity of one or more resources. Linear programming problems are generally solved by computer. Many linear programming packages are available. Most of them use the simplex method to solve LP problems by following the edges of the feasible region.

A wide variety of numerical optimization methods exists. The analyst may be forced to use one of them when the methods given earlier do not apply or do not work.

One numerical method is hill climbing. This is the numerical equivalent of calculus. It uses numerical approximations to the derivatives and moves around the solution space, "climbing the hill" of the objective function, until its approximations to the derivatives are zero within an acceptable tolerance. The process must be repeated with different starting points to make sure the overall, or global, maximum is found.

A second numerical method is the complex method of M. J. Box. It starts out as random search does, by choosing several random values of the decision variables and evaluating the objective function at them. Rather than continuing to choose more random points, however, this method uses the known values as a group to pick a new point to try. It tends to range widely over the solution space and then zero in on a maximum. As with hill climbing, it is necessary to repeat this process more than once to avoid settling on a local maximum.

KEY TERMS

Box's method
branch-and-bound approach
calculus
centroid
complete enumeration
complex method
constraint
derivative
equations of balance
Erlang distribution
exponential distribution
feasible region
global maximum
heuristics
hill-climbing
hyperexponential distribution
linear programming
local maximum
Markov process
modelers
numerical optimization methods
objective function
optimization methods
partial derivative
queuing model
queuing theory model
random search
renormalization
simplex method
solvers
sparse matrix
state transition
state transition matrix
state transition rate
state vector
steady state
utilization ratio

REVIEW QUESTIONS

1. What are the two basic approaches to mathematical modeling of a system?
2. What type of statistical distribution do both approaches assume for times between events that occur in the system? How can other distributions be handled?
3. What is being "balanced" in queuing theory equations of balance?
4. What mathematical structure is used to represent transition rates between states in a Markov model?
5. What is the basic calculation process for evaluating a Markov model?
6. Of the three approaches to modeling dynamic systems, which is most generally usable?
7. Of the three approaches to modeling dynamic systems, which makes it easiest to evaluate the effect of a change in mean interarrival times?
8. What is optimization? Why is it used in decision support systems?
9. What types of optimization problems can complete enumeration deal with? Give an example other than the ones mentioned in the text.
10. How does random search differ from complete enumeration?
11. What types of optimization problems can calculus deal with?
12. State the conditions that a problem must satisfy if linear programming is to apply.
13. What is the most common method for solving linear programming problems called? Briefly, how does it work?
14. When and why would you use a numerical optimization method?
15. Which nonnumerical method does hill climbing approximate?
16. What is one problem that arises when using the hill-climbing method? How could you deal with it?
17. Illustrate Box's method using three points on the upper half of a basketball (or a similarly shaped surface).

EXERCISES

1. Solve the queuing theory equations for the telephone system on page 348. It's easiest if you ignore the second equation of balance, using the first and third together with the condition that the state probabilities must add up to 1.
2. The following exercises extend the telephone system queuing model on page 348.
   a. Modify and solve the numerical model on page 350 for the case where a second person will wait for the phone, but one who arrives with two people waiting will leave. Does your solution suggest what the results might be if arriving customers never left, but joined the line no matter how long it was? (Many real systems, such as exit toll booths on a congested highway or box office lines for popular attractions, behave this way.)
   b. Modify and solve the symbolic model on page 351 for the same case as part *a;* that is, the waiting line must be two customers long for an arriving customer to leave.
   c. Modify and solve the numerical model on page 350 for the case where half the customers who arrive when the phone is in use (state 2) stay and wait, but the other half leave for another floor. Hint: If the average customer interarrival time is 10 minutes, what is the average interarrival time of customers who are willing to wait when the phone is in use?
   d. Solve part *c* using the symbols on page 351.
   e. Solve the numerical model for the case where all customers will wait if the phone is busy and nobody is waiting, and half will wait if there is already one person waiting. Your answer should be between the result obtained on page 351 and your answer to part *a.* Why?

3. Time the intervals between arrivals at a facility such as a mall, store, or dormitory, to the nearest second, for half an hour or until you have 100 data points. Pick a time of day when people do not bunch up and form lines at the entrance. Avoid periods when external factors affect arrival times, such as when a class changes or meal times at a dorm. Compare your data to the exponential distribution.

4. Develop a spreadsheet model of the pay phone problem. Put the average time between arrivals and the average length of a telephone call in visible cells, clearly labeled on your spreadsheet. Display, in other clearly labeled cells, (*a*) the percentage of time the phone is busy and (*b*) the percentage of customers who walk away. (This equals the percentage of time that the phone is busy with someone waiting.) Try the following cases. Print out and submit your results.

   a. Arrivals every 10 minutes, call duration 5 minutes. (This is the same as the example of Section 9.1.)

   b. Arrivals every 10 minutes, call duration 0 minutes. (Although the answers should be obvious once you see them, limiting cases are a valuable test of any computer program.)

   c. Arrivals every 10 minutes, call duration 1 minute.

   d. Arrivals every 10 minutes, call duration 9 minutes.

   e. Arrivals every 10 minutes, call duration 10 minutes. What is going on here? Explain.

   f. Arrivals every 10 minutes, call duration 15 minutes. Again, what is going on here? Explain.

   g. Arrivals every 10 minutes, call duration –5 (yes, negative 5) minutes. What does your result tell you about your spreadsheet model?

   Your instructor may also ask you to print your spreadsheet in the mode where it displays formulas, with column widths sufficient to show both computation formulas in full, and/or to submit your spreadsheet electronically (on diskette, as an attachment to an e-mail message, or in any other way he or she requests).

5. Keep track of day-to-day weather transitions in your area for a few weeks. (If necessary, extend the definition of "rain" to include other forms of precipitation such as snow. If your weather doesn't vary much in the current season, use a daily paper to track the weather in a locale where it varies more.) Determine the Markov process transition probabilities for this locale as in Figure 9–5.

6. Consider the choice of time step for a Markov model of the pay phone problem. Based on transitions out of state 1, it was concluded on page 356 that the upper limit for the length of a time step is 10 minutes. Is this still true if you consider all three states? If not, what is the upper limit on time step length?

7. Put the state transition probabilities of the telephone system on page 348 over one minute into Markov process transition matrix form. Assume the system is initially idle. Carry the process through five steps with a calculator. If you did not do exercise 5, use a one-minute time step. See how close your final result comes to the result obtained on page 351.

8. Write a computer program to carry out the arithmetic of exercise 6. Run the Markov process for 60 steps, or one hour. Print out the state probability vector every 10 steps. See how close your final result comes to the theoretical solution. Then, run your model until all three state probabilities in one iteration are identical to those of the prior iteration to at least four decimal places. How many iterations did you need to reach this degree of convergence?

9. Justify the statement on page 360 that decision trees support the complete enumeration approach.

10. You must optimize a function that meets the mathematical conditions for using calculus, but the equations are far too complex for you to deal with. You know, because of the nature of the problem, that the optimum is not in the neighborhood of any constraints on the decision variables. Compare and contrast (*a*) hiring a calculus expert, (*b*) random search, (*c*) hill climbing, and (*d*) Box's method to carry out this optimization. Is the Kepner-Tregoe method (Section 2.7) suitable for choosing one of these four methods? Why or why not?

11. Your factory produces wind-up toy trucks, wind-up toy cars, and nonmotorized toy cars. Each wind-up toy uses a motor, which is identical for cars and trucks. Each toy truck uses a truck body. Each toy car uses a body, which is identical for wind-up and nonmotorized cars. Either type of car can be decorated with "Super Slammer" trim to increase its selling price. The trim, like the body, is identical for wind-up and nonmotorized cars. You wish to allocate resources to the five types of toys so as to maximize your profit.

    a. Assume you have a finite number of parts (truck bodies, car bodies, motors, and Super Slammer trim kits) on hand and that the profit you make on each unit is independent of production volume. Does this problem meet the criteria for linear programming? Why or why not?

    b. Now assume the price you receive for each unit is independent of production volume, but production costs are subject to a "learning curve." That is, as cumulative production volume goes up, production cost per unit drops. Does this problem now meet the criteria for linear programming? Why or why not?

    c. What optimization method would you choose to solve the problem of part *b?* Would your answer differ if this were a one-time problem, or a recurring problem that had to be solved, with different numbers, every week? Why or why not? Discuss briefly.

12. Would you (assuming you didn't have to do it as a classroom exercise or want to do it to learn programming or for intellectual challenge) write your own computer program to solve a linear programming problem? Why or why not? Relate your answer to the discussion of packages versus custom programs on page 367.

13. The formula

$$z = 10 - x^2 - y^2$$

describes a paraboloid, centered at the (x, y) origin, with a maximum value of 10 at $(x = 0, y = 0)$ and dropping off as one gets further away from that point. Write a computer program that uses Box's method with a four-point complex to find its maximum:

    a. With no constraints. (You should find the maximum at or near the origin, with an objective function value of approximately 10.)

    b. With the constraint $x \geq 1$. (Since the constraint keeps you away from the function's true maximum, your answer should lie on or near it.)

14. You are considering what holiday presents to give your loved one. You have put together a tentative list: a partridge in a pear tree for the first night of the holiday, two turtle doves for the second night, three French hens for the third, four calling birds for the fourth, five gold rings for the fifth, etc. Each gift has a cost (which generally goes up through the sequence) and an impact on your loved one's feelings toward you (which goes up initially, then tends to level off, and eventually decreases as he or she wonders what to do with large numbers of geese a-swimming, maids a-milking, lords a-leaping, etc., after the novelty wears off). You wish to decide how far through the sequence to proceed for optimum effect. Which optimization methods would you use? Why?

REFERENCES

On Queuing Theory and Markov Processes

ASMU87   Asmussen, Soren. *Applied Probability and Queues.* John Wiley & Sons, New York (1987).

COOP81   Cooper, Robert B. *Introduction to Queuing Theory,* North Holland, New York (1981).

GNED89   Gnedenko, B. V., and I. N. Kovalenko. *Introduction to Queuing Theory* (2nd ed., translated from Russian by Samuel Kotz). Birkhauser, Boston (1989).

GROS85   Gross, Donald, and Carl M. Harris. *Fundamentals of Queuing Theory.* John Wiley & Sons, New York (1985).

HALL91   Hall, Randolph W. *Queuing Methods for Services and Manufacturing.* Prentice-Hall, Englewood Cliffs, N.J. (1991).

HILL90   Hiller, Frederick S., and Gerald J. Lieberman. *Introduction to Operations Research* (5th ed.). McGraw-Hill, New York (1990).

ISAA76   Isaacson, Dean L. *Markov Chains, Theory and Applications.* John Wiley & Sons, New York (1976).

SAAT83   Saaty, Thomas L. *Elements of Queuing Theory with Applications.* Dover, New York (1983).

On Optimization

BOX65   Box, M. J. "A New Method of Constrained Optimization and a Comparison with other Methods." *Computer Journal* 8, no. 1 (April 1965), pp. 42–52.

CALV89   Calvert, James E., and William L. Voxman. *Linear Programming.* Harcourt Brace Jovanovich, Orlando, Fla. (1989).

ERMO88   Ermoliev, Y., and R. Wets, eds. *Numerical Techniques for Stochastic Optimization.* Springer-Verlag, Berlin and New York (1988).

GASS90   Gass, Saul I. *An Illustrated Guide to Linear Programming.* Dover, New York (1990).

MALL75   Mallach, Efrem G., and Paul D. Berger. "Decision Trees with Continuous Distributions." *Operations Research Quarterly* 26, no. 2, part i (1975), pp. 297–304.

NEMH88   Nemhauser, G. L., and L. A. Wolsey. *Integer and Combinatorial Optimization.* John Wiley & Sons, New York (1988).

RICH73   Richardson, Joel A., and J. L. Kuester. "The Complex Method for Constrained Optimization" (Algorithm 454). *Communications of the ACM* 16, no. 8 (August 1973), pp. 487–489.

SCHR86   Schrijver, A. *Theory of Linear and Integer Programming.* John Wiley & Sons, New York (1986).

SHEN89   Shenoy, G. V. *Linear Programming Methods and Applications.* John Wiley & Sons, New York (1989).

SHER74   Shere, Kenneth D. "Remark on Algorithm 454." *Communications of the ACM* 17, no. 8 (August 1974), p. 471.

CASE

Fort Lowell Trading Company
Credit Card Policies

The following Wednesday, Miguel and Elizabeth returned to FLTC headquarters building to meet with Rob Fernandez, manager of accounting information systems. Rob's area was responsible for the applications which processed credit card applications and billing. As the two arrived at the area where his office was located, they heard cheering and applause. Then they noticed that the reception area was decorated with streamers and balloons.

"What's happening?" Miguel asked Joe Two Crows, whom he recognized in the group. "We just got here," he added by way of explanation.

"Oh, we do this every time we have an excuse for it," he responded. "It's a nice break from coding or whatever. Today we're celebrating Rob's engagement. That's him over there," he said pointing to a man cutting pieces of cake and passing them around on paper plates.

"Is that Rob Fernandez from accounting systems?" asked Elizabeth. "He's the person we're supposed to meet with this afternoon."

"Yes, it is. Grab some cake when it comes your way and I'll introduce you as soon as this is over. Won't be more than another couple of minutes now. You missed his speech. Too bad—it was really hilarious!"

A short time later, after Elizabeth and Miguel had a chance to wipe the cake crumbs from their faces, Joe ushered them into Rob's office. "Ah, you must be the two students from Sabino Canyon College!" he welcomed them. "Come right in! I see you already know some of our people."

"Yes, we've been coming here for several weeks now," Elizabeth confirmed. "It's quite an eye-opener to see things in the real world, not just the classroom. Too bad we weren't here to find out about today's celebration. We might have come a few minutes earlier. Joe said you gave quite a talk."

"It's supposed to go with the occasion," Rob explained. "Whoever gives us the excuse for a party is supposed to say something. Mostly I talked about how my fiancée and I met—it was a real case of mistaken identity that worked out in the end. That's her over there, in front of San Xavier del Bac," he said as he pointed out a picture on a shelf behind his desk. "We're going to get married there in September. Besides the history, it's convenient for her relatives in northern Sonora to drive to."

"But enough of that," he continued, changing the subject. "I was hoping that some of your classroom stuff might come in handy today. Do you two know anything about credit cards?"

"You mean like Visa, MasterCard, American Express, and so on?" Miguel asked.

"Yes, but I'm more concerned with our own Fort Lowell Trading Company card. It looks like this," he said, taking a card with a picture of a tall saguaro cactus in the Arizona desert from his wallet. "It's good in all our stores and for catalogue orders. We also give people an extra 2 percent off any order if they use it when they order from our Web site. We might not keep that up forever. Mostly we want to generate interest in the Web site at this point."

"Besides that 2 percent, why would someone use one of your cards?" Miguel asked.

"That's one aspect of what I wanted to talk about. Actually, there are a few reasons you might use one—besides that desert picture. You get on our mailing list for special sales, our credit terms are better than most other cards, sometimes you get a few months of interest-free payments, it doesn't use up your credit limit on other cards if that's a problem, and there's no fee. Still, it's hard to compete with bonuses like airline frequent flyer miles, credit toward your next new car, free gasoline, or doubling the manufacturer's warranty like some of the major cards will do. And *that* is why we have a problem."

"Why is that a problem?" asked Elizabeth.

"Because more and more of our best customers are using the other cards. The ones who are left using our cards are the ones who don't pay their bills on time or who are worried about maxing out their other cards. In short, they're the high-risk credit users. Our loss percentages have been going up. Nothing to really worry us yet, but not a good sign. We're looking for ways to analyze that so we can evaluate different credit policies if we want to."

"And how did you think we might be able to help?"

"Well, it seems to me that there must be some way to analyze what will happen with different credit card policies—different criteria for accepting applications, different minimum payments, different interest rates, and all that."

"Did you have anything specific in mind?" Elizabeth asked.

"I did, actually," Rob smiled. "I was reading an article recently about how one of the big California banks evaluates its loan portfolio and it sounded like we might be able to do something like it. They used something called a Markov process. Have you guys heard of it?"

"As a matter of fact, we were just reading about them last week!" Miguel responded with enthusiasm. "They sounded like one of those theoretical things with zero usefulness. Now you're telling us that this California bank actually does use them?"

"Either that or the writer was lying," Rob laughed. "He said they started by defining the different states a loan could be in. They all start in something called 'standard.' Mostly they stay there until they get paid off. Sometimes they go to 'substandard' or 'default.' Most of the defaults come from substandard loans but some go straight there. There were a few other states too, that I don't remember, but that was the basic idea. Anyhow, it seemed to me that if it helps them evaluate loan policies, it might help us evaluate credit card policies. What do you think?"

"I'm not sure I know yet," Elizabeth said thoughtfully. "Off the top of my head, it doesn't sound like the kind of system we talked about in class. Those all stabi-

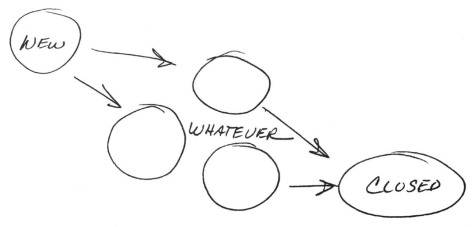

FIGURE 9–13 Rob's Sketch

lized at some kind of average state we could look at and say 'this is what it generally settles down to.' Bank loans sound more like something that starts in one place and ends up somewhere else: paid off or defaulted. Maybe credit cards are in between?"

"There might be something here, though," mused Miguel. "At any moment you've got accounts in maybe half a dozen different states—too new to tell, paid up, making minimum payments on time, paying late, closed, whatever. You'll have to tell us what they are," he said to Rob. "And you probably have some statistics on how many of your accounts go from each of those to each other one in a given month—are months the right time frame here?—so we could draw them like this—oops!" Miguel paused as he stared at a sketch he had started to draw.

"What was the 'oops?' " Elizabeth asked.

"Look at this circle over here," he said, pointing to the lower-right corner of his sketch. "That's where an account is closed. There are ways into that state but no way out. So, sooner or later, all the accounts will end up there. That's the steady state but it doesn't seem too helpful."

"That's what happens in real life to any given account," agreed Rob. "Except, first, we really care what happens on the way, and second, we get new ones all the time to offset the ones we lose. Could you recycle the closed accounts into new ones?

"I don't know about that . . . I really don't know, I really don't know. Like I'm taking this for the first time, right? Let's think about it: Is there any kind of steady state here?

"Yes, there is," stated Rob. "Like we were saying, accounts come and go, but the percentages stay the same unless we change our policies or something else happens. So if we knew the percentages that would go bad over a year, or how many would pay over time, we could figure out what we were making or losing on our credit card operations. Then, if we could do that for each policy change that someone suggested . . ."

"Right," Elizabeth interjected. "All we'd need is estimates of how each change affects the state transitions. Like, if you ask for bigger minimum payments or up the interest rate, do more people pay on time or do more people just stop paying at all? And, what about the extra profit the store makes selling things people wouldn't have bought in the first place if they didn't have this card? And . . ."

"Whoa, whoa there!" laughed Rob. "It sounds like you guys are onto something! Why don't you take this memo here—it's got some of the numbers about our current situation—and see what you can come up with. Say we get together again this time next week to look at it?"

"Sure thing—if the cake comes from the same bakery!" Miguel laughed. "See you then!"

FIGURE 9–14 **Excerpt from Memo**

All accounts start in No Experience status. They stay there for four months.

All status from there on is based on the previous four months' experience. The most recent month counts 31%, the others 26-23-20% going back. Whatever situation counts for the highest percentage with these weights is the account status:

- Paid in full.
- Partial payments, minimum or above, made on time.
- Late payment.
- Nonpayment.

The first three months most everyone's on good behavior. We get 65% full payment, 35% partial payments on time. Exceptions are negligible.

After that about 90% of the ones who have been paying in full keep on paying in full. The rest go equally to the other three.

Of the ones who make partial payments 70% keep making them. 20% pay off their bill. 5% go to each of the others.

Of late payers, for 60% of them it's a one-time miss and they go back to what they were before. 30% keep paying late. 10% miss the next one completely.

Of the ones who miss, half make a partial payment on time on their next bill. 30% pay off in full, 10% pay late and 10% miss the next one too.

A warning letter is sent after two months of nonpayment. Charge privileges are suspended after three months of nonpayment.

An inquiry letter is sent after three years of account inactivity. A postage-free reply card lets the holder ask to keep the account open. That restarts the three-year clock. If there's no response, if the card comes back with the "no" box checked, or if the letter is returned by the post office as undeliverable for any reason (including forwarding time expired) the account is closed.

Please feel free to contact me if you have any questions about this data.

EXERCISES

1. Read the memo excerpt in Figure 9–14. What six states can an account be in? Draw a state transition diagram. Indicate the transition probabilities from each state to each other state on a month-to-month basis. You will have to modify the information in the memo in two ways to do this. One has to do with the three-month initial period:

   a. Assume that one-third of the accounts in this state move out of it each month. This is statistically true even though it does not follow the progress of individual accounts correctly. That's one difference between Markov process analysis and queuing theory on the one hand, simulation on the other: Here we're concerned with the statistics, not with individual accounts.

   b. Assume that accounts that return to paid-up status after missing a payment go back in the appropriate proportions, but don't try to follow individual accounts. The reasoning is the same as with the previous point. As long as the right number of accounts go back to each state it doesn't matter (for Markov process purposes) which accounts they are. In fact, in this type of analysis we can't distinguish individual accounts. We only deal with fractions of the total population.

2. Modify the account state diagram to follow Rob's suggestion of recycling closed accounts into new ones to keep the system from converging into closed accounts and nothing else.

3. Construct a state transition matrix using the diagram in your answer to exercise 2.

4. Using a computer, take this state transition matrix through 1,000 iterations or until the state vector stabilizes. See what fraction of the accounts is in each state.

5. Assume that each fully paid-up account is worth $50 to FLTC per year, each account that makes partial payments is worth $100, each account that misses payments is worth $20 and each account that fails to pay costs the firm $200. If FLTC has a total of 10,000 charge customers, what is the total value (or cost) of the program per year?

6. What type of information would you need in order to evaluate alternative credit programs in terms of this same measure?

7. Assuming that the total value of the program per year is an appropriate measure for FLTC to optimize, which of the optimization methods discussed in this chapter (if any) would be suitable for doing so? Assume you have the information necessary to evaluate any given program as in exercise 6.

CHAPTER 10

Group Decision Support Systems*

CHAPTER OUTLINE

Introduction

In the last chapter we saw that group decisions differ from other types in the need to communicate during or about the decision-making process. DSS were originally designed to support an individual's decision-making process by allowing the user to access data or model the expected outcome of decisions. They were not designed for multiple individuals who had to communicate and collaborate to solve a problem jointly. The unique and differing communication factors in group decisions have, however, led to the development of DSS that accommodate these communication factors and are designed specifically to support decisions made at the group level. Such DSS are called group DSS, or GDSS. They are becoming in-

---

*The author is delighted to acknowledge the major contributions of Dr. Reza Barkhi to writing this chapter.

creasingly important in business. Since you'll probably run into one (or several) GDSS on the job, it's important for you to learn about them now.

CHAPTER OBJECTIVES

After you have read and studied this chapter, you will be able to:

1. Define group decision support systems (GDSS).
2. Explain why group decision support systems have become important.
3. Discuss the types of activities that groups carry out and how they differ from individual activities.
4. Identify the types of group decision support systems that exist.
5. Explain what media richness is and how it affects group DSS design.
6. Describe groupware and how it relates to group decision support systems.
7. Explain what electronic meeting systems are and how they can be used to support group decisions.
8. Discuss how work flow systems fit into the group DSS picture.
9. Describe some features of illustrative group DSS products.

10.1 WHAT ARE GROUP DSS?

A **group decision support system (GDSS)** is a decision support system whose design, structure, and usage reflect the way in which members of a group interact to make a particular decision or type of decision. It supports group decision processes that include communication, file sharing, modeling of group activities, aggregation of individual perspectives into a group perspective, and other activities that involve group interaction.

This definition goes beyond simply stating that the GDSS is used by more than one person. Suppose a group of factory managers—the stockroom supervisor, the milling room supervisor, the assembly supervisor, the paint room supervisor, the shipping supervisor—got together to choose a factory floor layout. They could look at DSS printouts that analyze bottlenecks and production levels for different floor layouts and choose the best. This would be a group decision where each member uses a DSS. However, the DSS would not be a group DSS because there is nothing about it that reflects the group nature of the decision-making process. An individual decision maker could use the same DSS equally well.

A different GDSS for this situation might use computers on each of the five supervisors' desks. The GDSS would ask the stockroom supervisor to input information relative to stockroom size, layout, and other requirements. It would also ask the other four supervisors for information related to their functions. The GDSS would be programmed to accept only appropriate inputs from each supervisor. It would then merge the inputs provided by each group member, analyze overall factory productivity, and propose solutions to the unique problems that each supervisor faces. And it would print different reports for each supervisor, each report relevant to the decision that the supervisor has to make. This conceptual system would be a GDSS. The decision-making task hasn't changed. The decision-making process, and with it the appropriate computer support, has. The GDSS has integrated the business tasks by considering the business processes as a whole. It has also incorporated different perspectives into the decision process.

The GDSS in this example is far from the only possible type of GDSS. However, the basic concept—that the GDSS is designed and developed with explicit awareness of the overall group decision-making process—applies to them all. A GDSS is a DSS with capabilities designed to support the processes needed for group activity. You'll read about several examples of commercially available GDSS later in this chapter. Lotus Notes®, a groupware product, will also be discussed later in this chapter and can also be a GDSS, depending on how it is set up, since Notes is adaptable to many uses.

10.2 WHY GROUP DSS NOW?

Two sets of factors have led to the recent explosion in GDSS: organizational factors and technical factors. Whereas each might suffice to lead to increased use of GDSS by itself, together they make it inevitable. The underlying fact here is that most organizational decisions involve more than one person; that is, they are group decisions. Organizations make decisions in groups both for task-related reasons and organizational reasons.

- *Task-related reasons* have to do with the functional requirements of making a decision. For instance, it may be that no one person has the necessary expertise or knowledge to make it.
- *Organizational reasons* have to do with reflecting people's desire to be involved in the decision. People may be unhappy to be shut out of a process they see as affecting them, or involvement in a decision may increase their buy-in and willingness to carry it out.

Both of these factors are becoming more important, as you'll see in the next sections. Task-related reasons are becoming more important because, with the explosion of specialized knowledge, it's increasingly unlikely that any one person will have all the necessary knowledge for any nontrivial decision. Organizational reasons are increasing in importance because the trend throughout the last few centuries has been an increase in people's desire to, and ability to, influence their own destiny.

You have probably studied, or will study, the subjects of the overall benefits of groups and how groups function in your organizational behavior courses under the heading "group dynamics." For that reason, we won't take them up here. If you're not reasonably current on them, though, you might want to take out your old textbook (or borrow one, if you don't have one) and familiarize yourself with the concepts or refresh your grasp of them.

10.2.1 Organizational Reasons for GDSS Growth

The key organizational factors that support the growth of GDSS are changes in the way management makes decisions and changes in organizational culture. Management decisions at the dawn of the 21st century require the participation of many more people than they did earlier. This results from several factors, including:

- More complex decision environments, which require the multiple perspectives of different people.
- Specialization of decision makers, making it unlikely that one person will have the required knowledge to solve a problem alone.
- Emphasis on time as a competitive resource, forcing multiple decision makers to break tasks into smaller subtasks and solve those subtasks in parallel.

Changes in organizational culture have led to increased use of participatory management methods. Whereas top managers could once rule by decree, today many feel a need to rule by consent of the governed. This, too, results from several factors including:

- The increased need to make a job fulfilling and make it satisfy workers' needs for self-actualization [MASL43], rather than merely satisfying their physical survival needs (which are largely taken care of in today's industrialized nations).
- The desire to achieve benefits of participative management such as improved morale and decision acceptance by all group members. Improved morale arises largely from removing the negative sense of being shut out. Improved decision acceptance comes from the positive sense of having participated.
- To overcome the shortcomings of group meetings such as "groupthink" and dominance by one or a few individuals, whose personalities may affect a decision more than the merits of their suggestions.

Groupthink   A common problem in group decision making is **groupthink:** the tendency of group members to fall into similar thought patterns and to disapprove, implicitly or explicitly, of opinions that do not conform to these patterns. Group decision support systems can help overcome groupthink where it is an obstacle to reaching good decisions. They do this by making it less threatening for group members to violate group norms by stating new opinions or by disagreeing with them. In some cases they do this by providing anonymity to opinions. Even where they do identify the person associated with an opinion, both research and experience have shown that people are more willing to state their views candidly when typing at a computer terminal than across a conference room table. Group DSS can also help by enabling junior members of a group to state their opinions before they know what senior members think, which is difficult in a face-to-face meeting.[1]

10.2.2 Technical Reasons for Group DSS Growth

Technical factors support the growth of GDSS because new technological advances make it technically and economically feasible to develop GDSS tools. Wide area telecommunications links, a necessity for many group DSS, are becoming less expensive. Fast (56,000 bits per second and up) telecommunication links, needed for rapid transfer of graphics or video, are becoming more widely available. More organizations have gateways and local area networks to bring these

---

[1]The understanding that this is of value is not new. Over two thousand years ago justices of the Sanhedrin, the highest court of the post-biblical Jewish kingdom in Palestine, gave their opinions in reverse order of seniority so junior members of the court would not be influenced by their senior colleagues.

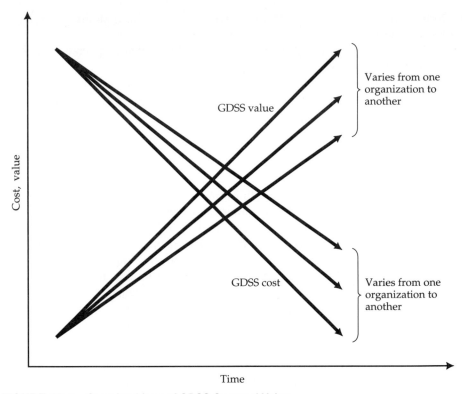

FIGURE 10–1 Crossing Lines of GDSS Cost and Value

high-speed links to decision makers' desktops. Networking standards, some of them related to the subject of open systems that we discussed on page 184, make it easier for computers of various types to share data with each other. Software firms, motivated in part by increased availability of the supporting infrastructure, are increasingly offering tools and packages to support interactive group processes.

10.2.3 Putting the Factors Together

The growth and acceptance of any technology depends on its perceived value exceeding its cost. The new organizational and management environments make GDSS a more valuable tool today. The new technical possibilities have reduced the cost of providing GDSS. As firms find it increasingly affordable to satisfy an increasingly important need, they are adopting GDSS rapidly. Figure 10–1 shows this.

10.3 GROUP VERSUS INDIVIDUAL ACTIVITIES

The key difference between group activities and individual activities is this: for individuals to accomplish their task in group activities, they must interact with other individuals in the group.

Interaction may be required for various reasons. The knowledge necessary to accomplish a task may be distributed among the group members. A task can be divided into several subtasks, which are each assigned to an appropriate person. Each member carries out a subtask and generates whatever intermediate results the subtask calls for. The members then work together to integrate these intermediate results and synthesize the overall solution. The synthesis requires members to coordinate their decision-making activities with each other. This type of interaction is not required when a single decision maker is involved.

In implementing this process in practice, splitting the overall task into subtasks is unlikely to create subtasks that map precisely into the knowledge of individual group members. This means that group members, in working on their subtasks, will have to request help from others. Therefore, each decision maker, in addition to having domain knowledge, needs to know who in the group may have the knowledge to help him or her: A GDSS can help here. A group directory can, for example, provide information about the group members, their skills, and other resources. Members can use this service to send requests for help to a specific member, or they may broadcast request for help to all members of the group via e-mail lists or a discussion group.

When the knowledge that group members require is in electronic form, each group member may grant other members the access rights to his or her knowledge base. In a higher form of information sharing, group members can publish what they have learned to make it directly accessible over an internal network—often called an *intranet,* when it is accessed through the same interfaces as the World Wide Web.

The design and implementation of a GDSS is more complex than that of a (nongroup) DSS. For example, consider the motivation of group members to cooperate—a problem that does not arise with nongroup DSS. Incentives built into a GDSS and its surrounding work environment may promote competition or cooperation among group members. If group members are motivated to cooperate, they will tend to share truthful information as they collectively try to solve a problem. If they are motivated to compete, they may engage in untruthful information exchange, making the GDSS less effective [BARK95]. Given that the design of incentive systems plays a crucial role in the effectiveness of the GDSS usage, you should pay particular attention to the incentive system as you introduce GDSS in your organization. If you want members to cooperate, then you should design incentive systems that are conducive to cooperation. For example, if you want to encourage people to publish what they know on an intranet, make sure people know they will be rewarded for becoming recognized as reliable sources of useful information [MALL98]. If your incentive system is conducive to competition, you will have to pay particular attention to the degree of truthfulness of the information that is exchanged between group members.

Members of a group may also take "free rides" from other members. For instance, a group member may fail to respond to a request, knowing that someone else will respond sooner or later. This sort of behavior is sometimes less immediately obvious in a GDSS setting than in a face-to-face setting. It is, hence, important to devise an incentive system that makes free riding costly in a GDSS setting. Such problems do not arise with nongroup DSS. In an environment where people are motivated to publish what they know for use by other group members, free rides are punished by the organizational system.

10.4 MEDIA RICHNESS AND TASK TYPES

Group decision making involves exchanging information among group members. Group DSS involve, therefore, exchanging information using computer and communication technology. If we are going to do this well, we must match the technology to the specific information exchange requirement. Technologies vary in their information communication characteristics. In order to choose the right one, we need to understand how the desired characteristics relate to the information exchange task.

10.4.1 Richness

Media richness is defined as the potential information-carrying capacity of a data transmission medium [LENG83]. The richness of the communication media used in groups may determine how information is processed. Figure 10–2 shows the spectrum of communication media, from high to low richness. The richness of a communication medium is measured by the number of available communication channels as well as the immediacy of feedback that is provided to decision makers [DAFT86]. Face-to-face communication is high in richness because it allows simultaneous display of multiple communication cues such as the words used, body language, facial expressions, and tone of voice of the speakers. Facial expressions and tone of voice used in verbal communication convey information that provides immediate feedback. With feedback, it is easy to gauge understanding and correct interpretations. Electronic mail is lower in richness than electronic chat, and electronic chat is lower in richness than face-to-face communication. You can see where the other media fall along this spectrum. Be sure you understand why they fall where they do.

In order to use this richness information, we must now classify decision-making tasks because different types of media, specifically differing in their richness, may be appropriate for different types of tasks. For example, a medium of low richness may be effective for making a transaction via an ATM or expressing opinion about a nonemotional subject, and will probably be more efficient than using a high-richness medium for that purpose. Negotiating the fate of nations is more effective

FIGURE 10–2   Communication Medium Richness Table

High
| face-to-face
| video
| audio
| real-time electronic chat
| electronic mail
Low

when national leaders meet face-to-face (rich media) than when they use electronic mail (low richness)—so they often find it worthwhile to fly several thousand miles to make this possible. Many people will purchase a pair of trousers or a sleeping bag on the basis of a Web page or printed catalogue description, but few would purchase a house (a more significant decision) without seeing it in person (higher richness). How can we categorize decision-making tasks so as to select the appropriate media for sharing information?

10.4.2 Task

There are many ways in which group activities can be classified. Figure 10–3 shows one useful categorization. McGrath calls this diagram a **circumplex.** GDSS designers have used McGrath's classification frequently to design GDSS to match

FIGURE 10–3 Group Task Circumplex
Source: From [MCGR84].

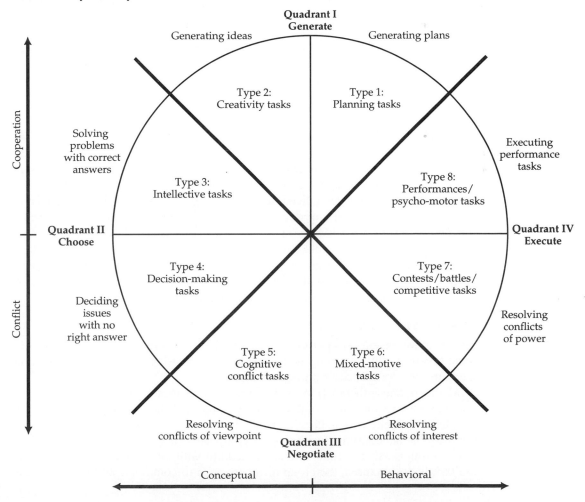

task requirements. This classification identifies two dimensions and four basic task types to create eight classes of tasks. Of the two dimensions, one dimension has a continuum that ranges from cooperation to conflict. The other ranges from behavioral (involving physical actions) to cognitive (involving mental activity and information). The four basic task types are to **generate,** to **choose,** to **negotiate,** and to **execute.** Each is subdivided into two on the basis of one dimension of the circumplex, thus creating a total of eight task types.

- *Generate tasks* are further classified into those that are associated with generating plans (*planning tasks*) and generating ideas (*creativity tasks*).
- *Choose tasks* include tasks that have a correct answer (*intellective tasks*) and those that involve issues without right answers (*decision-making tasks*). Note that McGrath's definition of a decision-making task doesn't correspond totally to the more general definition of a decision as used in this book. We include some decisions that have right answers under the "decision" umbrella, recognizing that it isn't always easy to find the right answer even when it is known to exist.
- *Negotiate tasks* include tasks where members have to negotiate to resolve conflicts of viewpoints (*cognitive conflict tasks*) and those where members have to negotiate to resolve conflicts of interest (*mixed-motive tasks*).
- *Execute tasks* involve physical activity. Since DSS are used to enhance cognitive ability rather than physical dexterity, we will not elaborate on the tasks that fall in the *Execute* quadrant.

Other task classifications exist. One is a categorization as simple or complex. This is determined by the range of solution options, also referred to as the size of the search space. Large search spaces are associated with complex tasks, small search spaces with simple ones. In a group setting, the interaction requirements between individuals may also be an indication of task complexity. DSS and GDSS are typically more useful for aiding decision makers faced with more complex tasks [GALL88, BUI90].

Group tasks can also be classified into structured versus unstructured, much as we classified decisions overall on page 42. Structured tasks are predictable, repeatable, and lend themselves to algorithmic solution methods. Unstructured tasks are one-of-a-kind and do not lend themselves to algorithmic solution methods.

10.4.3 Task and Media Fit

Now that we have a sense of task types and media richness concepts, we can put them together. This matching will guide you in choosing a good communication medium for a specific decision support task.

Media richness theory [DAFT86] suggests that groups that are faced with a complex task require rich communication media and those that are faced with a simple task require communication media low in richness. If the task can be structured so that an algorithm facilitates the group activities, the need for communication is diminished so a communication medium with low richness is sufficient. If the task is unstructured, the group members need to communicate to correct their divergent interpretations and define objectives. Here, a communication channel that is high in richness allows members to obtain immediate feedback and arrive at a more accurate interpretation quickly.

McGrath and Hollingshead [MCGR93] used media richness theory to hypothesize what type of media best fit each type of task. For example, they propose that idea generation tasks are best performed if the medium is not too rich (e.g., computer-mediated communication) whereas negotiation tasks are best performed when the medium is high in richness (e.g., face-to-face). The fit between a task and a medium is referred to as **task-media fit.** Experimental research has found that idea generation tasks result in a higher number of ideas when the medium is low in richness (electronic media) than when it is high in richness (face-to-face media). Barkhi [BARK95] showed that face-to-face media result in better decisions than does computer-mediated communication for tasks that involve negotiation.

Determining the correct richness of its communication media is an important aspect of designing a GDSS to implement in any organization. Making the choice correctly often runs counter to the intuitive assumption that more richness is always better—that videoconferencing is better than audio teleconferencing, etc. If your organization is implementing a GDSS that allows members to communicate, you should provide video teleconferencing if the group is engaged in, for example, negotiation. If it is engaged in an idea generation task, however, video teleconferencing may be unnecessary; it may even hinder group work. Something along the lines of a discussion group, which provides a written record of what others have suggested, allows time to consider their suggestions and provides a way to add to the discussion without peer pressure. It may also work better as well as being less expensive.

10.5 TYPES OF GROUP DSS

Given that background, it's time to get into GDSS themselves. Much as we categorized DSS in Chapter 4, we can categorize GDSS in terms of how they deal with the content and the information flow of decisions. Figure 10–4 shows the two-dimensional spectrum that results from these two classifications. The content axis starts with the DSS hierarchy you read about in Chapter 4. We have added a "content-free" zero level to this hierarchy. This level is meaningful because GDSS with no decision-making content can be of use if they perform a useful function along the second, information flow, dimension. A videoconferencing system is an example of such a "content-free" GDSS. A content-free DSS for use by a single individual, by contrast, would be pointless.

The information flow axis shows the degree to which the GDSS is aware of how the group works and supports that style of work directly.

Level 1 along this axis consists of **connection management systems.** Dealing with information flow at this lowest level consists of providing a physical mechanism through which people involved in a decision can communicate. A network operating system such as NetWare provides this at a local level. So do WAN architectures and the Internet over wider areas. A system that does no more than this is

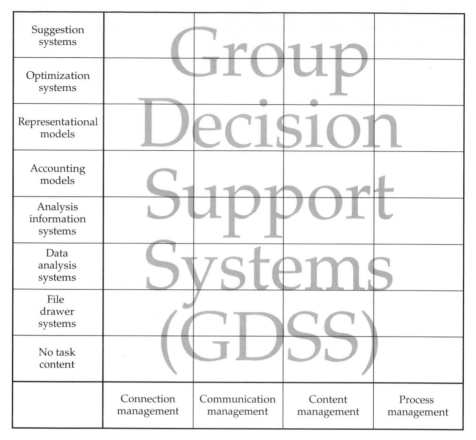

	Connection management	Communication management	Content management	Process management
Suggestion systems				
Optimization systems				
Representational models				
Accounting models				
Analysis information systems				
Data analysis systems				
File drawer systems				
No task content				

FIGURE 10–4 **Two-Dimensional GDSS Spectrum**

not a true GDSS, but this level anchors the spectrum at one end and underlies the more sophisticated capabilities of the higher levels.

Level 2 provides for **communication management.** This enhances the information flow by means of facilities to store messages, reply to them, forward them with comments, and so forth. Common examples of communication management software are electronic mail packages and discussion groups.

Level 3, **content management systems,** provides intelligent routing whereby the system knows where a document goes after its current user finishes with it, or where a message should go once it is entered. It is not necessary for the user to specify "send this to Chris" or "this is my vote on the current question." The system has the necessary information to handle the message correctly and will do so. Decision conference systems, which you'll read about later in this chapter, are examples of content management systems. A GDSS at this level does not take an active part in deciding how the decision-making process should proceed. Its actions are standardized.

Level 4, **process management,** takes an active part in the decision-making process, often by considering the content of the information in the flow in deciding what to do with it. A level 4 system might "know," for example, that hiring decisions above a certain salary must be approved by a division vice president but that those below this amount need only go as far up as the employee's department manager. In an electronic meeting, a level 4 system could decide who should have the virtual "floor," perhaps based on prior communication patterns, or advise participants on the best conflict resolution strategy to apply in a particular situation.

Other authors provide different views of this taxonomy. These views are important because they define other ways to combine GDSS which have common characteristics. These common characteristics can be useful guidelines for choosing a GDSS approach or product. In addition, you may encounter these other taxonomies in your reading.

One such taxonomy is from DeSanctis and Gallupe [DESA87]. They define GDSS level 1, level 2, and level 3. To avoid confusion between their numbered levels and ours, we will use the term *D&S level* from here on to refer to their levels. D&S level 1 GDSS "provide technical features aimed at removing common communication barriers." D&S level 2 provides "decision modeling and group decision techniques aimed at reducing uncertainty and 'noise' that occur in the group's decision process." D&S level 3 GDSS "are characterized by machine-induced group communication patterns" and control "the pattern, timing or content of information exchange." Figure 10–5 shows how these categories overlap the ones we presented earlier.

DeSanctis and Gallupe focus on the higher levels of the communication axis, which is appropriate in studying what is possible with GDSS. They do not bother with details of the task axis, because it is not unique to group DSS and because it has already been studied extensively. As they write, "Although support of the cognitive processes of individual group members may be included in a GDSS, the primary aim of the group component of the system must be to alter the structure of interpersonal exchange. It follows that GDSS research must be deeply concerned with the nature of communication in the group" [DESA87].

Another set of concepts that maps into our two-dimensional grid comes from Jay Nunamaker and his colleagues [NUNA91]. They call the vertical axis of our grid the task axis and the horizontal axis the process axis. Each axis is divided into support and structure. Task support corresponds to data-oriented DSS. Task structure, above it, refers to the use of models in DSS. This term fits since a decision must have structure if we are to develop a model for it. Similarly, process support refers to the communication infrastructure among participants in a group decision, whereas process structure means any techniques or rules that direct the pattern, timing, or content of this communication. Figure 10–6 shows how this two-by-two grid provides a higher level view of our categories.

It is, of course, possible to characterize group decision making (and group DSS) in several other ways: for example, by the size of the decision-making group. We won't cover all of the possibilities here because, although they are important for research, they tend to be less useful to information systems developers

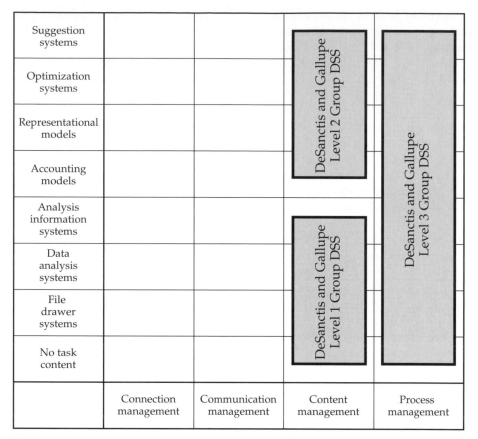

	Connection management	Communication management	Content management	Process management
Suggestion systems				
Optimization systems				
Representational models				
Accounting models				
Analysis information systems				
Data analysis systems				
File drawer systems				
No task content				

FIGURE 10–5   Two-Dimensional GDSS Spectrum with D & G Overlay

and users than the groupings we have discussed. (Some of them are quite useful in other contexts, of course. You have probably studied, or will study, them for this reason in organizational behavior courses.)

10.6 GROUPWARE

The term **groupware** came into popular use in the early 1990s. It is related to, but not identical with, group DSS. Groupware is the technology that groups use. The field that studies how people use groupware is called computer-supported coopera-tive work (CSCW). Groupware is defined in [ELLI91] as

> computer-based systems that support groups of people engaged in a common task (or goal) and that provide an interface to a shared environment.

Calendar programs are a common elementary groupware application. Such programs keep track of each group member's scheduled commitments. When it is necessary to arrange a meeting, each participant's schedule is instantly available

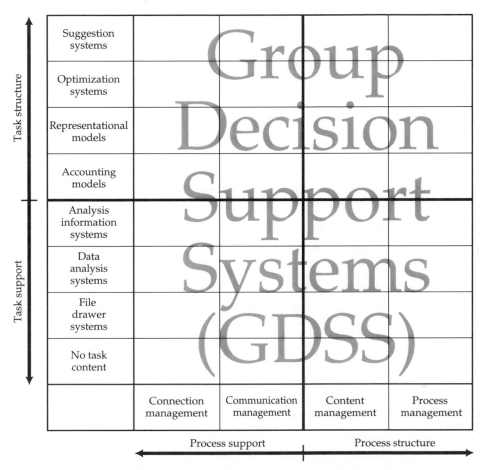

FIGURE 10–6 **Two-Dimensional GDSS Spectrum with Nunamaker Overlay**

and the most convenient time can be chosen. Whereas some programs merely display individual calendars in an easy-to-scan parallel format, most can find and suggest times at which a meeting can be held. When a calendar program is integrated with electronic mail capabilities, it can notify required and optional participants of meetings, schedule conference rooms and other required resources, collect confirmations, and generally simplify the process of meeting administration.

Given a group that is willing to keep their schedules on a computer for all to see—this is a behavioral, not a technical, issue—a calendar program can be a genuine time saver. Is it DSS? Probably not, though it is certainly groupware. The concept of groupware, then, covers more than a strict definition of GDSS would. We can view their relationship as in Figure 10–7. However, groupware facilitates the work of the group. It helps a group reach decisions more quickly, easily, or inexpensively than it otherwise would. We can be aware of the distinction and still discuss groupware as a useful component of a total system to support decision

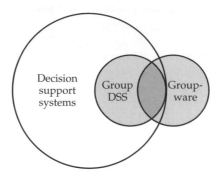

FIGURE 10–7 Relationship Among DSS, GDSS, and Groupware

makers. Most group DSS that you develop will incorporate some groupware components to smooth the overall work of the group.

Categories of groupware products include

- Electronic mail and messaging such as cc:Mail by Lotus and Microsoft Mail/Exchange.
- Conferencing tools such as ShowMe 2.0 by Sun Solutions and LinkWorks by Digital Equipment Corporation (now part of Compaq Computer).
- GDSS tools such as GroupSystems V by Ventana.
- Group document handling tools such as Face-to-Face by Crosswise and MarkUp by Mainstay Software.
- Workflow tools such as Workflow Analyst by ATI, FlowMark by IBM, and In-Concert by the vendor of the same name.

Some products, such as Lotus Notes, may fit into more than one category because of their flexibility and the wide variety of features they provide.

Once you select an appropriate groupware package for your organization, you have to implement it in your organization and make it a success. This is often not a simple task, but the following guidelines should help you achieve success with groupware. (You should not be surprised to find that these guidelines resemble those for implementing DSS, in Chapter 7, and for implementing data warehousing systems, in Chapter 15.)

- Find a groupware champion—a person of high stature in the organization who is willing to put his or her personal prestige on the line in support of the groupware project. (You'll read more about the need for this person in the context of executive information systems in Chapter 12.)
- Get a high level of commitment from top management.
- Pick a pilot project that has high visibility and financial impact, using a group that is supportive of both technology and innovation.
- Listen to the people involved in the pilot project, and do not be afraid to make changes they suggest.
- Plan and manage for change.
- Do not expect that introducing groupware will be a cure for all problems that your organization faces.

		Time	
		Same	**Different**

Place	**Same**	No-tech: meeting room
		
		Low-tech: overhead projector
		High-tech: conference room
		   support system
			No-tech: physical (cork and
			   thumbtack) bulletin board
			Low-tech: none
			High-tech: single-user computer
			   with shared files for
			   nonconcurrent use

	Different	No-tech: none
		Low-tech: telephone
		High-tech: teleconferencing
		   systems
			No-tech: mail
			Low-tech: fax
			High-tech: electronic bulletin
			   boards, electronic mail

FIGURE 10–8 Group Communication Grid

10.7 GROUP DSS IN USE TODAY

Several categories of group DSS are in use in the late 1990s. This section explores some examples.

10.7.1 Electronic Meeting Systems

Group decision-making situations vary by whether the decision participants are *in the same place* and whether they work on the decision *at the same time.* Since each questions has two possible answers (yes or no), there is a two-by-two grid of possibilities as shown in Figure 10–8. A great deal of work has been done to determine how computers can best support group decisions made in these different modes of cooperation. This categorization is important because the nature of the required support tools (computers, storage devices, display devices) depends on a group's position in this communication grid.

Many decision-making groups operate in different positions on this grid at different times. In one mode of operation, a group of people based in different locations gets together at the same time in the same place once, at the start of a long decision process, to establish personal relationships and ensure that all group members are working on the same overall task. Group members then return to their regular work locations, where they carry out their assigned tasks. This part of the process involves work at different locations and perhaps at different times. Depending on the nature of the decision and on the cost of bringing the group together again, there may be additional face-to-face meetings later.

Same time/same place meetings can be facilitated by an **electronic meeting room** (or **electronic boardroom** or **war room**) as shown in Figure 10–9. Such a facility typically has a microcomputer for each participant, connected by a high-speed local network. (You can read about LAN requirements for electronic meeting rooms in [DENN91].) There is also a large screen video display, located where it can be seen by all participants. A meeting **facilitator** guides the electronic aspects of the meeting. The facilitator can, among other things, view any participant's computer display and show it on the large screen. Conventional audiovisual

FIGURE 10–9   Electronic Meeting Room
Source: Photograph by Bob Mahoney. Supplied courtesy of IBM.

devices, such as overhead projectors and flipchart stands, are also available (sometimes a high-tech solution is more trouble than it's worth!).

Electronic meeting room software includes tools for planning the session, such as a tool by which group members can propose agenda items. During a meeting, the software can organize and structure members' comments. After the meeting, its recorded data serves as an organizational memory to ensure that comments are not forgotten. Thus, it supports primarily the process-related aspects of group decision making. Task-related support is limited to data retrieval and use of simple calculation tools.

An electronic meeting can proceed in the three styles described in [NUNA91]: **chauffeured, supported,** and **interactive.** In chauffeured style, the display screen is controlled by one person. It provides an electronic blackboard with effectively unlimited memory. Group communication remains primarily verbal. In supported style, all group members can write on the blackboard. Communication is partly verbal and partly electronic. In interactive style, the most highly computerized, hardly anyone speaks.

Nunamaker et al. found that the benefits of electronic meeting support grow as the group becomes larger, independently of the meeting style. However, the negative aspects of electronic support—for example, most people can talk faster than they can type—depend highly on the meeting style. The highly computerized interactive mode had the greatest drawbacks with small groups but did not get worse as the group got larger. Chauffeured style worked quite well with small groups but was ineffective with large ones. Supported style was between the two. Thus, they feel that "interactive styles will be preferred for larger groups, and supported or chauffeured styles for smaller groups."

A second level of electronic meeting support is provided by what Kraemer and King [KRAE88] call a **decision conference.** Starting with the electronic meeting room as its technical foundation, a decision conference facility adds task support tools. (An interesting application of decision conferencing, in which a nonprofit organization achieved impressive results on a budget using borrowed university facilities, is described in [QUAD92].)

One type of task support tool consists of voting support. This is appropriate when the decision-making group is large, such as a legislature. Voting support can include simple tabulation, averaging, evaluating preferences on a scale (say, 0 to 100), and the Delphi method.[2]

VisionQuest from Collaborative Technologies Corporation, Austin, Texas, is representative of decision conference products. Several others are available, such as Team-Focus (essentially IBM's version of VisionQuest), and OptionFinder. Decision conference products typically run on microcomputer workstation systems: one for each participant and one, a powerful file server with video projector, for the facilitator. They typically support group tasks of brainstorming, organizing the ideas generated, voting, evaluating the alternatives, and action planning. In brainstorming, decision conferencing tools initially give each participant a blank screen on which to enter ideas. As soon as the participant transmits an idea to the file server, he or she gets a new idea entry screen—but this time with one of the other participants' ideas, chosen at random and anonymous, at the top. Over time the random selection of other participants' ideas grows, giving the participant the inspiration of the other participants' thoughts but with no censorship, no time pressure, no way to identify the originator of a good or bad idea, and no need to compete with others for the floor. (These systems use a low-richness medium for this task, even though all participants are in the same room at the same time and could discuss the issue face to face. It just works better.)

Most decision conferencing systems support multiple voting methods: rank ordering of alternatives, yes/no, true/false, agree/disagree, score on a 10-point scale, percentage, and multiple choice. These can handle most voting situations that arise in practice. As is brainstorming in these systems, voting is anonymous. A junior accountant can give the CFO's ideas thumbs down without incurring corporate wrath. When votes are anonymous, personality and power issues do not arise. Everyone gets involved, including those who don't normally speak at meetings or who find it difficult to disagree with what has already been said.

Decision conference support software can also include analytic decision-making tools such as decision trees, influence trees, utility models, cost-benefit analyses, spreadsheet models, and on up to detailed models developed specifically for the purpose of making a particular decision or type of decision. Special considerations also apply to the user interface of such a group decision support system, as detailed in [GRAY89].

---

[2]Many present-day legislatures, including the U.S. Congress, use electronic devices to improve the speed and accuracy with which an otherwise conventional vote is recorded. These, however, fall below the threshold of what we call GDSS here.

Electronic meeting room and decision conference concepts can be extended directly to situations in which the group members participate at the same time but in different locations. If the different locations consist of multiple group sites—for example, part of a corporate planning group located at each of three divisional headquarters—the physical facilities at each location can resemble those of a central meeting place. A large display screen at each site can echo what is being displayed on the screen at the facilitator's location, via either a data link or a television camera and videoconferencing methods. Given sufficient high-speed communication bandwidth, a multisite meeting can take place practically as if all the participants were in the same room—though if any participant were to look up from the screen, he or she would see only part of the group.

When a meeting involves people who participate at different times, the potential for interactivity disappears. Participants read (or see, or hear) what others have done, mull it over, and respond. Simple meetings of this type take place on electronic bulletin boards. The software that maintains an electronic bulletin board is called a **bulletin board system** (BBS). In its simplest form, an electronic bulletin board is a sequential file of messages that any participant can read and append to. Most BBS allow a message to be identified as a response to an earlier message. This permits a reader to follow one thread of a discussion without being distracted by other threads. The USENET discussion groups (called **newsgroups**) on the Internet have operated in essentially this way for years. Most newsgroup-reading software, including the newsgroup modules of all popular Web browsers, can organize the messages by thread so readers can read related messages as a group.

Beyond the basic BBS capability, many decision support tools for same-time meetings remain useful in the different-time situation. Models are also useful in different-time meetings: having one model for the entire group has the advantage that all members are, so to speak, singing the same music.

The Delphi Method   The **Delphi method** [TURO96] is a useful different-time decision support method that is well suited to computer support. Its traditional application, which dates back to the 1960s at RAND Corporation [DALK70], was to obtain a consensus of experts on a forecasting question: "In what year will 50 percent of Swiss homes have picture telephones?" or "What percentage of patients, given this treatment, will be free of all symptoms within two weeks?"

Delphi was originally a paper-and-pencil system, though computers add new capabilities to the concept and are the standard communication method today. Its essence is a communication structure aimed at producing a detailed critical examination and discussion of a subject, often leading to a recommendation or decision. It is in this context that Delphi and DSS, specifically GDSS, converge.

The asynchronous nature of a Delphi process enables group members to participate when they want to, how they want to, and—importantly—*if* they want to. This last point is important because a decision process involves several stages, as you learned in Chapter 2. Different stages require different abilities. When a Delphi process is applied to a decision-making situation, each group member can participate in the parts where he or she feels most comfortable. In fact, different parts of the process can proceed in parallel. (This was not possible in the earlier paper-

and-pencil process, where the clerical aspects of coordination forced activity into formal question-and-answer rounds, but is perfectly practical with computer support.) This is an advantage over the "everyone in the same room" decision situation, where everyone involved in the process proceeds through it at the same rate, and those who cannot contribute to the aspect of the issue that is under discussion at the moment cannot do anything at all.

The essence of Delphi is posing questions or topics to group members, organizing their responses, and making the organized responses available to the group for further consideration. Participants are usually anonymous, which removes many barriers to free expression of ideas, though pen names can be used to enable group members to associate a contribution with the same person's earlier statements.

One application of the Delphi method is to obtain an expert forecast of some unknown but important decision parameter. Here, the group is typically asked one question—for example, how will introduction of our Model 200 affect demand for our existing Model 100 product? The group is asked to quantify their estimates and also to state any assumptions they are making and any uncertainties they have. The group can then discuss the assumptions and uncertainties, removing some as issues and highlighting the rest as critical to the forecast. After the uncertainties have been identified as reflecting either true uncertainty on the part of the entire group or unresolvable differences of opinion among subgroups, the entire group can revisit its earlier estimates in the context of these assumptions and the discussion that has gone on. The result is usually a better forecast, with deeper understanding of the issues, than averaging the initial estimates or any other simple procedure would have provided.

In another type of application, Delphi can be applied to an entire decision-making situation from recognition of the problem through evaluation and selection of the desired solution. Here some individuals could be working on decision goals while others are exploring options and their consequences. Here a human moderator is needed to organize the contributions and reflect them to the group in a coherent manner. Computers can do the job for simple, structured Delphis, but not for more complex situations.

Constructing a full Delphi process to support a major decision is a task for experts who have studied the method in more depth than we can go into it here. The concept of using a computer to facilitate structured, asynchronous interaction is often useful, though. (A discussion group is asynchronous, but unstructured.) Consider using it whenever you face a group decision situation in which differences must be aired and the reasons for disagreements discussed openly.

10.7.2 Work Flow Systems

When group work involves repetitive activities, the flow of work is known in advance and hence may be automated. A **work flow system** [MCCR92] (also written as **workflow system,** as one word) can be thought of as "intelligent electronic mail:" the system "knows" what the flow of information in a decision-making situation is supposed to be and routes information accordingly. This corresponds to either level 3, content management, or level 4, process management, of the group DSS hierarchy.

Most work flow systems are built on the foundation of an electronic mail system. They typically route work using **forms** and **scripts.**

A form corresponds to a paper form: a travel authorization, an insurance claim form, a purchase order form. Knowledge workers in the organization can read the form and, if authorized to do so, modify it by entering new data or altering existing data. When a user has finished with a form for the time being, he or she notifies the system. The work flow system then looks at the script associated with the form to decide what to do next.

A script defines the routing of the form. If the script is fixed, the work flow system is a level 3 system. If it can adjust its behavior on the basis of the form's content, it is a level 4 system. A typical script from [XENA92] might be

> If the purchase order amount is greater than $20,000, then send it to Jones; otherwise, if it's from a computer equipment vendor [this would be determined by the contents of some field, perhaps used as a key to access a database], then send it to Smith, otherwise, send it to Johnson.

The major characteristics of work flow development tools are [FERR92]

- They can move about various types of objects such as forms, documents, technical drawings, fax messages, photos, and artwork.
- They can route information objects automatically from person to person according to a programmed plan.
- Information can be processed at any point. Application developers have flexibility in the type of processing they specify.
- Tracking can show who has done what and where things are being held up.
- Information is, as noted previously, typically moved using electronic mail.

Thus, forms and scripts can support virtually any structured or unstructured business process that a systems analyst can describe.

Several workflow products are on the market today. They vary widely in their capabilities, not in the sense of one being 20 percent better than another, but in addressing different aspects of the work flow in an organization. For example,

- BeyondMail (Beyond, Inc., Cambridge, Mass.) can use scripts to filter the electronic mail a person receives. By searching for words in the text of messages, it can delete them, file them, or forward them to someone else—or, of course, leave them for their addressee to read. BeyondMail users can attach images, stored as binary files, to the routed messages.
- WorkFlo (FileNet Corp., Costa Mesa, Calif.) works in conjunction with that firm's imaging products to take image processing a giant step beyond just recording, storing, and communicating graphic information. Using OCR techniques to interpret the scanned image of a paper form, it can determine the content of a data field and use that value to route the form.
- Cooperation (NCR Corp., Dayton, Ohio) can record the steps that a user carries out in performing a computer-based task. It can use this record to automate the execution of the same task in the future.

- WorkMAN (Reach Software, Sunnyvale, Calif.) is able to "leapfrog" a person if a form sits too long on his or her desktop. While not appropriate to every situation, this capability can unstick a document moving up the chain of command if someone in the middle is on vacation or otherwise unavailable for an extended period of time.
- TeamRoute (Compaq Computer, previously Digital Equipment Corp., Maynard, Mass.) is designed to work with that firm's products for client/server computing. (You read about client/server computing, which partitions a task into components for execution on different computers, on page 171.)
- InConcert (InConcert, Inc., Cambridge, Mass.), which we discuss in Section 10.8.3, is an object-oriented solution for complex, production-level work flows.
- Notes (Lotus Development Corp., Cambridge, Mass.), which we discuss in Section 10.8.2, has work flow management capability among its other features.

In choosing an application to automate via a work flow system, Ferris suggests these candidates:

- Manual systems in which different people or departments complete different parts of a multisection manual form. For example, in insurance claim processing, one person certifies that a policy is current and another determines the amount of damages that were incurred.
- Manual systems where multipart forms are used, especially if participants do their tasks only at intermittent times that aren't easily scheduled. For example, corporate travel authorizations must be approved by several levels of management (question: what is the decision here?) and then go to the employee, his or her manager, the accounting office, and the firm's travel agency.
- Projects that require bits of information from many people. An example is a product specification that is distributed widely for comments.
- Front-ending production databases for either query or report generation. A form with an appropriate database accessing script can be an easy-to-use way to extract desired information with no technical expertise.

Work flow systems facilitate information, when compared to traditional communications where one must find out who has information, request it, and finally (hopefully) get it. They move power from the person who has information to the person who defines the processing of a given task. Moving power even further, so that a person who needs information has the power to get it, requires the cultural change that you read about near the end of Section 10.3.

Work flow systems are often associated with image processing.[3] It is incontestable that many work flow applications, such as those involving reproductions of paper forms or where some of the information to be routed is pictorial in nature,

---

[3]One reason is that one of the earliest successful work flow products, FileNet's WorkFlo, was developed by an image processing vendor and sold in conjunction with its imaging products.

are often well supported by imaging technology. However, the two concepts are separate and should be considered separately.

10.8 GROUPWARE PRODUCTS

The next three sections describe three categories of group DSS and provide example products of each category.

- *Collaborative authoring.* DOLPHIN and MERMAID help a group of writers and reviewers agree on the content of a document.
- *Document management and more.* Notes, from Lotus Development Corporation, makes sure that information gets to all interested parties and is organized properly for their needs when it arrives.
- *Workflow management.* InConcert, from InConcert, Inc. (a Xerox New Enterprise company), a work flow management system supports structured processes as well as dynamic changes that result from running instances of processes.

10.8.1 Collaborative Authoring: DOLPHIN and MERMAID

Group authorship of a document is common. You have probably written joint term papers or group projects. You will find the same situation in the business world. Few corporations let one person write a press release, marketing brochure, or magazine article and send it to the public with no review by others. Instead, such documents must pass careful review by experts on technical, marketing, legal, and strategic issues. The document is changed until all are satisfied.

The task involves a great deal of coordination and often negotiation. For example, if two reviewers disagree on how a section should be changed, the author must either shuttle back and forth (logically, if not physically) between them or bring them together to reach a compromise. Choosing the appropriate wording for a published document is a decision. This decision can be aided by suitable data-oriented computer support. This computer support can provide the DSS benefits of improved quality, improved communication, and often learning and training. By eliminating the need to track down people and have them available for discussions at the same time, collaborative authoring systems can save time. As a valuable byproduct, they can also save substantial quantities of paper.

DOLPHIN, from the German firm GMD, is a software system that supports collaborative authoring in a distributed or face-to-face meeting environment. It supports the phase of collaborative writing that requires intense communication and negotiation, and provides audio and video channels for distributed meetings. DOLPHIN provides a large number of functions and capabilities to make collaborative authoring easier. It provides multiple cursors to show who is working on what part of the shared document. The software also allows group members to access a shared workspace from remote sites, exchange annotations, and engage in discussions. It uses replication to replicate the changes and utilizes "locking" in the transaction-processing sense to control concurrency.

FIGURE 10–10   **Display Example in a Five-Party Conference Connecting the United States and Japan**
Source: From reference SAKA96.

Authors in a group need to access and modify documents concurrently. The environment should address issues of concurrency while enforcing minimum restrictions on the authors. That is, authors working on different parts of the document should be able to do this without any problems, while those who may be working on the same part of the document should be prevented from destroying the constantly evolving work of others. This is done by concurrency control, similar to what you learned about transaction processing in your introductory MIS studies, and replication.

MERMAID (Multimedia Environment for Remote Multiple Attendee Interactive Decision-making) is a multimedia and multiparty desktop conference system developed by Nippon Electric Corporation (NEC) (see Figure 10–10). MERMAID supports a wide range of cooperative work in a distributed environment, including collaborative authoring. Multiple geographically distributed decision makers can simultaneously view and process information in text, graphics, images, handwriting, voice, and video. The system has been used for such tasks as remote technical discussions, software development by groups whose members are distributed, joint system design, and joint document editing.

MERMAID can accommodate wide area networks and multiple local area networks using any networking technology. The system provides a multiwindow user interface with pull-down and pop-up menus that can be controlled by using the mouse and keyboard. This provides a friendly user interface and makes it easy for nontechnical office workers to collaborate using this program. When application programs execute any input from any participant, the executed results appear identically at all sites. Hence, executed results are simultaneously shared among all participants.

Multiple authors can co-edit documents in real time using the shared-document editor while they can have a conversation using the video- and audio-enabled conferencing facility. User experiences reported show that users prefer voice first, then written media, and last video for real-time computer supported effective collaboration [SAKA96]. This suggests that the type of collaboration involved in joint authorship does not require a rich communication medium. The task may involve idea generation more than negotiation. The limited uncertainty can be resolved using voice and text.

In terms of our GDSS categories, a collaborative authoring tool is a content management system. It knows a great deal about what is done during document editing but does not try to guide the process on its own. On the task side, it is a file drawer system: It can retrieve documents and display them but has no capabilities for analysis or modeling. (Given the task it is designed to help with, these capabilities probably wouldn't be useful.) A collaborative authoring program can be a worthwhile investment for businesses that rely heavily on group review of centrally written and controlled documents.

10.8.2 Lotus Notes

Since its 1990 introduction, Notes from IBM subsidiary Lotus Development Corporation has become the most popular groupware application. Indeed, to many people it defines the category. One reason is the marketplace impetus it received from an early order for 10,000 copies from one of the "Big Six"[4] accounting and consulting firms, Price Waterhouse. At the 1990 list price of $62,500 for 200 single-user licenses, that would represent over a $3 million purchase. (Given the size and visibility of PW's commitment to a brand-new and then unproven product, it is reasonable to assume that they received a substantial discount.) Subsequent large orders, some of them much larger, from other major firms such as Metropolitan Life Insurance and Arthur Andersen have combined to give Notes more corporate penetration and visibility than any other group computing application.

What is Notes? In its simplest form, Notes is a way to organize documents and make them available to groups of people. It consolidates the tools that groups within an organization need to communicate and collaborate effectively. Some people think of Notes as a document database for tracking applications. It is not a true relational database because it does not allow the user to enter data in a field in one file and then use that same field in another. Hence, changes made to one record do not automatically update all instances of that entry throughout the system. Because Notes databases may store information redundantly, applications that require the storage and manipulation of extremely large number of records are not well suited to Notes. Notes can store compound documents and do periodic, but not immediate, updates. Hence, Notes is not a good candidate for applications that require instant updating such as airline ticketing. However, Notes allows users to store unstructured information. This is valuable because most of the "soft" information in an organization is unstructured.

---

[4]Now "Big Five" as the result of the subsequent merger of Price Waterhouse with Deloitte & Touche.

Although not designed as a work flow product, Notes offers many features, such as serial routing and status checking, to make it usable in work flow applications as well. Notes macros can create rule-based work flow routing and management. Notes has been categorized as software for information sharing or for collaborative computing; however, it goes beyond that. An excellent definition comes from Jesse Berst in [BERS92]: "an environment for building information-sharing applications on networks." He goes on to explain that Notes is built around four core technologies: security, compound documents, replication, and development tools.

Compound documents are the basic component of the Notes database. A compound document consists of many types of information: data (structured text or numbers organized into named data fields), free-form text, graphics, and sound (with available add-on software to augment the basic package).

Notes is built around a distributed, **replicated database** (that is, several copies of the database exist in different locations) whose contents are available to all users. Replication is fundamental to the operation of Notes. Each user accesses a copy of the Notes database stored on his or her local server. Any changes or additions made by that user go into the local copy. Many organizations, however, have more than one server. These servers may be permanently linked via suitable wide area connections or, in a common situation, may be connected to each other only from time to time. When that user's server connects to other servers in the overall corporate network, the servers compare information on documents that have been changed or added since each database was updated. If one copy has been updated it replaces the older copy or copies.

What happens if two Notes users update the same document at the same time, each on a different LAN? This creates a **replication conflict.** Notes keeps both copies. The one that has been changed the most times since the previous replication is considered the original. The other is considered a response to the original and is marked with a special symbol next to its name. A user with suitable access privileges (the author of the document, or any other user with at least editor-level access) who sees this conflict flag can merge the differing versions into one, deleting the other. This new version will, through the replication process, then be distributed to all Notes servers on the network.

Development tools allow a Notes system to be customized to the needs of a particular organization. Customization involves **forms,** through which information goes into a Notes database, and **views,** through which it comes out.

Forms consist of static text, graphics, and fields. Fields can contain several types of data: number, text, rich text (formatted with character styles such as italic letters), time/date, and more. They can be specified as entered by the user (editable later or not), as computed and saved with the document, or as recomputed each time the document is displayed. Each type of field has a great deal of formatting flexibility.

Views allow users to view the summary of documents in the database, sort them based on a sort criteria, and select a particular database to view its contents. Each row in a view typically represents a document. Each column in a view can either be a field in the document or a formula that computes a value. Columns

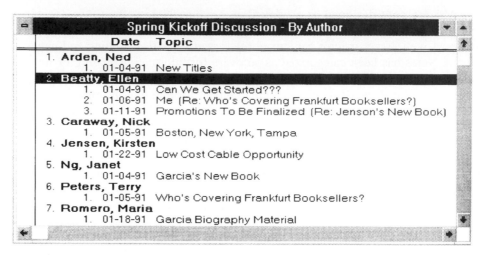

FIGURE 10–11 Lotus Notes Database Design Manual
Source: Courtesy of Lotus Development Corp. Lotus Notes is a registered trademark of Lotus Development Corp.

may overlap in a categorized view such as in Figure 10–11. This document is sorted and categorized by author name. The name Ellen Beatty appears once, with all her documents listed below. A mouse click will display the entire text of any desired document.

In addition to formatting, views have selection formulas. **Selection formulas** define the set of documents that Notes will include in the view. A user can thus opt to see only documents that apply to the Acme Corporation as a supplier, include the word *capacitor,* and were written since April 10th.

Formulas, used as selection formulas, as the basis for computed fields, and in several other contexts, provide Notes with considerable application development power. A **formula** is, in effect, a computer program that is invoked when the Notes user takes a specified action such as opening a view. Formulas can perform calculations, organize data, transform data, take different actions depending on the content of a field or of some other variable in the environment, and more. Although it would probably not be a good idea to process accounts receivable or compute stresses on a mechanical linkage via Notes formulas, it wouldn't be impossible.

Security is mandatory in sharing data over a network. If a product such as Notes is widely used, some of the information in its database will be confidential, to be seen only by a few of the many registered Notes users on the net. Accordingly, Notes incorporates several security features including **access control lists** (by individual, department, work group, or division, with seven levels as shown in Figure 10–12) and encryption (of individual fields or entire documents).

With the explosive growth of the Internet, Notes has long provided a capability to access the Internet and browse Web pages via a Notes server called InterNotes.

Rank	Access Level	Description
1	Manager	Can perform all operations: read, write, and modify data, forms and views; assign and modify all security controls. Default level for person who creates the database. Only level that can delete the entire database.
2	Designer	Can perform any operation on the database except modifying security controls or deleting the entire database.
3	Editor	Can read, write, and modify the content of any document in the database but cannot alter database structure or functionality (forms, views, etc.). Can remove the encryption from any document for which he or she has the encryption key.
4	Author	Can read and write documents. Can edit documents that he or she originally composed.
5 (tie)	Reader	Can read, but not enter or modify, documents.
5 (tie)	Depositor	Can enter, but not read or modify, documents.
7	No access	Cannot access the database for any purpose.

FIGURE 10–12 Notes Access Control Hierarchy

Starting with Release 5, the Notes interface has been modified to resemble the standard Web interface closely—requiring some relearning on the part of experienced Notes users but making it more accessible to the tens of millions of Web users who have never used Notes. A user at a Notes workstation can open Web pages and download files from FTP sites. Notes contains built-in mini programs that have specific functions to collect pages from the Web for off-line reading, and keep regular tabs on certain pages so that Notes can automatically notify the user if the pages change. Lotus Notes complements the Web by providing enhanced security, improved document authoring support, replication and mobile support, full text retrieval, improved application development support, integrated document database management, and workflow management, within the familiar Web environment.

The emergence of such tools as Sun's Java language brought Web application development to an acceptable level for client/server applications. Notes followed with the introduction of LotusScript, a version of Basic with object-oriented extensions. Combining LotusScript capabilities with InterNotes enables organizations to build Web-enabled applications within the Lotus Notes environment, taking advantage of Notes security, database replication, and other features. Notes work flow can accept input from remote users with Web browsers that are not based on the Notes platform by using InterNotes Web Publisher. Such browsers may also act as clients for accessing Notes server databases. Web Navigator allows users to search the Web and extract information in a way that is natural for Notes users.

Developing complex Notes applications using capabilities such as these calls for specialized training and expertise. Defining a database, creating views, and creating forms with complex formulas calls for skills that the average end user is not likely to possess. However, users with suitable training can create simple Notes databases for use within a small work group, can modify existing forms to meet their personal needs, and—perhaps most importantly—can see the value of new Notes applications and describe those applications to MIS specialists.

In terms of our GDSS spectrum with the categories shown in Figure 10–3, a Notes application can range up to a data analysis system on the vertical axis and to a content management system on the horizontal axis. (In theory it could go higher on the vertical axis, but if nontrivial modeling is called for, Notes is probably not the best choice of software.) A specific Notes application and database might be at a lower level.

10.8.3 InConcert Work Flow

InConcert Inc.'s InConcert [MARS97] is a work flow management system for complex production-level work flows. The InConcert work flow engine provides the platform for building specific applications that help groups work together to solve a problem. Companies such as the publishers of *TV Guide* magazine use In-Concert to manage processes with thousands of steps and hundreds of users.

InConcert's work flow system is adaptive. It lets managers and knowledge workers manage their work in a varied and constantly changing business environment (see Figure 10–13). InConcert uses its object technology to associate an unlimited number of attributes and external data with processes and tasks. These attributes provide placeholders for information that will become part of the processes as unanticipated change affects the processes. This lets InConcert adapt its behavior to changes in the work environment.

InConcert operates in a client/server environment. The package includes the server software, the client software, the developer's kit, and the optional tools and add-on modules. The client/server architecture is a three-tier architecture. Those tiers are (1) client software, (2) server software, and (3) database management system. Users interact with the client applications that access workflow services over the network to communicate with the server. The server interprets the requests from the client and executes the appropriate action. If the client's request is for access to the database, the server translates the requests into SQL statements appropriate for the relational database management system. Clients are used to build the process, design the user interface, and manage the process.

InConcert code is written in the C++ object-oriented programming language. The key object classes that make up the building blocks of the work flow applications include processes, tasks, roles, and data references. Tasks are the units of work that make up the processes, roles connect the tasks to the people who perform them, and data references associate documents and data. Developers can define subclasses of any objects and attach new attributes to these subclasses.

InConcert provides security by restricting access to the users who do not have the appropriate access privileges. A system administrator can assign different access privileges to users based on their needs. The process designer who is the owner of specific objects may grant access permissions to the objects.

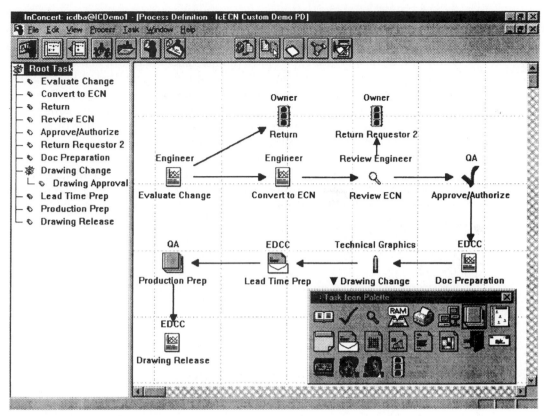

FIGURE 10–13 InConcert Screen
Source: Courtesy of InConcert, Inc.

It is not hard to define a work flow to InConcert. The first step in defining a process is to define the tasks in it. To do this, in turn, one sets task attributes by selecting the task and then opening an Attribute window to assign values to its attributes. Standard available attributes for a task include role, pool, priority, due date, duration, perform conditions, auto activate, application, process, and process owner. Most of these names are self-explanatory. For example, the *role attribute* indicates who will perform the task, the *pool attribute* identifies a group of users who have some common characteristics (e.g., skill set), and *duration* is the amount of time that the designer anticipates the task will take to complete. *Perform conditions* determine the route the process will take, while *auto activate* specifies if the subtasks of a task should activate without explicit participation of the task owner.

Once the tasks comprising a process are created, the system developer defines the routing by drawing arrows to represent dependencies between the task icons. Rules may define conditional routing based on task attributes. Composite conditions can be defined, using logical operators such as AND and OR.

Unlike other work flow products that check conditions for routing a task after it is complete, InConcert checks to see if the conditions for starting a task are satisfied.[5] For example, suppose that either task B or task C follows task A, depending on the value of a calculation that A performs. In most other systems, a rule associated with the definition of task A could state, "When this task is completed, if the value of attribute X is greater than 5, then route to task B; otherwise, route to task C."

In InConcert, the *receiving tasks* hold the conditional activation commands. A rule would be attached to task B that could read, "Start if the value of attribute X of task A is greater than 5." (The rule would not activate the task until task A is complete since the value of attribute X would not be defined until then.) Another would be attached to task C: "Start if the value of attribute X of task A is not greater than 5." Although this may be more work intensive because two rules must be defined instead of one in this example, it can provide more flexibility in how the rules define work flows.

InConcert is a process management system along the horizontal axis of the GDSS hierarchy. With its database accessing capabilities, it can be at least a file drawer system on the vertical axis. Depending on the particular application and the degree of customization that was applied, it may be higher than that.

SUMMARY

A group decision support system is a DSS whose design takes into account how people work together in reaching a decision. They can help with at least four types of group tasks: generating ideas, solving problems with correct answers, deciding issues with no "right" answer, and resolving conflicts of viewpoint.

Group DSS are becoming more prevalent for several reasons. One is that modern management methods have increased the importance of group decision making. Another is that the technical infrastructure for communication within the organization, including desktop access to organizationwide networks, is becoming more common.

Group decision support systems can be at any level of the seven-level hierarchy given in the previous chapter. In addition, they vary along a second, information flow, dimension. Along this dimension they can provide connection management, communication management, content management, or process management capability. While this is not the only possible view of GDSS, other views can be mapped into it.

Media richness theory suggests that groups that are faced with a complex task require rich communication media and those faced with simple tasks require communication media that are low in richness. Richness is defined in terms of the available number of the communication channels, the capacity of each channel, and the speed of feedback provided through the channels.

---

[5]If you are familiar with expert systems, you may recognize this as, in essence, the difference between forward and backward chaining.

McGrath and Hollingshead use media richness theory to suggest task-media fit hypothesis that proposes what type of media best fit each type of task. Task-media fit suggests group members engaged in negotiation would be better served if their communication channel is rich (i.e., face-to-face or video) while group members engaged in generating ideas may do better if the communication channel is less rich.

Groupware is a broader concept than GDSS. It incorporates all types of software designed to facilitate the work of a group, including aspects of its work that do not correspond to decision making.

Electronic meetings provide an important type of group decision support. These facilitate same time/same place group decision making. An electronic meeting can operate in chauffeured, supported, or interactive style. Task support tools can be added to an electronic meeting room to create a decision conference facility. Networks can extend electronic meetings and decision conferences to multiple sites. The Delphi approach is a useful way to structure asynchronous communication for a decision-making task.

Work flow systems are designed to reflect the flow of information in a group decision-making process. They use forms to carry the content of a decision being made and scripts to control the flow of these forms in an organization.

Sample group decision support products include—among many others— DOLPHIN and MERMAID to help writers and reviewers agree on document content; Lotus Notes, which organizes information and routes it to interested parties; and InConcert, from InConcert, Inc., which manages work flow.

KEY TERMS

access control list
bulletin board system (BBS)
calendar programs
chauffeured (meeting style)
choose (task type)
circumplex
communication management systems (GDSS type)
communication medium richness
compound document
connection management systems (GDSS type)
content management systems (GDSS type)
decision analyst
decision conference
Delphi method
electronic boardroom
electronic bulletin board
electronic meeting room
electronic meeting systems
execute (task type)

facilitator
forms (for entering data into Notes); (for work flow systems)
formula (in Notes view)
generate (task type)
group decision support system (GDSS)
groupthink
groupware
image processing
interactive (meeting style)
media richness
meeting facilitator
negotiate (task type)
newsgroup
process management systems (GDSS type)
process structure
process support
replicated database, replication
replication conflict
scripts (for work flow systems)
selection formula (in Notes view)
supported (meeting style)
task-media fit
task structure
task support
views (for extracting data from Notes)
war room
work flow systems (also as one word: *workflow* systems)

REVIEW QUESTIONS

1. What is a group DSS? How does it differ from a nongroup DSS?
2. What are the organizational factors that have led to increased use of group DSS?
3. What are the technical factors that have led to increased use of group DSS?
4. What is groupthink? How can its impact be reduced?
5. What are the eight types of group tasks? With which can group DSS help? What is the common characteristic of these tasks?
6. What are the two dimensions along which we can characterize group DSS? Which of these does not apply to other DSS? What are its four levels?
7. What is media richness? Why is media richness important to the design of group DSS?
8. What is groupware? How does it relate to group DSS?
9. Describe an electronic meeting system. For what types of decision-making tasks might it be useful?
10. What are the three electronic meeting styles of operation?
11. What is a decision conference facility? How does it differ from an electronic meeting room?
12. Define electronic bulletin board.

13. What does a work flow system do? What are its key characteristics?

14. Define script and form in the context of work flow systems.

15. Describe the major capabilities of Lotus Notes. What are its formulas good for?

16. Describe to a CEO why you may need both Lotus Notes and a collaborative writing tool such as MERMAID.

EXERCISES

1. Place each of the following GDSS in the appropriate squares of Figures 10–3 and 10–5:
   a. InConcert from InConcert, Inc.
   b. The second (group-oriented) version of the factory supervisors' DSS on page 385.
   c. A college admissions office system. It provides all admissions staff members with access to applicant records, lets them make comments on the applicants which other staff members may read, records evaluations (two evaluations, for academic and nonacademic factors, both on a scale of 1 to 5), and provides a summary of all evaluations to date.

2. You are writing a group term paper with two other students. Some parts, such as the introduction and conclusions, must be a joint product. Other parts will be written by one of you but reviewed by the others and, in some cases, used by the others as they write their parts. All parts must be merged before you submit the paper: in some cases section by section, in other cases (such as the bibliography) line by line. The three of you live and eat in different buildings. You have (except for the course that requires this paper) different class, activity, and work schedules. Discuss how DOLPHIN would support this group task. What capabilities would your ideal groupware tool for this task have, that it does not?

3. Use your library's automated search facility to find articles on Lotus Notes in the recent business literature. (Search for both "Lotus" and "Notes" rather than the phrase "Lotus Notes," as the words may not appear in precisely that form. For an example of why this is so, see the first sentence of the Lotus Notes section on page 408.) Find at least three add-on software packages that work with Notes. What capabilities do they add to it that it did not originally have? How would these capabilities be valuable in group decision making?

4. Consider the following three group decision-making situations:
   • Four instructors are teaching a business strategies course as a team. Each is responsible for a particular aspect of the course: marketing, finance, organizational behavior, and information systems. The four must jointly assign a grade to each student. Each instructor grades weekly homework assignments and hour exam questions in his or her area. A few assignments involve two areas, but never more than two, and are graded jointly by both instructors. (Because of time constraints in grading finals, no final exam questions are graded jointly, but the final includes questions from all four areas.) The term project involves all four areas and receives one grade. The instructors must also agree on grade adjustments for class participation and similar nonquantifiable factors.
   • A jury of 12 people, chosen with no regard for computer expertise, must reach a verdict in a technical trial. The defendant, being sued for infringing on the plaintiff's software patent, claims the patent is invalid because the patented method was already in general use when the patent was applied for. If this is true, the defendant will prevail. Both sides have brought forth experts who have explained, at great length and with many references to technical concepts, why their side's position is correct.

- The board of directors of the Starbyte Micro Users' Group (SMUG) is planning an annual meeting of this 10,000-member organization. They must choose a place (city, then specific exhibit facilities and hotels), dates, theme, and more. Some of these are partly fixed: The city must be large enough to have the required space and cannot be near one in which the group has recently met, the meeting must take place between late September and mid-October. Some may be interrelated: a desired hotel may be available only on one set of dates within that period. The board of directors consists of 10 employees of organizations that use Starbyte Micro computers. No two work in the same organization. All know each other from years of SMUG work. They come from all parts of North America (Mexico City to Edmonton). While their employers support SMUG, it is in everyone's interest to minimize travel and face-to-face meetings. SMUG has a small paid staff, shared with several other similar organizations, which can carry out specific tasks involved in arranging meetings and can get specific information as requested, but it cannot make decisions of this or any other type on its own.

  For each of these decisions:

  a. Which of the four quadrants of Figure 10–8 (same or different time and place) could this decision be made in?

  b. Describe a possible content management GDSS that could support this decision.

  c. Describe a possible process management GDSS that could support this decision.

5. ATM machines have eliminated the need to have face-to-face communication to perform many banking transactions. This change has replaced a rich channel (face-to-face communication) with one that is much less rich (character terminal with minimal keyboard) without impacting the customer's ability to perform the task or satisfaction with its outcome—indeed, customers are often more satisfied because the transaction is carried out more quickly. Identify two other business tasks for which a rich communication channel has traditionally been used but which do not require one. For each, suggest a reasonable substitute with less richness that can support the task.

6. Your company has five manufacturing plants, seven warehouses and one product. Each plant has a production capacity, a different unit cost of production, and a manager who decides how many units to send to each of the warehouses. Each warehouse has a total demand, given by the manager of that warehouse. Shipping cost depends on the distance from plant to warehouse.

   You are to design a GDSS that allows five plant managers, in each of their different locations, to collaborate to find a solution to the overall problem: How many units should each plant send to each warehouse so as to minimize the total cost to the company as a whole? You should design a GDSS that helps managers provide information and find a solution that minimizes the costs. The collaborative workspace should have the appropriate richness for the task. Since a wide range of systems could meet the functional requirement, picking appropriate richness is an important part of your answer to this question.

   You may assume the total production capacity of all five plants is at least equal to the demand of all seven warehouses. If it is greater than total demand, some plants will be asked to produce less than their capacity. (Some plants may not be asked to produce any product at all. When this happens in the real world, factories are closed.)

   a. Draw the plant managers' input screen, the warehouse managers' input screen, and the output screen of your system, and describe how your system would work.

   b. Given all the required data, does this optimization problem meet the requirements for a linear programming solution? Why or why not?

7. Members of the Harwich University Concert Band and Choir want to raise money to support their forthcoming concert tour to Austria and southern Germany. Would a decision conference system such as VisionQuest be helpful? Why or why not?

8. Search the Web for references to *groupthink* in the context of support for the Vietnam War among U.S. President Johnson's advisors in the late 1960s. How did groupthink manifest itself there? What were some of its consequences? Could group DSS have affected the situation? If so, how? If not, why not?

REFERENCES

BARK95   Barkhi, Reza. "An Empirical Study of the Impact of Proximity, Leader, and Incentives on Negotiation Process and Outcomes in a Group Decision Support Setting," unpublished doctoral dissertation, The Ohio State University (1995).

BERS92   Berst, Jesse. "Deciphering Lotus's Notes." *Computerworld* 26, no. 20 (May 18, 1992), p. 36.

BUI90   Bui, T. X., Sivasankaran, T. R. "Relation between GDSS Use and Group Task Complexity," Proceedings of the Twenty-third Annual Hawaii International Conference on System Sciences vol. 3. IEEE Computer Society Press, Los Alamitos, Calif. (1990), p. 69.

DAFT86   Daft, Richard, and Robert H. Lengel. "Organizational Information Requirements, Media Richness and Structural Design." *Management Science* 32, no. 5, (May 1986), p. 554.

DALK70   Dalkey, N. C. "Use of Self-Ratings to Improve Group Estimates." *Journal of Technological Forecasting and Social Change* 1, no. 3 (March 1970).

DENN91   Dennis, Alan R., Tom Abens, Sudha Ram, and Jay F. Nunamaker Jr. "Communication Requirements and Network Evaluation within Electronic Meeting System Environments." *Decision Support Systems* 7, no. 1 (January 1991), p. 13.

DESA87   DeSanctis, Gerardine, and R. Brent Gallupe. "A Foundation for the Study of Group Decision Support Systems." *Management Science* 33, no. 5 (May 1987), p. 589.

ELLI91   Ellis, Clarence A., Simon J. Gibbs, and Gail L. Rein. "Groupware: Some Issues and Experiences." *Communications of the ACM* 34, no. 1 (January 1991), p. 39.

FERR92   Ferris, David. "Work Flow Applications Simplify Office Processes." *Network World* 9, no. 27 (July 6, 1992), p. 31.

GALL88   Gallupe, R. B., G. DeSanctis, and G. W. Dickson. "Computer-Based Support for Group Problem Finding: An Experimental Investigation." *MIS Quarterly* 12, no. 2 (1988), p. 277.

GRAY89   Gray, Paul, and Lorne Olfman. "The User Interface in Group Decision Support Systems." *Decision Support Systems* 5 (1989), p. 119.

KRAE88   Kraemer, Kenneth L., and John Leslie King. "Computer-Based Systems for Cooperative Work and Group Decision Making." *ACM Computing Surveys* 20, no. 2 (June 1988), p. 115.

LENG83   Lengel, Robert H. "Managerial Information Processing and Communication-Media Source Selection Behavior," unpublished doctoral dissertation, Texas A&M University (1983).

MALL98   Mallach, Efrem G., and Dorothy Eastman. "Four Modes of Organizational Network Usage: An Information Management Framework for Organizational Assessment and Choice Management." *Proceedings.* Information Resources Management Association International Conference, Boston, Mass. (May 1998), p. 249.

MARS97   Marshak, Ronni T. "InConcert Workflow." Patricia Seybold Group's *Workgroup Computing Report* 20, no. 3 (March 1997), p. 2.

MASL43   Maslow, Abraham H. "Theory of Motivation." *Psychological Review* 50
(1943), pp. 370–396; reprinted with minor changes in his *Motivation and
Personality,* Harper Bros., New York, (1954).

MCCR92   McCready, Scott C. "Work-Flow Software." *Computerworld* 26, no. 44
(November 2, 1992), p. 85.

MCGR93   McGrath, Joseph Edward, and A. B. Hollingshead. "Putting the 'Group' Back
in Group Support Systems: Some Theoretical Issues About Dynamic Processes
in Groups with Technological Enhancements," in *Group Support Systems*
(L. M. Jessup and J. S. Valacich, eds.), McMillan, New York (1993).

MCGR84   McGrath, Joseph Edward. *Groups: Interaction and Performance.* Prentice-
Hall, Englewood Cliffs, N.J. (1984).

NUNA91   Nunamaker, Jay F. Jr., Alan R. Dennis, Joseph S. Valachich, Douglas R.
Vogel, and Joey F. George. "Electronic Meeting Systems to Support Group
Work." *Communications of the ACM* 34, no. 7 (July 1991), p. 40.

QUAD92   M. A. Quaddus, D. J. Atkinson, and M. Levy. "An Application of Decision
Conferencing to Strategic Planning of a Voluntary Organization." *Interfaces*
22, no. 6 (November–December 1992), p. 61.

SAKA96   Sakata, Shiro, Kazutoshi Maeno, Hideyuki Fukuoka, Toyoko Abe, and Hiromi
Mizuno. "Multimedia and Multi-Party Desktop Conference System:
MERMAID as Groupware Platform," in *Groupware and Authoring* (Roy Rada,
ed.), Academic Press, New York (1996), p. 345.

TURO96   Turoff, Murray, and Starr Roxanne Hiltz. "Computer-Based Delphi Processes,"
in *Gazing into the Oracle: The Delphi Method and its Application to Social
Policy and Public Health* (Michael Adler and Erio Ziglio, eds.), Jessica
Kingsley Publishers, London (1996).

XENA92   Xenakis, John J. "The Ultimate in Teamwork: Groupware." *BCS Update* 15,
no. 1 (January 1992), p. 6.

CASE

Fort Lowell Trading Company
Using GDSS?

Early Tuesday morning, Stan James, Sr., relaxed with a glass of tomato juice in the
first-class cabin of America West flight 2606 from Miami to Phoenix. He didn't
like to get up that early—he had to be at the airport at 7:30 for an 8:00 A.M.
flight—but this was the only nonstop from Miami to anywhere in Arizona. Fortunately, a company car and driver could meet him at Sky Harbor airport in Phoenix
and have him at FLTC headquarters in plenty of time for an important board meeting that afternoon. With any luck, he'd be back in the Everglades with his wife,
searching for that rare variety of anhinga, by Thursday.

Although this was only the second time that Stan Sr. had interrupted a vacation
for a board meeting, he thought, "With this Internet I keep hearing about, I ought to
be able to do this without being in Tucson." Not pleased that he had to lose valu-

able time during the best season to find the bird he and his wife sought, he opened a business magazine that another passenger had left in the seat pocket. The theme of the issue was "Can Technology Replace Meetings?"—an odd topic for in-flight reading, since so much of any airline's revenue comes from carrying people to and from meetings, but, after all, it wasn't the airline's choice of reading material.

An article about video teleconferencing caught his attention first. The author, identified as working for PictureTel, discussed how it could facilitate meetings where participants were in different geographical locations. "It would be nice if we didn't have to meet personally for all the board meetings," thought Stan. "If I was there on a TV screen, would that work? Would I be able to convince people effectively, if it came to that?" His thoughts ranged over the ways people communicate today. "What makes videoconferencing, face-to-face interaction, audio conferencing, and e-mail different from each other?" He continued reading the magazine until the familiar refrain, "Please return your seat backs and tray tables to their full upright positions . . ." came through the overhead speaker.

The Airbus 320 banked low over the South Mountains to approach Sky Harbor from the west, landed smoothly, and taxied to the gate. Stan Sr. folded the magazine into his briefcase. As he walked out of the terminal to the waiting FLTC limo, he recognized his usual driver and Niels—who often came to meet him when Stan Jr. was busy—but not the young man and woman talking with Niels.

Niels answered his unspoken question as soon as the two had greeted each other. "Stan, I'd like you to meet Elizabeth and Miguel from Sabino Canyon College. They're doing a project, studying our information systems, this term. I needed to spend some time with them today and the ride up here was the best time for all of us. I didn't think you'd mind—in fact, I thought you might enjoy talking with them."

"Pleased to meet both of you," said Stan as he shook hands with the students and all five got into the car. "As it happens, you might be just the people I'm looking for today. Ever read this thing?" he asked, pulling the magazine out and showing them the cover.

"Gee, sir, I'm afraid not . . ." Miguel ventured sheepishly.

"Don't worry about it, young man. Neither do I. That is, I didn't until I found this issue on the flight in this morning. It talks about using technology to replace meetings, so we could make decisions while I'm in Florida. Ever run into *that?*"

"Putting it that way, it sounds more familiar," Miguel smiled. "We've studied some ways of doing just that. What do they say in the magazine?"

"I highlighted a few good quotes," Stan responded. "How's this: 'a technological solution that breaks geographical barriers between group members to create a distributed meeting.' Aside from board meetings, I was thinking about how all our divisions order things independently. Usually that's a good idea, but sometimes we place six small orders instead of one big one. That's not the real problem, though. Central purchasing usually catches those. The real problem is that sometimes we place six small orders for things that are just a tiny bit different in ways that they don't have to be. Purchasing doesn't know if wider ribbing at the waist of a sweater is important to New Englanders or just what someone picked at random. If we could agree on even half of these things, we'd save a bundle. Can technology help us get together?"

"I'd think so," Elizabeth suggested. "Maybe the buyers for each merchandise category could get together electronically before the orders go in. If they all put their ordering plans in some database where everyone could look at them ahead of time, it shouldn't be that hard for each one to go through the other lists and see if they want the same thing, something close enough that they could switch to the same thing, or maybe even something close that has to be different but if they went into the supplier at the same time with both orders . . ." She paused to catch her breath in midsentence to see both Stan Sr. and Niels nodding agreement. The rest of the trip down Interstate 10 passed quickly as they discussed the details of how such a system might fit into the FLTC environment and the way people work at the firm.

Back in the office, Niels and the two students sat in his office. Niels turned to them and said, "Looks like the 'old man' is really turned on to this group technology stuff. It's not my area, but I was in the car when he talked about it so he probably expects me to do something with it. The first step is to sit down and figure out just what. Let's see when we can have a meeting." With that, he asked his secretary to set up a meeting with Dottie Eastman, Kareem Davis, and Joe Two Crows to discuss group decision-making technology.

The secretary came back in about 10 minutes, frowning. Dottie was out of town, visiting technology vendors in California, and wouldn't be back for a week. In four days Kareem was to leave for Prague, Warsaw, Budapest, and Moscow to evaluate FLTC's expansion potential in eastern Europe. He wouldn't return for another two weeks. By then Niels would be on the East Coast for a week. When he returned, Joe was scheduled to leave for his annual visit to all the FLTC regions, including a sampling of stores in each. This trip was to evaluate how the store information systems performed last year and find out about any problems, so they can be rectified. This trip always took three weeks. Thus, the four could not get together for another two months! "Do you want me to set up a meeting for then, Niels?" the secretary asked.

"No, let's hold off on it for a while," he responded. "I'd like to talk to Joe and find out if his schedule is still at all flexible before we look for alternatives." Turning to the two students, he said "Isn't this another perfect example of the problem? I mean, all I want to do is meet with three other people, plus the two of you if you can make it, and it takes two whole months! Now *that* is what I call frustrating," he concluded angrily. Then his face lit up. "You've been spending most of your time looking at what we do with information technology and learning about it. Think you're up to making some recommendations now?"

"That's a tall order!" was Miguel's response. "I mean, we've learned about some groupware and work flow systems, and we know about some of the packages on the market, but we're not really experts."

"Yes," Elizabeth agreed. "We've seen some textbook solutions but I don't see yet how these real problems would fit into them."

"I know, I know," Niels nodded. "You didn't come here as experts and we're not paying you the big bucks experts would get. Still, nobody here is an expert on this stuff either. So, to repeat my question: think you're up to making some recommendations now?"

"We'll give it a shot," Elizabeth answered for both of them. "Just so you don't expect us to come back next week with a program that's ready to install!"

"Agreed. If you come back next week with anything, it will be that much more than we have now."

The two students looked at each other. "We'd better go now," said Miguel. "We have some serious Web surfing to do this evening if we're going to come up with anything at all in that time frame."

EXERCISES

1. What are the problems FLTC has with group work that are discussed in the above episode? Which of these, if any, relate specifically to decision making? Write a decision statement for those problems for which it is possible.
2. Using the Web, find one commercially available package that could help FLTC deal with each of the problems you identified in exercise 1. (If you did not do exercise 1, your instructor will identify specific group work problems to use.)
3. What additional capabilities, if any, would help the packages you found in exercise 2 provide a better solution to FLTC's problems? Define each as specifically as you can. (Assume you are telling a programmer what the new programs, which are to provide those capabilities, will have to do.)

Expert Systems

CHAPTER OUTLINE

Introduction

Businesspeople, indeed people in all walks of life, often call on experts to help them make decisions. A college student may go to a faculty advisor for help in choosing courses. A homeowner may go to a lawn care expert for help in diagnosing and eliminating a condition that is damaging the grass. Businesspeople rely on experts to choose computer systems, to select appropriate corporate tax strategies, to set the price they will pay for a company in a related line of business. The list goes on.

Each of these experts calls on years of experience to make his or her recommendation. These years of experience make it unnecessary for the expert to start analyzing every problem from basic principles and proceed from the ground up. Instead, the expert instantly recognizes features of the problem that have appeared many times before and can apply rules that have worked in those cases. The result is faster and better problem solving than a nonexpert would provide.

If we could take these same rules and put them into a computer, the computer could in principle do exactly what the expert does, recommend the same decision the expert would. That's the idea behind expert systems. While they're seldom perfect, since it's not possible to capture every single facet of an expert's knowledge, they can improve the decisions of nonexperts in a wide variety of situations. In this chapter you'll learn how they do it and when to use them.

CHAPTER OBJECTIVES

After you have read and studied this chapter, you will be able to:

1. Define artificial intelligence (AI), and describe the five major topics of AI work.
2. Explain what expert systems are and how they work, including their major components.
3. Discuss how expert systems handle uncertain information by using confidence factors.
4. Describe how fuzzy logic can help model the way people make decisions.
5. Discuss the basic development approaches to expert systems and explain how to choose one.
6. Describe the types of decision support tasks expert systems are likely to be helpful with.
7. State what sort of human experts you'll need in developing an expert system.
8. Explain why expert system technology is useful in DSS, with its advantages and disadvantages.

11.1 ARTIFICIAL INTELLIGENCE

The concept of a "thinking computer," much like HAL in the movie *2001: A Space Odyssey,* is fascinating—and, to many people, more than a little frightening. As the 21st century opens we are still far from developing a true thinking computer. The problems turned out to be far more difficult than anyone imagined when research in this area began forty years ago. Still, progress is being made in the field of **artificial intelligence (AI):** making computers perform tasks which, if we saw them performed by a person, would lead us to believe that person was behaving with intelligence.[1] (This definition is a moving target: applications that were in this category twenty years ago, or even more recently, are commonplace today.)

The field of artificial intelligence encompasses several areas. Some, like teaching a computer to play chess, have little direct application to business, and yet the knowledge gained in studying those problems leads to better business systems down the road. Other fields are usable today. More will be over the next few years. Relevant facets of AI include the following:

• **Robotics.** Developing computer systems that can perform physical tasks on the basis of general instructions about what to do, rather than specific commands

---

[1]This definition is generally credited to Marvin Minsky of MIT.

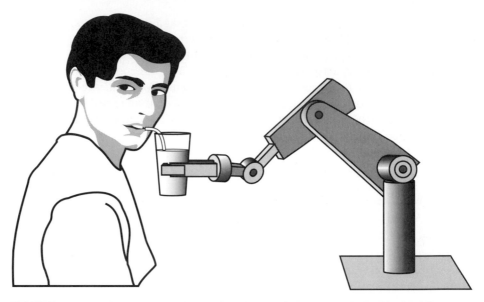

FIGURE 11–1   **Voice-Activated Mechanical Arm Assisting a Physically Disabled Person**

about how to do it. Robotics has applications in manufacturing, equipment maintenance, and carrying out any physical process that people find dangerous, boring, or beyond their physical capacity (see Figure 11–1).

- **Machine vision.** Making it possible for computers to recognize objects by "seeing" them through one or more TV camera. Optical character recognition (OCR), a practical reality today for most typed or printed documents, is a step in the direction of more general machine vision.

- **Understanding language.** Figuring out what is meant by a phrase, command, or sentence. There are systems today that can interpret queries such as, What did we sell more of last month than in October? to retrieve information from a database. Although such systems don't retrieve different data than an SQL query would, they can help decision makers by reducing the technical expertise required to retrieve it.

- **Recognizing speech.** Translating sounds into character strings. Wide availability of computer speech recognition might do away with much typing. Today's systems can recognize words if the vocabulary is small, if they have been trained to recognize the voice and pronunciation of the speaker, or if the speaker pauses artificially between words. This technology is advancing rapidly.

    Recognizing speech is not the same as understanding language. Speech recognition is concerned with turning sound waves into words. Language understanding is concerned with turning words into meaning. The two can complement each other (some degree of meaning can help distinguish between words that sound similar), but they are basically separate activities.

- **Neural networks.** Computer programs designed to mimic the way the human brain processes stimuli. The logic of a neural net is in the connections among electronic "neurons." Nets are "trained" by giving them thousands of examples and telling them when their random connections give the right answer—thus strengthening and preserving the connections in use at that time, while the ones that give rise to wrong answers are changed. Once trained, neural networks excel at finding patterns in masses of data and in determining which objects best match particular patterns. Because one important application of this capability is in finding information among the mass of data in a data warehouse, we'll discuss neural networks in more detail in Chapter 14. (Neural networks reflect *machine learning,* which could be considered as a separate aspect of AI, as a broader category, or as a technology within several AI application areas.)

* **Expert systems (ES),** also called **knowledge-based systems** or **rule-based systems.** Information systems that apply the reasoning process of a human expert to new situations. Such systems are especially useful in decision making. For that reason, we'll devote most of the rest of this chapter to them.

11.2 EXPERT SYSTEMS: THE BASIC IDEA

You arrive at your apartment at night. You are hungry. You have 59¢ in your wallet. The bank is closed, the nearest ATM is not within walking distance, the buses have stopped running, and your car is in the shop. You have spaghetti and a jar of sauce in your kitchen cabinet. You also have homework due tomorrow and a message on the answering machine that says "call Mom." What do you do?

You might put water on the stove for spaghetti, call Mom while it's coming to a boil, and put off the homework until after dinner (or during dinner, if you don't mind tomato sauce stains on your notes). Yet reaching this decision was not simple. Why, for example, didn't you go to a movie? Partly because 59¢ won't pay for a movie, partly because you're hungry, partly because of the homework, partly because of Mom's message. Putting these together to decide what to do, and in what order to do it, involved a series of logical (in the mathematical sense, at least) reasoning steps.

One of your rules might be expressed formally this way:

If I am hungry, my first action will be to obtain food.

That, in turn, can lead to analyzing your options for obtaining food, which in turn might suggest that cooking spaghetti is the most practical under the circumstances. The entire set of these rules, if you could express them, would explain how and why you made the plans that you did.

An expert system is an information system that follows human lines of reasoning, expressed in rules such as the one above, to arrive at a conclusion from known facts.

A Simple Expert System   Consider a system that can follow three rules:

1. If orders can be satisfied within a normal work schedule, then the factory should operate 40 hours next week.
2. If orders cannot be satisfied within a normal work schedule and overtime has not been scheduled, then schedule overtime work.

3. If orders cannot be satisfied with a normal work schedule and overtime has been scheduled, then notify customers that orders will be delayed.

This system shows the fundamental features of all computerized expert systems:

1. Someone must determine the objectives of the system, the concepts it will deal with, the ways it will represent knowledge, and the rules that apply to its decisions.

Someone chose to develop a system to recommend whether or not overtime should be scheduled and when to notify customers that their orders will be delayed. Someone also decided that the important factors in this situation are whether the factory can meet demand with and without overtime, and that these can be represented by yes/no truth values.

Note that this person also decided that different amounts of overtime, outsourcing some of the production, among other possibilities, are not options. Knowing where to draw the line is an important consideration in designing any expert system—indeed, in designing any information system at all. We don't know, from the information given here, if this decision was made correctly.

2. The rules are general. They do not describe a specific situation.

The same three rules apply whether the factory can satisfy demand or not, whether overtime has been scheduled already or not. However, they may lead to different recommendations at different times.

3. In a specific situation you will have, or be able to get, the facts you need in order to apply the rules.

You know, or can find out, if the factory can meet customer demand for its products. You know, or can find out, if overtime has already been scheduled.

4. While the rules may change, the basic reasoning process remains the same.

The words *if, then, and,* retain their meaning, and the methods of logical reasoning remain the same, when we apply them to different rules for different situations.

These characteristics lead to the block diagram of a computerized expert system or knowledge-based system as shown in Figure 11–2. It consists of these parts. The **knowledge base,** also called a **rule base,** contains the problem-solving expertise of the system. In most business-oriented expert systems, this expertise is expressed as rules in the form IF (some condition) THEN (some conclusion). Rules stated in this form are called **production rules.** The conclusion of a rule may establish other facts that the system will use in subsequent rules, or may lead directly to user output.

The **inference engine** is a computer program that applies the problem-solving knowledge (the rules) in the knowledge base to known facts. An inference engine is a general-purpose program that is not written specifically for one problem or problem area. It can work with any set of rules and facts it is given.

The **user interface** is a program that requests information from the user and sends output to the user. Most user interfaces provide a way for the user to ask an expert system how it arrived at a given conclusion or recommendation, or why it wants a particular piece of data.

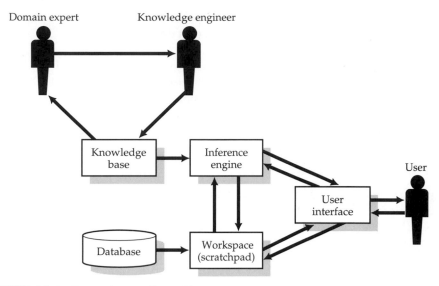

FIGURE 11–2 Expert System Block Diagram

The **workspace** is an area in computer storage where the expert system stores the facts it has been given about a situation and any additional information it has derived thus far. The workspace is also called **blackboard, scratchpad,** or **working storage.**

An optional database supplies facts that apply to one situation (and therefore should not be in the rules), but which the user does not know or which can be supplied more easily by electronic means. Expert systems used for decision support often use databases.

Human beings are also involved with any expert system.

The **user** is the person whose problem the system is to solve. He or she can use the system in any of the usage modes discussed on page 149.

The **subject matter expert** (also called a **domain expert**) and the **knowledge engineer** contribute to the development of the expert system but in general do not use it after it is developed. The subject matter expert contributes expertise in the field of the system but may not know how expert systems work. The knowledge engineer is trained both in eliciting information from subject matter experts and in encoding that knowledge in a knowledge base. In complex expert systems, the knowledge engineer may be assisted by (or may have to be) a **programmer.** At the other extreme, given a simple system and a suitably inclined subject matter expert, it may be possible to dispense with the knowledge engineer entirely.

An expert system cannot do anything that a conventional computer program could not do. The advantage of the expert systems approach is that, in separating the rules in the knowledge base from the inferencing logic that operates on them, it separates parts of the program that have different characteristics and call for different skills. That separation makes the system easier to change and expand, makes it easier to follow the reasoning process of the system, and lets each human and each part of the system do what he, she, or it does best.

Expert Systems and DSS   Expert systems are not an alternative to DSS. Rather, expert systems are a technology that is often useful in constructing a DSS. The question is not Should we use a decision support system or an expert system? Rather, it is Should we use the expert system approach as part of this DSS? The criteria you'll read about later in this chapter will help you make this decision.

11.3 CONFIDENCE FACTORS

Experts are not always sure of their conclusions. "It looks like your valves," a mechanic might say. "But it might be your piston rings." You may have heard a doctor say, "It looks like strep, but we'll have to do a throat culture to make sure." If experts are subject to this sort of uncertainty, why shouldn't computer systems that mimic their reasoning also be?

Or a person listening to a radio forecast of cloudy weather might decide to carry an umbrella. The uncertainty here is in the source of our knowledge, which is not 100 percent reliable.

Or a faculty member might advise a student, "All other things being equal, marketing usually works out best for first-semester juniors in MIS, but business law can be OK too." A travel agent could tell a New Jersey customer, "Hawai'i would be perfect, but you'd also like Grand Cayman. The flight is shorter and less expensive, and you wouldn't have jet lag from a five-hour time change." There is no uncertainty in these cases. However, there are multiple satisfactory answers. In situations like these two, a human expert can often provide a relative ranking of those answers.

Expert systems handle these situations by using **confidence factors** or **truth values.** A confidence factor is a numerical value associated with a variable that indicates the degree to which the system treats that variable as true. "True" in this context may mean "correct," as in an engine problem diagnosis, or "applicable," as in a course selection recommendation. Lack of absolute correctness, in turn, may be because of uncertainties in our reasoning process (again, as in engine diagnosis) or in our input data (as in our decision to carry an umbrella).

Another possibility is that we are uncertain about a fact because the fact itself is not precisely defined. In the sentence, "Today is warm," there is no universally agreed-upon cutoff point for "warmness." Whether or not a day is warm depends on the person making the assessment and on his or her concept of what is typical for that locale at that season. **Fuzzy logic,** which we discuss further on page 432, is used to handle this kind of uncertainty.

Where Confidence Factors Come From   An expert system can obtain a confidence factor to associate with a piece of knowledge in one or more of three ways:

- A user can enter the confidence factor to be associated with an input value. The answer to "Do you plan to retire at 65?" in a financial planning system might be, "Yes, there's a 75 percent chance that I will." The 75 percent here is the confidence factor even though the speaker didn't call it that. (Most real people wouldn't use the phrase *confidence factor* in everyday speech, even in a business situation.) This approach is appropriate when confidence in the input data is the issue, as with the decision to carry an umbrella after hearing a forecast of cloudy weather.

- A confidence factor can be obtained from a database. (This is in a sense a form of user input, since the data in the database had to come from somewhere.) In the database of an expert system used to recommend cars to prospective purchasers, a Toyota Camry might have a "sportiness" rating of 4; a Honda Accord, 5; and a BMW 328i sedan, 8 on a scale of 1 to 10. These ratings could be used to steer customers who want a sporty sedan to BMW, whereas those who value the different advantages of Toyota or Honda would be pointed in their direction. Both these sources of confidence factors are useful when multiple alternatives are to be ranked.

- A rule can incorporate a confidence factor into the logic of an expert system. Such a rule might be

IF *age* < 30 AND *height* < 70″ AND *weight* > 300 THEN *likes_beer* = yes, with a confidence factor of 85%

This approach is commonly used in problem diagnosis systems, where known symptoms may suggest a probable diagnosis without confirming it absolutely. It is also useful in ranking alternatives when the ranks are independent of input data.

- Confidence factors can be propagated forward from one rule to another. Suppose we have a rule

IF *time_to_retirement* < 5 years THEN *investment* = bonds

If we have previously determined *time_to_retirement* to be less than five years with a confidence factor of 75 percent, this rule will recommend buying bonds with the same confidence level of 75 percent. The impact of a 75 percent confidence level on the system's ultimate investment recommendations depends on whether other investment alternatives had higher or lower values.

The simplest way to deal with confidence factors is through traditional probability theory. In this approach, we (or our expert system) treat the confidence factor associated with a fact as the mathematical probability that the fact is correct. For instance, we might say that a particular patient has appendicitis with a probability of 0.9. Probability theory also lets us combine confidence factors when a conclusion depends on a combination of conditions. For instance, suppose a rule says, "Take the train if your car is low on fuel or if the highway is congested." If you feel that each event has an 80 percent probability of being true, an expert system can combine these probabilities to conclude that taking the train has a 96 percent probability of being the better decision.

However, probability theory is not always the ideal way to deal with confidence factors in expert systems. For one thing, it does not make it easy to change confidence factors in a controlled fashion. Suppose an expert system has determined that a patient has Disease X with a confidence factor of 80 percent. To resolve the diagnosis it recommends a new test, which the attending physician arranges to have performed. The result of this test will either confirm or refute the preliminary diagnosis. We would like to set the resulting confidence factor to 0 or 100 percent directly, not fool around with artificial probabilities to force that result.

As a result, most expert system development tools incorporate a variety of ways to handle confidence factors. Should you be involved in an expert system development project, your system's requirements in this area will help you choose the most appropriate tools.

11.4 FUZZY LOGIC

Fuzzy logic [ZADE65, ZADE83] is an approach to dealing with imprecise knowledge in a precise way. Where a confidence factor states, in effect, "I believe this fact to have a 70 percent probability of being true," fuzzy logic states, "I believe this fact to be 70 percent true." The two phrases sound nearly the same, but their meanings are quite different. In the first case, the fact itself is either true or false (or will be at some future time). We don't know which, so we take a guess and apply statistical reasoning to our guesses. In the second case the fact may be, literally, 70 percent true. The examples in the next two paragraphs will clarify this.

If you are asked, "Is there a box of cereal in your kitchen cabinet?" your answer may have a 60 percent confidence factor because you're not sure. Perhaps you don't remember. Perhaps you knew that there was none this morning, but that your roommate planned to buy some and usually shops before this time of day. In any case, there either is or is not a box of cereal there. The uncertainty reflects your knowledge of the situation, not the contents of the cabinet. The same applies to estimates of future facts: What will inflation be next year? Will it rain tomorrow? Will I pass my DSS course? When the time comes all these questions will have definite answers. We just don't know them yet.

However, if you are asked, "Is the person next to you tall?" you might be uncertain because *tall* is not precisely defined. Most people would agree that a North American male of 6 feet 9 inches (2.05 meters) is tall but one of 5 feet 2 inches (1.57 meters) is not. What, though, of 6 feet 4 inches? 6 feet 1 inches? 5 feet 11 inches? 5 feet 9 inches? As one goes down the scale, the degree of tallness decreases. At some point it drops to zero. Many other terms are subjective as well: Is a development project "risky?" Is an engine temperature "high?" Is a job candidate "well-educated?" Is travel time from a factory to a proposed warehouse location "short?" Is a swimmer "fast?" Are the residents of a postal zone statistically "upper class?" The list is endless.

Fuzzy logic provides a rigorous mathematical method of dealing with subjectively defined terms. It represents them via data elements that have partial membership in sets. A North American man of 5 feet 9 inches (1.75 meters) has at most about a 10 percent membership in the set of tall men. Rules such as "If a man is tall, then he should play basketball," interpreted via fuzzy logic, would yield only a weak recommendation in his case. Such an expert system might recommend that he find a sport better suited to his stature.

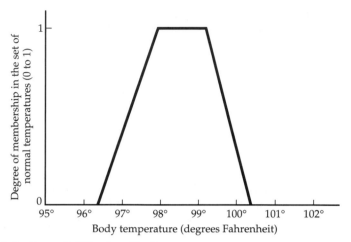

FIGURE 11–3 Fuzzy Set Membership Curve

Fuzzy logic–based expert systems can use modifiers to qualify relationships further. A rule might read, "If a man is very tall . . ." or ". . . rather tall . . ." or ". . . somewhat tall. . . ." The term "very" in this context might mean 90 percent set membership, and so on. Combining terms defined in this way can be handy for selecting the best fit to a combination of factors. Suppose, for example, we wanted to select all the apartments in our rental database that have "nice" buildings and are "close" to a bus stop. Fuzzy logic would let us pick out an apartment that is not too close to a bus stop, if the building is really fantastic, as well as one in a so-so building if the bus stops right in front of its door. If we define fuzzy set member-ship properly, this selection process can mimic human reasoning quite well.

Numerical factors can be translated into set membership grades via curves, such as the one shown in Figure 11–3. That curve shows one person's belief that a body temperature is "normal" based on a given, and accurately known, thermome-ter reading. (Normal body core temperature is usually taken to be 98.6 degrees Fahrenheit or 37.0 degrees Celsius.) A temperature of 100 degrees Fahrenheit, about 37.8 degrees Celsius, has some degree of membership in the set of normal temperatures but not much. A diagnosis that depends on normal temperature in this case would not have high credibility associated with it.

Fuzzy set membership grades should not be interpreted as probabilities. If one event has a 20 percent probability and a second has a 60 percent probability, the second event is three times as probable as the first. However, suppose one man is assigned 20 percent membership in the set of tall men and a second is assigned 60 percent membership. This does not mean that the second man is three times as tall as the first. More likely, the first is about 5 feet 10 inches and the second is a little over 6 feet.

Fuzzy set membership grades do not necessarily add up to 1: A 5 foot 10 inch man may have 20 percent membership in the set of tall men, 10 percent member-ship in the set of short men, and 90 percent membership in the set of men of medium height. The more height categories we have—very tall, medium-tall, medium-short, etc.,—the higher the sum of his set memberships will be, as each new category adds to the total. The purpose of fuzzy set membership grades is to allow us to rank entities or events relative to each other. They handle this job quite nicely.

The advantage of fuzzy logic for expert systems is that it matches the way human experts think about many important problem areas. "Low" blood counts, "good" high school grades, and programming language "expertise" are all matters of degree. The degree to which a situation has certain characteristics is often an important factor in a decision about that situation. Were we to deal with situations such as these via conventional logic, we would have to divide each parameter of interest into multiple categories: five for height, three for speed, and so forth. We would then need, potentially, a rule for every combination of parameter values: 15 rules for just these two parameters. The number of rules we would need in order to get a good match to the way humans deal with such data would get out of hand quickly. By using fuzzy logic, we effectively divide each parameter into an infinite number of categories. The rules of the expert system can carry out calculations based on membership grades without having the number of rules explode geometrically. That simplifies an expert system a great deal. ("A great deal" is a fuzzy concept, too.)

11.5 EXPERT SYSTEM DEVELOPMENT TOOLS

11.5.1 Shells

An inference engine, as we mentioned on page 428, can work with any set of rules we give it. The rules make the difference between one expert system and another. To the commercial user, it's the rules of the expert system that provide the business benefit or the competitive advantage the user hopes to obtain. Given these facts, many software firms have developed prepackaged inference engines to which a user can add any desired set of rules. A prepackaged inference engine is called an **expert system shell,** or (when context makes the meaning clear) simply a *shell.*

Each shell has a language in which its rules must be written and includes a user interface framework. User interfaces vary in their sophistication, from simple text-based systems through graphic output to completely mouse-and-menu-driven systems. The nature of the operating system under which an expert system shell runs may determine, and will at least influence, the user interface that the shell provides.

Many shells provide complete expert system development environments, including text editors for the knowledge base, while others rely on the user to have a text editor or word processing package available. Shells may also provide interfaces to popular database packages and spreadsheets, plus additional features to support application integration with other aspects of a complete DSS.

The syntax that a knowledge base developer must use varies from shell to shell. Figure 11–4 shows the three-rule factory overtime knowledge base, which you saw on pages 427–428, in three versions for two popular desktop microcomputer expert system shells: once as it would be written in VP-Expert, twice for two approaches to Level5, and once in Exsys.[2]

The second version of the Level5 knowledge base, shown in Figure 11–4C, was deliberately written to parallel VP-Expert in its structure. (Figure 11–4B is closer to the way a Level5 user would normally write it.) You can see some differences among the knowledge bases. These differences include the following:

1. A VP-Expert consultation is controlled by a series of programlike commands in its "ACTIONS block." Level5 does not use a similar set of commands, so all its action must take place within rules. That's why each Level5 rule in Figure 11–4B has a command to display output but the VP-Expert rules don't. We got around this restriction in the second Level5 version, in Figure 11–4C, but we had to add a new rule and a new goal to activate that rule. Exsys automatically displays any CHOICES that a rule concludes are true.

FIGURE 11–4A   **VP-Expert Form of Simple Knowledge Base**

In VP-Expert

```
!This knowledge base deals with overtime scheduling

ACTIONS
DISPLAY "I will tell you what you should do."
FIND activity
DISPLAY "You should {activity}.";

RULE 1
IF meet_demand_without_overtime = yes
THEN activity = schedule_a_normal_work_week;

RULE 2
If meet_demand_without_overtime = no
AND overtime_scheduled = no
THEN activity = schedule_overtime;

RULE 3
IF meet_demand_without_overtime = no
AND overtime_scheduled = yes
THEN activity = notify_customers_about_late_shipments;

ASK meet_demand_without_overtime: "Can factory meet demand at 40 hrs/week?";
ASK overtime_scheduled: "Has overtime been scheduled?";
CHOICES meet_demand_without_overtime, overtime_scheduled: yes, no;
```

[2]If you're familiar with Exsys, you know that you don't enter this listing directly as you would with either VP-Expert or Level5. Instead, Exsys creates it from rules and other entities that you enter individually. In doing so, it adds extra spacing, separators, etc., to make the listing easier to read. These have been removed here to fit the entire listing onto one page.

In Level5

```
TITLE Knowledge Base to Recommend Overtime Scheduling DISPLAY

                      I will tell you what you should do.

1. Recommendation is found


RULE 1
IF factory can meet demand without overtime
THEN Recommendation is found
AND DISPLAY "You should schedule a normal work week.".


RULE 2
IF NOT factory can meet demand without overtime
AND NOT overtime is scheduled
THEN Recommendation is found
AND DISPLAY "You should schedule overtime.".


RULE 3
IF NOT factory can meet demand without overtime
AND overtime is scheduled
THEN Recommendation is found
AND DISPLAY "You should notify customers about late shipments.".


TEXT factory can meet demand without overtime
Can the factory meet demand at 40 hrs/week?


TEXT overtime is scheduled
Has overtime been scheduled?
```

FIGURE 11–4B   **First Level5 Form of Simple Knowledge Base**

2. VP-Expert's goals are determined by the FIND command. Those of Level5 are listed in an outline form. That gives Level5 more flexibility in controlling the simultaneous search for several goals and in defining subordinate goals to be sought depending on which top-level goal is satisfied. (The simple knowledge base of Figure 11–4 doesn't make full use of this capability.) Exsys goals are implied by the rules. The search strategy specified at the beginning of the knowledge base determines how rules are selected for testing.

3. VP-Expert uses only character string variables, so the user's responses must be compared with "yes" and "no." Level5 also supports Boolean variables, which are a better choice in this case. They are inherently true or false so no comparison is necessary. Level5 also supports attribute variables—variables whose values are chosen from a predetermined set of possibilities. We used these in the second Level5 version of the knowledge base. (Like most programming languages, it also supports numeric variables, but we didn't need those here.) Exsys also supports multiple variable types, but in this case we are only using qualifiers that can take on values from a specified list (here, Sufficient or Insufficient). These behave more like VP-Expert variables whose input values are

In Level5

```
TITLE Knowledge Base to Recommend Overtime Scheduling DISPLAY

                 I will tell you what you should do.

ATTRIBUTE activity

1. Recommendation is found
   1.1. Recommendation is displayed

RULE 1
IF factory can meet demand without overtime
THEN Recommendation is found
AND activity IS schedule a normal work week.

RULE 2
IF NOT factory can meet demand without overtime
AND NOT overtime is scheduled
THEN Recommendation is found
AND activity IS schedule overtime.

RULE 3
IF NOT factory can meet demand without overtime
AND overtime is scheduled
THEN Recommendation is found
AND activity IS notify customers about late shipments.

Rule 4
IF Recommendation is found
THEN Recommendation is displayed
AND DISPLAY "You should [activity].".

TEXT factory can meet demand without overtime
Can the factory meet demand at 40 hrs/week?

TEXT overtime is scheduled
Has overtime been scheduled?
```

FIGURE 11–4C   Second Level5 Form of Simple Knowledge Base

constrained by the CHOICES statement in Figure 11–4A, though there are technical differences between the two approaches.

The above three differences have a unifying thread: Level5 offers capabilities that VP-Expert does not, but these make Level5 more complex to use for simple knowledge bases where VP-Expert would suffice. Moving up the scale, the capabilities of Exsys exceed those of Level5. As you might expect, that also makes it somewhat harder to learn and use.

4. There are several cosmetic differences among the knowledge bases. Level5 keywords must be in all uppercase letters, whereas VP-Expert and Exsys are

```
Subject:
Factory overtime scheduling

Author:
Efrem Mallach

Uses all non-redundant rules in data derivations.
Probability System: 0 (false) or 1 (true)

QUALIFIERS:

1 Factory capacity WITHOUT overtime is
Sufficient
Insufficient

2 Factory capacity WITH overtime is
Sufficient
Insufficient

CHOICES:

1 Schedule overtime work
2 Notify customers of late shipments
3 Schedule a regular work week

RULES:

RULE NUMBER: 1
IF:
        Factory capacity WITHOUT overtime is Sufficient
THEN:
        Schedule a regular work week - Confidence=1
RULE NUMBER: 2
IF:
        Factory capacity WITHOUT overtime is Insufficient
   and  Factory capacity WITH overtime is Sufficient

THEN:
        Schedule overtime work - Confidence=1

RULE NUMBER: 3
IF:
        Factory capacity WITHOUT overtime is Insufficient
   and  Factory capacity WITH overtime is Insufficient

THEN:
Notify customers of late shipments - Confidence=1
```

FIGURE 11–4D   **Exsys Form of Simple Knowledge Base**

case insensitive. Level5 rules end with periods, those of VP-Expert end with semicolons, and those of Exsys are entered into a dialogue box where entry is terminated by a mouse click or the Enter key. Level5 and Exsys allow spaces within variable names, while VP-Expert uses underscores where a human would normally put a space between words. Level5 uses the keyword "TEXT" where VP-Expert uses "Ask," and Exsys implies the question in the structure of a rule. Taken as a group, these differences and others like them can make knowledge bases developed with different shells look quite different, even though they are nearly identical in everything that matters.

The overwhelming majority of commercial expert systems are developed with packaged expert system shells. The job of developing a new inference engine is so large, the business benefit of having a unique inference engine (as opposed to unique expert system rules) so small, that firms with a bottom-line focus hardly even find it worthwhile to develop their own inference engine.

If you are faced with an expert system development project on the job, you will in all likelihood use a shell as well. The characteristics of commercial expert system shells change rapidly. Most of the features that matter to a knowledge base developer would not show up in a summary table. For example, the way different shells handle goal setting could make a big difference in the ease of setting up a particular knowledge base, but any approach can in principle handle nearly any situation. You can proceed as follows:

1. *Scope out your system in general terms.* How many rules will it have? (You won't know exactly, but you should be able to say "tens," "hundreds," or "thousands.") Will it access an existing database or a new one? How many people will use it and how often? Will they share a database? Will it require graphical output? Does the nature of its user community impose special requirements on its explanation interface? Will its user interface have other special characteristics? Do you expect it to use backward chaining, forward chaining, or both? Will it require frames to represent its knowledge?
2. *Determine any constraints on the platform you must use.* If constraints exist, they will limit your choices to shells that run on that platform. If there are no constraints, you may have a personal preference that is suitable for the application. If you don't, you can probably at least determine the general type of hardware and software platform your system should use on the basis of the discussion on page 189.
3. Based on the characteristics of your expert system and the hardware you expect to use, *specify what you require of a shell.* Factors to consider include:
   - *Embeddability.* The ability to embed an expert system developed with the shell in an overall application written in another language, usually a 3GL.
   - *Rapid prototyping.* The ability to get a prototype of an application running quickly and add features to it later without rewriting what exists.
   - *An explanation facility.* Enables users to find out how the system reached its conclusions or why it wants a particular piece of information.

- *Forward and backward chaining.* Forward chaining starts with what is known and works forward to what can be concluded from this knowledge. Backward chaining starts with the goal ("What should the factory manager do?" in our simple expert system) and works back, obtaining information as needed to figure out its recommendation.
- *Confidence factors.* The more sophisticated the shell, the more approaches to confidence factors it will support and the more flexibility it will give to users who want to define their own methods. VP-Expert, at one extreme, supports only confidence factors that range from 0 to 100 and has only one way of combining two confidence factors for each possible situation. If you don't want to take the smaller of two confidence factors when two conditions are combined via AND, VP-Expert isn't for you. Most other shells offer more options in this regard.
- *Linkage to databases.* The importance of this factor varies from one ES to another, and is usually an easily answered "yes or no" issue, but some type of linkage is often needed. If you expect to use the same shell for several projects, keep database linkage in mind even if your first expert system won't use a database.

4. *Investigate the shells available for that system or that class of systems.* Sources of products to investigate include software directories, trade press ads, magazine and newspaper articles and reviews, computer vendor or retail store sales representatives, and members of user groups.

   Your employer may have already standardized on an expert system shell. If that is the case, evaluate it before you look for alternatives. Most corporate standards allow exceptions if the chosen product is demonstrably unable to meet a specific need—but be sure of your ground before you ask for a waiver!

5. Evaluate the shells you have identified versus your list of requirements. If none meet your needs you can keep looking, broaden your hardware options, or write your system from scratch. If you pick the third option, the next section is for you.

11.5.2 Languages

There are several reasons why one might develop an expert system without using a commercial shell. These reasons include:

1. No commercial shell meets the requirements. This is unlikely, unless one is constrained to use rare hardware or the expert system needs are unusual in some other way.
2. To learn about expert systems by building one from the ground up. This is a noble goal, often best achieved via a computer science course in expert systems. You will be in an excellent position to benefit from such a course after finishing the course you are taking now.
3. The expert system is a small part of a larger application, which is to be written in some other language, and it's easier to write inference routines in that language than it is to interface the rest of the application to a shell. (If the expert system is large or complex, it is probably easier to use a shell and interface the two parts.)

4. The programmer already knows another language and doesn't want to learn a shell. This may be a good reason if the expert system and its logic are simple, or if the programmer knows an AI-oriented language such as **LISP** or **Prolog.** Otherwise, the effort of learning a shell will more than pay for itself in reduced knowledge base development time.

5. Because the resulting system must be portable across multiple platforms, which do not all support the same shell or compatible shells. (If the user community is small and is not already committed to multiple platforms for other reasons, it may be less expensive to buy new equipment for some users than to reject the shell approach for this reason.)

6. For improved performance. This is seldom valid even though the people who cite it believe it is true. The performance-critical portions of commercial shells are carefully coded by experts using efficient tools and algorithms. Anyone coding his or her first inference engine is unlikely to do a better job.

In these situations your choice is between specialized languages designed for AI and general-purpose languages meant to be used across a broad spectrum of application areas. The advantage of a specialized language is that, once mastered, it permits you to express expert system concepts quickly and concisely. However, the two most widely used AI languages differ in their underlying concepts from languages you are likely to use in other applications and may seem strange at first. General-purpose languages have the advantage of familiarity. The basic concepts of using any procedural language will be familiar to you if you have learned to program in any other, even if you do not have experience with a particular one. In terms of reason number 3 for not using a shell or package, the overall application will almost certainly be in a general-purpose language such as Pascal or C.

Most expert systems deal with symbolic knowledge that is often represented in the form of lists. The suitability of a language for developing expert systems therefore depends in large part on how well it deals with symbolic data and with lists. Specialized AI languages handle this well—in fact, the very name of the LISP language stands for LISt Processing—but not all general-purpose languages do. Pascal, C, and C++ all have the efficient pointer-handling capabilities that list manipulation requires. FORTRAN, BASIC, and COBOL do not. Pointers can be mimicked in these languages by indexing into arrays. This is awkward and artificial, leads to code that is difficult to maintain, and is often inefficient as well.

Handling knowledge effectively also requires the ability to manipulate structured data and sets. FORTRAN and BASIC fall down in the area of data structures, but COBOL, Pascal, C, and C++ all have facilities for this task. COBOL falls down in set handling relative to the others.

The choice, therefore, usually comes down to Pascal, C, and C++. It can be based on what programmers are familiar with and what runs on the available hardware. All have been used extensively for expert system development with good results. Using C++ is particularly appropriate when object-oriented programming techniques are to be used.

If you are developing an expert system that is to be integrated with an existing application in, say, COBOL, one of your choices will be to use COBOL (or whatever). This is not out of the question. Good expert systems have been built in COBOL, FORTRAN, and almost every other language. However, you might first want to see if the main application can call and exchange data with routines written in a more suitable language. If it can, you will probably do better to use a more appropriate language for your expert system work.

11.6 CHOOSING A GOOD EXPERT SYSTEM APPLICATION

As you learned in your introductory MIS course, three criteria determine the desirability of developing any information system: its technical feasibility, its operational feasibility, and its economic feasibility. These apply to expert systems as well.

> *Technical feasibility* asks: Can the desired system be developed using technologies available to our organization, including those we might be willing to buy?
>
> *Operational feasibility* asks: Will the system work with our people, within our organization? An information system that forces the steps of a task to be carried out in a specific order might meet with resistance in a firm whose staff is used to a different order or more free-wheeling individual flexibility. An information system that is perceived as taking away the "fun" parts of a person's job will likewise not be well accepted.[3]
>
> *Economic feasibility* asks: Will the benefits of the system justify its costs?

These factors apply to any information system and hence to any decision support system. Here, these factors can lead us to guidelines that will help tell us whether a candidate expert system is likely to work out well, or if we should try to solve the underlying decision support problem via other technologies.

Successful expert system applications usually have most of the following characteristics. If your candidate application is missing one or more, it might still be a good use of expert systems technology—but you should look carefully at the missing piece or pieces to make sure.

It is convenient to divide the selection characteristics into (a) the characteristics of the problem to be solved (see also [HOLS88] on this aspect) and (b) the characteristics of the human experts who solve the problem or make the decision now, and who would have to support any expert system development project.

Problem-Related (Task-Related) Criteria

1. *The task should typically take human experts from several minutes to a few hours to solve.* This time includes only actual problem-solving time, not waiting time. If it takes 48 hours to get the results of a cell culture that a physician needs in order to make a diagnosis, that time does not count as time that the physician spends making the diagnosis.

---

[3]Word processing centers, in vogue in the late 1970s, failed for this reason. Sitting at a word processor all day was cost effective but lacked the variety of traditional secretarial positions and led to poor morale. Operator turnover was high. Most firms that tried this approach abandoned it quickly.

Problems that an expert can solve in a minute or two are usually not worth the effort of developing an expert system. If a nonexpert needs help, a one-page paper checklist will usually do the job.

This rough lower limit on problem complexity is an economic feasibility issue and may be overridden in exceptional situations. For example, American Express uses an expert system to help make credit granting decisions that an expert can decide in a few minutes or less. However, due to the number of authorizers at American Express, the volume of calls they handle, the level of turnover (which leads to a low average of expertise) and the economic impact of a bad decision, the system is fully justified economically. In addition, the training benefits of this system add value.

Longer problems, those that take a human expert a day or two, are beyond the practical size for expert system development today. This is a technical feasibility issue. There is no fixed absolute upper limit, but tackling a problem that takes a human expert a half day or more to solve will be a large expert system development project. It should be attempted only by people who have experience with smaller projects and know what they're getting into.

2. *The task must involve only processing information and cognitive skills.* In other words, we have to be able to solve the task by putting data into a computer and getting data out of it. Physical activities are ruled out. A task passes this test if it can be solved by a human expert over the telephone.

Of course, an expert system can be hooked up to another computer system to carry out a physical process. Using an expert system to determine the mix of end products into which crude oil should be refined, then using a process control system to open valves and adjust temperatures, is entirely feasible. The output of the expert system itself, though, is not adjusted valves. The expert system's output consists of instructions to the process control system.

The information used in the task should be primarily symbolic (character strings) or logical (true-false). Tasks that involve primarily numerical calculations or massive databases are better handled via other programming methods.

3. *The task must be carried out often.* This affects economic feasibility. If the task doesn't arise with reasonable frequency, system payback—which is related to usage frequency—will be low, while the development effort will still be substantial. As with any economic feasibility issue, high desirability on other criteria can outweigh low frequency of use.

4. *The task must be reasonably stable.* The task must remain unchanged for at least as long as it will take to develop the expert system and obtain the desired benefits from it. This does not mean that the precise problem to be solved can never change. Were that the case, we would solve that problem once and be done forever. It means that the rules for solving the problem must remain valid. A system to recommend a driving route across town during rush hour must be able to cope with various points of origin, destinations, traffic and weather conditions, but the task is still stable in the sense that the network of roads and their desirability under different conditions remains the same. The system might need to be rewritten if a new vehicular tunnel was built under the central business district, or if flying automobiles became practical.

This criterion also does not mean that the task can't change at all. Computer vendors often use expert systems to configure the systems they sell. Their product lines change regularly. New components are continually being added. Some of these simply create new records in a product database, but others require new rules. In either case, the problem changes slowly enough for the solution approach and the bulk of the existing rules to remain useful.

5. *The task must involve only explicitly visible knowledge, not "common sense."* Some solution processes involve common sense, which we usually don't realize we're using. Suppose a mechanic, trying to see why an automobile engine won't turn over, discovers concrete in one cylinder. Even though the mechanic has never seen an engine with concrete in a cylinder before, was not specifically trained to deal with this situation, and cannot find it in a troubleshooting manual, he or she will waste no time in deciding what the problem is. How? Common sense. An expert system, unless someone prophetically put in the rule "IF there is concrete in a cylinder, THEN . . ." would be at a total loss.

6. *The required knowledge must be within an acceptably narrow area.* Efforts to program a wide range of information into an expert system, while not provably impossible, have not yet met with commercial success. Most narrowly defined business problems deal with a few dozen related concepts. (They may deal with many more data elements. The same concepts, such as "current price," "annual dividend," and "earnings per share," apply to every stock traded on every major market.) Systems whose anticipated scope is much broader than this should be approached as research projects.

7. *The necessary data must be available to the system.* Tasks that rely on data already in the computer have an edge over tasks that require a great deal of data to be entered. The cost of entering new data enters into economic feasibility: If it costs more to enter the necessary data than an optimal solution is worth, even a free system is not economically justified.

8. *The task must have financial importance to its sponsor.* This is, obviously, also a key factor in determining economic feasibility.

9. *Test cases must be available.* No information system can be developed if it cannot be tested. There is an important additional condition for expert systems. While testing most computer programs can rely heavily on test cases used by the developers in the development process, expert systems must also be tested on a range of cases that were not part of the knowledge acquisition stage. Using only test cases that were used in the development process can result in a "self-fulfilling prophecy" and a system that is useless when faced with new situations.

10. *We should be able to tolerate errors in system output.* As we've seen, expert systems are "brittle:" their performance falls off rapidly as we leave their intended area of application, rather than degrading gradually. Severe errors thus often arise without warning. One classical example is of a system that diagnosed bacteria-related blood diseases. Since it tried to interpret every deviation from "normal" in terms of blood bacteria, it reported a serious blood infection when faced with normal advanced pregnancy.

Expert systems used for decision support, rather than decision making, satisfy this criterion by submitting their output to a human who reviews it before making the decision. In other situations, checks and balances are built into the process at a later stage. A system that creates an occasional improper computer configuration may be acceptable because its mistakes will be caught, at the very latest, when someone turns the computer on and tries to boot it up. If the benefits of the system outweigh the cost of fixing these goofs—which may be the case if the computer goofs less often than people would—it should still be used.

Being able to tolerate occasional output errors doesn't mean "expert systems don't need to work." If they don't do better most of the time than their unaided users would, they're useless.

Expert-Related Criteria

The preceding criteria described suitable tasks for expert systems. We also need one or more experts. The following list of criteria complements the list of task-related criteria by describing what is required of the experts.

1. *We must be able to tell who the experts are.* Sometimes we can see who performs best and agree that those are the experts. Extensive data are available on the historical performance of various investment advisors, though their historical track record (when the market was driven by one set of factors, which a given expert understood well) may not be a good guide to the future (when a different set of factors may affect its performance).

   In other situations, such as medical diagnosis, solid information about which doctors are right more often is difficult to come by. (While certification in a specialty helps, there are far more certified physicians in most specialties than true experts.) We must then rely on secondary evidence, such as acceptance as experts by physicians in other medical specialties, or abandon the expert system approach.

2. *Experts must perform the task substantially better than nonexperts.* If the reasoning process of an expert is no better, or not much better, than that of a nonexpert in terms of results achieved, there is no point in cloning an expert's knowledge. We might as well let novices deal with the decision, as they will do almost as well. Several studies have concluded that "expert" stock recommendations perform, in the long run, about as well as choosing stocks by throwing darts at the stock market listings in the newspaper. If this is true (other studies have reached the opposite conclusion), it suggests that stock selection is a poor task for an expert system.

   The meaning of "substantially" depends on the situation. Is 99.9 percent performance substantially better than 99 percent? In some cases it may represent only a trivial 0.9 percent improvement. In others it may represent a reduction in the error rate by a factor of 10. A person planning an expert system must decide what the appropriate interpretation is for the situation at hand.

   This factor combines with task-related factors, such as frequency of use and financial impact of a good decision, to determine the economic benefits of the system in question.

3. *One or more experts must be available to work on the system.* If we want to mimic the reasoning of a human expert, it follows that we must have one to observe. The characteristics we would like this expert or experts to have, beyond simply being expert, are discussed further on page 447.

4. *The human expertise must be scarce.* "Scarce" can refer to absolute scarcity; for example, there are simply not enough blood disease experts in the world to deal with the demands on their services. Given the nature of this expertise, if a worldwide crash program to develop more blood disease specialists were to start tomorrow, it would not pay off for a decade.

Scarce can refer to economic scarcity. American Express could hire all the expert credit authorizers it needs if it paid them as much as it pays a senior vice president. It has chosen not to do so. It therefore does not have as many expert authorizers as it could use. That is a big part of the reason it developed an expert system to help its authorizers.

Scarcity may also reflect difficulty in getting human experts to accept the conditions under which work must be done, if they involve inconvenient schedules, remote locations, or hazardous environments.

Finally, expertise might be available at present but not in the future, as when the last technician who understands an old diesel locomotive model is about to retire but many of those locomotives are still chugging along on small regional railroads.

5. *Experts must agree on the solutions.* This means broad, general agreement. It does not mean that the experts must follow identical methods in reaching solutions (they often don't) or that they must arrive at identical solutions every time (ditto). It means that, by and large, they must agree on the characteristics of a good solution versus a bad one. Two competent faculty advisors may recommend different schedules for the same junior MIS student, but each should agree that the other's suggestions are within reason.

In most cases this criterion requires the experts to agree on the data required for a solution, on the general approach to the solution, and on the factors that determine if a solution is valid or not. This is true even if the experts' solutions themselves are slightly different.

Keeping the Criteria in Perspective   The above criteria, assembled from several lists proposed by experienced expert system developers and researchers, represent an ideal situation. Some of them, clearly, are "musts:" if you can't get a human subject matter expert, the idea of developing an expert system doesn't make much sense. Others are more in the nature of "wants:" financial importance, for example, is a relative term, and can be overruled if a task is sufficiently important for some other reason.

Figure 11–5 relates the criteria both to the three feasibility concepts—technical, operational, and economic—and to whether they are "musts" or "wants." In the case of wants, it indicates whether they are usually of high or moderate importance. The figure has check marks in a few places we didn't discuss above, especially in the operational feasibility column. These marks reflect second-level im-

		Feasibility			Importance
		Technical	**Operational**	**Economic**	
Task-related criteria	Size	√ (high)		√ (low)	Want-M
	Cognitive	√			Must
	Frequency			√	Want-M
	Stability			√	Want-H
	Visible logic	√			Want-H
	Narrow scope	√			Want-H
	Available data	√	√	√	Must
	Importance		√	√	Want-M
	Test cases	√	√		Must
	Error tolerance		√		Must
Expert-related criteria	Recognize	√	√		Must
	Much better		√	√	Want-H
	Available	√	√	√	Must
	Scarce			√	Want-M
	Agree	√	√		Want-H

FIGURE 11–5 Categorization of Expert System Development Criteria

pacts. Getting data into a system, for example, may raise operational feasibility issues, but they will usually not be overwhelming.

Lists such as this, as Krcmar [KRCM88] points out, are meant to apply when an expert system is being considered as the entire solution to a total problem. However, as he states, "Most successful ES in business are embedded in some larger context and . . . they often do not provide coverage for all tasks involved."

In other words, an expert system might often be a good solution for part of a problem even if the problem as a whole does not meet the above criteria. Krcmar recommends splitting the overall task into smaller parts. The system planner can then apply criteria such as those above to the individual parts, also considering the new issues of integrating the parts into an overall DSS.

11.7 FINDING THE EXPERT(S)

At least one competent, willing, and cooperative expert must be available to develop an expert system. If such an individual cannot be found, an expert system cannot generally be developed—no matter how desirable it might be in terms of other criteria. (One exception: If enough test cases are available, it may be possible to derive rules from them. This approach, called **induction,** underlies the data mining concept we'll discuss on page 542.)

A subject matter expert must be chosen carefully. Good experts have the characteristics listed below:

1. *They must be experts.* One criterion listed on page 445 for using the expert system approach is that we must be able to tell who the experts are. The person or people we choose as models for our expert system must fit the definition of

experts as it applies to their field. Where a field is changing rapidly it is important to choose experts who are up to date, not those whose reputation was established in the past but who may not be current with the latest approaches.

2. *They must be willing to be "cloned" by the computer.* Some experts take pride in this opportunity. Others see it as a threat to their control over what their firm does in their area of expertise.

3. *They must be able to spend substantial time on the project.* "Substantial" refers both to the fraction of their working day they will often devote to it and the number of weeks or months for which they will be involved with it.

4. *They should be personally cooperative and easy to work with.*

5. *They should be interested in computers or at least intrigued by the technology.* Many discussions with them will relate to how the computer follows (or doesn't follow) their rules and how it handles its input data. Curiosity about this side of the project motivates experts to participate in this type of discussion and helps them contribute to it, even if they are not computer professionals themselves.

One Expert or Several?   Using a single expert eliminates conflicts but may not ensure the best results. Expert systems tend to be "brittle:" They work well within their range of expertise but may fail drastically the instant they pass their limits. Sets of rules derived from different human experts tend to have different areas of applicability and follow different lines of reasoning. They will therefore have different limits. When a problem passes outside the limitations of one expert, thus invalidating one line of reasoning the expert system might follow, other lines of reasoning derived from other human experts may still apply. The performance of such a system can therefore degrade gracefully as it leaves its primary focus.

Other advantages of using just one expert are cost and time savings. Where system sponsors agree that one expert's knowledge will suffice, there is no need to waste these by using several. The other side of this coin is that one expert's time may be limited. If the approaches of several experts are sufficiently similar, this bottleneck can be relieved by using more than one.

If it has been decided to use several subject matter experts rather than one, they can be shadowed individually or solve problems as a group. Watching each expert individually and combining their methods in the system usually works better than gathering them into a group and asking them to develop a composite approach. Gathering them together may present logistical problems and will result in one compromise solution rather than displaying the spectrum of possible approaches. Even when logistics permit assembling all the experts in one place, group dynamics can cause problems that most subject matter experts and knowledge engineers are ill equipped to deal with. The experts may spend more time arguing over how to solve a problem than actually solving it. Such problems can derail a project before it truly starts.

There are, however, situations where the experts should be assembled and work as a group. This may arise where the process of developing an expert system is intended to standardize the experts' approaches, where it is necessary to bring them into agreement and the development project is a convenient way to do this, or where synergy among the experts makes the solution better than any one of them could develop individually.

If the knowledge of several experts is combined in one system, the system can attempt to combine all their knowledge in solving every problem or can select one line of reasoning based on the specific problem. An expert system can combine several experts' knowledge by assigning a confidence factor (see page 430) to the result obtained through each line of reasoning. Where different experts' lines of reasoning reach the same conclusion, the confidence factors will be merged and the system's conclusion will have a high confidence factor. Where the experts would disagree, the expert system will offer several conclusions, with a low confidence factor for each.

If each expert's line of reasoning is best applied to a specific part of the problem domain, the system can select one of them after a few general questions determine the domain in which the task at hand falls. A system that recommends vacation destinations may incorporate one travel agent's knowledge of Hawai'i and another's knowledge of the Alps. Once the system has determined if a prospective vacationer wants to surf or to ski, the rest of the consultation will use either the first or the second expert's rules.

11.8 EXPERT SYSTEMS AND DSS

Expert systems reproduce the reasoning process a human decision maker would go through in reaching a decision, diagnosing a problem, or suggesting a course of action. In terms of the categories in Section 4.2, this makes expert systems process-oriented DSS. They could be descriptive or normative, depending on whether their rules are based on what people do, or on what people should do. (What experts do is often what nonexperts should do. In this case we can take the expert system as reflecting a normative decision model.) In the DSS spectrum of Section 4.1, most expert systems are suggestion systems, as their output is a suggested course of action.

Expert systems can also incorporate databases and models, as used in other types of DSS: Databases, as noted previously, can supply facts that are unavailable to (or not easily entered by) the user. American Airlines uses an expert system to schedule aircraft maintenance. This system uses a database to look up flight schedules in order to get aircraft to maintenance centers at the right times in the course of normal flight operations. A system for investment decisions could be linked to a database of current stock prices and corporate earnings reports. While a stockbroker could look up this information on a printed page or via a separate query system, and type it into a DSS, automating this step makes the system easier to use. If the number of stocks being considered is large, automatic data transfer—a type of system integration, which we'll discuss in Chapter 16—can make the difference between a practical system and a useless one.

Models are implicit in many ES, but they are process models as we defined the term on page 301, not system models. Consider an expert system used to diagnose problems in automobile engines. One rule might be "If cylinder pressure is below

X psi, then check the valves." This rule is based on the process that a subject matter expert follows, not on a mechanical model of automobile engines that shows a cause-and-effect relationship between worn valves and low cylinder pressure. The effect of the two approaches might be identical but the content of the computer program is quite different. This lack of "deep knowledge" on the part of an expert system often makes them **brittle:** They fail dramatically when they are faced with a situation (such as concrete in an engine cylinder, the example used in discussing problem-related expert system criterion 5 on page 444) that was not foreseen when their rules were written.

System models can be included in DSS as supporting components for calculations that the decision process requires. A model in this context is essentially a complex, time-consuming arithmetic operation. Instead of adding a group of numbers, the numbers might be used as parameters of a simulation run. The net effect, that we supply input to a calculation and use its output, is the same in either case. An expert system used to help select an advertising program could use a consumer responsiveness model in this way.

Once the data retrieval and system modeling parts of a decision-making process have been automated, all that remains is applying human expertise to the results. Expert systems allow us to capture, within limits, this expertise. For that reason they are becoming more and more popular in DSS applications. The following factors, based on a list by Pfeifer and Luthi [PFEI87], suggest the types of DSS for which expert systems are likely to be suitable versus those for which they are not.[4]

- ES are generally used by nonexperts. If a decision is to be made by an expert, the help of an ES, which mechanizes the reasoning process that an expert performs without such help, will be less useful.
- An ES is generally considered successful if the quality of its recommendations approaches that of the human expert. Other DSS are considered successful only if they permit the expert to achieve better decision quality than he or she could without the system. This point relates closely to the previous one: A system to be used by nonexperts can improve their decision quality while remaining below the quality that a human expert could achieve. A system to be used by experts, if it achieved lower quality than the expert could achieve unaided, would be useless.
- ES are generally applied to recurring problems. This is also true of model-oriented DSS, and for the same reason. Both ES and model-oriented DSS incorporate a great deal of information about the task to be solved. This means their development requires substantial effort, most or all of which applies only to this specific task, and limits their flexibility to deal with other tasks.

Other types of DSS, especially data oriented, are more generally applicable. It may be worthwhile to develop them without knowing exactly what decision will arise, as long as one knows that some decisions within their general area are

---

[4]Our interpretation of these factors differs from that of Pfeifer and Luthi. They took the factors as distinguishing ES from DSS. Our definition of DSS is broader and encompasses many ES applications, so we take them as distinguishing ES from *other types of* DSS.

sure to. Data-oriented DSS are therefore usually more helpful with one-of-a-kind decisions.

- ES are generally applied to tactical, low-level problems. Other types of DSS are generally used to support strategic decisions. This point is related closely to the previous one. Low-level problems tend to recur often enough, with different parameters each time, to justify building a system to deal with them. Strategic decisions, by contrast, tend to be one-of-a-kind. They cannot be predicted far enough in advance, and in enough detail, to enable us to formulate solution methods and build those methods into an information system.

    This point also relates to the acceptability of an expert system that falls short of the decision-making capability of an expert. A firm will rightly insist on having its most capable employees make far-reaching strategic decisions. It may not have this luxury with respect to operational decisions that must be made repeatedly by many people in many locations. Bringing these decisions closer to the level that an expert would achieve may be the best for which an organization can realistically ask.

- ES are generally applied to fairly structured tasks. This is consistent with the fact that we must be able to document the reasoning process involved in their solution. Unstructured tasks are better suited to other types of DSS.

The above factors characterize the DSS situations to which expert systems are well suited. Pfeifer and Luthi's list also includes these two differentiating factors that characterize expert system technology rather than the decision-making situation:

- In an ES, the representation of knowledge is separated from the program that processes that knowledge. Specifically, the expert's understanding of how to solve a problem is encoded in rules. These are distinct from the computer program that follows the rules' reasoning. Other types of DSS generally integrate the two into one program or a set of programs. This is the key feature of ES technology that distinguishes it from traditional computer programming.

- The ability to explain its reasoning is inherent in the knowledge-and rule-oriented structure of an ES. Other types of DSS either do not have this ability or must have it explicitly added to them via additional program code.

The nature of expert systems suggests where you should think about applying them to your decision support systems. Look for a recurring decision that experts make well, but which must often be made by nonexperts. If enabling these nonexperts to make this decision better is of economic value, consider making an expert system a component of your DSS.

11.9 PROS AND CONS OF EXPERT SYSTEMS

Expert systems can provide substantial benefits in some DSS. At the same time, no tool is perfect for all applications. Attempting to apply expert system technology outside its area of applicability is, at best, a prescription for wasting time and effort. At worst, it can result in a system that does not achieve its objectives when other, perhaps simpler, approaches would have achieved them.

Advantages of Expert Systems   Expert systems, in effect, clone human expertise and put it in a computer. This immediately suggests the following benefits that they can provide, compared to asking human experts to carry out the same tasks:

- They can solve problems more quickly than humans could, given the same data. It might take a moderately fast computer a minute or two to go through information that would take a person a few hours.
- Their output is consistent. They don't get tired, impatient, or angry. This can help standardize multi-individual decision making.
- They can be replicated as needed with minimal lead time and at moderate cost. Human experts often need years of training and experience. Then they retire or quit.
- They don't cost money when they're not being used. People expect a regular paycheck.
- They can free up human experts to do other tasks, such as concentrating on the few problems that really require their high level of expertise.
- They don't mind working in locations that people find inconvenient or hazardous, or taking on repeated tasks that people find boring.

In addition, the specific technology of expert systems yields these benefits, compared to developing a program with identical inputs and outputs through conventional programming methods:

- They can be expanded by adding more rules as the organization gains experience in using them. Since their rules are modular, it is easier to add rules to the knowledge base of an expert system than it is to add comparable code to a traditional computer program.
- They can train novice problem solvers in the techniques used by experts.
- While this training is going on, they can raise the problem-solving ability of novices closer to that of the experts.
- In some cases, where an expert system integrates the knowledge of several experts, they may be able to do better than any one expert could alone.
- From the computer programmer's point of view, separating the expert's knowledge into modular rules reduces the chance of development errors and improves the maintainability of the system.

Drawbacks of Expert Systems   No technology is perfect for all applications all the time. Limitations of expert systems, of which prospective developers and users should be aware, include:

- Their domain of expertise is usually narrow. They are developed to solve specific problems and are not useful for any other purpose.
- They cannot apply common sense, only their rules. (We humans often don't realize how much general knowledge, or common sense, we use implicitly in decision making.)
- They are brittle at their limits. People recognize when they are reaching their limits and respond appropriately. Expert systems don't. They simply follow their

rules and may recommend inappropriate actions, often without recognizing that they have done so. It can be said that their performance "falls off a cliff" at their limits rather than degrading gradually.

- They may be costly to develop: not for the hardware (which is increasingly inexpensive) or for the software tools (ditto), but for the time of the human experts and other people involved in the process.
- One or more expert must be on hand to contribute to the project for an extended period of time. Even if willing experts can be found, and even if their cost is affordable, this commitment represents time during which they are not solving problems or are solving them more slowly than they could otherwise. When an expert's problem-solving ability has a clear present value and the possibility of developing an expert system is still conjectural, this can be a major barrier. (See exercise 7 at the end of this chapter for an example of this.)

Given these pros and cons, you can see that some applications are good for expert system technology while others aren't. Use this list on the job to help make this decision.

SUMMARY

The field of artificial intelligence (AI) encompasses several areas, including robotics, machine vision, understanding language, speech recognition, neural networks, and expert (or rule-based, or knowledge-based) systems. Of these, expert systems are the most useful in DSS overall.

Expert systems express a human decision-making process as rules a computer can follow. These rules are derived from the knowledge of human subject matter experts, often with the assistance of knowledge engineers. A specialized program called an inference engine then processes these rules to reach a conclusion, in the process obtaining data either from its user or from a suitable database. The rules are thus separated from the program that processes them, facilitating later expansion of the rule base. Intermediate results are stored in a workspace, and the conclusion is ultimately reported to the user via the system's user interface. Most expert systems can also explain to their users why they require an input data item or how they reached their conclusion(s). In terms of DSS categories, expert systems are usually suggestion systems.

Much of the information expert systems deal with is not absolutely certain, for a variety of reasons. Expert systems use a variety of methods for dealing with uncertain information. One is by attaching confidence factors to data. These indicate the degree of certainty associated with an input item or a data element in the workspace. Confidence factors of multiple input data items and rules can be combined to yield the confidence factor of a conclusion.

Fuzzy logic is another approach to uncertain data. It is designed to deal with concepts whose definition is inherently imprecise, such as "low inventory turnover." Fuzzy logic mimics the way people often deal with such concepts. It allows an expert system to have far fewer rules than would be needed if such a concept had to be divided into many levels for proper analysis.

Expert systems are usually developed using preprogrammed shells. A shell provides an inference engine and a user interface. The system developer need only write the rules in the language (often much like a programming language) that the inference engine understands. If it is necessary to write an expert system from scratch, without a shell, the specialized languages of LISP and Prolog have been developed specifically for artificial intelligence applications. Alternatively, a general-purpose language such as Pascal, C, or C++ can be used.

Certain conditions must be met for a problem to benefit from the expert system approach. The task itself should take from several minutes to a few hours to solve; it must involve only cognitive knowledge (and only explicit knowledge in a narrow area, not common sense or broad general knowledge); it must be important enough (considering both economic impact of the decision and the frequency with which it is made) to justify the investment, test cases must be available for it, and the overall decision-making situation must allow for errors in system output.

We also need suitable subject matter experts to develop an expert system. For this, we must first be able to tell who the experts are. They must perform the task significantly better than nonexperts, they must be available and willing to be cloned, they must be willing to work on the system (and, ideally, sufficiently interested in computers to be motivated in that direction), their expertise should be scarce (or there's no need for the system), and they must, in general, agree on the solutions. If time and resources permit, it may be useful to work with multiple experts—to get the benefit of slightly different opinions, or to take advantage of different areas of expertise.

Expert systems are usually applicable when a DSS is to be used by nonexperts, where the quality of their recommendations approaches that of an expert, and for tasks that are low level, recurring, and well structured.

Expert systems have many advantages over human decision makers. They solve problems quickly, don't get tired, will work anywhere, and can be replicated at low cost. However, they are limited to a single domain, tend to fail drastically when a problem is outside that domain, and don't always signal when they are taken beyond their limits. Their development also requires a considerable time investment on the part of subject matter experts. Since these people are scarce and their time is valuable, asking them to cooperate in developing an expert system is not a trivial matter.

KEY TERMS

artificial intelligence (AI)
brittleness (of an expert system)
confidence factor (also truth value)
expert system (ES) (also knowledge-based system, rule-based system)
expert system shell
fuzzy logic
induction
inference engine
knowledge base (also rule base)
knowledge engineer

LISP
machine vision
neural network
production rule
programmer
Prolog
robotics
speech recognition
subject matter expert (also domain expert)
understanding language
user
user interface (of expert system)
workspace (also blackboard, scratchpad, working storage)

REVIEW QUESTIONS

1. What are the basic subsets of the artificial intelligence field?
2. How do expert systems arrive at their conclusions?
3. Are the rules of an expert system written to apply to a specific situation, or are they general so they apply to many situations of the same type?
4. What are the inference engine and the workspace of an expert system?
5. How do expert systems cope with situations when the user isn't sure of something that the system needs to know?
6. How would your statement, "I sure have a lot of homework this week!" relate to fuzzy logic?
7. What is an expert system shell? What are its basic components?
8. Why would you possibly *not* use a shell to develop an expert system?
9. Name two programming languages designed for the field of artificial intelligence.
10. What kind of DSS is an expert system (usually)?
11. What kind of tasks are expert systems usually applied to? (Give at least three task characteristics.)
12. State at least 10 advantages of expert systems over human decision makers, and at least five disadvantages they have versus human decision makers.
13. What are the three types of feasibility that must be considered in evaluating any information system application?
14. What do we have to know about the availability of human experts before we embark on an expert system development project?
15. When is it a good idea to use more than one subject matter expert in developing an expert system?

EXERCISES

1. You work for a car rental firm with offices at major airports and at downtown locations throughout North America. One of the problems it faces on a regular basis is rate setting. Rates are influenced by many factors, including the type of car, demand for specific types of cars in specific locales (a convertible is more likely to command a high price in Florida than in North Dakota in January, Massachusetts renters tend to like compact cars more than Texans), the time of year (including holidays), specific situations such as

sports championships that affect local demand, competition, temporary situations such as a glut or shortage of cars at one location, promotional programs (often run in conjunction with an airline), and more. Your firm currently sends out general guidelines to each of its offices and lets the office manager set specific rates for his or her location. Your boss has suggested that an expert system might be able to do a better job.

   a. Based on the criteria in this chapter, do you feel this is a good expert system application or not? Justify your answer.

   b. Write three rules this system might be able to use, in English using the *if-then-else* form of the example on pages 427–428. You don't have to be an expert on the car rental business. Just make them look reasonable.

   c. Give two data items about which the user of this system might not be totally certain and for which the system would therefore have to use confidence factors.

   d. Who do you think should be the user of this system: someone at headquarters, who could determine rates for all offices and send them out, or each office manager to set the rates for his or her location? Why?

2. On page 439 you read, "The job of developing a new inference engine is so large, the business benefit of having a unique inference engine (as opposed to unique expert system rules) so small, that firms with a bottom-line focus hardly even find it worthwhile to develop their own inference engine." Relate this statement to Figure 6–1. Does it confirm or conflict with what was recommended there?.

3. Consider an expert system that your college could use to advise juniors and seniors concentrating in MIS or computer science about course selection for their next semester.

   a. Write (in English, using the *if-then-else* form of the example on pages 427–428) three rules this system could have in its knowledge base. Make them appropriate to the MIS or computer science curriculum at your college or university.

   b. Who do you think the user of this system would be? (There are many correct answers to this question. You must pick one before you can answer the next one properly.)

   c. What is one item of information that this user would have to supply?

   d. What is one item of information that this system could obtain from a database? From which database would the system obtain this information? (If you're not familiar with the specific databases your institution has, make reasonable assumptions about databases that most universities have these days.)

   e. Who might you choose as a subject matter expert to develop this system? Do you see any value in talking to more than one expert? Why or why not?

4. Interview a person in a profession that involves problem diagnosis: a physician, a mechanic, a repair person for electronic equipment. Discuss one or two recent problems that this person faced. Write down some rules the expert followed in diagnosing these problems in the form of if . . . then . . . else . . . . Try to obtain a complete sequence of rules that the expert would use to solve an entire (simple) problem.

5. Would the following DSS applications be good uses for expert systems, assuming one could be developed? Why or why not?

   a. Choosing a recreational sailboat. The sponsor is a boat dealership, which sells (and whose customers buy) sailboats frequently.

   b. The same system, but now the sponsor is a weekend sailor who buys a new boat every two to five years.

   c. Analyzing geological data to determine if there is likely to be oil under the surface in a given location.

   d. Determining the type of punishment (prison, suspended sentence, probation, community service, fine, etc., including various combinations) and magnitude (length of sentence, amount of fine, etc., as appropriate to each type of punishment) for a convicted offender.

6. Find a review of an expert system shell, or a comparative review of several expert system shells, in a newspaper, magazine, reference service volume, or Web site. What characteristics did the writer consider important? What features of the shell did the writer like or dislike? What did the review say about the shell's, or shells', handling of confidence factors? For what applications did the writer recommend using it or each of them?

7. The world's only expert in disease X can treat eight patients per day, about 20 percent of the 10,000 people who contract X worldwide each year. She can cure all the patients she treats. The disease has a 50 percent mortality rate with the best care available elsewhere. A computer scientist has asked her to cooperate in developing an expert system to treat X. He feels, after some study, that any physician following the system's recommendations will have a cure rate of 75 percent. While the specialist participates in the project— estimated to take three months—she will only have time to treat four patients per day. It is also possible that the expert system will turn out to be useless (that is, its use will not improve the 50 percent cure rate of today's widely available treatments). The computer scientist thinks this is unlikely but admits he doesn't really know and can't know without developing the system and testing it.

    a. How many lives will the expert system save per year if it works as the computer scientist hopes it will?

    b. How many people will die because the specialist can't treat them while the system is being developed, who would have been cured if she had been treating eight patients a day instead of working on the system? Assume the estimates of development time and of the physician's ability to treat patients during this period are accurate.

    c. Do you feel the specialist should agree to be the subject matter expert for developing this expert system? Justify your reasoning.

    d. Read the box "Who Is Liable? Just Ask the Experts" at the end of this chapter. Suppose the system is developed, a doctor uses it, and the patient dies. This doctor tells the patient's family, "I would have used treatment A, but I used treatment B instead because the system suggested it." The family then sues the specialist for negligence. Does this possibility affect your answer to part *c*? What would you recommend the specialist do to protect herself?

REFERENCES

ALEX91   Alexander, Michael. "Who Is Liable: Just Ask the Experts." *Computerworld* 25, no. 15 (April 15, 1991), p. 20.

HOLS88   Holsapple, Clyde W., and A. B. Whinston. *The Information Jungle.* Irwin, Homewood, Ill. (1988).

KRCM88   Krcmar, Helmut. "Caution on Criteria: On the Context Dependency of Selection Criteria for Expert Systems Projects." *AI Magazine* 9, no. 2 (Summer 1998), p. 109; reprinted in *Developing Expert Systems for Business Applications,* John S. Chandler and Ting-Peng Liang, Eds. Merrill Publishing, Columbus, Ohio (1990), p. 296.

PFEI87   Pfeifer, R., and H. J. Luthi. "Decision Support Systems and Expert Systems: A Complementary Relationship?" in *Expert Systems and Artificial Intelligence in Decision Support Systems.* D. Reidel Publishing, Holland (1987).

ZADE65   Zadeh, Lofti A. "Fuzzy Sets." *Information and Control* 8, no. 3 (1965), p. 338.

ZADE83   Zadeh, Lofti A. "The Role of Fuzzy Logic in the Management of Uncertainty in Expert Systems." *Fuzzy Sets and Systems* 11, no. 3 (1983), p. 199.

CASE

Fort Lowell Trading Company
Designing the Warehouse

If you haven't read it yet, read the Fort Lowell Trading Company episode in Chapter 8 for the background to this discussion.

"It really has gone great so far, Dottie. And we never could have done it without your support," said Miguel as they left her office. They had just updated her on the progress of their term project and their plans for the next few weeks. From there Dottie's secretary escorted them to the marketing planning area, where they knocked on Leighton Chen's office door.

"You said something last time that intrigued us," said Elizabeth after the three exchanged greetings. "Do you remember when you talked about those 'rules of thumb' that tell you how to design a warehouse?"

"Yes, I do," recalled Leighton. "I think I said they go back several centuries. The European traders of the sixteenth and seventeenth centuries were probably the first ones to look at warehouse design in any sort of serious way, though they weren't the first to have warehouses. Some of their buildings are still standing, you know. Ever visit Norway?"

"Can't say as I have," Miguel answered as Elizabeth nodded agreement.

"Well, I did, a few years back," Leighton continued. "It was a great trip, though a lot of people were surprised to see me. Most Americans who visit Norway want to see where their ancestors came from, so they don't get too many tourists with Chinese grandparents! Anyhow, I visited the old Hanseatic League warehouses in Bergen. They're a tourist attraction now. One difference from today is that the chief trader and the clerks were expected to live there. The clerks didn't have much room, probably because every square inch they used took space away from storing the goods. I'm not big by U.S. standards, but I don't think I could fit into those beds. The trader had more space—he was kind of like a partner in the firm and it was enough hardship for him to be away from home.

"Anyhow, to get back to the point: about these rules. One is that you put fast-moving items in the most accessible locations. That one's easy: We know how fast different items move and we know how long it takes a forklift to get to any given spot from the order assembly area or the receiving dock.

"A second rule is to put items that tend to be ordered or shipped with each other near each other. You go down one side of a row on the lower shelves, then you come back along the upper shelves, then you repeat the process on the other side of the row."

"You said 'that tend to be ordered or shipped with each other.' Which matters more?" Miguel asked. "Coming in the same shipment, or going out in the same order?"

"That's a good question, and the answer is 'we don't know.' Sometimes they're the same. Sheets and pillowcases tend to go together in both directions. But"—Leighton paused briefly as he searched for a good example—"candles and candlesticks, for instance, don't. The candlesticks come in with other housewares. Should we put them with housewares, to make it easier to shelve them when they arrive, or near the candles? Or, can we get the best of both world and put candles next to housewares? Sometimes that works, sometimes it doesn't.

"In general," he continued, "most items tend to arrive in larger batches than they go out in. So we access them more times for shipping than we do for receiving. This suggests we ought to put the candlesticks near the candles even if that puts them far away from the other housewares that arrive with them. But that rule's not an absolute.

"There are other rules like these. You generally want so many forklifts for so many aisles, the capacity of a conveyor is so many items per hour and so on. They don't tell you all you need to know, but they're a start.

"Anyhow, I was reading something last week about 'expert systems.' The article said they could take rules like these and actually tell you what to do in a specific situation. Do you think they'd help here? Would they be better than the simulation I'm working on?"

EXERCISES

1. Do you think it would make sense for FLTC to develop an expert system that would recommend how to design its Calgary warehouse? Why or why not?

2. Suppose the question were about a warehouse consulting firm developing an expert system that could recommend how to design a variety of warehouses for a its clients under a variety of different conditions. Would it make sense then? Why or why not?

3. Suppose FLTC decides to proceed with such a system. (While you may have answered exercise 1 with "no," the potential availability of free labor in the form of Sabino Canyon College students might affect their decision.) How would you suggest they find a good subject matter expert to use in developing this system?

Who Is Liable? Just Ask the Experts

Who is liable if a doctor follows the advice of an expert system and a patient dies as a result? Does it matter if the same system has also saved the lives of hundreds who would have died without it? The following article from [ALEX91] pursues some of these issues.

DAMAGE CAUSED BY KNOWLEDGE-BASED SYSTEMS COULD LEAD TO LAWSUITS THAT TARGET EVERYONE INVOLVED

Here is a quick multiple-choice test: If a knowledge-based or expert system failed in some way and caused personal or economic injury to an individual or organization, who would be the likely target of a liability lawsuit?

A. The developer who created the system's shell.
B. The expert who supplied the system's knowledge base.
C. The user who placed too much faith in the system's output.
D. All of the above and probably a number of others to boot.

The correct answer is *D,* according to several legal experts.

"I would sue everybody, jointly and severally," said David Newman Jr., an attorney and associate professor of electrical engineering and applied science at George Washington University.

A lawsuit based on injury caused by a knowledge-based or expert system has yet to make it into court, but the legal community "is just waiting for a case to happen," Newman said.

UNAWARE OF RISK

Designers of expert systems and end users who rely on their efforts are unaware of the risk they face should the system fail. Vendors who create the system's shell are also at risk even though they have little control over how the system is sued or who uses it, the legal experts said.

"If you're designing a system that is going to be used for an application that has significant exposure to damage or loss, you have a degree of responsibility of identifying how the knowledge system is put together," said Richard Bernacchi, an attorney and computer law expert at Irell & Manella in Los Angeles.

"The system designer and users can protect themselves to some extent by documenting the care they take in selecting a product before putting it to use. That care should include a complete evaluation of the product and a reference check with current users. 'Let the buyer beware' applies in this area like any other," Bernacchi said.

Despite the liability risk, sellers and buyers are not particularly cautious when working with expert systems, said Larry Harris, founder and chairman of AICorp., a Waltham, Mass. based developer of knowledge-based system tools.

"Someone has to get burned first" with legal action before attitudes change, he said.

The liability issue is a concern to the industry in general but probably affects designers of vertical applications more than the developer of the tools used to create the system, Harris said.

Who Is Liable? Just Ask the Experts (continued)

"It is not different than writing a medical book," Harris said. "I don't think that a doctor can sue the author of a medical book; it is still the responsibility of the doctor who makes the diagncsis."

Such disclaimers would probably not prevent a lawsuit or hold up in court, legal experts said. The vendor could be liable in ways never before imagined: end users could attempt to use the product in unforeseen ways or simply decide not to take training courses offered by the vendor, for example. In either case, the vendor could be in the docket alongside the other defendants, according to legal opinion.

TAKE PRECAUTIONS

There are precautions that vendors should consider, Bernacchi said. "One thing that would help considerably is to document the testing process." A show of reasonable precaution will help offset any legal action.

Even so, legal experts said, it is only a matter of time before a malfunctioning knowledge-based system triggers a lawsuit. When that happens, everyone involved in the creation of the knowledge-based system could face the prospect of legal action.

The suit could be on several grounds, ranging from breach of contract to negligence. "Would I win on every ground?" Newman asked. "It doesn't matter. If I win on one, I would get whatever I went after for my client."

The liabilities will also vary according to whether a knowledge-based application is determined by the court to be a good, a service or a combination of the two.

"That can make a difference in the sense that some jurisdictions have different ground rules whether certain principles apply in the case of service as opposed to product," Bernacchi explained.

Source: From [ALEX91]. Used by permission.

EXERCISES

1. What is it about expert systems that creates liability issues that do not arise with other computer programs? If you wish, use this example: two programs, one an expert system and one not, to tell a firm where to drill for oil.
2. Show this article to a business law instructor or attorney. Obtain his or her reactions to the points it raises. If someone harmed by an expert system asked that person's advice on whom to sue, what would he or she recommend?
3. You are developing an expert system to advise business students on course selection. Poor advice can prevent students from obtaining courses they want, lower their GPA (potentially harming their chances of admission to the graduate school of their choice or of obtaining a desirable job), and, in extreme cases, delay their graduation. What precautions should you take to limit your legal liability for such consequences?

DATA WAREHOUSING

CHAPTER 12

Data Warehousing and Executive Information System Fundamentals

CHAPTER OUTLINE

Introduction

As you read in the quotation from Barry Devlin on page 95 in Chapter 3:

> Data is what the information systems department creates, stores and provides. Information—data in its business context—is what the business needs.

A **data warehouse** can be thought of as the place the information systems department puts the data that is to be turned into information. Unfortunately, one can't just dump masses of data onto a disk drive and expect it to be usable, any more than one can dump raw food onto a stove and expect a gourmet meal to emerge. Food must be prepared, cooked, and arranged on plates before it is served.

Data, too, must be properly prepared, organized, and presented to its users if it is to be optimally useful. The place this is done is usually called a data warehouse. Data warehouses have become increasingly popular since the mid-1990s, for good reason: They provide an effective way for end users to handle their own needs for decision-making information. Because of their importance in data-oriented DSS, the rest of this book is devoted to them.

Executives are the top management of any organization. Their decisions are important enough to justify computer support. Their decisions are typically unstructured, making those decisions well suited to data-oriented DSS such as data warehouses. Since there are few executives and the organization can justify spending a lot of money to meet their needs, they had data warehouselike systems for years before data warehouses, indeed the very term *data warehouse,* came into general use. Today those systems, called *executive information systems (EIS),* are seen to have much in common with data warehouses, but there are also some differences. Because they're tied so closely to data warehouses, we'll discuss them in this chapter as well.

CHAPTER OBJECTIVES

After you have read and studied this chapter, you will be able to:

1. Explain what a data warehouse is and why a business would use one.
2. Describe the major components of a data warehouse and how they interact with each other.
3. Show how data warehouses have come into prominence recently.
4. Explain who executives are and how their decision making needs differ from those of other employees.
5. Describe executive information systems (EIS) and executive support systems (ESS), and how they support executive needs.
6. Explain why executives use EIS.
7. Understand the characteristics and features of executive information systems.
8. Predict and plan for the issues that arise when an EIS is introduced into an organization.
9. Take steps to ensure a successful EIS implementation.

12.1 WHAT IS A DATA WAREHOUSE?

At MediaOne, Inc., the marketing, finance, and operations groups were all jostling for information to better market the company's growing array of products and services. It needed to get a better look at how it was spending its money, who was buying its products and how well it was servicing its customers in an increasingly competitive market [MALL97].

Executives at Idaho Power Co., a Boise, Idaho-based utility company with 400,000 customers, needed a better way to understand the 2.5 million rows of information in their database [MALL97]. At Toyota Logistics Services, Inc., a subsidiary of Toyota Motor Sales, U.S.A., business analysts required quick, easy, and direct access to data in order to continuously reduce costs and vehicle delivery lead times [REDB97]. Sears, Roebuck & Co. is betting on technology to provide the tools it needs to leverage reams of information tucked away throughout the giant retail chain [CAFA95].

The common thread to meeting these diverse requirements, as well as those covered in more depth in the cases in the last part of the Appendix, is the **data**

Data Warehousing Fills CVS Prescription

For the IS managers and business decision-makers at CVS/Pharmacy, building a data warehouse was more than an attempt to gain a strategic advantage—it was a matter of survival.

Howard Edels, MIS senior vice president, said CVS had nowhere else to go: Changes in the health care system made information that could cut costs vital. "This project is critical to this company's future," he said.

After completing the first phase of its data warehouse, CVS is already reaping just that kind of data, according to Edels.

For instance, CVS can now analyze when stores are busiest and which stores sell the most of what kinds of retail items and prescriptions, according to Shafi Shilad, MIS vice president for pharmacy systems. CVS can also verify HMO-based prescriptions on-line.

"In the old days, we would say, 'If your store has X amount of [total] sales, this is what you will carry,' or 'If you fill X number of prescriptions, this is what you will carry," Shilad said.

The data CVS is collecting and analyzing also helps set staff schedules, and Shilad is working on applications to control inventory store by store.

That's in the near term. Edels said CVS envisions being able to market specials to individual consumers based on their buying patterns, make more use of less costly generic drugs, send customers reminders about taking medicine that could keep them out of the hospital and even offer pharmacists' services for a fee.

Norton Greenfield, president of Implements, Inc., a consultancy in Wayland, Massachusetts, said CVS' project "is exactly typical" of strategic data warehouse projects. "There are enormous paybacks in being able to see the business in a way that you didn't before," he said.

Source: From [GOLD96]. Used by permission.

---

warehouse. But what is a data warehouse? Here are a few definitions. First, the classical one due to William Inmon, who pioneered the concept and popularized the term:

> A subject-oriented, integrated, non-volatile and time-variant collection of data in support of management's decisions. [INMO96]

What do the terms in this definition mean?

- "Subject-oriented" means the data are organized by business topic, not by customer number or some other key (which may be the right way to organize, for example, transaction data).
- "Integrated" means the data are stored as a single unit, not as a collection of files that may have different structures or organizations.
- "Nonvolatile" means that the data don't keep changing. New data may be added on a scheduled basis, but old data aren't (as a rule) discarded.
- "Time-variant" means that a time dimension is explicitly included in the data so that trends and changes over time can be studied. This does not mean that data elements change over time, as your checking account balance would in your

Moen, Inc.

As technology jargon goes, data warehouse is relatively colorful, conjuring up images of shelves stacked high with information that knowledge workers pick off from aisles below. But Andy Sills, Moen, Inc.'s CIO, was having a hard time bringing the metaphor to life for the company's business executives.

"We talked about a data warehouse for over a year," says Sills, but we weren't able to paint a clear picture of its potential value to our executive staff."

Moen, a $600-million plumbing fixture manufacturer based in North Olmstead, Ohio, had been relying on IS mostly to fetch paper-based reports on sales trends, customer profitability and other key performance indicators. Five power users also knew how to coax reports out of the Amdahl mainframe using Focus, a report writer from Information Builders, Inc.

Sills was convinced a data warehouse with desktop access tools would provide more timely and accurate decision support information. But without buy-in—both literal and figurative—from top management, the project wasn't going anywhere.

Tired of talking, Moen's CIO decided to show them. In September 1994, Sills and his manager of information resources, Mark Zozulia, built a prototype warehouse for sales history data, using evaluation software and hardware from a couple of vendors. They then brought in the executives and sat them down for a demo.

Jaws dropped when the executives saw sales history data displayed for the first time in a graphical format. Sills and Zozulia invited attendees to fire some questions at them to test the system. One vice president wanted to see sales by day for the month of October. After a few keystrokes, the answer appeared. Normally, it would have required hours if not days to produce.

"It didn't take a lot of selling on our part for them to see what a difference the system could make," Zozulia says. Indeed, during a subsequent private showing of the prototype, Moen's president asked, only half jokingly, "Where do I sign?"

Source: From [MCWI96]. Used by permission.

---

bank's operational database. (Many data warehouses also have a geographic dimension to them.)

And some other definitions from other authoritative sources:

A single, complete and consistent store of data obtained from a variety of sources and made available to end users in a way they can understand and use in a business context. [DEVL97]

A data store for a large amount of corporate data. [BIGU96]

The data warehouse provides access to corporate or organizational data; the data in it is *consistent;* the data in it can be separated and combined by means of every possible measure in the business; it is also a set of tools to *query, analyze,* and *present* information; it is the place where we *publish used data;* the quality of the data in it is a *driver of business reengineering.* [KIMB96]

The focal point for dissemination of information to end users for decision support and management reporting needs. [SOFT95]

The data . . . and the process managers . . . that make information available, enabling people to make informed decisions. [ANAH97]

Data Marts

A related concept to a data warehouse is a **data mart.** A data mart is a smaller version of a data warehouse, typically containing data related to a single functional area of the firm or having limited scope in some other way. Data warehousing expert Claudia Imhoff puts the difference this way: "A data mart is based on a set of user requirements" [IMHO99].

A data mart can be a useful first step on the way to a full-scale data warehouse. Since a data mart has, by virtue of its size, more modest hardware requirements than a full data warehouse, it can also be extracted from a data warehouse and placed on a local server for use by members of a work group when its contents suffice for their more limited needs. Alternatively, a data mart can be derived from a data warehouse as an easier-to-work-with subset. A data mart that is derived from a data warehouse is called a **dependent** data mart. One that is derived independently from operational data is called an **independent** data mart.

These definitions are quite different on the surface.[1] Yet several common threads emerge from reading them as a group:

1. A data warehouse contains a lot of data. Some of the data comes from operational sources in the organization. Some of it may come from outside the organization.
2. The data warehouse is organized so as to facilitate the use of this data for decision-making purposes.
3. The data warehouse provides tools by which end users can access this data.

As long as these three points—content, organization, and tools—are clear in your mind, you can use any definition you like or make up your own.

The term *data warehouse* comes, as you probably would have guessed, from the centuries-old concept of a warehouse in general. The analogy is apt. Goods are entered into a conventional warehouse after they are inspected and found suitable for their intended uses. Once there, they are organized so as to be accessible when needed. Items that are likely to be required together are grouped for efficient access. The warehouse system includes capabilities for retrieving items that are known to be there or for checking to see what items of potential value happen to be there. In addition, the warehouse has the necessary associated capabilities to tell people what it contains and to exercise management control over these valuable assets. As you'll soon see, each of these characteristics of a physical warehouse has a corresponding characteristic in a data warehouse as well.

---

[1] In fairness to Joseph Bigus, who wrote the second, we should point out that he defined "data warehouse" in passing, on the way to discussing something else.

12.2 WHO USES DATA WAREHOUSES?

If we look at the three characteristics of a data warehouse just above, we might conclude that the ideal data warehouse (or data mart) user is something like this:

1. This person's job involves drawing conclusions from, and making decisions based on, large masses of data.
2. This person doesn't want to (or can't) get involved with finding and organizing the data for this purpose.
3. This person also doesn't want to (or can't) access a database in a highly technical fashion.

These conclusions would be correct. There are many people with these characteristics in the business world. That makes for millions of potential data warehouse users and a correspondingly large impact of data warehousing on businesses of all types.

We must, of course, never lose sight of cost. Data warehouses are not free. In addition to the three characteristics above we should add a fourth:

4. This person's, or the sum of these people's, decisions have enough value to the organization to justify the data warehousing effort.

Data warehouses have zoomed from nonexistence to popularity and hype since 1995. (It's not a coincidence that the data warehousing references at the end of this chapter are more recent than that.) We'll look at the reasons for this in the next section. Meanwhile, however, you should be aware of the human tendency to apply the solution of the moment to every possible need. We forget that other tools exist and have their place as well. As the old adage says, "When all you have is a hammer, everything looks like a nail." Some people *don't* need a data warehouse. For example,

- Anyone whose job involves dealing with individual data records, even if they are extracted as needed from a large amount of surrounding data. They are better served by conventional DBMS.
- Anyone whose job includes updating the organizational database, not just looking at what's already in it. They need the operational database. It's important to keep the distinction between an operational database and a data warehouse clear in your mind.
- Anyone whose information needs are so unstructured that they don't fit the data warehouse framework.
- Anyone with the technical skills to delve into complex SQL queries and the inclination to use them. (These people may use a data warehouse database but not data warehouse access tools.)

There are millions of people in these categories as well, especially the first three. This means that data warehouses aren't the universal solution to all of a business's information needs. Understanding what they are, and how they work, will help you develop the right information system for your organization's needs—not the system that happens to be popular at the moment.

12.3 WHY DATA WAREHOUSES NOW?

The need to analyze historical data is not new. Nearly two centuries ago, Wellington prepared for the battle of Waterloo by studying Napoleon's earlier tactics. In the past this need was satisfied by laborious manual analysis or, more recently, by programmed reports produced from mainframe files and databases. Why were data warehouses not used?

The reasons have to do primarily with technological evolution. As is often the case, hardware and software go hand in hand. The hardware capability to do something leads a few forward-thinking people and organizations to experiment with that capability, often at considerable cost. Their success motivates other organizations to imitate them and to request products that will enable them to do so more easily. This real or potential demand, in turn, motivates software developers to develop products to make this capability available to a wide user community. Some of the interlocking factors that worked toward data warehousing include:

1. A data warehouse requires huge amounts of storage. Until this was available at reasonable cost, data warehouses were simply not practical.
2. Going through this amount of data for anything but simple access and trivial analyses requires massive computing power. Steadily dropping costs in this area, with the speed of a microprocessor typically doubling every 18 to 24 months (often referred to as "Moore's Law," since this growth rate was first publicly pronounced by Intel cofounder Gordon Moore) have made the necessary processing power widely available as well.
3. Until the storage capacity and the processing power to deal with it were available, there was no motivation for software firms to develop the data organization and access tools required. Without these tools, which spread the programming cost of a data warehouse over many organizations, any data warehousing effort would require a great deal of custom programming—placing it well out of reach for all but the very largest organizations, and often not cost justified even for them. (A positive answer to "Can we?" may not imply a positive answer to "Should we?")
4. Much data warehouse development also went together with the development of multidimensional databases. While these, as you'll see in the next chapter, are not the only way to build a data warehouse database, they helped get the ball rolling. Multidimensional databases also require high-capacity storage devices and powerful processors.
5. In addition, human and general business factors played a part. With users becoming increasingly self sufficient in computing, they wanted direct access to the data they needed in their work. Increasing time pressure, resulting from a host of business and economic factors, made it important to obtain faster access than traditional printed reports could provide.

Once the initial capabilities were available in about 1994, many organizations began to experiment with data warehouses. Some of these experiments were successful and conferred a major strategic advantage on the companies that made them. Others, as one might expect of any new technology, were less so. Naturally, the successes were publicized while the failures were "swept under the rug." The result, which again is typical of many new technologies, was a wave of hype that led to unreasonable expectations and a sense that here, at last, was the answer to management's information needs. Today the hype has largely worn off. Realism, as it should and always eventually does, set in. Data warehouses are recognized as a major type of information system that has real value for supporting many types of decisions in many organizational settings. You are sure to see, use, and be involved in many data warehouse projects over the course of your career.

12.4 DATA WAREHOUSE CONCEPTS

The essence of a data warehouse is, as you've seen, a large database containing business information that end users can get at. For example, a data warehouse might contain one of the following:

- Store sales information by product, region, and time period.
- Medical insurance claim information by city, age, occupation, and type of policy.
- Credit card usage information by cardholder income, age, sex, marital status, and type of residence.
- Advertising medium information with costs and audience demographics.
- College applicant information by SAT score, high school GPA, athletic activities, other extracurricular activities, . . .

As you can imagine, the possibilities are endless. Managers, planners, and other knowledge workers in nearly every type of organization can use information that could be in a data warehouse. It remains only for the organization to find the information, put it in one place, organize it for rapid access (sorting and totaling 25 million poorly organized records is not an interactive activity!), and integrate the result with suitable end-user analysis tools.

Justifying the Data Warehouse Before planning any data warehouse, it is important to build the business case for the data warehouse project. This does not necessarily mean a dollar (yen, euro, etc.) figure associated with tangible benefits or an internal rate of return calculated to three significant digits. The business case must, however, state such things as the types of data to be included in the data warehouse, the kinds of decisions that will be made with the aid of that data, the way those decisions are made without the data warehouse, and how decisions made with it (presumably better decisions) will benefit the organization.

If the benefits cannot be quantified, it should at least be possible to quantify some associated parameters: "optimize an advertising budget of $4 million per year," "minimize discounts from full fare, which are currently $200 million per year," "choose suppliers whose products result in the fewest warranty claims, which currently cost us $25 million per year to handle." None of these statements says anything about how much the data warehouse will benefit the organization, but all provide information through which top management can calibrate the scope

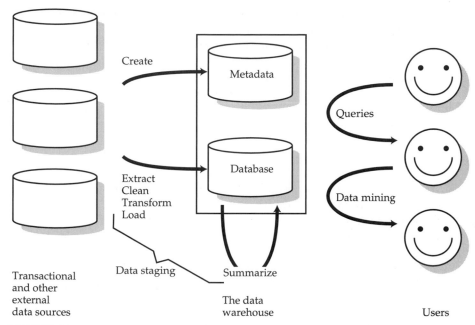

FIGURE 12–1   Data Warehouse Architecture

of its benefit. In the case of the last example—warranty claims—top executives now know that the benefit can't possibly exceed $25 million (nothing will ever totally eliminate warranty claims) but could well be a large fraction of that amount. This lets them put the data warehouse project in a business perspective. We'll take a more detailed look at justifying data warehouses in Chapter 15.

The Data Warehouse Architecture   You read on page 164 that an overall system architecture is important to any DSS. This is equally true of a data warehouse. This section covers the major elements of any data warehouse. This will let you see how the pieces of the puzzle fit together before we go into the details in the next few chapters.

Figure 12–1 shows an overall architectural diagram of a data warehouse system. The major elements of a data warehouse, and the major external entities with which a data warehouse interacts, include:

1. The transaction or other operational database(s) from which the data warehouse is populated. External data is also fed into some data warehouses.

   A key point to remember here is that transaction data feeds the data warehouse. The data warehouse gets a copy of the transaction data. It does *not* store transaction data directly. You wouldn't process payroll, handle a savings account deposit, or manage your inventory with a data warehouse.

2. A process to **extract** data from this database, or these databases, and bring it into the data warehouse. This process must often **transform** the data into the database structure and internal formats of the data warehouse.

3. A process to **cleanse** the data, to make sure it is of sufficient quality for the decision making purposes for which it will be used.

4. A process to **load** the cleansed data into the data warehouse database. The four processes from extraction through loading are often referred to collectively as **data staging.**

5. A process to create any desired **summaries** of the data: precalculated totals, averages, and the like, which are expected to be requested often. These are stored in the data warehouse along with the data imported from internal and external sources.

6. **Metadata,** "data about data." It is useful to have a central information repository to tell users what's in the data warehouse, where it came from, who is in charge of it, and more. The metadata can also tell query tools what's in the data warehouse, where to find it, who is authorized to access it, and what summaries have been precalculated.

7. The **data warehouse database** itself. This database contains the detailed and summary data of the data warehouse. Some people consider metadata to be part of the database as well. Others consider metadata to be outside the database. We'll put metadata outside the database, but it's a question of preference, not of right or wrong. Either way, metadata are part of the data warehouse.

   Because the data warehouse isn't used for processing individual transactions, its database doesn't have to be organized for transaction access and retrieval patterns (one record at a time, using any of several keys). Instead, it can be optimized for the very different access patterns used for analysis.

8. Query tools. These usually include an end-user interface for posing questions to the database, in a process called **on-line analytical processing** (**OLAP**). They may also include automated tools for uncovering patterns in the data, often referred to as **data mining.** A given data warehouse must have at least one of these two types and may have both. Shaku Atre's article, "Problem-solving," discusses the difference and some of its implications.

9. The user or users for whom the data warehouse exists and without whom it would be useless.

The same architecture applies to a data mart, though each individual component would be more modest in scope. A data mart typically has fewer data sources because it deals with one subject area, meaning fewer data transformation issues to deal with and fewer (if any) conflicts among the sources—different names for the same data element, different data elements using the same name, different values for what should be the same data, and so forth. Since it is smaller, it is less demanding of computing resources, making performance tuning and optimization less critical. Since its user community will be smaller, it will require less training and support. All in all, a data mart is an easier proposition than a full data warehouse even though its architecture is the same at the block diagram level.

Another approach to data marts treats them as more-accessible subsets of the overall data warehouse. In this approach, a subject area subset of the full data warehouse is extracted and transferred to a separate database. This database may be on a different server, perhaps local to its intended user community. Or the smaller data

Problem-solving

Do I need to improve business operations or analyze and project trends?

That is one of the questions you must answer before you build your data warehouse. You can't decide after you've built it, because each warehouse requires different tools and approaches. And besides, to convince management of the warehouse's utility, you first need to know what business problem you're trying to solve.

Operational data warehouse applications provide decision-makers with information that helps them monitor and control the company. For example, a utility company could use accounting information in a data mart to plot spending over the course of the year to find opportunities for cost reductions. Such applications use tools such as agent technology query and reporting tools and online analytical processing and multidimensional databases.

Analytical or data mining applications, meanwhile, use sophisticated software to help staff members come up with insights about a company's customers, processes and markets. For example, a company might study its customer base and identify new niche audiences for its products. Tools used here include statistical analysis tools, discover-based data mining tools and visualization tools.

These categories are distinct, but companies often confuse them. When companies build a poorly defined data mart or data warehouse that delivers technical capabilities that aren't tied to solving a particular business problem, the resulting system usually isn't very good at either analysis or operational monitoring.

AVOID VAGUENESS

All too often, companies simply put the technical capabilities in place and expect that their purpose will emerge after they're put to work. Some say vagueness is necessary because business users don't know in advance what kinds of questions they'll need to ask.

But much of that vagueness could be avoided with better planning and IT's insistence (backed up by senior management) that nothing can be built unless and until it addresses specific business issues.

Source: From [ATRE98]. Used by permission. You can find the entire column by searching *Computerworld*'s Web site, *http://www.computerworld.com,* by title, author, and/or publication date. If you just search for Ms. Atre by name, you will find many of her other insightful articles on different aspects of data warehousing.

---

mart may simply be able to respond more quickly to queries that fall within its scope, as well as giving its users a simpler view of the data because many extraneous data fields have been eliminated from it. In this situation the overall data architecture may include many data marts, all fed from the central data warehouse database.

The next chapter, Chapter 13, will focus on the first six of these items: the data warehouse database and everything that goes on to create it. The one after that, Chapter 14, will discuss item 7: getting useful business information out of the data warehouse. Chapter 15 will discuss the implementation issues that arise with data warehouses. You'll notice strong similarities between it and Chapter 7, where you read about the implementation issues of any decision support system. Finally, the Appendix presents some real-world data warehousing cases—somewhat along the lines of the mini-cases on CVS and Moen you read at the beginning of this chapter, but with more depth.

Data Warehouse or Data Mart?

Alice LaPlante [LAPL96] offers this checklist to help decide if an organization should pursue a centralized data warehouse or a data mart strategy:

If you answer "no" to most of these [seven] questions, then a data mart, not an enterprise-wide data warehouse, is probably in your future—with the strong caveat from the experts that some enterprise-wide architectural guidelines and goals are recommended.

- Is it possible for managers and users from different divisions or business units to agree on basic definitions of such things as "customer," "sales" and "profit?"
- Are they likely to successfully negotiate priorities regarding (a) which data belongs in the warehouse, (b) how far back the historical data should go, (c) the level of summary?
- Is the business problem that the enterprise warehouse is intended to solve clearly defined? (Or, for "no:" is the value it will provide dramatically less obvious for the enterprise than for specific business units or departments?)
- Is there significant synergy or overlap in the customer base, geography, culture, product lines and business strategy of the various divisions, units and departments?
- Will it be feasible to get approval from a central authority for the large amount of funding—typically, millions of dollars—that an enterprise warehouse will require?

Source: From [LAPL96]. Used by permission.

12.5 EXECUTIVE INFORMATION SYSTEMS

EIS and Data Warehouses   You've read that data warehouses can require massive computer resources: terabytes of data, powerful computers to analyze databases of this size, and complex software to combine analytical power with ease of use. This combination wasn't affordable enough before the 1990s to make data warehouses available to all those who can benefit from their use. However, the benefits of providing **drill-down** data access and analysis were evident before then. Systems to provide those benefits were developed as far back as the 1970s. The biggest differences between those systems and today's are as follows:

1. Because mass storage was considerably more expensive than today, earlier systems did not provide the level of detail typically found in a data warehouse. This limited the purposes for which they could be used.
2. Because providing access to them (including the processing power required for effective access) was more expensive, and the more primitive software then available required customization for each user, their use was typically restricted to a few people at the very top of an organization.

Since the people at the top of an organization are known as *executives,* such systems came to be called **executive information systems (EIS).** As the forerunners of data warehouses, EIS have much in common with other types of decision support systems you already know about.

EIS are still found in many organizations. Properly designed and implemented, they can provide a more focused, easier-to-use information capability than a data warehouse. Also, EIS typically present current data (as of, at least, the end of the previous day) while many data warehouses have a more historical orientation for in-depth analyses. Many organizations still use EIS for these reasons, though a data warehouse could handle some (perhaps most) of their uses. Some EIS have expanded to support a wide range of users. These may be referred to as "everyone's information system" or some other play on the acronym *EIS* that reflects their wider audience.

Executives are responsible for coordinating the activities of different parts of the firm and for setting its long-term strategic direction. Carrying out these responsibilities, which by their nature cannot be delegated, requires them to make important decisions. EIS provide them with the information systems support they need to do this.

The Executive's Job   Viewed in the abstract, **executives** are simply one end of a continuum that begins with first-level supervisors and continues upward from there. However, when a certain level of management is reached—the precise level varies from organization to organization, indeed from person to person—a manager's perspective changes.

The most significant change is from a functional to a cross-functional perspective. Ideally, everyone in an organization should always have the good of the entire organization at heart. In practice, it seldom works out that way. Engineering managers think about engineering, production managers think about production, marketing managers think about marketing. Even those whose jobs cross functional lines, such as product managers who pull together the engineering, manufacturing, and marketing aspects of one product, tend to think about "their" product independently of—often in competition with—the others.

An executive's view is broader. Some of the motivation for this changed perspective is financial. Top executives are often compensated in part on the basis of overall corporate or divisional performance. Engineering vice presidents will not try to cut the marketing budget if the size of their next bonus depends on successful marketing. As the saying goes, "There are no prizes for plowing a straight furrow if the crops don't come up." Other reasons for their broader view include the team-building effect of executives' close daily interaction with the heads of other functional areas and their personal involvement in broad, cross-functional decisions.

There are also differences in perspective that *are* properly seen at the end of a continuum. Decisions made at the top of an organization are typically, relative to decisions made at lower levels, characterized by

- Being less structured.
- Being less repetitive, hence less predictable.
- Having impact over a longer time period.
- Having a broader impact across parts of the organization (this and the previous point correspond to *strategic* decisions in the terminology of Chapter 2).

- Using more aggregated data and less detail data.
- Using more data from outside the organization.
- Requiring communication with more people.

This does not mean that all executive decisions have every stated characteristic or that no lower-level decisions have any of them. Some executive decisions have a short-term impact. Sometimes lower-level professionals make decisions that rely largely on external data. However, these are the general trends. Executive decisions tend to have more of these characteristics, more often, than do decisions made at lower levels.

An EIS can be expanded to become an **executive support system (ESS).** An ESS incorporates additional capabilities, such as a rapid interface to an electronic mail system or to an officewide appointment-scheduling calendar. A complete executive support system may also include modeling and/or expert systems capabilities, which go beyond the pure EIS and bring it closer to the OLAP concept in this respect. An ESS, while potentially more valuable to its users than a "mere" EIS, requires a strong EIS as its foundation.

What Is an Executive Information System?   Since executive decisions have the above characteristics, information systems to support those decisions must be designed to accommodate those characteristics. Consistently with that list, a DSS for executive use should generally be:

- Cross-functional, rather than limited to a single aspect of the organization, since an executive's perspective is cross-functional.
- Data-oriented, since the executive's decisions typically do not have much structure and are usually not repeated regularly enough to justify developing complex models.
- Summary in nature, since most executive decisions do not require the use of much detail. (Some executives like to see it, or at least to know it's available.)
- Graphically oriented, since graphs can provide sufficient precision for most purposes when detail is not needed.
- Communication-based, both to obtain data from outside the organization and to facilitate exchanging information with people inside it.
- Highly customized or customizable to the executive's individual preferences.

Why Use an EIS (or ESS)?   Executives have many reasons to use an EIS or ESS. An information system for their needs ought to reflect the needs of the executives who will use it. If it doesn't, executives will be more vocal about their displeasure, quicker to discard it, than lower-level managers would have been. One list of reasons for using an EIS, from [GULD88], includes:

- To solve specific problems in either decision making or control.
- To boost the executive's personal work efficiency.
- To facilitate change in the organization: either strategic change or reorganization.
- To "send a signal" to subordinates.
- To gain computer literacy. (Were Gulden and Ewers writing today, they might not have found it necessary to make this last point.)

These go beyond the reasons for using a data warehouse. This difference reflects the broader responsibilities of executives versus those of typical data warehouse users, not a real difference in what the system must do. A data warehouse is an excellent foundation for an EIS, however. As Inmon puts it [INMO96, Chapter 7]:

> The data warehouse is tailor-made for the needs of the EIS analyst. Once the data warehouse has been built, the job of the EIS is infinitely easier than when there is no foundation of data on which to operate. . . . With a fully populated data warehouse in place, the analyst can be in a proactive stance—not an eternally reactive stance—with regard to meeting management's needs. The EIS analyst's job changes from that of data engineer to that of doing true analysis, thanks to the data warehouse.

The reason for which an executive wants to use an EIS or ESS leads directly to the capabilities that the system must provide. Gaining computer literacy might call for allowing the user to manipulate data directly, perhaps by providing a spreadsheet or query capability. Sending a signal may require little beyond highly visible use of something—nearly anything. Facilitating change generally involves communication capability. Boosting personal work efficiency, and solving specific problems, depend on software tailored either to the executive's existing work bottlenecks or the specific problems in question. This is the usual reason for data warehouse development.

As EIS expert James Wetherbe points out [WETH89], finding out what executives want isn't quite as simple as asking them. Executives can't articulate their needs any more than DSS users can. With DSS, as you saw on page 261, prototyping is a big part of the answer. Prototyping works with EIS as well, but it must be approached differently. One cannot usually get a top executive to sit down for half a day each week trying out options, waiting patiently for a developer to modify a line of code here or tweak a screen there. Multiply the time investment that traditional prototyping demands of prospective users by the number of top executives in an organization and the approach quickly becomes impractical.

EIS Characteristics   Several features are common to most EIS and to every package used as a basis for EIS development. After each bulleted point, the paragraph below relates the EIS features to the corresponding aspect of a data warehouse.

- The database includes what Rockart and Treacy [ROCK82] called the **data cube:** historical information broken down by descriptive variable, time period, and business unit (product line, geographic division, or whatever else is appropriate.) For instance, an executive should be able to review sales volume (the descriptive variable) of product X (the business unit) for the last 12 months (time periods).

  An EIS database should go beyond the internal data cube, which tends to be internally focused. Much of the real value of an EIS comes from accessing external data. The cube is still an appropriate way to visualize some types of external data, such as market share by competitor, price segment, and (again) time period.

  The data cube, a term commonly used in an EIS context, corresponds closely to the multiple dimensions along which a data warehouse database is organized.

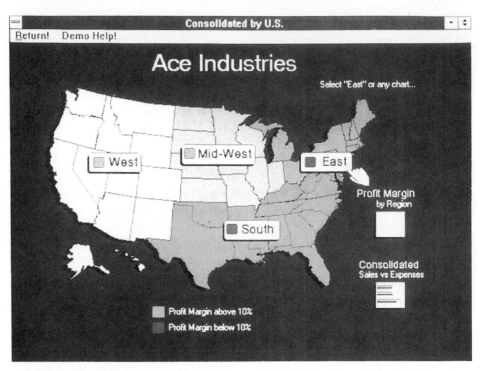

FIGURE 12–2   EIS Screen Shot with Map

- Graphical user interfaces (see page 235) let executives select the areas they want to review. Figure 12–2 shows a typical EIS screen. The P&L Review button, if clicked, might show a map of the United States indicating the sales regions for which P&L data are available. Each region is defined to the EIS as a **hot spot.** A mouse click on any part of this map can bring up data for the region in question. Other options, accessed via other hot spots on the screen, might include more detailed geographic analyses, analyses by product, and whatever else the data cube supports. Still other hot spots, usually identified by suitable graphics, access additional capabilities such as electronic mail or the user's personal appointment calendar.

    Again, the ease of use demanded of a data warehouse leads to graphical user interfaces there as well.

- Positional input (typically via a mouse) is provided to activate the hot spots. A keyboard is still present, however, as some types of input are best entered this way. (Entering an e-mail message by pointing at letters on a screen is not a constructive way for high-paid executives to spend their time.)

    The same is true of data warehouses.

- Users can **drill down** through interesting items of data in increasing levels of detail. An executive who needs more information on sales in the Western region might be able to get a breakdown by product, by sales office, or any other category that the data cube supports. A well-designed EIS screen will indicate what information is "drillable."

  Data warehouses offer this capability as well: The user might start with a precalculated summary or two, then move on to new requests which could not have been foreseen in advance.

- They can be set up to highlight a user's **key performance indicators** as soon as they are turned on. A financial executive might want to see data on stock price per share, inventory turnover, and interest rates as soon as she arrives at her desk. A manufacturing executive would care more about the latest production and quality control reports. An EIS can accommodate either.

  The user of a data warehouse query tool can store queries that address important factors to that user and reissue them easily. This is not exactly the same as customizing the initial screen, but accomplishes much the same thing while requiring less individual support.

- Exceptions are highlighted by the use of color.[2] Red often indicates that an item is below its acceptable performance limit. Most EIS allow the designer to specify tolerance levels for exception conditions. The EIS package uses these levels to apply color (or shading, blinking, boldface text) dynamically, depending on the value of a data item when the screen is created. A given item may appear in yellow one day, in red or green the next, based on changes in the database.

  Data warehouse analysis tools use color extensively as well, in the same ways and for the same reasons. There is an example of this in Chapter 14 on page 529.

- The delivery vehicle is typically a microcomputer linked to the corporate database. Terminals driven by a central computer generally do not provide the easy-to-use interface that executives insist on. What's more, the computational effort of providing even a part of that interface can be carried out far more cost-effectively on a micro.

  Most data warehouse analysis tools operate in client/server mode, with the user's desktop microcomputer serving as the delivery vehicle there as well.

In addition to internal corporate information, many EIS also access two other types of information. This type of information is not highly structured and does not usually find its way into data warehouses.

- "Soft" information, such as comments, opinions, and predictions [WATS92]. This type of information, in text form that can be searched via key words or linked to fields in the database, can help executives spot trends and understand what is behind the numbers. Figure 12–3, from [DIX92], shows the types of information

---

[2]Keep in mind, however, the cautions about color stated on page 239.

Hard ←						→ Soft
Financial statements	News reports	Schedules	Explanations	Predictions	Opinions	Rumors
Statistics	Industry trends	Formal plans	Justifications	Speculations	Feelings	Gossip
Historical information	Survey data		Assessments	Forecasts	Ideas	Hearsay
			Interpretations	Estimates		

FIGURE 12–3 Spectrum of Hard versus Soft EIS Information

that executives can access via an EIS. You can see that the soft information, while its accuracy varies and it is not standardized in content or format, can be of great importance in making strategic decisions.

- External information, that is, information not available from internal corporate databases. This includes, for example, news reports on a firm's industry and its competitors. Public databases provide the full text of leading papers such as the *New York Times* and the *Wall Street Journal* within 24 hours of their publication, often sooner. Earnings data, market research data, and government economic data are likewise available. (Much of this information is "soft" in the sense of the previous paragraph.) EIS can be programmed to access these news services automatically on a periodic basis, load reports of a particular type or about a particular subject, and make them available through the standard EIS interface.

EIS Design Approaches   Leading EIS packages operate in either of two ways within the above general parameters. In one approach, the executive's workstation operates on-line to the database that drives the EIS. In the other, the workstation accesses a predetermined, often summarized, selection from that database. Most EIS development packages were originally written to work in one way or the other, but have since been enhanced to support both. The choice today thus depends on how the system can best meet its users' needs.

In the **on-line** mode of operation, the EIS is essentially an easy-to-use query system tied to a database. A user request for sales data for the Chicago office would create a database query to retrieve the desired information. This information would then be displayed in tabular or graphical form as appropriate. The query itself is coded ahead of time by professional programmers, usually as a template into which EIS software can insert parameters based on the specific request. For instance, an EIS might have a prewritten query to obtain sales summary data for any region. It would fill in a specific region before sending the query to the database. Systems of this type can be linked directly to the live corporate database or to a static data warehouse.

In **off-line** mode, a wide range of possible queries is issued to the database during a period of light system load such as the wee hours of the morning. Data are extracted and screens prepared for display. Those screens are stored in a screen library, which the EIS accesses. That library can be kept at the central system or sent to the server of the LAN to which an executive's desktop computer is attached. It can even be loaded to a laptop computer, useful for users who would like to review data while traveling. When a user asks for specific information, the corresponding screen is retrieved immediately from the EIS screen database and displayed. No computation is required, other than interpreting the condensed form in which the screen is stored. (Storing the color of each dot on a large screen, multiplied by the number of screens involved, would occupy an unacceptable amount of disk space.)

The EIS Sponsor Whether the EIS is intended strictly for top executives, for anyone in the firm who has an interest in its subject matter, or somewhere in between, it is unlikely to succeed unless it has a powerful **sponsor** or **champion.** As Thomas McCarthy of Bankers Trust Company writes in [MCCA92]:

> A champion is the executive who says, "I want this!" (occasionally accompanied by fist-pounding on the table). "I'm interested" or "why don't we take a look" aren't good enough to indicate the level of commitment required. . . . Would-be EIS initiators and project managers should be absolutely certain in this regard. . . . Without a *bona fide* EIS champion, the successful implementation of an EIS is an immensely difficult undertaking.

As Rockart and De Long explain [ROCK88], the sponsor of an EIS has three responsibilities that generally cannot be delegated:

1. To make the initial request for the system. Even if the motivation comes from elsewhere, the sponsor must put his or her name and prestige behind the formal request. This is a one-time effort that takes little time.
2. To stay on top of system development, providing overall direction and feedback on specifics. This takes an ongoing commitment of time and energy.
3. To communicate strong and continuing interest to those who must support, who must contribute to, or who will be expected to use the system. This is an ongoing effort as well, though it does not require large amounts of dedicated time.

When the EIS sponsor is a chief executive, the second of these responsibilities may become too time-consuming for him or her to carry out properly. In that case some of this responsibility (but only this one!) can be delegated to what Rockart and De Long call an **operating sponsor:** a trusted subordinate, recognized as representing the executive sponsor, and typically having a high level of personal influence or authority in the organization as well. When an operating sponsor is present, Rockart and De Long use the term **executive sponsor** for the person called simply a *sponsor* above.

Employee Resistance to EIS EIS allow their users to sit in the executive suite and drill down to increasing levels of detail about organizational activity. The CEO of a global corporation might, for example, compare sales across the firm's four worldwide sales divisions. If North America is under-performing the other three, this executive could then look at the four regions on that continent. With the laggard identified, the president might now look at the six districts in that region. The low sales office in the poorest-performing district comes in for further scrutiny. Finally, one poor salesperson is singled out for a personal "WHAT IS WRONG WITH YOU?" message from this remote, august personage.

This is an extreme (and extremely unlikely) scenario, yet fear of it is normal. To guard against this fear, many EIS can be configured with limits on drill-down. A typical limit is three levels. The above CEO, were such a limit in place, would not be able to look below a North American region in person. To get data from inside the region, he or she would have to request the data from someone such as the regional sales director. This intermediary would be better known to the regional staff. An inquiry from him or her will therefore be less threatening to an individual salesperson. The regional director would also be more aware of unique situations that may not be obvious in the raw data, such as a salesperson's recent return to work after surgery. Such limits, if well publicized, can help prevent EIS-related morale problems.

SUMMARY

A data warehouse is a collection of a wide variety of corporate data, organized and made available to end users for decision-making purposes. A smaller collection, usually relating to one specific aspect of an organization, is called a data mart.

Data warehouses are used by managers and knowledge workers who require access to this data for analyzing the business and planning its future. These needs are usually unstructured, often unpredictable. The data warehouse provides flexibility to meet those needs. Knowing what these needs are, and how the data warehouse will meet them, is a critical first step in any data warehousing project.

Data warehouses have come into use primarily because inexpensive, high-capacity mass storage makes them possible. This hardware development has led to the availability of the necessary software and user motivation as well.

The data warehouse itself consists of multiple elements. The operational databases that feed it are at one side, the users who access it at the other. In between are the data warehouse database and a metadata database that describes the content of the data warehouse database. These are connected by processes which extract data from the operational databases for the data warehouse database, transform it and clean it as required, create any desired summaries, and create the necessary metadata.

An executive information system is an information system that provides information to top executives to support their decision-making needs. An executive support system adds communication and analysis capabilities to the underlying executive information system.

Executives' decision support needs differ from those of lower-level managers because executive decisions are typically less structured, less repetitive, more strategic, less detail-oriented, and more externally focused than those of other managers. These factors lead to common requirements that apply to most or all EIS: They should be cross-functional, data-oriented, summary in nature, graphically oriented, communication-based, and customized to the needs of the individual executive.

In line with these needs, most EIS incorporate a historical *data cube,* have a graphical user interface with positional input to activate *hot spots,* provide a *drill-*

down capability, use color, and are accessed via a microcomputer. In addition, many incorporate both "soft" information and external information. EIS can operate in either of two modes: directly on line to their database or via prestored screens.

Reasons for using executive information systems include solving specific problems in decision making or control, boosting the executive's personal work efficiency, facilitating change in the organization, sending a signal to subordinates, and gaining computer literacy. More and more systems are going beyond these original reasons and providing EIS-type support to many nonexecutives, as the type of information contained in an EIS can be valuable to other decision makers as well.

EIS developers must be conscious of (a) the need for a committed EIS sponsor, (b) the likely high cost of the EIS, (c) potential management resistance to the EIS, and (d) potential employee resistance to the EIS. To deal with these factors and implement a successful EIS, you should identify a sponsor, identify your sponsor's motivations to use an EIS, define your expectations within your corporate culture, pick one or a few initial topics that are important to your sponsor and do them well, define your data and communications requirements, make sure enough resources are in place, pick packages to support your EIS, develop a prototype, and prepare to offer the necessary user training.

KEY TERMS

champion
cleanse (process in preparing data for a data warehouse)
data cube
data mart
data mining
data staging
data warehouse
data warehouse database
dependent (data mart)
drill down
executive
executive information system (EIS)
executive sponsor
executive support system (ESS)
extract (as a verb; process in preparing data for a data warehouse)
hot spot
independent (data mart)
key performance indicator
load (as a verb; process in preparing data for a data warehouse)
metadata
off-line (EIS)
on-line analytical processing (OLAP)

on-line (EIS)
operating sponsor
sponsor
summary (type of data in data warehouse)
transform (process in preparing data for a data warehouse)

REVIEW QUESTIONS

1. State three characteristics of a data warehouse.
2. Contrast the characteristics of people who would use a data warehouse and people who would not need one.
3. What are the two basic hardware advances that made data warehouses practical?
4. What provides input to the data warehouse? Uses output from it?
5. What three things must be done to data before loading it into a data warehouse?
6. How might a university admissions office use a data warehouse?
7. What is an executive? A nonexecutive? Give two typical position titles for each.
8. How does the executive's viewpoint typically differ from that of a nonexecutive?
9. How do executives' decisions typically differ from those of nonexecutives?
10. What is the difference between an EIS and an ESS? What do they both have in common?
11. What characteristics should an information system for executives' use possess?
12. Why do executives use EIS (or ESS)?
13. What features are common to most EIS?
14. What is the data cube?
15. What is "soft" information? Why is external information often soft?
16. How do the on-line and off-line approaches to EIS design differ?
17. What is an EIS sponsor? Why is it important to have one?
18. Why might some managers resist an EIS? Some nonmanagement employees?
19. List several steps you can take to increase the likelihood of a successful EIS project.

EXERCISES

1. It is 10:21 on a Tuesday morning in early June in an automobile manufacturer's planning department. Parts must be ordered for the initial run of next year's models, to be produced over the summer for shipment to dealers by September. Since none of these cars is being built to a customer order, cars will be built to general customer preferences as best they can be determined. Other factors include (a) a desire to provide each dealer with a range of vehicles to show when the new models are introduced; (b) the historical sales patterns of different dealers—a dealer in an upscale suburb and one in a rural town might get different selections; and (c) a desire to mix the selections sent to dealers in the same geographic area so they don't all have identical cars on their lots.

   Dealerships are independently owned businesses that place orders with the manufacturer for cars they expect to be able to sell. Therefore, each dealership makes the final decision as to what cars it wants. However, the manufacturer feels it can provide dealers with guidance to suit their orders to customer preferences. This would help dealers, who will benefit from a more attractive selection of cars on their lot, and the manufacturer, by systematizing its early production runs.

   How could the manufacturer use a data warehouse in this situation?

2. Suggest one decision for which each of these types of organizations could use a data warehouse. Be specific as to both your decision statement and the types of information you would want to get out of the data warehouse in order to help make that decision.

   a. The central body of a worldwide religion with houses of worship in many countries.

   b. A provider of Internet access services to individuals and small businesses.

   c. The public relations department of a $10 billion per year information technology firm that makes a wide range of computer and communication products.

3. Using your library's computer-based information retrieval system or the Web-based search facility of a publication that tracks the information system field, search for the term *data warehouse* by year for 1993 through the present. If you limit your search to certain journals or in any other way, use the same limits on each year's search. Count the number of references, articles retrieved, or another measure of how much the system returned. Plot your findings on a graph. Then do the same for the term *data mart*. What can you conclude from the results?

4. You work for a nationwide chain of retail stores selling men's shirts. You are developing a data warehouse for its buyers to use. Define at least six dimensions that its database (which you can think of for this purpose as an EIS data cube; see page 479) could have.

5. Your college or university is implementing a data warehouse to help students select courses for each term. The data warehouse is to be available to all students from their Web browsers. You have been asked to join the student advisory board that will define the data warehouse in detail.

   a. List six pieces of information that you would suggest including in the data warehouse.

   b. State one item of information you would personally like to have when you make course selection decisions, but which (for ethical, privacy or similar reasons) you feel should *not* be included in this data warehouse.

   c. Give two queries that students might pose to the data warehouse. Draw pictures of screens showing how you think the answers should look.

6. If an EIS is a type of DSS, where does it fall in the seven DSS categories?

7. Page 478 gives a list of reasons why executives use EIS. Relate each reason to the DSS benefits in Chapter 1 on page 17.

8. Consider developing an EIS for the top management of your college or university.

   a. Who would your target users be? Be specific. Use actual names and titles: "Chancellor Hogan, Provost Rudenstine, Dean DiLuna . . ."

   b. Whom would you try to get as your sponsor? From what you know (or can find out) of this person, how responsive do you think he or she would be?

   c. What sort of information would you make available through the EIS? (Think about the key issues that top administrators face.) What summaries would you provide? Would each be a table, a graph, or the user's choice of either format?

   d. Would up-to-yesterday data suffice to drive this EIS, or would it need on-line access to the current database?

   e. Would you put any limits on what top administrators could see in terms of student data? Faculty/staff personnel data? Other types of data?

   f. What sort of external databases could be useful for your EIS? (You may want to use your library resources to find out what kinds of public databases exist.)

   g. What telecommunications capabilities would your EIS call for? Beyond them, what could you usefully add? (Find out what facilities, such as electronic mail, exist at your institution today, and how much the top administrators use them.)

REFERENCES

On Data Warehousing

This list includes books on data warehousing cited in the next three chapters, as well as specific papers and articles cited in this chapter. These books are collected here in order to have all the references in one easy-to-use list.

ANAH97   Anahory, Sam, and Dennis Murray. *Data Warehousing in the Real World.* Addison Wesley Longman, Reading, Mass. (1997).

ATRE98   Atre, Shaku. "Problem-solving." *Computerworld* 32, no. 3 (January 19, 1998), p. 71.

BIGU96   Bigus, Joseph P. *Data Mining with Neural Networks.* Wiley, New York (1996).

BRAC96   Brackett, Michael H. *The Data Warehouse Challenge.* Wiley, New York (1996).

CAFA95   Cafasso, Rosemary. "Sears Mines Data with Multidimensional Tools." *Computerworld* (June 26, 1995), p. 65. In addition, one of Sears's data analysis software suppliers has (in mid-1999) a case study on this application on their Web site, http://www.hysoft.com/cs_sears.cfm

DEVL97   Devlin, Barry. *Data Warehouse—from Architecture to Implementation.* Addison Wesley Longman, Reading, Mass. (1997).

GOLD96   Goldberg, Michael. "Data Warehouse Fills CVS Prescription." *Computerworld* (April 1, 1996).

IMHO99   Imhoff, Claudia. "Will the Real Data Mart Please Stand Up?" *DM Review* 9, no. 3 (March 1999), p. 12.

INMO96   Inmon, William H. *Building the Data Warehouse* (2nd ed.). Wiley, New York (1996).

KIMB96   Kimball, Ralph. *The Data Warehouse Toolkit.* Wiley, New York (1996).

LAPL96   LaPlante, Alice. "What's Best for You?" *Computerworld* (June 24, 1996); p. DW/6.

MALL97   Malloy, Amy. "Data Mart Dynamics." *Computerworld* (September 22, 1997), p. 99.

MATT96   Mattison, Rob. *Data Warehousing: Strategies, Tools and Techniques.* McGraw-Hill New York (1996).

MCWI96   McWilliams, Brian. "Case Study: Moen, Inc." *Computerworld* (July 29, 1996), Part II (Data Warehousing supplement), p. DW/6.

REDB97   Red Brick Systems, Inc. "Solutions Profile: Data Mining and Data Warehousing," advertisement to *Computerworld* (1997).

SOFT95   Software AG. "The Decision-Maker's Goldmine: The Data Warehouse," advertising supplement to *Datamation* (March 15, 1995), p. S6.

THOM97   Thomsen, Erik. *OLAP Solutions.* Wiley, New York (1997).

On Executive Information Systems

DIX92   Dix, Lory Zottola. "A Bunch of Softies." *Computerworld* 26, no. 42 (October 19, 1992), p. 105.

GULD88   Gulden, Gary K., and Douglas E. Ewers. "The Keys to Successful Executive Support Systems." *Indications* 5, no. 5 (September–October 1988), pp. 1–5; also in slightly different form as "Is Your ESS Meeting the Need?" *Computerworld* 23, no. 28 (July 10, 1989), pp. 85–88.

MCCA92   McCarthy, Thomas M. "Tales from the EIS Trenches" (in "The Expert's Opinion" section), *Information Resources Management Journal* 5, no. 1 (Winter 1992), pp. 35–38.

ROCK82   Rockart, John F., and Michael E. Treacy. "The CEO Goes On-Line." *Harvard Business Review* 60, no. 1 (January–February 1982), pp. 82–88. (Previously made available in similar form under the same title as Working Paper no. 67, Center for Information Systems Research, M.I.T., Cambridge, Mass., April 1981.)

ROCK88   Rockart, John F., and David W. De Long. *Executive Support Systems.* Dow Jones-Irwin, Homewood, Ill. (1988).

WATS92   Watson, Hugh J., Candice G. Harp, Gigi G. Kelly, and Margaret T. O'Hara. "Soften up!" *Computerworld* 26, no. 42 (October 19, 1992), pp. 103–104.

WETH89   Wetherbe, James. "Getting It Right the First Time." *Computerworld* 23, no. 28 (July 10, 1989), pp. 89–91.

CASE

Fort Lowell Trading Company
Planning the Data Warehouse

From their earlier meetings with Niels Agger, Miguel and Elizabeth knew he had been reading about data warehouses and liked the concept. They had encouraged him to start developing a small one using a sample of store data. They were quite pleased, then, when he opened their discussion during the walk to his office with "Well, I've decided to take your advice and start moving on this data warehouse thing!"

"Oh? What was the clincher?" asked Miguel.

"A couple of things, actually," Niels responded. "For one, every retail business magazine seems to have an article on this stuff! You never know how much is really going on and how much people are talking about what they'd like to do someday, but if there's that much talk we can't afford to fall too far behind.

"Reason number two is that we keep running into decisions that a data warehouse might really help with. Remember when we were talking about our Web site?[3] Well, if we had a good data warehouse we might be able to answer some of those questions instead of just taking a wild guess.

"Finally, Jim Atcitty, one of our marketing planners, sat down with me at lunch yesterday and we started talking about it. He had just read one of those magazine articles, too. One thing led to another. By the middle of the afternoon I had offered him a job in my group setting one up! How would you like to meet him?"

"We sure would! Is he in his office today?"

"Better than that. He's in mine!" Niels laughed. "I knew that's what you'd say, so I invited him ahead of time."

As they turned the corner into Niels's office, Elizabeth and Miguel saw an unfamiliar face across the familiar piles of clutter. Niels introduced him as they entered: "This is Jim Atcitty, the marketing planner I was telling you about. Jim, meet Elizabeth and Miguel."

---

[3]This discussion took place in the episode of Chapter 3.

"A pleasure," said Jim, extending his hand to the two. "I'm not sure what I've just gotten myself into here. I've read a lot about what our competitors are doing with data warehousing but I don't know anything about how they're doing it. Perhaps you can help me get started."

"What are your thoughts so far?" asked Miguel.

"Well, from what I've read, it's a good idea to start small. I've seen the term 'data mart' for a small data warehouse, but I'm not really sure how it's different from a big one except for size. And I'm not sure exactly what we we'd save by doing one first—wouldn't all the pieces have to be there anyhow?"

[Unfortunately, it was necessary to change recorder tapes while Miguel and Elizabeth answered Jim, so their answer was lost. See exercise 1 at the end of this episode.]

"As I was saying," Jim continued, "my background is market planning, so that's my bias toward where we should start. I'd like to be able to look at trends in who's buying what, where, how much and how often. Other folks probably want to look at trends in more detail to figure out if they should order more teal-green sweatshirts or brown ones, but that's not me."

"Those people do matter down the road, though," Niels pointed out. "We want to do a better job of breaking down our catalogue mailing lists, figure out how our Web customers are different from our catalogue customers or our store customers, and a whole lot of other things."

"Right," agreed Jim. "I didn't mean that those things aren't important or that we won't do them. I just wanted to explain where I was coming from, what my biases are and what, if it's up to me, we'd probably start with."

"I don't think either of us was really confused about that," Miguel said to make sure there were no misunderstandings. "You have to start somewhere, after all. Planning is as good a place as any. When would you see the project getting under way and what do you plan to do next?"

"Assuming I take the job," Jim laughed, adding "which is a pretty good bet or I wouldn't be here talking to you, I'll transfer over here in about a week. There are a few things I have to clean up first but nothing major that other people can't pick up. Then, I'd . . . I'd . . . You know, that's a real good question. What *would* I do?"

EXERCISES

1. Answer the question Jim asked right after he was introduced to Elizabeth and Miguel: Why would it be quicker and easier to develop and implement a data mart than a full data warehouse?

2. In response to Jim's last question, what are three things he should do with regard to this data warehousing project when he starts his new job?

3. Read Shaku Atre's article on page 475. From what you know of Fort Lowell Trading Company and its needs, which type of data warehouse—improving business operations or analyzing and projecting trends—would you recommend they start with?

The Data Warehouse Database

CHAPTER OUTLINE

Introduction

All the definitions of a data warehouse in the previous chapter focused, at least in part, on it as a collection or a store of data. Given this fact, it stands to reason that the way in which we organize the data will have a major impact on the value of the database. Proper data organization is a requirement if its users are to be able to get the data they want in a reasonable time frame.

Given the size and scope of many data warehouses, proper organization is a non-trivial issue. It is one thing to isolate the relevant quarter of a 1-megabyte (MB) database, divide its records into 10 categories, and total the Amount fields in each. A desktop computer can do this in a fraction of a second. If the database is 1 gigabyte (GB) instead of 1 MB, the same analysis would take a substantial fraction of an hour. And if it's 1 terabyte (TB), well below what is considered a "large" warehouse today? Given the structure of most desktop databases, it would be impractical to carry out even this simple calculation in a suitable time frame for business decision making. Trend analyses, correlations—all these are out of the question. If we want to accomplish these things we must resort to new techniques for organizing our data and pay careful attention to the way we apply these techniques.

After you study the material in this chapter you'll understand the issues involved in database creation for data warehouses and be in a better position to make informed choices in this area.

CHAPTER OBJECTIVES

After you have read and studied this chapter, you will be able to:

1. Describe four kinds of data that data warehouses use.
2. Explain ways in which the database needs of a data warehouse differ from those of transaction processing applications.
3. Show how a relational database can be organized for a data warehouse.
4. Explain the concept of a multi-dimensional database and why they are well suited to data warehouses.
5. Choose the right database structure for a data warehouse.
6. List the stages involved in getting data into a data warehouse and explain what each stage consists of.
7. Describe three types of metadata and how each type works.

13.1 CONTENT OF THE DATA WAREHOUSE DATABASE

If you look at Figure 12–1 again, the data warehouse architecture diagram, you'll see that the database has a central place in the data warehouse. The very name *data warehouse* focuses on its storage function, in that a warehouse is a place to store goods or materials until they are needed for the next step of a business process.

Another reason for focusing on that data warehouse database is that it typically represents most of the effort involved in developing a data warehouse. Experts regularly mention figures of up to 80 percent. This gives the database a great deal of leverage in the data warehousing project overall.

Third, the content of the data warehouse database defines what the data warehouse will be able to do. It is fairly easy to replace one analysis tool with another if it turns out that the first doesn't handle pivot tables easily or can't produce a desired type of graph. It is more difficult to change the content of a database that has been loaded with 5 TB of data and is updated nightly via a well-standardized procedure.

Finally, as the old saying goes, "garbage in, garbage out." Without high-quality data as its base, it is impossible for a data warehouse to provide useful information.

The data warehouse database is, as we noted in Chapter 12, separate from the organization's transaction databases. There are [BOWE95] three reasons for this:

- It is difficult to optimize data organization for both short transactions and large reporting tasks.
- Users need a consistent source of data for analyzing the business, not one that changes from moment to moment.
- Transaction data is usually organized by application, so that transactions can touch only the data they need and get out of the way as quickly as possible. Decision support data should be organized by subject to give users a more integrated view.

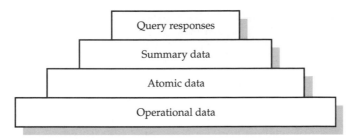

FIGURE 13–1   Four Data Levels

The data warehouse environment contains four levels of data. These levels, shown in Figure 13–1, comprise the following:

1. Operational data—that is, the data that come into the data warehouse from the operational databases of the organization. These are not part of the data warehouse itself but are fundamental to it. Data warehouses could not exist without operational data to feed them.

   Example: My checking account balance, right now, is $1,862.37.

2. **Atomic data warehouse data.** Atomic data consists of individual data items. This is the lowest level of data in the data warehouse. All data warehouse functions start with atomic data or with data derived from atomic data. Atomic data often correspond to transaction data with the addition of a time dimension. This is the level at which data are fed into the data warehouse database from the operational databases of the organization.

   Example: My checking account balance at the end of May was $1,236.98.
      . . . at the end of April was $326.03.
      . . . at the end of March was $3,004.81.
      . . . at the end of February was $2,661.90.
      . . . etc.

3. **Summary** data warehouse data. Analysts often have enough insight into the expected uses of a data warehouse to know that certain summaries will be needed on a recurring basis. Those summaries can be calculated ahead of time and stored in the data warehouse database for recall as needed.

   Example: At the end of May we had 11,276 customers in ZIP codes 01800-01899.
      At the end of April we had 11,098 . . .
      At the end of March we had 11,034 . . .
      At the end of February we had 10,847 . . .
      Etc.

4. Answers to specific queries. These are usually created as needed and stored only until the user who requested them is finished. If a user wants to keep them, that user's microcomputer usually has facilities for storing them, such as pasting them into a spreadsheet or a memo. The data warehouse itself isn't concerned with them.

Example: Our customer base in ZIP codes 01800-01899 grew by 3.95 percent during the three months from March through May.

Example: Our customer base in ZIP codes 01800-01899 grew 52 percent faster in the past three months than it did in ZIP codes 01700-01799.

In other situations, queries may be treated like summaries: If the data warehouse designers expect a given query to be needed often, they may arrange to have the answer precomputed and stored for instant retrieval. Unless a data warehouse database is truly large and the need for a specific query truly frequent, though, this usually isn't worth the effort.

Database design for data warehouses is concerned largely with the second and third of these items. The first, as noted above, is not part of the data warehouse itself. The fourth is not stored in the data warehouse database even if it is stored by query software, which is part of the data warehouse overall. The database must be designed to facilitate creating it, not to store it. Storing the results of specific queries, whether in the data warehouse or at the user's desktop, is a capability of the query software—not of the data warehouse database.

Most of this chapter is concerned with the second item on the above list, storing atomic data (individual data items derived directly from operational databases or other data sources). Summaries, which depend on high-quality atomic data for their creation, are covered starting on page 511.

Another type of data that is part of the data warehouse environment, but which we have defined as being outside the data warehouse database itself, is **metadata**—data that describe the data warehouse database content. We'll discuss metadata in more detail starting on page 514.

13.2 DATABASE STRUCTURES

As you know from the discussion of databases in Chapter 6 and from your prior coursework, the value of data depends on accessibility and usability. These, in turn, depend in large part on the way the data are organized in storage. Proper organization makes data easy to locate and quick to retrieve. Poor organization, on the other hand, can make data hard to locate and can make retrieval take an unacceptably long time for practical decision-making use.

Different database structures are used for data warehouses than for other types of processing because their requirements are different. The database structures described in Chapter 6 evolved primarily to meet the requirements of transaction processing. It is a tribute to the ingenuity of programmers, to the performance of modern computers (enabling them to deal with inappropriate data structures while still delivering acceptable responsiveness) and to critical user needs for decision support information that they can be used in the DSS environment as well. However, the DSS environment, and especially the data warehouse environment, differ from transaction processing. Some of the differences that affect database structures are shown in Figure 13–2. While there are gray areas between the two categories and occasional exceptions to these generalizations, the figure does represent the usual tendencies.

Characteristic	Operational (Transaction Processing) Need	Data Warehouse (DSS) Need
Volatility	Dynamic	Static
Currentness	Current	Historical
Time dimension	Implicitly "now"	Explicit, visible
Granularity	Primitive, detailed	Detailed and derived summaries
Updates	Continuous, random	Periodic, scheduled
Tasks	Repetitive	Unpredictable
Flexibility	Low	High
Performance	High performance mandatory	Lower performance often acceptable

FIGURE 13–2 Database Requirement Differences Between DSS and TP

For these reasons the hierarchical and network database structures, which you read about in Chapter 6, are unsuited to data warehouse applications. The same cannot be said of the relational structure which you also studied there. With suitable indexing and performance tuning, by an experienced database administrator or by automated tools, it can handle data warehouse applications quite well. However, it is not the only choice for this application. A new structure, quite unsuited to transaction processing, has emerged: the multidimensional database. This organization suits some data warehouses especially well, so we'll cover it here.

13.2.1 Organizing a Relational Data Warehouse

Consider a pet store with three salespeople that sells four different types of pets. We could record data on the number of pets of each type, sold by each salesperson during a time period of interest, as follows:

	Cats	Dogs	Fish	Gerbils
Adams	3	12	5	4
Baker	2	4	22	5
Carstens	6	2	3	16

There are two types of data in this example, as well as all the others in this book and in life: dimension data and fact data. This concept is independent of the structure in which the database is stored: relational, multi-dimensional, or anything else. However, it is most important to understand the distinction when dealing with a relational database because the analyst must set up the tables in a suitable fashion there. Multidimensional databases, which we discuss in the next section, handle these issues automatically.

- **Dimension data** are the dimensions along which data can be analyzed. In the pet store, we can analyze sales data by salesperson or by type of pet. Therefore, "salesperson" and "type of pet" are dimension data.

    Time is a dimension data element in most data warehouses: How do the three salespeople's trends in cat sales compare over the past 26 months? We passed over this in the above example by saying "during a time period of interest," but real data warehouses must deal with time explicitly.

Fact Data	Dimension Data
Millions or billions of rows	Tens to a few million rows
Multiple foreign keys	One primary key
Numeric	Textual descriptions
Don't change	Frequently modified

FIGURE 13–3 Differences Between Fact Data and Dimension Data
Source: From [ANAH97]. Used by permission.

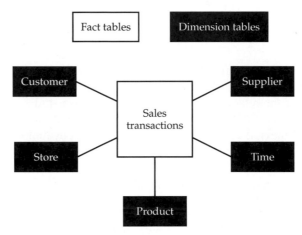

FIGURE 13–4 Star Schema

Dimension data are usually a key to the fact data in a relational database, though a single dimension data element is probably not a complete key to a fact record by itself. It requires a combination of keys to access a fact record. If the fact record represents atomic data, the complete key may involve all the dimension data elements.

Dimension data change as the business changes and user requirements for analysis change. It is important to plan for this change. Fortunately, since the volume of dimension data is usually a small fraction of the entire database, accommodating change is not costly.

- **Fact data** are what we know about what happens along these dimensions. In the pet store, it is a fact that Adams sold three cats during the period covered by our data. The number of pets sold by each salesperson is the only element of fact data in this example. Fact data constitutes the majority of the data in the typical data warehouse.

Fact data tend to be stable over time. For this reason, it is important to get the right fact tables into the data warehouse database from the start.

Figure 13–3, from [ANAH97], shows some of the differences between fact data and dimension data. If we put the fact table in the center of a diagram with the dimensions surrounding it, we have a figure such as Figure 13–4 that resembles a star. This logical structure, which is common in relational data warehouses, is called the **star schema** database design.

Salesperson	Pet Type	Week	No. Sold
Adams	Cats	April 20, 1998	3
Adams	Dogs	April 20, 1998	12
Adams	Fish	April 20, 1998	5
Adams	Gerbils	April 20, 1998	4
Baker	Cats	April 20, 1998	2
Baker	Dogs	April 20, 1998	4
Baker	Fish	April 20, 1998	22
Baker	Gerbils	April 20, 1998	5
Carstens	Cats	April 20, 1998	6
Carstens	Dogs	April 20, 1998	2
Carstens	Fish	April 20, 1998	3
Carstens	Gerbils	April 20, 1998	16
Adams	Cats	April 13, 1998	4
Adams	Dogs	April 13, 1998	10
Adams	Fish	April 13, 1998	7
Adams	Gerbils	April 13, 1998	5
Baker	Cats	April 13, 1998	6
Baker	Dogs	April 13, 1998	2
Baker	Fish	April 13, 1998	17
Baker	Gerbils	April 13, 1998	6
Carstens	Cats	April 13, 1998	4
Carstens	Dogs	April 13, 1998	6

FIGURE 13–5 Fact Table for Pet Store Data Warehouse

In the example in the figure (also from [ANAH97]), all of our information about business entities such as products, stores, customers, and suppliers are in the dimension tables at the sides of the diagram, as is time information. The store hierarchy that groups stores into regions would be in the store dimension table, and so on. If we have information that is specific to each store, such as the name of its manager or its address, that would also be in the store table.

The center table has information about transactions: Customer W bought Product X, made by Supplier Y, in Store Z, at Time T. Here we could also store information about the price, method of payment, and anything else we wanted to record about the transaction. If we want to find out what the patterns are in spending by individual customers, or if there are trends over time in sales of products made by Acme Industries, this is where we have the connections that permit the analysis.

We can make the concept of the star schema more concrete with a specific example. Suppose we use the pet store example, with the addition of time information for each sales period. The fact table for this data warehouse might look like Figure 13–5 (plus many rows not shown, of course). This data warehouse could have dimension tables for salesperson, type of pet, and time—the three types of dimension data in it. In this case we might want to analyze pet sales as a function of salesperson characteristics. Do salespeople who drive sedans or SUVs sell more fish? Do those who live in houses or apartments sell more gerbils? Whereas a sample of three salespeople isn't large enough to draw meaningful conclusions, the concept would apply equally well to a store with 3,000. This type of information is subject to abuse, but it can also be helpful in understanding the interpersonal

Salesperson	Car	Hair Color	Residence
Adams	Sedan	Red	Apartment
Baker	Sports car	Gray	Trailer
Carstens	SUV	Black	House

FIGURE 13–6 Dimension Table for Pet Salespeople

dynamics of the sales process and in identifying areas for potential improvement. A dimension table to support such analyses might look like Figure 13–6.

A dimension need not have an associated dimension table. Some dimensions don't have additional data associated with them. For instance, suppose product color is a dimension in a data warehouse. (This is often an important dimension for analyzing customer preferences and planning future orders.) Unless we were interested in who supplies different colors of paint or the chemical composition of dyes, the color dimension would not have a dimension table.

13.2.2 Multidimensional Database Structures

Take another look at the pet store data on page 497. We can see by a brief inspection that each salesperson tends to sell a particular type of pet more than the other types.

There could be several reasons for this. It might be coincidence. Perhaps other salespeople, knowing (for instance) that Carstens is a gerbil expert, send customers who ask "do you sell gerbils?" in her direction. Perhaps they tend, for whatever reason, to stand near where a given type of pet is found. It is also possible that each salesperson tends to suggest his or her favorite type of pet to customers who come in with no preference, in the process perhaps selling a pet that is not well suited to the customer and also not maximizing store revenue. (All else being equal, dog sales are more profitable than gerbil sales, but satisfied gerbil buyers who return for food and accessories and recommend the store to their friends are more profitable than unhappy dog buyers.) Whatever the reason, once we know what is happening we're in a position to investigate, find out if there is a problem, and deal with it if necessary.

We could represent the same data in a relational table, as in Figure 13–7. (This is the same table as the first 12 rows of Figure 13–5 without the time column.) The relational structure requires a row for each combination of parameters. The order of the rows is irrelevant. This is both a strength and a weakness of the relational approach: a strength because it provides the ultimate in flexibility to store and access data, a weakness because the DBMS must in principle search all the rows to find what the user is looking for.

This relational database layout and the simple 3 × 4 table contain the same data, but it's harder to see the pattern in the relational table. It's harder even though we've organized the relational table to make it as easy as possible. Each salesperson's records are grouped together, and the pet types are in the same order, alphabetical order, for each salesperson. If the rows of the table had been in random order—they could just as well have been, since row order has no inherent significance in a relational table—it would have been difficult to see the pattern.

Salesperson	Pet Type	No. Sold
Adams	Cats	3
Adams	Dogs	12
Adams	Fish	5
Adams	Gerbils	4
Baker	Cats	2
Baker	Dogs	4
Baker	Fish	22
Baker	Gerbils	5
Carstens	Cats	6
Carstens	Dogs	2
Carstens	Fish	3
Carstens	Gerbils	16

FIGURE 13–7   Relational Fact Table for Basic Pet Store Data

Now, suppose that the data, instead of representing a pet store with three sales-people and four types of pets, represented a wall covering store chain with 40 stores in six districts, hundreds of products in dozens of categories that differ in material, size, color, and more, with weekly data going back two years, and more—the conceptual merits of the multidimensional approach become clearer.

Much of the data used for business decision making is inherently dimensional. Fortunately, computers respond to a multidimensional presentation of data nearly as well as people do. A **multidimensional database (MDDB),** also called simply a **dimensional database,** reflects the multidimensional characteristics of data internally. It stores data in a giant **hypercube.**[1] This structures the data so we can find what we need easily: just go down to the third row and over to the fifth column. By storing the data in the form of a multidimensional array rather than as separate tables, we make it easy for the computer to locate any item of interest. It is also easy to calculate totals, averages, and so forth, on any desired dimension, since the locations of systematically related data in the database follow a regular pattern. An MDDB can retrieve related data elements (for instance, all blue cotton button-down shirts irrespective of size, store, and date of sale) quickly.

Of course, the data aren't actually in a hypercube because disk drives don't have four or more physical dimensions. A hypercube is just the conceptual structure. Think about how a two-dimensional matrix is laid out in a computer's memory, which is a linear (one-dimensional) structure. The matrix is mapped into the linear structure as in Figure 13–8. A multidimensional database works the same way. The disk addresses of the records change in a systematic way as the dimension variables change so that it's easy to find the record or records corresponding to a desired set of dimension data.

---

[1]A *hypercube* is the extension of a cube to four or more dimensions. While people have trouble visualizing hypercubes, their mathematical description is straightforward. For example, a line has two "corners," a square has four, and a cube has eight, so a four-dimensional hypercube has 16. Using similar reasoning, this hypercube has eight "sides," each of which is a cube touching six other cubes.

$$\begin{pmatrix} A & B & C \\ D & E & F \\ G & H & I \end{pmatrix}$$

(a) conceptual structure (two-dimensional)

(b) representation in memory (linear)

FIGURE 13–8 Matrix and Mapping into Linear Memory

You may be asking about now, What if we had put all the pets sold by each person in that person's record in a relational database? Wouldn't that give us the advantages you claim the multidimensional structure has, without having to invent a whole new way to store data? In other words, couldn't we do this with a relational table?

Salesperson	Cats	Dogs	Fish	Gerbils
Adams	3	12	5	4
Baker	2	4	22	5
Carstens	6	2	3	16

Now, it's easy for people to see what was going on and it's not difficult to calculate totals for each pet type. Calculating total pets sold by each salesperson, however, would be more difficult in standard SQL. (The standard SQL sum function totals a given field such as Cats or Dogs across multiple selected records. It can't total fields with different names across each record.) Trying to represent more dimensions this way rapidly becomes an exercise in futility. With a multidimensional database, it's just as easy to sum across the table (how many pets of all types did each salesperson sell?) as it is to sum down it (how many pets of each type did the entire sales force sell as a group?).

Extending the Basic Multidimensional Concept Some data require "don't know" cells. For example, consider a shirt where we know everything but its collar style. If we include it in our database with "don't know" for collar style, it will still be counted in analyses by color, size, and fabric. It's also sometimes useful to have a cell for "other," as in a store where most shoppers come from a few nearby towns, which are all listed individually, but some don't.

Multidimensional databases can get large quickly. In many situations most of the cells at the atomic data level are empty. For instance, a store may stock several hundred different types of men's shirts but sell only a few dozen a day. Dimen-

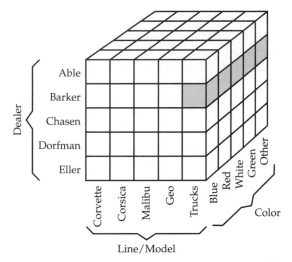

FIGURE 13–9   Database with Barker's Chevrolet Not Selling Trucks

sional database management software uses special techniques to store **sparse data** efficiently. These techniques may negate some of the performance advantages of the dimensional structure, as they make it necessary to deviate from the simple consistency of a uniform data array.

As a compromise that can save most of the unused space with minimal performance impact, some MDDB software compresses large areas of empty space but not scattered individual empty cells. In Figure 13–9, the shaded slice through the cube would be empty if Barker's Chevrolet dealership, as a matter of business policy, had chosen not to sell trucks. If we add more dimensions to this example— name of salesperson, time periods, and so forth—the space savings become still larger. In many applications, large database sections such as this, where the underlying nature of the business ensures that they will always be empty, provide the major opportunities for space savings.

13.2.3 Choosing a Structure

Either the relational or the multidimensional database structure can represent any collection of data we want. We will never be able to state, "We must use structure X here because the other one can't do what we want it to." The choice should be made on the basis of how well the data and our application match each structure. These will, in turn, determine ease of use and performance.

Size of the database is an important factor in the structure decision. As a rule, a multidimensional database of a given size will answer queries more quickly and generally be more responsive than a relational database of the same size.

The catch here, however, is those four little words "of the same size." The same amount of raw data does not, unfortunately, lead to the same size database in both organizations. A multidimensional database tends to be larger than a relational database for a given quantity of raw data. And, as the database grows, the multidimensional database grows proportionately faster.

For small data warehouses—data marts—the performance advantages of a multidimensional structure are more than enough to outweigh the impact of its somewhat larger size. As the data warehouse grows, this is no longer the case. The crossover point depends on a host of factors, including the number of dimensions in the data warehouse data, the number of summaries to be precomputed (see the next section), and the specific products being compared. As of this writing, it is usually in the vicinity of 50 GB. This leads to the following rules of thumb. Keep in mind that evolving technology, in both multidimensional and relational databases, may change the situation in a short time.

- Below 25 GB, multidimensional databases will be faster and the cost of the additional storage they require will be small. Relational databases should be used only if it is desired to use the operational database as a data warehouse as well.
- Above 100 GB, multidimensional databases will probably be unacceptably slow and the cost of their additional storage will be substantial. Relational databases are more practical. If subsets of the overall database can be defined and loaded into data marts, using a multidimensional structure for them may offer "the best of both worlds."
- In between there is a broad area where the right answer is not obvious. The specific situation will have to be analyzed. Expected database growth, and the availability of tools within the organization to work with one type of database or the other, are key considerations.

Another consideration in choosing between the two database organizations may be the computing power relationship between the client and server systems in a given organization. A multidimensional database tends to put more of the analysis workload on the server. A relational database, as a rule, gives the client more to do. If prospective data warehouse users already have high-end systems on their desktops, a relational data warehouse database may allow them to take full advantage of this hardware while minimizing the investment on the server side. If the existing desktop equipment is less capable, a more server-centric system (such as multidimensional databases typically are, though some relational database analysis tools can also be configured to do much of their work on the server side) may make companywide upgrades unnecessary at the cost of a somewhat more powerful server.

A second issue in data warehouse database design is where to put the database. Most data warehouses operate in client/server mode, so that the database can easily be shared by multiple users but much of the analysis and user interface work can be done on the user's desktop. You read about the major alternatives in this respect in Chapter 5. Here, it is important to keep in mind that the structure decision and the location decision are largely independent of each other. You may choose to locate the data warehouse database on the corporate mainframe, on a separate server dedicated to this application, or on a Web server accessed via the Internet or an intranet. The structure issues remain the same in any of these cases.

13.3 GETTING DATA INTO THE DATA WAREHOUSE

As you recall from the discussion of data warehouse architecture on page 473, there are several stages in moving from operational data to data warehouse data: extraction, transformation, cleansing, loading, and summarization. A given software tool may combine two or more of these steps—transformation may be done during extraction, for example. Cleansing and transformation may be done in either order. In general, though, the steps are performed in this order.

13.3.1 Extraction

Some of the data elements in any operational database can reasonably be expected to be useful in decision making, but others are of less value for that purpose. For example, it may be relevant that a customer used an American Express card or a personal check to pay for a purchase, but there is probably no reason to store the card number in a data warehouse. In a manufacturing analysis application the customer-visible information about products being produced may be relevant, but the internal manufacturing details (which milling machine was component 27C machined on, at what time, and by which machinist?) are not. In other situations, especially in data marts, only some types of information apply to the subject area of the database. For this reason, it is necessary to **extract** the relevant data from the operational database before bringing it into the data warehouse.

Many commercial tools are available to help with the extraction process. The user of one of these tools typically has an easy-to-use windowed interface by which to specify the following:

- Which files or tables are to be accessed in the source database?
- Which fields are to be extracted from them? This is often done internally via the SQL Select statement, though many extraction tools hide the complexity of the SQL from the person defining the extraction.
- What are those fields to be called in the resulting database?
- What is the target machine and database format of the output?
- On what schedule should the extraction be repeated? While initial database loading is a one-time operation, regular updates are a common practice.

Figure 13–10 shows a representative screen from a data extraction program, in this case Data Junction from the Austin, Texas, firm of the same name.[2]

Commercial extraction packages generally offer long lists of database formats that they accept as input and can produce as output. (The input list and the output list are usually different, since some common formats in transactional databases would not be chosen for use in a data warehouse and vice versa.) Alternatively, if an organization has few data formats and some of these are unusual, it is not difficult to write a custom extraction program.

---

[2]Several figures in this and the next chapter are screen images from commercial data warehousing software. While we are grateful to their vendors for making the figures available, no endorsement of these packages is implied. In choosing software you should always evaluate what is available at the time you make the choice in the context of your specific needs.

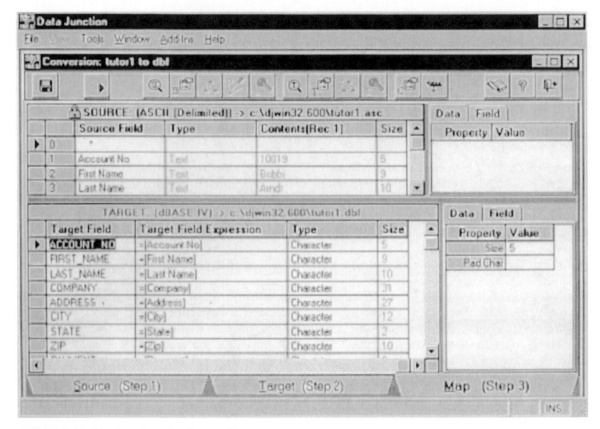

FIGURE 13–10 Data Junction Screen Shot

13.3.2 Transformation

The people who defined an organization's operational databases over the years had many priorities. Compatibility with the requirements of a future data warehouse, the very concept of which would have sounded like science fiction not too long ago, was probably not one of them.

Therefore, those who would develop a data warehouse based on these databases today are typically faced with inconsistencies among their data sources. As you read in Chapter 3, inconsistency is an indicator of poor data quality. In the case of multiple input sources to a data warehouse, inconsistency can sometimes make data unusable. **Transformation** is the process of dealing with these inconsistencies.

One type of inconsistency is a naming inconsistency. It is common for a given data element to be referred to by different data names in different databases. Employee name may be *EMP_NAM* in one database, *name* in another, and something else in a third. A field called *emp_id* in one place may be *SSN* somewhere else. The address component that most people in the United States refer to as a *ZIP code* (also often written *Zip code* or *zip code,* which are sufficiently different to confuse some software) is universally a *postal code* throughout the rest of the world.

What's more, the same data name may refer to different data elements in different databases. The data name *name*—a bad choice in most applications, since so many business entities have names—might refer to an employee name in one database, a customer name in another and perhaps the name of a boat somewhere else. While you might argue that nobody would call a data element simply *name,* because these problems are so obvious, what of *product_source?* Does that refer to the manufacturer of a product, the distributor from which it was purchased, or to the warehouse from which it was shipped to our customers? The real world is, unfortunately, full of poorly chosen data names that can't be changed now. One set of data names must be picked for the data warehouse and used consistently in it.

Once all data elements have the right names, they must be converted to common formats. The conversion process may encompass the following:

- Character sets must be converted ASCII to EBCDIC or vice versa. (Although this may affect the sorting sequence of data elements, that is usually handled in loading rather than now.)
- Mixed-case text may have to be converted to all uppercase for consistency. (This may seem to be a step backwards, but it is much more difficult to automate correct conversion in the other direction. Programming a computer to capitalize the fourth letter of MacDougall, but not of Machiavelli, is not worth the effort in most data warehousing situations.)
- Numerical data, in formats from fixed decimal to floating-point binary, may have to be converted to a consistent data type. Once so converted, the binary representation of (for example) 64-bit floating-point data varies from computer to computer, as does the order of bytes in a multibyte decimal number (high-order or low-order byte first in memory). Fortunately, algorithms for these conversions are well known.
- Other types of reformatting may be required. For example, there are several common ways to write dates using the standard human numbering for year, month and day—DD/MM/YY, MM/DD/YY, YYYYMMDD, to give just three—plus those formats used by different computer systems or DBMS internally (such as a positive integer representing seconds past midnight on January 1, 1904). Since time is a key dimension in many data warehouse applications, these must be converted to a common representation.
- Measurements may have to be converted: English measurements to metric or vice versa, times of international financial transactions to a common time zone from each office's local time, currency to a common unit such as Euros or U.S. dollars.
- Coded data must be converted to a common form. The categories *male* and *female,* for example, may be represented that way in one database, as *M* and *F* in another, *0* and *1* in a third, and *1* and *0* (in the other order) in a fourth.

All of these transformations can be automated. Most data extraction packages can handle the simpler cases just by being told to do so, and provide "hooks" via which user-written routines can be accessed to deal with the more complex ones. When such a package is used, the transformation takes place as part of the extraction process. Still, the two activities are conceptually different.

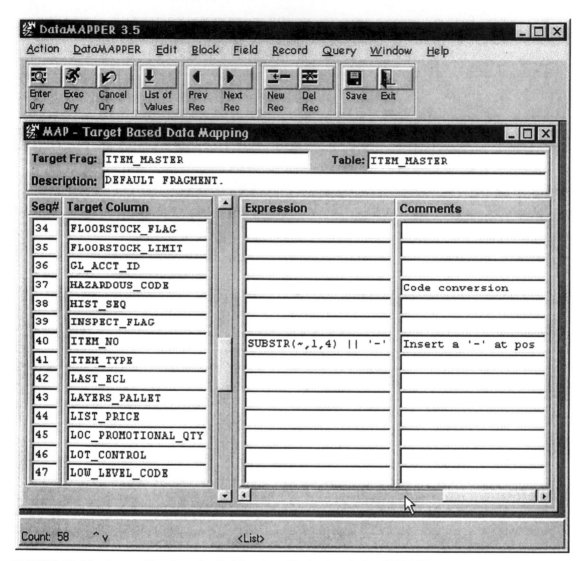

FIGURE 13–11 Screen Shot from Applied Database Technology's DataMAPPER
Source: Copyright Applied Database Technology. Used with permission.

Figure 13–11 shows how one data movement tool, DataMAPPER from Applied Database Technologies, sets up conversions. This figure shows how the data element ITEM_NO is reformatted by inserting a hyphen after the first four characters of the source. It also contains, in the Comments column, an indication that code conversion is required for the data element HAZARDOUS_CODE. (The specifics of that conversion are defined on a different DataMAPPER screen.) Coding these transformations requires computing skills somewhere between those of a spreadsheet user and those of a professional application developer. Learning them is well within the ability of a business analyst or a motivated "power user."

Other transformations create new logical views of the data. These may involve

- Separating parts of a field into two or more fields. A shoe size of 9C (in the U.S. system) may occupy a single field in the operational database, since each shoe size is a distinct inventory item with its own stock-keeping number. The best representation in a data warehouse could be in two fields, one each for length (9) and width (C). This would enable planners to analyze shoe width trends across all lengths or vice versa.
- Combining two or more fields of a record into one. Information that is one logical unit may have been split over multiple fields in a database for technical or historical reasons. This is especially common when a database is in use for a long time and there are significant changes in the business during this period.
- Combining fields from multiple records into one record. This may be done when the information an organization has about a single entity is spread over more than one database. For example, a hospital may have some information about patients in a medical database and other information, about these same patients, in an accounting database.

Sometimes data from two or more sources may conflict. In this case it is necessary to establish **data primacy:** which source should be considered the "database of record" with respect to which fields. This is often a matter of common sense. In an insurance application, a customer address is more likely to be current in a billing database (from which bills are issued every month) than in a policy database (which recorded the address when the policy was first issued and may not have been updated since). This could be considered an aspect of data cleansing, the subject of the next section, but is discussed here since it is performed when the records are combined.

13.3.3 Cleansing

As you know from Chapter 3, information quality is a key consideration in determining the value of that information. Information of high quality leads to high-quality decisions. Information of low quality leads to the opposite. Since organizations that go to the trouble and cost of developing a data warehouse are interested in improving their decisions, it follows that they should also be concerned with the quality of their warehouses' content. This is of particular relevance when the data warehouse is to be analyzed by automated data mining methods (see the next chapter) but applies to user-guided analyses as well.

The world is full of well-documented instances of data warehouses leading to poor (in retrospect, often absurd) conclusions. As Chase Manhattan Bank vice president Mike Eichorst says [STED97]: "The norm is that you find things that are bizarre, and 99.9 percent of the time they're also untrue." The reason is often poor information quality in the data warehouse database. The same source gives two examples of poor information quality leading to erroneous conclusions:

- Because data had been posted incorrectly, Chase got a faulty reading on the average balances of some credit card customers.
- Because a file was sorted incorrectly, Epsilon, a contract marketing firm in Burlington, Massachusetts, found that the best predictor of interest in a client's upcoming marketing campaign was customer ID number.

In another situation, many babies at Brigham and Women's Hospital in Boston were classified as female when their sex was simply not known to the person entering the data. This was because the hospital, originally founded solely for women and still serving primarily female patients when it first computerized its medical records, had set the default value for sex in the patient record to "F." This led to some head-scratching on the part of medical insurers' claims processing staff, who were asked to approve charges for some of these infants' circumcisions.

Finally, an insurance claim processing office in Wisconsin was found to have an unusually high ratio of broken legs to all claims. It was found that the claims adjusters in that office, to save time, were leaving nearly all Condition fields in claim forms at their default value of "broken leg." They had learned that the company will pay a broken leg claim as readily as any other type, so they chose to increase their claim processing productivity by not bothering to enter what the claim was for. Needless to say, this made analyses of injury type trends worthless.

It is a fact of life that large corporate databases have errors. Thomas Redman, who has studied this subject extensively, states that reported error rates range from 0.5 percent to 30 percent [REDM98]. He continues:

- Unless an enterprise has made extraordinary efforts, it should expect data (field) error rates of approximately 1–5 percent. (He defined the error rate as the number of erred fields divided by the number of total fields.)
- "That which doesn't get measured, doesn't get managed," so the enterprise should expect that it has other serious data quality problems as well. Specifically, employees are bedeviled by redundant and inconsistent databases and they do not have the data they really need.

The developer of a data warehouse is not usually in a position to change the quality of its underlying historic data, though a data warehousing project can put the spotlight on data quality issues and lead to improvements for the future. It is, therefore, usually necessary to go through the data entered into a data warehouse and make it as error-free as possible. (Note that the last sentence does *not* read ". . . and make it error free.") This process is known as data **cleansing** (sometimes data **cleaning**).

Data cleansing must deal with many types of possible errors. (Larry Greenfield [GREE97] lists 26 types and confesses that his list is not complete.) These include missing data and incorrect data in one source; inconsistent data and conflicting data when two or more sources are involved. All must be dealt with.

Many types of data cleansing can be automated. Direct mail firms have done this for decades. It is important to their business, since duplicate mailings to the same person (perhaps with minor variations in spelling) cost money and do not increase sales. (They may even decrease sales, as some people get upset at multiple copies of "junk mail.") Also, people like to see their names and addresses spelled correctly, so errors in these can reduce the effectiveness of a sales letter. Figure 13–12 shows a screen from SmartScrub, a component of the Data Quality Workbench package from Dataflux Corporation (Research Triangle Park, North Carolina). You can see a number of rules entered into the boxes to ensure a certain level of data quality. As

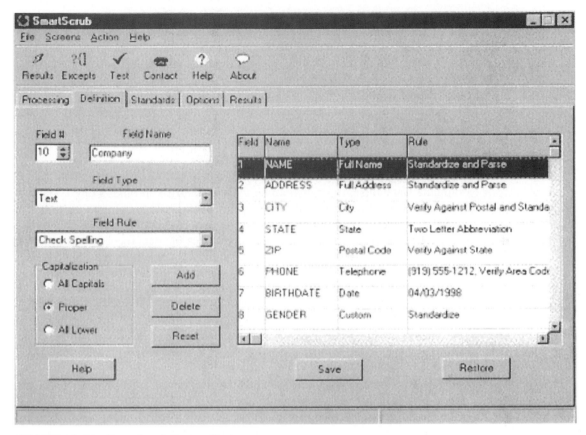

FIGURE 13–12 SmartScrub Screen Shot

one example, the city name, postal code, and telephone area code are cross-checked for consistency.

Data cleansing software can often suggest areas to check for poor data quality even if it can't figure out how to fix them. It does this by finding high correlations among two or more data elements and suggesting that the exceptions may be errors. For instance, if 99+ percent of the addresses having ZIP code 95014 have state code CA, it may suggest that the few with state code VA are wrong. (*V* is next to *C* on a standard keyboard, and *VA* is also a state code so it would pass a simple validity check.)

Other types of data quality checks cannot be automated. A computer can't know if I earn $5,000, $50,000, or $500,000 per year, though an expert system with information on my job and lifestyle might be able to figure out that the middle figure is closest. In these cases a manual procedure is required:

• Take a sample of the data and analyze it manually for quality. Standard statistical quality control techniques can help determine an appropriate sample size and appropriate quality levels to use as evaluation criteria. A small sample must be of higher quality than the target in order to provide high confidence that the database overall meets the target level, because a small sample may have gotten high-quality records by chance. A larger sample, while it will take longer to analyze, can provide this confidence at a lower quality level that is closer to the target level.

- If any fields or data sources show significant quality problems, assess whether or not they will impact the decisions with which the data warehouse is to help. Some types of errors, annoying though they may be in other contexts, will have no impact in this sense. They can be left alone.
- If it is felt that the quality problems will impact decisions made with the aid of the data warehouse, try to determine the source of the problem, any systematic error types, and how to correct them. It may be possible to correct them by using a different, more reliable data source. An expert system may also be able to help with some cleansing, if only by rejecting implausible data records so they do not interfere with the analyses. If all else fails and it is essential that the data be of the highest quality, manual review may be needed. Hopefully this will only apply to a minuscule fraction of the database.

To conclude this subject, Larry Greenfield [GREE97] offers these thoughts:

- Be prepared for a lot of tedious work. Probably the most important "tools" for solving these problems are a sharp eye and endurance for checking an abundance of detail information.
- You may spend much more time checking for errors than cleaning up errors. Most of these errors do not jump out at you.
- The errors of inconsistency are the most difficult to handle. (At least that is my experience.)
- The complexity of a data warehouse increases geometrically with the number of sources of data fed into it. Having to reconcile inconsistent systems is the reason. For example, if it takes 100 hours to reconcile data from two source systems, you can expect that it will take on the order of 400, not 200, hours to reconcile data from four source systems.

13.3.4 Loading

Once these steps have been successfully performed, it is finally possible to load the new data into the data warehouse database. This may be a complete load, as when the data warehouse is first created or if it must be restored after a crash. More often, it is a partial load that adds recent data to the database.

Loading often implies physical movement of the data from the computer(s) storing the source database(s) to that which will store the data warehouse database, assuming it is different. However, this movement will often have taken place earlier since data are often moved to the target computer as part of, or immediately after, the extraction step.

The most common channel for the data movement process is a high-speed communication link. High-speed links using local area technology are inexpensive if the two systems are located near each other. Organizations large enough to have them geographically separated are also usually large enough to have high-speed wide area links in place. Most systems housing operational databases are set up as servers or can be with little effort. It is then a relatively simple matter for the system housing the data warehouse database, or another system that is controlling the load operation, to act as a client and request the necessary data.

For the initial loading or when suitable communication links are not available, magnetic tape is an alternative. (The high-capacity removable storage devices such as Zip drives that are common in the microcomputer realm, typically storing 100 MB to 1 GB, are not widely used on large systems. In addition, they are far from "high capacity" in the enterprise-level context of a corporate data warehouse. It would be as impractical to load a large data warehouse via Zip drives or similar media as it is to do a complete backup of a 6-GB desktop computer disk drive onto diskettes.) Thus, at the end of the cleansing step, we have data ready to put into the data warehouse database itself. Every DBMS normally used to support a data warehouse has an import function that can carry out this process. Most extraction, transformation, and cleansing packages can convert data to the native formats of the more popular DBMS directly.

It may be necessary or desirable to close off access to the data warehouse when the loading is taking place. This is not usually a burden, as the time taken by an incremental update is small and it can take place during periods of little or no data warehouse usage. Full data warehouse database loads are sufficiently rare that users can be warned about them ahead of time and work around them if necessary. It may be possible to keep small data marts based on the old database operational while the loading is taking place, switching to the new database when it is ready. Keeping the entire old data warehouse database available during the reload may not be possible, since few organizations have enough spare mass storage space for two copies of a large data warehouse database plus the workspace needed for the loading process.

13.3.5 Summarization

On page 493 we noted that summary data is one of the levels of data in a data warehouse. Once the data warehouse database has been loaded it is possible to create these summaries. Summaries must usually be re-created after every incremental update, as any changes in the underlying data may impact them. It is usually more time consuming to go through the new data and figure out which summaries are not impacted than it is to create all of them. The exception is historical time-period summaries for periods entirely in the past, the data of which do not change.

The database designer must answer an important question before any summaries can be calculated: Which summaries should the database store? Like many other information systems decisions, this choice involves trade-offs. In this case they are as follows:

In Favor of Storing Many Summaries
- Queries that use the prestored summaries can be answered quickly.

In Favor of Storing Few or No Summaries

- Calculating summaries requires computer time and resources.
- The summaries occupy space on a mass storage device.
- Someone has to figure out which summaries to prestore.
- Someone (perhaps the same person) must define the summaries to the data warehouse software.

Since there are four drawbacks but only one advantage in the above lists, one might think that data warehouses should never calculate summaries. This is not the case, however. Let's consider the drawbacks in more detail to see how important they are.

Calculation time. Summaries can generally be calculated at times when the computer would otherwise be idle or nearly so. There is no incremental cost involved in using available CPU cycles for this purpose.

Storage space. Summaries are normally a small fraction the size of the data warehouse overall. The incremental cost of storing them is therefore a small fraction of the total data warehouse storage cost.

However, the more dimensions the data warehouse has, the greater the storage impact of summaries in a multidimensional structure. Consider the pet store database on page 495. We could augment it by adding summary totals by pet type and sales representative, as shown next.

	Cats	Dogs	Fish	Gerbils	Total
Adams	3	12	5	4	24
Baker	2	4	22	5	33
Carstens	6	2	3	16	27
Total	11	18	30	25	84

Here we have added eight cells (seven for one-way totals, one for the grand total) to the original 12 data cells, or about 67 percent additional space. But suppose we had a third dimension to the database, pet color (brown, black, other). We would then have 36 raw data cells but a total of 45 summary cells: 33 one-dimensional totals, 11 two-dimensional totals, and a grand total. This is 125 percent of the original database. Since a real data warehouse would have more records per dimension, the percentage of space occupied by summaries would be smaller, but the trend would be the same. You can see how, with the multidimensional structure, summaries can quickly escalate the total size by one or more orders of magnitude beyond what the raw data would occupy.

Furthermore, sparse raw data makes the impact of summaries even larger because summaries tend to be less sparse than atomic data. Suppose Adams sold no gerbils, Baker sold no cats, and Carstens sold no dogs or fish in a given week. In the two-dimensional database we would then have eight nonzero data cells (versus the original 12), but we'd still need eight summary cells. The three-dimensional database is even more likely to have sparse atomic data. Perhaps Baker does sell a

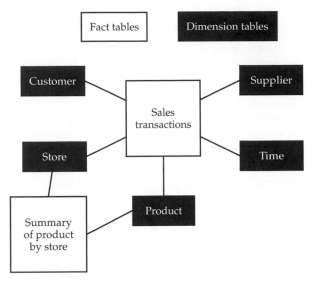

FIGURE 13–13 **Star Schema with Summary**

cat or two in most weeks, but chances are he doesn't sell at least one of each possible color. Therefore, while "Baker/Cats" is usually nonzero, at least one of "Baker/Cats/Black," "Baker/Cats/Brown," and "Baker/Cats/Other" would usually be empty. So, at the same time that having more dimensions increases the number of summary cells, it also increases the fraction of zero cells in the raw database. The percentage size impact of summaries therefore increases even more quickly than the pet store example would suggest.

Planning and defining the summaries. These are one-time costs. ("Defining" in this context refers to defining the summary to the computer program that will create it, not writing down what it is. That's planning.) These costs must be weighed against users' time saved every time a query that uses a prestored summary is invoked. If a summary will be used many times, the total user time saved will outweigh the analyst's time used in defining it. If it will be used infrequently, it's probably not worth the effort.

In a relational database, summaries are stored in separate tables with which the appropriate dimension tables can be matched. Suppose we wanted to add totals of products sold by store (for all suppliers, times, and customers) to the star schema of Figure 13–4. We would get the structure of Figure 13–13.

To take a more concrete example: Suppose we have the pet store relational data warehouse organized in a star schema, with its central fact table as shown in Figure 13–5. One summary we might reasonably want is pets sold by week by all salespeople. This summary table would look, in part, like Figure 13–14. (Be sure you see where all the numbers in its rightmost column come from.) Rows of this table could be associated with corresponding rows of the fact table or of either

Week	Pet Type	No. Sold
April 20, 1998	Cats	11
April 20, 1998	Dogs	18
April 13, 1998	Cats	14
April 13, 1998	Dogs	18

FIGURE 13–14   **Summary Table of Pets Sold by Week**

dimension table (pet type or time) by matching entries in their respective Pet Type and Week columns. This allows us to perform joins or to navigate the database in either direction. By going to the fact table, we can **drill down** into the data: to find out, in this case, how sales for a given week break down by salesperson. By going to the dimension tables, we can get further information about either of the dimensions represented in this summary.

An important type of summarization is **aggregation.** An *aggregate* is a set of elements along some dimension of the database. Stores may be aggregated into regions; days aggregated into weeks, months, and quarters; products into categories. Figure 13–15 shows a screen used in defining an aggregation—in this case locations, where cities are aggregated up to states, regions, and a total for all cities—using Syntagma Designer, a product of Relational Matters of Guilford, England.

13.4 METADATA

The Greek prefix *meta-* means, among other things, "along with" or "beyond." Applied to the subject of this chapter—data—we might think metadata would refer to something that goes along with data or is beyond data. We would be correct. In the data warehousing context, **metadata** means "data about data." Metadata are *data that describe the data in a data warehouse.* Metadata are required if people are to be able to access the data in a data warehouse. Without quality metadata, useful data analyses (such as those you'll read about in the next chapter) just can't be done.

Metadata can exist in any of three forms: human metadata, computer-based metadata for people to use, and computer-based metadata for the computer to use.

13.4.1 Human Metadata

People always have some sort of metadata in their heads or in their files. A person seeing the field name MANUFACTURER in a database of appliance store sales would probably reach the obvious conclusion. If this field has values such as GE, Panasonic, and Sharp in the first few records of the database, the assumption would be taken as fact. A business analyst might proceed to tabulate sales by manufacturer on this basis. The metadata, in this case, is the analyst's knowledge of what a "manufacturer" is in the appliance store context, and his or her familiarity with the names of some large appliance manufacturers through personal experience on the job or as a consumer.

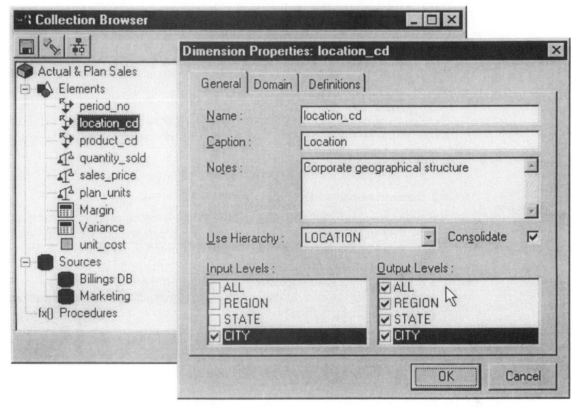

FIGURE 13–15 Defining an Aggregation
Source: Copyright Relational Matters. Used with permission.

Depending on human metadata, however, can cause several problems:

1. The "natural" assumption isn't always this obvious. It may sometimes be wrong. Suppose the field name, instead of MANUFACTURER, had been SUPPLIER. Does this refer to the manufacturer of the unit, or to the distributor from whom the store received it? In the absence of other information (such as another field named MANUFACTURER in the same record, which eliminates one of the two options) it's hard to tell. The user may not make the same assumptions as the person who set up the database. What is worse, two users may make different assumptions—and may not even realize that a different interpretation from theirs is plausible.

2. The same item, even if we can figure out what it is supposed to represent in the real world, can represent that business entity in different ways. Does SIZE in a shoe sales database reflect only length (9, $9\frac{1}{2}$, 10, etc., in the U.S. shoe sizing system) or width as well (with 9A, 9B, 9C, etc., considered different sizes)? Do we record the type of credit card a person used for payment (Visa, American Express, etc.) or derive it, if necessary, from the first few digits of its number?

3. There is no way to tell reliably that two data items, having different names in different files, refer to the same business entity. Is PAY_RATE in one file the same thing as SALARY in another, or are they different?

4. There is no systematic way to record information about how a data element is stored. Are family names truncated after 15 characters? Can they be stored with special characters (the period and space in "St. James," the apostrophe in "O'Neill," the hyphen in "Rimsky-Korsakov") or as letters only?

5. There is no way to specify validation rules to be applied to data when entered (a U.S. postal or ZIP code must consist either of five digits or of five digits followed by a hyphen and four digits), access or security controls, or other information about the data.

13.4.2 Computer-based Metadata for People to Use

To deal with these and similar issues, data warehouse developers often store this descriptive data in its own database. This provides a comprehensive guide to the data resource: a consistent way of recording the information, available to all those who might need it, and where important information will not be left out (or, if it is, at least that its absence will be noticed). According to [BRAC96], such a **metadata warehouse** can contain (assuming that a common data architecture for the data warehouse has been defined):

- A lexicon of common words used in formal data names and prominent data name abbreviation schemes.
- The data description, data structure, and data integrity rules of the common data architecture.
- Definitions of classification schemes for data in the common data architecture.
- A thesaurus for identifying data that exist in the common data architecture.
- A glossary of business words, terms, and abbreviations that support use of the data resource.
- An inventory of data maintained by various organizations, with cross-references between them and the common data architecture.
- A directory of organizations maintaining data, with contacts in those organizations for obtaining additional information about existing data.
- Data translation schemes between data variations to support data sharing within and between organizations.

Fortunately, most of this information is readily available as a data warehouse is developed. It is only necessary for the developers to have a place to store it as they encounter it, to recognize the need to do so, and to carry out the process.

Metadata for human use need not be in any particular format. Each of the above items lends itself to storage as a character string. These should be stored in a database with an easy-to-use search facility so that any desired item can be located quickly.

13.4.3 Computer-based Metadata for the Computer to Use

Some of the above metadata items have implications for the data warehouse database. If they are stored in a well-structured, computer-readable form, they can be

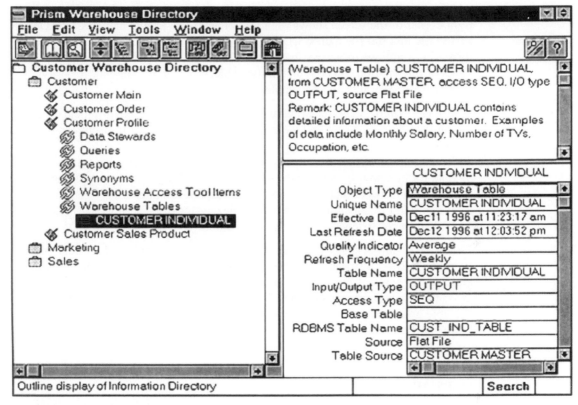

FIGURE 13–16 Metadata
Source: Copyright Prism Solutions. Used by permission.

read by a DBMS and can smooth the interface between a data warehouse and its users. With computer-readable metadata, for example, a user could search for the business term *volume,* obtain a list of data elements whose text description contains that word, determine by examining those descriptions that SALES_REVENUE is the desired element, and select it for analysis with a click of the mouse. In other areas, such as validation and security, computer-based metadata can go a long way to ensuring that the rules as described to the users are enforced by the information system as well.

A database containing computer-usable metadata is often referred to as a **data repository,** or just **repository** for short when the context makes it clear what type of repository is meant. The software that manages the data repository software is called, logically enough, **repository software.** In many situations, the software and its associated data are a single unit for all practical purposes. In that case the term *repository* may be used, informally, to refer to both together.

Figure 13–16 shows a repository screen, in this case from Warehouse Directory (Prism Solutions, Sunnyvale, California). The left side of the figure shows how the data table now being looked at, named CUSTOMER INDIVIDUAL in the data warehouse database, fits into the overall data warehouse database. The bottom-right corner of the screen shows where it comes from: a table named CUSTOMER MASTER in a flat file named CUST_IND_TABLE. The top-right corner gives information required to access the source data and tells users, in plain text, what kinds of information can be found in this table.

There are several benefits to implementing a repository:

1. It enables information sharing across multiple software environments, including database managers and the types of analysis tools we'll discuss in the next chapter.
2. It integrates the logical and physical aspects of the database. By contrast, metadata for human use focus on the logical aspects. They must be supplemented by data directories or dictionaries to define the physical database.
3. It facilitates the documentation of complex systems.
4. It ensures consistency across the organization.

The state of metadata products in 1999 is improving rapidly. Products such as Warehouse Directory can share metadata with other repository products and with the types of analysis products we'll discuss in the next chapter. This is a necessity in many organizations, where standardization on a single product is not always possible and may not even be a good idea. The metadata components of database products, however, are usually limited to storing the computer-related aspects of data and are not shareable across different DBMS.

SUMMARY

The data warehouse environment involves operational data (not actually part of the data warehouse, but important to it), atomic data, summarized data, and answers to specific queries. All are important in planning and designing a data warehouse.

An important part of data warehouse design is choosing an appropriate database structure for it. The structures used for transaction processing may not be well suited to data warehouses because the requirements of the two types of computing are quite different from each other. Data warehouses usually use either the relational structure (which can also be used for transaction processing and which is described in Chapter 6) or the multidimensional structure.

A relational database used in a data warehouse is usually organized in star schema form. Fact tables, in the center of the star schema, record information about individual activities such as business transactions. Dimension tables record information that applies to one or more, but not all, of the dimensions of the data warehouse database.

A multidimensional database stores data in the form of a hypercube, the extension of a cube to more than three dimensions. This structure has advantages over the relational structure because it maps more naturally into the way people think of most data warehouse data and becomes large more quickly than a relational database as the amount of data in a data warehouse increases. Whereas space-saving methods exist, they may negate some of the efficiency advantages that the basic multidimensional structure offers. For this reason, very large data warehouses tend to use the relational structure.

Data are brought into a data warehouse in a five-step process. The steps are

1. Extraction, in which the desired fields are selected and extracted from the operational database.
2. Transformation, in which data from all sources are given common formats and names.
3. Cleansing, in which erroneous data is (to the extent possible) corrected.
4. Loading, in which the cleansed data are loaded into the data warehouse database.
5. Summarization, in which any desired summaries of the data warehouse data are precalculated for later use.

The entire data warehouse database is described by metadata, which means "data about data." The simplest form of metadata is simply recorded by people on paper. Storing the metadata in a well-structured computer file or database makes it easier for people to find what they are looking for and increases the likelihood that database designers will pay attention to it. A third stage is to store the metadata, still in a computer file, in a way that database management software can use it to access the data warehouse database.

KEY TERMS

aggregation
atomic data
cleansing (or cleaning)
data primacy
data repository (or repository)
dimension data
dimensional database
drill down
extract
fact data
hypercube
loading
metadata, metadata warehouse
multidimensional database (MDDB)
repository software
sparse data
star schema
summary, summarization
transformation

REVIEW QUESTIONS

1. List the four levels of data in the data warehouse environment. Which two of them are in the data warehouse database?
2. Complete this sentence: The two fundamental types of data in a data warehouse database are _____ data and _____ data.
3. Why is the *star schema* called by that name?
4. State an advantage of the multidimensional database structure over the relational database structure for data warehousing applications.
5. What is one reason you might choose a relational structure over a multidimensional structure for a data warehouse database?
6. List the five steps that must be performed in taking data from an operational database source to a data warehouse database.
7. Give an example of a situation where data transformation would be necessary in preparing data to be loaded into a data warehouse database.
8. What is data cleansing? Why is it necessary?
9. What physical medium is usually used to transfer data into a data warehouse database?
10. Why should a data warehouse database store summary data?
11. Define *metadata* and give three reasons why it can be useful.

EXERCISES

1. Your college or university is designing a data warehouse to enable deans, department chairs, and the registrar's office to optimize course offerings, in terms of which courses are offered, in how many sections, and at what times. The data warehouse planners hope they will be able to do this better after examining historical demand for courses and extrapolating any trends that emerge.
   a. Give three dimension data elements and two fact data elements that could be in the database for this data warehouse. Draw a data cube, similar to that of the Chevrolet dealerships in Figure 13–9, for this database.
   b. Suggest an aggregation that could apply to one of the dimension data elements.
   c. State two ways in which each of the two fact data elements could be of low quality in some respect. (There are a total of four answer items to this question, two per data element.)
2. On page 500 we wrote, "trying to represent more dimensions this way quickly becomes an exercise in futility." Extend the pet store example of that section to include data from the most recent four months. Diagram the resulting relational record you would need and draw how the new data might be represented in a multidimensional database. Discuss, but do not diagram or draw, what would happen to each structure if you also wanted to record the color of the pet sold (black, brown, gray, or other.)
3. On page 507 one example of low data quality leading to data warehouse analysis problems read, "because data had been posted incorrectly, Chase got a faulty reading on the average balances of some credit card customers." Chase Manhattan Bank could have made (but, fortunately did not) wrong decisions if it had trusted the data warehouse output completely. For example, if it had been reviewing these customers for possible credit line increases, it could have increased the credit lines of customers who did not earn such an increase, thereby losing money when those customers used their new larger credit lines and then didn't pay their bills. Give three other poor decisions that this error could have led to.

4. You have decided to prepare a budget for the next 12 months based on your actual expenses for the past 12. You need to get your expense information into what is in effect a data warehouse, which you plan to put into a spreadsheet for easy sorting and analysis.
  a. What are your information sources for this data warehouse?
  b. Describe how you would carry out each of the five steps of data preparation for a data warehouse database, from extraction through summarization. If a particular step does not apply, say so and justify your statement.

5. Using the automated search tools of your choice, find out more about the Metadata Coalition. Write a report on this group, listing your sources. (Your instructor may give you length limits, format requirements, and other directions.) In addition to describing briefly what the Metadata Coalition is and giving some of its background, answer the following specific questions:
  a. What are its objectives?
  b. Do you think these objectives are important? Why or why not?
  c. What other relevant objectives, if any, do you think it should have that it does not have?
  d. Do you think it will be able to meet its objectives? Why or why not?

6. Connoisseurs of single-malt Scotch whiskies classify them by color, nose, body, palate, and finish. There are 8 to 19 possible values for each. For example, color is evaluated on a 14-point scale from "wyne" (lightest) to "sherry" (darkest). Researchers [LAPO94] have published a database of 109 such whiskies (http://alize.ere.umontreal.ca/~casgrain/en/R/scotch.html). Each whisky has been evaluated for all five parameters. In addition, the geographic coordinates of each distillery have been recorded, as well as a complete matrix of the distance from each distillery to the others. You can also find out the current selling price of whiskies of various ages from each distillery by calling beverage distributors.

   You suspect there may be patterns in this data that will enable you to identify underpriced whiskies—those that share important characteristics with expensive ones but cost much less. You further suspect that, if you can do this, you will be able to figure out a way to profit from your discovery. You would like to use a data warehouse to aid your search. Lay out the dimension and fact tables you would use in a relational database for this purpose. (You might not necessarily want to use all the data you have or can get.)

REFERENCES

Many of the books listed as general references at the end of Chapter 12 discuss data warehouse databases in detail. Those references are not repeated here. If a book cited in this chapter is not in the list that follows, you can find it there.

BOWE95 Bowen, Barry D. "Weighing and Making the Right Decisions." *Sybase* (Winter 1995).

GREE97 Greenfield, Larry. "An (Informal) Taxonomy of Data Warehouse Data Errors." (August 28, 1997). Available on-line: http://pwp.starnetinc.com/larryg/errors.html

LAPO94 Lapointe, F.-J., and P. Legendre. "A Classification of Pure Malt Scotch Whiskies." *Applied Statistics* 43 (1994), p. 237.

REDM98 Redman, Thomas C. "The Impact of Poor Data Quality on the Typical Enterprise." *Communications of the ACM* 41, no. 2 (February 1998), p. 79.

STED97 Stedman, Craig. "Data Mining for Fool's Gold." *Computerworld* (December 1, 1997), p. 1.

Fort Lowell Trading Company
Designing the Data Warehouse Database

Elizabeth and Miguel returned to Fort Lowell Trading Company the following Thursday to meet with Jim Atcitty. As he placed his ID card over the familiar reader to admit them to the MIS area, they noticed an unusual key chain hanging from it. Elizabeth, mustering all her courage, pointed to it and said, "That looks like a microchip. Where did you get it?"

Jim smiled softly as he showed her the key chain. "Yes, this side's a microchip," he verified. "An Intel 486, as it happens. This is getting old! This other side, here"—he turned the small block of Lucite over—"is a Navajo blanket woven in the pattern of its circuits. Intel commissioned a weaver to make it. Then they gave the blanket to AISES—that's the American Indian Science and Engineering Society—to hang in its headquarters in Colorado. They presented the blanket at the group's meeting in San Jose in—it was in '93 or '94, I think, and they showed a video of the weaver at work on it. Everyone who was there got one of these key rings. It has a special meaning to me because the weaver is a distant relative of mine on my mother's side."

As he reached the end of what was, for him, an unusually long speech, the three reached the MIS conference room. "I've got an office down here now," Jim explained, "even though I work for Niels. I've got so much to learn about the technology. Sitting with this group seemed like a good way to learn it."

"What kinds of things?" asked Miguel.

"You name it!" Jim laughed. "I mean, I'm OK with my PC, but we're talking about stuff that's so far beyond what a PC can do that it's a different world. Almost as different as what I found when I left the reservation for college. I mean, like I used to think a 50-meg file was big—real big. Down here they don't even try to estimate file sizes that close! If it's not multiple gigabytes, it doesn't show up in their space utilization reports. It just goes under 'other.' It looks like I'll have to start thinking like that in the data warehouse business."

"Yes, that's what it seems like from what we've read," Miguel agreed as the three sat down at one end of the conference table. "Have you started to look at what would go into those gigabytes yet?"

"A little bit," answered Jim. "Like I said the first time we met, I want to look at trends in what kinds of customer we have, what they're buying, and where and how they're buying it. So I came up with a picture that looks sort of like this."

With that Jim took a pad of paper that was on the conference table and sketched Figure 13–17. "This is about what the data warehouse I'd need might look like," he said. "Like Niels said, other people might go for something else, but we have to start somewhere. Does it make sense to you?"

"From what we know, which isn't much, it does," said Elizabeth after examining Jim's sketch. "You've got three dimensions along the sides and something in the middle. What do you think that something is?"

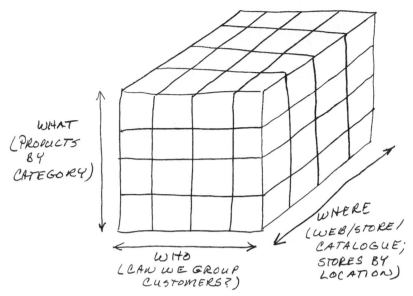

FIGURE 13–17 Jim's Data Warehouse Concept Sketch

"I'm not entirely sure about that," Jim said. "It could be a transaction number, so we could see what products were bought at the same time. We have transaction numbers for everything and they're all unique. But I'd also like to save information about how they paid, whether they used discount coupons, whether it was on sale, and stuff like that. Can this do that?"

EXERCISES

1. An important dimension is missing from Jim's sketch (Figure 13–17). What is it? (As it happens, the three participants in this episode thought of it too, about two minutes after we left them.)
2. Consider Jim's final question. "Can this do that?" To be specific, can a data warehouse database store the type of information Jim is talking about?
3. Jim said, toward the end of the episode, that Fort Lowell Trading Company transaction numbers are unique. He presumably based his statement on the two facts that (a) transaction numbers are supposed to be unique, and (b) the numbers are generated automatically by computers.
   a. What could make transaction numbers nonunique? (While it is tempting to say "nothing," experienced professionals working with real organizational data report that this idealistic view of the world is overly optimistic.)
   b. If a small fraction of the transaction numbers were duplicates, how might using them as is in a data warehouse harm FLTC? In other words, what would be the business implications of this specific instance of poor data quality?
   c. What automated checks could conceptually be performed (don't worry about whether a specific software package can perform them) to deal with this possibility?

Analyzing the Contents of the Data Warehouse

Introduction

A data warehouse is useless unless its content can be brought to bear on business issues. It may stand in splendor, a testimony to the data-gathering capabilities of an organization's MIS staff; it may occupy gigabytes or terabytes of disk space; but it is just a monument to technology unless it can be brought to users to answer their questions. There are two approaches to getting useful business insight out of a data warehouse.

One approach is user-guided analysis. The user says, "Show me how X varies with Y," and the computer does so. Having seen that answer, the user asks another question, and so on, until the desired level of insight is achieved (or time runs out, or it becomes clear that the available data won't provide it).

A second approach is data mining. Here, the user in effect points the computer at a database and asks, "What's in there?" There's more to it than that—one must usually tell the data mining programs what inputs to consider and what kinds of patterns to search for—but that's the general idea.

These approaches are complementary. Each has its place. When you finish this chapter, you'll have a good feel for what each can do.

CHAPTER OBJECTIVES

After you have read and studied this chapter, you will be able to:

1. Compare and contrast the two basic ways to analyze data warehouse data.
2. Describe how a user-guide (OLAP) analysis might proceed.
3. Explain the three ways data warehouse databases store OLAP data.
4. Follow several guidelines for selecting an approach to OLAP.
5. State the ways in which OLAP products resemble each other—and in which they differ.
6. Explain what data mining is and what all approaches to it have in common.
7. Describe how the CART, statistical analysis, neural network and nearest neighbor approaches to data mining work.
8. Use the concept of "lift" in determining the business benefits of a data mining analysis.

14.1 ACTIVE ANALYSIS: USER QUERIES

Many decisions can be made well on the basis of a series of questions (**queries**) and answers. Consider the following scenario from the planning department of an appliance manufacturer. A planner, working in mid-November, wants to determine the mix of vacuum cleaners to produce for next year.

1. The planner realizes that the first decision is the total the firm will make in each of its major product categories: upright and canister cleaners. She asks for a trend line of sales of these two types over the past three years. Her computer responds with Figure 14–1.

   The figures for the past two years and for this year through October are historical data. They are summarized from tens of thousands of individual transactions. They are stored individually in the data warehouse because they can be analyzed in several other ways as well. The November and December figures that went into this year's total include firm retail orders and forecasted sales, with a higher fraction of firm orders for November than for December. (In order to focus on the content without distraction, this sequence of figures was created with a spreadsheet program. You'll see many screen shots of commercial OLAP products later in this section.)

2. She extrapolates the curves approximately, keeping in mind that the approximate nature of any planning process does not justify several significant digits of accuracy. She decides that 1.5 million canister cleaners and 0.8 million upright cleaners are a good starting point for the plan.

3. The second basic product decision is the fraction of canister cleaners that will be equipped with power brushes for better rug and carpet cleaning. (All but the two least expensive canister models have power brushes.) She asks for a breakdown of canister sales with and without power brushes. The computer displays Figure 14–2.

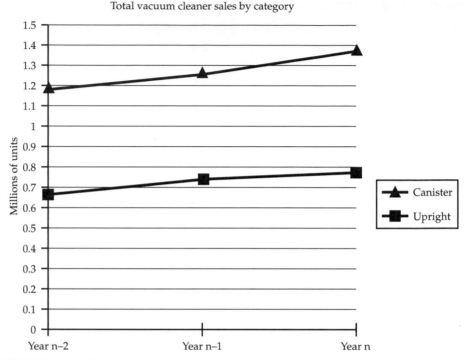

FIGURE 14–1   Sales Trends of Upright and Canister Cleaners

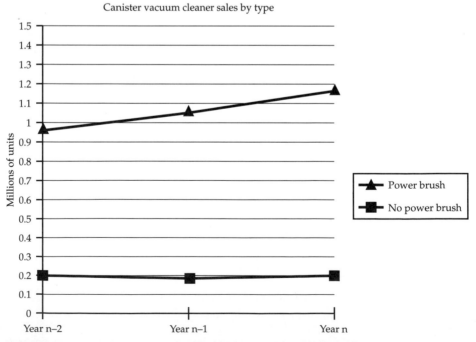

FIGURE 14–2   Sales Trends of Canister Cleaners with and without Power Brushes

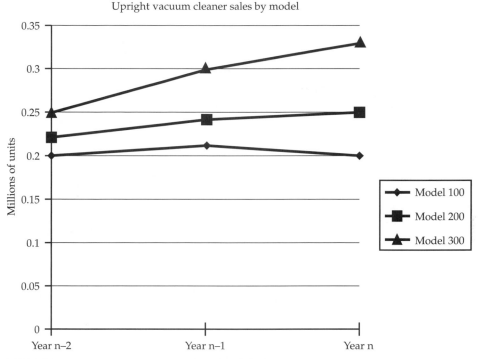

FIGURE 14-3 **Sales Trends of Upright Cleaners by Model**

4. She realizes that the number of customers buying canister cleaners without power brushes is holding steady while those with power brushes are becoming more and more popular—perhaps, she thinks, explaining in part the flattening in upright cleaner sales. (The primary strength of an upright vacuum cleaner is its carpet-cleaning capability, which is the big advantage of adding a power brush to a canister cleaner.) She decides to hold next year's production of canisters without power brushes at this year's sales level, 200,000 units, with the balance of 1.3 million having power brushes.

5. She now switches to uprights to plan the breakdown by model. The firm's three models of upright cleaners haven't changed much in the past three years, so a trend analysis should be meaningful. It is shown in Figure 14–3.

6. There is a slight trend toward more expensive models, which she could put into her plan for next year. That would create a breakdown of 200,000, 250,000, and 350,000 from bottom to top.

   However, the planner knows the product line will change. The most powerful motor, unique to the top model in the past, will be put into the middle model as well, in response to competitive moves. The top model will remain the only self-propelled cleaner (a slight push or pull on the top of the handle engages the wheel drive). But, some customers who chose that model only for its motor, and who don't care about self-propulsion or would like to save

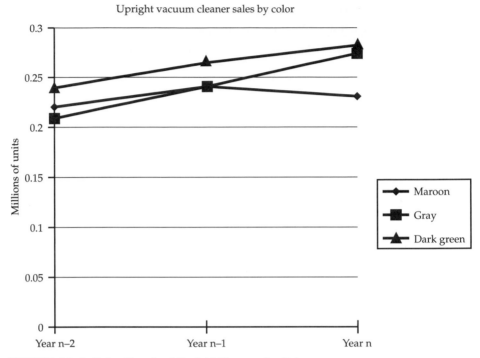

FIGURE 14-4   **Sales Trends of Upright Cleaners by Color**

money, will now buy the middle one. In the absence of relevant historical data, she decides to move 10 percent of the top model forecast to the middle one. Her final figures are therefore 200,000, 285,000, and 315,000.

7. Since she is working with the upright cleaners, she decides to select their color breakdown next. She obtains sales data for upright cleaners in the three available colors, maroon, gray, and dark green, as shown in Figure 14–4.

8. On an educated hunch, she now asks the computer to show color preferences by model for the last year. This is where the capability of OLAP tools to group and correlate data really shines. This table format is called a **pivot table.** The pivot table of Figure 14–5 was created automatically by the Excel spreadsheet program from the raw data in Figure 14–6. It's easier with most full-fledged data warehouse analysis programs, and Excel couldn't handle a database with several hundred thousand rows, but the concept is the same.

9. Instead of being split approximately evenly across the three models, she sees what seems to be a relationship between color trends and models. The values in each 3 × 3 section of the pivot table are largest, for all three years, along the di-agonals from the bottom left to the top right. Buyers of the top model strongly prefer green to either of the other two colors. The middle model sells best in gray, and the bottom of the line in maroon. To help her see if this is a fluke or a

Year	Model	Dark Green	Gray	Maroon	Grand Total
Year n	Model 100	0.05	0.06	0.09	0.2
	Model 200	0.07	0.012	0.06	0.25
	Model 300	0.16	0.09	0.08	0.33
Year n total		0.28	0.27	0.23	0.78
Year n-1	Model 100	0.05	0.06	0.1	0.21
	Model 200	0.07	0.1	0.07	0.24
	Model 300	0.15	0.08	0.07	0.3
Year n-1 total		0.27	0.24	0.24	0.75
Year n-2	Model 100	0.05	0.05	0.1	0.2
	Model 200	0.06	0.1	0.06	0.22
	Model 300	0.13	0.06	0.06	0.25
Year n-2 total		0.24	0.21	0.22	0.67
Grand total		0.79	0.72	0.69	2.2

FIGURE 14–5   Sales Trend Pivot Table of Upright Cleaners by Model and Color

Year	Model	Color	Sales
Year n-2	Model 100	maroon	0.10
Year n-2	Model 100	gray	0.05
Year n-2	Model 100	dark green	0.05
Year n-2	Model 200	maroon	0.06
Year n-2	Model 200	gray	0.10
Year n-2	Model 200	dark green	0.06
Year n-2	Model 300	maroon	0.06
Year n-2	Model 300	gray	0.06
Year n-2	Model 300	dark green	0.13
Year n-1	Model 100	maroon	0.10
Year n-1	Model 100	gray	0.06
Year n-1	Model 100	dark green	0.05
Year n-1	Model 200	maroon	0.07
Year n-1	Model 200	gray	0.10
Year n-1	Model 200	dark green	0.07
Year n-1	Model 300	maroon	0.07
Year n-1	Model 300	gray	0.08
Year n-1	Model 300	dark green	0.15
Year n	Model 100	maroon	0.09
Year n	Model 100	gray	0.06
Year n	Model 100	dark green	0.05
Year n	Model 200	maroon	0.06
Year n	Model 200	gray	0.12
Year n	Model 200	dark green	0.07
Year n	Model 300	maroon	0.08
Year n	Model 300	gray	0.09
Year n	Model 300	dark green	0.16

FIGURE 14–6   Raw Data for Figure 14–5

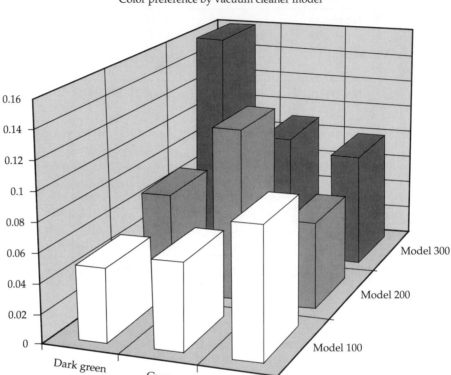

Color preference by vacuum cleaner model

FIGURE 14–7 **Sales Graph of Upright Cleaners by Model and Color**

real pattern, she asks for a graph of the data in the pivot table. Figure 14–7 shows this graph for Year *n*. Similar graphs for the other two years, as well as comparable graphs for canister vacuums, confirm this aspect of customer preferences for color by price range. Although the charts don't look exactly the same—for one thing, there are five models of canister cleaners versus only three of uprights—the pattern is similar. More expensive models sell better in green, less expensive cleaners in maroon. Gray is preferred in the middle. She therefore decides to plan production of upright vacuum cleaners as follows:

Model	Dark Green	Gray	Maroon	Total
Model 100	50,000	50,000	100,000	200,000
Model 200	75,000	140,000	70,000	285,000
Model 300	155,000	85,000	75,000	315,000
Total	280,000	275,000	245,000	800,000

10. She continues the process for the five models of canister cleaners: three with power brushes, two without. The resulting plan, she feels, will be close to actual retailer demand for the year. While the plan will still be fine-tuned as the year progresses, a plan that is close to eventual orders can save a great deal of money. A planning process that can create such plans enables a firm to economize via volume purchasing and longer, more efficient production runs.

Later, distribution planners will use the same data warehouse to analyze shipments from each regional distribution center. This will enable the firm to match the inventory of each center to user demand in its region. If planners conclude that people from the western part of the country like maroon vacuum cleaners more than customers in other regions based on orders coming into the western warehouse from the retailers it supplies, it will receive more than a proportional share of maroon vacuum cleaners. This, in turn, will reduce the frequency of stock-outs and back orders, thus reducing costs and increasing customer satisfaction.

This is an example of using a data warehouse for user-guided analysis. The data warehouse analysis software "slices and dices" the content of the data warehouse database to answer specific questions. The user chooses each question after examining the results of its predecessors, generally going into deeper and deeper detail (**drilling down**) until the necessary decisions have been made. This mode of operation is often referred to as **on-line analytical processing (OLAP).** One definition of OLAP, from [OLAP95], is

> A category of software technology that enables analysts, managers, and executives to gain insight into data through fast, consistent, interactive access to a wide variety of possible views of information that has been transformed from raw data to reflect the real dimensionality of the enterprise as understood by the user.

OLAP is the approach of choice when the user has a concept of what he or she is looking for. The concept may be quite specific, as in the above example: "Show me total sales of canister and upright vacuum cleaners for the past three years." Or, it may be more general where a user does not know where an investigation may lead: "Cross-tabulate product color by region." The next question in either case is still unknown at this point. It will depend on the patterns that emerge from the opening query, if any. If no patterns emerge the user may rephrase the query, proceed with a different line of inquiry, or decide that it's time for lunch.

14.1.1 OLAP Example

Figure 14–8 shows a typical OLAP screen, this one from BrioQuery Enterprise from Brio Technologies. This screen shows sales changes from one year to the next for a computer equipment distributor, by type of store. In the original color screen, items that had a unit sales decline of 20 percent or more are shown in red. If you look closely, you will see that the entries for electronics stores for the first two quarters appear as a shade of gray, rather than black, in the figure. Items that had an increase of 75 percent or more for the corresponding quarter year-to-year are shown in blue on a yellow background. The background appears as a light gray background in the book. The user is able to specify the ranges for each type of visual highlighting and what the highlighting should be.

			1994	1995	% Increase
			Units Delivered	Units Delivered	Units Delivered
CD-ROM Drive	Computer	Q1	150	310	**107%**
		Q2	225	280	24%
		Q3	275	285	4%
		Q4	320	410	28%
	Discount	Q1	30	260	**767%**
		Q2	75	285	**280%**
		Q3	220	290	32%
		Q4	115	300	**161%**
	Electronics	Q1	150	10	−93%
		Q2	140	20	−86%
		Q3	130	215	65%
		Q4	130	320	**146%**

FIGURE 14–8 **BrioQuery Enterprise Sample Table**
Source: Copyright Brio Technologies. Used with permission.

Suppose the analyst seeing this screen wanted to rotate the quarterly breakdown so that the quarters appeared across the top, under the years, rather than down the side. He or she could grab the tab under the Quarters column with the mouse and rotate that column, while holding down the mouse button, up and to the right. The result would then look like Figure 14–9 (which also differs from Figure 14–8 in that it shows the entire BrioQuery window, not just the table, and that it shows sales by product category, not store type).

In addition to tables such as those shown in Figures 14–8 and 14–9, BrioQuery Enterprise and most other OLAP products can also produce output in the form of a graph, much as a spreadsheet program can show data in tabular form or in many graphical formats. Figure 14–10 shows a graph giving both the store type breakdown of Figure 14–8 and the product category of Figure 14–9, for a single year. Having the capability integrated into the OLAP package makes it easier to use in some situations than going back and forth between an OLAP package and a spreadsheet.

14.1.2 OLAP Software Architecture

Demand for OLAP capabilities increased rapidly during the last half of the 1990s. Software vendors of all types tried to capture a share of this growth market. It is not surprising that they all approached it from the perspective of their existing products, much as early automobiles resembled stagecoaches if a stagecoach company built them or heavy bicycles with more wheels if they were built by a bicycle factory. Three approaches, all supported by contemporary software packages, are

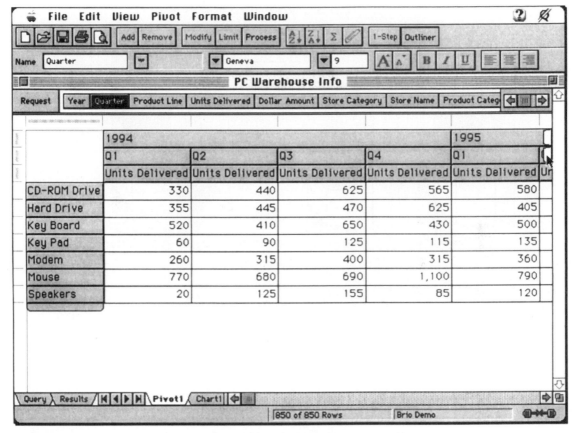

FIGURE 14–9 BrioQuery Enterprise Sample Table with Quarters across the Top
Source: Copyright Brio Technologies. Used with permission.

shown in Figure 14–11. The three approaches, corresponding to the numbers in the figure, are as follows:

1. Storing OLAP data in a multidimensional data warehouse such as you read about in the last chapter. This is the most natural form for most OLAP use. However, getting the data into this form requires more work than either of the other approaches, and it does not always provide adequate performance with very large data warehouse databases.

2. Storing OLAP data in a relational database, which is able to produce multi-dimensional views of its contents. The user, be it human or another program, can't tell this approach from the previous one. The difference is that the work of creating the dimensional view is done when the request is received, not when the data is stored. This approach is often called **ROLAP** for **relational OLAP.**

3. Storing OLAP data in a conventional database (typically, but not necessarily, relational) and sending it in that form to a program that can provide users with a dimensional view. The pivot table function of Microsoft Excel is of this type. It is probably the most widely used multidimensional data analysis product,

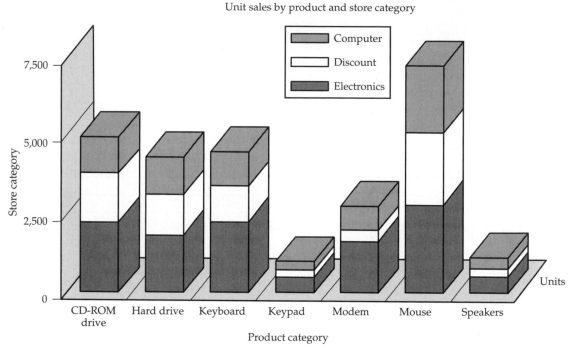

FIGURE 14–10 **BrioQuery Enterprise Sample Graph Screen**
Source: Copyright Brio Technologies. Used with permission.

despite being awkwardly grafted onto a two-dimensional spreadsheet foundation, simply because so many people have Excel. (Figure 14–5 is an example of this function's output.)

Most OLAP software, whichever approach it follows, is designed to work in client/server mode. The data warehouse database is on one computer, and the user sits at another that provides the user interface. Whether the majority of the analysis work is done on the client or the server varies with the product and, for some products, with the way they are set up.

OLAP is often associated with nonrelational databases—in particular, with multidimensional databases such as those you read about in the last chapter.[1]

---

[1] The term *OLAP* was first used by Edgar F. Codd, who also originated the relational database concept, in an August 1993 technical paper written for Arbor Software. Since Arbor was a supplier of OLAP products that use multidimensional databases, Codd defined the term so as to require this type of data storage. He was then publicly criticized for the technological equivalent of defining an automobile as "a self-propelled passenger road vehicle with the letters 'F-O-R-D' on the back." In response to this justified criticism he later withdrew many restrictive, technology-specific aspects of his original definition. This did not stop vendors of multidimensional products from using the concept as first put forth.

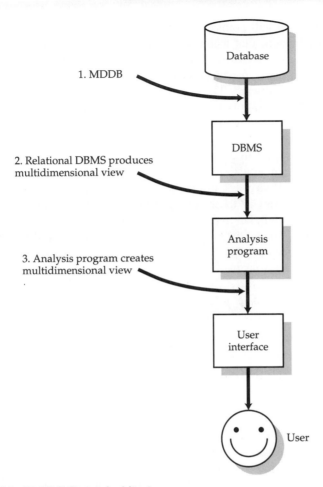

FIGURE 14–11   OLAP Software Architectures

OLAP is an approach to data analysis, not a supporting technology. The end user cares only that the technology provides the capabilities in which he or she is interested. Whether these are achieved via one type of database or another is less important—if it is a consideration at all. However, you should expect to hear the term *OLAP* used with a specifically nonrelational connotation—especially, but not only, by vendors of nonrelational OLAP products and people whose experience is primarily with such products.

The fact that users care more about results than about internals does not stop proponents of each approach from claiming that it is the only approach to make sense. Those who favor multidimensional databases will point to improved performance on queries that fit the multidimensional structure. Those who favor relational databases will point to the existing operational database and organizational familiarity with that technology, as well as the tendency of multidimensional databases to slow down with very large data warehouses. Those who favor letting a spreadsheetlike product create a dimensional view will point to end-user comfort with that software. The pages of data warehousing magazines and the Web sites of OLAP vendors bristle with claims of superiority and thinly veiled innuendo against anyone who might dare to disagree with the writer or the Web site sponsor.

As you might expect in this type of situation, everyone is right. The trade-offs that apply in different situations favor different approaches. What's more, any approach can be made to work in nearly any situation—sometimes at the cost of extra effort on the part of those setting up the system, sometimes at the cost of extra hardware to run it, but made to work in any case. Its users, seeing that the approach they chose meets their needs and provides the desired business benefits, will become convinced that they chose wisely and will defend their chosen method. In a few years, as the industry gains more experience with the technology and can put it in perspective, the debate will undoubtedly be put on the shelf together alongside the debate over round versus rectangular holes in punched cards. Meanwhile, be sure to evaluate vendor claims in the context of a particular situation. A few guidelines that may help you select an approach are

- If the database will be used heavily for regular and repeated OLAP analyses, the overhead of creating a multidimensional database will probably be more than repaid in time savings thereafter.
- If the OLAP analyses are concentrated on the content of one existing database, it is probably a good idea to use the existing database if at all possible. If that database is relational, it will normally be possible to use it.
- In this case, if the load is too heavy for the existing server or if a static snapshot of the database is required, copying the operational database onto another server in the same form is probably much easier than transforming it into multidimensional form. If the OLAP load is light and small variations in the database from one query to the next are acceptable, it can probably be accessed where it is.
- If the number of dimensions is small and the client computers are powerful, loading operational data into spreadsheets that create a multidimensional view will probably work well.
- If the number of dimensions is very large, the multidimensional database approach will increase storage requirements drastically. This is true even if the raw data are stored in an efficient form for a sparse matrix, as precompiled summaries at various levels can also be quite large. In this case a relational database will usually be a better choice.

These guidelines do not provide a single answer for every situation you could encounter. However, they are a start. If you understand the approach to trade-offs that underlie them, you will be able to continue the analysis in the context of a specific need.

14.1.3 Web-based OLAP

A category of OLAP products that began to emerge in 1997 is **Web-based OLAP (WOLAP).** These products allow users of Web browsers or network computers (see p. 178 if you're not familiar with network computers) to access and analyze data warehouse data. WOLAP users may not actually be using the Internet-housed World Wide Web. Security issues deter many organizations, quite reasonably, from putting their valuable data on display at a corporate Web site. Even if passwords are used to limit access, it is an opportunity for a security breach. More likely, an *intranet* will provide users with access to internal data while using familiar Web browsers and protocols.

A WOLAP system is still an OLAP system operating in a client/server model. The user can't tell a WOLAP screen, such as the one in Figure 14–12 depicting Business Objects' WebIntelligence program, from that of a client-based OLAP program. However, the limitation to Web-based operation limits client functionality to what Web browsers or their equivalent can be expected to do. This leads to two possibilities:

- The analysis can be done entirely on the server, with the results converted to HTML and sent to the client for display.
- The analysis programs can be written as Java applets, JavaScript code, or any other form usable by most browsers, and downloaded as needed. That is how WebIntelligence created Figure 14–12. (This particular screen shows a user defining a table that will show automobile sales revenue for the year by category and region.)

Either approach is independent of client architecture. As long as the client has the necessary Web software and is attached to a suitable network, it can use any version of Windows, the Mac OS, or any other environment of the user's choice. WOLAP also eliminates the need to install a software package on the user's computer, with the attendant issues of administration, upgrades, and more.

Although the surface similarity between the acronyms ROLAP and WOLAP seems to suggest that these are alternative approaches to OLAP, that is not the case. ROLAP refers to the nature of the underlying database—in this case relational. WOLAP refers to the way in which analysis software is structured and executed—in this case via the Web or a Weblike intranet. The WOLAP concept says nothing about how the data warehouse database is structured. WOLAP applications can work with any type of database they are programmed to use: relational, multidimensional, or perhaps something else yet to be invented.

14.1.4 General OLAP Product Characteristics

There are many OLAP products on the market. The number is increasing steadily as the size of the data warehousing market grows and it thus becomes more attractive to software vendors. (This market stage is usually followed by a shakeout stage, in which some firms merge, others fail, and still others discontinue unsuccessful

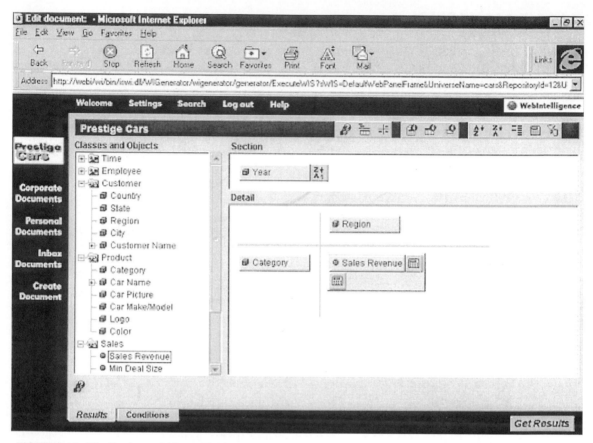

FIGURE 14–12   Business Objects WebIntelligence Screen

products, but as of 1999 any shakeout is still in the future.) Fortunately for the prospective user, they all share some common characteristics:

1. They can access data stored in any popular database. Where their basic architecture (see preceding section) does not permit them to access the data directly, they provide importing facilities to convert data to a suitable format.
2. They all allow the user to specify which data elements will be extracted from the data warehouse for analysis. This is usually done via a point-and-click or drag-and-drop interface such as that shown in Figure 14–13. The user need only drag data elements from the list across the top into the appropriate section of the schematic table at the bottom right.

   In this case the list of data elements across the top of the window was preselected to offer those needed for sales analysis. If desired, BrioQuery Enterprise and most other OLAP programs can go into the source database, or to a repository, and show the user all the data elements that are candidates for selection. The user can then select all or a subset for inclusion in the current set of analyses.

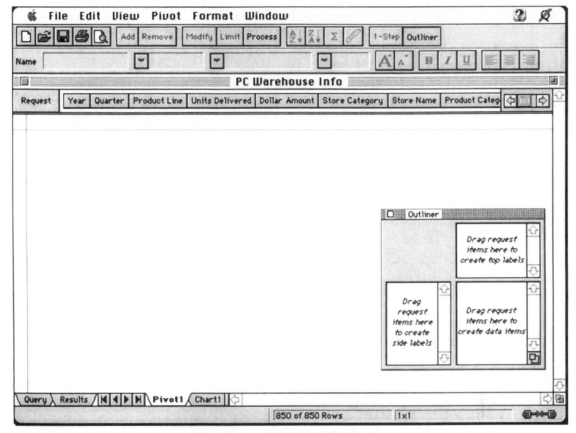

FIGURE 14–13 WebIntelligence Pivot Table Category Selection Screen
Source: Copyright WebIntelligence. Used with permission.

3. They all allow the user to select a subset of the data for analysis, such as "all association members in states coded WA, OR, ID, MT, and WY."

4. They all permit the user to define tables with multiple breakdown levels along the horizontal and vertical dimensions, such as the tables shown in Figures 14–8 and 14–9.

5. They all permit the user to create graphs from the data, in a variety of standard formats such as column charts, bar charts, and pie charts.

6. Having created whatever tables or charts the user requires, they all allow the user to drill down for more detail. Figure 14–14 shows two graphs created by BusinessObjects Explorer. The first shows revenue for a three-year period by year. The second drills down to show revenue for the third year by quarter.

7. They all provide a user interface that runs on the user's desktop under one or more popular desktop GUIs.

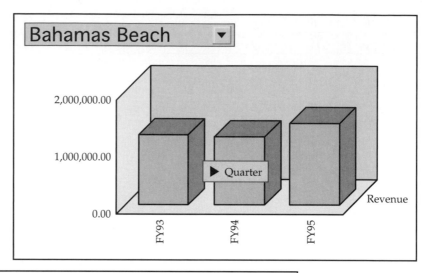

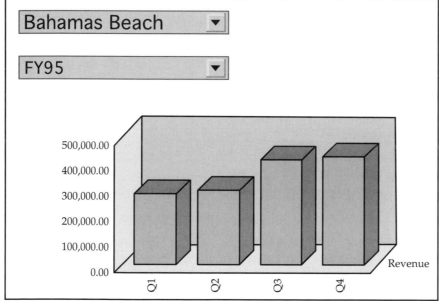

FIGURE 14–14   **BusinessObjects Explorer Drill-Down Example**

Within this overall framework, products differ in a variety of ways. As with any other software purchase, it is important for prospective OLAP software buyers to understand their needs before embarking on product selection.

1. As noted on page 533, their underlying data architecture may vary.
2. The specifics of their capabilities in all the above areas vary. One may support only Windows 98 and its successors, whereas another may support additional

platforms such as Windows 3.x, Windows NT, OS/2, Mac OS, UNIX/Linux, or Web browser access. One, especially if offered by a DBMS vendor, may require data in other formats to be imported into that format, while another may be able to access data in many DBMS directly.

There are often trade-offs in these characteristics. A product that can access data stored in a wide variety of databases may not be able to create a wide variety of chart formats. Or, a product that excels in all areas may have a high price tag.

3. Along similar lines, some products may offer features that go beyond these areas. For example, SmartMart from Information Builders uses an expert system to estimate the resource usage of a query before it runs. It can then accept or reject the query based on resource thresholds for the time of day and the user or user's department. If an extra feature such as this were essential to getting the job done, it would have been in the list of general characteristics. It's not essential, but it's often useful. Its value must be assessed on a user-by-user, case-by-case basis, especially if it involves trade-offs with other desirable product characteristics.

As another example, consider the pivoting in Figure 14–9 that followed the query response in Figure 14–8. Querying is not unique; every OLAP product does it. Pivoting is not unique; spreadsheets do it. Combining the two into one product, however, is not universal [OSTE99]. If a potential OLAP user wants to do both, he or she must weigh the value of being able to do both with a single product—and what other compromises choosing such a product will entail.

4. Some products offer close integration with familiar desktop tools such as the Excel spreadsheet package. Figure 14–15 shows the BusinessQuery package from Business Objects loading data into an Excel spreadsheet. The product name and sales revenue information came from a data warehouse database. The sales quota information presumably came from another source. The difference, percentage difference, and total calculations are easily done in Excel, as are the titling and formatting of the table.

5. Vendor characteristics are always a consideration. Some firms prefer to have the confidence of dealing with large vendors even if this means compromises in product capabilities. (This is not to suggest that the products of large vendors are always deficient, just that large vendors are sometimes chosen for reasons other than product excellence.) Others prefer the technology edge that may come from a small, innovative vendor focused on only one type of product. It is important for the individual making a selection recommendation to understand his or her organizational culture in terms of this and similar factors.

6. Another nontechnical factor is standardizing an entire suite of data warehousing products on one vendor's offering versus picking "best of breed" products from multiple vendors. The first approach may involve product compromises, as no single supplier is likely to have the best product in all areas. The second forces the user to integrate products which don't always work together as well as they are supposed to. As in the previous point, different organizations have different preferences in this regard.

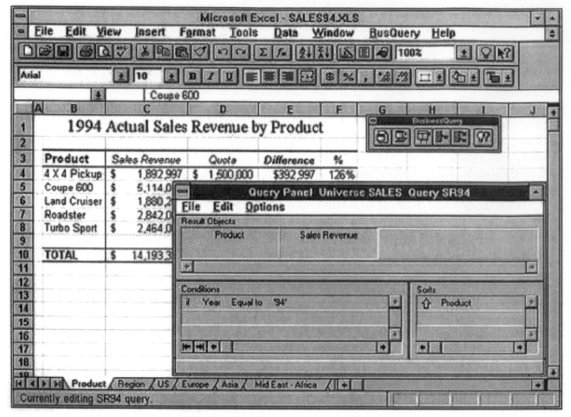

FIGURE 14–15   BusinessQuery Placing Query Data into a Spreadsheet
Source: Copyright Business Objects. Used by permission.

14.2 AUTOMATED ANALYSIS: DATA MINING

Data mining is a totally different approach to analyzing the content of a data warehouse. Bigus [BIGU96] defines data mining as "the efficient discovery of valuable, non-obvious information from a large collection of data." He goes on to say,

> The operative word in this definition deals with the "discovery" of information from data. . . . I am not talking about queries where the user already has a suspicion about a relationship in the data and wants to . . . check or validate a hypothesis. . . . Data mining centers on the automated discovery of new facts and relationships. . . . data mining [sifts] through the vast quantities of raw data looking for the valuable nuggets of business information.

In data mining, as opposed to actively user-guided data analysis, *the computer does the work.* The user need only tell the computer what he or she wants to find out in the analysis. For example, an actuary at a medical insurance company might ask, "Of all the information we have on our policyholders, what are the major factors that predict whether or not they will submit a claim in the next 12 months?"

The U.K. information technology analysis firm Bloor Research [CORY98] contrasts the two via these example queries:

OLAP Query	Data Mining Investigation
Which customers spent most with us in the past year?	Which types of customer are likely to spend most with us in the coming year?
How much did the bank lose from loan defaulters in the past two years?	What are the characteristics of the customers most likely to default on their loans before the year is out?
What were the highest selling fashion items in our London stores?	What additional products are most likely to be sold to customers who buy sportswear?
Which store/location made the highest sales in the past year?	In which area should we open a new store next year?

Compared to user-guided analysis, data mining has these pros and cons:

Advantages of Data Mining
- The computer does the work, so the user doesn't have to. The user need only turn the computer loose (with suitable software and enough parameters to guide the investigation, of course) and come back later to see what it found.
- The computer is not burdened by the user's preconceived notions of what relationships are likely to exist in the data. It may therefore find unexpected relationships, some of which could be of value.

Disadvantages of Data Mining
- An unguided search through many gigabytes or terabytes of data can keep the most powerful (i.e., expensive) computers busy for a *long* time. Serious data mining is not a job for whatever PC happens to be idle at the moment.
- Although valuable relationships may be found, they may be buried in a mass of irrelevant ones. Some of these irrelevant "findings" may be statistical coincidences in the data. Others may reflect poor data quality in the database.
- Even when a potentially valuable relationship is found, it may not be obvious what to do with it (or practical to do anything with it).

Data mining is cost effective in a wide variety of situations. It has been used successfully, for example, in the following situations:

- Finding relationships among the items purchased by people in a single visit to a store. Here, the reasoning goes, if people often buy A and B in the same visit, placing them in proximity might increase the sales of one or the other.[2]
- Finding relationships among items purchased by people in successive shopping trips. For example, people who purchase a barbecue grill may be candidates for

---

[2]In one often-cited example, disposable diapers and beer were paired in convenience store purchases (where such stores can sell beer). The usual interpretation is that the buyers are preparing to spend the evening with an infant. If the two are near each other, shoppers who came for diapers (presumably a necessity) will see the beer, hopefully purchasing it more frequently than if they had not seen it.

What companies are mining for

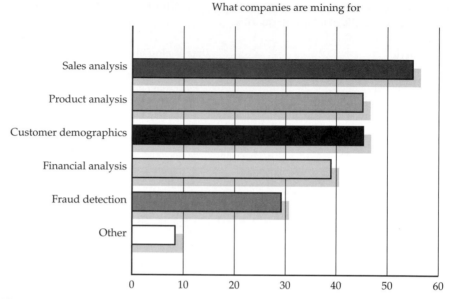

FIGURE 14–16   **What Companies Are Mining for**

charcoal or fire extinguishers. A store that knows this can offer coupons for discounts on those items. This is not as profitable as selling them at full price, but it's more profitable than having a competitor sell them.
- Fraud detection in credit card use. How do the spending patterns of card thieves tend to differ from those of legitimate users?
- Risk analysis for insurance policies. What combinations of policyholder characteristics increase, or decrease, the likelihood of future claims or fraud?
- Medical diagnosis. What symptoms, which may not have a known common cause, tend to be found with each other—and with what underlying medical conditions?
- Identifying customers who are likely to switch to another supplier. This function allows a vendor to make these customers special offers to induce them to remain, within the legal limits for preferential treatment of one customer over another.

When the information systems magazine *InformationWeek* surveyed 150 information technology managers [FOLE98] to determine what their firms are using data mining for, they found the results shown in Figure 14–16. Not surprisingly, the top three items all fall into the overall area of marketing and product planning. (The sum of all answers exceeds 100 percent because multiple responses were allowed.)

Several approaches to data mining are in use. Most "industrial-strength" data mining packages support more than one, as different approaches work best for different data sets. The following sections discuss some of the major ones.

All these approaches have certain factors in common. These are as follows:

1. The database supporting the project must be large enough to identify the desired relationships. A sampling of 10, 100, or even 1,000 customers will proba-

bly not suffice to identify anything useful. (One bank reportedly found a high correlation between being a physician who owns a Porsche and early withdrawals from certificates of deposit—only to learn that this "discovery" was based on one doctor who had done it twice in his life.)

2. The database should be partitioned in advance into two randomly selected subsets. The first is used for training, the second to verify that what the training has discovered is actually useful.

3. One must always be on the lookout for extraneous factors. For example, a project aimed at identifying employees who are likely to retire in the next 12 months might find that retirement is strongly related to hair color. A high fraction of employees with white or gray hair retire, but a much smaller percentage of those with black, brown, or blond hair. This is obvious, once you think about it, but may not be quite as obvious in other situations.

4. A data mining project may be guided by a known target for example, the search for applicants likely to succeed in an MBA program, or for customers likely to switch. In other cases it may be an expedition into the unknown.

14.2.1 Creating a Decision Tree

In creating a **decision tree** (also known as a **classification and regression tree [CART]** in this context) the data mining software first looks for the most important factor in determining the outcome about which we seek information. It then proceeds to the second most important factor and continues until "enough" (typically user-chosen with a reasonable default value) factors have been identified.

Suppose we, the MBA admissions committee of a selective business school, are selecting the applicants to whom we will offer admission. We have, for purposes of this example, two pieces of information about each applicant: undergraduate GPA and GMAT test score.[3] We also have historical data about students who have been admitted in the past: these two items, and whether or not they completed our program successfully. While real MBA admissions committees look at several factors beyond these two numbers, they will serve to show how a data mining program creates a decision tree.

We can plot all previous students on a chart such as the one shown in Figure 14–17, where a plus sign (+) represents a graduate and a dash or minus sign (–) represents someone who started our program but for any reason did not graduate. The chart ranges from 200 to 800 on the GMAT axis, as it is scored over this range, and from 2.0 to 4.0 on the GPA axis, as most U.S. undergraduate programs grade to a maximum of 4.0 and require a 2.0 on this scale for graduation.

Looking at this chart, we can see that neither GPA nor GMAT score is a good predictor of success. However, the combination seems useful: most of the successful students were in the top right triangle of the chart, most of the unsuccessful ones in the lower left. If we had more than two factors to consider, though, it would be difficult to visualize the data in this fashion.

---

[3]Graduate Management Aptitude Test, a multiple-choice examination administered by Educational Testing Service of Princeton, N.J., designed to predict success in MBA and similar programs.

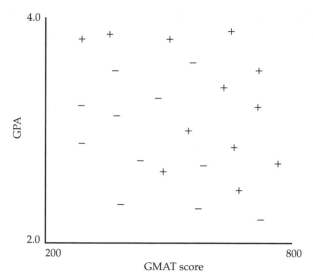

FIGURE 14–17   MBA Data

The decision tree approach to data mining starts by identifying the most important factor in determining success. Here it is GPA. About three-quarters of the students with GPAs of 3.0 or above succeeded in finishing our program. Conversely, most of those with lower GPAs did not. The program tries different dividing points—3.0, 2.9, 3.1, etc.—to find the one with the greatest power as a predictor of success. The result is Figure 14–18.

Having done this the program does not stop. For each half it now looks for the second most important factor. In this example, the only remaining factor is GMAT score. It turns out that, while most students with GPAs under 3.1 did not graduate, those who also had GMAT scores over 570 usually did. Conversely, while most students with GPAs of 3.1 or higher did graduate, most of those in that group who also had GMAT scores of 500 or below did not. The result is to divide the overall space into four sections as in Figure 14–19. Given this information, we can look at a new application and assess, based on the statistics of previous students, whether or not that person is likely to graduate.

The decision tree created by the data mining program could be represented in text form, using the Structured English approach you may have studied in a systems analysis and design course, as follows:

```
IF GPA > 3.1
    THEN IF GMAT > 500
        THEN SUCCESS IS PROBABLE;
        ELSE SUCCESS IS NOT PROBABLE;
    ELSE IF GMAT > 570
        THEN SUCCESS IS PROBABLE;
        ELSE SUCCESS IS NOT PROBABLE.
```

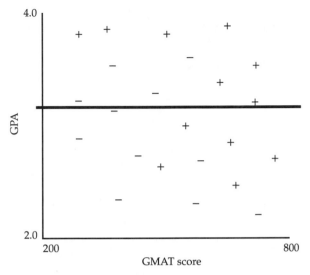

FIGURE 14–18   MBA Data Separated by GPA

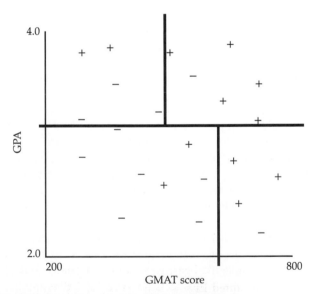

FIGURE 14–19   MBA Data Separated by GPA and GMAT

14.2.2 Correlation and Other Statistical Analyses

One problem with decision tree analysis is that it looks at each factor in isolation and creates a sequential chain of reasoning from known data to the desired conclusion. Sometimes it is not one individual factor that matters, but two or more factors in combination. MBA admissions people know this; a higher GMAT score can offset, as an indicator of predicted success, a low GPA and vice versa. They

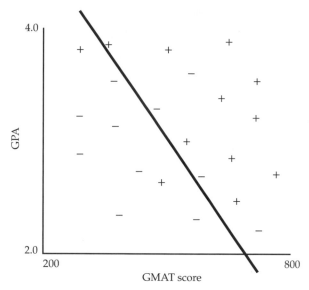

FIGURE 14–20   MBA Data Divided by Sloping Line

therefore often use a composite number that gives equal weight to each. It is calculated by multiplying the GPA (converted to a 4.0 scale if necessary) by 200, for a maximum of 800, and adding it to the GMAT score, which already has a maximum of 800. The resulting sum, with a maximum of 1,600, is often called the "applicant figure of merit."

A data mining program that looked for the best statistical dividing line between successful MBA students and unsuccessful ones might find the line shown in Figure 14–20. This line corresponds, approximately, to a figure of merit of 1,150. It slopes down by more than 45 degrees, suggesting that for this particular program the GMAT score is of more predictive value than the applicant's undergraduate GPA. The standard figure of merit, which is designed for ease of computation, intuitive appeal, and wide use by many colleges, is not as good a fit to this particular collection of data.

In a real situation many other factors would be taken into account. Some, such as the quality of personal essays, are hard to quantify. Others, such as years of full-time work experience, can be quantified easily. Many MBA admissions officers feel that work experience enhances one's prospects for success. A data mining project would be able to determine if this is so—and, if it is, how much each additional year of work can offset lower-than-desirable figures on the other quantitative factors.

14.2.3 Neural Networks

Computer science has taken two approaches to making a computer behave with what appears to be intelligence.[4] One is the expert system approach you read

---

[4]This sentence, which follows Minsky's definition of artificial intelligence near the start of Chapter 11, is phrased to avoid the philosophical question of whether they actually *are* intelligent.

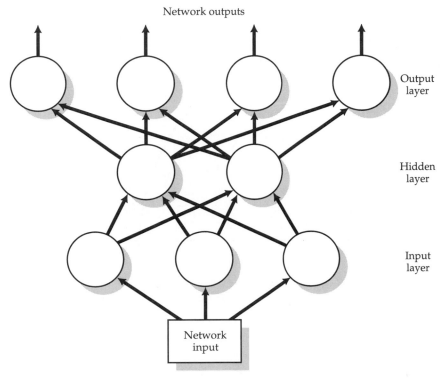

FIGURE 14–21   **Conceptual Structure of Neural Network**

about in Chapter 11—figuring out the rules that guide human behavior, then representing those rules, in a totally different form, in a computer program. Neural networks exemplify a second approach. They try to mimic the way human and animal brains function—first learning from experience how to deal with certain types of situations, then applying this learning to new situations of the same type.

A **neural network** consists of multiple, interconnected cells whose behavior is based on the neurons that control the behavior of humans and animals. Each neuron receives signals from system inputs or from other neurons. Based on the signals it receives, it generates an output, which it sends to system outputs or to other neurons. Figure 14–21 shows the structure of a neural network. As you might expect, the cells and their interconnections are usually simulated by suitable data structures and variables whose values change over time.[5] The methods are the same as those you studied in Chapter 8. At each step, each neuron sends a data value to the other neurons to which it is connected, as defined by the tables that control the simulation. In the next time step, each neuron collects its inputs, figures out what its output should be, and

---

[5]Researchers have built neural networks in which neurons are physical entities wired to each other. The difficulty of constructing and modifying a physical network, together with rapid improvement in microprocessor price-performance, have made this approach irrelevant in commercial practice.

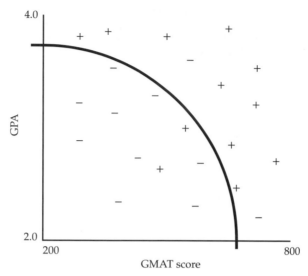

FIGURE 14–22   **MBA Data Divided by Neural Network Curve**

sends that output on to the next level. The process continues until the output emerges (or, with some network types, stabilizes).

Suppose we gave a neural network our MBA student data. It might well find that the best dividing line follows a curve such as that of Figure 14–22.

The challenge of developing a neural network to identify patterns is figuring out how to connect its neurons. The basic approach involves making a random set of connections, trying out the resulting network, and seeing if it produces useful outputs. If it does, the connections in it are given high scores. If it doesn't, they are given low scores. The process is repeated with many other sets of connections. Over time, some connection patterns tend to accumulate high scores while others don't. The high-scoring connections are reused in new network designs while the low-scoring ones are discarded. Eventually, if all goes well, the network improves to the point where it provides a useful analysis capability.

This procedure is known as a **genetic algorithm** because it resembles the way biological genetics works: the scoring for results corresponds to survival of the fittest, while the mixing of high-scoring connections corresponds to the mixing of parental genetic material. Genetic algorithms also incorporate the capability for statistical mutations, preventing them from getting permanently bogged down with one set of "chromosomes" and never improving beyond what that set makes possible.

A practical drawback of neural networks is that they can't tell us how they reach a conclusion. (As you know, the outcome in a real project with a dozen or more factors is not as instantly evident as the curve in Figure 14–22.) It is one thing for an MBA admissions officer to tell an applicant, "We're sorry, but data for 10 years tells us that students with your combination of GPA and GMAT have a very low success rate." It's far less effective to say, "We're sorry, our neural net-

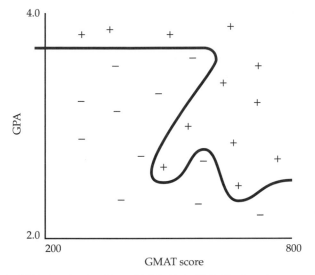

FIGURE 14–23 MBA Graduation Data Divided into Neighborhoods

work said you're not likely to make it, and we don't know why." In other situations, it may be mandatory to explain why a credit or insurance application was rejected, to prove that no illegal or unethical factors were considered in the rejection. No matter how effective neural networks are in such cases, they may be operationally unacceptable.

14.2.4 Nearest Neighbor Approaches

A fourth approach involves finding old cases that are close to each new one and assuming its outcome will match the majority of those neighbors. This can be done either on the fly, by looking for neighbors each time a new case comes along, or in advance, by predetermining the regions within which old cases tend to have one outcome or another. This is called the **k-nearest neighbors method (k-nn),** where k is the number of neighbors to look at for each point. This approach is also referred to as **memory-based reasoning,** because it is based on remembering where other points fall in the database. By contrast, the other methods develop partitioning rules by looking at old examples, but once the rules have been developed they don't need to remember the original examples any more.

Figure 14–23 shows how this approach might work with the MBA data. The line runs roughly along the previous two but bends in some rather surprising ways where the other methods smoothed it out. In this case the bends are probably an artifact of the small number of data points in the figure. We should normally have many more data points than this before embarking on any real data mining project. With more points we'd expect a smoother curve.

The number of neighbors to consider, k, is a parameter in this type of analysis. (As you would expect, most programs provide a reasonable default setting.) Using too few neighbors can create small regions where a random cluster of anomalous results distorts the outcome.

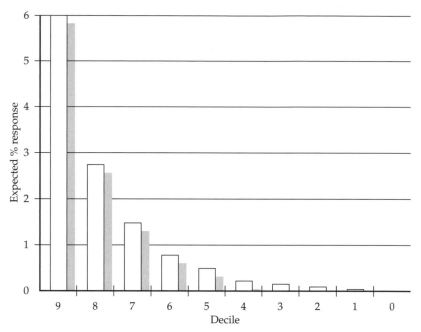

FIGURE 14–24   **Expected Charity Appeal Response Rates by Decile**

Another concern with all memory-based reasoning methods is that they depend on having a suitable measure for the "distance" of one point from another. It is easy to gloss over this concern with our simple two-dimensional MBA example because we subconsciously associate the concept of mathematical distance with physical distance on the page and don't even think about this as a possible problem. When points are defined by multiple measures whose numerical scales cannot easily be compared with each other, though, defining distance appropriately may take considerable thought and experimentation.

14.2.5 Putting the Results to Use

When there are more than two factors, it is usually possible to divide the set of subjects into more than two categories. If we were assessing likely response to a direct mail charity appeal on the basis of demographic factors, we might divide the total prospect base into four quartiles or 10 deciles. We could then plot the expected response rate of each decile as in Figure 14–24. The leftmost column in the graph represents the most likely people to contribute to our cause, down to the rightmost column representing those who are least likely. Clearly, we expect a better return from sending our letters to the people toward the left side of the graph than from those to their right. How far over should we go, though? Should we concentrate on the top decile, the top three, or perhaps all 10?

The answer depends on the business situation. Suppose each appeal letter costs us a total of $2 to print, address, stuff, and mail. Suppose, too, that the average contribution we receive is $100. As long as the expected response rate of a group is over 2 percent, we should mail the letters.

The average response rate to charity appeals mailed to the population at large, as fund-raisers know, is well below 2 percent. However, careful targeting can improve this rate dramatically. This phenomenon is known as *lift*. In the data mining context, **lift** is the ratio of the response rate (or whatever we're trying to find) within an identified part of the data set to that same parameter in the population at large. If the top decile for our appeal is expected to have a 6 percent response rate, whereas the population overall is expected to have a 1.2 percent response rate, the lift is 5. For the charity appeal we're considering here, we should start on the left and continue through any groups with a lift of 1.667 or more—the ratio between 2 percent, our breakeven point, and 1.2 percent, the expected average response rate. This means using the two leftmost deciles in Figure 14–24.

In data mining, high lift is good, as it means that the data mining process has identified factors that affect the outcome. The higher the lift, the higher the business value of the model. A model with no lift at all—that is, a model that has no ability to predict which members of the overall population are more or less likely to behave in a desirable or undesirable fashion—is of no business value at all. Conversely, a model that could distinguish between the two population subsets with total accuracy would be valuable indeed. Data mining technology isn't there yet, but it's moving in that direction.

SUMMARY

As you learned in Chapter 12, there are two basic ways to analyze the content of a data warehouse: on-line analytical processing and data mining.

On-line analytical processing, or OLAP, requires the user to ask a series of questions to be answered using data from the data warehouse database. A range of OLAP products is available today. Some store data in a multidimensional database. Some store data in a relational database which produces a multidimensional view of its contents. Others import data into a program, such as a spreadsheet program, which creates the required multidimensional views itself.

Most OLAP products operate in client/server mode. The server can be accessed directly over communication lines. Alternatively, it can be accessed over the Web and can present its results in Web browser format. This increasingly popular approach is known as Web-based OLAP, WOLAP for short.

All OLAP products can access (directly or indirectly) data from most popular database management programs. They let their users select subsets of the data for analysis, by data field and by selection of specific values in a data field. They let users break the data down in a variety of tabular and graphical analyses, drilling down to increasing levels of detail. They vary in cost, in the platform(s) they run on, and in the specifics of how, and how well, they provide each of these capabilities.

The second approach to analyzing the content of a data warehouse is called *data mining*. In data mining, the user specifies what he or she wants to find out and on what he or she wants the answer to depend. The computer, equipped with suitable software, goes to work and does the rest. Data mining can provide valuable insight that people would otherwise not have, though it is important to be on the lookout for "results" that arise from random statistical coincidence or poor-quality data.

Data mining approaches include classification and regression trees (CART), which identify causative factors in order from the most important on down; correlation and other types of statistical analysis of the data; neural networks, which attempt to "evolve" a set of interconnections that will find the desired separations in the data; and nearest neighbor approaches, which assume that a new case will behave in the same ways that similar cases have behaved in the past.

A good data mining project will divide the business entities in the data warehouse database into sections that vary significantly along a dimension of value to the organization. Some sections will score high on this dimension while others will score lower. The ratio of one section's score on this dimension to the average score of the entire database is referred to as *lift*. The lift of the highest-scoring section in a data mining analysis is a measure of the business value of the project.

KEY TERMS

classification and regression tree (CART)
correlation
data mining
decision tree
drill down
genetic algorithm
k-nearest neighbor (k-nn) method
lift
memory-based reasoning
neural network
on-line analytical processing (OLAP)
pivot table
query
relational OLAP (ROLAP)
Web-based OLAP (WOLAP)

REVIEW QUESTIONS

1. What are the two basic approaches used to analyze a data warehouse database?
2. What must you have, in addition to a data warehouse with a suitable database and the necessary hardware/software, before you can use OLAP?
3. What types of output can OLAP software provide to its user?
4. What kinds of databases can OLAP software use?
5. What is WOLAP? When and why would an organization use it?
6. How does data mining differ from OLAP?
7. What are four key considerations in any data mining project?

8. What are four different approaches that data mining software uses to find relationships in its data? Describe each briefly.
9. State one significant disadvantage of the decision tree approach to data mining.
10. What is lift? Why does it matter?

EXERCISES

1. You are analyzing the vacuum cleaner sales data in the scenario on pages 525–531 when you notice from Figure 14–4 that sales of dark green and gray cleaners are rising while those of maroon cleaners are dropping or holding steady. However, you do not know if this is because customer color preferences are shifting, or because customer model preferences are shifting toward the top of the line and maroon is most popular on the bottom model.
   a. What are the business implications of this question? That is, what might the manufacturer do differently, depending on how the answer comes out?
   b. What queries might you pose to your sales history database to help answer this question?
2. Why do you think on-line analytical processing is called that? What does each of the words in this term contribute to its meaning?
3. Like most other businesses, airlines derive most of their revenue from a small fraction of their customers. They go to great lengths to identify these customers and reward their loyalty through free travel, upgrades to first class, distinctive luggage tags that allow early boarding, special telephone lines for reservations and information, and other "perks." Airlines may have as many as three "elite frequent flyer" levels, typically reached after flying 25,000, 50,000, and 100,000 miles in a calendar year with that airline.

   Airlines are, naturally, concerned that these valued customers might switch to a competitor. If they could identify elite frequent flyers likely to defect they could offer these people additional benefits. The cost of these benefits would be prohibitive if offered to many people, but they would be worth this cost if they enabled the airline to retain a substantial fraction of the elite frequent flyers who would otherwise leave.

   The airline you work for wants to use data mining to uncover the characteristics of frequent flyers who switch the majority of their travel to a competitor. They have records that enable them to identify the travel patterns of these people in detail prior to their switch, as well as their participation in other programs (staying at specific "partner" hotel chains, and other such information) that give them credit with your frequent flyer program. They have comparable data for travelers who continue to fly with your airline. They suspect that there are patterns hidden in this mass of data that will enable them to characterize past defectors and thereby to identify those who are most likely to defect in the future. You have been assigned to carry out this data mining project.
   a. Is this a suitable application for data mining? Why or why not?
   b. Which of the methods of Section 14.2 would you try first? Why?
   c. Assume the airline has 500,000 elite frequent flyers in its database, that each of them flies an average of 30 segments per year, and that the airline keeps details of their flight history for four years. (One flight segment is defined as boarding to leaving a flight with one number. A trip from Philadelphia to Seattle with a plane change in Chicago is two segments, even if the Chicago–Seattle flight stops in Denver.) About how large is their frequent flyer history database? (You will have to make several assumptions; state them clearly. It may help to know that every airport with scheduled commercial service is identified by a unique three-letter code.)

d. Suggest four different dimensions along which to partition this database.

e. What are some factors that could make the results of this data mining project less meaningful than the airline might wish?

4. Using the Web, identify five data mining products from different suppliers. Find out which data mining methods each of them supports.

5. Reread exercise 6 of Chapter 13 (page 521). You have now constructed your database of Scotch whiskies and are ready to analyze it.

a. Would you use OLAP or data mining for this project? Why?

b. What types of relationships would you be looking for? Give two examples of relationships you might look for (OLAP) or hope to find (data mining). (For example, is there a relationship between the latitude of a distillery and the color of its whisky? Don't use that one as one of your examples.)

6. Refer to Figure 14–24. The percentages corresponding to the columns, from left to right, are 6, 2.75, 1.5, 0.8, 0.5, 0.2, 0.14, 0.08, 0.02, 0.01. Using the results of its data mining project, the organization has decided to send out its mailing to just the two highest deciles as described at the end of Section 14.2. Without the data mining project, it would have sent the mailing to everyone on the list. Suppose the data mining project cost $20,000 to carry out. How large must the *entire* mailing list be to justify this cost?

REFERENCES

Many of the books listed as general references at the end of Chapter 12 discuss data warehouse databases in detail. Those references are not repeated here. If a book cited in this chapter is not in the list that follows, you can find it there.

BIGU96   Bigus, Joseph P. *Data Mining with Neural Networks.* McGraw-Hill, New York (1996).

CORY98   Cory, Thérèse. *Business Intelligence through Data Mining.* Bloor Research, Milton Keynes, U.K. (1998).

FOLE98   Foley, John, and Joy D. Russell. "Mining Your Own Business." *Information Week,* no. 673 (March 16, 1998), p. 18.

OLAP95   OLAP Council, The. "Guide to OLAP Terminology." (January 1995). Available on-line: http://www.olapcouncil.org/whtpap.html

OSTE99   Osterfelt, Susan. "Suite Success." *DM Review* 9, no. 3 (March 1999), p. 18.

CASE

Fort Lowell Trading Company
Using Neural Networks for Market Segmentation

Much of the background for the conclusion of this episode is from [BIGU96, Chap. 9].

It was a warm day, even for Tucson, when Miguel and Elizabeth arrived at the FLTC Information Systems department for their scheduled meeting with Kareem

Davis, director of marketing planning. Since the three had already met there was no need for introductions. Kareem greeted them at the lobby, pressed his employee ID to the reader by the door to admit them to the IS office area, and led them down the corridor to the right. "It sure is nice to get in here where it's air-conditioned," Miguel commented.

"That's one benefit of working in the computer area," agreed Kareem. "We can't let the mainframes overheat, and our offices are cooled by the same chilled water. Sometimes it even gets too cold, especially after we move office partitions. Then we have to rebalance the system to match the new air flow patterns."

"Do you use a computer for that?" asked Miguel.

"No, just a couple of old guys who know this stuff cold, if you'll pardon the pun. They come in, hold their fingers in the air, maybe measure a few things, adjust some vents and everything's fine again. Takes 'em 10 minutes to do it, but it probably took 'em 20 years to learn how. I don't know what we'll do when they retire. Maybe one of those expert systems we talked about last time?"

With that the group entered Kareem's office and sat down. "Anyhow," he continued, "the reason I wanted to chat with you today is about this catalogue promotion we're planning."

"How so?" Elizabeth asked.

"Well, what we used to do was to pick some things to promote in our seasonal catalogue. We'd try to get enough variety to have something for just about anyone. We'd have a couple of home things with a southwestern flavor, some clothing items that would depend on the season, an electronic gadget or two, some outdoorsy stuff, and who knows what else. We'd put these on the cover, price them specially for this promotion, and Stan Junior would talk about them in that folksy letter he writes for the first page.

"For the past few years, we've been doing regional versions of the catalog. Like, we weren't selling much ski wear in Florida, but we still wanted to promote it in Colorado. This helped a bit. We can track how the promoted items sell versus the rest of the catalog, and it went up. Not much, but since it was pretty much a freebie it was worth doing.

"Now I'd like to try to see if we can do better than regional catalogs. I mean, overall, New Englanders are different from Midwesterners in what they buy, but there are some folks in Vermont who buy like people from Wisconsin and vice versa. We have huge amounts of data on what our catalog customers have bought in the past. If we can figure out what each customer is like, we should be able to tailor the catalogs better than just treating everyone in a region like a bunch of cloned sheep."

"What kind of data do you have about your catalog customers?" Miguel asked.

"We give each customer a number when they first order from us," Kareem began. "Then they use that number when they order again. If they don't have it, it comes up on the order screen as soon as they give us their name and address. So we can track what they've ordered since we started doing this in 1989. We have records of every single thing that every catalog customer has ordered, by catalog number.

"We also have more data on some of our customers. The ones who apply for a store charge card fill out a form with some basic info like annual income. Ditto for the ones who sign up for our repeat customer programs. We also sent a question-naire to a sample of our customers a while back asking for more of this type of in-formation. We don't have demographic info on all our customers, though. Finally, we can plug their addresses into a system that will tell us average income levels, education, and so on in that ZIP code or a smaller area, but those are just averages. Better than nothing, I suppose."

"That makes me wonder about a couple of things," Elizabeth commented. "One, how much data are we talking about here? And two, do the catalog numbers in your database correspond to anything that makes sense to the business?"

"Good questions, Elizabeth, real good ones," said Kareem while nodding ap-provingly. "Let's take your second one first because it's easier.

"The short answer to that, unfortunately, is 'no.' There is absolutely no system to assigning catalog numbers. It's like street numbers in Tokyo. Did you know they assign those numbers as they issue building permits? House number 1 is the oldest on the street. It might not be anywhere near house number 2 or 3. Our cata-log numbers are like that. If Item 30621 is a can of Texas chili powder, 30622 might be a coffee grinder, and 30623 could be a hat. Fortunately, we have a couple of other databases that match catalog numbers to product categories down to sev-eral levels of detail. You have to do some joins to get there, but we know how.

"As for the amount of data: it's big. Figure a million orders per year on the av-erage, about a thousand bytes per order, that's a gig of data each year. Times about 10 years, more or less, is 10 gig. It's growing at more than a gig a year now be-cause we're running at well over a million orders per year today."

"Is this data all on-line?" Elizabeth asked.

"Fortunately, no," Kareem smiled, "given how crowded our disk space is. Most of it is on mag tape in the archives. We keep the last two years on-line so our opera-tors have a little customer history when they take an order. For the rest, we have a small customer number lookup table with the date of the last order and info on the credit card they used for it. We could find room for the whole file in the mainframe disk farm if we needed to, but it's not the kind of thing you'd put on your PC!"

"There must be some way to shrink that . . ." Miguel wondered.

"There are a few possibilities," Kareem agreed. "We could do an age cutoff—ignore anyone who hasn't ordered from us in, say, three years. We might still want to use the older data on people who are current customers, so we don't want to just toss every record that's more than three years old. We also might want to ignore anyone who just ordered one item one time. You can't get much of a pattern out of one order. We could even cut sharper than that—maybe analyze only if we got at least two orders for at least three items total. Our customers follow the old 80/20 rule: 20 percent of them account for 80 percent of our volume."

"Do you think new purchases will follow the same rule?" Miguel followed up. "In other words, if you can segment your top 20 percent and target them better, do you think you'll get 80 percent of the benefit that segmenting all your customers would give you?"

"Probably," Kareem mused. "At least it's a smaller problem so it would be eas-ier to start that way. If it pays off we can go after the rest of it. Anyhow, does this sound like a reasonable thing to do?"

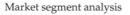

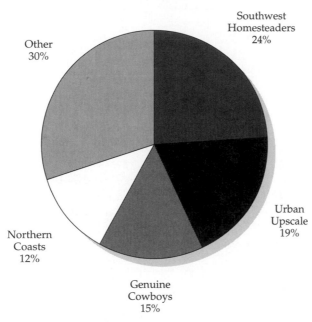

FIGURE 14–25 **Major Customer Categories**

"It does," Elizabeth responded. "It sounds like a perfect application for a neural network that would look at the data and try to find patterns in it."

"Are those for real?" asked Miguel. "Aren't those like trying to make an ant's brain out of a computer program? I mean, I read about them in my dentist's office once, and they sounded kinda like science fiction."

"They've had their ups and downs," Elizabeth confirmed. "But they seem to be pretty good at narrow problems like this. I mean, you can define a dozen or so inputs that you want it to look at, and ask it to come up with half a dozen or so categories—that's doable. I think you need something our professor called a feature map. He said that just about any neural network package ought to be able to give you one."

Two weeks later.

"Well, we did it," said Kareem after the three sat down in his office. "We pulled out a subset of our database, about one gig worth. Then we replaced all the catalog numbers with top-level categories from our merchandise database—stuff like sporting goods, women's clothing, entertainment electronics. Then we went into that database with a neural network analysis program and asked it for a feature map. We got four groups that look like so." With that he pulled a computer-generated pie chart (see Figure 14–25) from a desk drawer and passed it across his desk to Elizabeth and Miguel, adding, "Don't pay much attention

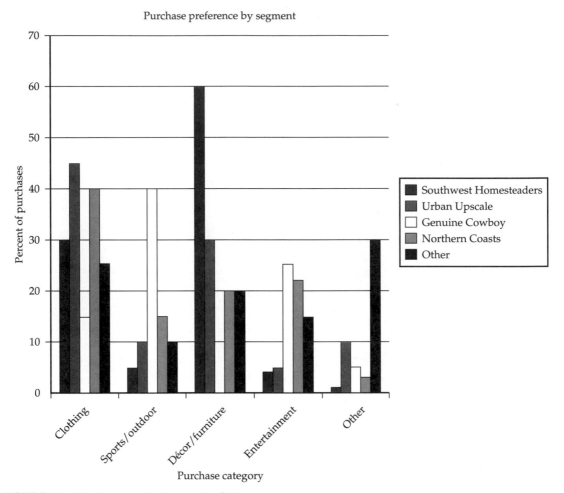

FIGURE 14–26 Purchase Preference by Category

to the labels. They're just something I put down for now so I could tell which slice is which.

"Then," Kareem continued, "we plotted their purchases in each category and got this," as he reached back into the same drawer and pulled out another chart (see Figure 14–26). "So what does it all mean?

"It means," Kareem answered his own question, "that we have four different kinds of customers here. We tried asking for five, but two of them came out so similar that we figured four is the right number. This one here," he said as he pointed to a tall column on the chart, "spends three times as much as our average customer on home goods with a southwestern flair. They're the ones I labeled 'Southwest Homesteaders,' but these folks are from all over the country. Maybe they used to live around here but we don't have any way to find that out. Anyhow, regional catalogs won't hit them, but a target mailing will. And we also have a handle on their age, their education, and some other bits like that, so we can target people who don't have a purchase history with us."

"How do you plan to use this information?" asked Elizabeth.

"Elizabeth," Kareem responded, "*this is a gold mine!* Each of these groups has its favorite categories. We can mail a catalog to this group and put southwestern home goods on the cover. You know, mesquite wood for grilling, wind chimes with Kokopelli playing his flute, tile house numbers, that sort of thing. They'll eat it up! I'll bet you both dinner at Scordato's that we can do 10 percent more business on the promotional items with these categories."

"It's a bet," smiled Miguel. "Not that we think you won't get the 10 percent— but we could both use a good meal!"

EXERCISES

1. Would the expert system approach be a good way to develop a computer program to balance a heating, ventilation, and air-conditioning system? Why or why not?
2. What could six dimensions of the database be for Kareem's investigation?
3. How could you apply the decision tree method to Kareem's problem in this episode? (You will have to be a bit creative. Don't worry if it's not a perfect match. The neural network approach, which they used, is usually best in situations like this.)
4. Estimate how much a 10 percent increase in business for catalog promotional items (not all the items in the catalogue, just the promotional ones) would be worth to FLTC. You have some of the necessary information in this episode, but you will have to make assumptions about several others. While you should try to make reasonable assumptions, your reasoning process is more important than accuracy.
5. Suppose you know, as Kareem now does, which subsets of your existing customer base have purchase preferences in each of four categories. How could you use this knowledge in selling to potential customers who are *not* in your customer files?

Constructing a Data Warehouse System

Introduction

The technology of a data warehouse, which you've studied in the last three chapters, is only part of the story. Technology—whether for a data warehouse or for anything else—is of no value unless it's brought to bear on organizational needs. As you already know, both from your prior study of MIS and from Chapter 7 of this book, bringing technology to bear on business problems is not a simple process. It involves many steps, which must be carefully thought out in advance. Some of these steps require more applied psychology than they do information systems knowledge. All, however, are important.

What you learned in Chapter 7 about implementing decision support systems applies equally to those DSS that are data warehouses. However, if you know that a DSS will be a data warehouse, you are armed with additional information, which can help you apply the general statements of Chapter 7 to your specific situation. This chapter will do just that.

In addition, this chapter has some material on project management (under "Developing a Project Plan," page 573) that could have fit equally well in several other places in this book. It's here because you need to know it in order to develop a project plan for a data warehouse. However, as you read it, keep in mind that it applies equally to all other types of decision support systems—indeed, to most information systems of any type.

CHAPTER OBJECTIVES

After you have read and studied this chapter, you will be able to:
1. List the stages of a data warehousing project.
2. Justify a data warehouse, in terms of both tangible and intangible benefits.
3. Obtain user by-in and overcome resistance.
4. Develop a project plan that describes what will be done, when, and with what resources.
5. Describe what a project leader does and what tools he or she uses.
6. Compare and contrast two basic approaches to building a data warehouse.
7. Explain the major architectural options for a data warehouse.
8. Use several experts' suggestions to make a data warehousing project successful.

15.1 STAGES OF THE PROJECT

Any information system project beyond the very smallest should proceed in a series of planned stages. These stages are generally taken to be the ones shown in Figure 15–1 (which you saw earlier as Figure 7–1), with many possible variations on the theme. Each stage is followed by a management review of its results. This review will usually authorize the team to proceed to the next stage. However, two other outcomes are also possible: direction to redo some of the work just completed (which may, in turn, require revisiting still earlier stages) or a decision to

FIGURE 15–1 Project Stage Diagram

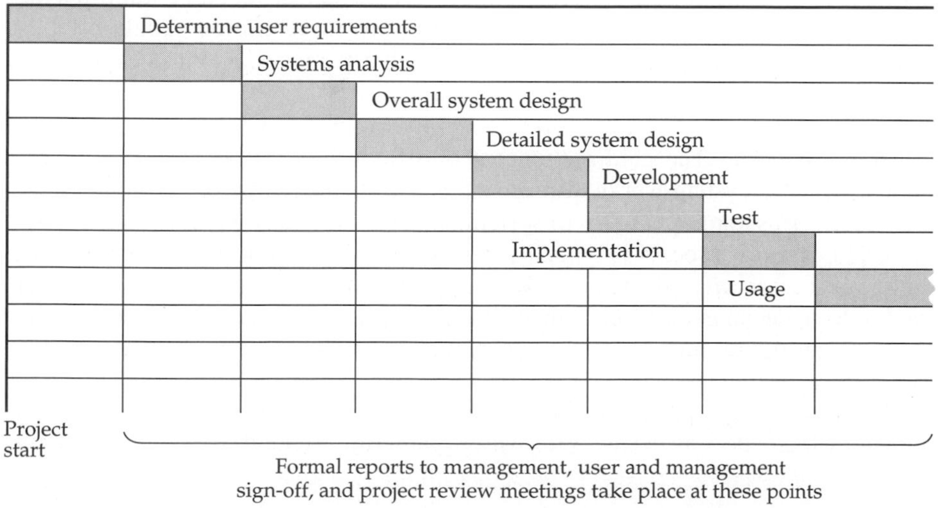

Formal reports to management, user and management sign-off, and project review meetings take place at these points

terminate the project. In addition to these reviews, there is a continuing need for regular discussions and updates for users, for the management of the data warehousing team and usually for the top management of the organization. These are some of the keys to success in any data warehousing project. We'll present some thoughts on them, as well as the suggestions of a well-known data warehousing expert, in Section 15.5.

The following subsections explain how the stages apply to a data warehousing project.

Determine User Requirements   The basic **concept definition** of the data warehouse will probably have evolved through a series of informal discussions. It is now necessary to describe it on paper, so that the people charged with carrying out the feasibility study will know what they are studying the feasibility of. Try to keep this document to a single page—ideally, a page with lots of white space.

A **feasibility study** is often part of the initial project effort. As you know from your earlier MIS studies, and as we mentioned briefly in Chapter 11 on choosing a good expert system application, organizations must consider three types of feasibility in deciding to proceed with an information systems project: technical feasibility, operational feasibility, and economic feasibility. The technical feasibility of a data warehouse isn't usually a real issue any more, though unusual file types on the input side may pose a problem. We'll discuss economic and operational feasibility in Section 15.2.

A key consideration in project feasibility is its schedule, since we can't evaluate a system's benefits unless we know when they'll be available. Therefore, a project plan in terms of activities, resources, and time is an important output of the feasibility study. You'll read about the data warehouse project plan in Section 15.2 as well.

People who look at potential user requirements for a data warehouse typically end up with a list of potential applications that is far too long for the initial project. Expect this. A data warehouse is an evolving system, not something that is put into its final form initially and stays there until it is scrapped. Its application list will grow gradually. The feasibility study or initial project definition should establish approximate priorities, so users will know which capabilities they can expect early and which will follow along later.

System Analysis   The guiding concept of **system analysis** is an effort to learn how a business system works at present, so that its operation can be improved in the future. This applies equally to system analysis for a data warehousing application. The business process is typically a decision-making process. The systems analyst must learn what decisions are being made, what information is needed to make those decisions, and how that information is used. Once that is known, the analyst can figure out how a data warehouse can support the people who make those decisions.

The methods of systems analysis do not change when they are applied to data warehousing. The four basic information gathering methods—reading, observation, discussions, and questionnaires—are still used. Discussion is the primary one, however. Reading tends not to be helpful, observation can't tell a systems analyst much about a decision-making process, and questionnaires don't provide the required depth.

Questions to ask at this stage (from Chapter 4 of [POE96]) include:

- How does the user do business?
- How is the user's job performance measured?
- What attributes (in terms of information) does the user need?
- What are the business hierarchies that apply to these attributes?
- What data do users use now, and what would they like to have?
- What levels of detail or summary do the users need?

The situation is different when the data warehouse is designed to support decisions that aren't being made, or when its purpose includes data mining. Then there is no "present mode of operation" to analyze. Instead, the analyst must figure out how an activity could best be performed in the absence of any existing methods to use as guides. The process in this case is the same, but the results are more conjectural. It is wise in such a case to err on the side of providing too much data, in case the initial concept turns out to have missed an important item or two.

The prototyping approach is, as you read in Chapter 7, often a good way to elicit user requirements for a data warehouse. The danger here is the third item listed under "Disadvantages of Prototyping" on page 263. A prototype of a data warehouse will not be connected to all its operational data sources. The work of data cleansing, transformation, and so forth will still remain to be done when the prototype is shown to users for their reactions. Those users, if they do not have a technical background, may not realize how substantial an effort this can be. It is important not to raise expectations through the finished user interface of the prototype (it will be a finished user interface, since it will probably be that of one or more commercial OLAP packages) that cannot be fulfilled in practice until much more work has been done.

System Design (Overall and Detailed)   System design focuses on the elements of the data warehouse that you read about in the previous two chapters: the database and data analysis. It includes activities such as choosing a database structure, laying out the database in terms of that structure, defining how data will be mapped and transformed from all its sources to the data warehouse database, figuring out when and how the data warehouse database will be updated, and answering the myriad other questions that will come up when a programmer sits down at a keyboard and asks, "What should I do?

There's no need to repeat the last two chapters here. However, we haven't taken up two design-related issues yet: the overall data warehouse architecture and the order in which data warehouse components should be integrated. We'll discuss those topics in Sections 15.3 and 15.4, respectively.

Development (Programming and/or Systems Integration)   Like system design, **development** relates to the technical aspects of a data warehouse which you've just studied. Unless one is writing custom file extraction software or the like, systems integration is likely to play a bigger part in the development effort than programming is. (Case 9 of the Appendix, "HFS: Mega-Warehouse as Marketing Tool," describes a situation in which custom programming was part of the job.)

In planning what should be developed first, keep in mind what you read in the section on determining user requirements: a data warehouse is an evolving entity. Focus on the set of initial capabilities that were defined there, perhaps modified in light of what the project team has learned in the meantime. These initial capabilities should be meaningful to the target user community but should not take any more time than necessary to put in place. If users see useful output, they will want more. If they see useless output or no output at all, they will have a very different reaction.

Poe suggests [POE96] allowing extra time for this phase for an interesting reason. Whereas the activity of developing or integrating analysis tools, defining useful database "slices," and defining reports may not be complicated, this is the stage at which data quality issues will become obvious. You will probably encounter problem areas that slipped through the prior testing but show up when people first look at the system output. It will take extra time to correct these problems.

Testing   Since most elements of a data warehouse are normally purchased as packages, testing them as individual components isn't usually part of the user organization's job. This is not to say that bugs won't turn up—they often do—but any testing process a user organization is likely to devise will not be as thorough as the testing that the packages have already been through, and is therefore unlikely to find them. Rather, the **testing** task of the user organization consists primarily of verifying that the purchased components all work with each other and with the organization's databases. This is necessary for these reasons:

1. Vendor testing must be spread over a wide range of environments. For instance, a data analysis or data mining package vendor must test it with several different DBMS. Testing to verify that it works with one specific DBMS is of necessity a small subset of its overall testing. Therefore, one can't expect a vendor to test such a program with any specific DBMS as thoroughly as one might wish.
2. No purchased package can ever have been tested with the user's specific databases, even if it has been tested with other databases that use the same DBMS. Small differences, such as using an obscure feature in an unusual (but legitimate) way, can uncover bugs that have gone unnoticed to that point.

The sequential nature of data warehouse processes lends itself to a sequential testing process. First the output of source file extraction is checked to make sure the right records were extracted and were given the right field names. Next, transformation and cleansing are verified to work properly. The contents of the data warehouse database are then checked against the source data to make sure the entire loading process worked. Analyses whose answers are known can then be tested. Data mining is harder to verify, as one doesn't know in advance what the answer is supposed to be, but data mining exercises on small subsets of the data warehouse can be checked manually to provide assurance that the system interfaces are operating correctly.

Implementation (Rollout and Conversion) The **implementation** process, including rollout and **conversion,** is the same for data warehouses as for any other data-oriented DSS. You learned about that process in Chapter 7.

Usage (Ongoing Maintenance, Enhancement, and User Support) Ongoing **maintenance, enhancement,** and user **support** are the same for a data warehouse as they would be for any other information system of comparable scope, complexity, and size of user community.

15.2 THE PLANNING STAGE

Several activities must be performed before the first line of code is written, database record is defined, or vendor presentation is scheduled. Hopefully, by this point there will be at least one top corporate manager who has shown interest in the data warehouse and will function as an executive **sponsor.** Having such a sponsor provides some official sanction for the project and makes it easier to carry out the steps that come under the heading of **project planning.** Planning must include the following items:

15.2.1 Justifying the Data Warehouse

As you probably learned in your introductory information systems course, information systems are justified on the basis of their benefits to the organization. These benefits can be tangible or intangible. **Tangible benefits** are those to which we can assign a dollar (or other currency) value. **Intangible benefits** are those, such as improved communication within a work group, to which the organization cannot assign financial value. Giving employees Web access, for example, doesn't usually save money, but businesses that provide such access assume that it has *intangible* benefits—that the corporate bottom line is somehow better off with this access than it would be without it. We just don't know exactly why or by how much.

Tangible Benefits Data warehouses offer tangible benefits in terms of improving the productivity of decision makers. Devlin offers [DEVL97, p. 338] an approach to figuring the approximate value of this added productivity. Although the specific percentages he uses will vary from case to case, the general approach is widely applicable. He proceeds as follows:

1. Assume that the users in question spend 50 percent of their time working with the type of information a data warehouse could provide. (The rest of their time is in meetings, working with other types of information, and doing the myriad of miscellaneous tasks any knowledge worker performs.)
2. Of this 50 percent, 80 percent is spent searching for, acquiring, and analyzing the available data. The remaining 20 percent is used in the real work of understanding and decision making.

3. A data warehouse would help primarily with the searching, acquiring, and analyzing stage. Devlin states that potential improvements are from 10 to 40 percent, depending on the complexity of the task and the analysis facilities of the data warehouse. A typical improvement of 25 percent is a reasonable assumption.

4. Combining these figures yields an overall 10 percent improvement in the productivity of these decision makers. Because the total cost of an experienced professional to an organization can easily reach or exceed $100,000 per year, this productivity improvement is worth $10,000 per year, per employee of this type, to the firm.

Parsaye and Petrie [PARS98] give a sample calculation for the value of a data mining project. They describe a hypothetical sales campaign intended to solicit new customers. It was, in the absence of data mining methods, to be aimed at a list of 250,000 white-collar professionals in the United States, aged 30 to 40 and earning at least $70,000 per year. Following a data mining analysis, the campaign was targeted at a different list, also of 250,000 people: sales professionals, aged 45 to 55, in the western United States, who earn at least $65,000 per year. In other words, the people in the new target group were older, were more focused professionally and geographically, and earned slightly less money.

Based on a test mailing, they figure that their example marketing campaign would have a 2 percent response rate for the original list, 4 percent with the benefit of the data mining analysis. (This corresponds to a *lift* of 2 in terms of the concept described on page 553.) They go on to assume, again from the test mailing, that the respondents from the original list would generate an average sales volume of $2,000 with an average profit margin of 3.5 percent, but those resulting from the data mining list would generate an average sales volume of $2,500 with an average profit margin of 6 percent.

Based on these numbers, Parsaye and Petrie calculate that the originally planned sales campaign would lose $250,926 in the first year, though it would turn profitable after that and would have a positive NPV of $822,449 after five years. The campaign whose planning benefited from data mining, however, would return $813,889 in the first year and have a positive five-year NPV of $5,414,065. While this example and its numbers are hypothetical, they are realistic. The methodology can be often applied, with different numbers, to actual situations.

Another important type of tangible benefit is the value of better decisions. Suppose a bank wants to reduce its losses due to loans that are not repaid. Each such loss is the result of a bad lending decision. Suppose the bank loses $2 million per year for this reason. With a data warehouse it would be possible to analyze the characteristics of defaulters with the goal of identifying them before the loan is made and not lending them money. If the bank estimates that this use of a data warehouse would reduce bad loans by 10 percent, with no corresponding reduction in the lending rate to people who do repay on time, it would be worth $200,000 per year.[1]

---

[1]It is easy to reduce bad debts to zero by not lending *any* money. A lending policy that is too restrictive can be worse for a bank than one that is too open.

Intangible Benefits   The above approaches may be inapplicable or may not yield enough tangible benefits to justify the data warehouse. Barry Devlin, who offered the example of tangible benefits used (slightly modified) as the first example above, goes on to write on the following page of [DEVL96]:

> In general . . . cost avoidance . . . does not provide sufficient savings to justify the investment required. . . . Rather, it is necessary to focus on the changed ways of doing business that the warehouse enables, and the benefits that accrue from them, in order to justify the implementation cost.

In that case an organization must evaluate the intangible benefits of the project as well, or turn it down as not economically justified.

Intangible benefits in this context are, however, only intangible in the sense that they cannot be assigned a dollar value ahead of time. As Stephen Cranford writes in [CRAN98], "The information and knowledge supplied by a data warehouse are not ends in themselves, but rather a means to achieve specific outcomes, such as increased revenue or productivity, lower costs or better customer service." The intangible benefits of a data warehouse must eventually translate into financial benefits such as these, or they are not benefits at all.[2]

International Data Corporation carried out an extensive study of data warehousing projects in 1996. (Increased experience with data warehousing, lower costs in all areas of information processing, and enhanced data warehousing tools have all improved the picture since then, so their results can be viewed as a lower bound on what a similar study would find today.) They found [GRAH96] one of the most powerful business benefits to be that

> . . . decision makers are finally properly equipped to attack problems in any business process. Whereas many other technologies enable managers to automate business processes, data warehousing provides the ability to thoroughly understand them and pinpoint necessary changes. It is the tool that managers can use to uncover the proverbial story which is trapped in their organizational data. . . . The true benefits of the warehouse lie in the decisions that it enables.

IDC also identified these additional types of intangible benefits:

- Managing the total customer relationship/opportunity.
- Creating value-add for the customer.
- Building empathy.
- Reacting quickly to volatile controls and opportunities.
- Managing both the macro and micro perspectives.
- Improving managerial ability.

These categories correspond to every one of the DSS benefits you read about in Section 1.4, with the exception of improving individual efficiency. That benefit of a data warehouse is one of the tangible benefits discussed in the previous section.

---

[2]Companies do (and, in this author's opinion, should) engage in activities such as charitable contributions that benefit society at large but do not directly improve the financial standing of the firm. Societal benefits, however, are not generally used to justify specific information systems projects.

Other data warehousing experts have different, but largely similar, lists. For instance, Kelly gives three key result areas [KELL94, p. 129]: identifying prospective customers, optimizing asset utilization, and providing flexible responsiveness to competitive actions. The first of these maps directly into IDC's first point; Kelly's third point is in effect IDC's fourth; and his second point relates to several of IDC's items. Others have still different breakdowns.

The point here is not that one list is right and the others are wrong. The point is that data warehouses can benefit organizations in a wide variety of ways. It is not important to put those ways into properly labeled pigeonholes. It *is* important to look at all aspects of an organization when we assess the intangible benefits of a data warehousing project. In all likelihood, it will turn out to have far-reaching benefits to many more parts of the organization than one might at first have expected it to.

The Bottom Line   In the final analysis, intangible benefits usually predominate in the predevelopment planning of a data warehouse. The IDC study cited above found that the 62 data warehouses it studied provided an average return on investment of 401 percent over a three-year period. More than 90 percent of the organizations studied reported three-year ROI in excess of 40 percent, a respectable return by any standard. What's more, these results

> . . . were consistent across the entire sample of companies that ranged from small warehouses measured in megabytes to warehouses topping a terabyte in size, supporting user communities ranging from 3 to 1,300, in a broad range of industries across North America and Europe. [GRAH96, pp. 5–6]

Thus, while organizations must often justify their data warehouse investment on the basis of benefits that cannot be quantified in advance, the record shows that these benefits do appear, and are financially significant, in the vast majority of situations. A data warehousing project in 1999 need not be an act of faith.

15.2.2 Obtaining User Buy-in

If you studied systems analysis, you know that it is important to obtain user buy-in before developing any information system. There are, of course, degrees of importance. You already know from Chapter 7 that user acceptance is more important for DSS than it is for operational transaction-processing systems. This holds for data warehouses, since they are a category of DSS, as well. Full support from the prospective user community is a critical success factor for any data warehouse project. The importance of obtaining user buy-in is due to several factors:

1. As you have just read, data warehouses are often developed in part under a *Field of Dreams* philosophy: "Build it and they will come."[3] Benefits are often intangible, even conjectural. Top management will not continue to allocate re-

---

[3]So called after an early-1990s movie of that name, in which the lead character (played by Kevin Costner) hears these words in a vision telling him to build a baseball field in a remote location.

sources to a data warehousing project if it keeps hearing from its prospective users, "Why are you pouring money down that rat hole?" Strong user support is necessary if a data warehousing project is to obtain the necessary resources and cooperation.

2. Data warehouses do not fundamentally change the way decisions are made. They change the way information to make decisions is obtained. If users don't consider the new ways of obtaining information a meaningful improvement over the old ones—in terms of ease of use, response time, quality of information, or some other factor they care about—they won't use the data warehouse. They will simply use their older ways of obtaining information, which have stood them in good stead for years. A data warehouse that is not used is not a successful data warehouse.

3. Most MIS departments have historically focused on functional applications and databases. (Some MIS departments are even organized so that different groups of people, under different managers, and working in different locations, develop applications for finance, marketing, manufacturing, etc.) A data warehouse must often integrate data from several of these. The ways in which users want to view the integrated data will probably not match the way the data were viewed in their separate sources. It is necessary to spend considerable time with users, understanding their perspectives, if the data warehouse database is to combine them in a usable way. Without full user support for the data warehouse project they will not spend this time with its developers.

User support is separate from top management (executive) support. Executive support is often a key factor in getting a project started. (You read about this in the section on EIS in Chapter 12.) One reason for this is that executives tend to have a strategic, cross-functional view that matches the data warehousing approach, so they would find the concept attractive while many employees with narrower job perspectives would not. However, once the project has been kicked off, user support is the more important of the two. Executives will generally not stop a project that has strong user support, except in the most dire financial exigency, but users won't hesitate to derail a project they consider useless no matter how strongly top management wants it.

15.2.3 Overcoming Resistance to the Data Warehouse

As Niccolò Machiavelli pointed out centuries ago—and as we mentioned in Chapter 7—few people have much to gain from change, but many have much to lose from it and will resist it tooth and nail. Rockart and De Long point out [ROCK88] that the same is true of executive information systems, which, as you know, are closely related to data warehouses. One way of assessing the likelihood of resistance is by the grid in Figure 15–2, which they credit to Gary Gulden of Index Group. This grid shows people who are familiar with a business (or think they are!) resisting such systems more than those who don't know the business well and aren't afraid to admit it. This is because people who don't know a business see clear benefit in a system that will help them understand it better. Those who do know it see a potential threat in bringing everyone else up to their level of

		Familiarity with the Business	
		High	**Low**
Perceived need for change	Low	resistance	attraction
	High	indifference	desire

FIGURE 15–2 2-by-2 EIS Attitude Grid

knowledge or, worse, having their colleagues and managers find out that they don't know so much after all.

Most resistance will come from people in the top-left quadrant of this grid: those who are familiar with the business and who don't see why anything has to change. This resistance can come from four groups of people, each with their own reasons. These groups are as follows:

1. Staff personnel who feel threatened in their roles as "gatekeepers" of critical corporate data. This type of resistance can be overcome through education, showing them that their skills will still be valuable—indeed, may become even more valuable. This process is culture dependent and can take several months of careful, sensitive effort.

2. Subordinate managers who fear giving others too much visibility into their operations, perhaps because they don't want to be "hassled" with detailed questions. Sensitive limits on the use of internal data can be an effective way to deal with this form of resistance. It can also be overcome by top management fiat, but that is a last resort: It can hurt morale and may simply push the resistance underground.

3. Line or staff managers whose resistance is based on the sentiment, "The business is doing fine, why change?" "This system is all costs and no benefits for my group," or "Others won't have the context to understand the data we send them." This type of resistance can often be dealt with openly, by discussing how the system can benefit the people in question or by adding features that will benefit them.

4. Knowledge workers who don't want to use the technology themselves but fear they will be pressured into using it or suffer from not using it. It may be best not to force them to use it. If the data warehouse is truly valuable, they will soon realize this and get on board.

None of these approaches to overcoming resistance is perfect. All require compromises on everyone's part. Your sponsor often has a key role to play in this area and should be willing to play it. Fortunately, the value of data warehouses in business is becoming less of an issue with every day that passes. You will have supporters as well as resisters in any data warehousing project. While it is important to understand the reasons for resistance so as to deal with them effectively, the fact that we have not devoted equal space to data warehousing supporters in this section should not lead you to believe that resistance is all you will find.

15.2.4 Developing a Project Plan

A project plan describes three things:

1. What will be done—that is, what tasks the overall project consists of.
2. When it will be done.
3. What resources will be used for doing it.

Tasks   **Tasks** (or activities) are the basic units of work used in project planning. Schedule and resource information, the other two basic items of a project plan, must relate to activities. The description of each task must state what is being done and how one will be able to tell that the task is complete—that is, what its **deliverables** will be. If a task is expected to take longer than a few weeks, it is helpful to plan intermediate milestones that can be used to detect any deviations from the planned schedule at an early date.

The description of each task should also state the dependencies of the task. Some dependencies will be within the project. For instance, testing can't start until there is something to test. Other dependencies may be external to the project, such as delivery of a server from a hardware vendor. Knowing the chain of dependencies of a project allows managers to focus their attention on items that, if not completed in a timely fashion, will delay the availability of the entire data warehouse.

Schedule   **Schedule** can be stated in absolute terms ("Monday, March 14th") or in relative terms ("Two weeks after the T1 line is up"). In general, a relative schedule is all one can realistically create. Tasks are usually given calendar dates despite this. These are more meaningful to most people and create a vision of when the entire project might be completed or when certain capabilities might be available. It is important to remember that these dates are just estimates. The completion date of any given task depends on everything that must be done before that task.

Resources   The key **resources** used in creating a data warehouse are people, hardware, and software. All of these must be arranged for and scheduled to be available for the required fraction of their total available time, for the duration of the project.

Several types of people are needed to complete a data warehousing project. Griffin suggests the following in [GRIF98]:

- Business analysts, responsible for identifying and defining the warehouse purpose and target user group, and ensuring that the warehouse meets the organization's strategic business objectives.
- Data architects, responsible for defining data collection, transformation, distribution, and loading, as well as defining the data models that are the foundation of the warehouse.
- Information systems services staff, responsible for testing tools and assessing the need for expansion of the warehouse.
- End-user support staff, responsible for allowing user reporting and access, as well as user training and support.

- Leadership and management, responsible for sponsoring the warehouse and making it a priority with the organization, developing project plans and ensuring that the warehouse remains aligned with business needs.

Resource requirements are usually converted to financial terms when planning a project. Unless this is done, the cost of a project cannot be stated and a well-thought-out decision to proceed with it cannot be made. Expressing resource requirements in financial terms by time period creates a project **budget.** This budget can, in turn, be used to monitor project spending and take action if it appears to be getting out of hand.

The Project Leader   The person whose job it is to coordinate all the tasks on a project is called the **project leader** or **project manager.** He or she is the lowest level manager whose responsibilities include the entire project. If a project is large, there may be lower level managers who report to the project leader, but they will be responsible only for parts of the project. If a project is small, leading it may not be a full-time job. The project leader may be responsible for other projects as well, or may also have a technical role in the project.

Project managers use a variety of charts to plan the coordination of project tasks, to monitor their progress, and to adjust project activities if conditions change. Two key types of charts are schedule bar charts (often called **Gantt charts,** after Henry Gantt who pioneered their use in project planning) and network charts (often called **CPM** or **PERT charts,** acronyms for two ways of using them to predict project duration).[4] Figure 15–3 shows a **schedule bar chart,** and Figure 15–4 shows a **project network chart,** for a sample project. The numbers over each box are the estimated duration of that task in weeks.

The heavy line starting with the coding of Module A and running through the tasks along the top of the CPM chart is the **critical path** of the project: the sequence of tasks which cannot exceed their estimated durations without delaying completion of the project as a whole. Adding the durations of these tasks suggests that this project cannot be completed in less than 13 weeks. Figure 15–3 shows it taking 14 weeks because it is planned for only two programmers (Henry and Susan). If the organization were to assign three programmers to the project, so that Module C could be coded without waiting for Henry to finish coding Module A, the project could be completed in one week less. One benefit of charts such as these is that they enable managers to see these relationships and make the trade-offs that are most appropriate in a given situation.

Project management overall, and software project management in particular, are professional fields of their own with too much content to cover here. Many successful project leaders achieved that status through hard work and observing other project leaders, often combined with painful failures (their own or others') early in

---

[4]*CPM* stands for Critical Path Method, *PERT* for Program Evaluation and Review Technique. Their most important difference is that CPM uses a fixed duration to plan each task, while PERT uses a statistical distribution of expected durations based on pessimistic, most likely and optimistic estimates.

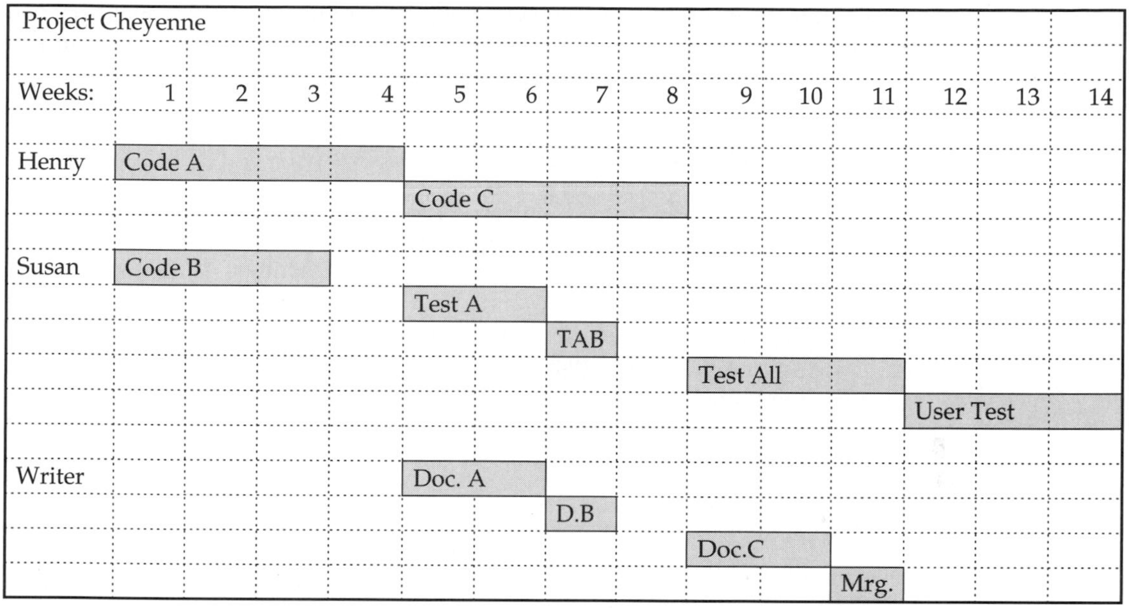

Project Cheyenne
Weeks: 1 2 3 4 5 6 7 8 9 10 11 12 13 14
Henry
Code A
Code C
Susan
Code B
Test A
TAB
Test All
User Test
Writer
Doc. A
D.B
Doc.C
Mrg.

FIGURE 15–3 Gantt Chart

4
Code A
2
Test A
3
Code B
1
Test A+B
4
Code C
3
Test all
2
Document A
1
Document B
2
Document C
1
Merge document
3
User test

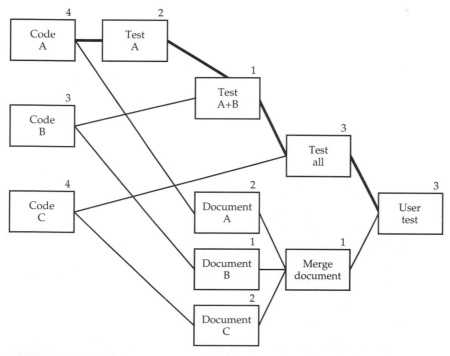

FIGURE 15–4 CPM Chart

their careers. If you'd like to accelerate your preparation for project management, many colleges, universities, and commercial training firms offer courses in this area. There are many books available on the subject as well.

15.3 DATA WAREHOUSE DESIGN APPROACHES

There are two approaches to developing the data warehouse. It is necessary to decide which one of them will be used. Kelly [KELL94] calls them the data-driven approach and the application-driven approach to constructing a data warehouse.

In the **data-driven approach,** which can be thought of as a bottom-up approach to populating the data warehouse, developers select successive data sources to add to the data warehouse database. An organization might, for example, start with the billing data of a particular service that the organization offers. Next, it might add billing data for other services or other data for the same service. Eventually all the data sources will be covered and the data warehouse database will be complete.

In the **application-driven approach,** which is more top-down, the first applications for the data warehouse are identified. These will typically require data from several operational systems. The necessary data sources are identified and loaded, with cleansing and transformation as required, into the data warehouse database. Subsequent applications add more and more data sources to the mix, until eventually, as with the data-driven approach, all the data sources are covered and the data warehouse database is complete.

The Two Approaches Compared The data-driven approach to building a data warehouse has the advantage that each stage is technologically simple. It deals only with the mapping of one file or database type to the data warehouse database. Each additional data source is added only after its predecessor has been handled.

Its disadvantage is that data sources are unlikely to map neatly into business queries. The first subset of the data warehouse database is unlikely to be of much use to anyone, as it will only be able to deal with queries that could already have been handled within the confines of one existing database. Whereas it may be a valuable technical proof-of-concept, offering it to users as a useful tool will produce yawns and may generate skepticism about the worth of the data warehouse project overall. Presenting easily obtained information in a "prototype" will create lack of support for expanding the system. A limited pilot may give the impression of "that's all there is" without creating the vision of data warehouse capabilities that will generate full support. (Burkan makes the same point for EIS in [BURK91].)

The application-driven approach has the advantage of providing useful business information from the first stage on. However, this stage will take longer to reach (than it would with the data-driven approach) because the activities required to reach it are more numerous and complex. The two can be combined as follows:

- The development team can present an application-driven face in discussing data warehouse availability with its users, but use something like the data-driven approach for internal development. This is not to suggest attempting to fool users into thinking it isn't going on—just to present it as a development approach, not a delivery approach.

- Initial applications can be chosen in part on the basis of the data sources they require. Applications that require few data sources, or that require data sources which happen to share a DBMS, can be done first. Subsequent applications can be chosen, again in part, on the basis of how well they take advantage of data sources already being brought into the data warehouse.

15.4 THE ARCHITECTURE STAGE

Before one can begin actually constructing a data warehouse system it is important to have an idea of where one wants to end up. This is, of course, not unique to data warehouse systems. The same could be said about setting up a spreadsheet, building a house, or buying a bus ticket. However, having a solid architectural foundation is more important for information systems than for most other objects whose failure does not pose a safety risk. You read about the benefits of an information systems architecture in Chapter 5. Such an architecture is necessary, in part, because *no other human activity combines the overall complexity of an information system with the need for correctness in the tiniest detail.*

The size of a data warehouse, the level of effort that goes into creating it (much of which would be wasted if it does not live up to expectations), and its complex internal and external interfaces make the need for an overall defining architecture particularly acute here. A data warehouse effort that does not begin by defining its overall architecture is doomed, if not to total failure, at least to depending on luck and probably spending more than necessary in the process.

15.4.1 The Data Warehouse Database

The most important part of the data warehouse is its database. It stays around longer than the applications, which will come and go over time. It determines the overall capabilities of the system: Anything not in the database can't be analyzed. And the quality of its content is arguably the most important factor in determining the value of data warehouse output. For those reasons, the architecture of its database is the most important part of any data warehouse architecture. You saw a conceptual database architecture for a data warehouse in Figure 12–1 on page 473. This conceptual architecture is not sufficient to guide a data warehouse implementation effort. It is too general, at too high a level. It is necessary to specify additional information at each level, corresponding to the four types of data you saw as being in the data warehouse environment, for example:

1. **Operational data.** The architecture must specify what operational data are to be brought into the data warehouse and by what means. It should also state how the quality of the imported data is to be ensured.
2. **Atomic data,** the foundation of the data warehouse. The architecture must specify where the data will be stored and how the data will be organized: in a relational database, a multidimensional database, or other. If the database is to

be distributed, perhaps with data marts in different parts of the organization, this should be documented. This part of the architecture document should also specify who (by job function and part of the organization, not by name) is responsible for data administration and database administration for the database, or, if applicable, for each part of it.

Some people suggest inserting an additional database layer between the operational data and the data warehouse database itself. Devlin [DEVL97] calls this the "reconciled data layer." This layer reflects the extraction, transformation, and cleansing processes. It combines the data so obtained into one coherent unit. The reconciled data layer is then organized into one or more databases that are used for actual analysis. It serves as the basis for summaries and for subset data marts. If a reconciled data layer is to be used, it should be specified architecturally here.

3. **Summary data warehouse data.** The architecture should specify which summaries will be maintained in the database on an ongoing basis. If any of these summaries are to be stored or managed differently from their underlying data (perhaps the atomic data are stored and managed within a division, but summaries are all kept at the corporate level), this should be stated.

4. **Answers to specific queries.** Since these are created as needed and not stored after their requester is finished, they are not part of the data warehouse database architecture. The way they are obtained is, however, part of the data warehouse architecture overall and must be specified for that reason.

In addition, we must not forget:

5. **Metadata.** The type of metadata that will support the data warehouse should be specified here. Even if an initial pilot implementation will not include the full metadata capabilities that are ultimately envisioned, having them in the architectural definition of a data warehouse will give everyone a clear picture of where that data warehouse is ultimately headed.

15.4.2 The Analysis Architecture

Once the database is in place, the data in it must be brought to its users and analyzed. Here the **architecture** must specify such things as

- What types of analyses are to be performed? Will the data warehouse be used for user-guided analysis, data mining, or both? An emphasis on data mining typically suggests a server-based data warehouse, but not necessarily. An emphasis on OLAP typically suggests client-centered analysis, but again not necessarily.
- Where will the analysis be done? Is the server expected to handle the job on behalf of the clients, or are the clients expected to do this? This decision has implications for the types of computers that will be required and for the processing power those computers will need.
- How many users will there be, and how often will they access the data warehouse? It is not necessary to have a precise answer to these questions—indeed, it would be unreasonable to expect one—but a rough estimate will help size the networks and server power required.

- Where will these users be? The answer to this question has obvious implications for the data warehouse network architecture. If an existing corporate network is to be used, it is important to learn as early as possible whether it will have to be upgraded to handle the additional data warehouse workload.
- What do we know about the existing computing infrastructure? If the firm has standardized on a particular type of desktop system or LAN approach, and is not planning to change it for other reasons, this will probably constrain the data warehouse. A constraint is not necessarily a problem—there are data warehouse analysis packages that run on all popular combinations of platform and LAN— but it should still be noted.

One reason the analysis architecture of a data warehouse is less important than its database architecture is that the analysis architecture is easier to change. If one doesn't like a query tool, one goes out and buys a different one. Unless there is something unusual about one's data warehouse database, the new tool will work with the existing data. If one doesn't like the underlying data, however, the effort required to change it is far greater.

15.4.3 Data Warehouse Hardware

There are several hardware options for a data warehouse, just as there are for any other decision support system. The unique characteristics of a data warehouse make the trade-offs in this case a bit different from other situations, however. The possibilities include the basic types of information systems you read about in Chapter 5. These apply to data warehouses as described below. The architecture of a data warehouse system should specify which of these technologies (more than one, perhaps) is or are to be used.

A Mainframe System   Those who use more "modern" types of computer systems often look down on **mainframe computers.** They consider microcomputers, UNIX workstations and servers, the Web . . . all as somehow better, often simply because they are newer, without serious consideration. Despite this common attitude, objective analysis tells us that a mainframe is often a good data warehouse solution.

A big part of the reason is that mainframe systems are designed for the rapid movement of large amounts of data. A transaction-processing application may involve a dozen or so disk accesses—reading indices, reading and updating data records, writing a transaction log or audit trail. Scanning a full-size data warehouse database, on the other hand, may involve millions. When databases scale up to multiple terabytes, the hundreds of parallel data paths in a large mainframe system provide performance that few, if any, other types of systems can match. A mainframe computer can therefore be an effective server in the data warehouse environment.

Mainframe computers (especially under IBM's OS/390, which controls almost all large-scale mainframes in North America and most of those in the rest of the world) also have software capabilities exceeding those typically available for other environments. Workload management software enables system administrators to define classes of queries, so that those that take several hours to complete will not impede the rapid execution of those which take several seconds.

Another advantage of the mainframe in the corporate environment is that the data are already there. It has been estimated that 70 percent of the enterprise-level data in the United States is stored in IBM System/390 and compatible (Amdahl, Hitachi Data Systems, etc.) computers. It may not all be on the same computer—many large organizations have multiple mainframe installations—but moving data among systems of the same type is simpler than moving it among systems of different types.

As long as the computer can handle the additional workload, and as long as the operational database can be used directly for data warehousing purposes, it may therefore be simpler to put the data warehouse where the data already are than to install a new system for the purpose. Even if the operational database is not suitable as a data warehouse database, perhaps because users want static "snapshots" of the data that remain stable long enough for a complete series of analyses, having everything on one system can reduce network loads, smooth data warehouse administration, and generally simplify life for all concerned.

A common argument against mainframes is that they cost more, per unit of processing capacity, than other computer architectures. This is undeniably correct. They may cost as much as 100 times more, if we consider only processing speed and compare them to desktop systems. However, it is usually not necessary to get an entire mainframe computer if one wants to use a data warehouse. It is more meaningful to compare the cost of the additional mainframe resources required to add a data warehouse application to an existing system, versus the cost of an entire computer of another type. This ratio will not be nearly as dramatic. Indeed, the cost factors—assuming good resource management, and considering that a desktop computer can't handle even a medium-sized data warehouse—may favor the mainframe.

Another argument against placing the data warehouse database on the corporate mainframe is that more and more data warehouse tools are being developed for UNIX and/or Windows NT servers. This is absolutely correct. However,

1. There remains, and will undoubtedly remain for many years, a wide variety of mainframe-based tools as well.
2. If the mainframe is the best place for the data warehouse database but the most desirable tools don't run on that platform, then either the database location or the tools will have to be a compromise. There is no avoiding that fact of life.

A Database Processor   Massively parallel systems (MPPs) are an effort to combine the cost-effectiveness of microprocessors with the power of a large system. Such systems, called **database processors** in this application, are an alternative to a mainframe for very large data warehouses. Building an MPP is not as simple as hooking a few hundred chips together, however. Taking advantage of this massive processing power requires internal data connection networks and hardware or software to manage their use. The result is a system priced in six or seven figures that has outstanding, but highly specialized, capabilities.

Compared to a mainframe, database processors can be more cost-effective when they are well suited to the application. However, they are subject to bottlenecks as a result of their internal connection networks. The nature of the bottleneck varies with the database processor in question. An organization that uses a database processor should expect to expend considerable effort in tuning the system to eliminate these bottlenecks.

Once this is done, a database processor can be a highly effective solution for a data warehouse database. Is it faster than a high-end mainframe, in terms of its ability to process queries against a 100-million-row table in an acceptable time frame? You will get different answers to this question from mainframe vendors (none of whom sell MPP database processors) and from database processor vendors (none of whom sell mainframes). As of 1999, both architectures are solving real-world problems on a daily basis for many users. They are also both evolving rapidly as technology forges ahead and new solutions are found to old problems. As a prospective DSS developer, you should be aware that both approaches to large-scale data warehouses exist. You should also be ready to evaluate them fairly, in the context of your organization, its needs, and whatever technology then exists, when the time comes.

A Dedicated Server   Data warehouses are often placed on a dedicated **server.** It has high-speed connections to client systems via local networks, fast (expensive) wide area networks, or (increasingly) the Internet. This approach has the advantage of creating a customized environment for the data warehouse database, allowing the organization to optimize the server for that task and that task alone.

Dedicated servers are usually multimicroprocessor computers running a UNIX-based operating system or Windows NT. Such systems tend to offer far higher performance per dollar than do mainframes or database processors. However, they are also more limited in their capabilities. Their internal data paths tend to be fewer in number, and individually slower, than those of a mainframe or database processor. One reason is that intense price competition in this market makes designers reluctant to add costly capabilities that most of their potential customer base doesn't need and therefore won't want to pay for. While large, powerful UNIX-based "superservers" do exist, they are not the servers one reads about with price tags in the middle four figures.

Using a dedicated server for a data warehouse allows the system to be tuned for the data warehouse application. This offsets, to a high degree, the value of mainframes' workload management software. In addition, there is a wider variety of data warehouse software available for UNIX-based and Windows NT-based servers than there is for mainframes. All in all, this approach is currently the most popular hardware approach for small-to-medium data warehouses (not the terabyte variety!). It will probably remain so for several years to come.

The Web   On page 537 you read about WOLAP, Web-based on-line analytical processing. In a sense WOLAP is complementary to the above approaches, not an alternative to them. To use the **World Wide Web** for this purpose one still needs a server to house the database; one still needs software to manage it. That server can be a mainframe, a database processor, or a smaller server of the multimicroprocessor variety. And one still needs analysis software that will display the results on the client system.

The differentiating factor here is in the implications of the choice for both the server and client sides of the network. With any of the conventional approaches, clients run application packages written for their instruction set and operating system. They also run network extensions to that operating system, such as Novell NetWare, which enable the client and server to share tasks according to the capabilities of each. The server may simply supply necessary data to the client, or may (depending on the software being used) carry out some or all of the analysis itself.

In the Web-based approach, client software has much less control over what goes on. All the work is done by the server, or by programs such as Java applets that are downloaded to the client by the server when the server decides to do so. The user is, for all practical purposes, communicating directly with the server via his or her Web browser. The browser knows how to follow hyperlinks to find the server, how to submit commands based on the content of form fields or menu choices, and how to interpret the Java (or other Web-oriented) language, but it has no built-in knowledge of data mining, OLAP, or any other aspect of data warehousing.

Summing Up   Each of the above approaches has its advantages and disadvantages. No one hardware platform is right for every situation or wrong for every situation. As with so many other issues in information technology, it is important to analyze the needs of the organization and make the right decision for that situation, at that time.

The architecture of a data warehouse, like that of any other information system, is a living document. It is first put on paper at a stage in the project when many issues are still undecided. For example, it may be known that a relational database will be used to store the warehouse data, but the choice among Informix, Oracle, Sybase, and DB2 may not have been made. Later the architecture will be more complete, but never static. It will change over time as new requirements emerge, such as a need for summaries, which could not have been foreseen, and new technologies emerge. The purpose of an architecture is to provide guidance to developers and information to users, not to put either group into a straitjacket.

15.5 HINTS FOR DATA WAREHOUSING PROJECT SUCCESS

Many sets of guidelines for data warehousing project success exist. Anahory and Murray [ANAH97] present a total of 145! All these sets are designed to help those responsible for a data warehousing project to bring it to a successful conclusion. Success in this case means that the knowledge workers of your organization use the system regularly and feel that it helps them do their jobs well. These steps can help you reach that desired state:

1. *Identify a sponsor*—ideally, more than one sponsor. If a single sponsor leaves, the system is likely to be orphaned. Aside from what that means to the organization, being associated with it under those circumstances won't help your career.

2. Once you have the sponsor's approval to proceed with data warehouse discussions, *start working on user buy-in.* You may, of course, have had informal discussions with prospective data warehouse users before this point, but executive sponsorship allows you to put more deliberate effort into them.

3. *Find out why your sponsor(s) and prospective users are interested in the data warehouse,* and what their motivations are. This information will help you design the data warehouse that they and other users need, not the one you *think* you would need if you had their jobs.

4. Based on this information, *pick one topic or a few topics that are important to your sponsor(s) and users.* Do those topics well. Having a useful tool early is better than having a complete tool later, or a broad but shallow one early.

5. *Recognize and respect the corporate culture.* Does it believe in centralization or in decentralization of authority? What are the power relationships between line and staff groups? Is it frugal—"lean and mean"—or willing to spend on appearances? A system that does not fit the culture cannot possibly succeed, whatever its theoretical benefits or technical merit.

6. *Define your expectations:* What people will use the system? How many of them? How will they use it? How will you know if it is successful? Establishing this vision will not control the future. Things change. However, success is next to impossible if you don't know what success consists of.

7. *Make sure enough resources are in place.* Most data warehouses require a substantial investment. This is especially true in large firms, which are not used to "shoestring" projects.

8. *Define your data requirements.* At the conceptual level, they will follow directly from the information your data warehouse will provide for analysis. As you know, few firms have a central database that contains all the required data in a consistent format that is usable by a data warehousing package. You will have to deal with data in incompatible files, data that isn't (yet) on the computer, and data that doesn't even come from within your organization.

9. *Define your communications requirements.* Where do the databases reside? How can they be accessed? What external databases must you access? Where are the executives? Are they networked—and, if so, how? What servers do their networks have in place, if any? What communication links exist among all these? Will their capacity suffice for the data warehouse load?

10. *Pick package(s) to meet your needs.* You probably studied package selection in your MIS course: developing checklists, issuing a request for proposals, evaluating responses, demonstrations or benchmarks, and so forth. The same process applies here. The Kepner-Tregoe decision-making method, discussed in Section 2.7, may help you.

    There will be trade-offs in package selection. For example, the package with the most features may not have the best user interface. The best package may turn out to be a combination of more than one package: perhaps one for in-depth financial analysis capabilities and another for its great graphics.

An Expert's Suggestions

Larry Greenfield, a data warehousing expert who maintains the Data Warehousing Information Center site (http://pwp.starnetinc.com/larryg/index.html) on the Web, has published his suggestions for a successful data warehousing project [GREE97]. Most of these have to do with the human aspects of planning and implementation. His suggestions are given in full here, in his words and unedited, and with thanks for his permission to print them. (Where he suggests a user-accessible automated directory to information stored in the warehouse, he's referring to what we called "computer-based metadata for people to use" on page 514.)

The following are some suggestions for the warehouse builder. These are points I rarely see discussed or I do not see discussed enough in the barrage of articles about data warehousing.

From day one establish that warehousing is a joint user/builder project.

Warehouse projects will fail if the builders get specs from the users, go off for 6 months, and then come back with the 'finished' project. Warehouses are iterative! (I think the word iterative means there are lots of mistakes in the projects.) Builders and users working with each other will not reduce the number of iterations, but it will reduce the size of them. By the way, see Peter Block's *Flawless Consulting* for a great discussion of how to bring about "joint" projects.[5]

Establish that maintaining data quality will be an ONGOING joint user/builder responsibility.

Organizations undertaking warehousing efforts almost continually discover data problems. Best to establish right up front that this project is going to entail some additional ongoing responsibility.

Train the users one step at a time.

Typically users are trained once. In several days they learn both the basics and intermediate and sometimes advanced aspects of using a tool. Slow down! Consider providing training initially in the minimum needed for the user to get something useful from the tool. Then let the user use the tool for a while (meaning several days, weeks, or months). Having basic training and some hands on experience, the user will have a much better context with which to grasp the next level. Also, once the basics and the next level are learned, keep training the users! After a year using the tool, schedule advanced training.

Consider doing a high level corporate data model/data warehouse architecture "exercise" in three weeks.

Actually, the key point regarding time is to "time-box" the exercise into a relatively short time. After about three weeks, the marginal benefits from additional time devoted to these types of exercises rapidly decrease.

The corporate model is going to identify, at a high level, subjects and relationships and most importantly, what are the chunks of information that it makes sense to deliver in different projects. The architecture part of the exercise to determine the dimensions, definitions of derived data, attribute names, and information sources that you will attempt to use consistently in your data warehousing efforts. The exercise also consists of coming to an agree

---

[5]The book Greenfield refers to is reference [BLOC81] at the end of this chapter.

---

11. *Develop a prototype and have some potential users try it out.* If the prototype is based on easily available data—perhaps using the data-driven approach to data warehouse development discussed on page 576—try to limit its exposure to people who are already enthusiastic about the data warehouse project so their enthusiasm will not be dampened by the prototype's limited repertoire.

An Expert's Suggestions (continued)

ment as to how to keep the corporate model up-to-date and how to make sure future data warehousing efforts pay attention to the architectural principles.

Implement a user accessible automated directory to information stored in the warehouse.

The majority of successful warehousing efforts I have seen included providing some means for the warehouse user to locate stored information. Most of the times this involved building a separate database with directory information. Note that the information catalog tools such as DataGuide are available if you do not want to build a custom solution.

Determine a plan to test the integrity of the data in the warehouse.

Do not underestimate the importance of user faith in the integrity of the warehouse data. Huge warehouse efforts quickly go sour if after system roll-out users find multiple mistakes.

A good investment of time in the initial stages of a warehouse project is for the builder and user to jointly determine what checks will be made on the warehouse data during development and what checks need to be made on an ongoing basis. The checks including tying warehouse data controls back to controls in feeder systems, checking the correctness of aggregation logic, testing whether classifications codes were assigned correctly.

From the start get warehouse users in the habit of "testing" complex queries.

Many people will assume that the query result is correct. At the very least, get the user in the habit of eyeballing the query or report to check if several records that should be included are, in fact, included and that several records that should not be included are, in fact, not included.

Coordinate system roll-out with network administration personnel.

Use of data warehousing systems can bring about some strange spikes in network activity. If you keep network administration people informed of the roll-out schedule, chances are they will monitor network activity for you and be ready to make adjustments to the network as necessary.

When in a bind, ask others who have done the same thing for advice.

People have been building warehouses for years. The Internet opens all sort of possibilities for asking whether someone has solved your problem already. By the way, if you take help from people off the Internet, try giving some of your knowledge back in return.

Be on the lookout for small, but strategic, projects.

Those of us in the IS profession often make the mistake of equating big projects with important projects. By big, I mean big in terms of time and effort required to complete and big in the amount of data stored. However, I have seen many highly valued "strategic" systems that have had quite humble beginnings. On the other hand, I have heard about many of the "galactic" warehouses costing millions of dollars that have failed.

Market and sell your data warehousing systems.

For the most part, use of data warehousing systems is optional. This means you have to identify the potential users of the systems, help them understand what are the benefits of the system, and then make them want to keep coming back to use the system.

From [GREE97]. Used by permission.

A data warehouse is, in a sense, always a prototype. It will keep evolving and expanding. However, it is important to make sure that the version first rolled out for widespread scrutiny provides real value to its users.

12. *Be ready to train the users, to support them and the system* for a long time to come. As they use the system, they will ask for more features, more analysis, and more data. Be ready to supply them.

> ## . . . And Another's
>
> Before planning a data warehouse or data mart, here are five things you should check off:
>
> ✓ A business sponsor—an IT customer who wants better information in a better form and who will provide experts to help you build a DW/DM.
> ✓ If your sponsor wants a DW/DM because of production problems, solve those problems where they exist. Warehouses can fail when they are conceived as work-arounds for deficiencies in the production system.
> ✓ A business case for the DW/DM—it shouldn't be funded by IT. Enthusiastic use by business people for good business reasons is the only justifiable metric.
> ✓ A good sense of the types of data your sponsor needs: type of data is what's important, not appearance. With good source data, you can format and deliver it anywhere. But you can't mine for gold in a sandbox and find anything but sand, no matter how good your mining tools are.
> ✓ An IS/IT commitment to permanently operate a different animal—a warehouse. It's not a production application. It has different users, operations and help requirements. Most importantly it has different growth characteristics—double or triple the number of users and usage within the first year is common.
>
> _____
>
> *From* [CLAR98]. Used by permission.

The power of any tool affects its complexity. One cannot pilot a Boeing 777 with the user interface of a tricycle, though Boeing 777s can be made more or less difficult to pilot. Well-designed screens will keep the need for technical training to a minimum, but they can never reduce it to zero. The technical sophistication of your user community will affect the design of your data warehouse.

SUMMARY

A data warehousing project, like any other project, proceeds through the stages of concept definition, feasibility study, system analysis, system design, development (programming and/or systems integration), testing, implementation (rollout and conversion) and ongoing maintenance, enhancement, and user support. These are not much different for data warehousing projects than for other types of information system development projects you may have studied.

Planning a data warehousing project should begin by justifying it. Information systems are justified on the basis of tangible and intangible benefits. Tangible benefits, such as saving the salary of another market analyst who would otherwise have to be hired, can be assigned a financial value, which can be compared with project costs. Intangible benefits, such as facilitating rapid response to competitive actions, cannot be assigned such a value but are also expected to benefit the firm in some way.

As a data warehousing project is being planned, it is important to obtain user support and to overcome potential resistance to the project. This support must be maintained for the duration of the project, until the data warehouse is in regular use and well accepted by its users.

Another part of planning a data warehousing project is developing a detailed plan for it. This plan must include descriptions of all the activities that will take place during the project. Each activity must be described in terms of what it is, what it will deliver on its completion, what other activities must be complete before it can start, how long it will take, and what resources it will require. Project managers use a variety of tools, including budgets, schedule bar charts (Gantt charts), and activity network charts (CPM and PERT charts) to manage activities and resources.

A data warehouse project can be approached on a data-driven or application-driven basis. In the data-driven approach, the data sources are built up, one by one. The data warehouse database contains, at any moment, just those data sources that have been brought into it thus far. In the application-driven approach, a sequence of data warehouse applications is defined and sources are brought in to support them. This requires more work before there is a usable data warehouse capability, but tends to provide capabilities that are more meaningful to data warehouse users.

Defining the architecture of a data warehouse is an important early stage in the project. The architecture of the data warehouse database is the most important part of the overall data warehouse architecture. This architecture must specify the sources of all data in the data warehouse, the atomic data which the data warehouse database will contain, the summary data it will contain, and the metadata that the data warehouse will use. The analysis architecture, which defines how the data warehouse will appear to its users, is less critical though never unimportant.

Several hardware approaches can be taken to a data warehouse. Most data warehouses use some variation of client/server computing. The server can be the existing mainframe system, usually shared with other applications; a specialized database processor; or a dedicated server of the "supermicro" variety—often with multiple central processing units for increased power. Another option is to deliver data warehouse data over the World Wide Web, with users accessing the data warehouse through their accustomed browser software. The choice among these approaches depends on the needs of the organization and the nature of its data warehouse.

Those responsible for a data warehousing project can take several steps to increase the likelihood of its success. These steps include making sure that one or more executive sponsors and the user community are supportive of the project; that their needs are well understood; that everyone shares a common vision of what to expect from the project; that the resources to support the project are in place; that the data, communication and analysis requirements of the data warehouse are well understood; that suitable software packages are chosen; that a prototype has been developed and shown to users to make sure the project is proceeding in the direction they expected; and that training and support are provided as needed.

KEY TERMS

application-driven approach (to data warehouse development)
architecture
atomic data
budget
concept definition
conversion
CPM chart
critical path
data-driven approach (to data warehouse development)
database processor
deliverable
development
enhancement
feasibility study
Gantt chart
implementation
intangible benefits
mainframe computer
maintenance
metadata
operational data
PERT chart
project leader (project manager)
project network chart
project planning
resource
schedule
schedule bar chart
server
sponsor
summary data
support
system analysis
system design
tangible benefits
task (activity)
testing
World Wide Web (as server)

REVIEW QUESTIONS

1. List, and describe briefly, the eight stages of any information systems project.
2. Why is module testing not usually part of the data warehouse testing process? What does the testing consist of instead?

3. What is the difference between a tangible and an intangible benefit? Which type is usually more important in justifying a data warehouse?
4. Give three reasons why user support is important for the developers of a data warehouse.
5. What types of people are most likely to resist a data warehousing project? What can be done to overcome this resistance?
6. What are the three basic elements of a project plan?
7. Describe two types of charts that project managers use.
8. Compare and contrast the data-driven and the application-driven approaches to developing a data warehouse.
9. What are the four types of data that the data warehouse architecture must specify?
10. Give five examples of things a data warehouse developer must know before specifying the analysis architecture of the data warehouse.
11. What is the most popular hardware platform for small to medium data warehouses today? Which two operating systems would it usually use in 1998? (Of course, a given computer wouldn't use both of them at the same time.)
12. What data analysis software would a client system run in the WOLAP environment?
13. What is a sponsor?
14. How can you find Larry Greenfield's complete collection of information on data warehousing?

EXERCISES

1. Read the case "MasterCard: Mining the Possibilities," Case 6 in the Appendix. Describe each of the eight stages (page 563) of that project in one brief paragraph. (The case does not give you enough information to describe all eight of them fully. Do the best you can, stating where applicable the information that is not available.)
2. One drawback of the testing strategy described on page 566 is that many of the items being used to verify correct system operation were not designed to be seen directly. For example, the output of cleansing and transformation was designed to be loaded into a data warehouse database, not to be shown to users. How serious a problem do you think this drawback (in general, not just with respect to this specific instance of its occurrence) would be? Why?
3. Consider the Parsaye and Petrie example of the tangible benefits of a data mining project on page 568. At the end of the example it gives five-year net present value figures. Discuss the quality of these figures in terms of the 11 information quality factors you read about in Chapter 3. (Since both NPV figures were obtained in the same way from the same set of assumptions, you need only discuss each information quality factor once. You don't have to discuss each factor once for the situation without data mining and another time for the situation with data mining.)
4. You are proposing, and attempting to justify, a data warehouse for a large public university. One of the key issues it faces is marketing: The better students tend to be drawn to the "name" private universities in the region and often do not investigate the quality of education that is available at the public institution. To help deal with this, the admissions office of the public university hopes to do longitudinal studies of its market. This would involve following applicants over time to try to characterize where they come from, which of them tend to be accepted, which of the accepted students tend to enter, and which of the entering students tend to graduate.

A data warehouse to support these analyses would combine information from existing admissions office files (which follow students from their initial information requests through entrance) and registrar's files (which follow students from entrance through graduation or withdrawal). It has been suggested that alumni files could be used as well, to provide career information on graduates.

Give three intangible benefits of this data warehouse. Be as specific as possible.

5. A development project consists of tasks A through K below. Each line also lists the tasks that must be completed before the given task can begin, and the time each task is expected to take. The project is complete when task K is done.

Task	Must Follow	Weeks
A	—	1
B	A	2
C	B	3
D	C	1
E	A	2
F	C, E	3
G	E	1
H	F	2
I	G	3
J	D, F	1
K	H, I, J	2

a. Draw a network chart for this project.

b. What is the minimum project completion time, assuming sufficient resources to perform all possible tasks in parallel? What is the critical path?

c. You have two people to work on this project. Their skills are interchangeable, so either can perform any of the tasks. Draw a Gantt chart for this situation. How long will the project take under these conditions?

6. Search the Web for material making a case that mainframes or database processors are good platforms for data warehouses. (Expect the person or firm putting this material on the Web to have an economic interest in the subject.) These pages will, in all likelihood, characterize the types of data warehouses for which they recommend such platforms. They may do this directly, by saying in effect, "This product is good for data warehouses that are X, Y, and Z," or indirectly, by giving examples of data warehouses for which they are well suited and letting the reader infer the common threads. What patterns did you find? What do you feel, based on this research, are the characteristics of data warehouses for which they would recommend such products?

7. Kelly does not use the terms *top-down* or *bottom-up* in describing the datadriven and application-driven data warehouse development approaches [KELL94]. Is their use here based more on the way they are used in a strategic business planning context or the way they are used in a software development context?

8. One of Larry Greenfield's suggestions for ensuring a successful data warehousing project is, "Establish that maintaining data quality will be an ONGOING joint user/ builder responsibility." Revisit the list of 11 information quality factors in Chapter 3. Put each information quality factor into one of four categories:

a. Does not apply to data warehouses in general.

b. Primarily the user's responsibility.

c. Primarily the builder's responsibility.

d. True joint responsibility. Both groups have a significant part of the job.

(Note that information quality overall is a joint responsibility even if you don't have any *d*s in your list, as long as there are both *b*s and *c*s in it.)

REFERENCES

Many of the books listed as general references at the end of Chapter 12 discuss data warehouse databases in detail. Those references are not repeated here. If a book cited in this chapter is not in the list that follows, you can find it there.

BLOC81   Block, Peter. *Flawless Consulting: A Guide to Getting Your Expertise Used.* University Associates, San Diego, Calif. (1981).

BURK91   Burkan, Wayne C. *Executive Information Systems: From Proposal Through Implementation.* Van Nostrand Reinhold, New York (1991).

CLAR98   Clark, Gary. "Before You Plan Your DW or DM." *DM Review* 8, no. 1 (January 1998), p. 20.

CRAN98   Cranford, Stephen. "Measuring, Managing and Retaining ROI." *DM Review* 8, no. 1 (January 1998), p. 16.

GRAH96   Graham, Stephen. "The Foundations of Wisdom: A Study of the Financial Impact of Data Warehousing." International Data Corporation, Ltd., Toronto, Ontario (1996).

GREE97   Greenfield, Larry. "Actions for Data Warehouse Success." (July 5, 1999). Available on-line: http://pwp.starnetinc.com/larryg/success.html

GRIF98   Griffin, Jane. "Staffing the Warehouse Project." *DM Review* 8, no. 1 (January 1998), p. 14.

KELL94   Kelly, Sean. *Data Warehousing: The Route to Mass Customization.* Wiley, Chichester, England (1994).

PARS98   Parsaye, Kamran, and David Petrie. "Measuring the Value of Mined Information." *DM Review* 8, no. 3 (March 1998), p. 44.

POE96   Poe, Vidette. *Building a Data Warehouse for Decision Support.* Prentice-Hall, Upper Saddle River, N.J. (1996).

ROCK79   Rockart, John F. "Chief Executives Define Their Own Data Needs." *Harvard Business Review* 57, no. 2 (March–April 1979), pp. 81–93.

ROCK88   Rockart, John F., and David W. De Long. *Executive Support Systems,* Dow Jones-Irwin, Homewood, Ill. (1988).

CASE

Fort Lowell Trading Company
Planning for Jim's Data Warehouse

Miguel and Elizabeth returned to visit Jim Atcitty a few weeks after they had discussed his data warehouse concepts.[6] He greeted them in the now-familiar lobby and escorted them to his office in the MIS area. Jim opened the conversation as soon as the three were seated. "You said you were looking for an update on what's been happening with the data warehousing project."

---

[6]See the episodes in Chapters 12 and 13 for this discussion.

"That's right, Jim," agreed Elizabeth. "It's getting toward the end of the term and we didn't want to leave without finding out where it was heading."

"Well, it's been a real education for me so far. I've been talking to vendors and reading as much as I can about what really happens when you try to build a data warehouse. Picked up a couple of books at the Barnes and Noble store on Oracle— you know, the big one just past Tohono Chul Park. I've found half a dozen Web sites on data warehousing, got a subscription to *DM Review,* and I gobble up *Computerworld*'s data warehousing section every week. I think it's about time to stop the book-learning and start to really do something!"

"So," asked Miguel, "is that your plan now? To really do something?"

"Before we actually do anything," Jim continued, "I have to come up with some cost and schedule estimates so that the folks with the budget can OK them. I'll also have to get a handle on what kinds of programmers we'll need, and for how long, so Dottie Eastman can put them on the project or we can go out and bring in some free-lancers."

"Do you think you'll have any trouble getting the OK?" asked Elizabeth.

"I'm not really worried about getting the resources to build something," Jim said. "Hosteen[7] Niels can sign off on that much. What concerns me more is, will anybody use it after it's built? Is there any real interest in this thing, or is it just an academic exercise? Nothing against academics," he hastened to add as he remembered that Elizabeth and Miguel were college students, "but you've both spent enough time around here to know that we have to make money."

"Well," reflected Miguel, "the last time we were here you sketched out a database design for us.[8] How many other people, besides yourself, Niels, and the two of us, have seen that sketch?"

"Quite a few, actually," Jim replied. "You know that I'm basically a market planner. So I know all the folks in the market planning department real well. I've talked to them about this project and the kinds of things we'd put in the data warehouse database. They all seem to think it's a great idea. They know we've needed something like it for a long time, that our competition is catching on to this techology, and we have to do it soon."

"How about folks outside the market planning group?" Miguel continued. "Have any of them been involved yet?"

"Not yet. Our first data warehouse will be pretty much just for market planning. We'll go out and get the data we need for that but not what we might need for other things. Once we get that one up and running, we'll think about what we can add to it that would make it useful for other people as well. We'll see what information they need to do their jobs. Then we can see what other data sources we'd have to plug in, or what other data we'd have to pull in from the sources we're already using, to give them what they need."

---

[7]A Navajo term of affectionate respect for an elder, literally meaning "grandfather."
[8]This visit is described in the Chapter 13 episode.

EXERCISES

1. Did Jim start talking to potential users of his data warehouse too early, too late, or at about the right time? Why do you think this way? What else should he do, if anything, to make sure he has user support for the project? (If you haven't already done so, read the FLTC case episode in Chapter 13 before you answer the last part of this question.)
2. In terms of Sean Kelly's two approaches to building a data warehouse—data-driven and application-driven (see page 576), which is Jim Atcitty using? Justify your answer.
3. Is Niels Agger a suitable executive sponsor for this data warehousing project? Why or why not?
4. Do you agree with Jim's assessment that he's done enough learning and it's time "to really do something"? Can you think of any sources of information he should use before "doing something," but (based on what he said here) he hasn't used yet?

SUMMARY

CHAPTER 16

Pulling It All Together: Systems Integration and the Future of DSS

CHAPTER OUTLINE

Introduction

In Chapter 1 you read many fine words about why DSS and data warehouses are useful. At that time you had to take this on faith. By now, however, you should have reason to know why this is so. You have seen how, in terms of technology and its relationship to human behavior, they benefit many types of organizations. And you have seen, in both real-world and the fictional but realistic FLTC case, how these benefits come to pass.

You now understand several related types of systems: traditional decision support systems, expert systems, group decision support systems, executive information (or support) systems, and data warehouses. Each type is useful by itself. Indeed, most real-world systems of all three types are built as separate projects. Yet organizations reap the greatest benefits from this sort of management support software when they are pulled together into a unified whole. This is the point of systems integration: pulling different systems, or parts of different systems, together to create a whole which is greater, in its value to the sponsoring organization, than the sum of its parts. While systems integration can be of value in many areas, not just in DSS, we'll focus on its use in a DSS context. We'll finish this chapter, and this book, with a few thoughts on where DSS is likely to go as you set out on your professional career in information systems.

CHAPTER OBJECTIVES

After you have read and studied this chapter, you will be able to:

1. Show how decision support systems, group decision support systems, expert systems, executive information system (or support) systems, and data warehousing systems relate to each other.
2. Describe a management support system and how it relates to the other types of systems.
3. Explain what systems integration is and why it is important, both to users and to decision support system specialists.
4. Compare and contrast the different types of systems integration.
5. Discuss current trends in systems integration, including the reasons users increasingly turn to outside systems integration firms.
6. Consider appropriate factors in selecting a systems integration firm.
7. Discuss some ways in which DSS are likely to evolve over the next several years.

16.1 COMBINING THE PIECES

In the late 1960s, as the cost of acceptably large magnetic disk drives dropped and immediate access to a database became practical, many information systems practitioners had a dream: the **Management Information System (MIS).** The MIS would provide managers with instant, up-to-date information on any business-related subject, processed and digested to their precise requirements. Truly, this would be the corporation of the late twentieth century.

Things didn't work out that way. Many organizations invested vast sums in pursuit of this dream. They often found themselves, as a result, with better access to more information than they previously had. But the payoff was less than they had hoped. The only remnant of the MIS concept today is the term: it is a common name for our field of study and, in many organizations, the title of the information processing group.

As we begin the twenty-first century, the technological capabilities that were to have gone into this MIS exist. We have access to data across a network. We can purchase a terabyte of storage for less than what a gigabyte cost then. We have easy-to-use financial modeling packages. We have graphs on demand, in our choice of formats and colors. What we do not have, as a single unified entity, is the MIS as a unit. Many experts believe that we never will, at least not with currently foreseeable approaches to computing. Yet we are now in the position of being able to create much of it, part of which we might now call a data warehouse: not by installing a standard package, or by developing a single, monolithic "megasystem," but by integrating the pieces we have, together with commercial application packages, into a single functional whole.

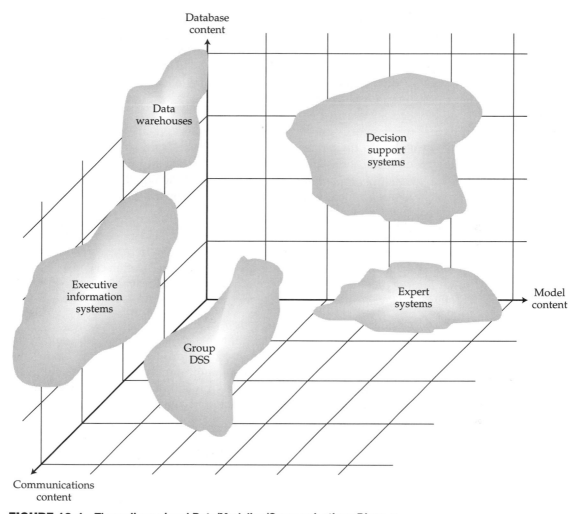

FIGURE 16–1   Three-dimensional Data/Modeling/Communications Diagram

We've discussed several of these pieces in the preceding chapters: decision support systems (DSS), group DSS (GDSS), expert systems (ES), executive information systems (EIS), the database and analysis components of a data warehouse, and variations on these themes. These types of systems all combine three characteristics to varying degrees: data, modeling, and communications. Figure 16–1 attempts, within the constraints of the two-dimensional printed page, to put each type of system in its appropriate place in this three-dimensional space. Note the following about each type:

• Decision support systems in the traditional sense incorporate varying degrees of database and model usage. However, their communications capability is incidental, usually limited to whatever is required in order to access the databases in question.

- Group decision support systems incorporate communications as an essential element. They also often incorporate a model, if only a model of how the group process is supposed to work. Their use of a database, however, is normally limited.
- Executive information systems focus on communications and data. Since their primary purpose is to support unpredictable and unstructured decisions, complex models are usually not found there.
- Expert systems focus on the model aspect: indeed, their essence is the process model built into their rules. Some use databases as a source of facts, others don't. Communications aspects tend to be incidental.
- Data warehouses focus on data with limited modeling. Their communication content is also limited, usually serving only to connect the client on the user's desktop to the server, which holds their database.

The "total MIS" must incorporate aspects of all these. Indeed, it must do more: It must bring them together into a unified whole. Such a system, even if it falls short of the 1960s' Management Information System concept, is often called a **Management Support System (MSS).** There are several good reasons not to call such a system a *Management Information System* or *MIS:*

- The term *MIS* has another meaning today.
- The objectives of an MSS really are different. We are not trying to computerize the world. We are trying specifically to support managers and other knowledge workers in their decision-making and communication tasks.
- The term *MIS,* used in this narrow context, might bring back memories of unfulfilled promises and thus turn people against a new, fully achievable, system.

A full management support system should include

- Access to internal databases reflecting the financial, marketing, production, R&D project, and so on, status of the organization.
- Access to external databases containing economic data, technology information, and the text of key business and industry publications.
- An easy-to-use interface by which any of these can be queried.
- Analytical capabilities to perform statistical and other analyses of the data so retrieved and to display it in tabular or graphical form.
- Modeling capabilities to help make decisions on the basis of these data.
- Communication capabilities to discuss and share this information with other managers in the organization.

The professional discipline that pulls elements of an information system together into a whole is called *systems integration (SI)*. We now discuss its impact on DSS. One note of caution: while the discussion of systems integration focuses on technical issues, the overall need to consider nontechnical ones during implementation never disappears! Refer back to Chapters 7 and 15 if you wish to refresh your memory on this point.

16.2 WHAT IS SYSTEMS INTEGRATION?

A decision support application is seldom useful in a vacuum. Some DSS, usually of the model-oriented sort, receive all their inputs directly from human users via a keyboard and return their outputs to humans via a printer or display screen. Those are, however, the exceptions. It is more common for a DSS to communicate in some fashion with other applications or computer systems: not necessarily to the exclusion of interaction with human users, but at least to supplement it. A data warehouse, for example, could not possibly exist without its data sources.

The ability of different applications or computer systems to communicate meaningfully with each other is not, unfortunately, automatic. Each subsystem, each part of the overall system, must be designed to provide the outputs that other subsystems need and/or to accept inputs that other systems can provide. Once this is done, technical issues of data representation, file structure, and database organization must be resolved. (The issues that arise in data transformation for a data warehouse, which you read about in Chapter 13, are a subset of the total problem.) Issues of data communication and networking must also be dealt with if, as is often the case, parts of the overall system reside on different computers. At a higher level, issues relating to the partitioning of an application across systems must be considered early in the application design stages.

Systems integration (SI) is the design and development of information systems that combine several hardware and/or software components to cooperate to carry out a joint task that would be beyond the capabilities of any one of them individually. This definition has a few points worth noting. First, SI is a *process.* It is an activity that takes place over a period of time. It is not a one-time event.

Second, SI can involve hardware, software, or both:

- At the software level, SI can mean enabling several software packages to cooperate on one computer.
- At the combined hardware/software level, SI can mean assigning one part of a task to one program on one computer and another part to another program on another computer. A DSS might obtain data from a mainframe database and manipulate it on a microcomputer. An organization could create a client/server application from components that may or may not have originally been designed to function in that mode. Combined hardware/software integration, usually involving data communication, is what most people think of when they use the term *SI.*
- At the hardware-only level, a user organization could buy a package that comes in parts intended to run on different, networked computers. Many packages designed for client/server operation work that way. The user doesn't have to integrate the software. The vendor has already done that. The user is still, however, responsible for creating the necessary communication link between the server(s) and clients.

Third, the statement "beyond the capabilities . . ." doesn't mean that the task must be beyond the capabilities of a single hardware or software component in principle. It might be possible, in theory, to design a single component to do the entire job. In the SI case, however, we didn't. We chose to combine several components. Doing that *is* SI. Whether or not another approach could have worked in principle—or might even have worked better in practice—is beside the point. It's like driving a car to visit your next-door neighbor. If you choose to drive a car, you're driving a car. Whether or not driving was the best way to go next door is a separate issue.

A similar definition comes from the Association of DAta Processing Service Organizations (ADAPSO). It defines SI as "the process of identifying and bringing together various technologies in order to define and deliver a complete information system that will fulfill specific design, operational, and/or management objectives."

16.3 A SYSTEMS INTEGRATION EXAMPLE

Consider a supermarket chain with electronic cash registers that read UPC bar codes on package labels. The cash registers look up product prices in files kept at a store controller. This is a high-speed microcomputer connected to all the cash registers. The store controller also collects data on each product's sales for inventory management and for management analysis.

Buyers and managers at chain headquarters must know how well each product is selling in order to plan orders from their suppliers. They can do this with a data warehouse that looks at recent sales trends. The data warehouse must also have information on prior years' sales, because many products' sales follow seasonal trends or depend on holidays. (A buyer who tried to predict U.S. sales of cranberry sauce in the last half of November by extrapolating from September and October would be in for a big surprise.)[1] It must also accept user input about planned sales and other promotional activities.

It is quite impractical for this data warehouse to use an in-store controller as its server. For one thing, that computer doesn't have the capacity; for another, it's in the wrong place; for a third, it doesn't have access to all stores' data; and finally, its software environment was not designed to support user applications. It is equally impractical to take a system that would be a good data warehouse server— most likely, a stand-alone system or part of the mainframe at corporate HQ—and expect it to control cash registers. Hence we need a network to connect the data warehouse server to the stores. We must also make sure our data warehouse can understand the data transmission formats used by the store controller.

A "low-tech" approach to accomplishing this end would be to obtain sales data printouts in every store, ship them to headquarters, and then key them into the data

---

[1]If you're not from the United States, the Thanksgiving holiday falls on the fourth Thursday in November. It is traditionally celebrated with a meal that includes cranberry sauce. More cranberry sauce is sold just before this holiday than during the entire rest of the year.

warehouse system. This would be labor intensive, time consuming, and error prone to the point of absurdity. It is not surprising, then, that before integrated DSS, supermarket managers made most of their own ordering decisions. They were often "helped" in this regard by "friendly" supplier representatives. Each of these representatives would suggest that ordering more of his or her product would be a good idea. No wonder that decisions were often not optimal. One store in a chain might have had a sale to get rid of surplus goods while another store, two towns away, was out of stock on the same item.

A modern supermarket chain would take a systems integration approach to this project. They would start with the existing store systems. These systems probably have some flexibility in configuring their data communication capability but are otherwise fixed. Along the lines of the recommendations for successful data warehousing projects in Chapter 15, they would also determine what the people at headquarters require of their data warehouse. This step of the project would tell them what has to be in its database. Next, they would choose either an existing database management system or a platform and DBMS to use in building the required new one. The DBMS would be chosen at least in part for its ability to interface with the query and analysis (OLAP) tools that the supermarket chain's managers will need.

The previous paragraph, by the way, glossed over a topic that is often a key issue in data warehouse development, because it does not arise in this particular example. That issue is *data availability*. What the data managers need in order to make decisions may not be available on any of the organization's computers. In that case the data warehouse (or, in general, DSS) developer must first determine whether the data in question—or alternative data, perhaps less ideal, but more easily obtained—can be brought into the system, and, if so, how. Until the developer knows where all the necessary data are coming from, proceeding with system development is a risky activity.

Having determined the end points of their system, store personnel would look for a data communication protocol and file format that are common to both the store controllers and the database environment. Should they fail in this quest, they would reconcile themselves to writing file conversion routines and look for, at least, a common data communication protocol. This search should succeed. Most systems that are candidates for use as data warehouse servers support a wide variety of communication protocols, and the people who develop store controllers know which protocols are popular. The data warehousing team would then be in a position to pull all the pieces together and bring consolidated sales data to decision makers' desks.

16.4 TYPES OF INTEGRATED SYSTEMS

There are, as we hinted in Section 16.2, several possible approaches to developing an integrated system. They differ along three principal dimensions, which we can portray as in Figure 16–2. The three issues that correspond to the three axes of this cube are described in the subsections that follow.

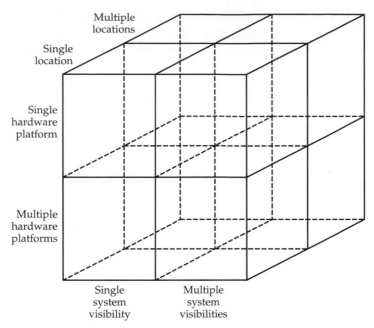

FIGURE 16–2 Integrated Systems Cube

16.4.1 Single System Visibility versus Multiple System Visibilities

Does the system appear to its user as one integrated system or as multiple systems with the ability to transfer data among them? This can determine how easy it is to use a decision support system. As a simple example, consider an integrated spreadsheet package such as Lotus 1-2-3 or Excel. It combines the ability to perform spreadsheet-style calculations with the ability to graph their output. Using such a system is easier than performing calculations in a spreadsheet, then transferring its output to a graphing package. Even if both packages support semi-automated data transfer approaches such as the On-line Linking and Embedding (OLE) of Microsoft Windows or Publish and Subscribe of the Macintosh, the user must still deal with two packages rather than one. This may be worth the effort, if the combination of two packages provides needed capabilities that no one available package supports, but it is still an added effort.

Executive information systems represent a situation where developers typically go to a great deal of trouble to provide single system visibility. EIS commonly allow the executive to access electronic mail, external databases, models, and more, all through a single interface. The trade-off is this: The executive's time is so valuable, that the added development effort needed to reduce his or her learning time is worthwhile. Web-based systems, where the user accesses the entire system via a browser program and has no direct contact with the server that does most of the work, are another example of this.

If the parts of a system are seldom or never used as a unit, creating single-system visibility may be a waste of time. In the supermarket example of Section 16.3, the people who update current selling prices in the store controller are not the ones who make purchase decisions. There is no need to provide the appearance of a single system in this case. The instore system and the data warehouse don't have to look integrated, as long as they can perform the required data transfers. It is often possible, and useful, to have each employee see a single system even if all employees don't see the same system.

16.4.2 One Hardware Platform versus Multiple Hardware Platforms

It is a fact of life that some applications are developed for some hardware architectures, whereas other applications are developed for other architectures. The user who wishes to use data from an existing mainframe database as input to a desktop publishing program on a microcomputer has no choice but to deal with two different platforms. In the supermarket example, using a single platform for both systems might have been a theoretical possibility but was not a practical one.

In other cases, using a single hardware and software platform is a practical option. Most types of software are available for a wide range of hardware platforms. In such situations, putting all parts of a total system on the same type of hardware, running in the same software environment (operating system, DBMS, etc.), will simplify the systems integration task.

The advantages of using compatible hardware may be a factor in package selection. Package A might be best for the job, but package B runs on the existing hardware. Package B will therefore be easier to integrate with other existing applications. We might select it for that reason. Is this a compromise? Yes, but either choice would be a compromise. (Most business decisions are compromises. That's why decision-making methods, such as those you read about in Chapter 2, exist.) The people charged with package selection must weigh the benefits of having the capabilities of package A against the costs of integrating it. These costs may include a delay in making any capabilities available, since package B could perhaps be brought up in a matter of days whereas package A would take weeks or months.

Using a combination of hardware platforms does not necessarily mean losing the benefits of a single, uniform system visibility to the user. Client/server computing allows the client to invoke the assistance of the server as necessary. The user interface is entirely through the client, though much of the application processing may take place on the server.

Client/server integration is common when specialized processors are used to perform a specific part of a complex task. High-performance supercomputers may be the best way to process a complex financial model. Supercomputers are unsuited to giving managers an easy way to access this model, and in any case would not be cost effective in end-user interaction. Integrating a microcomputer or workstation client with a supercomputer server is a way to get the best of both worlds.

Running software written for different architectures usually means using more than one computer, but it doesn't necessarily have to. It is possible for a computer to run programs originally written for a different architecture. This can be done via hardware or software, as follows:

- In the hardware approach, at the microprocessor level, the designer includes all of the necessary microprocessors in the system. This approach was widely used in the early 1980s when many different types of microprocessors were in use and the market hadn't yet determined which would survive. Today, it is usually found in Apple Macintosh computers or UNIX workstations that must also run Windows applications. The secondary processor lets users of such systems run Windows with good performance, giving them access to the wider range of applications available for that environment, without sacrificing the advantages that led them to obtain their system in the first place.
- In the software approach, a simulator program is written for the **host computer** to mimic what the central processor of the **target computer** would do: fetch instructions, analyze them for operation codes and operands, carry out the requested operation, and repeat with the next instruction. This is a slow process. It is practical only when the host computer is fast and there is a strong reason to need software written for a different system. Workstations and Apple Macintosh computers often use this approach to run Windows software today when maximum performance in Windows mode is not mandatory. Their central processing units (CPUs) are fast enough to provide reasonable Windows speed even with the overhead of simulation.
- As a compromise, instructions can be added to a CPU to make the simulation faster. If the instruction set to be simulated is known in advance, a few such added instructions can make a great difference in simulation performance. This approach, called **emulation** [MALL72, MALL75], involves both hardware and software. It is usually used as a transition tool from one generation of computers to the next. Emulation is found primarily in one place in the late 1990s: in Apple Macintosh computers that use the PowerPC microprocessor. Emulation lets them run programs written for the Motorola 68000 series microprocessors used in older models of that line.

None of these approaches is likely to surface as ideal in your next system integration job. Proceed under the assumption that, if software written for different architectures must be run, it will run on different computers. You'll be right more than 99 percent of the time.

16.4.3 One Location versus Multiple Locations

The complexity of system integration is affected by the locations of the systems to be integrated. Communications or networking of any type make the integration job more complex. The more complex the network, the more it increases the complexity of the integration task.

Systems that run on different hardware/software platforms almost always require some form of communication interface. (We discussed some exceptions in the previous section but, as we noted there, these are rare.) Integrating systems via data communications involves the communication protocol and data interchange at the application level.

Communication protocols are becoming standardized, but new ones emerge to handle new requirements and technologies as fast as the older ones turn into widely used standards. This situation did not stabilize in the first half-century of digital communications and is not likely to stabilize in the next. You will almost always be able to find a common local area or wide area protocol that all components of your system support. Difficulties will emerge only if your application is one of those that gives rise to the aforementioned new requirements. If you have to send full-motion digital color video in real time, traditional networking technologies won't do the job. Before committing to a critical corporate application that depends on unproven technologies, look for an alternative way to meet the business need.

Data interchange may be more of a challenge. Sequential text files can usually be sent without much difficulty. You may have to write conversion routines at one or both ends to get data into and out of a useful interchange format and a common character set, especially if you are integrating a mainframe-based application with other computers. Most mainframes use the EBCDIC character set, while most other computers use ASCII.

Even using ASCII does not guarantee compatibility. The ASCII standard specifies only 128 of the 256 bit combinations in a byte: 96 characters and 32 control codes.[2] The other 128 combinations are used differently on different platforms. They may represent accented letters; special characters such as curly quotation marks " " ' ', bullets •, and more; shapes for constructing graphs, or something else. Once one leaves Latin-based alphabets, more conversion is required, though fortunately the central standard-setting bodies of many countries have developed mappings of Greek, Cyrillic, and others into ASCII. Right-to-left alphabets, such as those of the Middle East, pose their own issues. And Asian alphabets such as Chinese or Japanese, with thousands of characters each, require 16 bits per character and are usually best left to specialists.

Even within the set of Latin-based alphabets, matters are not always simple. In some languages, accents are ignored in alphabetization; in others, accented letters are grouped after the nonaccented variety. Some other sequencing issues were discussed in Chapter 3 on page 113.

Graphics, geographic data, voice, and video are far more complex. There are few standards in these areas and none have yet received general support, though the Web is narrowing the options for some common data types such as bit-mapped graphics and video. It is often easiest to process graphical data as completely as possible on its originating platform and transmit it in a "lowest common denominator" format for screen display at the user's desk. (This is how Web browsers work.) In more complex cases, often involving multi-media, consider standardizing on one vendor's products across the board even if they are not ideal for some part of the overall requirement. If this would mean too much of a compromise in application functionality, prepare yourself for a big SI job.

---

[2]A few nonprinting "characters" such as <tab>, <space>, and <return> are in the control code portion of the ASCII character set. The effective number of characters is therefore a bit over 96.

The networking methods used in the World Wide Web are increasingly used as the basis for integrating systems in multiple locations. Users are, as you already know, comfortable with the browser interface. When all the systems being integrated are internal to the same company, the network often takes the form of an **intranet:** an internal corporate network which uses Web protocols but is not open to the Web user community at large. When an intranet is opened to a specific group of users outside the firm, such as suppliers, customers or business partners, it becomes an **extranet.**

16.5 TRENDS IN SYSTEMS INTEGRATION

Systems integration has grown in importance during the 1990s because information systems, and the issues surrounding information system development, are becoming more complex. Much of the reason for this, in turn, involves DSS.

When systems were used solely for transaction processing, a user organization could pick a computer and develop its information systems to run on that computer. Those information systems were not necessarily simple, but at least they were all in one place. With DSS, one often has a transaction processing database in one place and managers who require access to it on another system. DSS, by requiring data gathered in one place for one purpose to be made available in another place for another purpose, has driven the need for SI.

A second reason for the growing importance of SI is the proliferation of incompatible hardware and software throughout most organizations. Rapidly dropping prices have enabled every part of even a modest firm to obtain its own information processing capability. Proper corporate planning can keep this mixture under a semblance of control but has seldom, if ever, been able to prevent it from occurring. (Even if it is under control, a merger or acquisition can come along to upset the carefully planned applecart.)

Other widespread trends are also increasing the need for SI. On-line databases require the integration of data from multiple sources. (The need for on-line databases, in turn, is often driven by decision support requirements. It is hard to imagine a data warehouse without an on-line database derived from multiple sources.) Mission-critical systems that link firms with their suppliers and customers impose integration requirements. Attaching computers to functional devices such as cash registers and production equipment imposes such requirements also. In short, there are several driving forces in the expansion of SI.

SI allows an organization to accomplish information processing tasks that it could not have accomplished, or could not have accomplished cost effectively, otherwise. Because using multiple information sources together provides insights that no single one of them could provide by itself, the whole is worth more than the sum of its parts. The real value of an integrated information system is in bringing the parts together.

The major drawback of SI is equally clear if we think about it. The whole is also more complex than the sum of its parts. To integrate two components, an organization must first be able to use the two parts individually. It must then be able to connect them to each other so they can communicate. Finally, it must then be able to create a connection such that the resulting assemblage presents a single, or at least a consistent, interface to its users.

Major hardware and software vendors have developed architectures that attempt to unify their own products and make it easier to integrate them than to integrate products from multiple vendors. The intent is that a user who wishes to integrate a central computer with several workstations will find it easier to do so with a single vendor's products in these categories than with, say, an IBM mainframe and workstations from Sun Microsystems. On the software side, large vendors such as Oracle hope that its database management users will find it easier to use their data warehousing tools than to integrate another data warehousing vendor's. Most of these architectures embody a degree of openness: Their specifications are published so that other firms can develop conforming applications if they wish. Adopting a vendor's overall architecture, especially where it does not restrict the user to that vendor's products, can simplify many low-level aspects of the systems integration task.

One way or another, with a vendor architecture or the user's own, the user must pay to make all parts of its system work together. There are trade-offs in choosing the way its components will be integrated:

- A user may choose to obtain only compatible systems from the same firm. In this case the user pays via product compromises, since no single firm's offerings are best for every part of almost any large-scale, enterprisewide system. This approach corresponds to a home buyer choosing an existing house from those on the market at the time the choice is made. If they would have preferred a smaller dining room but a larger kitchen, they're out of luck.
- A user organization can perform the system integration task itself. In this case it pays by hiring (or engaging on a contract basis) the necessary specialized professionals, and by devoting management time and energy to supervising their work. This corresponds to a home buyer acting as general contractor and building a house: finding and hiring carpenters, plumbers, electricians, roofers, and so on.
- The third option is for the organization to call in a systems integrator. This corresponds to the home buyer hiring a general contractor to find and supervise the specialized workers. This approach generally involves a larger cash outlay than the previous one, but less time and energy on the part of management.

Systems integration requires skills that the average user organization does not possess—and does not need, at least on a full-time permanent basis. The average user organization therefore also usually does not have managers who understand these skills well enough to supervise them properly. As a result, many user organizations make the third choice and contract with specialized systems integration firms. You may well find yourself working with a systems integration firm as you develop a DSS on the job. In many cases your DSS will be one component of a larger system. Your employer will have engaged the SI firm, with its specialized skills, to develop some of the more complex pieces and to fit them all together.

**LEADING SYSTEMS INTEGRATORS
BY WORLDWIDE INTEGRATION REVENUE (1996)**

Company	SI Revenues
1. Electronic Data Systems	11,000
2. Digital Equipment Corporation	6,200
3. IBM	4,600
4. Andersen Consulting	3,450*
5. Oracle Corporation	2,800
6. Unisys Corporation	1,900
6. Hewlett-Packard Co.	1,900
8. Computer Sciences Corporation	1,300
9. Price Waterhouse	1,200
10. Ernst & Young	1,100
11. Deloitte Touche	967
12. Cap Gemini America	875
13. KPMG Peat Marwick	790
14. Shared Medical Systems	767
15. American Management Systems	733

Note: All figures in millions of U.S. dollars. Figures for some firms include both hardware and software revenue.

---

*Estimate by G2 Research, Inc.

FIGURE 16–3 Largest SI Firms

The preference of user organizations to go outside for specialized skills accounts for the dramatic increase during the 1990s in the number and size of firms offering systems integration services on a contract basis. According to the research firm Dataquest [VIOL98], systems integration was a $97.3 billion market in 1997 and was pegged to grow at 10 percent annually. What's more, these firms were responsible for well over an additional $100 billion of purchases on the part of their customers by recommending that they purchase specific software or hardware. Clearly, SI is big business—and it's getting bigger. The top fifteen systems integration firms according to *Computerworld* are listed in Figure 16–3.

The fifteen firms in Figure 16–3 did $39.6 billion worth of SI work in 1996. Other sources have different estimates: SI is often one of many corporate activities, it can be difficult to isolate from related activities because there is no universally accepted definition of what constitutes SI, and many SI firms do not disclose this breakdown publicly. All observers agree that the figure is large and growing.

Since strategic information systems often involve networking—how else can one communicate among the different parts of a large firm, or between a firm and its customers?—the growth in usage of strategic information systems has contributed to the growth in systems integration. To the extent that DSS are a part of strategic information systems, they, too, bear some responsibility for this phenomenon.

Hiring a Systems Integrator

Information technology executives, as Mark Fischetti reports in [FISC92], offer these guidelines for selecting an outside systems integration firm:

1. Before seeking outside help, define—*on paper*—the business problem you are trying to deal with. "If you can't write it down," writes Fischetti, "no one will be able to solve it."
2. Get ideas from colleagues, from other companies in the same line of work as yours, and by asking in user groups.
3. Get a list of each contender's experience and check references.
4. Test to see which of the contenders best understands your business. Knowing the technology is important, but not as important as handling your kinds of applications. Watch out for those who know the answer before they study the question, who try to sell a preset package.
5. Make sure the candidates are willing to work at your location, with your people. Eventually you will have to maintain the system. Make sure the SI firm is willing to transfer its knowledge to you for this purpose.
6. Try to reach a comfortable level of rapport with the finalists.
7. Draw up a written contract with specific milestones and timetables.
8. Form an integrated team that includes both your firm's employees and those of the systems integrator.

16.6 THE FUTURE OF DSS

We began this chapter with a look back at the management information system pipedream of the late 1960s. As we study decision support systems a third of a century later, we, too, can envisage the information systems world of the future. In some ways it resembles that MIS. In other ways it does not. As this book is being written, it seems likely to evolve in these directions.

DSS capability will become a standard and expected part of information systems. The history of information systems shows that new capabilities are first introduced as separate modules, then incorporated into "regular" applications. You've seen this in graphing. Once, creating graphs from data was the task of separate programs. Since the mid-1980s, people have assumed that their spreadsheet program will be able to handle most day-to-day business graphing needs. As companies develop new applications in the future, decision support needs will increasingly be taken into account when they are planned rather than being added on (more or less well-integrated) after the fact. This will impact the way databases are planned and organized, the way access to a system is controlled, the way an application uses standard interfaces, and the "open systems" approach to computing.

Decision makers will become more computer literate. You are personal evidence of this. It is impossible to graduate from a serious bachelor's or graduate program in management without having used computers and studied information systems. Most programs go beyond this. They incorporate industry databases and management simulation "games" into strategic planning courses, statistical analysis into market research courses, project planning tools into operations management courses, groupware technologies into organizational behavior courses, and Web-based research into almost everything. The managers you work with during your career will have a solid grounding in information technology and what it can do for them. They will increasingly be eager to cooperate in prototyping new applications to support their work.

Hardware technology will continue to evolve. This is not news. Each time "experts" predict that the end of rapid progress is at hand, something comes along to prove them wrong.[3] This will continue. While no one can predict the precise direction in which technology will evolve, we can be sure that its evolution will not stop. You must keep an open mind for new approaches and be willing to try them.

"New" software technologies will enter the mainstream. So-called "new" or "emerging" software technologies such as expert systems, voice recognition, and data mining have already proven their value in commercial use. Their first users were the "pioneers" or "early adopters" who first try any new technology: they gain the most if it succeeds, but lose the resources they put into the attempt if it doesn't. Then the bulk of the remaining organizations of the industrialized world got into line and adopted them.

User interfaces will continue to evolve. The 1990s saw a complete shift away from character-based user interfaces to GUIs. (GUIs were available in the 1980s, but neither the earliest Apple Macintosh products nor Microsoft Windows before release 3 were suitable for serious business use.) These are now being integrated with Web access. Many people, from grade school on up, who have little idea of what a computer is know how to "surf" the Web. Fueled by developments such as network computers, the Web browser interface will provide access to more and more applications.

Virtual reality, which gives the computer user a sense of being "inside" a system that exists only inside a computer, provides many potential advantages in viewing the results of a simulation or the data patterns inside a data warehouse. This technology is becoming easier to use, both for the developer who creates the virtual reality environment and for the user who later enters into it.

Pen-based computing did not take off as quickly as expected in the 1990s but is reality for specialized applications today. It is being rapidly enhanced by several vendors, large and small. Voice interaction is the foreseeable next step.

The job market for information systems professionals with a business perspective will remain strong. The intelligent use of technology has reshaped human enterprises for thousands of years. Farming technology reshaped the lifestyle of our hunter-gatherer ancestors. Printing technology, then telegraph and telephone technology, reshaped communication. Steam technology re-

---

[3]The head of the U.S. patent office in 1897 urged the government to shut that organization down because, as he wrote, "Everything useful has already been invented."

shaped transportation—after which internal combustion technology reshaped it again. Assembly lines reshaped manufacturing. (Today, many firms are reshaping manufacturing again by taking assembly lines out.)

Information systems technology offers more opportunities than any other to redesign business processes to achieve organizational objectives more effectively. There are two reasons for this.

1. The technology that is changing most rapidly always offers the most opportunities. Today, that is information technology.
2. Alone of all the technologies cited previously, only information technology can be applied to every area of every organization. Technologies such as assembly lines were limited in their areas of applicability: Information technology is not.

As a result, people who can harness that technology to the needs of the organization—people who understand both the technology and the business imperatives—will be those who create corporate success and are rewarded for creating it.

16.7 IN CONCLUSION

The 16 chapters you have just completed took you on a journey through the world of decision support systems: from the concepts of decision making, through the ways in which computers can support decision making, through some specific technologies (simulation, expert systems, data warehousing, OLAP, and data mining) that are used for this purpose. In this last chapter you looked at the ways in which the pieces can be put together and some directions in which the field may evolve in the future.

You are now ready to take what you know and put it to use. Your other courses have taught you, or will teach you, about programming languages, database management, and the other technologies that the modern information systems professional must understand. When you combine these with what you now know about DSS you will be able to make a real contribution to your employer's "bottom line."

Good luck!

SUMMARY

Decision support systems are not, by themselves, the answer to management's information systems prayers. They are an important part of the piece, as are executive information systems, expert systems, group DSS, and all the other elements of the corporate information systems picture. For management to obtain the maximum benefit from its investment in information systems, they must be combined into an integrated whole.

That integrated system can be called a management support system. Such an MSS would provide easy-to-use access to internal and external databases, to a variety of useful models, to analysis and display capabilities, and to communications networks.

The process of pulling disparate systems together into such a unified whole is called *systems integration.* Systems integration, or SI, can be done at the hardware level, the software level, or both. The resulting system can appear to its users as one system or as several, can run on one or on multiple hardware platforms, and can be in one location or in multiple locations.

Systems integration calls for the short-term use of skills that many firms do not possess. For that reason, information systems users with a need for SI often call on specialized systems integration firms. Using them does not necessarily represent an added cost to the user, since the user would otherwise have to assemble staff with those skills and also have to supervise their work with often-unfamiliar technologies. Systems integration firms are therefore growing rapidly.

Selecting a systems integration firm, if one is to be used, should be done as carefully as any other major corporate decision is made. The problem must be defined, each contender carefully evaluated, and references checked. The agreement with the SI firm must be based on a mutual understanding of the business problem and a sense of rapport, but must still include a carefully written contract.

Decision support systems will grow in importance in the future, as expansion and standardization of communications and distributed databases make information more easily accessible from the manager's office. New hardware and software technologies will make DSS both easier to develop and easier to use. The information systems professional who works in this area will find himself or herself a valuable, and valued, contributor to organizational success.

KEY TERMS

emulation
extranet
host computer
intranet
management information system (MIS)
management support system (MSS)
systems integration (SI)
target computer

REVIEW QUESTIONS

1. Of the three major components of most management information systems—databases, models, and communications—which do traditional decision support systems emphasize?
2. Which do group decision support systems emphasize? Executive information systems? Data warehouses?
3. What is a management support system?
4. Define systems integration.
5. What does systems integration have to do with MSS?
6. When doesn't it matter if the parts of an integrated system don't "look integrated"?
7. How can you run software, that was originally written for two different computers, on one computer? Give three approaches.

8. How are DSS contributing to the growth in systems integration?
9. What do specialized systems integration firms offer that information systems users find of value?
10. Approximately how large is the total U.S. systems integration market?
11. Will decision support systems continue to be used in the future?
12. Are decision makers becoming more, or less, computer literate? Why?
13. When will computer hardware stop evolving?
14. Can people find work supporting managers by developing decision support systems and data warehouses?

EXERCISES

1. Consider the supermarket systems integration example in Section 16.3. What type of decision(s) is (are) being made here? What type of DSS, in terms of the DSS hierarchy, is this? Is the statement that this DSS "most likely [runs on] a mainframe or large mini at corporate HQ" reasonable? Why or why not?
2. The supermarket example of systems integration in Section 16.3 said this about their approach to developing their data warehouse: ". . . they would also determine what the people at headquarters require of their data warehouse. This step of the project would tell them what has to be in its database." Which of Sean Kelly's two approaches to data warehouse development (see p. 576) does this statement imply?
3. Call the local sales offices of a few computer manufacturers or systems integration firms. (Use Figure 16–3, or a reference service in your college or university library, as a starting point for the names of SI firms.) Obtain their definitions of systems integration. Compare and contrast them with each other and with the two definitions at the start of Section 16.2. What common themes emerge from all their definitions?
4. The SoftWindows (Insignia Solutions Inc., Mountain View, Calif.) and Virtual PC (Connectix Corporation, San Mateo, Calif.) packages run on Macintosh computers. They mimic the behavior of an Intel-architecture microprocessor such as the Pentium and its successors, and of low-level portions of the Windows operating system. They also contain routines to convert file formats from those of one platform to those of the other, so that data can be moved between the two environments. (Similar programs exist for UNIX workstations.) They thus enable Macintosh users to run programs originally written for Windows. Where does this fit into the spectrum of approaches to running programs written for different computers, on page 606? How might you use such a program if you had a Macintosh database and a Windows cross-tabulation program which you wanted to use on the data in that database?
5. Pick a firm with which you are familiar. How could this firm benefit from pen-based computing? From voice recognition? From virtual reality? How could you combine these technologies with its existing information systems? How difficult a job do you feel this would be?

REFERENCES

COMP97 "In Search of Integration Gratification," *Computerworld* (July 28, 1997). Available on line:
http://www.computerworld.com/home/online9697.nsf/all/970812si_index

FISC92 Fischetti, Mark. "Hiring the Right Consultant." *Beyond Computing* (May–June 1992), p. 14.

MALL72 Mallach, Efrem G. "Emulation: A Survey." *Honeywell Computer Journal* 6, no. 4 (April 1972), pp. 287–297. Reprinted in *Advances in Microprogramming,* Efrem G. Mallach and Norman E. Sondak, Eds., Artech House, Dedham, Mass. (1983).

MALL75 Mallach, Efrem G. "Emulator Architecture." *Computer* 8, no. 8 (August 1975), pp. 24–32. Reprinted in *Advances in Microprogramming,* Efrem G. Mallach and Norman E. Sondak, Eds., Artech House, Dedham, Mass. (1983).

VIOL98 Violino, Bob, and Bruce Caldwell. "Analyzing the Integrators." *InformationWeek* (November 16, 1998), p. x.

CASE

Fort Lowell Trading Company
The Project Concludes

The first hint of something unusual was that Dottie Eastman greeted Miguel and Elizabeth in the Fort Lowell Trading Company headquarters lobby when the two arrived on Tuesday afternoon. After the start of the project someone else had usually brought them in. Dottie was always warm and often stopped to chat briefly, but the press of her other duties made it difficult for her to take the time to act as their FLTC escort.

"Surprise!" called out Niels, Ashwin, Vanessa, Chris, Bob, Joe, Leighton, Rob, Kareem, Jim, and the other Fort Lowell Trading Company staff members whom they knew as the two students entered the MIS conference room. The conference room was decorated with "Congratulations" ribbons. The table in the center had been covered with a paper tablecloth. It held a white-frosted cake, with a college graduation cap and diploma in dark blue icing under an excellent rendition of the Sabino Canyon College seal.

"We know it's a few weeks early, but we're not really worried about you two making it," explained Dottie. "Besides, with your project report due next week, you might not be coming back."

"How can you say that? How could we not come back?" asked Elizabeth, astonished. "And just drop everything? We have to see how some of those projects come out!"

"Well, we were hoping you'd say something like that," said Dottie. "Actually"— she paused briefly here—"we were hoping for a bit more. Do you two have jobs yet?"

"Sorry, but I do," answered Elizabeth with evident regret. "I interviewed with several companies that came to campus last semester, before this project started, and I accepted a job right around the beginning of this term. I'm supposed to start their training program in about two months."

"Well, Miguel, how about you?" Dottie followed up.

"You know, Dottie, I had been planning to go to graduate school and get my MBA. I've been accepted at ASU. I think I need more general business education to go with the technical stuff I've been focusing on until now. As soon as I got into Professor Kijewski's business strategy course, I realized that a few more electives in marketing and human behavior might have been at least as useful as the extra programming courses I took. If I get an MBA, I'll have the best of both worlds."

"Have you considered working for a few years and then going back for your MBA?" Dottie persisted.

"Now that you mention it, the MBA program people told me that most of their new students have three or four years of work experience, and that it helps them in the classroom. It might not be a bad idea. Can I get back to you on that next week?"

Cases

CHAPTER OUTLINE

Introduction

To really understand decision support systems, it is important to see real DSS in action. This Appendix will give you an in-depth look at several such systems. The first few cases relate to decision support systems in general, while the last few focus on data warehouses. As you read these cases, try to apply the principles you learned in the chapters of this book to these real-life decision situations and systems. The review and discussion questions that follow each case will help you do this effectively.

The use of cases that justify the choice of specific vendor products in this chapter, such as Oracle Corp. and Information Advantage in Case 6, is not an endorsement of those vendors at all times and in all situations. The reasons for which the firms in these cases chose those vendors were probably appropriate for their needs and for the state of vendor technologies at the times the decisions were made. Different organizations with different needs, or an evaluation performed when vendors are in different competitive positions, might properly make different choices. You should therefore not assume that the products used in these cases are necessarily the best products, or even suitable products, for you to choose on the job in the future.

CASE I OPTIONS PRICING WITH BLACK-SCHOLES

Most people think of investing in terms of buying a stock, holding it to obtain income from its dividends or selling it when its price has gone up. Some, expecting its price to drop, consider "short selling": selling a stock one doesn't own. Short sellers borrow the stock (usually on paper, through their broker) in order to have something to give the buyer. They expect to return the borrowed stock by buying shares on the market at a lower price later. Yet it is not necessary to buy, or to sell, shares of stock in order to speculate on future price changes. One can also buy *options:* the right to buy or sell shares of stock at a stated price until some stated future date.

Suppose you think the shares of Thompson's Trousers and Pizza (TT&P), now selling at $40 per share, will go up. You could buy 100 shares for $4,000—plus the broker's commission, which we'll ignore from here on. If you're right and the stock rises to $50 per share, you've made $1,000: 25 percent of your investment. If you're wrong and it drops to $30 per share, you've lost $1,000, again 25 percent.

Now suppose I own 100 shares of TT&P, and I *don't* think their price will rise. I could make a deal with you: You pay me $100 now, and I'll promise to sell you my shares at the current $40 price at any time you ask during the next 30 days. If they do go to $50, you make $900: the $1,000 increase in the price of the stock, less the $100 you paid me. That's less than you would have made buying the stock, but you only invested $100—not $4,000. Your return on investment has improved from 25 percent to 900 percent! (Had you invested your entire $4,000 and obtained this 900 percent return, your profit would have been $36,000. Of course, to do this you would have had to find someone with 4,000 shares who was willing to make the same deal I offered.) If the stock drops, you let our agreement expire at the end of the month since you can buy TT&P stock for less on the open market. In this case you lose your $100: less than the $1,000 you would have lost, but, percentage-wise, it is your entire investment rather than just 25 percent of it (or some other amount, depending on how far the price dropped). Figure A–1 shows your return on owning this option as a function of stock price changes. You break even if the stock goes to $41, as the $1 price increase multiplied by 100 shares balances the $100 you paid me. Figure A–2 compares the percentage gains or losses for the option and for buying the stock.

From my point of view, if the stock goes up, I lose the chance to sell my 100 shares at $50 per share since I've promised them to you (and, under those circumstances, you would want them). However, I have the $40 price I wanted plus the $100 you paid me, in effect selling my stock for $41 per share. If it goes down, I still own the stock and I also have the $100 you paid me.

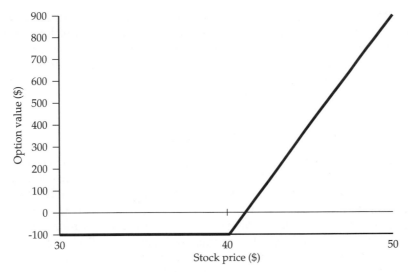

FIGURE A–1   **Return on Investment in a Call**

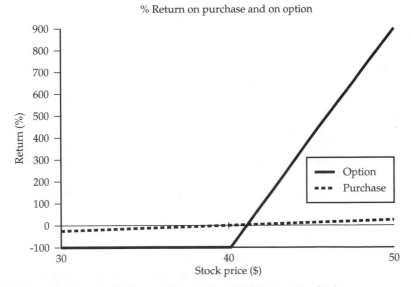

% Return on purchase and on option

FIGURE A–2   **Percentage Gains and Losses for Purchase and for Option**

In options terminology, you have purchased a *call* on my stock. A call is characterized by the type of security (here TT&P common stock), the number of shares (usually 100 shares, which is assumed from here on), the *striking price* (here $40) and the *expiry date* (here 30 days from now, but typically stated as a calendar date). I have *written* the call. A *put* is the opposite: Its writer promises to buy the stock, if asked to, at the striking price until the expiry date. The purchaser of a put typically expects the price to go down. Such a person wants to make money, or to be protected against loss, if that happens.

Investors don't have to find other individual investors who feel differently about a stock in order to buy or sell options. Puts and calls in shares of large firms are traded on major stock exchanges. Their price fluctuates with the price of the underlying security: a $40 call on TT&P stock is worth very little if the stock is now trading at $20, is worth something if it is trading at $40, and is worth at least $2,000 if it is trading at $60. (Be sure you understand why.) The value of a put, conversely, increases as the price of the underlying stock goes down.

An option does not represent any ownership in a corporation and therefore has no inherent value. Its value is transitory and can fluctuate dramatically in a short time. This provides investors with a great deal of *leverage:* They can make large amounts of money with a small investment, or they can lose their entire stake. Trading in investments where huge sums can be made or lost in a short time is not for the faint of heart. Doing it successfully requires both the right mental attitude and careful, objective analysis. Option traders, especially though not only at brokerage firms, use computers widely to support their decisions. They use computers to evaluate the desirability of writing or purchasing various options, or combinations of options, at certain prices. If they can find the right combination of puts and calls, they can often *hedge* one against the other and thus make money at little or no risk.

One approach to using computers is to develop and implement a mathematical model that calculates the price that an option "ought to" have. If it is offered on the market at less than this price, the investor or the firm will consider buying it. If it is being bought on the market at more than this price, they will consider writing it.

The quality of an investor's mathematical model is a key factor in his or her success in options trading. Suppose one investor's model calculates that the TT&P call I am willing to write for $100 is, based on the model, really only worth $80. That investor will not buy my call. If another's model suggests that it is really worth $120—based on what the model predicts, statistically, will happen to the price of TT&P stock over the next 30 days—that investor will buy my call. Both models will be right some of the time, wrong some of the time. In the long run, the set of decisions recommended by one model will turn out to be better than the set recommended by the other. One investor will ride in a chauffeured Rolls-Royce while the other will have to borrow bus fare.

The classical model for evaluating the value of a option is called the Black-Scholes (or Black-Scholes-Merton) model after its developers [BLAC72, BLAC73, also in most finance and investment texts]. Myron Scholes and Robert Merton were awarded the 1997 Nobel Prize for economics for it. (Their third collaborator, Fischer Black, had passed away two years earlier. Nobel Prizes are not awarded posthumously.)

The Black-Scholes model calculates the value of an option from these five factors:

1. The current price of the stock. This is really a convenient calibration factor. We could set it to 1 and normalize all other figures relative to it. Most people find it easier to deal with numbers that have a visible relationship to reality.

2. The striking price of the option.
3. The remaining time until the option expires: The further off the expiry date, the more the price of the stock is likely to fluctuate by then. If $100 is a fair price for a 30-day call on 100 shares of TT&P, a 60-day call is worth more.
4. The volatility of the stock price, expressed as the standard deviation of its annual rate of return. The more volatile a stock price, the more likely that fluctuations will carry it above the striking price. This factor has a great impact on option value and cannot be obtained directly from a stock price table. Estimating it requires good judgment. People who are good at this task can earn large amounts of money.

   The relationship between price fluctuations, as indicated by volatility, and option value is not linear. (This corresponds to Figure A–1 not showing a straight line.) TT&P stock is now trading at $40 per share. Suppose, first, it has an equal chance of trading at $50 or $30 per share in 30 days. Its expected value, the average of these two figures, is still $40. In the first case, a $40 call is worth $1,000 (the $10 price increase times 100 shares in the standard call). In the second case, it is worthless. The expected value of the call is therefore the average of $1,000 and $0, or $500. Now, suppose it is more volatile and has an equal chance of trading at $60 or $20 per share in 30 days. The expected value of the stock is still $40. However, the call is worth $2,000 in the first case, and is still worthless in the second. The expected value of the call has increased to $1,000. Calls on volatile stocks are therefore worth more than calls on comparable, but less volatile, stocks.
5. The current risk-free interest rate the investor can obtain, usually taken as the interest rate on government securities which mature at about the same time that the option expires. The higher this rate, the more valuable a call that lets the investor postpone paying the full price of the stock until the call is exercised. Given a high enough interest rate, a call can be worth something for this time factor alone even if the price of the underlying stock does not change by a penny.

The Black-Scholes formula for the value of a call is:

$$C = S_0 N(d_1) - \frac{E}{e^{rt}} N(d_2)$$

where

$$d_1 = \frac{1n\left(\frac{S_0}{E}\right) + \left(r + \frac{\sigma^2}{2}\right)t}{\sigma\sqrt{t}}$$

$$d_2 = \frac{1n\left(\frac{S_0}{E}\right) + \left(r + \frac{\sigma^2}{2}\right)t}{\sigma\sqrt{t}}$$

and the elements are defined as

C = value given by the model for a call option

r = riskless interest rate

S_0 = current price of the underlying stock

E = exercise (striking) price of the call

t = time to expiry, as a fraction of a year

σ = volatility, as standard deviation of the annual rate of return

ln = natural (base e) logarithm

e = 2.71728 . . ., the base of natural logarithms

$N(x)$ = the value of the cumulative normal distribution at x. This starts at 0 for large negative values of x, equals 0.5 for $x = 0$, and converges toward 1 for large positive values of x.

These formulas look forbidding. Fortunately for individual investors, they are pre-programmed into many investment planning packages. Investment analysts use models such as Black-Scholes in several ways:

1. *Directly, to calculate the value of an option.* This involves, as we mentioned, the difficult task of determining the stock's volatility. It can be approximated by calculating the stock's rate of return for each week in the past year and finding the standard deviation of these values, but that is at best an imperfect process. Once the value of an option has been calculated, the investor can decide to purchase, sell, or write an option by comparing its market price with the output of the model.

2. *In reverse, to solve for the volatility:* What volatility makes the current market price of an option precisely correct? The investor can then decide whether he or she thinks the stock's actual volatility is above or below this figure. It is often easier to make this judgment than to choose a volatility figure in the abstract. If an investor feels that a stock is more volatile than its current option price implies, then the option is worth more than its market value and should be bought.

3. *To compare the wide range of options that are traded in the stock of many large corporations.* These vary in their striking prices (typically every $5 or $10, depending on the price of the stock, in a range on either side of its current price) and expiry dates (typically at one-month intervals, about three months into the future). The Black-Scholes model can determine the volatility implied by the current market price of each option. An investment analyst can see if any of the options is priced inconsistently with the others. If one option's price implies higher volatility than the others, that option is (according to the theory) over-priced and should be sold. An option whose price implies a lower volatility than the others should similarly be bought.

In effect, the option trader is looking at the surface represented by options having different striking prices and expiration dates. In a perfect market these should form a smooth surface. Because of market imperfections there will often be an anomaly—a "bump" or a "dip"—in this surface. Figure A–3 shows such a bump, with the price

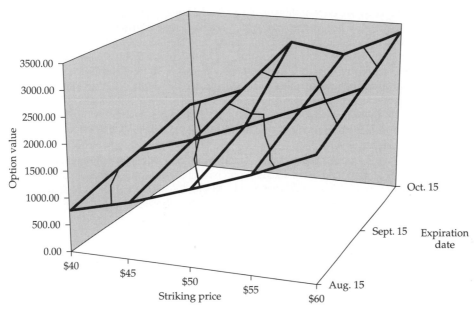

FIGURE A–3 **Option Price Surface with Bump**

for the October 15 option at $50 higher than the prices of the other options around it suggest it should be. The first person to notice this bump can sell that option. If this trader simultaneously buys options on either side of it (in this case, probably half that amount each of October 15 options at $45 and $55) there will be a nearly certain profit in the set of three transactions. However, the act of selling the option that is priced too high will lower its price. This puts a premium on being the first to notice it and to act on that information.

Black-Scholes is not the ultimate in option-pricing methods. For one thing, it treats stock motion as a random variable: It does not take into account whether the underlying factors favor an increase or decrease in the price of a particular stock. For another, it assumes that the risk-free interest rate is fixed until the option expires. Large investment firms start with Black-Scholes but move beyond it. The specifics of their most advanced models are closely guarded secrets. (You can read about one example in [CLIF92].) The "rocket scientists" who develop these models are among these firms' most highly prized, and most highly compensated, employees.

Questions

1. Consider the Black-Scholes model.
  a. Are the decisions it helps with structured, semistructured, or unstructured?
  b. Are they individual, group, or multi-individual decisions?
  c. Where would you put a Black-Scholes–based DSS in Alter's hierarchy?
  d. What are the benefits of a DSS that incorporates this model?
2. What database, if any, would be helpful to such a DSS that used the Black-Scholes model to support an investor? How would the DSS use it?

3. What type of hardware do you think is most appropriate for such a DSS?

4. You work in the MIS department of a Wall Street investment firm whose analysts use Black-Scholes or comparable models to evaluate and compare several call options. The options evaluated by one analyst at one time typically cover 10 firms whose current stock prices range from $20 to $120 per share. Options are traded at four to six striking prices per firm, at three expiry dates per striking price, for a total of 12 to 18 traded calls per firm or about 150 overall. Design a graphical screen display to convey as much important information as possible with a minimum of clutter. Use color if you think it can help, but in that case state how your system would support analysts whose color vision is impaired.

5. The Black-Scholes model uses a mathematical formula to calculate option values. Its ultimate purpose is to help users decide if purchasing a given option on the market is likely to yield a profit. One could also use the Monte Carlo method to simulate a large number of randomly chosen stock price fluctuation possibilities and make the same decision on that basis. Describe how that might work.

CASE 2 TRUCK BRAKE BALANCING

This case is summarized from [SMIT91].

Brake balancing is the art of adjusting the components of a truck's air brake system so they operate in unison with each contributing its share of the effort required to stop the truck. An unbalanced brake system causes the truck to handle poorly in emergencies and can cause other components of the vehicle to fail sooner than they otherwise would—often without indicating the root cause of their failure.

The importance of proper brake balancing grew dramatically during the years after the fuel crisis of the 1970s.[1] Trucks became more streamlined, reducing the braking effect of aerodynamic drag. Engine downsizing reduced its value in braking as well. Therefore, more and more of the stopping job was left for a truck's brakes.

An eighteen-wheeler truck has five axles, three on the tractor and two on the trailer (see Figure A–4). Each has brake pads, which come in a range of sizes with a range of friction coefficients. The brake balancer must determine the proper values for both of these for each axle. The balancer must also consider air compressors, the length of the air lines, the number and type of hose fittings, and relay valve activation values. Further complicating the process is that tractors and trailers do not stay together, but are exchanged frequently within a fleet. Balancing must therefore be performed on the fleet as a whole, or a tractor and trailer—each individually balanced—may be seriously out of balance when coupled together.

In 1988–89, Eaton Corporation, a major manufacturer of truck brake components, developed a computer-based system to determine the balancing parameters

---

[1]While the 1970s may be ancient history to most readers of this book, large trucks had been a stable technology for the preceding two decades. Individual components changed significantly, but overall truck design parameters and trade-offs did not.

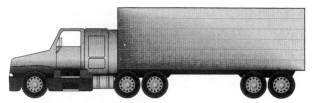

FIGURE A–4 Schematic of 18-Wheeler Truck

for truck brake systems. This system was innovative in its use of two types of AI technology: neural networks and expert systems. It works in three stages:

1. A knowledge-based preprocessor performs a preliminary checking function. It records data observed by the brake-balance technician regarding the manufacturer of the installed components, their sizes, and their condition. It then uses preliminary test results to verify that the tractor and trailer are individually balanced. There is no point in proceeding with the overall truck balancing process if this condition is not met.

2. Neural networks input graphs of brake pressure or temperature versus time and determine if each graph is "good" or "bad." A typical graph plots brake pressure over time when the brakes are applied. There are six lines on this graph, one for each axle and one for the truck pressure control line. Classification factors include both the overall shape of the curves and how well they match each other.

3. A knowledge-based diagnostic system accepts data from the preprocessor knowledge base, from the neural networks, and from a model of a truck. It produces recommendations for adjusting the components of the brake system together with explanations of the reasoning behind those recommendations. A typical explanation is

> The mismatched coefficients of the brake pads, combined with the oversized brakes and generally slow reaction of the brake system, will tend to cause the trailer brakes to do more work than the tractor brakes, creating excessive operating temperatures. In addition to wearing the brake pads prematurely, the brakes will quickly go out of adjustment, exaggerating the problem of a tardy brake system.

The knowledge-based components of the system were written using the LISP language and the KEE shell from IntelliCorp. They store data in frames.[2] Slots are inherited statically from parent to child, e.g., from trailer to axle. Values can be inherited dynamically in the other direction, from child to parent: once relay valve actuation values for both trailer axles are determined, a value for the trailer itself can be. Both knowledge-based subsystems together include a total of 120 methods

---

[2]A *frame* is a structured storage area in an expert system's workspace containing information about a given business object, such as a truck in this case. A *slot* is a place in a frame where a single data item is stored. The *inheritance* feature, which you may have also studied in the context of object-oriented programming, allows frames that describe related business objects to share slot definitions and data values in predetermined ways.

(procedures associated with frame slots, which can behave like rules) and 40 free-standing rules not part of any frame. They use both forward and backward chaining where appropriate.

Neural networks were used for graph analysis because they can recognize patterns better than knowledge-based systems.[3] The five neural nets were built with the Anza Plus board from HNC and its supporting software. (This board fits into an option slot of a workstation or microcomputer.) They use either three or four layers of neurons: an input layer, an output layer, and one or two hidden layers. The most complex network uses 11 neurons on each of two hidden layers and required a total of 50,000 iterations to converge to its final state with a training set of 129 example graphs. The simplest used three to five neurons on their single inner layer and converged after 1,000 iterations. Each of these networks is approximately 90 percent accurate in its classification of graphs: far better than either of two alternative approaches, a set of linear classifiers and a set of rules based on statistical data manipulation, could achieve. This is acceptable because there is some redundancy in the information contained in the five graphs. This allows the knowledge-based diagnostic system to correct a classification error made in any one of them. Also, an occasional balancing error on one rig in a large fleet is acceptable, as the system still performs better overall than all but the best few humans.

Interestingly, this 90 percent performance by the networks is higher than the system's developer expected. He surmises that, whether because of better design or better maintenance, today's truck brake systems are in better shape than were those of a few years ago when the training set data were obtained. Thus, he surmises, perhaps "some of the really awful tests that were seen in the training and test data won't be seen again." Training a neural network on examples that are more difficult than those it will see in real use is, he suggests, "a great trick if you can do it"—but one that can't be used in most practical situations.

The knowledge-based portions of this system were developed in less than four months: two months for knowledge acquisition and six weeks for design, development, and test of the computer system. The total cost of this work was approximately $30,000 but would have been higher were it not for the use of college juniors and seniors working on the system for academic credit. The neural nets took about five months to develop at a cost of $50,000. Adding the cost of hardware and software brings the total cost of this system to $105,500, not including the cost of deploying additional systems to the field. This is offset by savings of $100,000 in direct travel expenses by Eaton's expert, plus the value of his time and the morale benefits of his not having to travel nearly every week. The system is thus well cost-justified. An Eaton spokesperson cites these added benefits:

- Six times the former number of fleet brake balance appraisals can be conducted per year. As brake balancing is provided as a free service to large fleet customers to gain goodwill and hence do more business, this presumably spreads six times the goodwill.

---

[3]You can read more about neural networks on page 548.

- Extensive desk analysis is eliminated, thus giving the customer results in days or hours instead of weeks or months.
- The expert, freed from traveling to balance brakes, could be promoted to other, more challenging professional work. (Such a potential opportunity can be a factor in obtaining an expert's cooperation.)
- The system is valuable for training inexperienced staff members.

Questions

1. Which of the criteria for expert system development (Chapter 12) does this system meet? Had you looked at that list before reading the list of benefits at the end of the case, do you think that meeting those criteria would justify developing it?
2. What type of user interface would you recommend for this system? Why?
3. How do you think local brake technicians would react to the deployment of this system in their garages, if it were brought in without warning and they were simply told, "Use it!"? What steps would you take to ensure positive reactions on their part?
4. As mentioned above, much of the knowledge-based part of the system was developed by college juniors and seniors for academic credit after an experienced professional had designed them. According to [SMIT91], "They were relatively unfamiliar with programming, let alone LISP, KEE or AI." Do you think they should have received academic credit for this work? Why or why not?

CASE 3 ENTERPRISEWIDE GIS: BRINGING NEW DIMENSIONS TO DECISION MAKING

From [SYST94]. Used by permission.

For decades, government agencies and private companies have been building electronic information technology assets. These assets are integral to today's urban infrastructures along with buildings, public spaces, utilities, and transportation systems. In both the private and public sectors, information technology has substantially reduced costs and errors, and has improved many services. Still demands continue for lower costs, more efficiency, and better service. Fortunately, a rapidly developing form of technology, the geographic information system (GIS), enables these demands to be met in a novel way.

GIS Is Much More than a Map

A map represents a spatial model of the world. It is unrivaled in its ability to show spatial relationships—who lives next to whom, how to get there from here, and how much area is devoted to a given activity. Answers to these questions are fundamental to the management of the world's tangible assets. A GIS is a great deal more than a map, however.

The most commonly accepted definition of a GIS is *a computerized database management system capable of capturing, storing, retrieving, analyzing, and displaying spatial* (locationally defined) *data.* Many products exist that can perform some of these tasks. The unique power of a GIS resides in its ability to perform spatial analysis of the data it manages.

A GIS can perform several specific tasks:

- Create maps automatically from stored data, either onto a screen or various printers and plotters.
- Manage a database containing attributes of the features shown on the maps, such as who owns a piece of property or the age of an underground pipe.
- Keep track of the topological relationships among the points, lines, and areas or surfaces that represent the real-world features stored in the database. A feature-based GIS "knows" which power lines are attached to which poles, which streets are one-way or two-way, and which of two objects that occupy the same lateral position is on top of the other (e.g., a subway track under a street).
- Perform spatial queries and analysis. A GIS can handle data in locationally related ways, such as finding all the features of a certain kind within an area traced on a monitor screen, determining the shortest route between two points following the road network, or showing which areas would be flooded if water were to reach a certain depth.
- Combine existing features to create new ones. For example, elderly persons living alone, persons who do not own automobiles, and disabled individuals could be combined to create a new feature type: "persons likely to need assistance in the event of a hurricane evacuation."
- Maintain data integrity while updating and adjusting the spatial or attribute data associated with the features. For example, a house could be sold, renovated, or burned to the ground. In each case, the same mappable object would represent a transaction recorded in the data files of different departments: public records, building inspector, or fire department, respectively.

Benefits of an Enterprisewide GIS

Many enterprises have vast information resources, yet lack an efficient means to find needed information to complete a task or satisfy a customer's request. The reason for this is that nearly 90 percent of the information used in planning, analysis, and decision making still exists in the form of paper reports, maps, and aerial photographs, which are inaccessible to conventional database management systems.

Where database management systems do store public information, they are often physically separated by agency or department, or are structurally incompatible, making data collection and validation tedious and time consuming. In addition, often several departments maintain the same basic information, such as names and addresses of customers, thus duplicating each other's work unnecessarily.

A GIS can be the key to maximizing the value of existing information assets because it uses the common theme of location to tie both geographic and nongeographic information together. This approach succeeds because most information assets and business processes are nearly 90 percent location-based. An enterprisewide GIS relates mappable items (facilities, properties, administrative entities, natural features) to database files containing records of the transactions that apply to these items.

A GIS can be used to perform certain types of spatial analysis not possible with other types of software, for example:

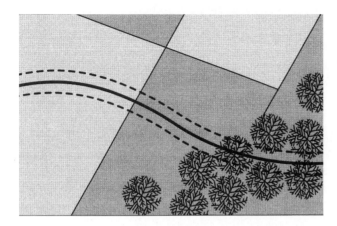

Buffer Analysis—If a new highway is constructed, how many acres of woods and how many acres of farm land will be lost?

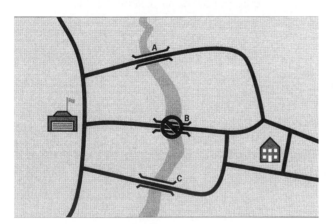

Network Analysis—If bridge B is closed during restoration, will bridge A or bridge C be best for travel between the firehouse and the school?

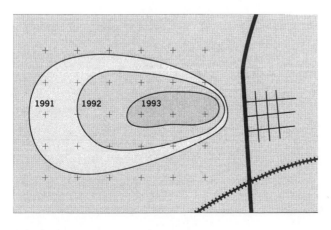

Time Series Analysis—If the areal extent of an underground oil spill is shrinking each year during cleanup, when will the spill be gone?

In a truly enterprisewide GIS configuration, users from throughout the organization access all information from their own workstations. Access can be regulated so that selected users, whether internal or external to the GIS owner, can access the data, and only permitted users can change data.

An enterprisewide GIS vision can provide critical benefits:

- Enhanced customer service through improved information delivery.
- Leveraging existing information resources through integration with the GIS.
- Improved geographic information access and data sharing.
- Effective management of multiple sources of geographic and nongeographic information.

In short, employing a GIS in an enterprisewide information technology solution can improve organizational cooperation, improve efficiency, and encourage more informed decision making. A GIS can be used in this way in many facets of an organization's operations, or shared by organizations with different responsibilities.

Achieving the Advantages

The starting point in engineering the enterprisewide GIS should be an objective assessment of the information needs from both departmental and enterprisewide perspectives. Questions to ask include:

- Are geographic and nongeographic data organized and accessible to all who should have them?
- Does the current information technology environment facilitate customer service?
- Does the existing information system support the GIS capabilities required to communicate with other organizations and clients?
- Is existing geographic information accessible in an open environment that leverages the value of other enterprise information?

How these questions are answered will determine the design of the enterprisewide GIS solution.

GIS systems already exist in many organizations in the form of departmental systems that meet a specific need, such as in a public works department or traffic management agency. Sometimes these existing systems can evolve into an enterprisewide solution. In other cases, they may be more effective by remaining as participating information systems within a broader solution. The issues and alternatives must be clear through careful analysis of the situation before attempting to prescribe a GIS solution.

Questions

1. Do you agree with the statement in the article that "most information assets and business processes are nearly 90 percent location-based"? Why or why not? Give an example of a business process that is location-based and an example of one that isn't. ("Location-based" in this context means the information asset is described by, or the business process uses, location information in a significant way. It does *not* mean that information is stored in a particular location or that a process takes place in a particular location.)

2. Give examples of two decisions that depend heavily on geographic data and a GIS could help with. Explain specifically how a GIS could help people make those decisions better than they could without a GIS.
3. The above article was, as you might guess, written by a firm that sells geographic information systems. (It did not attempt to hide this. *Systems* is published by Unisys for its customers and other interested parties. Product references found in the original article were edited out for this book.) It therefore does not discuss any GIS disadvantages. As you know, nothing is totally good. Every approach to information systems has its drawbacks. Every technology choice involves trade-offs. Suggest and discuss some GIS drawbacks and trade-offs.

CASE 4 FORT LOWELL TRADING COMPANY: DEVELOPING THE FINANCE DSS

This episode can be used in connection with Chapter 7. It relates to a different aspect of the chapter than the case episode located there.

Elizabeth and Miguel had talked with Vanessa a few times since their initial meeting in the FLTC information systems conference room. (You can read about that meeting in the FLTC case episode of Chapter 4 and about a subsequent meeting with Chris Demas in the episode of Chapter 6.) Contrary to what they might have initially expected, her meetings with the staff of corporate finance had gone extremely well for all concerned. Her obvious understanding of the finance department's needs, gained largely while working at Macy's, her willingness to listen, and the plain fact that she couldn't be blamed for the past all contributed to this.

It did not surprise them, then, that Vanessa was in a good mood when the two arrived at the FLTC lobby to discuss the progress of her project. "I just had the greatest session with Chris," she enthused, referring to Christopher Demas, manager of financial planning for the chain. "He had some really neat ideas about pulling interest rate forecasts off a bunch of Web sites and using the average to estimate where our line of credit costs would go for the next several months. I can tell you all about it. Want to head for the cafeteria and get a cup of coffee or something?"

"Sure, though something cold and fizzy is probably more my style," said Miguel as the three went through the double doors to the office area.

The Fort Lowell Trading Company cafeteria was a large, open area with a fine view of the Santa Catalina mountains north of the city. The three brought their drinks to a table next to the window, which was made of triple-glazed reflective glass to ward off the summer heat even though its position meant that the sun never hit it directly. As soon as they sat down, Elizabeth commented, "Well, Vanessa, you seem quite happy about how the project is going so far!"

"You could say that, I suppose," she grinned. "Is it that obvious?"

"Yes, it is," Elizabeth stated firmly.

Vanessa blushed slightly and changed the subject. "Anyhow, the meeting to approve the feasibility study is next Thursday. The development estimates so far are actually a bit under what they had guessed from those three other companies—

some new client/server development tools that weren't around three years ago will save us a bunch of time. So it's pretty much a given that we'll get the green light."

She paused to take a drink and realized that she might have come on a bit too strongly. "It's not that I'm so great, you understand. I don't want to sound like that. The finance system is really necessary—overdue, if you ask me—and I just happened to be in the right place at the right time. A lot of life is like that. Didn't Woody Allen say something like that?"

"Yeah, like 90 percent of life is just showing up or something," Miguel said. "What he didn't say is you have to know when to show up, and where."

"I guess I was lucky that way," Vanessa nodded. "But now the hard part starts. Talking to people and writing down what they say is fun, but making it happen is what pays the bills."

Questions

1. What development approach (see Chapter 7) would you recommend for developing the Fort Lowell Trading Company financial planning DSS? Justify your answer.
2. Assume that FLTC is developing, as part of this DSS, a module that compares alternative approaches to raising working capital or funds for expansion. It incorporates, among other features, three different ways to estimate future inflation rates and interest rate trends. Each of them may be appropriate for certain economic conditions and other assumptions. How should the user interface of this module differ, depending on whether it is to be used by someone in Chris Demas's department, who works with capital planning choices on a daily basis, or the firm's CFO, who usually works on other things but has a good understanding of finance issues? How would you design a user interface so the system could be used easily by either of them?
3. Consider the DSS development roles discussed in Section 7.2 in Chapter 7. How would each role apply to this DSS? (If any would not apply to it, say so and justify your position.)
4. Suggest a way in which FLTC's financial planning DSS could use virtual reality.

CASE 5 A WHOLE NEW BALL GAME (SORT OF)

From [KOCH99]. Used by permission.

The Supply Chain: Scouting

Between innings of the 1998 World Series, New York Yankees catcher Joe Girardi spent much of his time in the dugout thumbing through computerized "spray charts" that show where the San Diego Padres hitters hit the ball as well as graphics highlighting the weak spots in the strike zone so that he could call the appropriate pitches the next inning. "The Yankees started using the service in 1996, and they won the Series that year," says Randy Istre, whose Minneapolis company, Inside Edge, Inc., collects and sells information to the Yankees and other teams. The Yankees pay Inside Edge $41,000 per regular season for its service and half that much again if the team makes it to the playoffs. "The Marlins started using it in '97," continues Istre, "and they won the [1997] Series. The Tigers used it and went from the worst team in baseball in '96 to just under .500 in 1997. It makes us wonder if the power of this information isn't showing in some of the teams' results."

Istre's service isn't revolutionary, just more thorough. Advance scouting, that is, keeping track of what the other teams are doing, has been practiced haphazardly by major league teams for years. But tracking through a database the details of every pitch an opponent throws and everything a hitter does to defend himself is new and growing.

This is only part of baseball's larger quest to know all there is to know about a player, from the time he first cuts a wide swath through his high school and college leagues to the day he strides off the field of a major league ballpark for the last time. The teams contract with baseball-crazed programmers to create their own proprietary software to track every player's (not just their own) contract history, injuries, psychological makeup, and athletic strengths and weaknesses. All this information helps determine in what game situations he performs best and what types of pitches he likes (or hates) to hit (or throw).

But the information is most valuable in determining how much a player is worth. Baseball is becoming a game of payrolls as much as of hits, runs, and errors, where the teams with the most money get the best players. The ability to pull player history out of a database is one of the most valuable tools teams have in making trades and wrangling over contracts with players.

"Scouting is the most valuable application on the front end of baseball," says Bill Bolt, vice president of information systems for the Phoenix-based Arizona Diamondbacks (as well as for the NBA's Phoenix Suns). It's a three-tier system: amateur (high school and college), professional (minor league player development), and advance (competitive intelligence about other major league teams). Scouting applications track player development on all three levels, at a big cost for the teams, which support their own networks of (six or so) minor league clubs. Baseball players spend more time in development than almost any other pro athlete—at least two years in the minors before they hit the majors. So keeping tabs on everyone helps the teams reduce cycle time and expense.

"Most baseball people are still in high school when we start tracking them," says Bolt. "They're looking to get lucky on Saturday night, and we're looking to find a third baseman. Our bet is this kid will be valuable three to five years after we first meet him."

The teams pride themselves in gathering nuances, like personal presence on the field, and cross-references, like testimony from a Little League coach, about a player whom no other team is looking for. Each team's set of scouting applications is considered its information technology crown jewels, and IT leaders refuse to share their secrets with the press or each other—a collective sense of propriety that seems a little exaggerated.

"About 70 percent of the data entry fields in these programs are the same across all the teams, but there's 30 percent that teams try to make their own to look at things other teams aren't," says William N. Duffy, project manager for sports solutions at IBM Corp. Global Media and Entertainment Industry division in Atlanta. IBM is one of a handful of major vendors trying to crack the scouting application market. IBM scored with the New York Mets, but most team IT leaders sneer at the concept of a "packaged" scouting application.

"IBM tries to come in and say, 'Here's our view of baseball, and everyone should buy our application,' " rails one major league executive who speaks on the condition of anonymity. "But they don't know how the teams work. Each team does things slightly differently. It's true competitive advantage," he says.

Questions

1. What decisions are supported by information systems in the above article? Write clear decision statements for as many as you can identify.
2. Pick one DSS described in this case and state what it is. What type of DSS, in terms of Alter's categories (Section 4.1) is that DSS? Describe a different DSS, at least two levels away in his set of categories, that could help make the same decision. In your opinion, would it provide better or worse help? (Teams might be making the right decision not to develop it even if it would provide better help. Perhaps its advantages would not justify its development cost.)
3. Other parts of Koch's full article discussed the difficulty of getting experienced baseball scouts to use laptop computers, marketing programs to encourage fans to attend games, making team administration more efficient, and computerized control of a ballpark. Where, of all these, would you be most likely to find DSS? Why?
4. Do you feel IBM's package approach, as discussed in the last two paragraphs of the article, makes sense for this application? Use the concepts of Section 6.1 in your answer. Is this opposition to packaged applications consistent with teams' use of Inside Edge's services?

CASE 6 MASTERCARD: MINING THE POSSIBILITIES

From [MAYO96]. Used by permission.

Have you seen the credit card adorned with a reproduction of Winslow Homer's "Boys in a Pasture"? How about the one that promises to help save the rainforest? Or the one that lets you earn free goodies from Toys 'R' Us? Welcome to the bank card phenomenon of the 1990s—co-branding.

Like never before, traditional banking and credit institutions are teaming up with retailers, nonprofit organizations, airlines, gas companies and automobile manufacturers to offer consumers a new breed of credit card, one that gives something back. Because they are intent on racking up points for travel, hardware items or donations to their favorite charitable institutions, "consumers use a co-branded card differently than they use a regular credit card," explains Anne Grim, senior vice president of global information services at MasterCard International in Purchase, N.Y. "They treat it as a different financial vehicle, and they use it in places where they never used a card before."

Lending banks looking for leverage in an increasingly cutthroat and competitive market were, by the end of 1994, clamoring for access to data on purchasing trends to develop special offers and to analyze the new purchasing patterns spawned by this type of precision marketing. "In such a competitive environment, with big guys and little guys all going after the same [credit card] customers, those who are going to win in the long term are the ones who can adapt very quickly to changing patterns in customer behavior," says Ronald Zebeck, president of Finger-hut Financial Services Corp., which offers its own branded MasterCard to customers. (Fingerhut Financial is a subsidiary of Fingerhut Companies Inc., a retail and direct marketing corporation in Minnetonka, Minn.)

But MasterCard's core transaction-processing systems weren't built to support data mining and certainly weren't available for member banks to access directly. With 22,000 member financial institutions, some 452 million credit and debit cards in circulation and more than 13 million acceptance locations, MasterCard's IBM Corp. and NCR Corp. mainframes were already plenty busy processing requests for approval from merchants' banks and linking those requests to Master-Card member banks that issue cards to consumers. When member banks wanted information on the purchasing patterns of their cardholders, they had to request a report from MasterCard. Some information was simply unavailable. Other data had to be culled from several systems and prepared by internal staff. That process could take days or even longer and resulted in static, rather than dynamic, data. The company needed to develop a new system, and fast.

So, in the spring of 1995, MasterCard International embarked on an ambitious plan to build from scratch a data warehouse that could deliver purchasing data to the desktop at member banks. After securing top management's approval for the project, MasterCard rolled out the new service within a self-imposed (and, some might say, Draconian) deadline of five months. In just 150 days, the development team brought in vendors to develop various components of the system; built and populated a brand-new warehouse for one terabyte of data culled from Master-Card's transaction processing systems; integrated an end-user front end; and tested, debugged and delivered the service in beta to its first group of customers.

The result of MasterCard's efforts was Market Advisor; a data mining service that lets member banks recognize spending patterns, uncover opportunities for special offers by identifying unusual card-holder activity, compare the perform-ance of their cards against that of comparable lenders and more accurately track response to promotions. Market Advisor gives a competitive edge to its member banks, and it helps MasterCard move beyond merely offering transaction process-ing services to become an information provider. "There is an improved relation-ship between MasterCard and our partners when we're perceived as the most tech-nologically advanced," says Grim.

The new service is part of a trio of fee-based services that are accessed through MasterCard Online, an umbrella platform that features a graphical, point-and-click front end that runs on client workstations; security; support for standard e-mail protocols; and file transfer protocol telecommunications software that provides dial-up access to MasterCard's processing center in St. Louis and to multiple ap-plication servers around the globe. Users dial into MasterCard Online, and the server directs them to one of the three services—Market Advisor, the data mining tool for competitive analysis; Portfolio, a service that provides each member bank and merchant bank with a complete picture of its overall credit card business; and Match, an updated, real-time version of MasterCard's fraud detection system that runs off the company's transaction processing computers.

With Market Advisor, Fingerhut and MasterCard's other member banks can drill up or down on defined levels of data, sort and filter data according to predefined criteria, and use custom calculations to identify specific groups of spenders. Partners can analyze purchasing trends by merchant categories, geographic location or card performance and benchmark against other lenders' performance.

For Fingerhut Financial, Market Advisor serves two essential purposes, says Zebeck. First, it allows the company to increase efficiency and eliminate waste by offering promotions only to customers who are likely to be interested in them. "We want to avoid sending stuff about cars to people who live in Manhattan," he says. And second, it helps retain customers by enabling Fingerhut to present them with relevant, timely offers. "If we identify customers that have made a lot of television-related purchases, we can offer them a 5 percent rebate if they buy a large appliance, like a television, within a certain amount of time," says Zebeck. "With attrition rates in the double digits, even lowering that rate by two or three points is an accomplishment."

MasterCard succeeded in its efforts in such a short amount of time because it built a data warehouse for all the right reasons. "What drives a data warehouse is competition, the search for new business opportunities," says Neil Mendelson, senior director for data warehousing at Oracle Corp. in Redwood Shores, Calif. "This is not reengineering. This is not about doing more for less; it's about doing more." Data warehouses work best when they are attached to a specific business objective and definable goals, Mendelson says. "The objective was not to warehouse a whole bunch of data and then find out what to do with it. MasterCard started with something it thought was manageable and did it in a fixed amount of time."

MasterCard made the project manageable by following a master plan that could have come straight from an MBA textbook and, as Grim says, by putting in "lots and lots of overtime." The global information services group began the process by developing a clearly defined, highly specific set of business requirements and by getting all parties involved to agree on the deadline in advance. Next, a small group of executives from both the business and IT sides of the company identified technology able to fit together easily into a seamless system, from front end to back room, and chose vendors with proven track records for handling large databases and a willingness to work in cooperative, intracompany groups.

Selecting the database was one of the earliest steps in the development process, says Rob Reeg, senior vice president of systems development for MasterCard, and Oracle immediately came to the forefront. MasterCard had recently conducted a study of virtually every third-party database, and Oracle was recommended as the company's database of choice. For the data warehouse project, "we chose Oracle for its corporate expertise and the functionality that it brings to the table," says Reeg.

Picking a front end—a crucial piece since ease-of-use could make or break the success of the service in the field—was much more difficult, in part because there was a much vaster array of products from which to choose. The company decided on user query tools from Information Advantage Inc.'s DecisionSuite business analysis software. "We were originally looking at SQL reporting packages," says Reeg, "but Information Advantage had the abilities we wanted. It fit into our niche."

Market Advisor incorporates two of the four modules of Information Advantage's DecisionSuite line: Analysis, which MasterCard uses internally for authoring and report generation, and NewsLine, the data mining tool that represents the heart and soul of the system from the end user's perspective. NewsLine allows users to review reports and then drill down to gain new levels of detail on certain dimensions or change parameters on the fly (for example, comparing domestic U.S. performance to that of French, then English, merchants). The software lets users send electronic alerts to one another and forward live reports, complete with all assumptions and rules, which can then be further analyzed by the recipient.

From the outset of their relationship, MasterCard made it clear that it wanted to work with Information Advantage less as a vendor and more as a business partner, says Larry Ford, president and CEO of the Minneapolis-based company. "MasterCard came up to visit in January [of 1995], and we showed them our architecture and what we had in development," says Ford. "The architecture was stable; the [ability to handle] database volume was proven. Their question was, could we get NewsLine out in time to meet their very aggressive schedule?"

In addition to obtaining feedback from MasterCard and a select group of its member banks testing the NewsLine front end as it was being developed, Information Advantage had access to MasterCard's usability labs, human-factors specialists and other developers working on the warehouse's design. "With Information Advantage, it was a case of very frequent meetings. Their product [was changed] a lot during development," Reeg says of MasterCard's partnership strategy. "With Oracle, we actually had Oracle consultants on board working with our in-house data administrators."

"MasterCard came to Oracle in the very earliest stages of this project and treated us not as a vendor-supplier but as a partner," says Oracle's Mendelson. "We embarked with a shared set of goals and objectives rather than traditional objectives. The time frame otherwise would have been very much extended."

Such business partnerships were crucial to the fast turnaround time on Master-Card's warehouse project, according to Grim and Reeg, but they would not have been possible without teamwork of a different variety—a strong internal partnership between the business and IT sides of the company. At the core of this partnership was a small group of executives, including Brantley Orrell, at that time the senior vice president of global performance and tracking and now senior vice president of global brand development; Grim from global information services, which functioned as the "business owner" of the project, in charge of marketing, distribution and deployment of MasterCard Online; and Rod Mack and Reeg from global technology and operations. (Mack, the former senior vice president of system development, has since left MasterCard for AT&T Corp.)

From an IT perspective, development staffing for the project peaked at 17 people, including 10 to 12 programmers, four database administrators and a few data analysts, according to Reeg. Now that Market Advisor and Portfolio are up and running, Reeg estimates that there are about nine people dedicated to ongoing maintenance and development.

Lessons Learned

1. **BREAK THE RULES:** New technology often calls for breaking business rules. At MasterCard, standard procedures dictate that new business proposals include multiyear projections for technologies and costs. But new, rapidly changing technology like a data warehouse doesn't lend itself to five-year projects—"five to nine months is more like it," says Anne Grim, MasterCard's senior vice president of global information services and the main "business owner" of the data warehouse project. The upshot for MasterCard: Following an "education process" for senior management, Grim and her staff received permission to make financial and technological projections annually for the warehouse project.

2. **GET PERSONAL:** When deadlines are tight, there's nothing like "face time" to move a project along. With the business owners in New York and the project developers in St. Louis, the shortest distance between the two turned out to be not a network, voice mail, or conference call, but an airplane. "With so many [development] efforts going on in parallel, there was always some interaction needed. Telephone contact just wasn't sufficient," says Grim. To make sure the project stayed on track, Grim and other members of the business team spent three days a week in St. Louis for the five months of active development on the warehouse. "There was definitely some personal wear and tear that we hadn't anticipated," she says.

3. **SIZE MATTERS:** A database of more than a terabyte behaves very differently than one that's a quarter of that size. As MasterCard discovered, a very large database needs performance tuning on a daily basis, says Grim.

Nearly everyone involved in the data warehouse project, both internally and externally, was bolstered by MasterCard's unwavering business objectives for the warehouse. "The business side did a very good job of determining what the co-branded partners needed," explains Reeg. "Then we had a series of joint sessions with IT people plus business people, and we took them and translated them into technical specifications."

"The business requirements haven't changed in 18 months, which is pretty amazing," says Grim. "IT mapped out what data we needed and in what format we needed to see it, and then we just went from there." Such an ironclad business plan helped the team stay focused and move more quickly, Grim says. "There was room for [multiple] points of view, but everyone recognized there wasn't a lot of latitude for debate," she says. "When a decision had to be made, we said, these are the options, these are the pros and cons, now let's make a decision and move on."

Questions

1. The data warehouse in this case was used primarily for data mining rather than for user-guided analysis. Why did they choose this approach? In your opinion, was this a good decision?

2. Some of MasterCard's success in this case is due to the unusual, partner-like relationships that MasterCard maintained with its key software suppliers, Oracle and Information Advantage. Suppose the IS manager of a small firm, without the size or marketplace clout of MasterCard, read this article and approached these vendors (or any other vendors) and suggested the same mode of operation. They told him in effect "we can't afford to work that way with every small customer." What would you recommend he do to approach this situation as closely as possible?

3. The first "lesson learned" in the box at the end of the case suggests that five-year projections are not feasible for rapidly changing technologies. Why would a data warehouse be different, in this regard, from (say) the corporate Web site or any other innovative use of technology? What aspects of a data warehouse do you feel it should be feasible to project for five years?

CASE 7 CLOSE CALL CORP.: ANATOMY OF A FAILURE

From [PAUL97]. Used by permission.

Wasted time. Squandered money. Lost jobs. Ruined reputations. Jeopardized careers.

Project failures are the dirty little secret of data warehousing. Anyone who has spent time around data warehouse projects is likely to have chalked up a failure or two. The majority of those debacles can be attributed not to technology snafus but to lack of strong executive sponsorship and to poor management.

For many, being part of an abysmal data warehouse project is a rite of passage. But that doesn't make it any easier. The project manager and consultant who were central figures in the data warehousing effort at the company we'll call Close Call Corp. deserve credit for candidly sharing their experiences here. Through a spokesman, the CEO of Close Call—who pushed for the warehouse in the first place—declined to comment.

Because it's so hard to do data warehousing well, the kinds of things that went awry in this case study could afflict any implementation in any industry. Do not, therefore, assume your company is safe from a failure of this magnitude. If you look closely—and are honest about it—chances are you'll recognize some of the red flags raised here.

Editor's Note: All names in this case study have been changed.

The road to hell is paved with golf games. For the CEO of Close Call Corp., his trip netherward began with a day on the links in the fall of 1995 with a software vendor. At the time, the CEO was particularly vulnerable to a "business-transforming" pitch. He knew he needed to make technology changes—and fast. His teleservices company, which he'd founded with $200 in the 1970s and had grown into a modest empire worth $100 million, was at a crossroads. Intent on choosing the straightest push through a double-digit growth period, he was searching for technological help. So when the vendor tempted him with visions of integrated data flow and information on demand, the CEO couldn't resist.

Historically, Close Call's outbound (telemarketing) and inbound (catalog sales) business units had operated as totally separate companies. The company had recently gone public, and rapid growth was putting major pressure on its antiquated and proprietary systems. The vendor made a convincing case that a data warehouse was the answer to Close Call's prayers. Nothing to it, went the siren call, you can be up and running on a fully functional data warehouse in three to four months. The CEO began salivating at the thought of providing a unified view of Close Call's business data to its autonomous business units.

But with 1996 already shaping up to be a banner year for Close Call, the timing for a data warehouse project could hardly have been worse. The company was planning to expand from six call centers to 116, implementing new, open switching systems in the new centers to enable automatic dialing and call routing. In addition, information systems (IS) was updating all of Close Call's internal management systems by deploying new human resources and general ledger software.

When the CEO returned from his fateful golf game and sounded the call for a data warehouse, he ensured that 1996 would be a year to remember—but not for the reasons he'd hoped.

Unrealistic Expectations

The CEO expected the can-do culture that he'd nurtured from the early days of the company to carry it through this period of exponential growth and technological change. He believed that making all the systems changes—including building the data warehouse—in a very short time frame was just a matter of getting the right people for the job, according to a consultant we'll call Michael Farraday, co-founder of the data warehousing and decision support consulting firm that was called in to do the data warehouse design and data modeling. "He put decisions in place and said 'Go make this happen.' That approach had always worked in the past. But not this time," says Farraday.

Based on the few technology tidbits he had obtained from the software vendor on the fairway, the CEO was convinced he could have a 500GB production data warehouse up and running in four months despite the fact that the existing IS staff was already stretched to the limit. Before the project team was on board, he set the project deadlines and a budget of $250,000, the ultimate no-no, says Farraday, who has 12 years' data warehousing experience.

Because no one in-house had data warehousing experience or time to devote to the project, five outside people were hired. The outsiders included Manager of MIS Jackie Pemberton (not her real name), who was brought on in part to manage the data warehousing project, and a director of MIS, both of whom had proven data warehousing track records and a combined total of nearly three decades in the field. Pemberton was also put in charge of the general-business system software rollout.

Unrealistic time and resource allocations alone might not have grounded Close Call's data warehouse had the business ranks been clamoring for the information it could provide. But because they'd never been exposed to an analytical environment before, the users didn't know what they were missing. Indeed, the business unit managers were quite content with the canned reports they could get from a DOS-based Reflex database. The few who needed more analysis entered the report numbers into a spreadsheet and did rudimentary manipulations.

The lack of demand for a new reporting system foreshadowed a virtually insurmountable problem, says Farraday: Down the road, the users would not be willing to commit the time and effort required to make the warehouse a success. "The challenges go up dramatically if the data warehouse represents the first analytical environment," says Farraday. "[The users] never really understood what a data warehouse could do."

The Project Launch

The new director of MIS assembled the initial project team, consisting of Pemberton, two senior managers from sales and telemarketing and a database administrator as well as Farraday and another consultant from his firm. Pemberton, the director of MIS and the consultants pushed back on the scope of the project, the preset deadlines and budget, but the CEO stuck to his guns. Ultimately, he grudgingly accepted the idea of a pilot in five months rather than insisting on the full-blown production warehouse. But he never seemed to understand the magnitude of the undertaking, says Farraday.

From the start, the data warehouse lacked a clearly defined business objective, mostly because the users had never asked for greater analytical capabilities. Pemberton believed she would be able to articulate the business case herself after gathering detailed user requirements.

Early on, Pemberton met weekly with the director of MIS, who in turn met separately with the executive sponsors (the CEO and the CFO) every week. Only when things began to fall apart several months later did the four begin to meet face to face each week. Also, the general managers of the business units said they were too busy to get involved in the requirements assessment stage of the project. "The feeling was, 'go talk to my guys. They'll tell you what they need,' " says Pemberton. In retrospect, she says the director of MIS didn't reach out to the business users as much as perhaps he should have.

Despite the early uncertainties, optimism prevailed at the project launch. "[The director of MIS] had so much positive energy, I really thought together we could make this happen," says Pemberton.

Collecting User Requirements

Farraday and his consulting colleague saw the process of gathering user requirements for the warehouse as critical. Along with Pemberton, they embarked on three painstaking months of interviewing the key users as 1996 began. Instead of merely asking users what data they needed from a data warehouse, they invited them to talk in general terms about their jobs, homing in on how their job performance was evaluated and how they managed people.

Although the users complained that the interviews took too much time, everyone felt this stage had been a resounding success. In spite of the very separate business units, the team was beginning to build the consolidated picture of the business they'd need to begin constructing the warehouse.

Building the Business Model

As they collected user requirements, Pemberton and Farraday set about creating a business model that would capture the business professionals' requirements in their own terms. Independent of technology, this model would define the business dimensions (for example, looking at the business in terms of products, locations and time periods), attributes, relationships, facts and logical navigation paths, all of which would translate to the design of the warehouse. The challenge was to get the distinct and autonomous business units to settle on these critical definitions.

This, too, went much more smoothly than anticipated. "People from different groups were agreeing on things they had never agreed on before," says Farraday. The bad news was that the model revealed a highly complex set of business requirements and an inconsistent group of data "facts" that would populate the warehouse. Unlike a retail data warehouse in which the quantity of a particular SKU[4] sold at a particular time becomes an unalterable "fact," performance of customer service representatives—what Close Call was trying to measure—was much more subjective and obscure. Business managers had created their own customized spreadsheets into which they reentered the data they wanted to examine from the Reflex database reports. Because the managers looked at things differently (for example, some defined "revenues" as actual revenues, others considered them estimated revenues), defining fact groups therefore became a hellish ordeal that required sorting through literally hundreds of calculations based on subjective assumptions. This process alone took nearly a month, says Farraday, which meant the team couldn't start building the relational format and user interface. It was a delay the executive sponsors were not inclined to forgive.

Source Data Crisis

Then came the biggest blow to date. With the pilot deadline at hand, Close Call's IS veterans, who believed their jobs were threatened by the data warehousing project, finally admitted to the project team that there was no way to populate the warehouse. The only data available was basic customer and transaction information that had been captured by Close Call's proprietary telecommunications switching systems as a byproduct of call routing. Writing a program to extract that data for the warehouse would be too expensive and time-consuming even to consider. Clearly, the old switching systems in the original six call centers would have to be updated with open technology to capture the data for the warehouse electronically, says Farraday.

Panicked at the thought of breaking that news to the executive sponsors, the team jury-rigged a way to populate the pilot by parsing the DOS-based Reflex reports and manipulating the report data into a relational database format. But the handwriting was on the wall—without replacing the proprietary switching systems, there would be no data warehouse.

By this point, Pemberton and her team were in overdrive, working 15-hour days, six days a week. Twice-weekly trips to Close Call's other major corporate office in the next state also took their toll. "I was trying so hard, but it was an emotional nightmare," says Pemberton.

The Pilot

The pilot contained a small summary-level set of data that the team had manipulated and manually loaded into the database. After the pilot was complete in August, the team faced an unpleasant revelation. Even if there had been pristine source data, the users weren't having any of it.

---

[4]StockKeeping Unit, a unique identifier assigned to each different item a store sells.

"They said, 'You're giving me what I already had, and it's harder for me to get it and the data doesn't even match my hard copy,' " recalls Farraday. "We lost the users at that point."

The anger began to build and hit a crescendo in the executive suite. "They had wanted the production warehouse in place in four months and at the end of eight months we said, 'Here's your itsy-bitsy little one-page pilot, and guess what, you're not even getting your warehouse,' " says Pemberton.

It was all over but the shouting.

Crashing Down

A few weeks after the pilot debacle, Pemberton found herself with a new boss. The director of MIS, who had been promised the CIO spot, ended up with two new bosses, who shared the responsibilities of IS management as vice presidents of technology. To no one's surprise, the director of MIS elected to leave the company shortly thereafter.

Undaunted, Pemberton assembled a team of 57 IS staff and business users and in a few weeks created a detailed plan for reengineering the outbound business processes and updating their systems. With her heart in her mouth and passion still unspent, she presented her plan to the executives in October 1996, telling them it would take two years to reengineer before they could even begin the data warehouse. She said she believed nothing less than the survival of the company was at stake. Her words fell on deaf ears. "They said, 'Thanks for your work, but no thanks,' " says Pemberton. No one spoke in favor of her proposal at the meeting.

The Aftermath

Close Call's CEO canceled the data warehousing project in October 1996. Though it was hardly a shock, Pemberton was shattered. "I had never been involved in a situation where I failed at my job. I had gone in with such high hopes. I really wanted to give them a data warehouse," says Pemberton. In February 1997, she quit without a new job nor any prospects of one and took three weeks off to recover. (Pemberton reports she is now a senior data warehousing manager for another company and has just delivered a pilot of a data warehouse.)

From the CEO's point of view, the entire project had been a fiasco, says Pemberton. The anemic pilot was delivered four months later than the initial (highly unrealistic) deadline for the fully functional warehouse. Although the CEO had budgeted a paltry $250,000 for the project, the team had spent nearly $750,000 on hardware, software and services.

"Management finally said, 'We have spent a lot of money, and we have gotten no value,' " says Pemberton. "It was devastating."

Besides wasting money and time, the project cost Close Call 50 percent of its IS staff, about half of whom quit, according to Farraday. Today, Farraday reports that the company is reengineering its outbound business processes with an eye toward another data warehousing attempt. But in the meantime, Close Call's stock has taken a beating, losing more than two thirds of its value between October 1996 and September 1997. Farraday attributes the company's change of fortune to attempting too many technology projects at once. "They bit off way more than they could chew," he says.

So much for believing everything you hear on the golf course.

Questions

1. Consider the data warehousing project described in this case in terms of the data warehouse implementation recommendations of Chapter 15. What did the Close Call team do right? What did they do wrong?
2. Based on the information in the case, is there anything that Pemberton, Farraday, and their team could have done to make the data warehousing project a success? If not, why not? If so, what?
3. In the sixth case in this appendix, MasterCard built a data warehouse in five months. What factors made it possible for them to do it when Close Call couldn't?
4. You have just been offered a job to join a company and be in charge of its first data warehousing project. You have been told that the company CEO is solidly behind the project. What are three questions you could ask, based on Jackie Pemberton's experience in precisely that situation, to reduce your chances of walking into a guaranteed disaster down the road?
5. You are an experienced data warehousing consultant, much like Michael Farraday in the case. The director of MIS of a firm similar to Close Call has called you in and asked you to join the team on their first data warehouse project. He offered to pay your standard hourly billing rate for the time you spend on this engagement. You believe the project is unlikely to succeed. What do you do?

CASE 8 MAKING WAVES AT HELENE CURTIS

From [JOHN93]. Used by permission.

'Twas nearly the night before Christmas five years ago, and Joyce Young was despairing over her first client/server project.

The director of decision support systems at Helene Curtis Industries, Inc., in Chicago had just given 20 salespeople the pilot version of what later became a very successful sales automation system. She was out having a late dinner with Maria Borzych, her sales systems manager and the first employee to join Young's fledgling three-person department.

"Things were not good. We were so upset! We wondered if we'd have jobs when it was over," said Young, who can smile about it all now. "We were using all this beta stuff, and we became our own system integrators. It was awful."

Client/server computing arrived at Helene Curtis Industries not with a bang but a whisper—and long before it became a fashionable buzzword.

"From the very beginning, we had a great deal of involvement with our clients, the sales force," said Young, 40, whose background includes degrees in computer science and business administration plus five years of information systems consulting for KPMG Peat Marwick. "These are very aggressive people, and I had to coalition-build. I couldn't go to them and be 'Ms. Tech Wienie IS' and be successful."

That first client/server project—a circa-1989 sales information system that gave laptop PCs to 170 direct sales representatives and managers nationwide—is scheduled for its second-generation revamp next year. A new retail information system—the second major client/server project—began rolling out last month to 150 more members of the retail sales force. This time, Young's department put pen-based AST Research, Inc./Grid Systems Corp. palmtop computers in the hands of another set of sales reps.

The decision support systems group now counts 30 staffers among Helene Curtis's 137-person Business Information Systems Division. The handful of PCs kicking around when Young joined the company in 1988 is now a network of more than 700 desktops and 21 LANs.

For this $1.2 billion corporation, whose mainstay product lines include Suave, Finesse and Salon Selectives shampoos and conditioners, client/server has come to mean all forms of decision support for sales, marketing and finance. "The scope that my department has is very broad; we support everything that is not part of the data center or the transaction processing systems," said Young, whose budget this year is about $3 million of the overall $25 million IS budget.

Success has been one of Joyce Young's personal hallmarks. Now married and the mother of a 5-year-old son, she once considered careers in dress designing or professional dance. Her first job in the computer industry was as a programmer/analyst at the now-defunct[5] Sperry Univac Corp., where she began working with fourth-generation languages and modeling tools.

"Decision support systems were a big interest of mine from the days of the early PCs and LANs," Young noted.

The sales automation system that Young's department built at Helene Curtis gives the sales force daily access via laptops to constantly updated product and customer information that once took several weeks to assemble and distribute.

"Our system is very flexible and fluid in what data you pull up," said Paul Silverman, national field sales manager at Helene Curtis and an early evangelist for the technology. "That's a good deal of its power."

For example, a sales rep can fire up his laptop and ask for all customers with orders over $5,000 as of yesterday. Then he can query specific product distribution information for Suave and Finesse shampoos. When he later connects—through a dial-in modem—to the national database in Chicago, he will upload his latest information from the field and drop off requests for additional reports not included in his laptop database.

The laptops run several off-the-shelf software packages, such as WordPerfect Corp.'s WordPerfect, Lotus Development Corp.'s 1-2-3, Software Publishing Corp.'s Harvard Graphics, a Moditech Corp. electronic mail system and Dealmaker forms software from EASI Co.

---

[5]The article's author is in error on this point. Sperry Univac, whose MAPPER was an early 4GL, merged with Burroughs Corp. in 1986 to form Unisys. While Sperry Univac no longer exists by that name, in late 1999 Unisys is very much in business.

Empowering Business Managers

Direct and retail sales reps perform very different jobs at Helene Curtis.

Direct sales representatives—the ones with laptops—deal at higher corporate levels with the buyers for merchandisers such as Kmart Corp. Retail sales reps, on the other hand, work with individual retail store managers in the roughly 40,000 different drugstores, supermarkets and retail outlets in which customers buy Helene Curtis products.

The new palmpad-based retail system will give sales reps an automated way to collect data, an analysis tool to measure sales productivity and more disciplined planning methods for handling accounts at the retail store level.

"This kind of technology allows us to bring information to the retail sales reps that empowers them to become business managers," said Dan Glei, customer business development manager and a key user liaison between IS and the sales force. "They can analyze information they never had before and make better decisions because of it."

Edge on Competition

Making better decisions is an increasingly crucial skill in the viciously competitive hair care market, in which Helene Curtis rose from relative obscurity a decade ago to become one of Procter & Gamble Co.'s most significant rivals.

"Helene Curtis has been very innovative over the years in new product creation and very persistent in reworking brands and supporting them," said Diana Temple, an analyst at Salomon Brothers, Inc. in New York. "But their U.S. sales were off by 7 percent in the first quarter because of inventory reductions by retailers."

"They're not doing that well right now, but I'd guess they'd be doing a little more poorly if it wasn't for their great information technology," added Andrew Shore, an analyst at Paine-Webber Inc. in New York.

The new retail information system, which was three years in the making from inception to reality, has a "fairly near-term horizon for payback," Glei said. "We believe this will provide us with a very distinct competitive advantage."

One quick payback from the retail system, Young added, is that it will let the sales reps add one more store to their daily rounds—eliminating the need to hire more salespeople.

Powerful Analysis Tools

The combination of daily updates from the field with syndicated market data has proved to be a powerful tool for market analysis at Helene Curtis.

When competitor Unilever introduced a new shampoo called Rave, for example, the market research department at Helene Curtis assumed it was aimed at their Salon Selectives line. But an investigation and analysis indicated that the bargain-priced Suave line was the true target.

"We were going to take down the pricing on Salon Selectives as a reaction to Rave, but the system enabled them to avoid doing something very reactive and losing money," Young recalled.

The heart and soul of the decision support system lies within the 25G bytes of data stored in a relational database on a Teradata, Inc. system in the data center. It stores syndicated market data from A. C. Nielsen Co. about the $20 billion personal care products industry, as well as product information from the field and internal data on logistics, promotions, sales and order entry.

From that data warehouse, information is parceled out to a Sybase, Inc. relational database management system on several Sun Microsystems, Inc. servers and then further down to Novell, Inc. NetWare LANs, IBM-compatible PCs and Compaq laptops.

Now facing a bill of $400,000 to upgrade storage capacity on the Teradata system, Helene Curtis is actively considering other options for its next wave of technology purchases. The "Three Rs" at the firm now are "rehosting, rightsizing and reengineering," said Tom Gildea, vice president of business information services.

To identify the vendors that will become strategic partners in the future, a team of 25 IS managers and staffers recently visited several major system and software vendors. NCR Corp., Hewlett-Packard and Digital Equipment Corp all made the short list as potential partners.

"One thing we've discovered is that nobody has a complete solution out there," Gildea said. "I'm reluctant to say we're going to go to client/server everywhere because then everybody's got a hammer in their hand saying, 'This is what we're going to do,' " he added. "What I want people to do is sit down and develop intelligent applications for the business community."

No Easy Task

Although client/server systems ultimately provided tangible benefits for the company, there were unnerving pitfalls in the early days—from LAN configuration crises to distributed data synchronization problems.

One big mistake Helene Curtis made with the sales information system, for example, was overzealously distributing databases to the field. "We had the actual database running on the laptops, and it was just a nightmare to support," said Borzych, sales systems manager. "Because we have very sophisticated transactions going on here and sales territories realigning, we have as many as 500 customers that could change from one territory to another. Being able to keep those databases in sync and up to date was a logistics nightmare, as well."

Moving back to a centralized national database on the Sun servers—with only the easily refreshed data distributed on the laptops—was a change the sales reps welcomed because performance improved, Borzych said. "Now if they submit a report [request] at 11 a.m. and wait until 11:30 to pick it up, 95 percent of the time their reports are ready."

Aside from introducing a new type of computing to Helene Curtis users, decision support systems also pioneered a closer working relationship with users during application design.

"The crux of the success of Joyce's group is the heavy front-end involvement of users and people like me becoming part of their business," Glei said. "Joyce and her people work real hard to understand our needs and deliver on them."

Questions

1. This article was written before the term *data warehouse* came into general use (though it is used once, on page 649). What about it relates to data warehousing as we use the term today (besides being in a collection of data warehousing cases)? What about it doesn't?

2. The first sentence of the fifth paragraph in this case uses the word *clients*. Compare and contrast this use of the word with its use in the phrase "client/server computing," which appears frequently throughout the case.

3. The Helene Curtis database differs from most data warehouses in that it contains current, up-to-yesterday data for sales and order inquiries rather than being solely a historical repository for analysis. State three ways in which you think this difference made its development more expensive or complicated.

4. Do you think the Helene Curtis system was justified from a business point of view? Why or why not?

CASE 9 HFS: MEGA-WAREHOUSE AS MARKETING TOOL

From [VIJA97]. Used by permission.

If you think building a data warehouse for one company is hard, try building an integrated version for more than 10.

That's what HFS, Inc. in Parsippany, N.J., is trying to do.

The $10 billion holding company of national chains said it is nearing completion on a $5.5 million integrated warehouse that contains data on more than 50 million customers of HFS's brands worldwide. These companies include Avis, Inc., Howard Johnson International, Inc., Ramada International Hotels and Resorts, Century 21 Real Estate Corp., Coldwell Banker Corp. and Resort Condominiums International.

The project, which started in HFS's marketing department, was formally launched about 18 months ago and is expected to wrap up next month.

The objective is to use the consolidated information in new, highly targeted cross-brand promotions aimed at increasing the market share of each HFS brand.

By using the warehouse to provide a single view of customers and their buying preferences across all brands, the company theoretically should be able to target customers with promotional offers tailored to their specific profiles. For example, regular Avis renters could get special discounts at HFS hotels, or time-share purchasers could get special rates on Avis rentals.

Rewarding Loyalty

"The idea is to reward our customers for their loyalty and bring to the table additional offers at the right time and the right place," said Scott Anderson, vice president and chief marketing officer at HFS. "We think it is going to be a significant value-add to our business."

If HFS can pull it off, the company will have succeeded in doing what corporations everywhere are struggling to do: find a way to harness and shape vast amounts of widely dispersed enterprise data into a powerful business and marketing tool.

Such capabilities will be crucial for HFS, particularly in light of its recent acquisition by Stamford, Conn.-based direct marketing giant CUC International, Inc. One of the goals of that deal is for the companies to cross-market to one another's customers.

No decision has been made on if and how CUC systems will be merged with the unified HFS warehouse, Anderson said.

"Qualitatively, it is no different from what happens when two different companies merge with each other," said Ken Rudin, a partner at Emergent Corp., a consultancy and integrator in San Mateo, Calif. "You have two sets of data with entirely different personalities that you somehow [have] to merge with each other," he said. But in HFS's case, it is more like 15 different sets of data. And getting there isn't easy.

Building from Scratch

Integration of the type HFS is trying to achieve involves melding different databases, data models, product codes and data collection methods and then building a warehouse from scratch.

The HFS warehouse will be powered by Digital Equipment Corp. symmetrical multiprocessing Alpha servers running an Informix Corp. database engine. The data being fed into it comes form a mix of mainframe, Oracle Corp., Sybase, Inc., Informix and Microsoft Corp. SQL Server databases.

"Digital's 64-bit architecture, their scalability and their support for Very Large Memory provided what we were looking for from the hardware," said Clyde Bryant, manager of database technology at HFS.

The decision to go with Informix was made last year. Tilting the balance in its favor were its partitioning capabilities and features such as the 64-bit and large file support on the Informix 7.23 database, Bryant said.

The data comes from the tens of millions of customer transactions involving HFS brands every year. For example, HFS collects information from about 45 million room reservations, 15 million Avis rentals, 1.5 million real estate sites and about 2 million time-share reservations. To build the warehouse, HFS had to extract, clean, convert and move relevant data from each of these sources to the centralized database.

Fast Growth

The completed warehouse will start at a relatively modest 500G bytes but is expected to nearly triple to 1.2T bytes by early next year.

"It took almost a year of constant interaction with our brands just to decide what information we wanted to collect, how we were going to collect it and from where," Anderson said.

After testing many of the data acquisition and cleansing tools available in the market—and rejecting them for being too expensive or inflexible—the integration team finally decided to develop its own technology for collecting data from multiple sources and feeding the data to a central warehouse (see box at end of case).

Support Choices Were Critical

The centralized warehouse project, which was managed out of HFS's data center in Phoenix, was put together by its information systems staff and a group of systems integration firms.

They included Deloitte and Touche, System Research and Development, Inc. (SRD) and Digital.

"The project was bigger than the warehouse. We needed to find vendors who were willing to partner with us, understand our objectives and help us define our architecture," said Clyde Bryant, manager of database technology at HFS.

"Considering the sheer size and magnitude of this project, it was very important that we pick outside vendors that could support the management capabilities required" and understand our data warehouse architecture, Bryant said.

As project manager, Deloitte and Touche coordinated the effort, including day-to-day management. Lead integrator SRD helped with things such as data modeling and building front-end tools and user screens. Digital was the main technology provider and supplied its high-end 64-bit Alpha servers. Digital also worked with SRD to develop the warehouse architecture.

The result was HFS's proprietary "universal message format," which at a basic level defines what kind of information should get into the central warehouse. It also provides a standard set of specifications for exactly how the data gets mapped into the warehouse.

"The basic driver for anything like this is competition. If you look at the real estate business, for instance, our brands have about 25 percent of the marketplace. That means there's 75 percent of sites out there that don't have our flag. That's the opportunity we want to tap" with these technologies, Anderson said.

Questions

1. The typical real estate buyer sees Century 21 Real Estate and Coldwell Banker as separate chains of agencies with no shared corporate identity, and assumes that they compete with each other. (This is not to suggest that anyone in either organization would deny the shared ownership if asked.) How do you think such a person would feel if he or she found out, after buying a house, that the agent who sold the house, and the presumably "competing" agent whom they chose not to deal with, were in fact working for the same overall firm (HFS)?

2. Consider Cases 6 (MasterCard), 7 (Close Call Corp.), 8 (Helene Curtis), and 9 (HFS). What are two characteristics that the situations described in Cases 6, 8, and 9 (the success stories) have in common, but that the situation in Case 7 (the failure) does not?

3. The HFS data warehouse started at 500G bytes and was expected to reach 1.2T bytes in well under a year. By contrast, the typical new desktop microcomputer has a total mass storage capacity (in mid-1999) around 5G bytes. Any one file or database on that computer is much smaller than that. Thus, the HFS data warehouse is more than 1,000 times larger than what one would consider a "very large" database on a desktop system. Digital's Alpha processor chip, while faster than those used in business desktop systems, is less than 10 times faster. What characteristics of an Alpha server, and/or what factors not considered in the first part of this question, make it able to handle such a large database?

4. The problems HFS faced in trying to integrate multiple data sources into a single data warehouse are not unique to HFS. If it couldn't find a suitable product on the market, and solved the problems with its internally developed data acquisition and cleansing tools, their solution might be of value to other firms as well. As many companies have shown, selling software can be a very profitable business—and HFS already has the product. If you were the HFS vice president of business development, which of the following actions would you recommend HFS take with this software? Justify your choice.

   a. Do nothing; just use the software internally.

   b. Start a software division or subsidiary to market it commercially.

   c. Enter a partnership with Deloitte and Touche and/or SRD to market it.

   d. Sell the software to Informix, since it is designed to feed data into their database, and let them market it.

   e. Another strategy of your own devising.

5. A follow-up article [VIJA99] discusses what eventually happened to this data warehouse after the merger of HFS and CUC International. (The merged firm is now known as Cedant Corp.) Find this article on *Computerworld*'s Web site, http://www.computerworld.com, or in your library's paper or on-line collection. Which specific points from the original article, if any, worked out as hoped or planned? Which, if any, did not?

REFERENCES

BLAC72   Black, Fischer, and Myron Scholes. "The Valuation of Option Contracts and a Test of Market Efficiency." *Journal of Finance* 27, no. 2 (May 1972), pp. 399–417.

BLAC73   Black, Fisher, and Myron Scholes. "The Pricing of Options and Corporate Liabilities." *Journal of Political Economy* 81, no. 3 (May–June 1973), pp. 637–654.

CLIF92   Clifford, James, Henry C. Lucas Jr., and Rajan Srikanth. "Integrating Mathematical and Symbolic Models through AESOP: An Expert for Stock Options Pricing." *Information Systems Research* 3, no. 4 (December 1992), pp. 359–378.

JOHN93   Johnson, Maryfran. "Making Waves at Helene Curtis." *Computerworld Client/Server Journal* 1, no. 1 (November 1993), pp. 26–30.

KOCH99   Koch, Christopher. "A Whole New Ball Game (Sort Of)," *CIO* 12, no. 13 (April 15, 1999), p. 38.

MAYO96   Mayor, Tracy. "Mining the Possibilities." *CIO* Section 1, 9, no. 16 (June 1, 1996), p. 53.

PAUL97   Paul, Lauren Gibbons. "Anatomy of a Failure." *CIO Enterprise* (Section 2 of *CIO*), November 15, 1997, p. 55.

SMIT91   Smith, Michael Lawrence. "Cooperating Artificial Neural and Knowledge-Based Systems in a Truck Fleet Brake Balance Application," in *Innovative Applications of Artificial Intelligence 2*. Alain Rappaport and Reid Smith, Eds. AAAI Press, Menlo Park, Calif., and MIT Press, Cambridge, Mass. (1991).

SYST94   "Enterprise-wide GIS: Bringing New Dimensions to Decision Making." *Systems* (Unisys Corp.) 8, no. 1 (Winter 1994), p. 13.

VIJA97   Vijayan, Jaikumar. "Mega-warehouse Drives Targeted Marketing." *Computerworld* (August 18, 1997), p. 1.

VIJA99   Vijayan, Jaikumar. "A Data Warehouse, 18 Months Later." *Computerworld* 33, no. 10 (March 8, 1999), p. 44.

Index